*Recalling the Hope of Glory* deals expertly and thoroughly with worship in the Bible. What is most refreshing: it is not at all ideological. It contains no worship-war polemics, but just sets forth straightforwardly what the Bible says. People of all persuasions will find it valuable as a reference work. It also gives us a large perspective on worship that is likely to moderate the current discussion.

—JOHN M. FRAME
Professor of Systematic Theology and Philosophy,
Reformed Theological Seminary

Ross presents an in-depth analysis of biblical wisdom about worship from the book of origins to the anthem of the redeemed around the throne of the Lamb in glory. Along the way stereotypes are exploded, assumptions challenged, as the awesome, tri-personal God—Father, Son, and Holy Spirit—is shown to be the true object of all creaturely confession, adoration, and praise. This is not only a study of worship; it is a book designed to lead Christian believers into worship. I commend it heartily to God's people everywhere.

—TIMOTHY GEORGE
Dean and Professor of Divinity, Beeson Divinity School
Executive Editor, *Christianity Today*

This is a book that needed to be written a long time ago. *Recalling the Hope of Glory* is instructive, setting forth the biblical teaching on worship; practical, challenging the church to properly integrate biblical teaching into contemporary worship issues; and inspirational, bringing the reader to a posture and place of worship. This book should become foundational for the church.

—DAVID TALLEY
Associate Professor of Biblical Studies and Theology,
Talbot School of Theology

Allen Ross takes his readers back to the Bible itself to paint a colorful picture of worship that is spiritually vibrant, theologically sound, and focused on Christ. His passion for worship that glorifies God and his thorough knowledge of Scripture are obvious throughout. For the western church, which needs desperately to recover its biblical and theological roots, this book will be an extremely helpful resource.

—DANIEL I. BLOCK
Professor of Old Testament,
Wheaton College

It is remarkable that so many books about worship have so little to say about God. This book is a welcome exception. Through its patient reflection on specific biblical texts and themes, the book evokes a vivid awareness of the God of glory. By developing the theme of glory, the book hones a vision of worship that is at once luminous, transcendent, and inexhaustible.

—JOHN D. WITVLIET
Director, Calvin Institute of Christian Worship
Professor of Worship, Theology, and Music,
Calvin College

Stunning in scope, *Recalling the Hope of Glory* provides a historical-theological study of worship from creation to the new creation. The logic of Allen Ross's ranging exposition across the flow of biblical history will challenge every reader and grace every church, regardless of tradition. Here is dazzling substance for recovery of robust worship of our sovereign and holy triune God. Sure to be a standard work.

—R. KENT HUGHES
Pastor, College Church in Wheaton
Series Editor, Preaching the Word commentary series

The publication of *Recalling the Hope of Glory* is a splendid addition to the growing number of works on biblical worship. Not only is this work a comprehensive theological vision of creation, incarnation, and re-creation, it is also a genuine work of praise.

—ROBERT E. WEBBER
William R. and Geraldyne B. Myers Chair of Ministry,
Northern Seminary

# Recalling the
# Hope *of* Glory

### BIBLICAL **WORSHIP** FROM
### THE **GARDEN** TO THE **NEW CREATION**

## ALLEN P. ROSS

Kregel
*Academic & Professional*

*Recalling the Hope of Glory: Biblical Worship from the Garden to the New Creation*

© 2006 by Allen P. Ross

Published by Kregel Publications, a division of Kregel, Inc., P.O. Box 2607, Grand Rapids, MI 49501.

**Library of Congress Cataloging-in-Publication Data**
Ross, Allen P.
  Recalling the hope of glory: biblical worship from the garden to the new creation / by Allen P. Ross.
    p. cm.
  Includes bibliographical references and indexes.
  1. Worship—Biblical teaching.  I. Title.
BS680.W78R67    2006
264—dc22                                                    2006028903

ISBN 0-8254-3578-1

Printed in the United States of America

06  07  08  09  10 / 5  4  3  2  1

*For Jan,*
*whose insight and inspiration*
*made an immense contribution to*
*this book.*

# Contents *in* Brief

## Part 4: Worship with Sacrifice: The Establishment of Sanctity in Worship

## Part 5: Worship as Praise: The Provision for Celebration in Worship

## Part 6: Worship Reformed: Prophetic Rebukes and Reforms

## Part 7: Worship Transformed: The New Setting of Worship and the New Covenant

## Part 8: Worship in Christ: Patterns of Worship in the Early Church

## Part 9: The Perfection of Worship in Glory

## Part 10: Basic Principles for More Glorious Worship

# Contents

## Part 2: The Memory of Paradise

## Part 3: Worship with Proclamation: The Development of True Worship in a Religious World

## Part 4: Worship with Sacrifice: The Establishment of Sanctity in Worship

## Part 5: Worship as Praise: The Provision for Celebration in Worship

## Part 6: Worship Reformed: Prophetic Rebukes and Reforms

# Part 8: Worship in Christ: Patterns of Worship in the Early Church

## Part 9: The Perfection of Worship in Glory

## Part 10: Basic Principles for More Glorious Worship

# Preface

THIS BOOK IS AS MUCH THE product of my personal pilgrimage as it is years of study. I suppose growing up in a pastor's home had me thinking at an early age about what went on in public and private worship. But my experiences in that church, a German Baptist Church, were only the beginnings of a pilgrimage that has taken me through many denominations and many different churches within the major denominations. And in the process I have been exposed to the major forms of worship. Then, when I began to speak in different churches, I was able to see firsthand the great variety of activities that go under the heading of worship. My experiences with churches and my teaching in the areas of the Psalms, Leviticus, Jewish backgrounds to the New Testament, and studies in worship itself, inspired even greater research into the subject. This book has emerged from this lengthy process.

I have written this book to inspire and encourage Christians, and therefore congregations, to study Scripture more closely on this subject in order to discover all that worship can and should be. There are many good works on the various aspects of worship, but none that focus almost entirely on the biblical passages that are concerned with the subject. To study Scripture with such a designated purpose enables Christians to see how much the Bible has to say on the subject, and how far we are from exhausting all the revelation of God on it. I am not trying to get people to change their denominational affiliation, although that might happen; but I am trying to change their thinking on the subject of worship so that they might begin to follow more of the principles and patterns of worship that are found in the Bible, which various groups have implemented effectively. If people will study the Bible with this in mind, it will be a lifelong study, but it will be rich and fruitful—their worship activities will flourish in accordance with their discovery of what has happened in the history of the faith. Their worship will become much more glorious, and their spiritual service will be raised to a much higher level.

The focus of the book is primarily on communal worship, though most of the principles can be easily used in private worship as well. But since worship is a communal activity, all the private acts of devotion will find their greatest expression and their divinely intended purpose in the assembly of believers. And when communal worship is glorious, it will in turn inspire greater private worship.

There have been far too many people to enumerate who have inspired or helped in significant ways in the writing of this book—pastors, teachers, students, and congregations. But I would like to mention my students especially, for in taking the courses and interacting with the material as it was being developed, they proved to be a valuable testing ground. Especially, I would mention Ross and Lauren Blackburn, who have been such an encouragement to me for even getting started. I am grateful also to Beeson Divinity School, Samford University, Birmingham, Alabama, for its generous provision to enable me to finish the work. But most of all I thank my wife, Jan, who has been enthusiastic and encouraging about this project from its beginning and has contributed a good deal to the development of the ideas and the way they have been presented.

# Abbreviations

## Standard Resources

| | |
|---|---|
| ANET | *Ancient Near Eastern Texts Relating to the Old Testament* |
| BDB | Brown, F., S. R. Driver, C. A. Briggs. *A Hebrew and English Lexicon of the Old Testament.* |
| GKC | *Gesenius' Hebrew Grammar* |
| LXX | Septuagint |
| MT | Masoretic Text |
| TDNT | *Theological Dictionary of the New Testament.* |

## Rabbinic Literature

| | |
|---|---|
| *Ber.* | *Berakot* |
| *Dem.* | *Demai* |
| *Eduy.* | *ʿEduyyot* |
| *ʿEruv.* | *ʿEruvin* |
| *Kid.* | *Kiddushin* |
| *Makk.* | *Makkot* |
| *Meg.* | *Megillah* |
| *Mid.* | *Middot* |
| *Neg.* | *Negaʿim* |
| *Nid.* | *Niddah* |
| *Pes.* | *Pesaḥim* |
| *Shab.* | *Shabbat* |
| *Shek.* | *Shekalim* |
| *Sot.* | *Sotah* |
| *Suk.* | *Sukkah* |
| *Tos.* | *Tosephta (Tosefta)* |
| *Yad.* | *Yadayim* |

# Hebrew Transliteration Key

| Consonants | | Vowels | |
|---|---|---|---|
| א | ʾ | ◌ַ | a |
| בּ ב | b v | ◌ָ | ā |
| גּ ג | g | ◌ָה | āh |
| דּ ד | d | ◌ֳ | ă |
| ה | h | ◌ֲ | ᵃ |
| ו | w | ◌ֵ | ē |
| ז | z | ◌ֵי | ê |
| ח | kh | ◌ֱ | ĕ |
| ט | ṭ | ◌ְ | ᵉ |
| י | y | ◌ִ | i |
| כּ כ ך | k | ◌ִי | î |
| ל | l | ◌ָ | o |
| מ ם | m | ◌ֹ | ō |
| נ ן | n | וֹ | ô |
| ס | s | ◌ֳ | ŏ |
| ע | ʿ | ◌ֻ | u |
| פּ | p | וּ | û |
| פ ף | ph | | |
| צ ץ | ts | | |
| ק | q | | |
| ר | r | | |
| שׂ | ś | | |
| שׁ | sh | | |
| תּ ת | t | | |

accents ´

# Greek Transliteration Key

| | |
|---|---|
| α | a |
| β | b |
| γ | g |
| δ | d |
| ε | e |
| ζ | z |
| η | ē |
| θ | th |
| ι | i |
| κ | k |
| λ | l |
| μ | m |
| ν | n |
| ξ | x |
| ο | o |
| π | p |
| ρ | r |
| σ | s |
| τ | t |
| υ | u; *often* y |
| φ | ph |
| χ | kh |
| ψ | ps |
| ω | ō |
| ʽ | (rough breathing mark) h |
| ˋ ˆ ´ | (accents) ´ |

# PART 1

# WORSHIPPING *the* GOD *of* GLORY

# Introduction

THE WORDS OF WORSHIP FLOW so easily from our lips that we seldom stop to think about them: we casually talk about knowing the Lord; we say we talk to God and in one way or another hear from God. We attend churches on Sundays to have, as we say, fellowship with God and each other. There we celebrate the belief that he is our God with songs and hymns, but even these have become so familiar to us that our minds drift to other, more immediate concerns. And when we approach the Lord's Table, to eat with God as it were, we often do not have enough time to appreciate what it means. In short, our worship services have become time-bound and routine. We have been so successful in fitting God into our important schedules that worship is often just another activity. But it should be anything but routine and ordinary.

After all, this God we say we know is the sovereign Creator and Lord of the whole universe, the eternal and ever-living God, all wise, all powerful, and ever present. Our attention to the Lord must not be an ordinary part of life; our worship of him should be the most momentous, urgent, and glorious activity in our lives. But we rarely see the splendor, the beauty, and the glory of worship because we are not drawn out of our world enough to comprehend this God of glory; consequently, our worship is all too frequently unexceptional and at times irrelevant.

If we could grasp the incongruity of speaking so casually about God, we would be overwhelmed and could never again worship comfortably in the same ways. We would think it too demeaning for God and too flattering for us. On the one hand, here we are, finite human beings, concerned chiefly with staying healthy and making a comfortable living. We spend our days in familiar routines with an array of anxieties and uncertainties threatening our sense of security. We genuinely would like to focus on worship and service, but more immediate concerns occupy our time.

And on the other hand, there is God, the sovereign and ever-living Lord. He is the inconceivable and incomprehensible source of all existence; he is the invisible majesty who reigns on high. This God we claim to know is the one before whom thousands upon thousands of angels and archangels stand, never ceasing to laud and praise him as the holy and glorious majesty. This Lord merely speaks, as he did at creation, and myriads of angels wait to carry out his will. He is completely unique, truly glorious and incomparably holy—there is no one like him, anywhere, at any time. And there is no measure of the magnificence and beauty of his holiness, for all his works are amazing, good, and glorious. And we say we know him!

Moreover, by his greatness and because of his grace, this God created us humans out of the dust of the ground and made us as his image; he made a Paradise for us and promised us immortality and everlasting joy in his presence. And even though we, his creation, treated him as worthless and relegated him to an insignificant place in our all-important lives, he still desired that we be with him and he with us. Therefore, he set about with his plan to bring us to glory. Such was his preoccupation with us, such was his love for us—who are but dust and ashes—that he prepared this plan in ages past, revealed it century by century, and then at just the right time in human history came into this little world in human form to die a humiliating death in our place so that our indifference to and rebellion against him could be forgiven and that we might still live with him forever. This incarnate Lord, the Jesus we talk about as if he were just another man, albeit extraordinary and exemplary, is the one who made all things. And he is the one who is the radiance of the glory of the Godhead, and the exact representation of the divine essence. It is he who bears the world along on its course by his powerful command. It is he who someday will come in great glory and power to judge the living and the dead. And it is he who will make all things new, a new heaven and a new earth, in which righteousness and peace will reign undisturbed. There is no power in heaven, on earth, or under the earth that can change his plan, for all wisdom, knowledge, power, and dominion belong to him. Nothing occurs, or has occurred, or will occur, that he does not know perfectly well. And because of who he is and what he has done, there is nothing in all this universe that can compare with his unimaginable perfection, illimitable majesty, and incomprehensible glory. Our minds can scarcely begin to take it in.

And we say we know him! How can we claim to know him, whose ways have been from everlasting past finding out, whose essence is beyond anything mankind could construct, the one who is infinite?

Well, we do know him, in part. We know him because he chooses that we should know him and reveals himself to us. We know him if we are willing to receive his revelation. And as we come to know him more and more we discover how well he knows us. He knows us, little us; he knows all about us, our trivial activities, our chief concerns, everything we think or say or do, even every hair on our heads. He knows us personally, individually by name. He knows us because he wants to know us, and that is the wonder of it all. He knows us because he wants us to be with him throughout eternity, to have immediate access to him as in the beginning, to sing with angelic choirs in glory, and to reign with him forever. He knows us because he is our God.

How then can we talk casually of this Lord? How can we merely slot him into our fully scheduled lives? How can we think there might be more important things for us to do in life than to worship him? If we even begin to comprehend his glorious nature, we cannot. We will be caught away from our worldly experience and transported in our spirits to realms of glory. We will be overwhelmed by the thought of being in his presence, tremble at the thought of hearing what he has to say to us, and be amazed at the thought that we can speak to him and he will listen! How can we not desire to transcend the ordinary routine by entering his courts to praise and glorify him above the profane things we so eagerly value? Truly, if our worship, if our spiritual life, is going to rise above this earthly existence where our minds are fixed on mundane thoughts and our attention is given to mundane concerns, then we are going to have to begin to focus our hearts and our minds on the holiness and the glory and the beauty of the one we say we know and love.

Our churches do not always make this easy. All too often the heartfelt desires of the worshippers to see God in his glory are frustrated by meetings and programs that often get in the way and jar our spiritual sensitivities. This, in spite of the fact that churches are always trying to make worship more meaningful. But usually these efforts focus on new methods and different styles designed to make worship more lively and more relevant rather than on how to inspire worshippers to see the true and holy God of glory. In an effort to simplify things and make them relevant, the meaning and the mystery has been lost. As a result, in many services there may be almost nothing that is truly uplifting, moving, or even interesting. Efforts to improve worship often start with outbursts of energy and enthusiasm, but they have little lasting effect, and in time people are looking for other ways to do it, or for other churches that do it differently. This cycle indicates that worship needs constant attention—with a better focus. While many congregations are concerned enough to make the effort, there are too many that are satisfied that they have worship in good order and therefore think they need no reexamination. Sadly, some groups are not even touched by such concerns.

But there is evidence of an increasing interest in improving worship, judging from the amount of literature that has been written recently.[1] Will churches succeed in transforming worship for greater involvement of the people? Will churches improve praise and music with more relevant and meaningful material? Will they develop greater variety and spontaneity in their set forms and order of worship? No doubt what has been written recently on these kinds of details of worship will help bring about change; the more general works that try to capture the essence of worship and show how it has been expressed from the early church to the present are also helpful. But whether they will be able to break down the centuries-old barriers to more glorious worship remains to be seen.

For any significant change to occur in our worship activities, we have to get behind forms and methods and changes in style and focus on the biblical theology that informs worship, because one of the reasons, if not the main reason, for the lack of proper attention given to worship is the lack of a biblical, theological understanding.[2] That understanding must begin with a thorough study of the biblical text from the beginning of creation to the end of the age that traces the unfolding revelation of God's

---

1. A decade ago A. E. Hill listed some of the trends in worship renewal: an emphasis on personal piety and corporate worship, congregational participation through spiritual gifts, a return to the traditions of worship, a move toward holistic worship involving all the senses, the attempt to accommodate liturgy to the culture, a connection between worship and service, and a trend toward ecumenism. These beginnings need to be developed further, but with proper biblical and theological motivation (*Enter His Courts with Praise,* xxii).

2. Saliers says that one cannot divide theological thinking and liturgical participation. He is concerned with "continuing worship" as a form of theology, but approaches the subject liturgically (*Worship as Theology: Foretaste of Glory Divine,* 15).

design for communion with his people and the cumulative record of their appropriate responses to Him. Such a study will show how the patterns of worship have developed along with the outworking of God's plan of redemption, culminating with worship in glory in the presence of the glorified Christ.

Although the material for this study is vast and complex, the organization and presentation of it must be clear enough for churches to understand the abiding biblical patterns and principles of worship and to be able to examine what they are doing in the name of worship. When the matter is approached from the perspective of biblical revelation, the greatest changes in worship will take place in the hearts of the worshippers, which in turn will lead to the community's finding better ways of worshipping.

For worship to be as glorious as it should be, for it to lift people out of their mundane cares and fill them with adoration and praise, for it to be the life-changing and life-defining experience it was designed to be, it must be inspired by a vision so great and so glorious that what we call worship will be transformed from a routine gathering into a *transcendent meeting with the living God.* When that happens, then we will be caught up in our spirits to join the heavenly choirs of saints and angels who even now are gathered around the throne of God. Thereafter, our hearts and minds will be filled with the hope of glory so that we may truly love and serve the LORD in this life.

Without sustaining a vision of the holy Lord of glory, what some call the sublime "worship" very quickly digresses from the revealed design of worship that God desires and becomes routine, predictable, and even irrelevant. The starting point of any discussion of worship must be the object of worship, the Lord God himself, who is higher and more significant and far more glorious than life itself. This is the vision we need to inspire our worship; it is the vision that a world lost in sin needs in order to be reconciled to God.

In his discussion of this idea, John Stott writes that human beings are aware of a spiritual reality that is "awesomely vast" and transcendent but that they look for it in unlikely places:

> They seek it everywhere, through yoga, Transcendental Meditation, and other forms of Eastern mysticism; through sex, which

Malcolm Muggeridge calls the "mysticism of the materialist";
through music and the arts; through drug-taking and the "higher consciousness"; through modern religious cults and dangerous experiments with the occult; and through the fantasies of
science fiction.[3]

He draws this conclusion:

This quest for transcendence constitutes a challenge to the quality of Christian public worship. Does it offer what people are
seeking—the element of mystery, the sense of the numinous, in
biblical language the "fear of God," in modern language "transcendence," so that we "bow down before the Infinitely Great" in
the mixture of awe, wonder, and joy called worship?[4]

The answer to this question is "not very often."

---

3. John R. W. Stott, "The World's Challenge to the Church," 124. Bloesch also discusses
the importance of a proper perception of God in *Essentials of Evangelical Theology*,
1:24–50.
4. Stott, "The World's Challenge to the Church," 125.

# CHAPTER 1

# The Revelation *of* *the* Holy LORD God *of* Glory

## The Revelation

The greater our appreciation and apprehension of the majestic God whom we say we worship, the greater will be our reverence, adoration, and service. This is the effect that we find in the biblical records whenever people received fuller revelations of the God of glory. One primary example of this is in the account of the calling of Isaiah, which tells how the prophet saw a vision of the glorious, holy LORD that transformed him into a devout and dedicated servant. Isaiah saw the LORD

> seated on a throne, high and exalted, and the train of his robe filled the temple. Above him were seraphs, each with six wings: With two wings they covered their faces, with two they covered their feet, and with two they were flying. And they were calling to one another:
>
> > "Holy, holy, holy, is the LORD[1] Almighty;
> > the whole earth is full of his glory."
>
> At the sound of their voices the doorposts and thresholds shook and the temple was filled with smoke. (Isa. 6:1b–4)

---

1. The standard representation of the divine name Yahweh with the substitute title "LORD" will be followed in this book, apart from the places where the exact name "Yahweh" is required to understand the passage fully.

This overwhelming sight could not have been timelier. The beloved King Uzziah had died; but Isaiah now saw "the King" (v. 5). Earthly kings come and go, but the LORD sits enthroned forever. This heavenly king is not earthbound: he is not subject to the fears and failures of this life as are pagan gods and mortals; he is neither human nor the product of human invention. He is the Sovereign LORD God, the eternal King of Glory.

God's heavenly court was filled with angelic choirs that praise him endlessly for his holiness and his glory. Here Isaiah saw the seraphs, majestic angelic beings with wings and hands and voices, who are occupied with praising God.[2] These are either a form of cherubs or a separate order of angels; they have the appearance of fire and the function of praising God and supporting and guarding the heavenly throne.[3]

The glorious vision given to Isaiah enabled him to put into perspective the immediate troubles in his land and thus inspired the proper submission and adoration of worship. Consequently, this vision prepared him for the special task that God had in store for him. And likewise today, if people respond to the revelation of the Lord as did Isaiah ages ago, they too will be transformed into devout worshippers and dedicated servants. We may not see exactly what he saw; but we have far more revelation than he had. And the revelation that we have focuses on the same glorious LORD Isaiah saw.

## The Holiness of the LORD

The angelic praise Isaiah heard has become a standard acclamation among the faithful: "Holy, holy, holy[4] is the LORD of hosts."[5] And it will

---

2. The plural noun *seraphîm*, perhaps related to *sāraph*, "to burn," is often transposed into English as *"seraph,"* an angelic being. See Robin Wakely's study in *The New International Dictionary of Old Testament Theology and Exegesis,* 3:1289–91.

3. According to Ezekiel 1:10–28 and 10:2, 20, there were four creatures or *cherubim* at the throne of God. They were composite creatures with four wings, two of which extended up and supported the throne and two of which extended down to cover them. Their appearance was of burning coals of fire, and between them fire flashed back and forth. They were ever watchful (full of eyes) and always moving (with their wheels).

4. In the church this is often called the *trisagion,* "thrice holy" (*hágios* in Greek is "holy"). This will be discussed in the study of the early church, but for helpful information see Flusser, "Jewish Roots of the Liturgical Trisagion," 37–43; and Werner, "The Doxology in Synagogue and Church," 275–351 (esp. 292–307).

5. "Hosts" refers to angelic hosts, but may include earthly armies; they are all at God's disposal.

be their song when they join the angelic choirs in glory (see Rev. 4:8). The brief acclamation expresses the essence of God, who is praised and adored forever—he is incomparably holy!

What do we mean when we say God is "holy"? By itself the word translated "holy" *(qādôsh)* simply means "set apart, unique, distinct." Theologians have tried to improve on the translation, but we have nothing better than "holy."[6]

The word for "holy" has a wide array of uses in the Bible, but essentially it describes anything that might be set apart for a specific reason.[7] For example, a bowl set apart for use in temple ritual would be called "holy" and could not be used for ordinary or common meals (see Dan. 5:23). The understanding of the word is helped by a study of its antonym, "profane" *(khōl,* from *khālal),* which refers to anything that is common, ordinary, or secular—not set apart.[8] What is common may be good and useful in various aspects of life—but it is not "holy," or set apart for God's use.

To say that God is holy is to ascribe a uniqueness to him that is almost incomprehensible. It indicates that he is set apart from all that is creaturely and corrupt, that he is distinct from this physical and fallen world.[9] It affirms that God is not like humans, angels, false gods, animals—or anything in existence. In short, we may say that *there is no one like God,* even though that statement has the obvious limitations of

---

6. One suggestion is the translation "other." It does make people stop and think in a different way, but it too needs clarification. See further Otto, *The Idea of the Holy.*

7. Many words are etymologically related to *qādôsh,* "holy." There is the noun *qôdesh,* "apartness, sacredness," the nouns *qédesh* and *miqdāsh,* "sanctuary" and "sacred place" respectively, and place names like Kadesh, a sanctuary city. All these words in their contexts point to the meaning of separation from common use for a specific purpose.

  Of course the primary use of the word *holy* has reference to God. For example, *places* set apart for the worship of God were called holy. Similarly, *times* were declared holy when they were to be devoted to God. And *people* were set apart to God and his service; they were to be "sanctified" to God: "Be holy because I, the LORD your God, am holy" (Lev. 19:2; cf. 1 Peter 1:16).

8. According to the *American Heritage Dictionary, profane* is derived from a variant of the Latin *profanus, pro* meaning "before (outside)" and *fanum* meaning "temple"— outside the temple, i.e., secular. It has come to be used to describe vulgar and base things.

9. See further Trevethan, *The Beauty of God's Holiness.*

a negative sentence—it does not by itself say what he is. But when we describe the holiness of God, we must think of his uniqueness. Isaiah records God's own description of his holiness: "For this is what the high and lofty One says—he who lives forever [inhabits eternity], whose name is holy: 'I live in a high and holy place, but also with him who is contrite and lowly in spirit'" (Isa. 57:15). This is what makes communion with God so marvelous—he is high and exalted, separate and unapproachable, but he delights to dwell with us. It is the greatness of God that makes his grace so amazing; or to express it in terms of his grace, the way to God in the highest heaven is through the lowest contrition, for those of a contrite heart may know that God dwells with them, and they will dwell with him some day in the highest holy place. In Isaiah's vision this God is called "holy," incomparably holy, as the threefold repetition stresses.[10]

In what ways is God distinct (i.e., holy)? To answer this we have to think of the numerous attributes of God revealed in the Bible, for they represent God's holiness, or uniqueness, in specific areas.[11] For example, God is all-powerful (*omnipotent;* see, e.g., Gen. 18:14; Pss. 33:9; 115:3; Matt. 19:26). His power is revealed in his mighty acts, such as creation, salvation, and judgment. No one else has power like that, no one on earth or in heaven. Angels are created beings and not divine; humans are weak and frail; and the pagan gods, even with spirit forces behind them, are impotent and worthless. But God is different; he is not weak or dependent. So with respect to power, God is holy.

The Bible also reveals that God is all-knowing (*omniscient;* see Pss. 139:1–6; 147:4–5; Matt. 10:29–30; Rom. 11:33). He knows everything— he knows all that has happened, all that will happen, and all that could happen. No one else has that kind of knowledge. So, with reference to knowledge, God is holy.

God is also everywhere at once (*omnipresent;* see 1 Kings 8:27–29; Ps. 139:7–12; Jer. 23:23–24; Acts 17:27–28). Who in heaven or on earth can do this? Who can even understand it? So with regard to space, God is holy.

He is also eternal; he is without beginning and without end (Ps. 90:1–2;

---

10. With the threefold repetition of the word *holy,* some have suggested there is a hint of the fullness of the Godhead, especially in view of the later verse in Isaiah 6 in which "we" and "us" form part of the word from God. But to say Isaiah understood that would be difficult to prove.

11. See Packer, *Knowing God;* and Arthur W. Pink, *The Attributes of God.*

Isa. 43:10–13; John 1:1–2; Rev. 1:8, 17–18). He alone lives forever—in fact, he is alive in a sense that we cannot begin to understand, for he is the giver of life, the sustainer of life, and the restorer of life—he is life! In the aspect of time and eternity, he is holy.

God is righteous (Gen. 18:25; Pss. 7:9–12; 145:17). All his acts are right and just. He commits no iniquity and will leave no iniquity unpunished or any good unrewarded. People may have the capacity to do righteous things but not continuously or characteristically. And because their righteousness does not measure up to God's standard, they must admit that they are unrighteous next to him. The pagan gods were certainly not righteous; they had all the vices and imperfections of the people who served them. But God is perfect and right in all his ways; in this too he is holy.

Even when we consider the attributes that God shared with humans at creation, we find that there is still a vast difference. For example, God, who is merciful and compassionate, gave people the capacity to show mercy and compassion. But our mercy and compassion is limited by our human nature, and consequently we can only reflect these divine attributes in an imperfect way. If we continued down the list of all the attributes—his faithful love, goodness, wisdom, and the like—we would find the same thing. There is no one like him—he is holy.

So while the word *holy* retains the basic idea of being set apart, it takes on a greater, more positive meaning when it is fully understood in reference to God. Holiness is not one of many descriptions of God; it is the summary designation of all that God is and is known to be in contrast to all of creation.[12] Therefore, the Bible speaks of the holy LORD as the one, true and living God Almighty—not *a* god, not Israel's national god in competition with other national gods, and not one holy being among many, but *the* Holy LORD God, as we see in Isaiah 44:6–8:

> This is what the LORD says—
>     Israel's King and Redeemer, the LORD Almighty:
> I am the first and I am the last;
>     apart from me there is no God.
> Who then is like me? Let him proclaim it.
>     Let him declare and lay out before me

---

12. See Labushchagne, *The Incomparability of YHWH in the Old Testament.*

> what has happened since I established my ancient people,
>         and what is yet to come—
>     yes, let him foretell what will come.
> Do not tremble, do not be afraid.
>         Did I not proclaim this and foretell it long ago?
> You are my witnesses. Is there any God besides me?
>     No, there is no other Rock; I know not one.

The connotation of *holy* ultimately goes beyond negative descriptions to affirmations of positive power and perfection.[13] Accordingly, when anyone or anything is set apart to God, that person or object comes under the dominion of a power that is life changing, dangerous (if violated) or beneficent (if received).[14]

The revelation of the exalted holy LORD was given to Isaiah to change the way people respond to God for all time. That is why the prophet recorded his vision of the sublime[15] and the words of the angels around the throne, crying "holy, holy, holy." The impact of such a revelation is overwhelming: it causes people to tremble and fall down before him. The prophet and countless others after him have been inspired to devout service by the revelation of the power and perfection of the LORD.

## The Glory of God

In Isaiah's vision the angels also proclaimed, "The whole earth is full of his glory" (Isa. 6:3b). In the Scriptures the "glory of the LORD" is the most dramatic manifestation of the presence of the LORD. To talk about God's holiness is to speak of his essential nature; but to speak about God's glory is to declare his importance or the display of that importance in history and in creation.

The noun translated "glory" *(kāvôd)* is related to a verb "to be heavy" *(kāvēd),* which by extension means "important."[16] It can be used for the

---

13. Eichrodt describes it as a "marvelous power, removed from common life and bound up with particular objects." The connection of the word with the idea of morality came with the preaching of the prophets (*Theology of the Old Testament,* 1:271).
14. E. Jacob, *The Theology of the Old Testament,* 86.
15. The word *sublime* means "exalted, lifted up, preeminent."
16. The word can describe anything that is literally heavy, such as a man (1 Sam. 4:18) or a rock (Isa. 32:2); but it can also be used figuratively to describe blindness (eyes

human soul, that is, the real person, the essential life (Ps. 30:12).[17] In this sense *kāvôd* is what gives a person "importance." Everyone has this *kāvôd*, this inner glory or importance, but the LORD has a quality of it superior to everyone else.[18]

The word *glory* came to refer to all the trappings that reflect the importance or greatness of someone. Joseph, for example, told his brothers to inform their father of his glory (*kāvôd*; NIV: honor) in Egypt (Gen. 45:13). When this meaning is applied to the LORD, as in "the glory of the LORD," it refers to all the manifestations of his powerful presence, such as the stars of the heavens (Ps. 19:1), or the brilliant, luminous cloud at the sea and in the wilderness (e.g., Exod. 14:19–20, 24). Moses saw that, but still wanted to see God's "glory" (Exod. 33:18). He wanted to see past the bright cloud and the fire to the real person: "Show me your glory." The Greek version chose to translate this verse using a pronoun rather than *doxa*, the Greek word for "glory"—"Now show me *yourself*." This translation captures the precise connotation of the word in Moses' request.

When the Bible uses the word "glory" or "glorious" with reference to the LORD, it is basically saying that *he is the most important or preeminent person* in this or any other universe. And when the Bible refers to the "glory of the LORD," it is usually referring to all the evidence of God's preeminence. It may speak of him as the Creator by focusing on the heavenly hosts of stars and galaxies as the glory of the LORD; or it may reflect his powerful presence by displaying the brilliant luminous manifestations

---

that are "heavy"; Gen. 48:10), or unbelief (a heavy or hardened heart; Exod. 9:7), or wealth ("heavy" with silver and gold; Gen. 13:2). The related meaning, "important," arises because what has weight was perceived as important (like our idiom of "throwing one's weight around"). So things or places or people that are important, such as the temple (Hag. 2:3), or priestly robes (Exod. 28:2), or even a forest (Isa. 10:18), are described with words related to *kāvôd*. Paul captures this meaning in 2 Corinthians 4:17 with a word play based on the Hebrew background of the Greek words "the eternal *weight* of *glory*. A derived form has the meaning "to treat as important, to honor" (*kabbēd*). To honor the Sabbath day (Isa. 58:13) meant that people were to treat it as more important than the other days. Parents were to be honored, that is, given their proper (weight of) authority (Exod. 20:12). If people honor God, they will demonstrate his importance in their lives by obedience (Mal. 1:6) and praise (Ps. 50:15).

17. The word for "liver" in these languages is a related noun, for the liver is the heaviest organ and therefore thought to be the most important, or at least at the center of the human life.

18. Jacob, *The Theology of the Old Testament,* 88.

usually accompanied by angels; or it may refer to his mighty saving works as evidence of his glory, his true nature. All such manifestations are properly called "the glory of the LORD."[19]

To speak of God's "holiness" is to say that there is no one like him, that he has absolute power and perfection; to speak of God's "glory" is to say that he is preeminent in existence and that the whole universe is filled with evidence of his importance and sublimity. And while it would take some time to draw from Scripture all the details that describe the nature of the LORD, these two expressions, holiness and glory, have come to be used by the worshipping communities down through the ages to describe God's nature as praiseworthy, inspirational, and authoritative.

The New Testament records the final revelation of the sublime in the person of Jesus Christ, the Son of God, who, the writer to the Hebrews says, is "the radiance of God's glory and the exact representation of his being" (1:3).[20] John explains that although no one has ever seen God, the only begotten Son has revealed him (John 1:18). And John claimed that he and others were privileged to behold his glory (John 1:14). On the Isle of Patmos, John received the revelation of the risen Christ in glory, a vision that brought together the many revelations of the LORD given down through biblical history. In fact, when John reported how Jesus fulfilled the suffering servant prophecy recorded in Isaiah 53 as well as the ministry described in Isaiah 6, he explained that "Isaiah said this because he saw Jesus' glory and spoke about him" (John 12:41). It was the second person of the Trinity in glory, the preincarnate Christ, who was revealed to Isaiah as the holy LORD, high and lifted up.[21] And now that the Son of God has taken on mortal flesh (John 1:14) and fully revealed the Father (Matt. 11:27; John 1:18; Heb. 1:1–4), all true and complete worship must focus on the full revelation of God in Christ.[22]

---

19. See D. F. Coggin, *The Glory of God.*
20. Bloesch says that God's glory as the shining of his light in a dark world finds its fullest manifestation in his Son (*Essentials of Evangelical Theology,* 38).
21. Not only was the LORD high and lifted up in the vision, but at the cross Jesus was also lifted up to draw all people to himself. Even in his ignominious death he was exalted; thus, the essence of the sublime nature of Christ includes the glory of the cross.
22. Because Christ Jesus is the incarnate LORD God, the only true and living God, then it is impossible to conceive of worship without Christ. Worship that is not centered in Christ completely disregards the final and complete revelation of God in the new covenant.

But to the degree that a vision of the sublime has faded from the consciousness of religious people, adoration and reverence as well as obedience and service have also been diminished. For worship to rise above the clutches of a materialistic and secular world, the church must once again focus on such revelations of the LORD of glory. The revelations of glory revealed in Scripture will inspire all we do in the name of worship. Without them we, and our worship, will wither and fade; but with them we will be able to keep our eyes fixed on what is eternal (2 Cor. 4:16–18). And as we do so, we shall be changed into that glory, and all our expressions of worship will be more glorious (2 Cor. 3:18). Thus, properly motivated worship will be transforming.

## The Response to the Revelation

### The Immediate Response

The apprehension[23] of the revelation of the holy LORD God of glory will bring about an immediate response (Isa. 6:5), which, although varied from experience to experience in some of its outward expressions, is essentially one. Those who received such a glorious revelation were completely overwhelmed. After all, the visions were so glorious, so otherworldly, that mortals could hardly take them in. But what they had no trouble understanding in the light of those visions was their own frailty and sinfulness. When John on Patmos saw the vision of the risen Lord in glory, he fell to the ground as if he were dead (Rev. 1:17). Earlier revelations were not as complete as that which John saw, but they still were overwhelming. When Jacob awakened at Bethel from his vision of the LORD and the angels ascending and descending on the stairway, he was afraid. His immediate response was, "How awesome is this place! This is none other than the house of God; this is the gate of heaven" (Gen. 28:16–17). Then he responded with appropriate acts of worship. Job also was overwhelmed by a direct revelation from God and, although it was not a vision of the full heavenly court, he responded with reverential fear and self-disdain, or in the words of Isaiah, humility and contrition (Isa. 57:15). When God spoke out of the whirlwind, Job could only say, "I am unworthy—how can I reply to you? I put my hand over my mouth. I

---

23. The word *apprehension* captures both ideas of comprehending and accepting by faith what has been understood.

spoke once, but I have no answer—twice, but I will say no more" (40:4–5). Then after additional revelation he declared, "My ears had heard of you but now my eyes have seen you. Therefore I despise myself and repent in dust and ashes" (42:5–6).

Not only is there an acknowledgment of who God is, but there is also a confession. The prophet Isaiah was gripped with fear because he now realized his sinful condition. "Woe to me!" he cried. "I am ruined! For I am a man of unclean lips, and I live among a people of unclean lips, and my eyes have seen the King, the LORD Almighty" (Isa. 6:5).

Such revelations were not made to terrify or destroy people but to inspire them to greater devotion and service. And as we shall see, throughout the history of the faith there have developed a great number of appropriate responses to divine revelation, whether that revelation was as exceptional as one of these visions or simply the clear revelation of the written Word of God. Thus, in general terms, "worship" refers to the appropriate response to the revelation of the holy God of glory. More specifically, Christian worship, whether individual or collective, is the *structured and ordered expression of the proper response* of the people of God to the revelation of God in Christ. And in relationship to the whole life of faith, worship is actually the point of concentration at which the whole of the Christian life comes to ritual focus, for what we do in worship has a bearing on everything else we do in the faith, and how we live out our faith will impact our worship.[24] The Bible itself does not give a comprehensive definition of worship; it simply describes things that people have done or should do when they receive the revealing words and works of God.

In the Old Testament "worship" is the translation of a word that means "bow oneself down low to the ground" *(hishtakhăwāh)*.[25] The word can be used in secular contexts, such as in the accounts of Joseph's brothers bowing down to him (Gen. 37:10; 43:28). But its meaning in contexts where people bow before the LORD often includes more than the mere act of bowing to the ground. For example, in Genesis 22:5 it includes Abraham's plans to sacrifice; Abraham told his men: "We will worship and then we will come back to you." Also, Job's troubles prompted him

---

24. Wainwright, *Doxology,* 8. Some say that the whole Christian life is our worship. In one sense that is true, but the biblical language of worshipful acts is more specific.

25. The word has been traditionally connected to a root *shākhāh* (see BDB), but may actually be related to *khāwāh*. See Emerton, "The Etymology of *Hištaḥ͏ᵃwāh,*" 41–55.

to worship: he tore his robe, shaved his head, and falling to the ground he worshipped God (Job 1:20). The word also seems to have a wider reference in Exodus 24:1, where the LORD summoned of Moses and the priests and the elders to ascend the mountain "and worship from afar"; they were to participate in a number of acts of worship on Mount Sinai when the covenant was inaugurated. It also has a more general meaning in Exodus 33:10, which says that the people "stood and worshiped" the LORD from the doors of their tents. At Solomon's dedication of the temple, all the people "saw the fire coming down to the altar and the glory of the LORD above the temple," and they knelt "with their faces to the ground and worshiped and gave thanks to the LORD" (2 Chron. 7:3). Psalm 66:4 parallels the verb "worship" with singing praises.[26]

Likewise in the New Testament one key word for "worship" *(proskunéō)* also means "to bow down" (*kunéō,* "to kiss"). The word can be used for the simple act of kneeling before someone who is respected or revered (Matt. 8:2; 9:18). But it can also indicate the sense of full worship, as with the obeisance of the wise men before the holy child (Matt. 2:2, 8, 11), or when the disciples in the boat worshipped Jesus after he walked on the water (Matt. 14:33), or when the women clasped the feet of the resurrected Jesus and worshipped him (Matt. 28:9). This is the term used when Jesus declared that those who worship must worship in spirit and in truth (John 4:24). The word is used frequently in the book of Revelation, such as when the twenty-four elders fall down and worship the exalted Christ (4:10; 5:14; 19:4) and when the company of angels worship (7:11).[27]

The New Testament also uses *sébomai* for worship; it has the sense of giving reverential homage. The verb is used in Matthew 15:9 (and Mark 7:7), "They worship me in vain," indicating the honor the people gave with their lips (but not with their hearts).[28] When it describes the God-

---

26. The verb also can be used for the worship of false gods, for the same posture and accompanying mental and physical acts would be involved. It is used in the prohibition of idolatry (Exod. 20:5; Deut. 5:9) and reiterated with the confirming of the covenant in the land: "Do not invoke the names of their gods or swear by them. You must not serve them or *bow down* to them" (Josh. 23:7). The verb *bow down* signifies all that such an act would represent in worship.

27. It is also used in Revelation to describe unbelievers who worship demons (9:20), or those who had not worshipped the beast (20:4).

28. It too is used for false worship, as of the Greek goddess Artemis (Diana in Latin, Acts 19:27).

fearer or worshipper in the book of Acts, *sebómenos* refers to worship and
not just reverence. That it has something to do with exaltation may be
seen in the related noun *sebastós,* "reverend, august" (*augustus* in Latin),
which indicates an exalted place, usually a sacred place.

Thus both Testaments use words for bowing down and giving homage
to mean worship in general. To bow down before someone, a king or God,
is to show adoration, devotion, submission, and service; and by the physical act of bowing the object of the veneration appears higher and so is
exalted. And so when the Bible describes people bowing down before the
LORD, it usually means more of what that particular posture represents.
This was one posture that would be clearly understood.

## The Essence of Worship

The worshipful response to the revelation of the holy LORD God of
glory will have certain characteristics that may be exhibited in different
ways and with different levels of intensity. But they form the essence of
worship.

### Fear and Adoration

People respond differently to the mystery and majesty of God. On
the one hand when there is no appreciation of the mystery and majesty,
people are indifferent, curious perhaps, and at times irritated.[29] But the
positive reaction of wonder and reverence, which is the response of faith,
turns into acts of worship, for the revelation moves from evoking a sense
of fear and astonishment to one of self-abasement and adoration. Isaiah's
response was: "Woe to me! . . . I am ruined."

It is not surprising, then, that the expression "the fear of the LORD" is
used to describe the proper response of the worshipper. There are some
who are uncomfortable with the use of "fear" for worship, or "God-fearer"
for the devoted worshipper. But even the New Testament refers to the fear
of God as an essential part of piety and service (Matt. 10:28; Eph. 5:21; Heb.
12:28; 1 Peter 2:17; Rev. 14:7). Whenever we come into the presence of God
in worship and truly perceive who it is that we are worshipping, the natural

---

29. Meland's observations on how the scientific approach to life has dulled our sense of
    wonder, though dated, are still relevant today (Meland, *Modern Man's Worship*). The
    discoveries of science should increase our wonder over the power and the majesty of
    God.

response will be reverential fear. The absence of reverence in worship indicates that we do not think that God's presence is there in a special way.

The Old Testament word for fear *(yārē')* can mean "be afraid, stand in awe, reverence." Accordingly, that which is feared is referred to with forms of this word that mean "awesome, dreadful, terrifying." There is no problem understanding this meaning of fear or dread;[30] the difficulty is relating it to the positive meaning of "reverence." The English *revere* includes the ideas of regarding something as sacred or exalted, of holding something in deep and usually affectionate or religious respect, or of venerating. The religious sense does not eliminate the basic idea of fear but turns it into positive devotion. Like the Israelites at the base of the fiery mountain, we should shrink back from the Holy One because his power is terrifying—and yet we are drawn to him in adoration and wonder because his power is glorious. In worship we draw near to him because he has called us to draw near to him, and we want to be near him, but we do it with reservation and caution. On the human level the same tension between the two aspects of the word occurs, for people may be afraid of certain things and shrink back from them, but they are attracted to them as well—dangerous animals, tornadoes, or natural wonders. The presence of God is likewise both attracting and frightening.

For the sinful person who has every reason to fear God, the aspect of fear will be uppermost in the contemplation of God. But for the righteous person, who by God's invitation draws near to commune with God, the aspect of reverence will be uppermost, reverence tempered by the knowledge that he is the Sovereign Lord of all creation. When John saw Christ in glory, he fell at his feet as though dead; but then the Lord placed his right hand on him and comforted him in his presence (Rev. 1:17–18). The revelation of the nature of our Lord in glory ought to fill us with fear and wonder too, but that initial fear will turn to adoration and praise because he has made it possible for us to be with him.

### Confession and Commitment

If the revelation of God inspires fear and adoration, it also leads to spiritual renewal in the worshipper. Here is where the purpose of the

---

30. The basic meaning of the word is to express fear, or terror, as in life-threatening experiences (Jonah 1:5). This meaning also can be found in "religious" contexts, such as when people are afraid of the LORD's judgment.

revelation of the glory of God is realized, for the worshipper begins to participate fully in that glory. Fear and adoration alone do not constitute worship. Before the infinite God we must lose ourselves, for we are finite; but in his presence we find ourselves as we are renewed in our spirits daily (2 Cor. 4:16). Because the Holy One has made himself known to us in order to redeem us, and redeemed us in order that we might worship and serve him, we first must be conformed to his glory. At the outset there must be a personal acknowledgment, verbal or mental, of who this God is and of who we, the worshippers, are. This acknowledgment we call confession: we confess our faith in the Lord, and we confess our need of the Lord.

Isaiah's response was: "Woe to me!" When he saw the vision, he was filled not only with wonder but also with fear because in seeing the LORD in glory he was made fully aware of his sinfulness—he was unclean, with unclean lips, and dwelling in an unclean generation. His focus on his "unclean" lips was in contrast to the glorious words of praise that he heard coming from the lips of the angels; he realized that what passed from his lips was mundane and trivial. Conversely, it may also be said that those who never envision the holiness of the LORD never truly see themselves for what they are.[31]

Isaiah's confession of his unclean condition led to the removal of his impurity and his commission to service. Here, then, we see the spiritual progression that is to be reflected in true worship: *revelation:* the vision of the holy LORD of glory overwhelmed the prophet and uncovered his sinfulness; *cleansing:* his confession brought direct intervention from the LORD to remove the sin (6:7); and then *commitment:* once the prophet was cleansed from sin, he was able to hear[32] the word from God calling him to greater service. Isaiah's commitment was the proper and necessary answer to the point of the revelation: The LORD asked, "Whom shall I send?" and the prophet responded, "Here am I. Send me." Revelation demands a response; and commitment demonstrates that the worshipper has properly understood the revelation and desires to participate in it.

---

31. Tozer says, "A person who has sensed what Isaiah sensed will never be able to joke about 'the Man upstairs' or the 'Someone up there who likes me'" (*Whatever Happened to Worship?* 74).

32. The Hebrew syntax is very clear on the sequence here: *"then* I heard."

### Ritual Acts and Religious Observance

The worshipper is never to be a passive auditor of the words and the ritual of worship. Neither is worship to be a dry routine nor a formless ecstasy. It is designed for the consecration of all our faculties to God. Drawing near to God and receiving the revelation of God should inspire commitment to serve God.

Along with the word for "worship" ("to bow down"), we also find words for "serving," "keeping," and "ministering" used in contexts about worship. The verb meaning "to serve, do" *('āvad)* when used in religious settings, describes spiritual service in general but also specific duties in the sanctuary.[33] The verb for "to keep, observe" *(shāmar)*, when used in religious settings, refers to the keeping of religious practices, occasions, and institutions.[34] What these specific observations and duties are will be studied later. But the point to be stressed here is that genuine worship takes the form of spiritual service and religious practice. Accordingly, down through the centuries the faithful have used the word *service* to describe the order and intent of communal worship—the worship service—and the word *observance* to describe what practices are being followed. In the New Testament we shall encounter a word for the spiritual work or service of the people—*liturgy.*

A third word, meaning "to minister" or "to serve" *(shārat)*, is used for the work of priests and laity who serve at the sanctuary with the ritual, the incense, the music, or other activities (1 Sam. 2:11; 1 Kings 8:11; 1 Chron. 15:2), although it can be used for secular service as well. In the spiritual sense, it parallels the above words with its focus on service that is

---

33. The word emphasizes the submission and obedience of the servant to the will of God set forth in the religious rites and rules of the law (Josh. 22:5). It may be used for ordinary work (Deut. 5:13; Exod. 1:14), but it has a good number of uses for the service of God (Exod. 3:12; 4:23), showing absolute allegiance to God, sacrificing to him, worshipping him, and doing his will. Isaiah 19:21 uses the word in conjunction with serving the LORD with peace offerings. And Numbers uses the word for the work of the Levites and priests in the sanctuary (3:7; 4:23; 7:5; 8:11; 16:9; 18:6, 21, 23).

34. The verb *to keep* has a wide variety of uses, but in religious contexts it is used for keeping the commandments (Jer. 35:18), or the covenant and all its stipulations (Ezek. 17:14), or vows or religious duties (Deut. 23:21, 23). For further examples of religious uses, see Exodus 12:17; 23:15; 34:12; Leviticus 19:3, 30; Deuteronomy 5:12; Isaiah 56:4 (keeping Sabbaths); Exodus 23:15; 34:18 (celebrating Unleavened Bread); and Deuteronomy 16:1 (observing the New Moon and Passover).

the responsibility of the leaders of worship and caretakers of the sanctuary (see Num. 16:9; Deut. 10:8; 17:12).

The believer's response to revelation, then, leads to specific acts of devotion and service, and these specific acts and observances follow a variety of forms. They may be individual religious acts that are performed spontaneously, such as Jacob's worship at Bethel (Gen. 28:10–22). Or they may be organized ritual acts and regular observances of significant events that find their place in the life of the covenant community, such as thanksgiving convocations or communal meals. All churches have ritual of some kind, whether it is the way they have Holy Communion or how they conduct baptisms, ordinations, weddings, and the like.[35] The expression of their faith has been formed into various rites.

From the outset the ritual observances of the people of God have included certain features. First, at the center of worship is *sacrifice,* including the ritual representing atonement, gifts and offerings to express thanks and devotion, vows and dedicatory acts made secure at the altar, and other rites to perform and words to say. The ritual of sacrifice by no means disappeared with the New Testament, but it was transformed by the fulfillment in Christ.

Second, connected to sacrifice is *proclamation,* for a ritual act without appropriate words is open to any interpretation. The proclamation could take the form of invocations that properly identify the one being worshipped, creedal statements that might develop into full liturgy, public reading and declaration of the word of the LORD, or prophetic preaching based on the ritual with the intent to preserve and promote the faith. But in any case there must be proper and powerful words if the ritual act is to be understood. With the new covenant the content of all proclamation is made complete, and so it is imperative that the full revelation be used in the proclamation of the worshipping community.

Third, with the proclamation of the faith there is also *praise.* Whether the sacrifice focuses on the atonement provided by the Lord or the gifts presented to him, the occasion is naturally accompanied by praise. With the new covenant all forms of praise should be much more glorious than ever before in view of the full revelation in Christ, and the worshippers

---

35. All individuals have ritual as well, either in their daily routines or family traditions. There is something comfortable and reassuring about following familiar routines.

should be much more eager to praise in view of the nature of their salvation in Christ.[36]

Fourth, praise assumes there has been *prayer*, because the whole spiritual cycle moves from prayer to praise. If prayer is nonexistent, praise will be lost or, if routinely performed, hollow. Israel's sanctuary was a house of prayer because as people came together to worship, they came as a needy people with their prayers; and as they came to pray, others were there to give praise for answers to their prayers and to encourage those who were still praying. Worship without prayer would be unthinkable.

And fifth, worship included *covenant renewal*—some act of renewed commitment or dedication by the worshippers. This will almost always be a response to the Word of God read or expounded, but it will be inspired most by the dramatic celebration of communion with God. All of worship must lead to the transformation of the worshipper, who will then go out to serve the Lord in the world. Worship without significant service in the spiritual and physical needs of the community has fallen short of the divine plan.

The specific ritual acts and religious observances are designed to satisfy four basic senses of the human spirit as it responds to God. If it fails to do this, then it will be imbalanced if not deformed.

The first is the *intellectual sense*.[37] People must understand what the ritual acts mean. In Israel this understanding was to come from the messages of the prophets and the instruction of the priests; and in the church various leaders with appropriate spiritual gifts have been charged with the same tasks. Fulfilling this sense in worship demands the most preparation and the greatest clarity.

Understanding has two effects in worship: (1) it safeguards the expression of worship by ritual acts and religious observances from superstition and empty routine, and (2) it is the way by which worshippers learn how to relate the vision of glory to the reality of life. When they understand who the Lord God is, they realize that they live in a rationally ordered

---

36. But alas, it is missing, replaced by routine hymns and songs. D. Donnelly rehearses the familiar reasons for the absence of praise in "Impediments to Praise in the Worshiping Community," 39–53.

37. Services that focus on satisfying this sense more than the others are classified as "oracle" types (see Hislop, *Our Heritage in Public Worship*, 11).

universe, that the events of life have a reason, that there is a plan with a goal, and that outside the faith things cannot be fully harmonized.

The second sense is the *aesthetic sense.*[38] Ritual ceremony, symbolism, and the drama of reenactment in worship, have always been a part of religion.[39] When dramatic worship is combined with the proper reading and exposition of the Word, the impact is powerful and lasting. In Israel the worshippers were drawn into the worship in times of sacrifice and festival. They lived in booths, ate communal offerings, put blood on their doorposts, followed ritual processions, and performed a host of other dramatic and symbolic acts. They were not there to be observers.

And so, too, in the church drama and reenactment in worship are most effective in drawing people into the service and the spiritual life. Every church uses symbolism and ritual acts to one degree or another, whether in an elaborate formal service or on special occasions such as baptisms, weddings, funerals, dedications, sunrise services, musicals, children's plays—or the Lord's Supper itself.[40] The point is that people come out of themselves when they take part in some dramatic ritual. In those dramatic experiences they live out various aspects of their religious heritage again and again. And most of their actions are shared rather than individual acts, for they are a community.

This, then, leads to the third sense that worship should satisfy—the *corporate sense.* Worship was designed to be a communal activity, a time when the household of faith would assemble to praise God together, to pray for one another, to continue in the Word and encourage one another, and to commemorate together the sacrificial atonement that God provided to make them one. It is the participation in the ritual of the sacrifice that does the most for restoring the sense of community.

Under the influence of others, people act differently. If a group is evil, people can be easily influenced toward evil. But if the group is good, it can strengthen the goodness of the participants. This is why the psalmists desired to avoid the assembly of the wicked and to be with the congre-

---

38. See Susan A. Ross, "The Aesthetic and the Sacramental," 2–17; and Richard Viladesau, *Theological Aesthetics.*

39. The mystery or drama type of worship reaches back to the beginning of the church; the Eastern churches in particular follow this (Hislop, *Our Heritage in Public Worship,* 10–11).

40. See among others in the bibliography Stafford, *Christian Symbolism in the Evangelical Churches.*

gation of the righteous (e.g., Pss. 26; 42; 43). But communal worship also enables people to overcome their self-consciousness and their insecurity, for in the congregation their commitment to the faith is made courageous, as they become an important part of the visible corporate body. They realize how much they have to do with one another as the people of God as they gather together around the altar, become one in spirit as they pray for each other, encourage one another in praising and singing of their common faith, and are strengthened for their individual struggles in life as they hear testimonies and exhortations from others.

Accordingly, private worship or personal devotions, which are essential for the spiritual life, must lead into and find full expression in the assembly of the righteous, for private meditations must benefit others. This contribution to the spiritual life of others must not be lost in the emphasis on individual piety and personal responsibility; and it must not be excluded by the rigid uniformity of a service. Individuals have their unique roles in the work of the Lord; they are not to lose themselves totally in a crowd, but neither are they to function in isolation from the body. When the Israelites came together at the great convocations, the worship was greater and its benefits more lasting. The music was more glorious and the praising better than anything they had in their villages, and the prophetic messages were more powerful than the routine instruction and counsel of a local priest. Moreover, sharing the joys and sorrows of others was more readily facilitated by the larger company of believers with all their resources. And because believers still need such uplifting experiences, the New Testament warns people not to abandon assembling together (Heb. 10:25). After all, worship on earth is a prelude to glory when all the saints will be gathered together and will join the heavenly hosts in Paradise to praise and serve God forever.

Finally, there is the *moral sense*. Worship must develop this sense, otherwise the intellectual sense will become arrogance, the aesthetic sense will be entertainment, and the corporate sense an unguided assembly. Ethical and moral content must be clearly taught in the service, obviously present in the ritual and the ceremony of the service, and encouraged and inspired by the community.[41] In Israel it would have been hard to miss this emphasis even when the teaching was bad, for the ritual was

---

41. See Willimon, *Service of God*.

concerned with clean and unclean, holy and profane, and right and wrong. Everything about the formal worship service dealt with what was acceptable to God and of spiritual value for the life of the community. And even the glorious setting of the worship gave the sense that life had to be lived on a higher plane than that of the world with all its corruption.

In many congregations today the moral sense is addressed usually by communicating the Word of God for the purpose of meditation and of making decisions about what is righteous, just, honest, good, and compassionate. But all the other aspects of the worship must reinforce what the exposition of the Word seeks to do. In a word, worship must inspire a different ethic among the people, which in turn will have an impact on society.

But if the teaching only imparts information, and fellowship is equated with socializing, and the ritual acts are rushed and not explained, the moral sense will not be caught by the people. If worshippers leave a service with no thought of becoming more godly in their lives, then the purpose of worship has not been achieved. If they walk away from an assembly without a conviction that they need to conform their lives to Holy Scripture, even if it means changing their lifestyle, then worship has been perverted somewhere. For example, if people continue to be unkind, or mean-spirited, or self-centered, or immoral, then there has been a breakdown somewhere in the process. If they are not at peace with one another in the assembly, then they are not at peace with God and should not leave the sanctuary until they are. The clear teaching of Scripture is that genuine worship is life changing.

## Conclusion

Genuine worship is the natural and proper response to the revelation of the holy Lord God of glory. It will bring about reverential fear, confession, sacrifice, praise, and commitment. And when worship responds correctly to divine revelation, all four spiritual senses will be satisfied so that people will grow in grace and knowledge, live out their spiritual heritage, become one in the Lord, and walk in righteousness.

# CHAPTER 2

# Worship *as* Celebration

## The Need for a Working Definition of Worship

### Diverse Forms of Worship

In today's churches we have every form of worship from the very high church ritual to the very informal and unstructured assemblies. Most churches give attention to a number of the aspects of worship found in the Bible, which they may have perfected, but few if any give a balanced attention to them all. For example, some equate worship with liturgy and ritual—and it all runs smoothly and richly; but there may be no place for individual praise and thanksgiving and very little attention given to preaching or teaching. Or some may designate a time of singing songs and praises as their worship, leaving the impression that the rest of the activities of the service are not worship.

Most churches do not have a worship committee to evaluate what they are doing and ensure that all the needs of the people are being met. And there are scores of people who would love to step into more meaningful and glorious ways of worshipping if given the opportunity, but they are limited by their church's format.

But things can go too far in the other direction as well if churches simply give people what they want, that is, adapt worship to what is popular or appealing rather than instruct and inspire people in what they should want. This is the easiest thing to do; it is most often prompted by the desire to have a well-attended church. Accordingly, there may be a greater emphasis on making worship more enjoyable, more entertaining, and more attractive and convenient to modern Christians. While these efforts do have value in the whole ministry of the church (the festivals in Jerusalem were appealing), the form and substance of worship is not to be set by popular preference (in Israel that led to idolatry) but must draw people out of the world. In the final analysis we must recognize that entertainment is not worship, that simplifying and shortening sermons, music, and prayers weakens worship, and that good attendance does not in and of itself mean that worship is taking place.

In other churches the service may be predominantly filled with teaching or preaching. No one would ever fault the desire to instruct and exhort people from the Word of God. In fact, an emphasis on this may be refreshing to those who have grown up in services that had short, ten-minute homilies. But if the sermon fills up most of the time, too many aspects of worship will be crowded out, and as a result "worshippers" will become listeners and observers. The sermon, so important to worship, is not by itself worship.

On the other side, where formal liturgy predominates, all too often it is the sermon that has been crowded out, the time being given to other activities. Perhaps it is assumed that because the Word of God is behind the liturgy it therefore does not need much attention by itself. Whatever the reasons, a lack of biblical instruction, coupled with the absence of individual praise and thanksgiving, leads easily to routine and empty ritual. A church may have beautiful rituals and profound liturgy, but the perfunctory performance of the rites can be carried out with little worship taking place. It takes a tremendous effort by faithful worshippers to keep things alive for the benefit of their own worship when those who should be bringing it alive do not.

The popularly named renewal movement has been trying to bring life back into worship services. Now more and more frequently congregations are (literally) faced with "worship teams"—which actually are a number of singers and musicians—who function as leaders for the time of worship (the time of worship refers to the music and praise leading up to the rest of the service). The music is usually contemporary, and the praise brief exclamations. But these times of worship, even though involving the congregation, often follow a set pattern at a particular time in the service with repetitious songs. Thus, in fact, a new form of liturgy has emerged, which may be every bit as predictable and repetitious as prayer book worship. And the brief expressions of thanks between choruses are a far cry from the clear and rich praises and thanksgivings that the devout psalmists offered in the assembly of the righteous. Without solid biblical content in the music, in the readings, and in the sermon, it is no wonder that the church has produced a crop of inarticulate Christians.

It seems that churches have each gotten a few pieces of the biblical picture and made those their form of worship. Then, once their ideas of "worship" have been formed and defended, there is tremendous resistance to change, even if it is change that will improve and not replace what they are already doing. Some churches are very comfortable with the way that they have always done things and cannot imagine anyone else is right. Annie Dillard writes:

> The higher Christian churches—where, if anywhere, I belong—come at God with an unwarranted air of professionalism, with authority and pomp, as though they knew what they were doing, as though people in themselves were an appropriate set of creatures to have dealings with God. . . . In the high churches they saunter through the liturgy like Mohawks along a strand of scaffolding who have long since forgotten their danger. If God were to blast such a service to bits, the congregation would be, I believe, genuinely shocked.[1]

The task is for each worshipper and each congregation to develop worship as fully and meaningfully as possible, not necessarily to replace their tradition, but to embrace more of the biblical patterns and principles. This calls for a thorough study of passages that deal with the subject, careful planning and preparation with much prayer, and a regular evaluation of all that is being done.[2] Just as a sermon that has not been prepared will not be easy to listen to, or a choir number that has not been practiced will be painful to hear, so a worship service that has not been developed properly will be off-putting and distracting. Oh, the Spirit of God can rescue things from all of our poorly developed activities and use them to speak to people. But that does not justify the

---

1. A. Dillard, *Holy the Firm,* 60.
2. Most denominations have done studies in worship and may even review it frequently; they have also produced books that set forth their worship and their hymns. This is as it should be, of course. But all worshippers need to discover for themselves what worship is all about and how to improve it, and this must come from the Bible itself. After all, our worship of God must continue to develop throughout life.

poor efforts. God requires that everything we offer to him be the best that we can do.

It should be clear by now that the subject of worship is complex; it encompasses all the biblical information as it was revealed and developed over the centuries, and all the extrabiblical traditions and teachings down through the history of the faith. And because there are so many things that are part of what we call worship, it is very difficult to write a definition that is both clear and complete. If we try to cover all the ideas in a general way, our definitions will be too vague; and if we try to be too specific, we end up leaving too much out.

What makes the task of defining worship difficult is not only that the Bible includes so many things but also that its essential features were progressively revealed to and through various groups of believers over the centuries. A study of the subject, then, must trace worship through the Bible in order to uncover the patterns in their historical development and then identify the principles and acts that remain constant for worship in the church today. Some of the outer forms of worship may have changed over time, but the recurring patterns carry the principles forward to fulfillment in the New Testament.

What is needed in a thorough study of all the biblical material in sufficient detail to formulate the basic principles and patterns of worship, beginning with creation and culminating in glory, when worship will be perfect. The intent of this book therefore is to take the readers through the Bible so that they may see these patterns and principles emerge and in the process understand more fully their Christian heritage and thereby discover ways to improve their worship. This is not simply a theology of worship; it is an inductive study of the biblical material as it was revealed over time, for the purpose of identifying the abiding theological truths that must inform our worship today.

This kind of Bible study cannot be done quickly. In fact, there is so much material that it would take a lifetime to analyze it all and put it into practice. But that is how God planned it. For all believers it should be an ongoing study throughout their spiritual journey. But with each step on the journey, new insights will be gained into this life-changing subject of true worship.

## Diverse Definitions of Worship

Definitions are helpful in that they enable people to organize a complex body of material with a unifying statement or paragraph.[3] For worship we have an interesting array of definitions and descriptions, all of which are helpful in one way or another, but none of which is completely satisfying as a thorough *working definition* for biblical surveys such as this.[4] Some broaden worship to cover all of Christian activity.[5] Worship definitely has a bearing on everything we do, but the biblical text uses the words and descriptions of worship for the special acts of the people of God in private or communal devotion. Others focus on such acts but try to capture the idea of worship with easy-to-remember statements, such as "worship is praise," or "worship is the response of the creature to the Eternal,"[6] or worship is "a dialogue between God and his people,"[7] or worship is "a meeting between God and His people."[8] Of course, all of these statements are true; and they are designed to lead into discussions that elaborate on the details. But people often use the definition and forget the clarifying discussions. For serious, thorough study of the subject, people need to consult the Bible every step of the way; and a working definition that guides that study will prove most helpful.

The standard introductory books and Bible dictionaries do refer to worship acts. *Harper's Bible Dictionary,* for example, says that *worship* is the attitude and acts of reverence to a deity. The *New International Dictionary of the Bible* is a little more specific, saying that *worship* is "the honor, reverence, and homage paid to superior beings or powers, whether men, angels, or God."[9] In other words, worship involves an *acknowledgment* of the higher power or powers in word and deed.

These definitions are certainly more useful than the popular approach of explaining worship on the basis of the etymology of the English word

---

3. For some general definitions that have been used in the past, see E. D. Reed, "Questions People Ask: What Is Worship All About?" 68–74.
4. A working definition will not be a "bumper-sticker" type of statement. It will be more comprehensive, including all the major parts of the subject in order to give direction to the study of the subject.
5. Melton, *Presbyterian Worship in America,* 9.
6. Underhill, *Worship,* 3.
7. Huxtable, *The Bible Says,* 2.
8. Webber, *Worship: Old and New,* 11.
9. "Worship," in *New International Dictionary of the Bible,* 1,070.

*worship* from "worthship," meaning that worship is the acknowledgment of the supreme worth of God—God alone is worthy of our praise. But this does not clarify what worship is or what it does.

Schaper is more specific, saying that worship is "the expression of a relationship in which God the Father reveals himself and his love in Christ and by his Holy Spirit administers grace, to which we respond in faith, gratitude, and obedience."[10] Rayburn is more specific with regard to the object of our worship: "Worship is the activity of the new life of a believer in which, recognizing the fullness of the Godhead as it is revealed in the person of Jesus Christ and His mighty redemptive acts, he seeks by the power of the Holy Spirit to render to the living God the glory, honor, and submission which are His due."[11] While no one would argue with gratitude, honor, obedience, and the like, the details of what we are to render are only broadly referred to here.

If we want to be able to trace these specific details of worship, our best approach is to have a working definition based on what the Bible reveals about the requirements and responses that are the essential elements of worship. Individual worshippers and various groups could then use it to guide their Bible study of the subject. Once people begin to probe this matter of worship, they will discover a richness and a depth to their spiritual experience that they never imagined. Once they catch a vision of the risen Christ in glory and are transported to sing with angels, it will become harder and harder to remain in lifeless and uninspiring services.

## Developing a Working Definition

Any definition of Christian worship must be formulated within the framework of the Trinitarian nature of the faith. Our worship must be God-centered. This should be obvious, but we often lose sight of it and focus our attention on people. If worship loses its God-centeredness, it ceases to be a holy convocation and may become something akin to a common assembly, a rally, a theatrical performance, or an awards ceremony. This is not true worship. People should come away from a worship service with a fresh awareness of the majesty of God, with a desire to glorify God, and with renewed commitment to serve God.

---

10. Schaper, *In His Presence*, 13.
11. Rayburn, *O Come, Let Us Worship*, 20–21.

Second, worship must be in Christ, the Son of God, who came into the world and brought salvation to us. Because he is the full revelation of the Godhead and the one way of access to the Father, he must be the focal point of worship. If he is not and we try to worship God without reference to the divine Son of God, then we have failed to follow God's revelation through to its culmination in the plan of redemption. Believers should come away from a worship service with a renewed assurance of the grace of God through our Lord Jesus Christ, of forgiveness through his blood, of acceptance into his eternal kingdom, and with a fresh commitment to give him the preeminence (Col. 1:18).

Third, because the Holy Spirit is the one who enables all spiritual service, all genuine worship must be by the Spirit. Without falling into the error of denying the physical part of worship, we must recognize that worship is to be spiritual—inspired by the Spirit, empowered by the Spirit, genuine and life-giving because it flows from the Spirit. And as this happens, the Spirit will not draw attention to himself but will point to Christ, will not lead into error but into righteousness, and will not produce responses that are foreign or out of harmony with the Word of God but will empower the Word to produce fruit in the lives of the worshippers. When worshippers come away from a service that has been truly spiritual, they will come away with zeal to love and serve the Lord. It will not be contrived or forced, and it will not be momentary enthusiasm; rather, the Spirit will continue to work in them to produce godliness.

The following definition provides a concise statement of the essence of worship, followed by clarifications of how it is expressed in the acts of worship. It is designed to be the starting point for a thorough study on the subject of worship:

> **True worship is**
> > **the celebration of being in covenant fellowship with the**
> > **sovereign and holy triune God,**
> > > **by means of**
> > > > **the reverent adoration and spontaneous praise**
> > > > **of God's nature and works,**
> > > > **the expressed commitment of trust and**
> > > > > **obedience to the covenant responsibilities, and**

**the memorial reenactment of entering into
covenant through ritual acts,
all with the confident anticipation of the fulfillment
of the covenant promises in glory.**

The choice of the word "celebration" as the key word is appropriate.[12] The word captures all the festivity and the ritual and the praise that is present in biblical worship. And if the worship is led by the Spirit and in conformity with the Word, then the celebration will not deteriorate into pagan or worldly festivities.

It should be noted that a regular "worship service" *per se* is not commonly found in the Bible. Whenever believers assembled in sanctuaries, it was for different aspects of worship—sacrifices, festivals, covenant renewals, ordinations, prayer, and the like. These could be called services but are usually designated by their functions. There are only a few passages that lay out parts of the orders to be followed in certain "services" and words to be said. In the New Testament the Jewish believers in Jesus added to their temple and synagogue attendance the regular gathering together in homes for apostolic teaching, fellowship in Christ, the breaking of bread, and prayer. Then in Paul's letters we see descriptions of what the believers were doing when they came together in their assemblies. Accordingly the early church quickly developed various orders of activities that were followed in the assemblies, and much of this has remained through the centuries. But these too followed different patterns for different occasions.

Describing worship as a celebration does not nullify the fact that it is a service or that there are solemn and serious aspects to it. All worship is service to God, even though not all service is worship in the proper sense. Worship is service in that it is the obedient response to the revelation of the Lord God. The Psalms are filled with commands for the righteous to enter his courts with singing, or to give praise to him, or to bring the thank offerings to his altar. But worship is also service in that it will inspire spiritual growth and provide encouragement for faithfulness.

---

12. The *American Heritage Dictionary* defines the verb *celebrate* to mean: (1) To observe (a day or event) with ceremonies of respect, festivity, or rejoicing. (2) To perform (a religious ceremony). (3) To announce publicly, proclaim. (4) To extol, praise.

The idea of worship as celebration is governed by what is being celebrated—being in "covenant fellowship with the sovereign and holy triune God." The focus is certainly on the nature of the sovereign God of glory; but the glory of it all to us is that we have been brought into covenant with this God. Contemplation of such a God without a covenant might inspire awe and wonder but not celebration; and celebration of a covenant without any perception of God, with whom the covenant is made, would not inspire much awe and wonder.

This word *covenant* may not be familiar to some people. It refers to a treaty, a pact, or an agreement made between two or more parties. A covenant is usually based on some significant event in history and includes both the benefits and the obligations of the parties who enter into the agreement. People often entered into such treaties with other people, promising by solemn oath through ritual sacrifice to abide by the agreement. God used this well-known form to assure his people that he was their God and they were his people. So at Sinai, for example, he established a covenant with Israel based on the fact that he had redeemed them from bondage. By doing so he entered into a unique relationship with them. In that covenant he made promises to them, promises that were both temporal and eternal, and he swore by himself to fulfill them; but he also set forth obligations that they were to meet if they wanted to be his people and to enjoy his benefits. The agreement was then sealed by the shedding of blood in a sacrificial ritual. In the New Testament the eternal Son of God established the new covenant with believers and sealed it with his own blood, thereby making it an eternal covenant. This covenant, also referred to as a testament (hence, New Testament), promises salvation through the forgiveness of sins and all related blessings in this life and the next; but it also includes obligations for the recipients of the covenant to demonstrate their love and devotion to their covenant Lord. It is this union with God, this covenant that is sealed and secure through the sacrifice of Christ, that is at the heart of Christian worship.

Based on this focus of worship, our celebration is expressed in a number of ways (in the subpoints of the definition).[13] The first is "by the reverent adoration and spontaneous praise of God's nature and works." This

---

13. This working definition, then, has the advantage of giving the essence of worship and providing summary descriptions for all the individual activities that are included in it. A study group could easily develop this definition into a full outline of the subject.

would include the response of fear and adoration, the contemplation of the wonder and majesty of God, expressions of faith, doxologies, thanksgivings, hymns and songs of praise, and affirmations of compliance and commitment to the one true and living God.

The second way this celebration is expressed is "by the expressed commitment of trust and obedience to the covenant responsibilities." Part of communal worship is the renewal of the covenant, rehearsing its nature and renewing commitments to its stipulations. This presupposes the public reading of the Word, where we hear the responsibilities, exhortations and teachings on them, encouragement and approval for compliance with them, as well as opportunity for correction and amendment of ways. Worship should also provide opportunity for many of these duties to be performed—making and fulfilling vows, presenting gifts and thank offerings to God, and reconciliation with others. It should also inspire spiritual service, such as committing time and talents to God in faithful stewardship, sharing the faith with others, and ministering to the needs of people in the community. These are our covenant obligations.

The third way this celebration is expressed is by "the memorial reenactment of entering into covenant through ritual acts." The people of God preserve in their memory their entering into this covenant: on God's part the means was sacrificial atonement, and on their part the means was faith in and identification with the death of Christ. Baptism and Holy Communion are the main rites that Christ instituted for his church. And since ritual reenactment and meditation go hand in hand, relevant themes such as confession and forgiveness of sin, and reconciliation with God and one another, are all necessary parts of this aspect of worship.

But all such acts of worship would be uninspired and weakened, if not meaningless, without the vision of the hope of glory, the anticipation of the fulfillment of the covenant, both its promises and our perfection. As we worship we celebrate our salvation through Christ who will bring us to glory, we pray for that kingdom to come, we quicken our hope by praises and anthems that direct our thoughts to the next life, and through the ministry of the Word we build our faith in this eternal hope. In this light our worship, and the Lord's Supper especially, takes on eternal proportions, leading us to look forward to the heavenly union with Christ Jesus. As Charles Wesley wrote,

> Yet onward I haste
> To the heavenly feast:
> That, that is the fulness; but this is the taste;
> And this I shall prove,
> Till with joy I remove
> To the heaven of heavens in Jesus' love.[14]

So our worship must be eschatological.[15] It should not only prepare us to live and serve in this world in view of the coming of the Lord, but it should also celebrate victory over the world. And that victory over the world should find practical expression in demonstrating how the faith can transform the world and all its problems into what God had intended from the beginning. Thus, when some worship services regularly proclaim that "Christ is coming again," that proclamation should inspire the worshippers to take the revelation of the nature of God and the work of Christ and the powerful ministry of the Spirit and turn them into practical, relevant directives for Christian living that is above this present but temporary evil world system and into practical ministry to those who are in bondage to the world—and do it all with urgency.

It has been this hope of glory that has inspired the worship of God from the very beginning. And it has been characteristic of the faith that over the centuries as worship has developed, worshippers have carried forward the principles and practices of the faith. All our worship looks back and recalls the biblical and historical events that have shaped our tradition; but in recalling the principles and practices of those earlier stages in the household of faith, we also recall their inspiration for worship—the hope of glory. And it is our inspiration as well. Our worship after all is a celebration of the great works of our glorious Lord, especially his saving deeds, with a view to their fulfillment in glory. And if the aspects of the order of our worship form a reenactment of and response to God's plan of redemption, they are at the same time a foreshadowing and rehearsal for that time when we shall worship in the heavenly sanctuary

---

14. Charles Wesley, *Methodist Hymn Book,* vol. 3. (London: n.p., 1933), no. 406.
15. "Eschatology" is the study of last things, what the Bible predicts will happen at the end of this age and in the ages to come. Worship is eschatological in the sense that it looks to continue, with perfection, in glory.

with the angelic choirs. Until that time we are merely tuning our instruments;[16] but we may persevere in improving our worship by constantly recalling the hope of glory. In that way we may build on the glorious heritage that we have received so that in every way it may be even more glorious.

---

16. John Donne, cited in Lewis, *Reflections on the Psalms,* 97 (without reference).

# Conclusion *for* Part 1

WORSHIP IS NOT A CHOICE, but a divine imperative. God has been calling his people to worship from the beginning. Accordingly, Jesus declared that the Father was seeking true worshippers (John 4:23). Knowing the will of God in this matter, believers down through the centuries have been trying to appreciate and develop proper and meaningful worship practices. That is the task for every new generation of believers; and every generation must preserve the heritage that it has received and build on it. But at the heart of this effort is the need for believers to recapture the vision of the exalted and holy LORD of glory, that is, the sublime; for to the degree that worshippers apprehend the glory of the Lord, their worship will be purified of base instincts and elevated to the level of true and spiritual worship. Unfortunately, almost everything in our nature and in our world pulls us back from that; and without a good knowledge of the biblical revelation on the subject, worship becomes routine, centered on people and performances, and secularized. And the sense of celebration of being in covenant fellowship with the living God is lost.

How then shall we proceed to recapture this vision of the central focus of worship? One good way to start is with a regular meditation[1] in those passages that describe the glorious manifestations of the LORD, revelations and visions of the LORD in glory, passages like the transfiguration of Jesus, or the revelation of the risen Christ (Exod. 24; Isa. 6:1–3; Ezek. 1:4–28; Matt. 17:1–13; 2 Cor. 3:7–18; Rev. 1:9–20, to name but a few). These will effectively focus our thoughts on the God of glory and therefore the hope of glory. As this becomes a fixed part of our thinking, we can begin searching the whole revelation of God to discover the patterns of worship

---

1. As we shall develop later, meditation involves the careful study of the text, the memorization of the text, prayer to God about that text, and self-exhortation over the meaning of that text.

that will inspire us to greater glory in our worship. But unless we capture that vision, we will not be very successful. This book is designed to assist believers in their diligent study of the Word of God toward that end.

What will become evident in the process is that the biblical material is not so much concerned with particular styles and methods but with proper attitudes and expressions. Worship is a far more complex subject than we often realize, for we too often focus on simple "how-tos." The biblical patterns and principles leave open a wide range of ways to do things, allowing for diversity within the faith. Our own particular form of worship does not exhaust all the appropriate worshipful responses that we could make. In fact, this study will show how far we are from "perfecting" the worship of the holy God.

# PART 2

# THE MEMORY *of* PARADISE

# Introduction

God, by his powerful word, created the universe and everything in it. This beginning revelation of the Bible is clear enough, but understanding it is anything but simple—it is, in fact, beyond human comprehension. Moreover, the account of creation in Genesis was not written to answer all our questions about the beginnings of our universe; it includes just enough information to present its theological message. Its brevity and mystery are due in part to the fact that it was written in an elevated prose that comes close to being a hymn of creation.[1]

Genesis begins with the declaration that God created the heavens and the earth and then traces God's great acts day by day. It begins with the creation of light, the necessary beginning, for without the provision of light to dispel the darkness there would be no life. Immediately then God made divisions in creation, separating the darkness and the light and separating the waters below an expanse of air called sky from the waters above it. God appointed light-bearers in the heavens, the sun to have dominion over the day and the moon to have dominion over the night, along with the heavenly host of stars. He then gathered the waters that were on the earth together to make huge seas, causing dry land to emerge.

On this dry land lush vegetation began to grow, filling the earth with grasses and shrubs and trees. Furthermore, the land, the skies, and the seas were soon teeming with life that God created. But the crowning point of all creation was the formation of humans, male and female, to be the very image of God; these humans were to rule and have dominion over the earth. With this, all of creation was now perfect and pleasing to God.

---

1. It is not a hymn, of course. Compare its form with psalms of creation: Psalms 8; 136; 148; or with Proverbs 8:22–31; and even with Job 38. On the emphasis of God the Creator, see Habel, "Yahweh, Maker of Heaven and Earth," 321–27; and idem, "He Who Stretches Out the Heavens," 417–30; and also Vawter, "Yahweh," 461–67.

What power! What imagination! What a glorious Creator-God! No wonder the angelic hosts shouted for joy when the LORD laid the foundation of the earth (Job 38:4–7). And those heavenly choirs continue to praise him because he created all things and by his will everything exists (Rev. 4:11). Such is the greatness of the Creator.

When creation was complete, that is, when the heavens and the earth and everything in them had found their place in time and space, God entered into a season of refreshing celebration, what was called his *Sabbath* rest. Then began the Creator's full enjoyment of the perfect working of all his handiwork in undiminished harmony with his eternal plan—and he concluded that it was all very good. So God set that time apart to be a perpetual reminder of the bliss that the fulfillment of the plan of God brings.[2]

After this overview Genesis focuses specifically on the creation of Adam and Eve and the garden of Eden (2:4–25). This section tells how the LORD God formed man, gave him the divine breath that made him a living human being with the capacities to commune with God and keep his commandments, and provided a corresponding partner to share these capacities and responsibilities; by these capacities they were enabled to function as God's representatives on earth. It also tells of the provision of a Paradise in which they could serve God and enjoy his creation. The passage also records the divine stipulations they were to follow if they were to continue in that life.

These first two chapters of the Bible provide an unparalleled revelation of the LORD, who is the majestic and sovereign God of creation. This revelation is not only foundational to the faith but is also essential for worship: The LORD God alone must be worshipped because he is sovereign over all things—he was before all things, and by him all things exist. If the angels celebrated the work of creation with praise, then we who say we know God surely must also praise him for this work, especially since the world with all its sophisticated learning seeks to eliminate the idea of creation and thereby rob the Creator of his honor.[3]

---

2. See Weinfeld, "Sabbath, Temple and the Enthronement of the Lord," 501–12.

3. A common approach to these texts today is to take them as symbolic rather than factual. But as Hoekema observes, if it is all symbolic then we know nothing of how man fell into sin (*Created in God's Image*, 128). Accordingly, there would be no reason to praise God as the Creator or Redeemer, for there would be no basis for these ideas.

The faithful in Israel certainly praised God for creation in their hymns and psalms. They were aware of the bizarre ideas about creation in the mythological beliefs of the pagans, and in striking contrast to them they declared in their holy writings that everything was created by the decree of the one, true and living God.[4] The psalmist expresses this point precisely: "For he spoke, and it came to be; he commanded, and it stood firm" (Ps. 33:9). Here was the unambiguous witness to the sovereignty of God. And this focus on his sovereign Word also provided a powerful instruction for the worshipping community: if all of creation exists because of the decree of God, then the way to life and blessing in God's presence would also be through obedience to the Word of God. For example, the law of Israel said, "You shall have no other gods before me" (Exod. 20:3); and the account of creation made it clear that there were no gods before God, for everything that the pagans worshipped was made by him. How foolish it would be to worship the creation and not the Creator (see Rom. 1:25). Again, the law said, "You shall not make for yourself an idol ['graven image' in KJV] . . . You shall not bow down to them or worship them" (Exod. 20:4–5); and the account of creation reminded people that they themselves were the image of God. How foolish and how blind it would be to make a god after the image of a human (see Isa. 44:9–20)—God made people as his image. In similar ways all the stipulations of the law were based on the will of the Creator. Thus, all creation sings in response to the one who gave all things life.

---

4. Pagan creation myths include a cosmic battle among the various deities, resulting in the victorious deity creating the earth out of the carcass of another deity (see A. Heidel, *The Babylonian Genesis,* 3–10).

# CHAPTER 3

# The Memory *of* Creation

## Creation and Redemption

Creation has always been foundational to the faith of the worshipping community, not only because it displays the power and majesty of the Creator, but also because it provides the basis and even the pattern for God's great work of redemption. For example, in the judgment of the Flood and the redemption of the race through Noah, we find a "re-creation" theme: everything was put back under water as it had been in the beginning.[1] And then, after the world was purged, the dry land appeared as in the beginning; and eventually Noah, the new Adam, along with his family, started a new life—but now with grateful worship (see 1 Peter 3:20–22 for the use of this as an example of salvation). Some of these motifs also were used in the redemption of Israel from the bondage of Egypt: God used the sea to destroy wickedness and redeem his people so that they could emerge on the other side of the flood to begin a new life with worship and praise (see also 1 Cor. 10:1–4). Other writers of Scripture also used the language and the motifs of creation to describe God's saving acts. For example, the "Song of Moses" praised God as Israel's "Creator" because he redeemed them from bondage and formed them into a nation (Deut. 32:6). And the prophecies in Isaiah 45–49 frequently reminded Israel that the God who redeemed them was their Creator (Isa. 44:21–22). By "redemption" God "created" the Israelites as his covenant people.

With this association of creation and redemption in mind, we may identify additional motifs in the accounts. For example, just as the Holy Spirit was at work in the creation of life, so is he with salvation. Or again,

---

1. See Clines, "The Creation—Un-creation—Re-creation Theme of Genesis 1–11," 61–79.

just as God caused light to shine out of the chaos and darkness so that new life could be formed,[2] Paul declares, "For God, who said, 'Let light shine out of darkness,' made his light shine in our hearts to give us the light of the knowledge of the glory of God in the face of Christ" (2 Cor. 4:6). And just as God makes divisions between the light and the darkness, so he makes divisions for his people between good and evil, and clean and unclean (e.g., Lev. 11:8; 1 John 1:5b–7). God's work of redemption is in fact a new creation, for the Lord re-creates the spiritual life by breathing his Spirit into the human heart and making the redeemed conform to his image (John 20:22; 1 Cor. 12:13; 2 Cor. 3:18). Paul declares, "Therefore, if anyone is in Christ, he is a new creation" (2 Cor. 5:17a). Those who are new creations, that is, the redeemed, enter into God's eternal rest, that *Sabbath* rest that was first introduced at the culmination of creation (see also Matt. 11:28; Heb. 4:9). Again and again the motifs of creation are used in texts that pertain to redemption.[3] The worship of God, the Creator, is therefore also the worship of God, the Redeemer, for what God did in creation set the pattern not only for redemption but also for the worship of the redeemed.

And the goal of creation and redemption is communion with God. This communion finds its first expression at the culmination of the creation narratives, where the LORD God was present with his people in Paradise—the Garden of Eden. Adam and Eve could enjoy God's presence; they could walk with God, commune with God, and serve God with undiminished capacity in their garden sanctuary. Communion with the living God is at the heart of all worship; and where God is present with his people is a sanctuary.[4]

## The Creation of the Sanctuary

When *immediate* access to God came to an end because of sin, God provided a way for his people to enjoy *mediated* access to him. This was

2. For the different views of the passage, see my discussion on Genesis 1:1–3 in *Creation and Blessing;* also Waltke, "The Creation Account of Genesis 1:1–3," Part 3, 216–28; and Konkel, "בהו"[*bōhû,* "void"], 1:606–9. But see also Tsumura, "The Earth in Genesis 1," 310–28.

3. See J. G. Gibbs, "The Relation Between Creation and Redemption According to Philippians 2:5–11," 270–83; and idem, *Creation and Redemption.*

4. See Haran, "The Divine Presence in the Israelite Cult and Cultic Institutions," 251–67; and I. Wilson, *Out of the Midst of the Fire.*

most clearly laid out when God instructed Israel to build a sanctuary so that he could dwell in the midst of the people he had formed. And since it was to be built according to a revealed pattern (Exod. 25:8–9), it is no surprise that the instructions included many motifs and ideas from creation, notably Paradise. This was true not only of the tabernacle in the wilderness, but also of the Solomonic temple; and it is true also of the prophetic visions of the new creation yet to come.

Wherever God's presence dwells is a holy place, a sanctuary.[5] Therefore, when Israel's desert shrine was called a "dwelling place" for the LORD, it was not that God needed such a place but rather that the people needed a place that facilitated their access to God (see 1 Kings 8:27; 1 Chron. 17:4–6). Such a place had to preserve the holiness of God on the one hand and make allowances for the human condition on the other. Therefore, because the God who dwelt in their midst is holy and pure, the people had to be made pure and holy by some means in order to draw near. And since God's perfect work of creation was marked by sanctified rest, every time people entered the sanctuary they were leaving the work of the outside world, with all its conflict, pain, and death, to celebrate life and peace in a special *Sabbath.*[6]

God's dwelling place with Israel was holy in its physical layout. The shrine itself, the tent, was situated in a large courtyard, and it was divided into the Holy Place and the Most Holy Place. The entire courtyard was set apart from the world by a curtain partition. That outside world, creation at large, was contaminated and to a large degree alienated from God; but inside this special area was the domain of God preserved in a fallen world. All the people of God could enter into his courts to commune with him and worship him, provided they followed the prescribed orders. Only the priests could enter into the actual tent, the Holy Place; and into the Most Holy Place, the presence of the LORD, the high priest alone could enter on behalf of the congregation.

This sanctuary complex reflected the regions of original creation. The

---

5. Of course, God is everywhere. But the dwelling place for the LORD refers to the place God chose to be with and meet with his people in a special way. The word *mishkānôt* ("dwelling place" [plural], s.v. *shākan*) has traditionally been translated "tabernacle," referring to the tent spread over the wooden framework and walls of the holy place.

6. Every major assembly for worship was designated as a special *Sabbath* (see especially "sabbath of sabbath" [*shabbat shabbātôn*]) in Leviticus 23:32.

land outside the sanctuary represented the world of God's creation,[7] albeit contaminated by sin and death; the courtyard of the sanctuary corresponded to the region of Eden, the place of blessing and enjoyment for the people of God, provided their sin and defilement had been dealt with; and the sanctuary itself with its Most Holy Place recalled the Garden of Eden, the place where God walked (i.e., communed) with his people.

These correspondences between the regions of creation and the arrangement of the sanctuary bring to mind another similarity, that people are separated from God by their disobedience and defilement and are barred from the presence of God just as Adam and Eve were prevented from returning to the garden by the guarding angels. The only way back to God is through his provision of redemption so that people who once were alienated from God might enjoy restored communion with their Creator. And because this restored communion with God is not limited to a spiritual sense of fellowship with God but ultimately includes a full and eternal communion, spiritually and physically, in the very presence of the living God, the structure and substance of Israelite worship was designed so that people might trace the process of redemption in word and act from the place of sin to the glorious presence. So what do we find? Worshippers approached the sanctuary with reverence, responded to God's Word with confession and a commitment to obey, and then drew near to the divine presence through sanctifying ritual acts. Then they could celebrate being with God. Before sin entered the world, "worship" was in effect pure celebration, adoration, and enjoyment of God; but after sin entered the world, "worship" had to include the process of gaining access into the presence of God as a new creation for that celebration. And since the process was a provision from God's grace, it was received with thanksgiving and reverence by the worshippers. Their praise of the Creator now necessarily included praise for his new work of creation, redemption. And this will continue in glory: the angelic praise will still be for the Creator (Rev. 4:11), but with the saints present it will also be for the Redeemer (Rev. 5:9–10).

Accordingly, the setting for Israel's worship was designed to draw the believers back to that communion with God, time and time again, until they would finally be gathered into the presence of God in glory.

---

7. Deuteronomy uses lavish descriptions to present the land as blessed with the best of creation (see Deut. 8:7–9; 30:11–20).

With this in mind, everything in the sanctuary spoke of a re-ordered world with the Creator at the center, recalling the original creation, but anticipating what was yet to be in the world to come. Solomon took it to a grand scale, placing huge columns in front of the temple to represent the pillars of the earth (1 Kings 7:21), and a huge laver of water in the courtyard to represent the sea (1 Kings 7:23–26).[8] Levenson explains that the temple was the epitome of the world, a miniature cosmos; as such it was to communicate that in God's domain there is a peace, stability, and order.[9] The laver in this sacred world symbolized the containment of the chaotic seas, under the dominion of the LORD who was enthroned nearby in the Holy of Holies.[10] Even around the rim of Solomon's "sea" was arboreal and vegetation symbolism that reflected God's creation.

All of this greatly enhanced the Israelites' understanding of the one whom they were worshipping. The temple was not just another place of worship but a reminder of God's creation in its pristine order—a little Paradise. Like the Garden of Eden, the sanctuary was the place where heaven and earth converged—the LORD was in heaven, and he was also in his holy temple. Thus, Isaiah could stand in the earthly sanctuary, and peer into the heavenly sanctuary and hear the angelic choirs (Isa. 6:1–4; John 12:41). The heavenly place was the "spiritual" sanctuary, the ultimate reality; the earthly place was the "physical" copy, functioning in the reality of this life. Levenson explains: "The Temple and its rites, especially those of a purgative character, can be conceived as the means for spiritual ascent from the lower to the higher realms, from a position distant from God to one in his very presence."[11] The earthly place represented the heavenly because it participated in that to which it pointed.

---

8. See further Wylie, "On King Solomon's Molten Sea," 86–90.

9. Levenson, *Sinai and Zion*, 138–39.

10. The sea was considered a force of chaos, one that the pagans explained with gods or monsters and a cosmogonic battle. The Hebrew poets used some of their designations to teach that the LORD controlled these "seas" (Pss. 74:12–17; 89:9–11; Isa. 51:9–11; see for some details Wakeman, *God's Battle with the Monster*). Sarna cautions that the biblical fragments that seem to refer to these gods or to a cosmogonic combat myth have been included for metaphorical and polemical purposes and that those figures were never afforded divine attributes or said to form any challenge to the LORD (*Understanding Genesis*, 22–23).

11. Levenson, *Sinai and Zion*, 142. Levenson here draws on Paul Tillich, *Dynamics of the Faith* (New York: Harper and Row, 1958).

Along with these general observations on the way the sanctuary was a reflection of the setting and order of creation in a fallen world, the report of its completion strengthened this reflection by mirroring the language used to describe creation.

## The Construction of the Sanctuary

### The Arrangement of the Instructions

In the wilderness God instructed Israel on how to make the sanctuary, essentially a tent over a portable building made of interlocking boards.[12] But these instructions have some interesting parallels with creation.[13] Among the studies attempting to trace these parallels, P. J. Kearney focuses on the instruction section of Exodus 25–30.[14] Observing the introductory formula "Yahweh said to Moses," he was able to identify seven speeches giving instructions for the building of the tabernacle, the first six dealing with the work itself and the seventh an instruction to observe the *Sabbath* day.[15] So, there were six days to make the earth and six steps in the instructions to make the tabernacle; and then there was rest.

### The Completion of the Construction

#### The Plan

Even closer parallels with creation may be found in the section on the actual construction of the sanctuary (Exod. 35–40). Chapter 35 opens with a call to observe the Sabbath (vv. 1–3) and then gives instructions for the preparations for making the tabernacle, which is actually a sum-

---

12. Canaanite gods dwelt in tents (Ugaritic Tablet III K iii 18019; Aghat IID v 31–33), and the tabernacles were made with boards (Tablet V AB v 17). See Cassuto, *Commentary on the Book of Exodus,* 322–23; see also Clifford, "The Tent of El and the Israelite Tent of Meeting," 221–27.

13. W. P. Brown, *Structure, Role, and Ideology.* Leibowitz says, "Just as God created the world . . . , so is man called upon to use all the bounty with which God has endowed him—nature's resources, animal, vegetable, and mineral, and prepare for his presence a dwelling place on earth among the children of Israel" (*Studies in Shemot,* 2:697).

14. Kearney, "Creation and Liturgy."

15. The chapters have seven sections or speeches: the first speech (a long one) is Exodus 25:1–30:10, the second is 30:11–16, the third is 30:17–21, the fourth is 30:22–33, the fifth is 30:34–38, the sixth is 31:1–11, and the seventh is 31:12–17.

mary of the previous seven speeches (vv. 4–19). The account of the fulfillment of the instructions of chapters 25–31 begins with the report that all the congregation with willing hearts brought the supplies as a freewill offering (Exod. 35:20–29), thus fulfilling Exodus 25:1–7.

### The Agents

We are then introduced to the leaders and workers in the construction (Exod. 35:30–36:7). Bezalel and Oholiab were endowed by the Spirit of God (see 31:2) with the ability to do the work and instruct others. And the people who took part were all those whose spirits moved them to do so. Brown lays out the following parallel structure between these participants in the building of the tabernacle and the agents of creation: In Genesis God gave the commands, the Holy Spirit moved upon the creation, and the creation itself (the sea, the land, the trees, the living creatures) became a creating order, bringing forth life, so that the product was the creation of our world; in Exodus God again was the head of the hierarchy, giving the orders, Moses as the messenger assumed the divine role (according to Exodus 39:43 it was Moses who saw the work and blessed it), the Spirit moved upon the people, the new creation itself, inspiring them to produce the work so that the product was the construction of the sanctuary.[16]

### The Fulfillment

The detailed report of the construction is then recorded in Exodus 36:8–39:31. In these chapters we find interspersed seven times the expression "just as Yahweh commanded" (including 36:1; then also 38:22; 39:5, 21, 26, 29, 31). This correlation between the command and the fulfillment is reminiscent of the way Genesis 1 is written ("God said . . . and it was so"). This pattern reaches its culmination in Exodus 40 where we read that Moses did as Yahweh commanded (v. 16, repeated in v. 19). The statement that the glory of Yahweh filled the place (40:34–38) indicates divine approval—it was very good!

### The Completion Report

The wording used in the completion report for the tabernacle also

---

16. W. P. Brown, *Structure, Role, and Ideology,* 212.

parallels the completion report for creation.[17] In Exodus 39:32 we read, "So all the work on the tabernacle, the Tent of Meeting, *was finished.* The Israelites *did* everything just as the LORD had commanded Moses, so *did they.*"[18] And in Genesis 2:1–2 we read, "Thus the heavens and the earth *were finished* and all their vast array; by the seventh day God had *finished* his work which *he had done.*"

Then Exodus 39:43 says, "And Moses inspected all the work and *saw* that *they had done* it as the LORD had commanded; even so *did they.*" And in Genesis 1:31 we have: "God *saw* all that *he had done,* and behold, it was very good."

After the completion of the work, there was the blessing. In Exodus 39:43 we have the statement that "Moses *blessed* them" because they had done all the work of the LORD. And in Genesis 2:3 we have, "And God *blessed* the seventh day" because on it God rested from all his work.

And again, in Exodus 40:9 we read that the LORD instructed Moses, "And *you shall sanctify it . . .* and it shall be *holy.*" And in Genesis 2:3 we have, *"and he sanctified it."*

So there is a deliberate attempt to show that the construction of the sanctuary paralleled the work of creation, as if to say, this was God's new creation of his dwelling place on earth.

## Symbolism in Solomon's Construction

The account of Solomon's building the temple provides additional links with creation. It took Solomon seven years to build the temple (1 Kings 6:38); it took seven days for the divine King to create the world (Gen. 2:2). Moreover, Solomon dedicated the temple during the Feast of Tabernacles (1 Kings 8:2), a seven-day feast in the seventh month (Deut. 16:13); and his speech has seven specific petitions (1 Kings 8:31–53).[19] And when completed the temple was to be God's resting place (*m$^e$nûkhāh*, Ps. 132:13–14), reflecting how God rested on the seventh day.

---

17. Weinfeld thinks that this parallel between Genesis 2:1–3 and the completion of the tabernacle, when the LORD enters his resting place, is the best of all these connections. See "Sabbath, Temple and the Enthronement of the Lord," 501–12.

18. I have made the translations a little more literal in this instance and in other places throughout the book to show the exact correspondences that are there.

19. See Levenson, "Paronomasia of Solomon's Seventh Petition," 131–35; and idem, "Temple and the World," 275–98.

## Conclusion

The temple was to be the one place on earth where the people could enter into the rest of God and again be in the sanctuary where the LORD God dwelt. For the worshipper, entering the rest of God and entering the dwelling place of God were one and the same.[20] The *Sabbath* rest sanctified time and creation, and the dwelling place sanctified space and the history of redemption, or re-creation.[21] Like the Garden of Eden, the sanctuary was rich, and beautiful, and pure; and everything in it was in its proper place as God's presence would require. Like creation in general, the sanctuary was to be a world by itself, an ordered, supportive, and obedient environment where God dwelt. If we look more closely at the record of creation with this in mind, it will become clear that the Garden of Eden was a "sanctuary" with features and figures that subsequently adorned the sanctuary of Israel, the place of worship.[22]

---

20. See Ahlstrom, "Heaven on Earth—at Hazor and Arad," 67–83.
21. Levenson, *Sinai and Zion,* 145.
22. See G. J. Wenham, "Sanctuary Symbolism in the Garden of Eden Story." Wenham notes that we should not be surprised to see this aspect of the Garden of Eden, for Genesis 1–11 is filled with motifs about worship.

CHAPTER 4

# The Memory *of the* Center *of* Creation

## The Garden in Eden

In the center of God's creation, there was a garden; and although no sinful person since Adam and Eve has seen it, it remains in human memory as the epitome of beauty, tranquility, and fertility (Gen. 13:10). Genesis says, "Now the LORD God had planted a garden[1] in the east, in Eden; and there he put the human he had formed. And the LORD God made all kinds of trees grow out of the ground—trees that were pleasing to the eye and good for food" (2:8–9a).[2] This garden was to be the one place in the world where all the beautiful and beneficial gifts of God were concentrated.

When the end of the story tells how the sinners were not allowed to remain in this garden, we learn that there was something far more important about it than its beauty and fruitfulness, something spiritual. It was where the LORD God walked in the midst of his creation,[3] where the man and the woman had immediate access to God in a perfect environ-

---

1. The ancient idea of a garden would be an enclosed area containing a variety of plants, flowers, shade and fruit trees, fountains and pools of water, and birds and animals. It would usually be protected by a wall or hedge and entered through a gate. It was symbolic of nature re-ordered and perfected, or at least of creation cultivated aesthetically. Assyrian reliefs depict terraced gardens with large trees, water channels, and aqueducts, as well as small temples. See Cornelius, "גַּן" [*gan,* "Garden"], 1:875–78.
2. The name *Eden* has been taken to mean "pleasure," but it probably describes the place as fruitful. For the meaning of "lush fecundity," a sign of God's presence, see Millard, "The Etymology of 'Eden,'" 103–6.
3. The verb in Genesis 3:8 for "walking to and fro" is used elsewhere of the LORD's "walking" in the sanctuary (see Lev. 26:12; 2 Sam. 7:6–7).

ment—before they rebelled.[4] It was the place of God's presence on earth. Nothing else could account for the special life-giving properties of the garden—it was the "garden of the LORD" (Gen. 13:10). Later the place was called "Paradise" (*Paradeisos* in the Greek), a term borrowed from Persian that refers to the inner garden of the king.

This description of the garden has striking parallels with descriptions of the dwelling places of gods in other literature in the ancient Near East.[5] The Mesopotamian accounts preserve the memory of the place where their deities dwelt as a garden unparalleled in splendor, filled with beautiful and fertile trees, and rich with precious gems. And it too was the source of life-giving water, where the rivers and the primal deep converged. There on a cosmic mountain[6] the deity was said to meet with the divine council and issue decrees.[7]

In the Israelite tradition, Ezekiel 28:12–19 provides us with more details about the creation setting. In the process of denouncing the proud king of Tyre, the prophet uses language descriptive of creation and a fall in Eden:

---

4. The note that they heard the "sound of the LORD God walking about in the breezy part of the day" (Gen. 3:8) suggests a familiarity with his presence as well as something ominous after the sin (Wallace, *Eden Narrative*, 79).

5. See among the other works listed here, Cornelius, "Paradise Motifs in the 'Eschatology' of the Minor Prophets," 41–83.

6. See Clifford, *The Cosmic Mountain in Canaan*. Genesis does not mention any mountain with Eden, but Ezekiel 28:13 seems to do so (whether earthly or heavenly one cannot say for sure). But in prophetic passages Mount Zion, the dwelling place of the LORD, and its surrounding area, was expected to be like Eden (Isa. 51:3), a place of safety and security (Isa. 11:9). Features connected to the garden are also linked to Israel's holy mountain (see Ps. 48:2; Isa. 33:20–24; Ezek. 47:1–12).

7. Wallace suggests that some of the language of Genesis might be taken to mean that there was present in the garden a host of supernatural beings, if not a divine council, when God spoke to the sinners. He suggests that the expression in Genesis 3:5 "be like God" (*kē'lōhîm*) could be translated "like gods" because the form as usual is plural and because the participle following is plural: "knowers of (*yōd'ʿê*) good and evil." Genesis 3:22 says that God said, "they have become like one of *us*." Of course there are other, perhaps more compelling, ways to interpret these expressions; but it is still possible that angels (e.g., the cherubs) were there. Wallace (and others) makes further connections with Canaanite (Ugaritic texts) parallels where El ("God"—the high god) was said to make decrees from the cosmic mountain in the presence of the "sons of god," who in Canaanite texts are lesser deities but in the Bible angels (as in Job 1–2; see Wallace, *Eden Narrative*, 80–81).

You were the model of perfection,
   full of wisdom and perfect in beauty.
You were in Eden,
   the garden of God;
every precious stone adorned you:
   ruby, topaz and emerald,
   chrysolite, onyx and jasper,
   sapphire, turquoise and beryl.
Your settings and mountings were made of gold;
   on the day you were created they were prepared.
You were anointed as a guardian cherub,
   for so I ordained you.
You were on the holy mount of God;
   you walked among the fiery stones.
You were blameless in your ways
   from the day you were created
   till wickedness was found in you. . . .
So I drove you in disgrace from the mount of God,
   and I expelled you, O guardian cherub,
   from among the fiery stones.
                    (Ezek. 28:12b–16)

Some modern interpreters argue that Ezekiel was applying an old account of the creation and fall of man to this king, as if he were the one created and placed in Eden, to show that Tyre (the man and his city) was mortal after all. But older, traditional interpretations conclude that there is more—that in denouncing the evil king the prophet began to address the spirit-force behind him (as in Dan. 10:13), a spirit-force who was actually in Eden.[8] However the oracle is to be explained, the text de-

---

8. At the center of the issue is the identification of the "cherub" in Ezekiel 28:14. The traditional views were not contrived to fit an interpretation of prophecy—they follow the Hebrew text: "You were the anointed guardian cherub" (*'att kᵉrûv* [אַתְּ־כְּרוּב] *mim-shakh hassôkēk* [the feminine pronoun is rare for the masculine, but see GKC 32g]). The one to whom Ezekiel was speaking was the anointed *cherub*. Some, however, reject the Masoretic Text in favor of the Greek to obtain the reading "with" (*'et* [אֶת־]); this would avoid having the king referred to as a *cherub*. It would then mean, "the anointed cherub was with you" (see Leslie Allen, *Ezekiel 20–48*, 94–95; and Eichrodt, *Ezekiel*, 394). The MT reading is more difficult and still the better reading.

scribes Eden as a place rich with gems and gold, a place associated with the mount of God, a place where the anointed *cherub* walked in perfection and beauty until he sinned and was cast from the presence of God.

Other passages describe Israel's temple in terms reminiscent of the garden. The psalmist tells of the blessings believers receive there: "They feast on the abundance[9] of your house; you give them drink from your river of delights (lit., "river of *your delights*," *ʿǎdāneykā*, "your *edens*"). For with you is the fountain of life; in your light we see light" (36:8–9). The house of the LORD was like the Garden of Eden; it was where the people had access to God, received all the blessings of life, and feasted on the peace offerings and drew from the living water—but they were prohibited from entering the Most Holy Place, past the curtain embroidered with cherubs.

Also, in prophecies about the coming of the Lord, we have the same connection. Isaiah 51:3 foretells the restoration of the Holy City with these words: "The LORD will surely comfort Zion and will look with compassion on all her ruins; he will make her deserts like Eden, her wastelands like the garden of the LORD." Such fertility will be present because God will once again be in the midst of his people.

If these passages were the only ones that described Israel's sanctuary in terms of the Garden of Eden, we would have enough to say that Paradise was thought of as a sanctuary, and the sanctuary a Paradise, a place that was known as God's dwelling place on earth. Indeed, all the features of the garden are also represented in the sanctuary.

## Features of the Garden

### The River of Life

One feature of the garden was life-giving water. At first there was a subterranean source of water (*ʾēd*, "mist," NIV "streams") that used to go up from the earth and water all the fertile soil (Gen. 2:6).[10] Then the text

---

9. The word *fatness* (*déshen*) is used a number of times for the fatty ashes of the sacrifices in the sanctuary (Lev. 1:16; 4:12). Since the usage here is followed by "your house," the temple, that is probably its meaning—they eat from the sacrifices. It teaches that believers receive the best from the LORD.

10. For a study of the word, see Speiser, "*ʾĒD* in the Story of Creation," in *Oriental and Biblical Studies,* 19–22.

reports that "a river watering the garden flowed out from Eden, from there it was separated into four headwaters" (2:10). Although it is impossible to locate Eden, the four rivers indicate that it was somewhere in the area of the Fertile Crescent.[11] The Tigris and the Euphrates flow from the top of the Fertile Crescent down to the Persian Gulf. The Pishon went around Havilah, a general term that refers to parts of the Arabian peninsula as well as northeastern Africa, and the Gihon went around Cush, which may be Ethiopia or the Babylonian region of the Kassites.[12] If Havilah and Cush are located to the southwestern end of the crescent, and the Tigris and Euphrates flow from the northeast around Assyria to the southeast, then the center might have been in the middle of the crescent, perhaps even overlapping with the Promised Land (bounded by the river of Egypt and the Euphrates River). Be that as it may, the point is that a river of living water flowed from Eden, the presence of God, and separated into four rivers that flowed through the lands around it. From the garden God made provision for life.

The memory of a river of life was preserved in other ancient religions as well. According to texts from ancient Mesopotamia, the garden where the gods dwelt was the source of life-giving water. In Canaanite texts as well, the god El is said to have dwelt at the crosscurrent of the rivers of the deep.[13]

Interestingly, there are biblical texts that also associate a river of living water with the sanctuary city of Jerusalem.[14] Isaiah 8:7–8 describes an impending invasion of Assyrians in terms of a flash flood: the river Euphrates would overflow its banks and flood the land of Israel up to the neck (meaning Jerusalem). This was going to happen because the people had rejected the true source of their stability, the "gently flowing waters

---

11. Speiser suggests a location at the mouth of the Persian Gulf ("The Rivers of Paradise," in *Oriental and Biblical Studies,* 23–34). But this would mean the rivers flowed north.

12. *Gihon* is a fairly common word for a spring or river of water, since it is related to the word for "gush forth." It is not surprising then to see it used for a spring in the valley below the oldest part of the city of Jerusalem (1 Kings 1:33, 38); the name Gihon invites comparison of Mount Zion with Paradise.

13. But see also the Semitic motif of fresh water above the sky (D. Nieman, "The Supercaelian Sea," 243–49).

14. "Living water" is fresh water. Levenson notes that these texts reveal that only the water of life flowed here because the temple was the guarantee against chaos, i.e., the seas (*Sinai and Zion,* 152).

of Shiloah" (8:6). Shiloah was the pool that collected the water from the spring of Gihon in Jerusalem.[15] So the prophet used two rivers that originated in the remote past; one to represent the force of chaos, the invading army, and the other to represent tranquility, the provision of God. Shiloah was connected to the Holy City, where the LORD dwelt; it was a place that was safe and secure, a place where living waters caused the faithful to rejoice rather than fear the invasion, for with that water they could withstand a siege. However, by not trusting the LORD they rejected his provision of security.

Psalm 46, a psalm of confidence, also locates a river of water near the sanctuary. In contrast to the raging sea, the chaos in the world, the writer declared that the Holy City was a safe haven of peace and tranquility: "There is a river whose streams make glad the city of God, the holy place where the Most High dwells. God is within her, she will not fall; God will help her at break of day" (vv. 4–5). The reference is probably to the same fresh water flowing from the springs under the city of God; it was a symbol of God's provision of life and peace in the midst of chaos. Again, the provision of life-sustaining water in a time of siege would have been a great advantage; but the true source of security was the presence of the LORD, the one who gave this water of life. Like Psalm 36 with its allusions to Eden (vv. 8–9),[16] the river signified God's provision and protection flowing from his presence in the sanctuary.

Moreover, when the prophets foretold the dramatic changes that were to take place at the end of the age, they included the description of a river that would refresh the world so that it could flourish in paradisial splendor. Ezekiel foresaw water gushing out from under the temple and going eastward, miraculously flowing deeper and deeper until it filled the valleys and wadis, providing life to the desert regions so that the arid land could flourish and people could even fish from the once dead Dead Sea (Ezek. 47:1–12). Zechariah envisioned how at the coming of the LORD the Mount of Olives would split in two, and fresh, life-giving waters would

---

15. The Hebrew word *shilōakh* may have meant "sent," indicating the water came by a channel or aqueduct from the upper Pool of Gihon. The Greek is *Silōam* and *Silōa*. Today the pool is popularly known as Siloam.

16. The psalm makes several allusions to creation: God's judgments are a great "deep"; his provision of life as "a spring of life"; and his light as the source of "light and life." The use of the "river of your pleasures" makes the reference to the garden obvious.

flow from the house of the LORD, half to the Dead Sea, and half to the Great Sea (Zech. 14:1–21). And Joel, speaking of a time of eternal peace when foreigners would never again invade the land, tells of a fountain that will flow from the temple (Joel 3:17–18). Many would interpret these passages symbolically, but because of the details of the predictions and the connections to creation, it seems most likely that they are part of the new creation of this world (see also Rom. 8:22).

And this connection is carried forward to the vision John saw of the heavenly city coming down, lit by the presence of the LORD God himself: "Then the angel showed me the river of the water of life, as clear as crystal, flowing from the throne of God and of the Lamb down the middle of the great street of the city" (Rev. 22:1–2a). Again, many interpret this to be merely symbolic of God's provision of life.[17] It certainly is symbolic; but that does not rule out the possibility that there might be a physical reality to it, especially in the light of the other prophecies of the renewal of creation.[18] The connection to Genesis is clear enough: the revelation of the river of life draws upon the memory of the river of Eden as the source of life, indicating that in the glorious age to come the true Paradise will be revealed in the new heavens and the new earth.

## Gold and Precious Gems

In addition to the provision for life coming from the garden, we have the provision of wealth, and beauty, and brilliance.[19] Wherever the river flowed, the land was rich with the purest gold and with precious stones. First, we have *bᵉdōlakh,* possibly bdellium, but NIV interprets it as an aromatic, transparent resin, yellowish in color.[20] One clue to its appearance comes from the comparison with *manna* that looked like coriander seed (see Num. 11:7; Pss. 78:24; 105:40). Genesis also mentions the onyx

---

17. A biblical example would be John 7:38–39, where Jesus taught that the Spirit would flow like a river from the heart of the believer.
18. Symbols in the Bible can be both literal and symbolic. Perhaps the best example in early Genesis is the serpent.
19. Gispen, "Genesis 2:10–14," 115–24.
20. We are not sure of the precise meaning of some of these stones mentioned in the Bible because they are often mentioned without a description. For my purpose the exact nature of the stones is not that important; their association with the LORD is. I will normally use the English translations for the different gems found in the NIV but will add clarifications or adjustments along the way.

*(shōham)*, a chalcedony (a class of quartz crystal) often with milky white bands alternating with black (or red).[21]

The oracle in Ezekiel 28 adds to the description of the riches of Eden by listing additional precious stones associated with it. These included the ruby *('ōdem)*, topaz *(pit'dāh)*, emerald *(yāhălōm)*, chrysolite *(tarshîsh)*, onyx *(shōham)*, jasper *(yāsh'phēh)*, sapphire *(sappîr)*, turquoise *(nōphek)*, and beryl *(bār'qat)*.[22] Nine jewels in all were set in gold filigree to form the covering for the one who was in the Garden of God.[23] The jewels indicate a rich blessing from God, the best that creation contains. But it was all forfeited because of sin, which brought the expulsion from the "fiery stones."[24]

Interestingly, in the literature of the ancient world, precious gems were included in the gardens of the gods. In the *Gilgamesh Epic* of Babylon, there is a garden of jeweled stones (Tablet 9.4.44–46); in fact, the fruitful trees in the region are depicted as gems: the carnelian bears its fruit, and the lapis lazuli bears its fruit (Tablet 9.4.48–51).[25] These ideas indicate the richness of the dwelling place of the gods.

When we turn in the Bible to the record of God's instructions for the building and furnishing of the sanctuary, we find gold and precious gems

---

21. Cassuto takes the *b'dōlakh* as a gem (Greek: carbuncle, crystal) but says the identity of *shōham* is uncertain (*From Adam to Noah*, 1:77, 120).
22. Studies suggest the following descriptions or identifications. What is called the ruby may be closer to a dark carnelian, or a sardius like red jasper; the topaz is a green gem, perhaps peridot; the emerald is a very hard stone, perhaps a jasper; chrysolite may be the beryl, a sea-green color, perhaps feldspar, although some maintain that it is the golden yellow chrysolite; the onyx, as mentioned above, is a chalcedony, often with white bands alternating with black or red; jasper is an opaque quartz, red-yellow or brown; what is called the sapphire is probably lapis lazuli, azure blue with gold flecks (because the modern blue sapphire may have been too hard for them to engrave); turquoise may be turquoise but is more likely emerald or green feldspar; and the beryl is greener than the sea-green beryl, more like an emerald, although some suggest the word refers to a red carbuncle.
23. The LXX translation has all twelve stones that are found in the high priest's breast pouch, obviously supplying the missing three. See further on the stones, Yaron, "The Dirge over the King of Tyre," 28–57; and see McKenzie, "Mythological Allusions in Ezekiel 28:12–18," 322–27.
24. The "fiery stones" have been interpreted as gems by some and as angels by others. For detailed discussion, see further Habel, "Ezekiel 28 and the Fall of the First Man," 516–24; and Fensham, "Thunder Stones in Ugaritic," 273–74.
25. *ANET*, 89.

there as well. The people brought precious metals for use in different places in the sanctuary. Around the courtyard the implements were covered with silver; in the courtyard the furnishings were with bronze; but in the Holy Place everything was covered with gold, and, in the holiest place of all, the top of the ark of the covenant with the carved cherubs was made of solid gold. The increasing value of the metals corresponds to the increasing closeness to God. Later, when Solomon built the temple, he spared no expense but used vast amounts of gold, silver, bronze, and sparkling gems (see 1 Chron. 29:2–9).

For the priestly garments the people also were to bring, among other things, precious gems (Exod. 25:7; 1 Chron. 29:2). Two onyx stones were set in gold filigree and attached to the shoulder pieces of the high priest's ephod. On each stone were engraved the names of six of the tribes of Israel (Exod. 28:9–14; 39:6–7). Then four rows of three precious gems were to be set in gold filigree and attached to the breast piece or pouch that the high priest would wear (Exod. 28:17–20; 39:10–13). The stones on the top row were the ruby *('ōdem)*, topaz *(pit<sup>e</sup>dāh)*, and beryl *(bāréqet)*. The second row had the turquoise *(nōphek)*, sapphire *(sappîr)*, and emerald *(yāhǎlōm)*. The third row had three new stones: a jacinth *(léshem,* an orange color, perhaps amber), an agate *(sh<sup>e</sup>vô,* a variegated quartz), and an amethyst *('akhlāmāh,* a purple stone). And the bottom row had a chrysolite *(tarshîsh),* onyx *(shōham),* and jasper *(yāsh<sup>e</sup>phēh).* The names of the twelve tribes were inscribed on the stones the priest wore. When he entered the Holy Place to make intercession, it was as if the people once again entered the sanctuary of God, a place most fitting for all the precious gems.

When the prophets later wrote of the future glorious city and temple, precious gems were prominent in the description. Isaiah 54:11–12 records the revelation of God to the afflicted Holy City: "I will build you with stones of turquoise, your foundations with sapphires; I will make your battlements of rubies, your gates of sparkling jewels, and all your walls of precious stones." The city made with precious gems may be symbolic of the righteous people of God as many have concluded,[26] but that symbolic

---

26. The symbolism would indicate that this was to be a place characterized by purity, quality, and brilliance. Peter used similar imagery to declare that Jesus is the living Stone, the fulfillment of the prophecies about the Stone, and that believers are also living stones, built up into a spiritual house (1 Peter 2:4).

use would not necessarily preclude the future realization of a glittering central dwelling place in a rich new creation where the LORD would be in the midst of his people.[27] Similarly, John describes in more detail the heavenly city (Rev. 21:10–21).[28] While there are widely diverging interpretations over his vision, the inclusion of gold and precious gems[29] certainly links the passage with the Isaianic prophecy, as well as with the sanctuary and the garden. This revelation of the glorious creation to come may provide a glimpse of the spectacular aspects of that new creation, a creation characterized by an abundance of everything that is beautiful and prized, especially in the presence of the God of creation.

## The Trees of the Garden

The garden of Eden was therefore a place of beauty as well as a place of provision. And both of these aspects are further displayed by the fact that the garden was filled with every kind of tree that was beautiful in appearance and good for food. This was true in the pagan world as well. According to the *Gilgamesh Epic*, the dwelling of the gods was surrounded by all kinds of luxuriant trees (Tablet 5.1.1–9 [Assyrian Version]). It was in a forest that Gilgamesh and Enkidu battled Humbaba, whom the god Enlil put there to guard against trespassing humans (2.5.1–2).[30] And as already noted, trees in this region were depicted as gem-bearing "fruit" trees (9.4.48–51). The biblical record has no gem-bearing trees. But in the middle of all the trees of the garden there were two special trees, the Tree of Life, and the Tree of the Knowledge of Good and Evil.

---

27. In addition to the description of the city, Isaiah adds material about the people of the city in a way that indicates the subjects are distinct. It is interesting to note that the apocryphal book of Enoch describes seven mountains of precious stones that appear at the end of the heavenly firmament, one of which supports the throne of God and is covered with sweet-scented trees (18:6–9, 23–25).

28. Because the city is portrayed as descending like "a bride" (Rev. 21:2), many take the view that it is the church; but it is difficult to harmonize that interpretation with the end of the chapter, which says believers will enter the city (21:27).

29. John lists the gems in a different order and has four new gems. The analysis of the gems in the book of Revelation is a separate but related study. In spite of the variations, the point is that gold and precious gems are identified with Paradise and with the sanctuary.

30. For text and commentary, see Heidel, *Gilgamesh Epic and Old Testament Parallels*.

## The Tree of Life

The Tree of Life was designed to be a source of perpetual life.[31] This is clear from the fact that God prevented Adam and Eve from eating from this tree and living forever (Gen. 3:22). Apparently eating from it would have perpetuated life or, in some sense, preserved access to immortality.

In the religions of the ancient Near East, there were in the temple reliefs stylized sacred trees. And in Mesopotamian literature we read about plants that were believed to bestow immortality, or at least youth. Thus, in the *Gilgamesh Epic* the search for the sacred tree (or plant) of life is prominent.[32] Immortality was thought to be possible because the Babylonian hero Utnaphishtim gained it, though only by divine assistance and exceptional circumstances. Likewise in the *Descent of Ishtar* into the netherworld, there was a plant of life in addition to the water of life. But the quest for immortality required an ascent to the gods above or a descent to the netherworld below the sea.[33]

In some of the ancient texts, a sacred tree with healing powers grew in a place of abundance between the mouths of the two rivers. It was rooted in the subterranean water,[34] and its appearance was that of lapis lazuli. No one ever entered there except the gods Enki, Shamash, and Tammuz.[35]

In the ancient Near East, and still today, a clump of trees was a sign of blessing because it meant there was water—life! And apart from any

---

31. The syntactical construction of "the Tree *of* Life" should be interpreted to mean a tree that was life-giving, that which produced life.

32. See P. Watson, "The Tree of Life," 232–38; and Veenker, "Gilgamesh and the Magic Plant," 199–205; and see further, Paul, "Heavenly Tablets and the Book of Life," 345–53.

33. Such impossible journeys were unnecessary for Israel because God brought life to the people. They did not have to ascend into heaven to get it or cross the sea (death) to find it. It was revealed to their hearts in God's Word (Deut. 30:11–15). In the New Testament the message is that Christ is the one who both descended and ascended, and so it is he who brought immortality to us (Eph. 4:7–10).

34. The word *apsu* can refer to the cosmic sea, the subterranean water, deep water, or the netherworld. It was also used for the water basin in temples, a parallel to Solomon's "Sea" (*Chicago Assyrian Dictionary,* 1:194–97).

35. Astonishingly, the idolatry in Judah embraced the cult of Tammuz and the Queen of Heaven (Ezek. 8:14–18; Jer. 44:15–30). For more information, see Gurney, "Tammuz Reconsidered: Some Recent Developments," 147–60; see also Olyan, "Some Observations Concerning the Identity of the Queen of Heaven," 161–74.

pagan perversion, the tree was a symbol of life and fertility.[36] But it is no surprise that the Canaanites credited groves of trees to a local baal ("lord"), and ultimately to the god of fertility called Baal, and to the goddess Asherah.[37] A sacred tree was part of the fertility cult of Asherah, and sacred poles were erected to her on high hills or under spreading trees. The Israelites, of course, were forbidden to plant or set up an "Asherah pole" (Deut. 16:21), but they embraced the god Baal and the goddess Asherah and her cult object anyway (cf. Isa. 57:5; Hos. 4:13).[38] But when a statue of Asherah and her pole were set up in the sacred precincts (1 Kings 16:33; 2 Kings 17:10), reformers had to tear them down and burn them (2 Kings 23:4–7).

Given the memory of the Tree of Life in the garden sanctuary, as well as the significance of trees in the ancient world, especially the traditions of a "tree of life" in the temples, we are not surprised to see that the Tree of Life was also represented in Israel's sanctuary. It was symbolized by the lampstand. According to Exodus 25:31–40, this lampstand was to be a single shaft of pure gold, with six "branches" on it, three coming out each side and turning upward (v. 32). Each branch was to have three cups shaped like "almond flowers" with "buds and blossoms" (v. 33). And on the main stock there were to be four cups shaped like "almond flowers" with "buds and blossoms" (vv. 34–35). Seven oil lamps were then to be placed on the tops of the main shaft and the six upward branches. It was a stylized almond tree made of pure gold![39]

This golden "tree" represented God's provision of life; it stood inside the tent to light the way to God, its light also falling on the loaves of bread

---

36. In Israel the image of the tree of life was used metaphorically in wisdom passages without reference to pagan deities: wisdom is a Tree of Life because it too imparts life and leads to a long life (see Prov. 3:2, 18; 8:10–36; 9:11). Moreover, kings and their empires were often compared to trees in the ancient world; Assyria is compared to a magnificent tree in an enclosed garden, unrivaled even by the cedars in the garden of God and envied by all the trees of Eden (Ezek. 31:2–18). But because of its pride it was cut down.

37. See W. L. Reed, *Asherah in the Old Testament.*

38. It was this cult object that Gideon cut down. His father defended him by saying that if Baal did not like it, he could contend for it himself. So Gideon got the nickname Jerub-baal *(Y'rub-bá'al),* "let Baal contend" (Judg. 6:25–32).

39. See further C. L. Meyers, *Tabernacle Menorah,* 174–81. Why an almond tree? Perhaps it was because the almond tree was the first to blossom in the spring, the first to show life (as with Aaron's [almond] rod that bloomed).

that symbolized God's provision for life. The creation of light had been foremost in the provision of life in the beginning; the first rays of light made life possible (Gen. 1:3; Ps. 36:8–10). Because this lampstand preserved the memory of God's provision of the light of life, it had to be pure (solid gold) and its light timeless (it could never go out).

And then in John's vision of the age to come, there is a Tree of Life with leaves for the healing of the nations (Rev. 22:2). Whatever the spiritual and heavenly reality of this may be, it is clear that the elements of the garden have been brought forward to the future Paradise to show that the source of all life is with God. Participation in eternal life is promised to those who have saving faith: "I will give [permission] to eat from the tree of life, which is in the paradise of God" (Rev. 2:7). And in that glorious place the saints will know as they are known, for the law will be written on their hearts. But they will still attribute all wisdom and knowledge and glory and honor to God (Rev. 5:12).

### The Tree of the Knowledge of Good and Evil

The Tree of the Knowledge of Good and Evil was also in the garden, but it was off-limits to humans—the knowledge of good and evil belonged to God. He would reveal it when he wished, in the way he wished, and to whom he wished. The prohibition of this tree was a test of obedience, and so it naturally became the focus of the temptation. Eating from this tree, the appeal ran, would bring a special kind of knowledge, a knowledge that was the prerogative of divinity.[40] Such knowledge would bring power over life, the kind of power God has; in short, the temptation was to obtain the wisdom of God (cf. Gen. 3:6; Job 15:7–9; 40; Prov. 30:1–4).[41]

To try to wrest divine knowledge from God, or more specifically, in defiance of God, is to try to assert spiritual autonomy. Adam and Eve failed in this because they were, after all, dependent creatures; and for

---

40. See Oden, "Divine Aspirations in Atraḫasis and in Genesis 1–11." 197–216.
41. See W. M. Clark, "The Legal Background of the Yahwist's Use of 'Good and Evil' in Genesis 2–3," 266–78. There is also a strong contrast between the course of action in the garden and the teaching of wisdom literature. Adam and Eve wanted to be like God, so they disobeyed the commandments by eating from a tree that would make them wise; but in the end this produced evil so that they hid in fear of the LORD. Wisdom teaches that if people want to become wise they should begin with the fear of the LORD (Prov. 1:7), obey his commandments, and in the process they will become like God. See Forman, "Koheleth's Use of Genesis," 256–63.

trying to overstep their boundaries, they were expelled from the presence of God. Once outside the garden, they had to endure the limitations and hardships of life, which was a far cry from the divinity they had sought. Ezekiel 28 has the same message: the one who exalted himself in pride was cast down in ruins.

Pride prompted Adam and Eve to want to be like God, but the outcome of their hubris made it clear that they were merely human. The pagans may have promoted a confusing mixture of the human and the divine, but in the Bible whenever humans tried to appropriate divinity for themselves, God in his wisdom prevented it. They were not divine, and they could not become gods, or demigods—they were mortals.[42] The commandments in the garden should have told them this.

The Tree of the Knowledge of Good and Evil is unique to the biblical memory of Paradise—it had no symbolic representation in the sanctuary. So what, then, was the legitimate way for the people of God to gain the knowledge of good and evil? It was by knowing God's law and keeping his commandments. And, in the sanctuary the essence of that law was with God, in the Most Holy Place—inside the ark of the covenant. In the representative form of the two tablets, the law was preserved inviolable at the foot of the throne of God.[43] This told the worshippers that God possessed this full knowledge of right and wrong, and that their sin, far from demonstrating that they now had the knowledge, was evidence that they ultimately needed to seek him to learn what was good and what was evil.[44]

This tree appeared to be "good for food and pleasing to the eye, and

---

42. One of the clearest indications of this is the declaration that man by himself is not good (Gen. 2:18). Only God is complete in and of himself; only God is sovereignly independent of all creation. But neither the man nor the woman has that autonomy. To have a significant other, with whom one must reckon, and share, and who limits the grandeur of solitude that only God enjoys—all this is the definition of "not godly" and "not great" (see further on this theme Zornberg, *Beginning of Desire*, 15).

43. The lid of the box is called the "place of propitiation" (*kappōret*, s.v. *kipper*, "to atone"). Wycliffe called it the "mercy seat." But the ark is called the "footstool" in Psalm 132:7. The idea was that the Lord was seated enthroned above it; and the blood of atonement was sprinkled at his feet to atone for the violations of the law—which was represented by the tablets in the box at his feet (see Woudstra, *Ark of the Covenant from Conquest to Kingship*).

44. See Clines, "The Tree of Knowledge and the Law of God," 8–14; and W. M. Clark, "The Legal Background of the Yahwist's Use of 'Good and Evil' in Genesis 2–3," 266–78.

also desirable for gaining wisdom" (Gen. 3:6). And the psalmist says that the law of the LORD is perfect, making wise the simple, giving joy to the heart, and giving light to the eyes; it is more precious than gold (19:7–11). But in the garden the attempt to gain this knowledge of good and evil by disobedience brought death (Gen. 2:17). Likewise, any attempt by Israel to open the ark of the covenant brought instant death (see Num. 4:20; 2 Sam. 6:7).

So these two trees in the Garden of Eden were not forgotten in the formation of Israel's worship. True to the pattern of the garden, the aspects of the sanctuary made it clear that God is the source of all life, and that God has the knowledge of good and evil. He has made it possible for people to know the truth and receive eternal life by his grace. But none of this is possible apart from God, or in defiance of God.

## The Image of God

All ancient temples and sanctuaries had images of the deities that had dominion over them. Likewise the garden sanctuary of the LORD had images, but they were very different from what the pagan world later developed.[45] These images were made by God, not by people, for humans themselves were the image of God—living, breathing, thinking human beings. Because the "image of God" describes living human beings with spiritual and intellectual capacities and not carvings made of stone or wood, the description is essentially functional. When the LORD imparted his "breath of life,"[46] he was sharing with people some of his nature, giving them the capacity to represent him on earth.[47] They were then able to communicate with God, enjoy God, obey God, and serve God.[48]

This service of God is stated briefly in Genesis 2:15. Most translations of Genesis 2:15 say something like this: "the LORD God took the man and put him in the garden of Eden *to work it and take care of it.*" The usual in-

---

45. See Moran, "Creation of Man in Atrahasis: 192–248," 48–76.
46. A study of the usage of "breath" (*n$^e$shāmāh*) shows that it brings life (Gen. 2:7), spiritual understanding (Job 32:8), and a functioning conscience (Prov. 20:27). See T. C. Mitchell, "The Old Testament Usage of *N$^e$šāmâ*," 177–87.
47. Humans were enabled to produce life and thus reproduce the image of God. For a discussion, see Hoekema, *Created in God's Image,* 11–32.
48. God shared his "communicable" attributes, such things as love, mercy, compassion, wisdom, and the like; the "non-communicable" attributes—what he did not impart—would include omniscience, omnipresence, omnipotence, infinity, and sovereignty.

terpretation is that Adam was placed in the garden to work the ground.[49] One immediate difficulty with this is that according to Genesis 3:23 the LORD drove man out of the garden "to work the ground from which he had been taken." How is this kind of work a part of the curse if it was what man was created to do in the first place? There are several things in the passage that lead us in a different direction.[50]

### Placed in the Garden

Genesis 2:15 begins with the simple report that God put the man in the garden. But the choice of verbs for "put" sets the tone for the interpretation of the line, for it is a different word than the one translated "put" in verse 8. There the word was *sîm,* but here the verb used is from *nûakh,* "to rest," which in this passage has the sense of "set to rest." In biblical usage *nûakh* is often parallel to or equated with the main word for "to rest," *shāvat.* For example, the Bible says that the disobedient Israelites were not permitted to enter into God's "rest" (*mᶜnûkhāh,* Ps. 95:11); so the book of Hebrews says there yet remains a Sabbath rest, a *sabbatismós.* The noun "rest" (*mᶜnûkhāh,* s.v. *nûakh*) is also used in the description of the sanctuary of the LORD as his "resting place" (Ps. 132:14).

### Serving in the Garden

To understand exactly what the humans were placed in the garden to do, we need to survey how the two verbs, "work" and "take care of," are used in the Pentateuch. The first verb, "to work, do the work, serve," is *ᶜāvad.* As noted previously, it is used frequently for spiritual service, specifically serving the LORD (Deut. 4:19) and for the duties of the Levites (see Num. 3:7–8; 4:23–24, 26). Throughout Scripture the truly devout person is called "the servant of the LORD."

The other verb is *shāmar,* also introduced earlier. It can be translated "keep, observe, watch, guard," but its religious use is that of observing spiritual duties or keeping the commands (Lev. 18:5). It also is used for the duty of the Levites to guard the tabernacle (cf. Num. 1:53; 3:7–8 and

---

49. What that would mean in a perfect environment that was watered by the LORD's provision is hard to imagine. Thorns and thistles came up as a result of the curse.
50. Cassuto, *From Adam to Noah,* 1:121–23. Cassuto shows how a good deal of this material was already noticed in earlier rabbinic sources.

elsewhere for the expression "they shall keep the charge"*[wᵉshāmᵉrû ᵓet-mishméret]*).

In places where these two verbs are found together, they often refer to the duties of the Levites (cf. Num. 3:7–8; 8:26; 18:5–6),[51] keeping the laws of God (especially in the sanctuary service) and offering spiritual service in the form of the sacrifices and all the related duties—serving the LORD, safeguarding his commands, and guarding the sanctuary from the intrusion of anything profane or evil.[52]

An important consideration in regard to Genesis 2:15 is that the pronouns (translated "it") on the two infinitives ("to work *it* and to take care of *it*") are feminine *(lᵉ ᶜovdāh u-lᵉshomrāh)*, but the word "garden," to which they would naturally refer, is a masculine noun.[53] While this in itself might not be a major problem, it is another indication that something else may have been meant. Cassuto notes that in a number of places in the Pentateuch where parallel infinitive constructions occur, the form is spelled not with a feminine suffix attached but with an infinitive ending;[54] accordingly, if that was what had been originally intended here, the forms could be translated generally "for serving and for keeping."[55] Therefore, as Wenham observes, if the garden was an archetype or pattern of the sanctuary, then humans were the archetypical Levites.[56] Accordingly, Adam and Eve were created to serve the LORD, not the ground—they were like

---

51. The KJV gives a clearer translation for identifying the words in the English: "And ye shall *keep the charge* of the sanctuary. . . . behold, I have taken your brethren the Levites . . . *to do the service* of the tabernacle of the congregation" (Num. 18:5–6).

52. It is significant that the very next verse, Genesis 2:16, then provides the first commandments of God to be obeyed, using the very verb "commanded" *(tsiwwāh)*. Note also Midrash *Berashit Rabbah* 16.5, which mentions that these verbs denote the making of the sacrifices. Exodus 3:12 [NIV translates it worship, not serve] says they were to serve *(ᶜāvad)* God this way, and Numbers 28:2 says they were to take heed *(shāmar)* to offer the sacrifices.

53. Many commentators interpret it to be a reference to "ground" which is feminine, and not to "garden." But that referent is too far removed from the word.

54. The feminine pronominal suffix is a *qāmets-hēᵓ (-āh)*, with a dot *(mappîq)* in the *hēᵓ* to distinguish it from a normal vowel ending, the *qāmets-hēᵓ* vowel *(-āh*, or to distinguish it, *-â)*. In parallel constructions, the dot is not in the final *hēᵓ* and so simply forms an infinitive ending (see e.g., Gen. 1:29–30; Exod. 29:28; 30:18).

55. One would conclude that the MT assumed that the endings were pronominal suffixes and pointed them accordingly (see the full discussion in Cassuto, *From Adam to Noah*, 1:121–23).

56. G. J. Wenham, "Sanctuary Symbolism in the Garden of Eden Story," 401.

the priests who had the responsibility for the care of all the divine institutions in the sanctuary.[57] The man by himself could not do all that God required, and so the woman was formed to be his fitting complement. The description of her as "helper," which has been so shamelessly trivialized, completes the preparation of the image of God and emphasizes an equal share in fulfilling God's will on earth, specifically, worshipping and serving the LORD, ruling and having dominion over the earth, and producing life—not just physical life but eternal and spiritual life.[58]

All the details of the text then indicate that God created human beings to serve him in a spiritual capacity.[59] When they rebelled they were no longer able to do this as he had intended. Then the text uses the two key verbs with different connotations to reflect the change. The pair was expelled from the garden, now to *"work* (i.e., *serve) the ground"* (la *ʿăvōd* in 3:23), and in their place the cherubs were stationed to *"guard the way"* (*lishmōr* in 3:24) to the Tree of Life, for sinful humans could no longer have access to it.

The restoration to spiritual service could only come through the LORD's provision of a new beginning, through redemption. Thus, when God redeemed Israel and made them a kingdom of priests (Exod. 19:5–6), he was in essence re-making them as the functioning image of God on earth, for all who represent the LORD and do his will are fulfilling the design of the Creator.[60] But this spiritual restoration was provided fully in Christ. In the fullness of time God sent forth his Son into the world. This Son, Jesus, was revealed as the image of the invisible God (Col. 1:15), the likeness of God (2 Cor. 4:4), and the express image of the Father (Heb.

---

57. This would be the intended meaning of the text, not, as some suggest, an implication drawn from the original meaning of working the ground. They had a covenant of service or works with God that they were to fulfill. And because such a spiritual service ("serving") anticipated the forces of evil that were about, obedience to the LORD ("keeping") was absolutely essential. After the Fall the spiritual service would include atonement (as the Midrash included), purification, reconciliation, and instruction in holiness.

58. The description of marriage as "holy matrimony" should reflect what God had originally intended for man and woman, i.e., that they unite their capacities and characteristics into a spiritual union in the worship and service of the LORD.

59. Also in the Babylonian Epic of Creation, serving and guarding were the duties of the humans; they were created to serve the gods and guard heaven and sheol.

60. This application does not nullify the fact that all humans are the image of God—they have the capacity. But without spiritual renewal it is not functioning.

1:3). Only believers in Jesus Christ, those who are "in Christ," can attain the likeness of God (Col. 3:10). And this they do as they are conformed to the image of the Son (Rom. 8:29) through the Word of God (2 Cor. 3:18). Therefore, it is through the redeeming work of Christ that people can now realize what it means to be a kingdom of priests (1 Peter 2:1–10); now they can worship and serve as they were intended to do.

## Conclusion

The Garden of Eden was a sanctuary, the place where the people had access to the living God. And because God was there, every good and beautiful gift from God was also provided for their delight and benefit. In time Israel built a sanctuary and then a temple patterned after Paradise, not only to recall the memory of Paradise but also to rekindle the hope of glory in the Paradise to come. To remain in communion with this LORD of glory and enjoy his bounty, they simply had to serve him and obey his commands.

Thus it is in any sanctuary where the people of God gather for what they call a worship service. In their worship they should be reminded, either by the service or the surroundings, that they are entering into the presence of the Creator in a very special and spiritual way and that their place in his presence and their enjoyment of his provisions for life are available only through redemption. Their experience in worship should recall not only creation as they worship God the Creator but also redemption as they worship God the Savior. In this way they enter into communion with the saints of all ages awaiting the coming glory.

# CHAPTER 5

# The Perversion *of* Paradise

IF THE NARRATIVE ABOUT CREATION displays the wonders of Paradise where people had *immediate* access to the LORD God, the account of the expulsion of the sinners from that garden sanctuary reminds people that only through *mediation* can they draw near to the divine presence again. Genesis 3 begins with the interrogation of the woman by the tempter, which leads to death, and ends with the interrogation of the woman and the man by the LORD, which leads to life. But because of sin, all of life would now be different. And because of this, worship changed forever!

Here we see motifs that will become more pronounced in the biblical teachings about worship, for we are now dealing with the expulsion of sinners from the sanctuary and the gracious provision of their reconciliation to God. Now, in worship, that all has to be sorted out before worshippers can celebrate their covenant relationship with the holy LORD God. Here, then, is the message of the Bible in its primitive beginning. And this message has been preserved by the people of God in the drama of worship.

## The Serpent in the Sanctuary

After the words of life from the LORD, there were the words of death from the Evil One. The tempter shrewdly came in disguise, in the form of a snake, a subordinate creature over which Adam and Eve were to have dominion. And the way of temptation was to question the clear Word of God. It made no difference that the man had heard the Word from the LORD himself—Satan was clever enough to pervert it and discredit the LORD so that the pair thought it in their best interests to defy the Almighty. And ever since that fateful day the household of faith has known that the Evil One is always ready to deceive people over what God said, so that they will embrace unrighteous deeds—often with pious intentions (cf. 2 Cor. 11:13–14). The sanctuary, then, is not a safe haven where temptation and sin do not exist.[1]

Understandably the text is not concerned with a mere snake. How could a reptile know God's Word better than people and so cleverly destroy it in their minds? No, there was an evil spirit present in Paradise, one whom Revelation 12:9 identifies as Satan.[2] And ever since the beginning, the serpent has been associated with him as a reminder of the curse. It will remain that way until God renovates creation and renders the serpent and the Serpent harmless.[3]

In the ancient world, however, the serpent became an integral part of religion. Sacred snakes and serpent gods were considered not only forces of death but also forces of life and fertility. In Egypt good snakes and bad snakes guarded the sanctuaries and the mortuary temples, as the paintings in the tombs display. The pharaoh himself wore the image of the sacred cobra on his headdress. And in Canaan incense burners and other cultic implements were decorated with serpents, even in the Israelite period, indicating that many Israelites got caught up in the veneration of the serpent.[4]

One striking contrast with the biblical report comes from the Canaanite-Phoenician world. There was a mother goddess in the form of a serpent whose name, like Eve's, was connected to the word for "life," possibly meaning "life giving."[5] In the pagan world this serpent

---

1. In fact, the history of Israel and of the church record how much temptation to evil there has been in the teachings and practices of the so-called religious leaders. This has made discernment necessary for worshippers at all times.

2. Hoekema rightly affirms that the serpent is real and not simply some mythical symbol; it was used by Satan to deceive. This is the view held by H. Bavinck, Geerhardus Vos, John Calvin, L. Berkhof, E. J. Young, G. C. Aalders, C. F. Keil and F. Delitzsch, J. Fichtner, and many others (*TDNT,* 5:573). See Hoekema, *Created in God's Image,* 128.

3. Isaiah 27:1 predicts that at the end of the age when God judges the wicked (primarily in this passage the enemies of Israel, Babylon, Assyria, and Egypt) he will also destroy the evil spiritual force that coils behind the nations, described here as Leviathan, the gliding serpent, Leviathan the coiling serpent, and the monster of the sea. To Isaiah, the evidence of that victory will be the renovation of creation (Isa. 11:8).

4. See Joines, *Serpent Symbolism in the Old Testament;* and D. W. Young, "With Snakes and Dates," 291–314.

5. The name "Eve" is *Khawwāh,* or *Khavvāh* (חַוָּה), "life-giving." The name of the pagan goddess is formed with the same root letters, *KH-W-T,* but without the vowels written in the word (the Hebrew feminine ending *-āh* and the Canaanite feminine ending *-t* correspond), so we cannot be sure just how close the name was to the spelling of "Eve." For a full discussion, see Heller, "Der Name Eva," 636–56.

was worshipped as a mother goddess; but according to the Bible there was a woman who was the mother of all living—a human—who had been beguiled by the serpent, Satan in disguise. In the Bible the serpent was the agent of death, but in the Canaanite religion it was linked to fertility, the fertility ritual of the pagan "sacred marriage union," a ritual enactment of the sexual union of the gods, or of a god and a mortal. And in Mesopotamian traditions the sexual union of the gods took place in the sacred garden. Wallace connects this mother goddess of Phoenicia with Asherah in other Canaanite texts, because the gods are called the children of Asherah.[6] In the confusion of goddesses, she became equated with the goddess Qudshu ("holy one"), who was usually represented naked, standing on the back of a horse and holding lotus blossoms and snakes in her hands. Thus, several ideas from the beginning had found their way into pagan traditions but in a decidedly different context with very different meanings.[7]

Genesis simply reports the details about the people, their nakedness, desire, the provision of children, and the continuation of life in the face of death. These features may surface in fertility themes in pagan myths, but in Genesis they have none of the trappings of those myths. The Bible preserves the historical event. Wallace suggests that the narratives in Genesis were written in such a way that they made direct allusions to the Canaanite-Phoenician goddess Asherah, and in doing so they made it clear that what the pagans believed was the reverse of the biblical faith. According to the Bible, with the Serpent came conflict and death, as well as pain and suffering for the mother of all living in her childbearing. The Serpent was and is destructive. And so when Genesis recorded the details of the Fall, it intended the motifs it emphasized from the event to have a strong polemical effect—to destroy Canaanite and Egyptian beliefs. In Canaan the serpent goddess was worshipped as the source of life and fertility, but the faithful Israelites knew that it was the archetypical unclean animal that represented the spirit of disobedience and produced death

---

6. Wallace, *Eden Narrative*, 158.

7. Over the years there have been a number of attempts to find connections between Eve and the serpent. One was to point out that in some of the Semitic languages the word for the serpent is *khewyā'*, which looks and sounds like the Hebrew name for Eve *(khawwāh)*. The rabbinical literature plays on these words when it notes that "Eve became a serpent to Adam." There might be something to this if that word for "serpent" *(khewyā')* existed in Hebrew—but it does not.

and defilement.[8] In the world the serpent was a welcome part of sanctuary paraphernalia, but in Israelite memory the serpent was behind the expulsion of people from the garden sanctuary. And throughout Scripture the Evil One behind the serpent lurks behind all false worship, appealing to the baser instincts of mankind, ready to usher them into the realm of darkness. To regain access to the presence of God, where there is light and life, requires the complete reversal of all that the deceiver has wrought. The process of reversal began in the garden, but the struggle will not be complete until God makes everything new—after the final judgment.

The connection between the serpent and death appears frequently in Scripture. For example, in Numbers 21 we read how the murmuring Israelites were bitten by venomous snakes in the wilderness so that many of them died (v. 6). Moses made a bronze snake to represent the curse and put it up on a pole; those who by faith in the LORD's instructions looked to this symbol of the plague escaped death (v. 9). God was nullifying death from the snakes by lifting up this representation of the curse.[9] It is typical of human folly that the next we hear of the bronze snake is in 2 Kings 18:4.[10] When Hezekiah purged idolatry from the nation, he not only tore out the Asherah poles but also cut up the bronze serpent because the people had begun burning incense to it. Apparently it had been kept by the priests and placed in the temple as a commemorative piece. It did not remain a commemorative symbol, however, but had become an object of false worship. This is typically the way that the abuse of worship symbols develops.

Another example of the perversion of Israel's faith occurred with the last-ditch effort of the king of Moab to destroy the Israelites (Num. 25:1–15). Balaam could not curse Israel, so he counseled the king that seduction to fornication would bring them to ruin. And it started to work, as the people indulged in sexual activity on the steppes of Moab. It all took place at Baal Peor, a center of Baalism, making it plausible that the sexual

---

8. Modern writers who deny that the Bible is divine revelation see the popular religion of the Israelites, that is, their idolatrous practices, to be just as authoritative as the "book religion" of the prophets. To them these are simply different ideas about religion. See Dever, *Did God Have a Wife?*

9. The bronze serpent became a type of Christ, who would be lifted up to take the curse to himself so that those who look to him by faith might live.

10. See Joines, "Bronze Serpent in the Israelite Cult," 245–56; Rowley, "Zadok and Nehushtin," 113–41; and Wiseman, "Flying Serpents," 108–10.

activity was linked to a sanctuary.[11] Phinehas killed the most blatant violators so that the plague was stopped. But sexual activity associated with pagan idolatry became a snare to Israel. Jeroboam I allowed cultic prostitutes (called *qᵉdēshāh*) in the land and set up the Asherah poles (1 Kings 14:23–24). In spite of this corrupt influence on Israel's religious practices in the sanctuary, God would have none of it. The LORD God is one; he has no consort.[12] He was not involved with any sexual union in the garden. All of this was a pagan projection of human activities into the realm of the gods. Those who embraced it were deceived by the Evil One just as much as the first humans. Satan has always tempted people to set God's Word aside so that they would be free to live in defiance of what God prohibited—even while claiming to worship the God they will not obey.

The law went to great lengths to ensure that sexual activity, legitimate or otherwise, was kept out of the sanctuary. It also stressed that the priests were to make sure they covered themselves properly when moving about in the Holy Place (see Exod. 20:26; 28:42). What a contrast this was to Canaanite shrines, where sexual activity was common! As it turned out, even Israel's reforming kings and prophets armed with the law of God could not stem the tide of this perversion of worship with pagan gods and fertility rites, and it eventually destroyed the nation (1 Kings 15:12; 2 Kings 23:6–7).[13]

The witness of the Bible and the evidence from the pagan world clearly shows that Satan not only brought about the disobedience of Adam and Eve, but also set the pattern for the perversion of worship for all time. It remains a constant struggle for the faithful to avoid false worship practices that nullify God's Word and destroy communion with the Lord.

---

11. Likewise in 1 Samuel 2:22–25 we have a reference to the sons of Eli the high priest having sex with women at the entrance to the Tent of Meeting—the sanctuary of the LORD. This activity was no doubt linked to Canaanite ideas.

12. See Dever, *Did God Have a Wife?*

13. Amazingly, today the liberal mood is to restore the gods and goddesses that these re-forming prophets in Israel had removed. The argument is that early Israel had a richer religion before rigid monotheism set in; that rigidness remains a hindrance to the full and free expression of the human spirit. See Keel, *God, Goddesses, and Images of God in Ancient Israel.*

## The Savior in the Garden

The tempter may have raised questions about the meaning of God's words, but the LORD simply asked if the Word was obeyed. For God the main issue was straightforward: "Did you eat from the tree that I commanded you not to eat from?" And it is a similarly direct question that confronts every prospective worshipper who desires to draw near to God—"Did you keep my commandments?" This question, no matter how it is put, forms the necessary starting point of all worship ritual. And the proper response to the question, the acknowledgment "I have sinned; I have not kept your commandments," opens the way for the individual to find restored fellowship in the presence of the Lord. Thus, from the beginning we find perhaps the most fundamental element of worship in a fallen world—the acknowledgment of the need of reconciliation.

The sinners in the garden immediately heard the sound of the LORD God's presence, but it was a convicting sound. Thereafter in Israel the sanctuary became the place where the worshippers sensed the presence of the LORD; and it was in the sanctuary that the Word of the LORD most effectively uncovered their guilt and convinced them of their sin. As unforgiven sinners they could not participate freely in sanctuary worship (see Lev. 7:20–21; Ps. 51:16–17); but as confessing believers they would be restored to a proper relationship with God and be able to enter his courts once again.

This is the pattern in the history of worship. When people sin they forfeit access to the sanctuary, the place God chose to make his presence known, until the sin is dealt with.[14] In Israel's understanding, to be excluded from the temple for any reason was a living death.[15] Sinners had to confess that their disobedience separated them from God before they would be welcomed into his presence. Being separated from God because of sin was dangerous; it was only in God's presence that people found the provisions for life—there they could reenter "Eden" as it were, eat from the holy food and draw from the living water (Ps. 36:9–10) and find rest for their souls.

---

14. G. J. Wenham, *Genesis 1–15*, 86.
15. Even physical contamination meant exclusion from the temple. The poor Israelite with the incurable skin disease, for example, was barred from the sanctuary; he entered the realm of the dead and behaved as if in mourning (Lev. 13:45–46; Num. 5:2–4; see also 1 Sam. 15:35). But the diseased knew that when they recovered they were free to enter his courts again. The sinner's return to the sanctuary required more.

Therefore, the acknowledgment of sin brings reconciliation with God. When Adam and Eve admitted their sin, God replaced their temporary coverings with animal skins. By so doing he was revealing for all time the cost of sin—death. Later in the sanctuary the skins of animals from the sacrifices were to go to the priests (Exod. 28:41; 29:8; 40:14; Lev. 8:13). Clothing thus became a symbol of God's grace; on holy occasions the priests were to be appropriately clad in holy array (see again Exod. 20:26; 28:42), usually white linen to symbolize righteousness and purity before the LORD. No one could approach God unprepared; one had to be properly clothed to enter his courts to worship with the garments of holiness (see Pss. 110:3; 132:16). And in the world to come, we find the same symbolism, for John says that the saints will be clothed with white linens, that is, righteousness (cf. Rev. 19:7–8).

There is one final comparison between Genesis 3 and the later sanctuary—the cherubs. Even though Adam and Eve were clothed by the LORD, they could not return to the Tree of Life in the garden. At the entrance the LORD stationed these guarding angels with the flaming sword that flashed this way and that. In Israel's tabernacle and the later temple, symbolic representations of these creatures were everywhere to indicate that immediate access to the presence of God was restricted. On the curtain that separated the Holy of Holies from the Holy Place, large cherubs were embroidered (1 Kings 6:23–28). On the ceiling and walls of the tent were embroidered the cherubs, as a reminder that God's holy presence was guarded—that the people could not wander into his presence without mediation (Exod. 26:31; 1 Kings 6:29). And on the ark itself two cherubs were fashioned out of the gold to guard the throne of God (Exod. 25:18–22).[16] Even in the biblical revelations of glory, we find the cherubs present protecting the throne of God (cf. Ezek. 1:4–28).

Before sinful humans could again find access into the presence of God, there had to be a resolution to their dilemma. And in God's plan the sacrificial death of Jesus the Messiah, the divine Son of God, was exactly that—God's complete remedy for the race's complete ruin, what the ritual of Israel's worship had been anticipating for ages. The suffering of the Savior began in another garden, not Eden, but dark Gethsemane. And on

---

16. It is obvious that these embroidered and carved images did not constitute idolatry, for God instructed that these be made. The prohibition against making images was against making images for the purpose of worshipping and serving them.

the cross when Jesus tasted death for us all so that we all might have life, he opened the way of access to the Father. At that moment the veil in the temple with the embroidered cherubs on it was rent from top to bottom, symbolizing that those angels could step aside so that the people of God could approach the throne of grace with confidence.

The resurrection from the dead, the great sign of the completion of redemption, also took place in a garden. There the women met the risen Lord, first mistaking him for a gardener. But he was not the one who had been expelled from the garden to work the ground! He was the Lord of the whole earth, the King of Glory. Through his sacrificial death, he liberated us from sin and guilt and a miserable existence under the curse and restored us to a glorious life of worshipping and serving him.

And so worship in Christ now celebrates the glory of the new creation as well as the old creation; it glorifies the one who is the Redeemer as well as the Creator; and it finds in the garden sanctuary the pattern for worship and the symbolism for the spiritual life. And in his presence we find every provision for life and thus every reason to worship him.

# Conclusion *for* Part 2

THERE IS NO GOING BACK TO the garden of Eden. Instead, the path of salvation is the path to glory, to the heavenly sanctuary of God, of which the earthly Paradise was a manifestation. It is a place of exquisite beauty and perfection, where light and life proceed from God undiminished and where angelic choirs surround the throne and sing praises to the Lord because he created everything by his will. Into this heavenly sanctuary the righteous will go, joining the angels in giving honor and glory and praise to the Creator—and the Redeemer. It is this place that Jesus called Paradise.

The earthly Paradise remains a memory from the distant past, but a memory that helps us unlock some of the mysteries of the divine plan. We are left to ponder what once was—a place of pristine beauty and order at the heart of God's creation, a garden of delights for the enjoyment of the Lord's provision of life, and a sanctuary where humans enjoyed direct access to the living God whom they worshipped and served.[1]

As we recall the past, we enter into the joy of the first humans' privileges, we appreciate their hope of glory, and we understand their failure. In every age people have had to reckon with these things, for we all were barred from the presence of God because of our sin and were unable to work our way back. But when we confessed our sin, believing his Word, we were restored to fellowship with God—albeit a mediated fellowship due to the continuing presence of sin in this life and the constant temptation of the Serpent. Therefore, the memory of Paradise is in part a painful

---

1. Down through the ages many have used the garden for a means of meditation. Elaborate gardens were laid out in a pattern to reflect creation, using four sections to represent the main regions of the world and planting every kind of tree and plant that was available. Such "botanical gardens" reflected the beauty and order of the garden of Eden. See Prest, *Garden of Eden*.

memory because of what was lost, but it is also an inspiration to hope for things to come. The spiritual journey we are on means that as we identify with those who have gone before, we bring forward to our age the same hope of glory, where redemption will be complete and worship made perfect. If the memory of the past gives us a glimpse of the true Paradise, then our worship will be invigorated to lift us out of this world and into his presence, now in spirit, but at some glorious future day in complete reality.

# PART 3

# WORSHIP *with* PROCLAMATION

*The Development of True Worship
in a Religious World*

# Introduction

IF WORSHIP IS INSPIRED BY THE revelation of the Lord of glory, then it will flower into a life-changing communion with the living God that will ultimately be made perfect in glory. But for the present it takes place in the world, which has always been a very religious place, though not in the truly spiritual sense. Christian worship may take place in the world, but it is not the same as the worship of the world.[1] Most of the time it stands in stark contrast to the religious practices of the world.

True worship of the one true and living God must make its presence known if it is to offer people the opportunity to become part of the people of God who worship in spirit and in truth.[2] By making worship available in this way,[3] God is offering the people of the world the only way to fulfill the deepest needs of their lives—needs that they have sought to fulfill through various religious and secular activities, activities that may be primitive or sophisticated, perverse or pure, confused or intelligent, but ineffectual nonetheless (e.g., Isa. 57:9–13). And by inviting people to become worshippers, God is also giving them an opportunity to participate in the transformation of the world. He is offering them a real future![4]

By doing this, true worship also denounces pagan worship as a futile lie. If the worship of the world had been pleasing to God, there would have been no need for God to call people out of the world to form a holy

---

1. The word *world* has several meanings: it may mean the physical world that God created, the people who live in the world ("the world did not know him"), or the present evil system ("love not the world").
2. Webber also discusses how worship may identify with the world but is actually designed to transform the world (*Worship: Old and New*, 185–90).
3. The Father is seeking worshippers who will worship in spirit and in truth (John 4:23–24).
4. Allmen, *Worship: Its Theology and Practice*, 57.

nation. God simply could have dusted off one of the old pagan religions and made do with it as well as he could. No, pagan religions had become so defiled by the god of this world that the truth would not find a hearing in them. Instead, the LORD God set about to create a holy people who would worship in truth. He chose to reveal himself anew in a world that was loaded with ideas about gods; he chose to call people to start a new religion in a world that had scores of religions; and he chose to teach people how to worship in a world that thought it had worship down to an art, if not big business. Not surprisingly, from the outset people in the world saw this new worship as a threat because it uncovered the perversion and the vanity of their ways and called for exclusive allegiance to one sovereign, holy—but invisible—God.

Moreover, because pure worship celebrates a covenant made with the sovereign God of history, it anticipates the fulfillment of its promises at the end of the age. It proclaims not only the one true and living God but also his ultimate victory over all spiritual and physical forces. This aspect of the faith clearly trumpets the temporary nature of false worship, which from antiquity has been so preoccupied with securing the recurring cycle of life that it has provided no solution to the greater problems of life. It provided no way out of the struggle of life and death or of good and evil, only a continuation of these endless problems in the next life. But the true God has provided a way out, and true worship can therefore anticipate victory over evil and the resolution of life's problems in a whole new creation.

All of this means that the people of God must be able to distinguish true worship from the worship of the world. And this is not always easy to do because so many of the religious acts in pagan religions seem similar to, if not identical with, biblical acts of worship. One might be tempted to conclude, as many have, that they are simply different expressions of the same spiritual instincts and desires and therefore part of the truth, or in words that defy logic, another truth. But the difference is substantial—it is the difference between night and day, earth and heaven, a lie and the truth. It is for this reason that the proclamation of the truth is such an essential part of worship. Without it true worship would become hopelessly entangled with false worship (2 Cor. 6:14–18).

False worship was not a late development. From the very beginning of civilization, people began to worship what they perceived to be God or gods, and they quickly deteriorated into worshipping various creatures and forces instead of the Creator; as a result they engaged in all kinds of corrupt religious practices (see Rom. 1:21–32). But not everyone! God began to call out of the world a remnant of true worshippers (e.g., Gen. 4:26; 6:8–9), and with them he formed a covenant people who would be true worshippers and thereby begin to bring blessing to the world (Gen. 12:1–3). In the outward forms of their worship—sacrifices, burials, festivals and the like—there would not have been much to distinguish what the faithful were doing from what was going on in the pagan world, unless the difference was made clear.[5] Something had to be communicated.

While there are a number of ways that worship will be a proclamation to the world,[6] the most immediate and effective way is through the spoken word. This is why early on God invested the worshipping community with priestly and prophetic gifts (Gen. 20:7; Exod. 19:6; 1 Peter 2:9; Jude 14–15). If the people of God remained faithful to their calling and worshipped in truth, their worship would be a proclamation of the truth; but if they failed and brought corruption into their worship, then they would only convey confusion to the world. The prophets of Israel had to address this again and again, and so the worshipping community was constantly being called to repentance and reformation.

---

5. This was what made the test of Abraham so difficult (Gen. 22). It must have appeared to him that God was acting like the gods of Canaan. But it was a test to see if he would obey even if God seemed to be requiring something out of character with the faith (Crenshaw, "A Monstrous Test: Genesis 22," 9–30).
6. For example, in the celebration of Holy Communion we "proclaim the Lord's death until he comes" (1 Cor. 11:26b).

# CHAPTER 6

# The Religious World *in* Antiquity

IN ORDER TO APPRECIATE THE development of true worship in the world and to be reminded of the continuing need for clear proclamation, we must understand the world in which it began. It often comes as a surprise to find that all the ancient civilizations had highly developed, well-organized religious systems ages before Abraham came on the scene. But in spite of the outward similarities between those systems and Israel's, there were significant differences—differences that led the pagan religions to confusion and depravity in the name of worship. Because of such corruption in those polytheistic systems, the true faith had to come by divine revelation. And the content of this revelation had to be the regular and consistent proclamation of true worshippers, or their worship would soon be like the pagans' worship.

## A Survey of Worship in the World

### In Abram's Homeland

Ancient Sumer, the place from which Abram was called,[1] was a complex religious state where people worshipped many gods that embodied the earth's forces governing life and fertility. Although there were city gods, the important gods were cosmic, responsible for the universe and its cycles and laws. One trilogy was made up of *Anu* (heaven), *Enlil* (air),

---

1. This is the high culture of the lower Mesopotamian region at the end of the third millennium B.C. Abraham came from Ur (Ur III in archaeology). See Samuel Noah Kramer, *The Sumerians: Their History, Culture, and Character* (Chicago: University of Chicago Press, 1963); Helmer Ringgren, *Religions of the Ancient Near East,* trans. John Sturdy (Philadelphia: Westminster, 1973); and Samuel Noah Kramer, *History Begins at Sumer* (Garden City, NY: Doubleday, 1959).

and *Enki* (earth). Another was astral: *Namar* (moon), *Utu* (sun), and *Inanna* (Venus, also mother earth, fertility). These gods were given human forms, sexes, and families and differed from humans only in their immortality and power. Below them was a world of demons—good demons were protective; bad demons were restless spirits of the dead, dwelling in tombs, deserts, and darkness.

The center of all activity was the temple, because everyone served the gods. Sumerian temples were often built on platforms or terraces, and in the larger cities they were built at the top of terraced towers *(ziggurats),* representing cosmic mountains. A staircase connected the different levels, ascending to the top, which was the residence of the high god.[2]

Temple priests had numerous functions, including making offerings, divining, anointing, and wailing; some were singers and poets, and some were eunuchs and temple prostitutes who participated in ritual acts. Priests trained in magical arts were involved in overcoming bad demons with incantations and curses, especially where they had brought illness and uncleanness. They also wanted to peer into the future and thought that they could manipulate the divine powers.

Sumerian worship called for the sacrifice of sheep, goats, oxen, swine, birds, fish, grain, flour, bread, cakes, dates, figs, oil, honey, milk, wine, beer, garments, perfume, and a number of other things. And it included a number of festivals, notably the New Year Festival that included the celebration of the holy marriage, theoretically (at least), between the king and the goddess (or a priestess). There seems to have been a procession to the temple with rejoicing, sacrifices of animals, singing of love songs, and the culmination of the marriage. It was all intended to determine the destiny of the king and the stability of the coming year. A banquet concluded the festival with music, ritual enactments, hymns, and prayers.

Their ritual was concerned with the annual cycle of life, and there was no real hope of a life that would supercede this painful earthly existence. They knew of life beyond the grave,[3] but that life too would continue to be dominated by the gods.

---

2. Jacob's dream (Gen. 28) uses a word for "ladder" *(sullām)* that is related to the word for the staircase *(simmiltu)* of the *ziggurat.* But Jacob saw the real communication between earth and God.

3. Kramer, "Hades: The First Tale of Resurrection," in *History Begins at Sumer,* 155–69.

## In the Major Centers in the East

For the world of the Babylonians and Assyrians, we have much more material available—but it portrays the same darkened confusion.[4] Once again we find the ancient gods of heaven, air, and earth, called *Anu, Enlil* and *Ea (Enki),* as well as the gods of the moon, sun, and Venus, now called *Sin, Shamash,* and *Ishtar.* There were also national gods, *Marduk* for Babylon, and *Ashur* for Assyria, and various other gods for crafts and guilds (such as *Nabu* for writing and wisdom) or smaller ethnic groups (*Adad* for the Amorites). There was no shortage of gods.

There was no shortage of demons either. People believed that demons were the cause of their ills and at death hovered over bodies that were not properly buried. Only priestly exorcism could drive them away. Divination was based on the belief that the gods set destiny and let people know of their plans through signs (cf. Ezek. 21:21). But since destiny was not completely "fixed," divination warned of impending disasters so that they might be avoided. As a by-product of this interest, observatories were built to chart the stars and eclipses[5]—and the beginnings of astronomy, mathematics, and geometry emerged.

The temple staff was large. The king headed the ritual, but apart from this there was no hierarchy. Guilds of priests worked incantations, while others appeased angry gods with music and preserved the secret knowledge. There were singers, craftsmen, observers (divination), askers, ecstatic prophets, and castrated priests. There were also ranks osf female personnel, such as the "temple prostitutes," "infertile ones," "consecrated ones," and others "belonging to Ishtar." Most of the time priests attended to the gods, dressing the images, serving them food, burning incense to appease them, and pouring out drink offerings before their statues. Temple ritual included blood sacrifice, but there is some uncertainty over the meaning of the blood.

---

4. In addition to Ringgren, *Religions of the Ancient Near East,* see S. H. Hooke, *Babylonian and Assyrian Religion* (Oxford: B. Blackwell, 1962); H. W. F. Saggs, *The Greatness That Was Babylon: A Sketch of the Ancient Civilization of the Tigris-Euphrates Valley* (New York: New American Library, 1962); and Sabatino Moscati, *The Face of the Ancient Orient* (Garden City, NY: Anchor Books, 1960); and André Parrot, *Babylon and the Old Testament,* trans. B. E. Hooke (London: SCM Press, 1958).

5. G. E. Wright, *The Old Testament Against Its Environment,* 50–93.

Babylonian sanctuaries had the character of gardens and retained the step-tower structure *(ziggurat)*. The temple on top was a dwelling place for the high god, whose presence was represented by an image. Only at the great festivals could common people take part in the ritual and see the image.

Certain days were unlucky, and on them people abstained from many activities. The days of the new moon and the full moon (15th), later called *sapattu,*[6] were feast days, but the most important feast day was the New Year Festival *(akitu),* celebrated at the vernal equinox. It seems that the celebrations included a prayer to Marduk for mercy, making images, incantation at the rise of the constellation, reciting the *Epic of Creation,* purification of the temple, removal of the king's insignia to be laid before Marduk, striking the king, his negative confession, a blessing from the priest, and the restoration of kingship. There is also some reference to a procession, perhaps a cultic drama of Marduk's victory, or a sacred wedding.

Apart from such festivals, however, common religious life seems rather gloomy, and nothing better was promised for the next life. At death there was no recompense of good or evil, only the place of the dead enveloped in darkness below the earth. People still alive on earth could alleviate the sufferings of the dead through ritual, but if they forgot or if they did not bury the dead, then the dead would return in the form of demons and trouble them.

## In the Land Promised to Abram

The religious ideas and practices Abram met when he arrived in Canaan probably seemed far more base than what he knew in the East.[7] Canaanite religion was also a naturalistic polytheism; but as a system it often defies logic in that the functions, identities, and sexes of the gods

---

6. Scholars have noted some similarities between these workless days and the Israelite Sabbath.
7. See Albright, *Yahweh and the Gods of Canaan;* John Gray, *The Legacy of Canaan: The Ras Shamra Texts and Their Relevance to the Old Testament,* 2d rev. ed. (Leiden: E. J. Brill, 1965); A. S. Kapelrud, *The Ras Shamra Discoveries and the Old Testament,* trans. G. W. Anderson (Norman: University of Oklahoma Press, 1963); P. C. Craigie, *Ugarit and the Old Testament;* Bronner, *The Stories of Elijah and Elisha;* and Giovanni Pettinato, *The Archives of Ebla: An Empire Inscribed in Clay* (Garden City, NY: Doubleday, 1981).

seem to change. It contains elements of crudity, such as snake worship, male and female cultic prostitution, and child sacrifice, and at the same time some fairly sophisticated religious ideas.

In the pantheon El ("god") was supreme, although his position was later usurped by Baal ("lord"). Asherah was the wife of El (Asherah also refers to the pole used in fertility rituals). Baal was the cosmic force, the storm god as well as the god of vegetation (equal to Hadad, the Syrian equivalent of the Assyrian Adad). Astarte, his wife, was equal to Ishtar. Anat also was the wife of Baal and also called his sister. But from the existing texts it is difficult to piece together a cohesive interpretation.

Canaanite temples were built with several rooms, the idol occupying the innermost "holy" chamber. Open-air sanctuaries were often established near trees,[8] springs of water, or rivers. The use of high places was common; in fact, temples were usually built on the tops of mounds or hills, even within the cities. Baal's temple was said to be on Mount Zaphon in the north. But essentially, sacred standing stones, an altar, and a small enclosure were sufficient for a shrine.

There was a hierarchy of priests—high priests, ministering priests, sanctuary keepers, singers, male and female holy ones (prostitutes probably), craftsmen, and diviners. The priests offered sacrifices, animal, vegetable, and even human. Several of the names for sacrifices also appear in Leviticus—votive, peace, guilt, and whole burnt offerings, but there is no indication that any were for atonement.

Sacred prostitution apparently was common because the ritual was a fertility cult, designed to ensure fertility in the fields, flocks, and families through sympathetic magic. Some of the texts portray rather graphic rituals, with profane and even animalistic descriptions, included in Baal's function of propagating life.

The myths appear to describe a cosmic struggle between the gods, perhaps to be reenacted in the ritual. In the autumn Baal was killed by Mot ("death") and taken to the netherworld and guarded by Prince Yam ("sea") and Judge Nahar ("river"). As a result, death—winter—came to the earth. In the spring the goddess Anat descended to rescue Baal, hacking her way through defenders, wading through gore up to her hips. She

---

8. Abraham settled near the Oak of Moreh (Hebrew for "teacher") in the midst of the Canaanite territory (Gen. 12:6). This seems to be a Canaanite religious center for divination or instruction.

brought him back to the earth, and they ascended the sacred mountain and held a feast that was filled with debauchery.[9] With this ascendancy of Baal, springtime fertility returned. The Canaanites probably explained the cycle of life on earth with such seasonal dramas and hoped they would ensure the cycle for another year. Therefore, there was no conception of a final victory.[10] They believed in life after death, but the archaeological finds in tombs speak more of the continuation of life than the translation to a glorious existence.

## In the Land of Bondage

In Egypt the families from Abraham would have found a dark and sometimes grotesque religious world. Egypt's religious activities were very complex—an endless multiplicity of forms that are often obscure and contradictory. The earliest stages have deities in the forms of animals—oxen, sheep, dogs, cats, birds, serpents, crocodiles, and the like. Then gradually human images were made, but often with animal heads. For example, Horus was a human with a falcon head; Hathor had a cow's body and a woman's head. Thereafter gods with complete human forms appear.

Egypt also had cosmic deities. The earth was in the shape of a dish, floating on the water. It had a fertile valley at the center with mountains at each end, and the Nile gushing through at points in the valley. Above was the air. But all these parts were also divinities: earth was Geb, a god lying down; heaven was Nut, an arched goddess (or cow) over the earth; air was Shu, who holds up the sky; the sun was Re, who traverses the sky, leaving Thoth, the moon, in charge. In the myth the serpent lies in waiting at the setting of Re (the sun), and after a bloody struggle Re prevails (for another day). Wilson writes:

> For example, we should want to know in our picture whether the sky was supported on posts or was held up by a god; the Egyptian would answer, "Yes, it is supported by posts or held up by a god—

---

9. Psalm 93 may be a polemic against this mythic cycle, asserting that it is Yahweh who defeats the "sea," and that it is "holiness" that characterizes his "temple."

10. This is one of the major differences between the ancient myths and the Bible, for the biblical faith goes far beyond ensuring good harvests to ensuring the culmination of the ages in the coming of the Lord.

or it rests on walls, or it is a cow, or it is a goddess whose arms and feet touch the earth."[11]

The myths of the gods unfolded like human dramas. Osiris was the god of agriculture, and Isis was his wife. Set was jealous and killed Osiris. Isis then pleaded for him, and Horus, their son, avenged Osiris by killing Set. Of course, all of this was symbolic to the devotees. But even so, it stood in sharp contrast to a faith in one true and sovereign God.

The temple was the dwelling place of the god and the home of the priesthood. It had inner chambers for the statues of the god and outer areas for all the guilds of priests, the readers, purifiers, sacrificers, prophets, musicians, singers, concubines, and the like. The temple was the center of cultural life, especially for the scribes, who gathered to interpret, compose, and copy texts in their "holy writing" (hieroglyphics).

The priests, by and large, were the educated elite. They were led by a primate, at least in the later periods (about 1500 B.C.), who was the first prophet of Amon. The priests organized the pantheon and the laws of the universe, and they also warded off evils by curses and spells. In their regular task of ordering ritual ceremony, they would purify themselves and then enter the temple, breaking the seal of the holy place so that they could stand before the god, pray to it, wash it, clothe it, and burn its meal before withdrawing and sealing the place again.

There were also agricultural festivals to celebrate the fertility of the earth. Herodotus, in *The Histories* (2.60), described people on boats, women shaking rattles and men playing flutes, others singing and clapping. At their destination they offered sacrifices and celebrated with more wine than they drank all year. The festivals often included sacred drama in which devotees enacted episodes of the myth of Osiris and Set.

The many funerary temples in Egypt indicate how much the next life occupied their thoughts. That future life did not simply continue this life; it promised a definite resolution that included retribution for the deeds of this life. After death one stood before Osiris to give the negative confession ("I have not . . ."). The heart was then weighed: if it was sinless

---

11. H. Frankfort, J. A. Wilson, T. Jacobsen, and Wm. A. Irwin, *The Intellectual Adventure of Man* (Chicago: University of Chicago, 1946), 44–45. See also John Albert Wilson, *The Culture of Ancient Egypt* (Chicago: University of Chicago Press, 1951); and Manfred Lurker, *The Gods and Symbols of Ancient Egypt* (London: Thames and Hudson, 1980).

(lighter than a feather), the person entered the region beyond; but if guilty (heavier), the person was given over to forty-two judges, whose names said it all—"breaker of bones," "devourer of entrails," and the like. Egypt's belief in the next life left a lasting witness with the pyramids and tombs—the rulers and nobles spent their lives preparing them and preparing for them.

## A Comparison with Israel's Worship

All the evidence indicates that from the beginning people began to worship all kinds of forces and creatures other than the true LORD God, and over time they gradually developed what they must have thought were the higher religions—organized, elaborate, and meaningful. But they were grotesquely human, confusing, and corrupting. There was very little in them that was uplifting, transcendent, or glorious.

How are we to account for such elaborate and highly developed religious systems centuries before the Israelites were instructed in their faith and worship? Many scholars argue that Israel simply borrowed ideas from their pagan neighbors, cleaned them up for their newfound monotheism (which was also borrowed from Egypt), and then attempted to conceal their origin by attributing it all to direct revelation. There is, of course, no evidence for this. In fact, the theory runs contrary to the biblical witness that every time Israel borrowed religious ideas from her pagan neighbors it led them away from monotheism and toward the corruption of idolatry, never away from polytheism to a purer form of worship. But even more critically, it is hard to accept a theory that says that the whole religious system of Israel was simply borrowed from the pagan world and then artificially credited to God's revelation at Mount Sinai. Such a theory not only destroys the idea of revelation, attributing deception to the formation of the faith, but it also makes the true faith pagan in origin, invented for the most part by humans, and thus of no greater value than the false religions.

And yet, there are undeniable parallels between the patterns and practices of worship in Israel and those of the ancient Near East. One may conclude that when God revealed his plan for the worship of Israel, he chose to use a number of existing forms that the people would readily understand. God took old wineskins, as it were, and put new wine in them. But if the form and contents of Israel's sanctuary worship were to be patterned after the heavenly scene, as Exodus 25:8–9 says, and they still matched pagan forms, one must conclude that a certain amount of truth, or at least a proper instinct for religious matters, existed in the pagan systems prior to Sinai.

The most plausible way to explain the similarities is to attribute both to a common origin. In other words, the earliest descendants of Adam somehow had a basic understanding of and religious instincts for the setting and structures of worship as it was made known in the garden in the beginning; but as this memory was handed down from generation to generation, it changed dramatically to include an unlimited number of gods and goddesses that were all too human and a disturbing array of corrupting human activities. And yet the basic ideas of sanctuaries where the deity dwelt, seasonal rites of worship, sacrifices that were offered to the deity, and priestly attendants who served in the sanctuaries and organized ritual that included prayers, hymns, praises, and other forms stayed pretty much at the center of the religious systems.

The literature of the ancient Near East offers no explanation of the origin of sacrificial worship. But in the Bible we have some hints. Genesis 2 and 3 describe a garden sanctuary where God dwelt but where sinners could not dwell. Genesis 4 tells how Cain and Abel brought sacrifices in the appropriate season and how people began early on to proclaim the name of Yahweh, which at the least is an indication of organized worship. Genesis 6 tells of a corruption on earth by the "sons of God," which appears to be a polemic against the pagans' fertility customs. Then the book records Noah's sacrifice after the flood (Gen. 8), a ritual soon perverted in the pagans' telling of the story. Then the narrative jumps to the building of Babel and its tower to heaven (Gen. 11), the forerunner of the *ziggurat*. The biblical text clearly has a different concern than tracing the development of religions, but in the process of tracing what actually happened to God's creation, it reveals the events and beliefs that are behind those religious practices. A comparison of what the Bible does include with what we know of those ancient religions is sufficient to say there was a common origin. But as the apostle Paul says, although the ancients knew God, they chose not to glorify him and so exchanged the glory of the immortal God for images made to look like mortal man and birds and animals and reptiles (Rom. 1:21–23). It is still true that sinful humans prefer to construct their own religious systems rather than accept divine revelation.

The similarities also probably reflect a common human instinct for religious observances and practices, which are often an extension of human life in general—eating, drinking, living in houses, marrying. Many of the religious instincts of the pagans were valid—approaching the deity with a gift, having a special place where the deity could be found, or thanking the deity for the provision of rain and the harvests that resulted, to name a few. But in time their instincts seem to have influenced the religions to become too human, and the ritual became manipulative. Thus the differences between those religions and Israel's were far greater than the similarities.

The Bible also indicates that there was some kind of supernatural influence in the pagan world as well. The biblical writers did not hesitate to identify evil spiritual forces behind pagan kings and pagan ideas (cf. Ezek. 28:11–19; Dan. 10:13; 2 Cor. 6:14–18; 11:14; 1 Tim. 4:1; Rev. 9:20). We really cannot know just how evil forces have worked at this level, but we do have a few passages that hint at the connection. The book of Revelation tells us that idolatrous people worship demons or fallen angels (9:20) or possibly Satan himself, who can masquerade as an angel of light (2 Cor. 11:14). Much of this, of course, is shrouded in mystery, but the spirit of deception, appearing early in the garden, no doubt resided in the pagan shrines.

Something new and profound would have to be developed if true, spiritual worship was to exist in the world, and it would have to proclaim its new and unique ideas to the world if the knowledge of the true God was to be preserved in the earth.

# CHAPTER 7

# The Worship *of the* LORD *in the* Life *of* Abraham

## Abraham's Faith

### God's Revelation

When God called Abraham (Gen. 11:27–12:9; 15:7; Acts 7:2–4), Abraham's family was living in a major religious center and had a history of worshipping other gods (Josh. 24:2).[1] So Abraham would have known the religious traditions about Creation, the Flood, the longevity of famous ancestors, and the confusion of languages, as well as the practices common to most religions. These things had all been corrupted by pagan ideas to be sure, but people still knew that there were supernatural beings that controlled destiny, that there was life after death, that people were to serve the god(s), and that sacrifice, prayer, and even chanted hymns were the natural aspects of worship. The point is that a religious frame work was in place; all that was missing was the truth, and that came to Abraham by divine revelation.

That revelation from God made Abraham realize that there is only one sovereign God, and therefore only one way to worship. Accordingly, God called him to leave his old way of life and introduce the true faith to the world. The poetic form of his call emphasizes these two commands and their purposes: "*Go* . . . (in order that) I may make you into a great nation, and bless you, and make your name great; and *be* (so that you

---

1. There probably was a mixture of false religious ideas with whatever traditions about the true God that the family may have preserved (see remnants of the faith in Haran in Gen. 31:19, 34–35 [Woudstra, *Book of Joshua*, 344]).

my be) a blessing. And then I will bless those who bless you, but the one who treats you lightly I must curse, and all the families on earth will be blessed through you."[2]

Abraham obeyed the command of God and went (Gen. 12:4). Because he believed the word of the LORD (Heb. 11:8; Gen. 15:6), he left Ur for Canaan; and because he became a faithful believer in the sovereign God Yahweh, his worship was pleasing to God. It was true worship.

## Abraham's Belief

Before considering how Abraham obeyed the command to be a blessing, it will be helpful to reconstruct what Abraham believed, because his faith found expression in the way he worshipped. The narratives in Genesis give us this information.

### Yahweh Was the Living God

*He believed that Yahweh was the living God* in a way the pagan world could not imagine. Not only did Yahweh speak (Gen. 12:1; cf. 13:14; 15:4; 16:8–9; 21:12), but he also actually appeared (Gen. 12:7; cf. 15:1 [in a vision]; 18:1; 20:3 [in a dream to Abimelech]). He was truly alive.

### Yahweh Was the Sovereign God

*He believed that Yahweh was the sovereign God.* Abraham came to realize more and more the greatness of Yahweh, the Most High God; he was the Creator of heaven and earth (14:22), he provided water for them in wilderness places (16:7; 21:19), he controlled plagues (12:17), he could give the land to whomever he wished (13:15), he raised up nations and appointed kings (17:6), he judged nations (13:13; 15:14, 16; 18–19), and he protected his covenant (20:6) and his covenant people (15:1). In short, Yahweh could provide life (17:16)—and he could take it away (18:23).

### Yahweh Was the Righteous Judge

*He believed that Yahweh was the righteous judge* of the whole earth (18:25) who decreed blessings or curses in response to the way people acted. He was just in his decisions (15:16; 18:25) because he was able to discern the heart (18:13, 15). He would even spare the wicked for the sake

---

2. My translation here captures the sequence; see my full treatment of the structure in *Creation and Blessing*, 262–64.

of the righteous (18:26), even though the punishment for sin was death (20:3, 7).

### Yahweh Was the Gracious God

*He believed that Yahweh was a gracious God.* By grace God called Abraham out of pagan darkness and promised to bless him and his descendants (12:1–3; 15:4–7; 22:17). When he heard the cries of people in trouble (16:11; 21:17), he graciously met their needs (16:13). But most importantly, it was by grace that he credited Abraham with righteousness (Gen. 15:6; cf. Rom. 4:1–5, 16). Abraham knew that the covenant itself was a work of grace throughout (Gen. 15:7–21; 17:7–8). Abraham also witnessed God's grace in rescuing Lot (19:16) and his loving-kindness in leading the servant to find a wife for Isaac (24:7, 21, 27; see also 12:7).

### Yahweh Was the Faithful God

*He believed that Yahweh was faithful* in keeping his promises, first by the confirming appearance (12:7), and then by fulfilling the promise of a son (21:1–7). God was faithful also in preserving Lot in accordance with his word to Abraham (19:29), as well as in providing a sacrifice on Moriah (22:8).

What Abraham believed about God determined what he believed about people as well. He knew from the outset that people needed the LORD for blessing and protection, because they were frail and sinful—mortal, and not divine (18:27). He recognized that besides the "righteous" there were the "ungodly" (18:23), the people of the world who would receive God's judgment (chap. 19). And although people who feared the LORD were determined to obey him (20:11), even they would fail (chaps. 12; 20). But they, the "righteous," were called to be a blessing to the world (12:1–3), and so they were to be perfect (17:1), to keep the sign of the covenant (17:9), to protect the covenant (15:7–11), and to maintain righteousness so that they could fulfill their mission to the world (18:19).

When we gather the data from these passages, it becomes clear that Abraham knew and believed a good deal more than people often think.[3]

---

3. In John 8:56 Jesus said, "Abraham rejoiced to see My day, and he saw it and was glad" (NASB). The context indicates that "My day" refers to the manifestation of the promised Messiah. The most plausible occasions for this revelation would have been at the birth of Isaac when he rejoiced (Gen. 21:1–7), or at the sacrifice of Isaac, when he

So from the start he would have been able to proclaim in his worship the nature of the true and living God, the sovereign, righteous, gracious, and faithful Yahweh. His worship might have appeared to the pagans to be similar to their worship—but not if they listened to what he had to say.

## Abraham's Sacrificial Worship

God's revelation prompted Abraham's obedience, and that obedience was frequently demonstrated by the way he worshipped. That worship was the primary means through which Abraham would obey the command to be a blessing. His worship centered on sacrifice, but that sacrifice had to be properly explained if the world was to understand. This began immediately when Yahweh appeared to Abraham in the land of Canaan, and Abraham responded by building an altar (12:7), a practice that would be repeated throughout his life (12:8; 13:18; 22:9). There is no mention of a "sacrifice," per se, but we may assume that one was made on the altar,[4] for it would be expected that a sacrifice would be made on an altar (see Gen. 22:7).

Since sacrifice was an essential part of worship throughout the ancient world, it was the proper thing for Abraham to do to show gratitude and devotion to his God. But what exactly did those ancient sacrifices mean to him? The narratives leading up to the story of Abraham establish for us the basic principles about sacrificial worship, and they provide the background for Abraham's worship.

### Background of Sacrifice

#### The Offerings of Cain and Abel

Worship is the setting for Cain's murder of Abel in Genesis 4, as startling as that may sound. Accordingly, the chapter has a lot to say

---

foresaw the future provision of the LORD in that mountain (Gen. 22). Jesus' point is that he was the I AM before Abraham and that Abraham saw something of the greater sacrifice. Hebrews 11:19 explains that Abraham offered up Isaac because he believed that God was able to raise him up from the dead. Abraham believed in the creative power of God and that that power could somehow maintain Isaac as the promised seed even if sacrificed.

4. The word *altar (mizbēakh)* is related to the verb "to slaughter for sacrifice." An altar was the "place of the slaughtering the sacrifice."

about worship, but our primary interest here is with the sacrifices themselves.[5]

As the story begins, we are told literally that "at the end of days" Cain and Abel brought from their respective occupations gifts for the LORD. They apparently had been told that there was a God who made all things and who gave them life and that they needed to give him some token of their gratitude. The most natural way to do this was to bring a gift.

The kind of offering that they each brought (called *minkhāh*) was later legislated to be brought in gratitude and dedication (Lev. 2). Since this offering could be an animal or a basket of food products, it is likely that Abel's offering was accepted and Cain's was not because of the attitude of their hearts. The word order of the text has: "The LORD looked with favor on Abel and his offering, but on Cain and his offering he did not look with favor" (Gen. 4:4–5). Abel had faith, and so he was accepted—with his offering (Heb. 11:4). However, God saw something unsatisfactory in Cain, and so his offering was unacceptable. This gives the reader a preview of human worship in general: some people attend a service and are uplifted, and others who are there do not respond; some give to the Lord and are blessed, while others do it and are disgruntled. It is not the ritual that is at fault but the person. Thus, in this story we are dealing with two kinds of "worshippers." On the surface Cain's offering looked perfectly acceptable, but his heart was not in it. In fact, Cain simply brought an offering, whereas Abel brought from the "*fattest* of the *firstborn* of his flock." Abel went out of his way to please God, bringing the fattest of the firstborn to God, but Cain was simply discharging a duty. Cain thought that God would be satisfied with the performance of the routine, but he was wrong.[6]

Here is the first principle of sacrificial worship: people with a living faith make it their desire to please God. They come before God with their gifts, not because it is a duty to perform or because they think that God

---

5. Genesis 4 uses several motifs of worship, the offering *(minkhāh)* they each brought, the "fat" and the "firstborn," the "seasonal marker," and "the acceptance of the sacrifice" made by faith. The use of Levitical terminology stresses that Israel's ritual preserves much of what had been there from the beginning.

6. This reading of the case of Cain is confirmed as the evidence in the chapter continues to emerge. There is not a hint of sorrow, grief, concern, or repentance anywhere, only envy, anger, and strife. With a heart like Cain's, no offering made to God would be acceptable.

needs it, but because they know that they need God and need to acknowledge that he is the source of all life and goodness. It is not so much what
they give, but how they give themselves in worship, for the proper attitude in offering anything to God must be one of submission to the Lord.

### The Sacrifice of Noah

We also read how after the Flood Noah built an altar to the LORD
and offered burnt offerings (Gen. 8:20–21). When God smelled the sweet
aroma, he promised never again to curse the earth in this way but to
ensure that life in its seasons would continue.[7] Because God had spared
his family from the Flood and given them the opportunity to start life
all over again, Noah knew that it was right to bring a gift to the LORD as
an expression of gratitude and submission to God. This was the only appropriate response to God's grace and power. After all, God had revealed
and fulfilled his plan to preserve righteousness in the world by destroying
wickedness and by saving some and establishing them as a new creation.

By making a sacrifice Noah acknowledged how much he and his family
needed the LORD, expressed their submission to his sovereign will, and
proclaimed his grace in redeeming and restoring life (Gen. 6:8). Even
though the human heart was still evil, what began here became the wonderful prospect of worship, namely, that whenever confessing believers
expressed their faith and submission through sacrifice, God would smell
the sweet aroma and say again and again, "With this I am well-pleased.
Because of this sacrifice I will dwell with them and they shall be my people, and I will be their God; and their sins and iniquities I will remember
no more."[8]

## Abraham's Sacrifices

When Abraham built his altar to Yahweh (Gen. 12:7), it was no perfunctory religious act. Not only was it the spontaneous response of a
heart of faith to an amazing revelation from God, but it was also a sincere
act of worship, proclaiming gratitude to the one who had called him,

---

7. Here we also find motifs that would become prominent in Israel's worship: an altar,
   clean animals, a burnt offering, and a sweet aroma to God. The Israelites hearing this
   story told with these expressions would have recognized Noah as a true forbear of
   their worshipping community.
8. See Maurice, *The Doctrine of Sacrifice Deduced from the Scriptures*, 18–32.

devotion to the one who was now his God, and submission to the plan of the one who would bring blessing to the world. Worshipping God in this way was the most natural thing for Abraham to do because his heart was filled with joy and hope. And for all who witnessed it, the significance was not lost.

But would Abraham still show his submission to God in this way when the joy and the hope were threatened? Would he still surrender to God with a sacrifice if God asked him to surrender his dearest possession as the sacrifice, his only beloved son? And so in time God tested Abraham (Gen. 22:1).

The command was hard and painful. It called for Abraham to offer to God the very gift God had given him, the gift that had caused him so much joy and that had provided him with so much hope for the future. But there was no other way for Abraham to show his complete submission to Yahweh. By surrendering his beloved son to God, he would be complying with the divine will and acknowledging that Isaac belonged to God and not to him.

Of course, the act never came about—except in Abraham's heart as he raised the knife to slay his son, and in this sense the sacrifice was made. Abraham offered himself at the altar, his own will, his own desires, his own affections.[9] When this *real* victim had been slain, there was no reason to harm the boy. The ram that the LORD provided would be all that was needed now for the *symbolic* expression of Abraham's submission. Abraham learned that a pleasing sacrifice begins with the offering up of oneself. In that central act of sacrifice, the LORD God makes the worshipper like himself, for in the divine plan God would provide his own Son to be the sacrifice for us (Rom. 8:32).

It is no surprise that this chapter became a significant one for Israelite sacrificial worship. The Israelites knew that God had instructed them also to come to Mount Moriah, the temple mount according to the Chronicler, and offer their sacrifices there (2 Chron. 3:1). The faithful understood that the animal was merely a substitute, that they were surrendering themselves to God. And as they expressed their gratitude to God in this way, they would recall the motto: "In the mountain of Yahweh

---

9. This is the point the psalmists and prophets make in Israel's ritual: "Sacrifice and offering you [do] not desire . . . a body you have prepared for me . . . I have come . . . to do your will" (Ps. 40:6–8 [LXX]; cf. Heb. 10:5–7).

it will be provided"[10] (Gen. 22:14). They would also preserve the name to commemorate this truth: *Yahweh Yir'eh* ("the LORD will provide"). The Israelites went regularly to the holy mount, believing that God would provide all their needs. But they had to make their sacrifices first—their surrender had to precede his provision. That is the way faith works. When they made their sacrifices, they were not only expressing their gratitude, devotion, and surrender, but they were also expressing their faith that he would continue to provide. In much the same way, Jesus later would teach that to gain your life you must be willing to lose it. This is the essence of sacrificial worship—otherwise it is not sacrificial.

## Abraham's Proclamation at the Altar

### Proclaiming the Name of "Yahweh"

If Abraham was going to be a blessing to others, he would have to proclaim his faith to the world around him. Acts of worship are a form of proclamation only if they are understood. Accordingly, if Abraham's sacrifices had not been publicly identified with the person of Yahweh, they would have easily been identified by the people in the land as Canaanite.

Therefore, when Abraham built his altar to the LORD "he made proclamation of Yahweh by name" (Gen. 12:8; cf. 13:4; 21:33; 26:25). Since most English Bibles translate the Hebrew clause *(wayyiqrā' b<sup>e</sup>shēm Yahweh ['ădōnāy])* as "and he called on the name of the LORD," it is necessary to offer some clarification.

One standard Hebrew dictionary says the expression means using the name Yahweh in public worship.[11] But since the verb used *(qārā')* has a number of possible meanings ("call, call out, cry out, proclaim, read aloud, name, or summon"), English translations have to decide which is meant here. The most common view is to interpret it as referring to invocation or prayer, representing worship in general.[12]

If it refers to invocation, the interpretation would have to be adjusted a bit because "the name of Yahweh" normally refers to the divine attri-

---

10. The verb is "seen," although it can have the sense of "provide." But since Abraham said that "God will see to it," meaning "provide," this translation works well here to capture the significance.

11. BDB, 895, 2c.

12. S. R. Driver, *The Book of Genesis,* 71.

butes of Yahweh. "Yahweh" is the actual name; the "name" means the character or nature of Yahweh. So in passages where the expression is used for invocation, it would have the interpretive sense of "call on the basis of the nature of Yahweh" (cf. 1 Kings 18:24; 2 Kings 5:11—the first passage referring to the prophet's calling on God to answer with fire and the latter to calling on God to heal the visiting leper [cf. Isa. 64:7; Zeph. 3:9; Zech. 13:9]).

A number of biblical scholars, ancient and modern, have interpreted the expression in Genesis to refer to proclamation at the altar rather than invocation (see also Ps. 105:1).

In support of the idea of proclamation for this expression, we have a very clear usage in Exodus 33:19 and 34:5–8. The latter passage says literally:

> Then Yahweh came down in the cloud and stood there with him *and made proclamation of Yahweh by name [wayyiqrā' bᵉshēm Yahweh].*[13] And Yahweh passed in front of him and *made proclamation [wayyiqrā'],* "Yahweh, Yahweh, the compassionate and gracious God, slow to anger, abounding in loyal love and faithfulness, maintaining loyal love to thousands, and forgiving wickedness, rebellion and sin; and yet by no means will he leave the guilty unpunished, visiting[14] the sins of the fathers upon the children and upon the children's children to the third and fourth generation." Moses bowed to the ground at once and worshipped.

This passage says that Yahweh himself came down to meet with Moses on the mountain, and as Yahweh passed by he "made proclamation of Yahweh by name"—the exact same Hebrew clause that we have in Genesis 12:8. But with Yahweh as the subject of the verb, proclamation is clearly what is intended and not prayer. What is most helpful is that the content of the proclamation is recorded for us in the text—it is the clear proclamation of the nature or the attributes of Yahweh.[15] This proclamation came after the Israelites had rebelled with the worship of the golden calf.

---

13. NIV has "and proclaimed his name, the LORD."
14. NIV has "he punishes the children and their children for the sin of the fathers."
15. This is the "name of Yahweh." Isaiah 9:6 says, "[His name] will be called Wonderful Counselor, Mighty God, Everlasting Father, Prince of Peace." See also my discussion of "name," in *New International Dictionary of Old Testament Theology and Exegesis.*

Before renewing the covenant with them, Yahweh had to proclaim the kind of God he is. Moses fell down on his face in worship in response to the revelation. As Durham explains, the declaration of the nature of Yahweh makes it clear how bad their rebellion was and what the next step had to be—renewal of the covenant.[16]

From this revelation of God about his nature, there developed a fairly standard form of Israel's "confession of faith," which is reflected in several Old Testament passages where the attributes of God are enumerated (Num. 14:18; Neh. 9:17; Pss. 86:15; 103:8; 145:8; Joel 2:13; Jonah 4:2; Nah. 1:3).[17]

It is most likely that the sense of the clause as it is used in Exodus 34 is the same sense to be understood in the other uses in Genesis. Whatever else Abraham said in the worship at the altar, there was a similar proclamation about the nature of Yahweh. Such a proclamation of Yahweh as the one true and living God, revealed in his moral perfections, his absolute power and sovereignty, and his compassion and faithfulness, would be absolutely necessary to preserve the faith amid the confusion of pagan beliefs.

Earlier in Genesis 4:26 a slightly different form of the same expression is used to say that after the birth of Enosh "people began to make proclamation of Yahweh by name." That brief comment makes the observation that in the midst of and probably in contrast to all the advances of secular culture, there was the beginning of organized worship by devout people as a witness to the LORD. Von Rad says the verse claims that Yahweh worship was the primeval religion of mankind in general.[18] At least the verse is stating that faith in Yahweh took on a form of worship characterized by the proclamation of the nature of Yahweh as the true God. This was new in the biblical records, for before this there were only individual acts of worship. Now with civilization developing there was worship with proclamation. It is worship in, but against, the world. Franz Delitzsch says, "Then began the formal and solemn worship of God, the proclaiming (preaching) Church, hence the Church form of confessing the God of sal-

---

16. Durham, *Exodus*, 453–54.
17. Moberly convincingly argues that the list of attributes is clearly a development of the context; the list then originated in the narrative event (as the Bible presents it here) and is not a later insertion from creeds. Later, the list of attributes was adapted for use in worship (*At the Mountain of God,* 128–31).
18. Von Rad, *Genesis,* 109.

vation."[19] In view of the emphasis in the clause on "the name of Yahweh," meaning his nature, it would be hard to see how even an invocation could not have with it in some sense this idea of proclamation, perhaps not as strongly as "preached," but proclamation nonetheless.[20] H. C. Leupold observes that sacrifice made together with public invocation of Yahweh's name is "an act which could hardly be performed without proclaiming the works and character of Yahweh."[21]

Therefore, from the place of sacrifice[22] there issued forth the proclamation about the living God. When Abraham sacrificed to Yahweh, he proclaimed to all around him the nature of his God—who he was, what he was like, what he had done, and what he had promised. Such a clear proclamation would have prevented his sacrifice from becoming an empty or superstitious ritual, or from being misinterpreted as a Canaanite or pagan rite.[23] This sacrifice was different from their sacrifices: it was made to Yahweh to celebrate a personal relationship with the living God.

Thus, Abraham was a witnessing worshipper. But what impact did that proclamation have? There is a hint in Genesis 12:5 that the message was being heard. The text says that when Abraham came to Canaan, he brought "the people (or "souls," *hannéphesh*) they had acquired (lit. "made," *'āsû*) in Haran." It is likely that this refers to proselytes, people who heard the faith proclaimed and joined Abraham in his new life.[24]

The idea of Abraham's proclaiming his faith at the altar should not be surprising. Later, God said that Abraham was to have the responsibility of teaching righteousness to the nation (Gen. 18:19). And in a revelation

---

19. Delitzsch, *New Commentary on Genesis*, 204.
20. Luther's translation for Genesis 12:8 has "preached." This follows a number of commentaries and is fairly close to the mark of what Abraham was doing at the altar. Proclamation, however, can include more than a sermon that is preached.
21. Leupold, *Exposition of Genesis*, 421.
22. Genesis 4:26 does not actually say that the people making proclamation made a sacrifice, but the patriarchs did. And it is reasonable to suggest that sacrifice would at least be one occasion for the proclamation among the early descendants of Adam.
23. The text tells us that "the Canaanite was at that time living in the land," and that Abram settled near "the oaks of Moreh," a cultic center for Canaanite religion.
24. The expression would not refer to acquiring servants or slaves or to having children— Abraham had none. Cassuto says, Abram "began to proclaim in *Haran* the basic principles of his faith, and succeeded in winning for it a number of souls" (*From Noah to Abraham*, 2:320–21). Cassuto adds that the statement "and proclaimed the name of the LORD" alludes apparently to a proclamation and missionary work of this nature (ibid., 2:321).

to a pagan king, God designated Abraham as a prophet (Gen. 20:7). In that sense Abraham stood in a tradition that was already ancient, for the book of Jude (vv. 14–15) tells us that Enoch, the seventh from Adam, prophesied of the coming of the Lord with the angels to bring judgment on the earth. And Peter tells us that Noah was a preacher of righteousness (2 Peter 2:5).

Therefore, beginning with Genesis 4:26 and continuing through the history of the faith, true believers have proclaimed their faith to the world through their worship. With the call of Abraham to begin the covenant program of bringing blessing to the world, that proclamation became clearer, richer, and more powerful. And as we shall see, proclamation has ever since been an integral part of worship. Now in the worship of the new covenant the preaching of Christ crucified is the necessary correlative to celebrating Holy Communion. Whenever proclamation has been lost to worship, worship loses its way and becomes empty ritual. Both the drama of the ritual and the interpretation by the proclamation are necessary for the full worship of God. The Word gives the ritual meaning, and the ritual gives visible form to the Word.

## The Knowledge of "Yahweh"

Many scholars doubt that the ancestors knew the actual name "Yahweh"; they argue that the biblical text (which they say was written much later) simply added the name to the narratives to tell us that the God they worshipped and proclaimed was in fact Yahweh all along. The argument is based, in part, on a simplistic reading of Exodus 6:2–3: "I am Yahweh. I appeared to Abraham, to Isaac, and to Jacob as ʾĒl Shaddāy, but by my name Yahweh I was not known by them (or, I did not make myself known to them [*nôdaʿtî*])." But to say that the patriarchs knew the title ʾĒl Shaddāy but not the name "Yahweh" has several difficulties.[25]

First, since Moses needed to convince the elders that the God of their fathers had sent him to them, a new, previously unknown name, would not do. Second, when Moses asked what name he should give the people, God did not answer with the revelation of a new name Yahweh but with an explanation of that name. To understand "I am that I am" (*ʾehyeh*

---

25. For a more detailed discussion of this issue along with some archaeological evidence for the early use of the name, see my article, "Did the Patriarchs Know the Name of the LORD?"

*ʾăsher ʾehyeh* [Exod. 3:14]) the elders would have to have known the name Yahweh, for the explanation uses the first person singular form of the verb, and the name is the third person ("he is"). By using this play on the name, God was giving Moses the significance of the name for the immediate situation.[26] Moses did not need a new revelation but proof that he had met with Yahweh their God. Third, if the ancestors never knew the name Yahweh, then they had worshipped a no-name God, which is most unlikely. And fourth, there is evidence from the pre-Mosaic traditions that they knew and used the name Yahweh[27] in addition to other designations for God, including "God Most High," "Almighty God," and "Lord." For example, Abraham named the place of the sacrifice of Isaac: Yahweh Yirʾeh, "Yahweh will provide" (Gen. 22:14). The text records a straightforward report that he named the place using "Yahweh."

Also, in passages that record God's self-revelation, we find the name: "I am Yahweh who brought you out from the Ur of the Chaldees" (Gen. 15:7). If Abraham never knew the name, then this sentence was artificially included to explain that the God who made a covenant with Abraham was in fact Yahweh who made a covenant with Israel.

It is more likely that the name was used in the patriarchal period as many have acknowledged. Decades ago Ryle wrote that the writer of Genesis 4:26 taught that a form of the name Yahweh was known to historic antiquity.[28] Von Rad concluded that the "Yahweh cult" had roots that went back much farther than Moses, that Yahweh worship was the original worship.[29] And Gunkel said that the name was known in the earlier communities but not understood in its full sense.[30]

The interpretation of Exodus 6:2–3, then, must hang on the meaning of the verb "to know." The text is probably making a distinction between *earlier awareness* of the name and *later understanding* of it. Benno Jacob

---

26. See further M. H. Segal, *The Pentateuch*, 3–7.
27. Moses' own mother was named "Jochebed" (*yôkéved*), which combines the abbreviation of the name "Yahweh" with the word *kéved*, "Yahweh is glory." J. F. Ross, writing in the *Interpreter's Dictionary of the Bible*, defines the word this way as the most natural etymology but then withdraws it because that would mean that the name of Yahweh was known before the time of Moses: "Thus the priestly writer did not understand it in this sense." Incredibly, he finds a better meaning for the prefix of the name in an old Canaanite god YW, even though such a god probably did not exist (2:925).
28. Ryle, *Book of Genesis*, 83.
29. Von Rad, *Genesis*, 109.
30. Gunkel, *Genesis ubersetzt und erklart.*

paraphrases the verse this way: "I am Yahweh even though I have not allowed myself to be experienced by this attribute."[31] But that experience was about to take place through the deliverance by Moses. Jacob goes into detail to show that God "appeared" to the patriarchs as ʾĒl Shaddāy because the covenant was still in promise form. The speeches of promise were introduced with "I am ʾĒl Shaddāy" (17:1; 28:3; 35:11; 48:3) to show that God's power was behind the promises.[32] Now that the promises were going to be fulfilled with Moses, God would start using the personal, covenant name in his self-disclosure: "I am Yahweh."[33] The holy name with its fresh interpretation meant that God would now be with them in an even greater way, redeeming them from bondage and making them into a great nation.

In fact, God promised that when he redeemed the people, they would "know" (i.e., experience what it means) that he is Yahweh (Exod. 6:7). Knowing the name means experiencing the fulfillment of the promises. In Isaiah 52:6, Yahweh promised that when he delivered the Israelites from the Babylonian captivity, they would "know" his name. No one would claim that exilic Jews were ignorant of the name Yahweh. It means that when they were set free in accordance with the promise, they would truly know the meaning of the covenant name.

Therefore, when the ancestors made proclamation of Yahweh by name, they used the personal name to identify their God and rehearsed the characteristics of this God who had revealed himself to them. But they lived in the time of the promises. As the years passed there was so much more to proclaim because of all that Yahweh revealed through word and deed. And this is the way it has continued throughout the history of the faith. By the time of the fulfillment of the promises in Christ Jesus, the proclamation of the name of the LORD became rich beyond measure—yet without leaving the basic truths that were known from the beginning.

The same development could be illustrated from the Gospels. The disciples certainly knew the name "Jesus"; but after his death and resurrection, they truly came to know him and what that name meant.

---

31. B. Jacob, *Second Book of the Bible: Exodus,* 142–56.
32. The title "ʾĒl Shaddāy" has been traditionally interpreted to mean "God Almighty," based on possible etymology and early translations. But convincing etymological support for that meaning, or any of the more recent speculative meanings, is lacking.
33. Interestingly this formula was used in Genesis 15:7 because the LORD had fulfilled his promise to Abraham to bring him out of Ur of the Chaldees.

## Other Worshipful Acts That Proclaim the Faith

### Solemn Oaths

One clear public declaration of Abraham's faith came in the ritual of making oaths in the presence of people who served other gods. He solemnized his oath before the king of Sodom by invoking the name Yahweh as the Most High God (Gen. 14:22). Later, in his dealings with the king of Gerar, he also swore an oath (21:23–24). And then, as he sent his servant to find a wife for his son, he had the servant swear as well (24:3, 9). Using such oaths proclaimed the sovereignty of the LORD, because people swore by the highest power they knew. Those who witnessed these oaths realized that Abraham was swearing by all that was sacred to him.

### Tithes

Abraham paid tithes to Melchizedek (Gen. 14:20) as a public demonstration of his submission and gratitude to the LORD for granting him victory. It was generally conceded that victory was due to the victor's god fighting for him. So Abraham paid this tribute in the presence of his Amorite confederates and the king of corrupt Sodom. Abraham's devotion was exemplary in that he took nothing for himself except what should be given to the LORD in tribute.[34]

### Intercessory Prayer

Two of the most significant prayers of Abraham were intercessions. He first prayed for the LORD to spare the righteous people of Sodom (Gen 18:16–33) from the judgment, and then he prayed for Abimelech and his household to be restored to health and vigor (20:7, 17). By his intercession others could see that his God Yahweh was not just a tribal deity but was sovereign over all the people of the world and that faith in him could change their circumstances.

And this devout expression of worship was passed on to Abraham's servant. Following his master's instructions on how to trust the LORD for a successful mission to find Isaac a bride (24:12), he prayed for and received divine guidance. But most significantly when his mission was

---

34. Note, however, that this is not a normal tithing practice. Abram actually was tithing out of the spoils of war, things that formerly did not belong to him. It is still an act of submission and worship but not a sample of regular giving.

successful, he insisted on publicly declaring the faithful love of the LORD before receiving any hospitality. His devout faith was transformed into public proclamation.

## The Rite of Circumcision

When God made circumcision the sign of the covenant, he was establishing a regular ritual for the nation of Israel. Covenant signs were meant to proclaim the nature of the covenant and remind the participants of their obligations. Circumcision was a sign that the Israelites were set apart to the LORD as members of a covenant (Gen. 17:10, 24–27; 21:4), reminding them of the standard of holiness and purity in the family. In time the circumcision ritual became an integral part of the life of the worshipping community, who would hear the covenant proclaimed and see it sealed with the sign. In the New Testament the sign of the new covenant is the cup of Holy Communion—as often as Christians drink it they proclaim the essence of the covenant, the saving death of Christ.

## Commemorative Thanksgiving

Abraham frequently responded to the LORD with gratitude and adoration, falling on his face before him (cf. Gen. 17:3), or bowing to the ground (18:2), or rejoicing in his provisions (21:1–7). But one of Abraham's most significant thanksgivings took the form of the commemorative naming of "Yahweh Yir'eh" (22:14). Such namings were a sure way of keeping the name of Yahweh before the eyes of the world. With this proclamation a saying grew up that perpetuated the link between the name and Israel's worship on the temple mount.

## Burial with Faith

When it came time for Abraham to bury his wife, he chose to do it in a way that would perpetuate the faith. He bought a cave from the people who were living in the land (Gen. 23). Abraham was making it clear that no longer would his dead "be gathered to their ancestors" back in Padan Aram—the future was here, in the land that the LORD had sworn to give him and his descendants. This was a significant expression of his faith in the promise, and it too was done openly in the presence of Amorite and Hittite inhabitants of the land, who would have understood the significance. So the "world" made room for this devout man's convictions.

And down through history the funeral has provided one of the greatest opportunities to worship with proclamation to the world.

## Conclusion

Worship is the natural response to the revelation of the LORD, whether in word or act. This we have seen in the life of Abraham. Abraham built an altar to the LORD after the LORD appeared to him (Gen. 12:7–8). He built another altar after the LORD's word of promise (13:18). He paid tithes after the LORD gave the victory (14:20). He took an oath after the blessing of Melchizedek (14:22). He prepared the sacrifice and protected it after the revelation from God (chap. 15). He bowed to the ground after the LORD appeared to him (17:3). He circumcised in compliance with God's command (17:10, 23–27). He interceded after judgment was revealed (chap. 18). He interceded again after God directed Abimelech to him (20:7, 17). He rejoiced in the LORD after the fulfillment of God's promise (21:1–7). He swore by the LORD after the LORD gave him peace in the land (21:23–24). He "sacrificed" Isaac in obedience to the LORD's command (chap. 22). So as far back as the time of Abraham, worship was both *a spontaneous and an ordered response to divine intervention.* And Abraham's acts of worship, characterized by submission, dependence, and gratitude, *proclaimed* his beliefs to a watching world, a world that was familiar with the ritual acts but not the God being worshipped.

# CHAPTER 8

# The Worship *of the* LORD *in* Abraham's Descendants

## The Patriarchs

### The Worship of Isaac

#### *Prayer*

One of the most significant acts of personal worship recorded in the traditions about Isaac is prayer—significant because he did not make the same mistake his father made. When Isaac and his wife could not have a child, they prayed to the LORD and the LORD answered (Gen. 25:21). Then, when the pregnancy became difficult, Rebekah went to enquire of the LORD and was given an oracle. She may have gone to some holy place like Beerlahairoi (where God had heard Hagar in her affliction), or to a prophet (cf. 1 Sam. 9:9) like Abraham (Gen 20:7),[1] or to a priest like Melchizedek. In time "enquire" *(dārash)* came to refer to seeking the LORD with acts of worship; and acts such as fervent prayer in the sanctuary often became great sources of comfort and resolution (1 Sam. 1:3–11).

#### *Sacrifice with Proclamation*

Isaac made proclamation of the LORD by name (Gen. 26:25), just as his father Abraham had done. Thus the pattern continued: In response to the revelation of God, the faithful respond in worship with proclamation.

---

1. Even though Abraham's death is recorded before the record of the birth of Jacob and Esau, he lived fifteen years into their times.

### Oaths

Isaac also made a treaty with the Philistines just as his father had done (Gen. 26:12–33). The demonstration of his faith was the issue in what could have been an explosive situation. But the descendants of Abraham were to be a blessing to the families of the world, and Isaac would only be a blessing if he was able to exalt the LORD in his dealings with the pagan king. Abimelech saw the obvious blessing on Isaac from the constant supply of water he received and so sought a treaty with him to share the blessing. Isaac agreed to the treaty but made sure that the oath was in the name of the LORD, proclaiming by the transaction the correct interpretation of the blessing.

### Oracles of Blessing

Although rare, oracles proclaimed the faith in a powerful way. An oracle was no simple greeting or parental well-wishing; it was a revelation from God himself. In the patriarchal accounts, the head of the family who was the guardian of the covenant actually spoke for God (Gen. 27:27–29, 33, 39–40; 28:1–4; 47:10; 48; 49). When this happened it was a clear proclamation of the faith, and it usually prompted devotion and commitment. The fact that Isaac was shaken with fear (Gen. 27:33) when he realized that he had given the blessing to Jacob shows that he knew that God had overruled his intent to bless the wrong son. And what he had said could not be taken back—it was a word from the LORD.

Later in the worship of Israel, the main oracle of blessing from God would be pronounced by the high priest after the atoning sacrifice had been made in the sanctuary (Num. 6:22–27). This too was clearly a direct word from God, and not merely a benediction or greeting from the priest.

## The Worship of Jacob

### Worship at Bethel

Genesis 28:10–22 provides another important glimpse of patriarchal worship, now with more ritual acts than before. Here, too, worship was the spontaneous response to the dramatic revelation of God, now in the dream—there was a stairway between heaven and earth with the angels of God ascending and descending on it, and the LORD himself standing at the top of it confirming the covenant promises to Jacob. When Jacob realized the import of this revelation, he trembled with fear. God was in this place! This was none other than "the house of God," and this was "the gate of heaven"! Here, on this very spot, heaven and earth touched! Jacob's fear was properly directed by faith so that he turned that awesome place into a holy place. He had no animals and no altar, and so he stood the stone up and poured his oil out on top of it.

When someone saw a standing stone *(matssēvāh),* it was obvious that it had been placed in an upright position intentionally to arrest the attention of the onlooker. Standing stones[2] could be memorials for the dead (Absalom's in 2 Sam. 18:18),[3] legal boundaries or border markers (Laban and Jacob in Gen. 31:45–54), commemorative markers (Samuel's "stone of help" [called "Ebenezer," *'even hā'ēzer*] in 1 Sam. 7:12), or religious shrines marking out a sacred area where the deity could be found. The last two apply here.

The stone that Jacob stood upright had been "one of the stones" (Gen. 28:11) that he had found in the place. It became an altar when he stood it upright and poured oil on its top (v. 18). It is apparent from the way the text parallels the vision and the worship that the standing stone represented the stairway that Jacob had seen, with Yahweh standing at the top.[4] Thus, Jacob's acts recalled the vision of glory, and his pouring oil on the top of the stone set this place apart, that is, sanctified it, to the worship of the LORD who appeared at the top of the stairway. Pouring oil on the rock was also a sacrifice. It was a gift to be sure, but more importantly it was a symbolic act by which Jacob demonstrated his submission and devotion to the LORD. Later in Israel's worship, people would bring oil to the sanctuary (Lev. 24:1–9); and among other uses, it was used to consecrate everything for worship.

The actual place was formerly called Luz. But that is not as important as the new name it now received, Bethel, "the House of God," a holy place, a consecrated place of devotion, vows, and tithes, a place where the LORD appeared to the ancestor of Israel. Jacob had no congregation to join him in worship, but this proclamation by naming would invite worship on

---

2. C. F. Graesser, "Standing Stones in Ancient Palestine," 34–63.

3. Compare the stelae found at Hazor in a thirteenth century funerary shrine showing the forearms with hands up in a raised position (prayer or protection?).

4. For a good analysis of this passage, see Fokkelman, *Narrative Art in Genesis,* 46–81.

this spot in the years to come. It would remind subsequent generations that God had chosen it as his "house," a place where he might walk among his people. Thus Bethel would provide Israel with its first echo of Paradise within the Holy Land.

Holy places were frequently marked out by such namings. Later generations wanting to establish places of worship would be reminded by such names that God had revealed himself there in a special way, and to worship in a place where the greats of the faith had found God was also a way of experiencing in some sense community with former believers. When the Israelites settled in the land, Bethel became an important place for the spiritual life of the nation (Josh. 16:1–3; 18:11–27).

Jacob also made a vow (Gen. 28:20–22): If the LORD would indeed be with him[5] and be his God, then he would worship and serve him in the proper place (Bethel). This is the first report of a believer's verbal commitment to the LORD in response to his promises. It is a valuable lesson: God revealed his gracious promises in order to draw out the believers' devotion and alter their lives. In his vow Jacob also promised to give to God a tenth of all that God gave to him. He had just been promised divine provision, and the natural response of faith was to return a portion of that material substance to the Lord, the giver, as a token of gratitude.

### Invocation with Covenants

Among the several other worshipful acts of the descendants of Abraham, we read how Jacob and Laban marked out their border with a monolith and a cairn and then sealed the agreement by a sacrifice that was a shared meal (Gen. 31:44–55). What makes this a religious activity is that the LORD was invoked to watch between them so that they would not enter each other's territory and inflict further pain on one another. Once again the sovereignty of God was proclaimed through ritual; his power would make this treaty work (v. 29). Thus, the oath that Jacob took at Gilead was by "the Fear *(pakhad)* of his father Isaac" (v. 53), "fear" being a reference to God, the object of Isaac's fear and devotion.

---

5. The expression "The LORD be with you" has become a common greeting in the church. It expresses the idea that the LORD intervene in a special way to protect and provide.

### Rites of Confirmation

Once the patriarch was back in the land safely, some twenty years after he had fled, he built an altar at Bethel to commemorate God's faithfulness (Gen. 35:7). This act of worship was out of gratitude to God for
bringing him safely to his father's house again (cf. Gen. 28:20–22). Jacob
again set up a pillar as an altar, poured out a libation, poured oil on the
stone, and renamed Bethel (Gen. 35:14–15). He performed acts almost
identical to the former event to celebrate the fulfillment of the promises
God had made to him. Accordingly, Jacob named it "the God of Bethel"
(*'Ēl Bêt-'ēl*, v. 7) and "Bethel" (*Bêt-'ēl*, v. 15).

### Worship for the Journey

When Jacob traveled to Beersheba on his way down to be with Joseph
in Egypt, he stopped to make sacrifices to the God of his father Isaac (Gen.
46:1). The prospect of leaving home to go and live in another country is
no small concern. But such concerns are also opportunities to strengthen
and confirm one's faith. As a result of this act of worship, he received
the assuring word from the LORD that all was well. Worship calms the
troubled soul.

### Sacred Burials

When Rachel died Jacob set up a pillar and mourned for her (Gen.
35:20). But when Jacob died, there was a far more elaborate and solemn
burial procedure following Egyptian customs for the burial of great
men. Genesis 50:1–14 reports that Jacob was embalmed in Egypt (forty
days) and then mourned extensively (seventy days). The ensuing funeral
procession to Canaan with its lamentation and solemn ritual caught
the attention of the Canaanites (vv. 10–11) and led to a commemorative
naming: *'Āvēl-Mitsráyim*, "the Mourning of the Egyptians." It was a great
and solemn event witnessed by many along the way.

In all this Joseph made sure that the faith of his father was honored:
the burial took place in the land of Canaan, where the hope lay, that other
Eden, and not in the pagan world, what would become the land of bondage. What marked this out as a burial within the faith was not the special
embalming or the great lamentation but the fact that it took place in the
Promised Land. In following this plan, the significance would have to be
explained to all interested. One might have asked what difference it made

where one is buried. Well, it made a great deal of difference for people whose faith was in the future fulfillment of the covenant promises, a fulfillment that would not leave them in a grave in Egypt. And so Joseph too was concerned that his bones not be left in Egypt but be taken up to Canaan at the great exodus (Gen. 50:25).

Of course, people in the ancient world buried their dead with some hope of life beyond the grave—their religions promised this in some sense—so they buried their dead with religious ceremony. What distinguished the worship of the LORD from these pagan rituals was not so much the outward form but the truth of the faith. Yahweh was the one true and living God. Burial in faith in him offered more hope than burial with the beliefs of the pagans (cf. Pss. 49; 73). Only faith in the LORD could guarantee a future glorious life.

When believers die they are buried with hope in the promises of God, and the fulfillment of those promises demands life after death, a resurrection. Down through history Christians have preferred burial in "sanctified land," usually churchyards, as opposed to common burial spots. In one sense we might say it doesn't really matter; but in another sense it does—believers want everything about their death and burial to be distinctly "Christian," for their identity is with the church, their communion is with the saints, and their hope is in the resurrection and the fulfillment of the promises. How we die and how we are buried proclaim our faith to a world that has no hope. And the worship ritual that accompanies the burial of the faithful is one of the most powerful proclamations of the hope we have in the Lord, the hope of glory.

## Israel's Ancestors in Egypt

When we survey the worship of Israel in Egypt several centuries later, we are no longer dealing with a few people but with a vast number of families. And we are no longer witnessing several individual acts of worship but communal acts of worship that gain in intensity and content with every act of God. However, these people were in bondage in Egypt and not in the Promised Land where they could worship and serve their God freely; until they were free, their faith in the LORD had to sustain them. When God came to their aid (Gen. 50:25), he found a responsive community of people ready to believe, ready to obey, and ready to worship.

## Worshipful Responses to Revelation

In the misery of their bondage, the people of Israel cried out to God (Exod. 2:23); after all, God had promised to deliver them (Gen. 50:25). Therefore, when God heard their cries and sent the deliverer to them, they responded with eagerness and probably a good sense of relief. And even though they frequently faltered in their faith, their allegiance was clearly to the LORD.

### The Burning Bush

First, God had to prepare his deliverer, and he did so with an astounding revelation in the desert—all of a sudden a bush burst into flames, but it was not consumed (Exod. 3:1–3). This is the first revelation of the glory of the LORD in the book of Exodus. Manifestations of his glory continued to intensify until the whole top of Mount Sinai was ablaze with his glory, prompting fear and adoration in the people of God who had assembled at the foot of the mountain. But here, in a lonely spot in the desert, the sight of a burning bush captivated Moses. As he drew near, God stopped him in his tracks: "Take off your sandals, for the place where you are standing is holy ground" (v. 5). That little plot of sand was now holy ground because the Holy One himself was there, and no mortals may step on holy ground without humbling themselves in acknowledgment of God's holy presence. Scripture affirms again and again that to enter the presence of the holy Lord God is a fearful thing.[6] Moses now knew that the holy LORD God had found him and nothing would be the same again.

### Signs for the People

Moses was thereby given the commission to lead the people of Israel out of bondage—no small task. He would have to explain this revelation clearly and convincingly to the people to inspire their faith. To convince the elders and the people that this was of God, he was given the clear understanding of who Yahweh was and why he was about to do this (Exod. 3:14–15); and he was given confirming signs to perform before them as well (4:1–9).[7] His mission had to be seen by the people of Israel as the be-

---

6. The emphasis on God's holy presence and holy ground will be a major theme of Exodus, culminating in the establishment of the sanctuary. Michael Fishbane shows how Exodus 1–4 foreshadows Exodus 5–19 (*Text and Texture,* 75–76).

7. The signs, as well as the later plagues, were all designed to demonstrate the Lord's sovereignty over things that the Egyptians depended on and venerated (see Num. 33:4).

ginning of the fulfillment of the promises that Yahweh had made to the fathers, to Abraham, Isaac, and Jacob. And by the words from God that he proclaimed and the signs that he performed, Moses was able to convince them that Yahweh their God had sent him. When the people heard that the LORD had answered their prayer, and remembered his covenant with the fathers, and was about to change their destiny,[8] they bowed (s.v. *qādad*) their heads and worshipped (s.v. *shākhāh* in BDB) him (Exod. 4:31).[9]

## Sacrificial Pilgrimage

When Moses announced to Pharaoh that the Hebrews would be leaving Egypt, he did so in terms of their going to worship their God, because to worship is to acknowledge the highest authority. Moses demanded of Pharaoh that the people be set free so that they could go on a sacrificial pilgrimage *(khag)* to meet Yahweh their God in the desert (Exod. 3:18; 5:3). In other words, the purpose of their deliverance from the pagan world of bondage was to form a worshipping community. The implication of Moses' demand was clear to everyone: to go "three days" into the desert and to sacrifice "to Yahweh" clearly meant that their loyalties were with Yahweh, not the world or the world's king, especially one who claimed to be a god. By making this pilgrimage they would be proclaiming that Yahweh, not Pharaoh, was their God as well as their king. When they eventually did sacrifice to him, they would be expressing devotion and gratitude to him for delivering them from Egypt. Here was worship against the world, over the world.

This ancient and lasting significance of going to make a sacrifice to their God must not be missed. It meant that they had no higher authority to whom they owed allegiance. It also meant that they would not be coming back—and Pharaoh knew it. Thus he refused, claiming that he did not know this Yahweh. But he would come to know about him, both

---

8. The Hebrew traditionally was translated "visit" *(pāqad)*. When God "visits" someone, it is either for blessing or for cursing. That is why the essential idea is that of "changing the destiny through divine intervention." See my word study on this in *Creation and Blessing*, 736–40.

9. The two verbs could be translated separately (they bowed down, and they prostrated themselves), but since they are homonyms, they could be taken as a verbal *hendiadys* (one verb modifying the other). This would express one intensified idea: "they bowed low to the ground."

through the plagues and then the defeat at the sea. True worship cannot be suppressed for long by the world or by the tyrants of the world. When it comes to the question of allegiance, true believers will proclaim their devotion to the living God through worship.

## Passover

God's plan for the deliverance of Israel from Pharaoh's bondage would come with another sacrifice, but one made in Egypt itself—the Passover.[10] This ritual called for faith in the LORD's promise to save his people; if the people believed the word from God, each family would kill an animal and apply its blood to the doorway of the house (Exod. 12). The blood of the sacrifice protected them from the plague of death that filled the land, it redeemed the firstborn who would otherwise have died, and it hastened their escape while the Egyptians were in chaos. The faithful were then to eat the Passover meal in a certain way, each ingredient and each step carefully prescribed, and they were to eat it with unleavened bread because they had to be ready to leave.

That this ritual was to play a central part in the worship of the nation ever after is made clear by the instructions included in this chapter: it was to be a feast, a holy convocation, and a service for all generations (12:14, 25, 48). But it was for faithful members of the covenant. In the ritual the sacrifice became a communal meal with the people awaiting the deliverance from the LORD. At this early stage the Passover was instituted as a meal in the homes, a meal that was both joyous and ominous. Later it would be celebrated in part in the temple with great ritual and praise, without the urgency of being ready to leave. But from the beginning it was a ritual of worship based on faith in the Redeemer—and it never lost that meaning; it was a dramatic form of worship to be reenacted perpetually. Because of this it had to be accompanied by precise interpretive words that became a fixed liturgy over time, words that preserved the story and explained its meaning. Without this proclamation, people would think of it as just a good meal.

This feast is one of the richest celebrations of worship in history. To celebrate Passover was to rejoice over the deliverance from bondage, actual or realized. To explain what it all meant to the children was to proclaim

---

10. This ritual will be discussed more fully in subsequent chapters.

the wonders of the LORD's redemption from age to age. To eat the symbolic parts of the meal was to share in the experience of the beginning of the covenant nation. To apply the blood (later at the altar) was to demonstrate faith in the salvation of the LORD. To keep the Feast of Unleavened Bread was to acknowledge that a life of purity was to follow redemption. And to dedicate the firstborn to the LORD, the firstborn who did not die, was to declare that the redeemed belong to the LORD. And because the firstborn represented the whole nation, the redemption of the firstborn represented the redemption of the nation. So Passover became the beginning festival of the worship of Israel. All who would celebrate it in the years to come were to do it "as if" they had been in Egypt at that formative time.

Essentially, however, the ritual centered on a blood sacrifice in which an animal died and the human lived (cf. the same substitution in Gen. 22), and so it was a celebration of redemption and life. Its connection to the Exodus made it the celebration of victory over the world that worshippers ultimately must find. But this celebration also signified another step in the reversal of the curse in the garden: there the sinners were expelled from the presence of the LORD to serve the ground in order to survive in the world, but here the people of God were released[11] from bondage, where they served the world, to begin their journey back to enter God's rest; there the sinners could only look forward to death as a release from the curse, but here they escaped the judgment by the blood of a lamb and could look forward to life in another Eden.

Most biblically informed Christians will readily note the many parallels between the Passover and its fulfillment in the Lord's Supper. This is, of course, because the ritual had a prophetic element to it—it was typological of the death of the Messiah, the Lamb of God, whose blood was shed so that people everywhere might escape the judgment on the world.[12] Paul declared to the Corinthians that "Christ, our Passover lamb, has been sacrificed [for us]" (1 Cor. 5:7). Christians celebrate the fulfillment of the Passover in the rite of Holy Communion and the fulfillment of Unleavened Bread in holy living.

---

11. The verb *shālakh* is used in Genesis 3:23 for the expulsion from the garden and in passages in Exodus for "sending out" or "letting the people go" (4:23; 5:2).
12. Typology is a form of prophecy, indirect prophecy, in which people, places and events form divinely intended illustrations of a corresponding reality that will be the fulfillment.

## Celebrating Redemption

Exodus 15 records the song that Moses and the people sang after crossing the sea. It is a profound work, both in its poetical composition and its theology. In it the people praised the LORD for his greatness that he displayed in his victory over Egypt and for his loyal love that he displayed in the redemption of his people from bondage; they also expressed their confidence that God would guide them to his holy habitation, the land of rest where he would dwell among them and make them his inheritance.

Verse 1 says that Moses sang the song, and verse 21 says that Miriam, the prophetess, "sang in response" to his words (*ʿānāh*, "to answer," here means "to sing antiphonally"). Moses may have sung a line at a time, and then Miriam and the others repeated them (at least she repeated the main refrain). This song of praise was the natural and enthusiastic response of God's people to their marvelous redemption. This was no routine time of singing—they had just been miraculously delivered from death at the crossing of the sea! Their redemption was real and still vivid in their memory; they could hardly contain themselves now that there was the opportunity to celebrate their redemption and their freedom (cf. Ps. 126 and the unbounded joy of deliverance from the Exile).

Amazingly the form of the song (a hymn) is remarkably developed, raising for some the question concerning the composition of the piece. It is possible that the song may not have been in this exact form when they first sang it. Prayers and praises were often said spontaneously and then later put into a better form to be preserved in a book.[13] Yet, because the roles of the prophet and the musician often overlapped, as in the case of the Psalms, the song that Moses and Miriam sang may very well have been a prophetic work, inspired by God. In any case, the song indicates that the singing of hymns was known to Israel at this early stage, as it was to the cultures around them. The Israelites could sing—and sing they would now that they had a great reason to sing. Later, God would use David to develop this aspect of worship fully. The Song by the Sea (Exod. 15) is in many ways a foretaste of the songs of deliverance that would be sung for ages by the people of God, culminating in the new

---

13. The Song of Jonah (Jonah 2), while perfectly representing the experience, appears to have been put in its final poetic form later (certainly not in the fish) for the composition of the book. See also the beautiful form of Psalm 51 to express David's confession in 2 Samuel 12:13.

song in glory, praising the Lord who redeemed us by his blood (Rev. 5:9–10).

One part of this celebration at the sea was the dancing of Miriam and the women who accompanied her with timbrels and dances (Exod. 15:20). Dancing with musical accompaniment was a legitimate expression of praise in the believing community of the Old Testament. But how did dancing in praise of God differ from secular celebration? In order for dancing to be in praise of the LORD, it had to be inspired by some great or gracious act of God (and so natural and spontaneous), it had to communicate that God was being praised (and not be a performance), and it had to be consonant with purity and righteousness (not distracting or suggestive, and not mixing the sexes). This means that worshippers seeing the dance would be caught up in the praise of the LORD, not in the dance or with the dancer. It has always been very difficult to have sacred dance that meets these criteria. Sometimes when it is spontaneous, it is more effective than in a prepared "performance." But when such dancing is genuine in its praise of God, it can be beautiful and moving.

# Conclusion *for* Part 3

FROM THE VERY BEGINNING believers were identified by their worship. When they used religious acts and forms that existed in the world around them, they had to make it clear that they were worshipping the one true and holy LORD God of glory and that their use of these forms had a completely different content. They made sacrifices, set up pillars, commemorated holy places, swore sacred oaths, paid tithes, carried out ritual burials, and sang and danced in praise to their God. Every one of these acts was an act of worship that spoke to the world around them that they were a worshipping people. But what made their worship distinct and what clarified true worship to the world was their proclamation of "the name of Yahweh." That proclamation most naturally would be made at the altar, when they declared their faith, who Yahweh was, what he had done, and what he was about to do. Proclamation of the faith, however, also could be made through commemorative naming, oaths and treaty covenants, distinctive burial ritual, and celebration in song, all of which revealed the truth to the watching world. And certainly the proclamation of the faith is the boldest when it declares its true allegiance to the King of heaven, for such a proclamation sounds the death knell for the world and its false gods. Those who came into contact with this worshipping community would soon learn that the object of their devotion was the one true, living, and holy God, God of gods, King of Kings, Lord of Lords, Yahweh.

In the formative periods of the religious experience of Israel, there was no organized worship, no central sanctuary, and no standing priests. But all the main elements of worship had begun to appear. Each would be developed over the centuries to its finest expression. However, since from the beginning it was absolutely critical that the worship of the holy God be clearly distinguished from corrupt false worship, the common element throughout these early biblical narratives was the proclamation of the faith. In a world that is so pervasively religious, proclamation must characterize all acts of worship.

# PART 4

# WORSHIP *with* SACRIFICE

*The Establishment of Sanctity in Worship*

# Introduction

ISRAEL'S ANCESTORS HAD COME to know their God as the Sovereign Lord of heaven and earth (Gen. 39:2, 21; 41:37). He was not like the pagans' gods with their corrupt practices, for those gods were just like humans in their vices and virtues. Moreover, they were governed by magic and superstition and manipulated with ritual and incantation. No, this God, Yahweh, was truly holy for all the glory and the power in heaven and on earth resided with him. And amazingly he had promised by his covenant to be with his people and to make them into a great nation.

The Israelites in Egypt lived with the hope of this promise of his presence (Gen. 50:25). When the LORD did come to deliver the Israelites with great plagues and a Passover night that broke Egyptian resistance, they quickly learned just how dangerous it could be when God began to make his presence known in the world—dangerous, but yet miraculous and wonderful. Who of God's people would have it otherwise?[1] Moses, of course, hesitated at first (Exod. 3–4), but he soon learned that the LORD's presence with him would never let him return to his normal life. The divine persuasion began when he was warned that where God makes his presence known is holy ground (Exod. 3:5). People would learn that whoever dared to stand on holy ground, whoever entered that area of God's presence to worship him, could not do so on ordinary human terms, because it was no longer an ordinary place. Whoever entered into God's sacred precinct would have to conform to a kingdom that is not of this world.

Moses entered that sacred precinct, and through him God began the process of turning a vast number of people into a holy nation and a kingdom of priests (Exod. 19:5–6). What brought them together as the people

---

1. The terror of this thought was contemplated by David in Psalm 139:7–12.

of God and made them a holy nation was the presence of the LORD dwelling among them and sanctifying them. This is the glory of the covenant; and this is the memory of Paradise, now to be recalled in a defiling and dying world—God dwelling with his people, sanctifying and blessing them, and eventually restoring the world to himself through them. Since it would take the sanctifying presence of God to turn them into "the people of God," God first separated them from their bondage to the world and then led them to his holy mount, where they learned what it meant to have him in their midst as their God and King.

Meeting God at a mountain would not have seemed unusual to the people, for throughout the ancient world sacred shrines were built on the tops of mountains. The thought was that to meet with the deity one had to ascend from this mundane life to a more lofty place, a place where the earth reached up to the heavens. Mount Sinai would be forever remembered as a holy mountain because on it God chose to reveal himself. There was to be no doubt that this was the "Mount of God," for it was engulfed in terrific fire and smoke, and from the midst of it the people of Israel heard God's voice (Deut. 4:10–14).

Later, when Israel settled in the land, Mount Zion in Jerusalem became the holy mountain, much to the "dismay" of the other mountains in the land, as the poet put it (Ps. 68:15–18). Worshippers went up to Jerusalem to ascend that holy hill to worship the LORD in his sanctuary, because that was where he chose to make his dwelling place among his people (Ps. 132:13–18). This all would change, as we shall see, with the coming of Jesus the Messiah. No longer would it matter that one mountain was preferred over another (John 4:21), because worship would now be in spirit and in truth (vv. 23–24). And yet the symbolism of the mountaintop was not completely discarded, for Jesus ascended to a high mountain to be transfigured (Matt. 17:1–3). There, high above the world below, as it were, a few disciples saw him in his glistening glory and radiant beauty. Not only did that experience let them see the true glory of the Son lifted up on high, but it also rekindled their hope of entering into that glory. Later, when Jesus ascended to heaven, leaving the disciples standing there gazing up into heaven in amazement, it was from the top of the Mount of Olives.

Long before that ascension, Moses ascended Mount Sinai to receive the covenant with all its provisions for Israel's worship, especially the pattern of the sanctuary (Exod. 25:1–9). God did not need a house. After all, as Solomon later said, the heavens, even the highest heavens, cannot contain him, so how much less a temple (1 Kings 8:27)! It was the people who needed a sanctuary where they could come together and focus on him in their worship (vv. 29–30). Therefore, the tabernacle was to be made in such a way that everything about it reminded the worshippers of the majesty, glory, holiness, and beauty of the real presence of God.

Because this sanctuary was to be the one spot on earth where God's presence would reign supremely, it was to be like the heavenly sanctuary, where his will is done and he is the focus of all adoration and praise. Moreover, nothing incompatible with the holiness of God could be there—no diseased, or defiled, or sinful human could enter—unless God himself made that person fit to enter. From the beginning God had warned people that the one who sins must die. Only when such judgment was exacted could sin be removed. But how could that be done so that the sinner could still live to enter God's presence? God in his grace made the ritual of substitutionary sacrifice the way. Or, in New Testament terms, God found a way to be just and the justifier of many (Rom. 3:26). Of course, the Christian will anticipate that this gracious provision of sacrifice was made for Israel with the death of Jesus the Messiah in mind, as Israel's prophets foretold (Isa. 53:10).

From the beginning sacrifices had been an essential part of worship. But now, with the revelation at Sinai, God would make it clear to Israel just how essential they were and how precisely they had to be made (the law is filled with instruction on this aspect of worship). The devout would come into God's presence on the basis of the shed blood and would hear his word and share in his praises in his courts, and their worship would culminate in a communal meal in which they would celebrate being in covenant with the LORD. Sacrifice was the basis of the covenant, but sacrifice also was the heart of their worship; and it was all because of the presence of the Holy One in their midst. Their participation in worship at "the house of Yahweh" was not possible without sacrifice, but with sacrifice their worship was freeing and fulfilling. Because God's presence was a sanctifying presence, the faithful complied with the ritual to maintain their covenant relationship with him, to have access to his presence, and to become a holy nation in the world.

It was the centrality of the sacrifice that focused everyone's attention on sanctity by constantly reminding them of the holiness of the LORD and by providing them the only way of access into that holy presence. And even though sacrificial ritual came to an end with the inauguration of the new covenant, sacrifice remains the sanctifying center of worship. This sacrifice, of course, is the sacrifice that God has made for us in his Son, Jesus Christ our Lord, the sacrifice to which all these others were types or foreshadowings. Christ's sacrifice is the basis and the focus of our worship. Because of it Christ is the sanctifying presence in our worship, and by it Christ is the reminder of our need of sanctification as we enter a holy place—be it a formal sanctuary or a plot of sand in the desert—to offer our gifts, our homage, and ourselves to God.

# CHAPTER 9

# The Patterns *of* Worship *at* Sinai

AT THE HEART OF THE LAW IS the instruction about the sanctuary and the sacrifices for Israel's worship; but three narratives in Exodus prepare the reader for those instructions, just as the events themselves prepared Israel for the revelation: the meeting with God, the covenant with God, and the rebellion against God.

## Meeting with God at the Holy Mountain

With the bondage of Egypt already fading in their memory, the redeemed people of God made their way to Sinai to meet with their God (Exod. 19). But they could not have imagined what they were about to see on the mountain!

### The Indisputable Word from God

*Revelation*

The first clear indication of God's presence was his voice: "The LORD called [out]" (Exod. 19:3; or "proclaimed" *[qārāʾ]*). He reminded the people of all he had done for them (revelation begins with a self-disclosure and a report of God's gracious acts) and then charged them to obey him and keep his covenant (vv. 4–5). If they obeyed him, they would then be a kingdom of priests and a holy nation. The kingdom was God's, and it was to be comprised of priestly people who were living holy lives in God's service and enjoying access to him. It still is.[1] Today, as members of the new covenant, we are also "a chosen people, a royal priesthood, a holy nation, a people belonging to God" (1 Peter 2:9; Rev. 5:10).

---

1. See further R. B. Y. Scott, "A Kingdom of Priests (Exodus xix 6)," 213–19; Moran, "Kingdom of Priests," 7–20; and Torrence, *Royal Priesthood*, 14–22.

The calling for Israel to be "a kingdom of priests" was a call for them to follow Abraham in the role of witnessing worshippers. What the priestly order in Israel was to do for the nation, the nation itself was to do for the world: teach the word of God, make intercessory prayer (i.e., burn incense), and make provision for the people to find access to God through atonement (Deut. 33:9–10).[2] Thus, their spiritual service had to retain the elements of proclamation and prayer with the ritual acts at the altar. To do this they had to be "a holy nation," set apart from the rest of the world by their faith and their compliance with God's will. The law taught the people how to live as a holy nation and how to maintain their relationship with the holy God. If they failed in this, they would not be a blessing to all the families of the earth (Gen. 12:2).

### Response

When Moses, the mediator, presented the words of the LORD to the people (Exod. 19:7), their response was instant: "All that the LORD has said we are willing to do."[3] Here began a pattern that has been at the heart of worship ever since, namely, that the faithful respond to the proclamation of the word of God with a commitment to obey.

## The Vision of God

### Revelation

The second manifestation of God's presence in Exodus 19 was a visible one (v. 9). The people saw this great manifestation of his presence and heard the sounds and as a result were convinced of the divine origin of the law. God's people had to know that the words of Moses were in fact from God.

### Requirements

The LORD stated his requirements for people to approach him (Exod. 19:10–16): they were to be set apart by the ritual of washing and be spiritually prepared by the third day. Preparing to enter God's holy presence now involved more than removing shoes on holy ground! Setting oneself

---

2. See further Heinz, "Exodus 19:5 and the Mission of Israel," 239–42.
3. This translation of the imperfect tense captures the idea of their desire to obey and does not give the impression they were presumptuous.

apart to meet the LORD required focusing on spiritual things, and not on physical things. For example, they were to abstain from sexual relations. A similar instruction for special spiritual concerns was made by the apostle Paul for the church (1 Cor. 7:5). God also set boundaries around the base of the mountain so that the people would not come too close (Exod. 19:12–13). These instructions began to teach worshippers about the great privilege and the grave danger of coming into the presence of the holy God of glory: they were to draw near to him, but they were not to come too close. He was their redeemer, but he was also God Almighty.

### Obedience

Moses told the people what God had said, and the people prepared themselves to meet him (Exod. 19:14–15).

## The Power of God

### Epiphany

The third manifestation of God's presence was the most spectacular: there was thunder, lightning, a thick cloud, smoke covering the mountain, and a very loud trumpet blast. As the LORD descended in the fire, the whole mountain shook, and the sound of the trumpet grew louder.[4] Then they heard the voice of God speaking to Moses, warning the people not to break through to gaze on the manifestations, for that would be to treat it as a common spectacle (Exod. 19:16–25). Deuteronomy 4.11 12 recalls this incident:

> You came near and stood at the foot of the mountain while it blazed with fire to the very heavens, with black clouds and deep darkness. Then the LORD spoke to you out of the fire. *You heard*

---

4. Here is the origin of "epiphany," the miraculous appearance of God in the midst of the upheaval of natural phenomena. Epiphany language drawn from this revelation was used throughout the Bible to describe different kinds of supernatural intervention (see Judg. 5:5, 20; Pss. 93; 95–99; Joel 2:28–32; Rev. 19:11–16). The sound of a trumpet blast indicated to the people that this was not simply the phenomena of nature. The clear sound of the trumpet, growing louder and louder, marshaled their attention and proclaimed something significant was about to occur (see also the Feast of Trumpets, Lev. 23:23–25).

*the sound of words but saw no form; there was only a voice* (emphasis mine).

Fretheim says that this revelation served to convince the people of the reality of the presence of God in their midst and to clarify the role of Moses as intermediary before them.[5] Subsequent generations of worshippers would go to the sanctuary to hear from God, sometimes directly through a prophet, but usually through the reading of Holy Scripture. Based on revelations like this at Sinai, the faithful knew that the word they heard was from God.

### Response

The people trembled in fear (Exod. 19:16) and kept their distance. The events in this chapter do not actually describe full worship, per se, but we do see the beginning of it—the response of fear and devotion to the revelation of the living God that prompted the spiritual preparations to meet God.

In describing the spiritual realities of the new covenant, the book of Hebrews says that we "have not come to a mountain that can be touched and that is burning with fire; to darkness, gloom and storm; to a trumpet blast or to such a voice speaking words." But we "have come to Mount Zion, to the heavenly Jerusalem, the city of the living God" (Heb. 12:18–22). While we learn many important principles from the experiences of the ancient Israelites, we are reminded that as members of the new covenant we have gone beyond that and have a better relationship with God through Jesus the Messiah. Thus, our worship and service should be far greater now.

## Celebrating Covenant Peace with God

After the glorious revelation of the law, Exodus records the ratification of the covenant with a solemn assembly and ritual (Exod. 24). The form of that inaugural service set the pattern for subsequent worship services, especially those that would renew the covenant with God.[6] As Jantzen says:

---

5. Fretheim, *Exodus,* 220.
6. See further Nicholson, "The Covenant Ritual in Exodus XXIV 3–8," 74–86; and Vriezen, "The Exegesis of Exodus xxiv 9–11," 100–33.

The covenant ceremony is rich in meaning partly spoken and partly acted out. The words give the actions their focus and clarity of meaning; the actions give the words a depth and range of meaning that words can only hint at. For example, . . . When we see the blood, we see the very life fluid that only moments before flowed through the veins of these living animals, which then was separated into two halves and now covers the altar on the one hand and ourselves on the other. Through the words that have been exchanged (v. 7) and through the actions with the blood that surround these words and ritually "embrace" them (vv. 6b, 8a), the two parties to the covenant have entered into a bond of unity that suggests one covenanted divine-human life.[7]

## The Call to Worship

The inauguration of the covenant by sacrifice began with the LORD's calling Moses, Aaron, Nadab, Abihu, and seventy elders to come up to the mountain to worship (Exod. 24:1). The people were to remain at a distance, their leaders were to go up to the mountain, but only Moses the mediator could draw near (v. 2). By bowing to the ground at the proper distance, the people showed their reverence for God. The point is that worship is an obedient response to the call of God, whether that call should be as spectacular as this or come through fixed biblical commands. The New Testament continues the emphasis on calling people together to worship (1 Cor. 14:26; 16:1 et al.), warning them not to abandon assembling together (see Heb. 10:25; 12:28–29; 13:15–16).

## The Consecration of the People

Next came the consecration of the people for this service (Exod. 24:3–8). These steps set the pattern for all subsequent worship.

### Proclamation of God's Words (Exod. 24:3a)

Moses "told" *(waysappēr)* the people all the "words" *(devārîm)* of the LORD and all the "decisions" *(mishpāṭîm).*[8] Likewise the prophets later would declare God's Word, and that Word would be written down and

---

7. Jantzen, *Exodus,* 186.
8. These two nouns refer to the contents of Exodus 20–23, the "words" being the Ten Commandments, and the "decisions" being the case decisions.

deposited in the sanctuary for future reading. Likewise, the messages of Jesus were written down to become part of our Scripture.

### Response by the People (Exod. 24:3b)

The assembled worshippers unanimously ("with one voice") declared their willingness to obey. This is the proper response to the proclamation of God's Word.

### Recording the Law (Exod. 24:4a)

The laws that the people agreed to now had to be written down because they formed the heart of the covenant.

### Sacrifices by the People (Exod. 24:4b–6)

The next morning Moses built an altar and set up twelve pillars (for the twelve tribes). The people then offered burnt offerings to signify both their surrender to God and their acceptance by God (Lev. 1), and peace offerings to signify their peace with God (Lev. 3; 7).

### Reading the Covenant (Exod. 24:7a)

Moses took the "Book of the Covenant" and read it to the people. This verb *(qārāʾ)* refers to public reading; the word used in verse 3 referred to reporting what God had said. Both declaring the Word and then reading it formed the substance of the proclamation that was so necessary to interpret the rites they were performing.

### Response by the People (Exod. 24:7b)

Just before the ritual of consecration took place, the people once again expressed their willing compliance.

### The Consecration by Blood (Exod. 24:8)

Moses took the blood and sprinkled it toward (over *[ʿal]*) the people, perhaps on the representative pillars. He said, "This is the blood of the covenant that the LORD has made with you in accordance with all these words." By this ritual act the people were set apart to be the people of God, and by it God confirmed their agreement to live holy lives before him. Jacob says,

This was the first and primary pilgrimage festival, and the people appeared before God with sacrifices, which made his presence real to them. *Every subsequent* ḥag[9] *represented a renewal of this covenant;* the reading of the Torah during the *ḥag* of booths in the following year (Deut. 31:11) followed the example of the *reading of the covenantal document* during the first *ḥag* celebrated at Sinai.[10]

In the same manner that Moses inaugurated the covenant at Sinai, Jesus in the upper room inaugurated the new covenant with people who were likewise committed to following him, saying similarly, "This is my blood of the [new] covenant."[11]

## The Communication of God's Approval

### The Vision of Glory

According to Exodus 24:9–11a, the representatives of the nation "saw the God of Israel," and God did not raise his hand against them (it was believed that no one could see God and live [33:20]).[12] What exactly they saw is hard to say, but it was clearly much more than the phenomena of nature that they had seen (cf. how Moses was allowed to see more in 33:23). They were given an actual glimpse of God's glorious presence—they saw a pavement of sapphire stone, deep blue but transparent, like the vault of the sky, which may have been the foundation of the heavenly throne (Ezek. 1:26; Rev. 4:6), but they did not dare to lift their eyes higher.

No longer did they see smoke and fire and clouds or feel earthquakes as before when they trembled in fear (Exod. 19). Now they saw the tranquility of the heavenly scene with paved work like sapphire and the body of heaven in clearness, and above it they saw a vision of the God of Israel exalted in his glorious dominion. Now that the people were in covenant

---

9. The Hebrew word *khag* is the word for a pilgrimage to hold a sacrificial festival to the Lord.

10. B. Jacob, *Second Book of the Bible: Exodus,* 744.

11. The words will be discussed later; but see Jeremias, *The Eucharistic Words of Jesus,* 168–69, 218–25.

12. Cole says that no mortals can bear to see the full splendor of God; in the full revelation of the New Testament, it is in Christ that we see the Godhead revealed (*Exodus,* 187; see Heb. 1:3).

with God almighty, the terrifying features of his presence were gone—
they were at peace with God (cf. Isa. 44:22).

### Communion with God (Exod. 24:11b)

When they saw God, "they ate and drank." This is the second time we
are told that they saw God, the repetition underscoring that they actually
saw something, that this was not merely their imagination. God wanted
them to know that his presence was real. And because of that revelation,
they could celebrate with a communal meal from the peace offerings (see
Lev. 7:16–21). To eat the covenant meal in the presence of God confirmed
that they were at peace with God. And Israel's experience of a communal meal anticipated the Christian meal called Holy Communion. It too
would be a celebration by those who were at peace with God, a peace
made possible by the sacrificial death of Christ.

## The Hope of Greater Glory

The last few verses of the chapter report that the mediator was called
up higher to receive the tablets from the LORD (Exod. 24:12–18). Moses
entered into God's presence, and the "glory of the LORD" settled on the
mount. To the people it looked like a consuming fire on top of the mountain. They were left to wait for his return, and in time they began to wonder when that might be.[13]

Nevertheless, the glorious manifestations on the mountain signified
the authority of the Word of the LORD. The people would be hard pressed
to doubt their authenticity now that they had heard the voice of God and
had trembled at his presence, had seen him in his glory, and had eaten
with him in peace. The covenant with the living God was real! The promises were sure—and the stipulations to be obeyed.

## Restoring the Ruined Relationship with God

The third passage that prepares us for the instructions of the ritual
concerns the sin with the golden calf (Exod. 32). In spite of the dramatic
evidence of the divine presence, and in contrast to the glorious and holy
ritual on the slopes of Sinai, it was no time at all before the people vio-

---

13. Commentators for ages have observed that this passage provides a preview of the
    Mediator of the new covenant, who, having inaugurated the covenant in his blood,
    ascended with clouds into heaven with a promise to return.

lated the covenant by making an idol. The event marks a major turning point in the narrative—it is the fall of the nation into sin, reminiscent of the fall of Adam and Eve in Genesis 3. As in the garden, the LORD had just formed his new creation, promising his people a life of blessing and service in a fruitful land. But even though God was in their midst, they disobeyed his commandments and made an idol of gold to be the object of their festal gratitude. Because of that rebellion the threat of death hung over them until God set aside the judgment through Moses' intercession. In fact, from now on their access to God would require intercession because of their propensity to sin, a propensity that eventually prevented this generation from ever seeing the beautiful place God had prepared for them, because they died in the desert.

Like the first parents expelled from Eden, the Israelites would find access to the presence of God prevented by the cherubs, now in symbolic form, and would come to appreciate all the more why entrance into the sanctuary of God could be gained only through the prescribed ritual. Sacrifices and intercession now would be pursued with a sense of desperate urgency, at least by those who understood what sin did to their relationship with God. And those who followed it by faith would again catch a few glimpses of his power and his glory—and hope for a greater glory.

## Corruption of Worship

While Moses was on the mountain, the people corrupted themselves (Exod. 32:2–18) with celebration around a golden calf. No matter how they tried to explain it, their sin was nothing short of blatant idolatry, an idolatry that confused the worship of the LORD with pagan religion.

In Moses' absence the people wanted gods who would go before them (contrast Exod. 20:3–5), gods with a physical presence like the pagans had. And they wanted a festival—soon. Surprisingly, Aaron complied and made a molten calf out of the golden earrings the people brought. Then they declared, "This is your god, O Israel, who brought you up from the land of Egypt" (32:4 NASB). They thus robbed God of his glory—as well as the gold that was to be used for the tabernacle (25:2–3); and even worse, their inspiration was pagan, for in Egypt and Canaan the calf was venerated. After things had gotten out of hand, Aaron tried to turn the celebration back to God by building an altar and proclaiming that there would be "a festival to Yahweh" the next day (32:5). But their defection was not so easily reversed. The next day when the people offered burnt offerings and peace offerings, they sat down to eat and drink and then got up to indulge in revelry (32:6; contrast 24:11).

The existence of the golden calf, no matter how it was explained, destroyed any hope for pure worship. Therefore, God broke off the giving of the Law. After all, there was no reason to continue writing covenant stipulations when the first two had been openly disregarded. Furthermore, God expressed his anger by appearing to disown them: he told Moses, "*your* people, whom *you* brought up out of Egypt, have become corrupt" (32:7). This choice of wording reflected the words of their defection: "This is *your* god." If this golden calf was their god, then Yahweh could not be their God; if they persisted in this defection, there would be no covenant at all.

What their festival involved is hard to say. The NIV says they rose up "to indulge in revelry" (others: "to play" *[lᵉtsakhēq]*).[14] The context suggests that it was anything but a harmless festival and certainly not a holy celebration. At best it was profane and worldly, but at worst it was degrading and defiling.[15] At any rate, the central difference between this and proper festivities was the presence of the idol, for in religion the more base the focus of attention is, the more corrupt the festivities will be. This incident warns believers for all time not to mingle religious objects from pagan religions with the worship of God.

## Restoration Through Intercession

The complete destruction of the idolatrous people was averted only through the intercession of Moses (Exod. 32:11–14; 30–32).[16] His intercession displayed a self-sacrificing love for the people, for in it he not only disregarded his own interests but offered them to God. He did not for one moment excuse their sin, nor did he even ask for mercy for them; rather, he threw himself before God, willingly offering his life in their place. Moses thought only of the LORD's glory and of Israel's preservation.

The intercession was prompted by the unusual way that God announced his readiness to destroy the people. At first glance it sounds like

---

14. Although this word can be used of harmless activity, it can also be used of something problematic or sinister (Gen. 21:9) or of something sexually intimate (Gen. 26:8).
15. B. Jacob, *Second Book of the Bible: Exodus,* 941.
16. Deuteronomy 9:20 tells us that God was also angry enough at Aaron to kill him, but Moses interceded for him as well, and his life was spared.

he was resolutely prepared to annihilate the whole nation; however, he conditioned the punishment on Moses' agreement! He said to Moses, "Now leave me alone so that my anger may burn against them and that I may destroy them. Then I will make you into a great nation" (Exod. 32:10). The words provide the clue that something else was intended. If God intended to destroy Israel, he did not need Moses to step aside and leave him alone. But by telling Moses to do that, he was putting the destiny of the nation on Moses' back. He was prompting Moses to intercede. Childs observes that "God himself leaves the door open for intercession. He allows himself to be persuaded. That is what a mediator is for!"[17] Moreover, by promising to make Moses into a great nation, God was using the identical words that he had given to Abraham (Gen. 12:2), thus reminding Moses that this nation was the fulfillment of divine promises. He was giving Moses the strongest argument with which to oppose the divine threat.

Moses' intercession was intense; he lay prostrate before the LORD forty days and forty nights on behalf of the nation (Deut. 9:18, 25). This was no short and simple prayer. To Moses, nothing else mattered more than the future of these people as the people of God. He made three arguments in his intercession (Exod. 32:11–14).[18] First, he appealed to God's miraculous deliverance of Israel from Egypt, referring to them as *"your* people." Was that redemption for nought? Second, he called to mind how the Egyptians would ridicule God's destruction of his people and be able to show how untrustworthy God was (Deut. 9:28; Ezek. 20:14). And third, he appealed to the promises that God had made to the ancestors that were yet unfulfilled promises.

In his intercession Moses placed his own life in place of the people. He so identified himself with the people—which is the strength of intercession—that if they were to be destroyed, he was willing to die in their place (Exod. 32:32).[19]

---

17. Childs, *The Book of Exodus,* 567. B. Jacob adds that God could have closed the door, indeed slammed it as he did in Deuteronomy 3:26 when Moses asked permission to enter the Promised Land. But he did not do that here—he left room for the judgment to be averted (*Second Book of the Bible: Exodus,* 944).

18. Ibid., 568.

19. So also Paul: "I could wish that myself were accursed from Christ for my brethren, my kinsmen according to the flesh" (Rom. 9:3 KJV). Intercessory prayer does this; the real intercessor cannot pray and walk away.

God preserved the people alive, albeit purging the unbelieving rebels. God was not arbitrary in this.[20] He had intended to show mercy all along, but he had intended to show it through Moses' intercession. God not only ordains the end, but he also ordains the means to the end, and here the fervent prayer of a righteous intercessor was the means of his showing mercy. In the crisis that had arisen, everything depended on the mediator; and God in his grace had provided a mediator who could stand in the breach and plead his people's cause, not on the grounds of what they were, but on the grounds of who God is.[21] With that in mind, God remained faithful to his promises even when his people were unfaithful. In his intercession Moses counterbalanced Aaron's folly. As Childs says, "Aaron was too weak to restrain the people; Moses was strong enough to restrain even God."[22]

Moses then took God's side to purge the congregation of the real idolaters, the smaller group of ringleaders who would not stand with the LORD (Exod. 32:15–29). Now it was Moses' anger that raged as he entered the camp to deal with the apostasy.

Afterward Moses returned to the LORD to continue his intercession, this time for forgiveness and atonement for the sin (Exod. 32:30). His intercession was effectual, for the covenant promises were secured for the people. In his prayer Moses said, "If your Presence does not go with us (cf. Exod. 33:1–5), do not send us up from here" (Exod. 33:15). His prayer rightly expressed the faith of worshipping communities of all time, namely, that it is God's presence that is so desperately needed in this worldly pilgrimage.

Along with the guarantee of his presence, the LORD provided Moses with a grander disclosure of his nature (Exod. 34:5–7). Because of all that had happened, the people needed to have a clearer understanding of the nature of God if they were to remain loyal to him in the future. In fact, knowing the nature of their God would help them appreciate all the more the need for intercession on their behalf. So the LORD "made proclamation" of his name to Moses, saying:

---

20. The use of the verb "to repent, relent" (Exod. 32:14) is a frequent anthropomorphism in the text of Scripture. God has to communicate his warnings and his gracious dealings in ways that we humans can understand. It is "as if" he changed his mind. See H. Van Dyke Parunak, "A Semantic Survey of *NḤM*," 512–32.

21. Edward Dennett, *Typical Teachings of Exodus,* 357.

22. Childs, *The Book of Exodus,* 570.

Yahweh, Yahweh, the compassionate and gracious God, slow to anger, abounding in love and faithfulness, maintaining love to thousands, and forgiving wickedness, rebellion and sin. Yet he does not leave the guilty unpunished;[23] he punishes the children and their children for the sin of the fathers to the third and fourth generation.

Then Moses bowed to the ground and worshipped (Exod. 34:8). In this wonderful proclamation, we have the pattern for later creedal formulas—by enumerating the nature and the works of the LORD, it expresses the essence of the faith. It is no surprise that such a list of divine attributes was used frequently in biblical history to call to mind the historic faith in the LORD.

This sad chapter in Israel's history had a lasting impact on the people of God. Subsequent generations realized how idolatry in any form destroys fellowship with God and makes worship out of the question. But they would have to admit that all too often they were guilty of such disloyalties and that there was a constant need of a mediator who would intercede for them. As time passed and the nation sank deeper into apostasy, there was a growing conviction among the righteous remnant that they needed a mediator greater than Moses, one who could bring lasting forgiveness.

From the very beginning of the church, a comparison between the intercession of Moses and that of Jesus was made. In the New Testament Jesus the Messiah is the great Mediator of the new covenant. It is as if he came before the Father on our behalf to say: "Blot me out in their place." This is what happened, for Jesus made intercession for us with his own blood, as Isaiah predicted by writing, "He bore the sin of many, and made intercession for the transgressors" (53:12). In Exodus Moses is surely a mediator, but it is in the contrast between Moses and Jesus that we see the greatness of our Lord Jesus' mediatorial ministry.[24]

---

23. In this event God showed himself gracious by forgiving the people, albeit punishing those who stood in opposition to him.
24. For a description of the mediatorial work of Christ, see Dennett, *Typical Teachings of Exodus,* 364.

But why is this account located where it is in the book of Exodus, between the instructions for making the sanctuary (chaps. 25–31) and the report of the actual making of the sanctuary (chaps. 35–40)? Its placement underscores the truth that idolatry will destroy the sanctuary and all its service, or in this case the plans for it, and make the continued presence of God among the people impossible. Only restoration through intercession preserved the promise of the divine presence and allowed for the completion of the sanctuary.

What a fitting way to make the transition from the instructions for a sanctuary to its construction! Nothing else could have reminded people of the need for a sanctuary more than this event. No one needed a sanctuary more than these people, who came within a breath of being destroyed; no one needed a place where intercession could be made for them more than these people, who so shamelessly celebrated before an idol instead of God; no one—unless we look more closely at ourselves and confess that we too desperately need a place of atonement and a mediator to intercede for us. Nothing draws us to these provisions with more urgency and longing than our guilty fears brought about by sin.

# CHAPTER 10

# A Holy Place *for* Worship

IF THE PEOPLE OF GOD WERE TO be a holy kingdom of priests, then it was important for them to have a sanctuary for their communal worship and service. In such a place they would enjoy communion with the living God, a vital reflection of what the parents of the race had enjoyed in the garden.

Yet, as we have noted already, they were well aware that God was not limited to such a little shrine. Subsequent revelation would restate this point in a number of ways: God was the God of heaven (Dan. 2:18–19); he dwelt in the heavens (Ps. 115:3); his throne was in heaven (Ps. 11:4), and the earth was his footstool (Isa. 66:1); but God was also everywhere at once (1 Kings 8:27; Ps. 139:7). Nevertheless, the LORD had chosen to make his presence known to his people in time and at certain places; and at Sinai he instructed them to make a portable sanctuary where he could continue to make his presence known to them.

## The Heavenly Pattern

According to Exodus 25:8–9 the instructions for the tabernacle were of divine origin and not human invention. This holy place *(miqdāsh)* was to be made after the pattern of "the dwelling place" *(tabnît hammishkān)*[1] shown to Moses. What exactly God showed Moses on the mountain is difficult to say. The book of Hebrews offers some help by addressing the relationship between the earthly tabernacle and the heavenly sanctuary. It identifies the heavenly counterpart as the "true tent" that the Lord, not man, "pitched" (8:2). It explains that the earthly sanctuary was a "shadow" of heavenly things (v. 5), the "greater" tabernacle in heaven

---

1. The word *mishkān* is usually translated "tabernacle" or "tent." The verb *shakān* means "to dwell" or "to settle," and so the noun is literally "a dwelling place."

(9:11), and that the earthly things were "copies" *(hupodeígmata)* of the things in the heavens (v. 23) and that the Israelite Holy Place was a figure *(antítupa)* "of the true one" (v. 24). Thus, there is a heavenly sanctuary of some nature that is behind the giving of the instructions for the earthly tabernacle in the wilderness.

Furthermore, Revelation pictures a throne in heaven with a great rainbow around it like an emerald (4:2–3). This "throne room" is to be equated with the tabernacle's Holy of Holies because the ark of the covenant was called God's footstool (Ps. 132:7–8), indicating that God "sat enthroned" above its cherubim. John also saw a sea of glass like crystal before the throne (Rev. 4:6) and seven lamps of fire burning before it (v. 5). The seven lamps correspond to the lampstand in the tabernacle with its seven bowls, and the sea represents the laver, now calm as crystal, controlled and peaceful in God's perfect domain. The descriptions prompt us to think of physical objects, but we are most certainly dealing with spiritual realities that, unless described this way, would be beyond comprehension.[2]

The tabernacle language persists throughout the book of Revelation. It says that the Lord spreads his tent over his people (7:15), that there is a golden altar of incense before the throne that represents the prayers of the saints (8:3), and that fire is taken from the altar and hurled to the earth in judgment, becoming lightning and thunder and earthquakes (8:5). Later, when the temple is opened in heaven, there is revealed the ark of his testament (11:19), which in Revelation 15:5 is called the temple of the tabernacle of the testimony. So in the heavenly vision of Revelation, there are spiritual correspondences to the earthly objects.

Even though the exact reality of the heavenly place was, and still is, beyond comprehension, the old Israelite tabernacle did represent this heavenly sanctuary. Several clues in Revelation indicate that the reality is primarily spiritual, even though there would have been some form and substance suitable for glory.[3] In the book those who overcome will sit with God on his throne, a powerful way of saying that they will reign (3:21). Seven lamps represent the seven spirits (or sevenfold spirit) of

---

2. See Hughes, "The Blood of Jesus and His Heavenly Priesthood," 305–14.
3. Paul explains that there are spiritual bodies as well as physical bodies, so a spiritual reality may still be expected to have form and substance (1 Cor. 15:44; see also 2 Cor. 5:1–10).

God, indicating that there is a spiritual reality for illumination (4:5). The saints become pillars in the heavenly sanctuary (3:12). The golden bowls of incense represent the prayers of the saints (5:8), and a voice comes out of the horns of the altar (9:13). John's vision was symbolic of the spiritual reality of the heavenly sanctuary, but the symbols were the familiar ones God had used before to instruct Israel in building the earthly replica.

What this may mean, perhaps, is that what John saw on Patmos was comparable to what Moses saw at Sinai, albeit with fuller knowledge of the meaning due to the full revelation he now had of Christ in glory. Westcott says that the heavenly things on which Moses looked took for him a shape that could be reproduced on earth.[4]

But there is one further consideration that indicates the reality of the heavenly setting. When John saw the vision of the New Jerusalem coming down to the new earth, he described it as the tabernacle of God, for God would dwell with people who would have access to the city (Rev. 21:3, 26). There was no temple in this city, for the Lord God almighty and the Lamb were the temple (v. 22). The idea of a temple essentially represents God's dwelling with and among his people. While sin is in the world and even in worshippers in the world, God's presence must be veiled and access restricted. But when in the future glorious age all things are made whole, no such restrictions will be needed. God will dwell with his people without a restrictive temple in a new creation where everything will be glorious and beautiful and where people will have access to him. That will be Paradise.

All of this means that the building of the earthly sanctuary was no insignificant matter for Israel—or for us. Because it replicated the heavenly reality, it had to be prepared with precision and care. One might be inclined to minimize the importance of the tabernacle and the later temple for any consideration of what might be included in planning buildings for Christian worship, thinking that because they are in the Old Testament they are no longer relevant. But since the old sanctuary was patterned after heaven's eternal places, it remains relevant for our instruction. Its principles and purposes should help us think more seriously about what we construct for worship.[5] Worship or worshipful

---

4. Westcott, *The Epistle to the Hebrews*, 217.
5. See Hart, "Preaching the Account of the Tabernacle," 111–16; and D. Skinner, "Some Major Themes of Exodus," 31–42.

acts, of course, can occur in any setting; but when it is necessary to have a place for the congregation to gather to complete the acts of worship in communion, the surroundings must be given careful thought so that they encourage and enhance all the aspects of worship and focus the worshippers' attention on the Lord.

## The Purpose of the Tabernacle

The main purpose of the tabernacle was that the LORD might dwell among his people (Exod. 25:8), thereby giving a reality to the truth of his presence with them. That the LORD God was with them meant that he was near and approachable. However, the way that the tabernacle was constructed to reflect his holiness and majesty also meant he could be approached only through divinely regulated procedures, for the tabernacle with its curtains and quarters restricted the people from free access to God. The tabernacle, therefore, was designed both to reveal and to conceal the holiness of God. Access to him was controlled to prevent people from approaching holy things suddenly and irreverently (Num. 4:19–20; Lev. 10:1–2; 16:17; 2 Sam. 6:6–7). Israel Abrahams summarizes how access was controlled by the location of the sanctuary in the midst of the tribe of Levi, by its construction with an outer court, Holy Place, and then a Most Holy Place, and by the division of the people that allowed Israelites in the courtyard, priests in the Holy Place, and the high priest in the Most Holy Place.[6]

The New Testament writers saw in the sanctuary a prophetic type of the access to God through Christ Jesus. When the disciples heard the things Jesus was teaching and later came to realize the significance of his death, resurrection, and exaltation, they looked back into the institutions of Israel to see how God had prepared for the full revelation in his Son.[7] Guided by the Spirit of God, they perceived that the meaning of the tabernacle and its furniture and every act connected with them found fulfillment in the person and work of Jesus the Messiah.

For example, John writes that the Word, the Son of God, became flesh

---

6. *Encyclopedia Judaica*, s.v. "tabernacle," 686–87.
7. The study of biblical types has not received much attention recently. Older works, though at times excessive in their interpretations, do make the reader aware of this relationship between the Testaments: Habershon, *Study of the Types;* and Soltau, *The Tabernacle, the Priesthood, and the Offerings.*

and "tabernacled" among people on earth, his flesh being like a tent that covered the glory inside (John 1:14). And Jesus himself referred to his body as a temple (John 2:19): "Destroy this temple, and in three days I will raise it up" (KJV). The people thought he meant Herod's temple, but he was speaking of his own body as the true temple—as the resurrection made clear.[8] Hebrews also notes that the flesh of Christ was the corresponding reality of the temple curtain (Heb. 10:20), which when torn apart represented Christ's body being broken to provide access to God (9:8). Furthermore, when Paul says that God sent his Son to be a "propitiation" through his blood (Rom. 3:25), he was referring to the "place of propitiation" (usually translated "mercy seat") in the Holy of Holies. The New Testament fulfillment of such things does not diminish the theological significance of the Old Testament type in its setting; on the contrary, it greatly enhances it by revealing its corresponding reality in the revelation through Jesus the Messiah.

## The Nature of the Tabernacle

One begins to realize that people could not presume to determine how to approach God. God himself had to make the way clear by revealing the plans for the tabernacle. Because it was "the house of the LORD," the design had to stress the majesty, beauty, and holiness of God. So along with the practical features for approaching God, there was an increasing beauty and value to the parts of the tabernacle the closer one got to the divine presence. In the courtyard, bronze covered the altar, the laver, the utensils, the bases for the curtain posts, and the tent pegs. Silver was used for the hooks and bands on the posts; more silver was used for the actual sanctuary, for the bases of the frames of the tabernacle, the pillars for the veil, and the moldings in the court. But closer to the presence of God there was gold. Ordinary gold was used for the moldings, the rings and

---

8. But there was probably a double meaning in his words. The direct meaning was that his body was the temple, and although they would put him to death, he would rise from the dead. But the implied significance from the figure of speech is that when they destroyed his body they would actually be destroying their temple as well, for after the death of Christ, there was no real need for the temple and its ritual anymore. Moreover, in rising from the dead, Jesus would raise up a new temple wherein God would dwell, the church that he would build. Because of the resurrection of Jesus, the church was formed as the mystical "body of Christ," the temple of God by the indwelling Spirit (1 Cor. 3:16–17; 6:19; 12:27; 2 Cor. 6:16; 1 John 2:20).

staves of the ark, the table and the incense altar, as well as for hooks and bars and pillars inside the building. Fine or pure gold was used to overlay the ark of the covenant. The lampstand was to be fashioned out of solid gold. And the lid on the ark of the covenant, the place of propitiation, was to be a solid slab of pure gold.

The valuable metals reminded worshippers of God's exalted majesty and the beauty of his holiness. The most valuable metals of this world and the beautiful fabrics and embroidery work could only begin to reflect his glory. Because his presence was displayed in this way, it told the people that he was to be the central focus of their devotion, the object of their spiritual desire, and the transforming power in their lives. So the shrine dominated the camp not only by its central location but also by its great beauty and significance.

## The Parts of the Tabernacle

Just as the sanctuary was instrumental in attracting people to God, inspiring them to participate in the glorious worship assemblies, it also was functional in enabling them to draw near to his presence.[9]

### The High Altar

Basic to that provision was the place of sacrifice. In the courtyard the dominant feature was the altar for offerings, the first stop for the worshipper once inside the entrance (Exod. 27:1–8; 38:1–8). It was made of wood but covered with bronze to make it fire and waterproof, and it contained four stylized horns on the corners to secure the pieces in place and to symbolize that the sacrifices were efficacious (horns in the animal world represented power).[10]

---

9. This survey will move from the outer court to the Holy of Holies, tracing the approach to God; but the Bible begins with the ark and moves out from his presence. See further Roland de Vaux, *Ancient Israel*; B. A. Levine, "The Descriptive Tabernacle Texts of the Pentateuch," 307–18; and Ben-Uri, "The Mosaic Building Code," 36–39.

10. The tabernacle (and temple) faced east, allowing the sun to shine directly into the complex at the beginning of the day. The reason for this orientation is not given, other than it was common to face east. But given the pervasiveness of sun worship, one practical side of this is that people would have to turn their back on the sun to approach the LORD. Amazingly, Ezekiel witnessed the idolatrous priests turning their backs on the LORD to worship the rising sun (Ezek. 8:16).

The altar was an immediate and perpetual reminder that entrance into the presence of God was based on sacrifice. No one could come near God without atonement being made through the shedding of blood. Since that provision had to be available always, it was the duty of the priests to make sure that the sacrificial fire never went out (Lev. 6:8–13). They were to ensure that the way of access to God was always available.

Christian theology understands that the altar with the sacrifices prefigured the death of Jesus the Messiah, and therefore there is now no access to the Father apart from the shed blood of Christ, not now in worship, and not in the future in glory.

## The Laver

Worshippers and priests alike had to wash with pure water from the laver, a good-sized bronze basin and stand designed to hold a significant amount of water (Exod. 30:17–21). In practical use, sacrificial blood and earthly defilements were washed away here, but the laver symbolized a spiritual purification through the washing of water.[11]

In the New Testament washing with water was applied by Jesus in the Upper Room when he washed the disciples' feet (John 13). When Jesus found resistance from Peter, he said, "Unless I wash you, you have no part with me" (v. 8). And when Peter wanted more than his feet washed (v. 9), Jesus explained, "A person who has had a bath needs only to wash his feet" (v. 10). Regeneration is portrayed as being washed in the blood (Titus 3:5); but the cleansing from frequent defilements in the world, so necessary for fellowship and service, is portrayed by this washing with water.

## The Light

The tabernacle itself was a frame building covered with a tent. It had two rooms, the first and larger was the "Holy Place," and the smaller, the "Most Holy Place."[12] In the first room was the lampstand, made of solid gold in the form of one central shaft with six branches decorated with cups and almond blossoms—a stylized tree, recalling the Tree of Life in the garden (Exod. 25:31–40; 37:17–24). The seven lamps that burned with olive

---

11. The same symbolism has been retained in Judaism with the ritual bath, the *miqweh*.
12. The literal translation of "Holy of Holies" is to be interpreted as a superlative genitive.

oil had to be serviced by the priests daily to keep them burning to light the way to God, just as the Creator had provided the light of life (Ps. 36:9).

According to the New Testament, Jesus identified himself as the true light that reveals the way to the Father (John 8:12; cf. Isa. 49:6), the true light that shines in darkness, giving light to everyone who comes into the world (John 1:9). In the New Jerusalem the Lamb will be the light (Rev. 21:23). The New Testament teaches that the followers of Jesus are also to be lights in the world, continuing his work of bringing people to the true Light. So important was this motif in Scripture that in the letters to the churches in Revelation the symbol of the lampstand was used to refer to the functioning ministry of each church (1:20; 2:5).

## The Table

Across from the lampstand was a wooden table overlaid with gold (Exod. 25:23–30; 37:10–16). Each week twelve loaves of bread representing the tribes were placed on it, and frankincense was poured on top of them for a sweet aroma. The bread and the table signified communion with God. On the one hand, the bread was a thank offering from the tribes, a grateful recognition of God's provision of food; and on the other hand, the bread was a reminder of their dependence on God.

In the Gospel of John, following the miraculous feeding of the five thousand, and using the tradition of the manna, Jesus said that he was the provision of life that God had made for the people (John 6:32–59), the Bread of Life that came down from heaven. The message is a reminder that God has freely given us all things through Christ. Therefore Christians lay up before the Lord gifts of gratitude just as the ancient Israelites did.

## The Altar of Incense

Just outside the curtain that set apart the Most Holy Place was a wooden altar, the size of a small pulpit, covered with gold (Exod. 30:1–10; 37:25–29). The little altar was used for intercession: the priest would take some coals from the high altar and place them on this altar (the prayers were based on the sacrifices), sprinkle frankincense on them (the prayers would be pleasing to God), put blood on the tips of the horns of the altar (the prayers would be efficacious), and then, perhaps while seizing the horns, offer prayers to God for the people. Here, directly in front of the throne, but separated from it by the curtain, was the place of intercession.

Intercessory prayer was a regular ministry of the priesthood, and it is still a spiritual duty of the servants of God in Christian worship. Jesus is our Great High Priest who is in heaven today in the presence of the Father to make intercession for us based on his atoning sacrifice (Heb. 7:24–27). But the people of God are also to make intercession, especially as part of their priestly worship, for the imagery of the altar of incense is used in Revelation 5:8 for the prayers of the saints.

## The Ark of the Covenant

Inside the Most Holy Place was the ark, a box forty-five inches wide, twenty-seven inches deep, and twenty-seven inches high (Exod. 25:10–22; 37:1–9). It was made of hard wood overlaid with pure gold, and a ring or crown of gold trimmed the top of the box. Inside the ark were placed the two tablets of the law, some manna, and (later) Aaron's rod that budded. The lid on the box, a solid slab of gold, was known as the "place of propitiation" or "propitiatory" (*kappōret*, s.v. *kipper*, "to atone"). This ark was the footstool (1 Chron. 28:2; Pss. 99:5; 132:7–8; Isa. 66:1), and the glory of God hovered above it, signifying that he sat enthroned above the golden cherubim on the lid of the box (cf. Pss. 80:1; 99:1; 1 Sam. 4:4).[13]

The use of this ark clarifies the symbolism: during worship on the Day of Atonement, blood was sprinkled on the lid, the place of propitiation—at the feet of the Majesty as it were. Inside the ark was the law that revealed the knowledge of good and evil and the punishment for violations, but the blood sprinkled on the covering of the ark made atonement for the violations. The blood on the lid spoke of death. But inside the box the manna and the rod that budded spoke of life, the former for God's provision of life, and the latter as a symbol of new life.[14] And both forms of life were made possible by the death of the sacrifice.

In the New Testament fulfillment of these things, Paul declares that God set his Son to be the propitiation for our sins, so that through faith in his blood we might have the remission of sins (Rom. 3:25) and new life in him (5:17–19).

---

13. See Woudstra, *Ark of the Covenant from Conquest to Kingship.*
14. It is often taken as a picture of resurrection, for a dead stick began to blossom with almond blossoms as if it were again a living tree.

## Conclusion

God's desire to be among his people on earth required that a sanctuary be built in which he might make his sanctifying presence known. The sanctuary was necessary because of sin and made access to God possible. Thus, the tabernacle was not only the setting for worship, but it also revealed God's plan of redemption, a plan that was dramatically reenacted as people drew near to God through the ritual.

Because the tabernacle was God's plan, it was designed to find its fulfillment in the work of redemption. In the incarnation, when God the Son came into this world to dwell among people, his glory was veiled by the tent of his earthly body. Down through the ages believers have needed places to meet with God as a congregation in order to celebrate being in communion with him, and so in their structures with their furnishings and utensils they have often tried to signify what they believe and practice. Almost all churches have a specially prepared place to worship in their way, and most have furnishings and some symbols as well. If these have been prepared carefully and are used properly, they can be most effective in enhancing if not communicating the faith and worship of the church.

# CHAPTER 11

# Sacrificial Ritual

THE PROSPECT OF ENTERING THE presence of the living God was both thrilling and overwhelming for the devout Israelites. Just seeing the glory and the splendor of that place with all its bronze and silver and gold, the rich beauty of the priestly robes and the woven tapestries, and then watching the billowing smoke ascending from the high altar must have been breathtaking for the humble pilgrim. This was no ordinary place—nothing about it was common. This was the house of the LORD.

Accordingly, worshippers would have felt out of place, even though God wanted them there and they eagerly desired to be there. This tension would have been enhanced by the teaching of the priests that to enter the sanctuary they could have no sin, no defilements from the world, and no illnesses or impurities at all. Did this mean that no one could ever enter God's presence? On the contrary, the rules were designed to make the Israelites keenly aware of their need to follow God's gracious provision. Craigie says:

> The preparation for worship illuminates also the necessity for worship. On the one hand, we must live in such a way that we may prepare for worship with integrity, without hypocrisy; on the other hand, the introspection involved, prior to worship, clarifies beyond any doubt the need for forgiveness.[1]

When worshippers were reminded of the high standard of holiness, they did not despair; rather, they acknowledged their deficiency with contrition and humility and prepared to make the appropriate sacrifices. They would have rejoiced that they could yet celebrate communion with

---

1. Craigie, *Psalms 1–50*, 153.

the living God in the sanctuary, because what God's holiness demanded his grace provided.

In this section, we shall survey the various rites available to the worshippers and the occasions for their use.[2] We do not know exactly how the details worked out on a regular basis because we have no records of the day-in-day-out activities, only references to them in the Psalms and Historical Books. Leviticus 9 gives us the pattern followed on major holy days; whether over the years they did it carefully or fully we do not know. The Bible tends to record the great convocations more than the ordinary ones.

# The Sacrifices

## The Purification Offering

When worshippers came to the sanctuary, the first sacrifice that they brought was the purification offering (Lev. 4:1–5:13 and 6:24–30).[3] It covered any defilement that had occurred over the preceding weeks or months, as well as any sins committed unwittingly. When the offering was made for a sin, confession was required and forgiveness was granted. However, when it was offered for other reasons, such as a disease or a defilement, no confession was required and no forgiveness given.[4]

The ritual was very dramatic. For example, when the offering was made for the sin of a leader, the penitent would place one hand on the head of the animal, make confession of the sin, and then with the other hand slay the animal. A priest would catch the blood in a basin and sprinkle some of it seven times against the veil in the Holy Place, rub some of it on the horns of the altar of incense, where intercessory prayer would be made, and pour the rest of it out at the base of the high altar. The ritual for an ordinary member of the congregation was not quite as elaborate; some blood was put on the horns of the high altar, and the rest was poured out at the base. The animal was then burned on the altar, with some of the

---

2. For a more thorough treatment of this material, see my commentary *Holiness to the* LORD: *A Guide to the Exposition of Leviticus.*
3. This sacrifice traditionally has been rendered the "sin offering" because it was offered for sins and its name *(khattā't)* is translated "sin" elsewhere. But because the sacrifice covered more than sin, "purification offering" is a better title for it.
4. In the New Testament, for example, Mary fulfilled the days of her purification with this sacrifice after giving birth to the holy child Jesus.

meat given to the officiating priest to eat to signify that the sacrifice and therefore the worshipper had been accepted. For the poor who brought birds or a basket of gleaned grain, the ritual was even more simplified.

In the Old Testament forgiveness of sin was granted whenever confession was made (e.g., Ps. 32:5); the sacrifice symbolically completed the process, showing that forgiveness was based on the shedding of blood.[5] The confession without the ritual was incomplete, but the ritual without confession was worthless. In this way the Israelite experience is not unlike the Christian's. We also need to confess sins and acknowledge defilements in order to participate fully in the worship and service of the Lord. Participating in the rite of Holy Communion without making confession does not remove sins any more than offering an animal sacrifice in ancient Israel did. God forgives people when they confess to him. The ritual is the public expression of faith in the provision of forgiveness through the blood of the Lamb.

In Israel, if the sin was willful or premeditated, then no simple purification offering could be made. All the penitent could do was plead for mercy and wait for a word of forgiveness from God (cf. Num. 15:30–31; Ps. 51:16–17). According to Psalm 51, until David heard the word from God, he could not go into the sanctuary, he could not join the choirs in their praise and singing (v. 8), he could not teach sinners the ways of God (v. 13), and he could not worship legitimately (vv. 14–17).

If the people lived at a time when the priests were righteous and responsible, they would have been taught that the blood represented the life that had been forfeited because of their defilement and sin, that the blood put on the horns of the altar signified the powerful intercession of the offering, and that the parts being consumed by fire meant that God had accepted the offering. When the priests carried the remains outside the sanctuary, they would have been assured that their sin and defilement had been removed.

New Testament believers live in the fulfillment of the sacrifice of the Lamb of God who takes away the sin of the world (John 1:29–34). In New Testament terms, God made his Son to be "sin" for us, in order that we might become righteous (2 Cor. 5:21). So when Christians prepare

---

5. A person living far from the sanctuary might wait until the next festival when he would go up to Jerusalem.

to worship, they confess their sins with faith in the cleansing blood of Christ (1 John 1:7–9). This is the fundamental starting point of all spiritual preparation for worship.

## The Reparation Offering

Forgiveness is granted only if there is genuine repentance, and there are times when genuine repentance must be demonstrated by making things right. When this was so for Israel, they were obligated to follow the ritual of the reparation offering (*'āshām;* Lev. 5:15–6:7; 7:1–6).[6]

Here is how this would work. An Israelite may have defrauded a business partner in some way, and when he admitted his wrongdoing he had to repay the defrauded amount plus a fine at the sanctuary (20 percent). Most likely the sins covered by this offering would have gone undetected unless the guilty person came forward. In so doing, it would have been a clear indication of true repentance. The same procedure was to be followed if the guilty person had defrauded God: he had to repay the amount to the sanctuary along with the added penalty. The procedure for making restitution did not form part of the sacrifice; it was required before the sacrifice was made. Once things were made right, the animal sacrifice took on greater meaning because genuine repentance had been demonstrated.

The reparation offering taught the necessity of reconciliation between the guilty party and the one defrauded. Confessing a sin, even with the appearance of contrition, without attempting to make things right when they could be set right was, and is, a sham. Jesus said that before worshipping God people should leave their gifts at the door and first go and be reconciled with those who may have something against them (Matt. 5:23–24). Many sins cannot be made right, but those that can should be, otherwise worship is hindered.

## The Burnt Offering

Besides offering one of the sacrifices designated for the removal of sin and impurity, the worshipper had to offer an atoning sacrifice, called the "burnt offering" (*'ōlāh;* Lev. 1; 6:8–13) because it was completely burnt on the altar ("a total *[kālîl]* offering" [e.g., Deut. 33:10; 1 Sam. 7:9]). It sig-

---

6. This offering also has been called the "trespass offering" or the "guilt offering" because the word *'āshām* can be translated as "trespass" or "guilt" for the trespass.

nified that the worshipper had surrendered his or her life to God and that God had completely accepted the worshipper. In other words, any barrier that had existed was removed—there was full atonement. The sweet aroma of this offering would ascend to the heavens, signifying that God was accepting it and the worshipper with pleasure.

With these three sacrifices, but especially this last one, God provided atonement for the offerer. In the Old Testament, the word "atone" *(kipper)* was used primarily for the maintenance of a right relationship between the worshipper and God. It referred to the ritual by which all the barriers to access to God were removed and devout worshippers were free to commune with the holy LORD God. In the church this process of maintaining a proper relationship with God is called (ongoing or practical) sanctification, which means, of course, making someone or something holy. The word *sanctification* can refer to both the beginning of the relationship with God (what we call salvation) and its maintenance. Thus, the atoning death of Christ has not only brought us salvation, but it also continues to provide sanctification so that we may enjoy continued fellowship with God. The principle is the same in the new covenant as it was in the old: no one can draw near to God in worship apart from the blood atonement.

## The Dedication Offering

All who received this gracious provision of atonement realized that they belonged to God and owed him a debt of gratitude they could never repay. But God also opened a way for worshippers to pay that gratitude in token by the "dedication offering" *(minkhāh;* Lev. 2).

The grateful Israelite could bring a basket of fine flour, unbaked, mixed with olive oil, and accompanied by incense. A handful of the flour and the incense were burnt on the altar as the token of the worshipper's dedication to God, and the rest of it went to the priests for food. An Israelite could do the same using flour baked on a tray or in a pan, or with the firstfruits of the crop, parched grains or baked bread, or a basket of fruit. There also may have been a libation of wine that was poured out at the foot of the altar like blood.

The handful, the little token, of this dedication offering that was burned up was called the "memorial" *('azkārāh,* s.v. *zākar,* "to remember"). The word *remember* usually conveys more of what came of remembering than the mental reflection itself. It often includes the idea of acting upon what is remembered (as in, "O Lord, remember me"). Here the dedication offering "reminded" God of the worshipper's dependence and also reminded the worshipper that everything was due God. It was not a simple gesture. With this token the worshipper was in effect saying, "Here I am—everything I am and everything I have belongs to you, because it came from you. I offer this gift, this memorial, as a token of my dedication; I offer myself and all my substance to do your will" (cf. Ps. 40:6–8; see also 1 Sam. 15:22). If the worshipper did not make this dedication (or did not mean it), the ritual of the sacrifice did not achieve its intent.

The priests had the responsibility to make sure the worshippers understood all the aspects of the dedication offerings. They were instructed in the very details of what to say and do at the sanctuary (cf. Deut. 26:1–15 for the scripted ritual). They were to be told about the details, that the fine flour represented the purest and best of God's provision, that leaven and honey were corrupting influences and were to be kept out of what was given to God, but that salt was a preservative and signified the lasting bond of the covenant (and so, "the salt of the covenant").

Such a gift to God, a gift through which the worshippers dedicated themselves and their substance to the LORD, was seen as the natural response to God's provision of atonement with forgiveness. And so the apostle Paul, after explaining the many facets of the sacrificial death of Christ, exhorted believers to present themselves as living sacrifices to God (Rom. 12:1–2). Such dedication should flow naturally from the realization of what God has provided, and the renewal of this dedication should be a part of any worship service that remembers the sacrifice of our Lord Christ. Paul explains, "For [you] are bought with a price: therefore glorify God in your body, and in your spirit, which are God's" (1 Cor. 6:20 KJV).

Hebrews declares that the greatest dedication offering was made by Jesus himself, who presented himself to the Father in the body that was prepared for him to do the Father's will (Heb. 10:5–7). His dedication is the fulfillment of the dedication liturgy of Psalm 40:6–8 and therefore the pattern for all worshippers to follow.

## The Peace Offering

Now that communion with God was secured through the observance of the ritual God prescribed, the worshippers could once again "eat to their hearts content" in the presence of God, as Adam and Eve had been invited to do in their Eden. The "peace offering" (*zebakh sh'lāmîm;* Lev. 3; 7), the culmination of the sanctuary ritual, was the great communal meal.[7] It was not a sacrifice offered to make peace with God but one that was made to celebrate being at peace with God. It was a sacrifice offered in communion with God, not to establish or renew communion. In this sense it parallels the ritual of Holy Communion in the church as nothing else does; in Communion Christians eat the food from the Lord's Table *because* they are in covenant with him. This new covenant rite is a celebration of being at peace with God through Christ, and it is eaten in anticipation of the great celebration of eternal Communion in the glorious heavenly sanctuary (Matt. 26:29).

Thus, the important feature of the peace offering was that the sacrifice was a meal shared between God and his people.[8] The ritual of killing the animal and collecting the blood was repeated. But only the fat, kidneys, liver, and fat of the sheep's tail were burned for the LORD. The rest of the animal provided the meal for the worshippers, the priests on duty, and any others who were present. This means that the poor could eat in the sanctuary and share in the thanksgiving that was being offered (cf. Ps. 22:26). The peace offering was the only sacrifice the worshippers could eat. But they could eat! Eating in normal life was a sign of fellowship, but eating with God, so to speak, was truly amazing fellowship.

The instructed worshippers probably understood that burning the fat on the altar represented giving the best to God, that offering the visceral organs to God signified surrendering their wills to God,[9] and that giving the best cut of meat to the priests was their way to honor those whom God had honored in his house. The people probably needed repeated instruction in the necessity of purity for participation in this peace offering meal, because to offer the peace offering defiled was a sin and would incur a death penalty (Lev. 7:27).

This particular sacrifice looks not only at the culmination of the process of approaching God but also at the worshippers' celebration of being

---

7. It also has been called the "fellowship offering" and the "sacrifice of well-being," among other translations.
8. Recall that in Exodus 24 the leaders ate this sacrifice with God on Mount Sinai when the covenant was being inaugurated.
9. For a discussion of the words for heart, liver, kidneys and the like, see Wolff, *Anthropology of the Old Testament,* 10–65.

at peace through the communal meal. In Christian worship believers finally approach the Lord's Table, or the altar as some groups prefer to call it.[10] There they eat the "body and blood" of Christ as a witness to the fact that they have peace with God through the death of Christ. This is not a common meal; it is Holy Communion. To participate in this holy "meal" unworthily is unacceptable to God; some in the early church died prematurely because of this violation (see 1 Cor. 11:30).

## Purification Rites

People regularly found themselves in a condition that required purification and sanctification before they could enter the sanctuary. Their impurity was not necessarily a moral defilement, nor was holiness only understood as a moral virtue. It could be a condition that occurred unavoidably in the routine of living in this world. Nevertheless, to draw near to God in all his perfection required some form of purification.

### Washing with Water

On most occasions sacrificial worship was to be accompanied by a ritual washing with water, usually meaning that the person immersed himself or herself in clean water before participating in sanctuary services. Water purification was specifically required for people and objects, such as the officiating priest who contacted impurity (Exod. 29:4; 30:17–21; Lev. 8:6; 16:4); vessels, clothes, or people defiled by contact with unclean things (Lev. 11:24–25, 28, 32, 40; 15; 22:6); things that had been in contact with the sacred (Lev. 6:27); the man who led out the scapegoat and the man who burnt the sacrifices offered for sin on the Day of Atonement (Lev. 16:23–28); the participants in the rite of the red heifer (Num. 19:7–10, 20–21); and participants in and booty from holy war to be de-consecrated (Num. 31:16–24).

This washing with pure water made people aware of hygiene, of course, but its real purpose was symbolic of spiritual purification. It provided the ritual for moving something or someone from being classified as "impure" to "normal," or conversely, from being "holy" to "normal once again" (as when priests were finished with some of their sacred duties). As noted earlier, the New Testament uses this symbolism to signify cleansing from sin and defilement as well (Titus 3:5; John 13).

---

10. In the Old Testament the altar was at times called the table of the LORD (see Ezek. 41:21–22; Mal. 1:6–14).

## The Rite of the Red Heifer

The strange ritual of the red heifer was at one time a purification rite (Num. 19). A red heifer, without blemish and having never been yoked, was killed outside the camp by a layman. The whole carcass was burned, along with some cedar wood, hyssop, and red cochineal. Its ashes were collected and stored in a pure place. When needed, some of the ashes were mixed with fresh water to make lustral water for purifying anyone who had touched a corpse or a tomb or the house of a dead person (vv. 11–22). The rite seems to have been an ancient one that was used alongside the ordinary prescriptions of washing with water, and its features united the ritual of sacrifice with water purification.

## The Ritual of the Birds

Before people who had recovered from a serious skin disease could return to normal life, they had to go through a special ceremony with birds. A vessel was filled with fresh water, and a bird was killed over it so that its blood dripped into the water. Then, cedar wood, red cochineal, and hyssop were added to the water. Another bird, a live one, was pushed into the water and then released into the open country. After seven days the individual would have to shave the hair in the infected area, wash the clothes, take a bath, and be pronounced "clean" or normal by the priest (Lev. 14:2–9). This was then followed by sacrificial ritual for sanctification (using the reparation and burnt offerings), but in it the priest applied blood to the person's right ear, right thumb, and big toe to sanctify the whole life. He applied anointing oil for consecration.

This ritual adds the idea of removal to the purification. Running water, a living bird, and cedar wood all speak of life restored or preserved. The release of the bird in particular signified the removal of the impurity from the camp (similar to the scapegoat). Washing with water, sacrificial applications, and occasionally anointing with oil were used to prepare people who had been diseased for reentry into normal life.

# Tithing and Sacrificial Giving

In addition to the sacrificial offerings that were to be made, worshippers also were to bring their required tithes and freewill offerings to the sanctuary. On the surface tithing sounds like a very simple calculation—10 percent. But the laws for Israel's stewardship were more complex.

The regular tithes and offerings were legislated in Leviticus 27:30–31; Numbers 18:8–13, 19–32; Deuteronomy 14:22–23; 26:12–15; and Nehemiah 10:35–39. The people could not pledge their tithes (Lev. 27), for that would make it look like a freewill offering—they could not pledge what already belonged to God.

At the outset an offering *(t<sup>e</sup>rûmāh)* was given to the priests, either 10 percent or 2 percent. Then the standard tithe (10 percent) was paid to the Levites, covering all forms of income. But there was also a second tithe, a budgeted 10 percent to be spent in Jerusalem at the three annual festivals. Then, in the third and the sixth years of the seven-year cycle, a third tithe, properly known as the poor tax, was due. Thus, a faithful Israelite family could pay anywhere between 22 percent and 30 percent in a given year. Poor people would bring tithes as well, but they would have had to glean in the fields of willing rich people to have something to give to the LORD.

Above and beyond the yearly tithes, there were other financial obligations under the law. Fields were not to be planted in the seventh year, which meant that over a seven-year cycle people would relinquish up to one-seventh of their income. The same was true of the Year of Jubilee; accordingly, every forty-ninth year there would be little or no income, so people had to prepare for the loss of that amount too. But in the Jubilee all debts had to be canceled, possessions returned, and lands restored. Someone who had accumulated a good deal of wealth over a forty-year period might find Jubilee costly if the laws were obeyed.

To all this we must add the animal sacrifices. Three times a year the Israelites were to go to the sanctuary, and each time they were to bring a few animals and some foods per family. If they had major sins to deal with as well, the reparation offering would be a factor in what it cost to live under the law; it required a guilty person to restore what was defrauded and pay an additional 20 percent to the sanctuary.

Farmers were to leave the corners of their fields for the poor. How much of the field made up the "corners" depended on the generosity of the farmer. If they obeyed the laws, then the poor would have food and something to bring to the LORD.

Charitable gifts were also expected from the devout. The spirit of the law was to love the neighbor, take care of the widow and the orphan, and help the poor and the foreigner. These had no monetary values placed on them, but certainly would have cost something (e.g., the Good Samaritan). There was also the ruling that a rich and responsible relative would pay off the debts of his near kinsmen in order to keep the land in the tribe. This was not always charity; it could be a good investment. But no devout wealthy person could allow his relative to be sold into servitude.

Finally, people also made vows and freewill offerings, promising to give something to the LORD that was above what was required. Hannah's generous offering was the fulfillment of vows she made and the expression of her deep faith and gratitude. Moreover, even when worshippers wanted to praise the LORD, they would bring a peace offering, called the sacrifice for praise. If they simply wanted to declare their love for the LORD, then they would bring the same for a freewill offering. One simply did not think of going before the LORD empty-handed. The spirit of true worship is gratitude, and generosity is the evidence of gratitude.

All of this adds up to a sizeable financial responsibility for those under the law who professed to be righteous worshippers. But it was all necessary because the laws were part of a full socio-economic system, not just the support of a religious organization—although that would be no small task since the Levites who were to be supported were one-twelfth of the nation. This is why it is not easy to transfer the rules of tithes and offerings over to the church—a simple 10 percent is a small part of what Israelites paid. If people try to live under the law today, they cannot ignore all of these covenant obligations.

Even though Christians are not under Israel's law as their binding constitution, their obligations are not less than Israel's. To go back under the regulations of the law, even if possible, would be to go back under a whole system of life that is no longer in place. Yet what the law revealed about the will of God is still binding for instruction in righteousness (2 Tim. 3:16), that is, the spirit of the law remains; so giving, and giving generously, to the Lord and to the needy is part of spiritual devotion and worship. But the New Testament has a higher standard. Because we live in the fulfillment of the promises and have been sanctified before God forever by the one complete and sufficient sacrifice, *all our time* belongs to God, *all our talents* are for his use, and *all material possessions* are his. We are to live a life of total dedication to the Lord, being willing to give everything to him, willing to use everything for his glory. The point is that devout worshippers acknowledge through their giving that they owe everything to God, even though God in his goodness allows them to retain most of it for their use.[11] Those who refuse to give anything, or who give what is left over and unusable to God (Mal. 1:6–14), are not worshipping in spirit and truth.

## Conclusion

True worship is sacrificial—it costs. It cost our Lord his life on the cross as the perfect sacrifice that restored us to full communion with God. Thus our worship focuses on the sacrifice of Christ in many ways, just as Israel's worship was always with sacrifices. And just as every act of worship in ancient Israel required the people to bring sacrifices and gifts to God to express their gratitude and commitment to him, so too must we serve God sacrificially, not to obtain mercy, but to demonstrate our gratitude and devotion to him. Because he created and redeemed us, we owe everything to him. He asks only for a token.

---

11. This is the point of the message in Deuteronomy 8. God warned the people that when they settled in the land and became wealthy and comfortable they were never to forget that God gave them everything they possessed. If they did not give him the credit, he would take it all away.

# CHAPTER 12

# Qualified Worship Leaders

SINCE THE PEOPLE WERE CALLED to be a holy priesthood, they had to have divinely commissioned spiritual leaders to guide them in the way of worship and show them the way of spiritual service.

## Elders

The office of elder in Israel grew out of the recognition of elders in the families as the natural leaders of the people. Many of them began to serve in an official capacity when Moses needed help in administration and counseling. Those who were chosen had to be capable ("men of valor," *'anshê kháyil*), men who were wise and mature, who had strength of character and a record of significant influence in their families and in the communities. In other words, they had to be capable and respected. The elders also had to be fearers of God (*yir'ê 'ĕlōhîm*), that is, devout worshippers who obeyed the word of the LORD. They had to be truthful ("men of truth," *'anshê 'ĕmet*), leaders who in their lives were faithful to the truth and in their decisions trustworthy. Finally, they had to be impartial in their decision making; specifically, they had to reject bribes ("haters of bribes," *śōn'ê bátsa'* [see Exod. 18:21]).

The elders were distinct from the temple staff, but they functioned in conjunction with them, ensuring that the instruction of the temple was followed in daily life. Even in the wilderness they worked closely with Moses to teach the people, for when the Bible refers to the congregation that Moses addressed, it was probably these representatives who would then take the instruction to their families.[1] After the settlement in the

---

1. See G. J. Wenham, *Book of Leviticus*, 98. The "congregation" was a clearly defined group with representative functions; since each family was represented, the congregation could be equated with the nation. Logistics would make it impossible for Moses to instruct the entire nation at one sitting.

land, elders were to look after the administration of justice and the execution of the divine regulations (Josh. 20:4; Judg. 8:16; Ruth 4:2; Ps. 107:32; Lam. 2:10; Ezek. 14:1). But after the Exile they became more significant. In time synagogues were governed by elders; after all, elders were the rulers of the people, and their ruling consisted in interpreting the law, as it had from the time of Moses. In the church the role of "elders" became very important due to the influence of the synagogue.

## Priests

### Their Calling

In the earliest periods, the head of the clan functioned in the priestly capacity (Gen. 12:7; 46:1; Job 1:5). But the ancestors knew about official priests from the established cultures around them, such as Melchizedek (Gen. 14:18), or Reuel (Exod. 2:16–18), or the priests in Egypt (Gen. 41:45). For Israel's worship, it was not until a sanctuary was constructed that a priesthood was formed. And it was to be a glorious and powerful order because it communicated the holiness of God to the people.

Israel's priesthood began with Moses the Levite, since he instituted the office and inaugurated the ritual. God thereby established the priesthood in the tribe of Levi (Mal. 2:5). The family of Aaron, Moses' brother, was selected for the leadership of the priesthood (Exod. 4:14–17), while the other priestly families carried out the regular duties.

The priests were called to lead the nation in worship and service (Num. 1:50; 3:6–7).[2] In doing so they were to be mediators of spiritual life and peace with God (Mal. 2:5). Those who were faithful priests were given this life and peace, so that worshippers could see the faith lived out in them. Their primary task (as "messengers" of the LORD) was to teach people the word of the LORD (vv. 6–7), turning them to righteousness and leading them in proper worship (not as in 1:6–17).

The plan for the nation of Israel, therefore, was that there would be one high priest, a large number of properly prepared and recognized priests to minister to the nation, and then the nation itself to serve as a kingdom of priests in the world. A very similar pattern emerges in the

---

2. In addition to this system of Levitical families functioning as priests, there were also on special occasions non-Levitical priests, priests from one of the other tribes of Israel.

New Testament, where there is one eternal High Priest, Jesus Christ (Heb. 8:1–2), a large number of people called and equipped by God to lead the churches in their worship and service (some known as elders and some as overseers—Eph. 4:11–13; 1 Tim. 3:1–12; 1 Peter 5:1–4), and all the redeemed serving as a kingdom of priests (1 Peter 2:9).

## Their Consecration

Leviticus 8 records an elaborate ceremony of worship for the consecration of spiritual leaders. This "ordination" service was to be conducted in full view of the congregation, because they had to be sure that God was installing qualified people to be their ministers (Lev. 8:1–3). The following steps formed the dedication service.

### Washed with Water

The ritual washing with water (Lev. 8:6) symbolized that the minister had to be purified of all worldly defilement (cf. Isa. 1:16; John 13:8).

### Clothed with Priestly Robes

The priests were clothed with beautifully prepared robes (Lev. 8:7–9), because they were to give dignity, honor, and beauty to the priesthood, which was to communicate the glory of the LORD (Exod. 28:2). Each part of the clothing had a spiritual and practical significance (see Exod. 28; 39), indicating that the priests were to be properly equipped for the various functions of ministry. In the New Testament priestly believers, especially those called to lead worship, also must be equipped with the proper spiritual gifts, and the imagery of clothing is also retained: they are to be clothed with Christ (Rom. 13:14), good deeds (Col. 3:12), and with righteous acts (Rev. 19:7–8; cf. Ps. 132).

### Anointed with Oil

Anointing set the priests apart for service in the sanctuary (Exod. 29:7; 40:12–15; Lev. 8:10–13). For those who were actually believers, the oil represented the impartation of the authority and power of God through the Holy Spirit (cf. 1 Sam. 10:1; 16:3; Isa. 61:1; Zech. 4:14). Since the priests had been removed from common life to live out the sacred life, their life was to be on a higher level of holiness (e.g., Exod. 28:31–43; Lev. 10:8–11; 21:1–7). In the New Testament all believers are "anointed" with the Holy Spirit at regeneration (2 Cor. 1:21; 1 John 2:20); the sanctifying presence of the Spirit sets them apart from the world to a life of holiness and enables them to minister to one another and to the world (Rom. 12:1–8; 1 Cor. 12:12–31; Eph. 4:7–16).

### Sanctified by Sacrifice

The priests' consecration then continued with the atoning sacrifice (Lev. 8:14–21). No one could gain access to God without this, and that was especially true for the priests who were going to lead the people to God in worship. This is still true of the new covenant, in which the sacrificial death of Christ has sanctified us. It is impossible for those who have not been sanctified to lead the people in holy service, no matter what talents they might have.

### Consecrated to Service

The consecration proper (Lev. 8:22–30) was symbolically designed to inaugurate the ministry. The expression used for this is "filling the hand" with the sacrificial offerings (cf. Exod. 32:29; Lev. 8:33; Judg. 17:5–12). Moses put part of the meat into their hands and lifted them up before the LORD. This was the beginning of what they would be doing the rest of their lives. In churches that ordain, the custom today is to put Bibles, specifically New Testaments, into the hands of the ordinands, because that is what they will be about as they lead the people in worship and service.

The ceremony also involved Moses' daubing blood on the right earlobe, the right thumb, and the great toe of the right foot of the priests, indicating that their entire life had to be set apart to God—what they heard, what they did, and where they went. In fact, the whole ordination ritual was a reminder to all that God was to be glorified by those who would be drawing nearest to his presence (Lev. 10:3).

## Their Charge

### Teaching God's Word

According to Deuteronomy 33:9–10, there were three primary ministries of the priests. First, they were to instruct the people in holy living and spiritual service (Mal. 2:1–9). Since they were the teachers of Israel, they were responsible to maintain a knowledge of the law (Jer. 18:18) so that people could learn from them, either through their teaching or by asking questions.

At the end of the Old Testament period, teaching was open to anyone who studied, and so by the New Testament period official scribes and teachers of the law had become more prominent.

### Making Intercessory Prayer

The second ministry for the Levites was "burning incense," which was the accompanying ritual for making intercession in the sanctuary. This ministry complements the first, for intercessory prayer makes teaching effectual. While all believers can be involved in intercession (e.g., Ps. 20), the priests were to lead them in this spiritual service by going into the Holy Place to the altar of incense. The high priest even had the names of the tribes engraved on the precious gems that he wore on his chest so that as he drew near to the LORD he "lifted up" the people before the LORD.

### Providing Access to God

The third priestly ministry mentioned in Deuteronomy 33 was to make the atoning sacrifices. Priests were to keep the fire going on the altar for the daily sacrifices. In the ritual, they were to collect and sprinkle the blood in the appropriate place, wash all the parts and the instruments with water, and burn the appropriate parts of the offerings. All this necessarily involved their communication with the worshipper, pronouncing God's forgiveness or God's acceptance of the offering, giving counsel or instruction on reparations and vows, and declaring the blessing when atonement was made. In short, the priests had to ensure that people could get to God at any time through the provision of the sacrifice. This is a true worship leader.

### Taking Care of the Holy Things

The priests also were entrusted with guarding and caring for the sanctuary and all that was in it. In the wilderness the Levites encamped around the tent (Num. 1:53; 3:23, 29, 35), and Aaron's sons were posted at the entrance (Num. 3:38). When the shrine was to be moved, the priestly families moved with it and carried it (Num. 4:5–20; Deut. 10:8).[3] All the

---

3. In David's time Zadok and Abiathar were in charge of the ark (2 Sam. 15:24–29), but under Solomon only Zadok (1 Kings 2:26–27, 35; 4:1–2).

priests had a part in the daily routine of caring for the altar, trimming the
lamps, preparing the incense, serving as gatekeepers to meet and advise
the worshippers, and a host of other duties. In general, when they were on
duty in the sanctuary, they were to serve the LORD with all their duties
and to protect the sanctuary from defilement or misuse.

Now that Christ has fulfilled the sacrificial ritual of the old covenant,
worship and leading worship has been changed dramatically. There is no
longer a temple and no longer the ritual of animal sacrifice. However,
those who lead worship still must instruct people in all that Scripture
teaches about corporate worship as well as about individual spirituality
that prepares people for worship and service. They must guide the congregation in their intercessory prayers, and they must maintain the sacrifice of Christ as the center of worship with such clarity and power that
people are always directed to find access to God through him. As with
ancient Israel, all the people of God should seek to cultivate these spiritual services since they are a kingdom of priests. The serious problems
that have developed in worship are largely due to the failure of the leaders
or to the leaders' turning worship leadership over to those who may play
an instrument but are not qualified to do all that is required.

## Ministers

### Levites

The function of the Levites is perplexing. The Bible usually equates priests
and Levites. The whole tribe of Levi was set apart to carry the ark, serve
God, bless the people, and be priests (Num. 18:2–4; Deut. 10:8; 18:1). All
Levites, then, could perform priestly functions in the sanctuary. However,
there were simply too many of them to make this possible, and so unem-
ployed Levites were at times reduced to poverty. Deuteronomy lists Levites
along with the stranger, fatherless, and widow as charity cases (Deut. 12:12,
18–19; 14:27, 29; 16:11, 14; 26:11–13). But when a Levite came to Jerusalem
as part of a pilgrim worship journey, he was entitled to all the rights.

At the risk of oversimplifying a major issue, we may say that the Levites
were to be attached to Aaron and his sons to serve in the sanctuary. Levites
who were not priests were "given" by God for service. So the vast majority of the Levites were supporting ministers to the predominant priestly
families.

## Musicians and Singers

Beside the normal activities of the priests and Levites, there were other groups that served the LORD with music. As we shall see in the next part, David organized the Levites into their guilds of music and their specific functions in the ministry of the sanctuary. Musicians and singers from all the tribes were placed under their direction (cf. Exod. 15:20–21; Judg. 5:1–31; 1 Chron. 16:4–6; 25; Ps. 68:26).

## Ministering Women

That women served in leading worship has already been seen in the celebration of Miriam and the women in Exodus 15. Exodus 38:8 also speaks of the "women who served *(shārat)* at the entrance to the Tent" (see also 1 Sam. 2:22). No satisfactory interpretation has been presented for this, but Psalm 68:11 tells us that when the LORD gave the word, great was the company who proclaimed it. The word used in this text is a feminine participle, indicating that it was probably a company of women who proclaimed the message. The idea is one of celebration in the procession: when the LORD revealed himself, perhaps through conquest, it was declared by scores of women who proclaimed it, much in the fashion of Miriam and the women singing at the crossing of the sea, or of the women celebrating David's victories, or even in the New Testament of the chosen women proclaiming the word of the Lord through Gabriel to them (Luke 1). Women were actively proclaiming God's word in the congregation whenever there were such glorious reasons.

## Servants

Many other servants were used in the temple as well under the supervision of the Levites (Ezra 8:20). For example, Joshua 9:23–27 tells how the Gibeonites became woodcutters and water carriers in the sanctuary.

# Prophets

It is questionable whether the prophets were part of the temple staff. There are hints at some connections. For example, the Chronicler associated the priestly musicians Asaph, Heman, and Jeduthun with prophecy. But the word "prophet" (*nāvî*, "prophet") has a very wide usage; the Chronicler may have used its verb form to describe the inspiring singing, for "prophecy" and "singing" were at times used interchangeably (1 Chron. 25:1–6). And if we take the superscriptions of the Psalms seriously, then these folk prophesied by writing psalms. In fact, it was generally understood that poetry was more inspired than ordinary communication and therefore natural to prophetic speech.[4] Accordingly, most of the prophetic literature is written in poetic form.

There is sufficient evidence that prophets and priests worked together in the function of temple worship. Several of the prophetic works may have been written for liturgical purposes, books like Nahum and Habakkuk. Joel may have been delivered at a cultic ceremony; and Lamentations may have been written for religious services using laments and dirges. If there were "worship" prophets, then their functions would have been to explain the ritual, declare oracles from God, and lead the people in the liturgy. As early as Abraham, the prophet was considered to be more effective in intercessory prayer (Gen. 20:7). Samuel, Moses, and Jeremiah are preeminent in praying (cf. 1 Sam. 12:19, 23; Jer. 37:3). But anyone could pray or write compositions to be used at the temple.

The sanctuary and its worship[5] was the center of the faith for Israel. If the prophets, those men and women who spoke for God, were to address the household of faith, there was no better time or place than in the assembly. The prophetic messages were filled with references to the sanctuary and the ritual; they even quoted from its prayers, rituals, and liturgies. And the cult was significantly informed and directed by prophets.

Prophets and priests should have seen themselves as colleagues in God's service. But they were often at odds. The prophetic rebukes of corrupt worship are not to be construed as opposition to the priesthood as an institution. False worship, false priests, and even false prophets would be denounced alike (as we shall see in part 6). Prophetic reforms were designed to reinforce the ritual and the celebration so that it would be acceptable to God. They served a positive purpose for worship with their messages.

---

4. See Alfred Guillaume, *Prophecy and Divination*.
5. Modern writers use the word *cult* for religious activities. This is not to be confused with "occult," which has a different etymology and meaning.

# Conclusion *for* Part 4

WORSHIP HAD ALWAYS BEEN understood to be a response to the sovereign God of creation, but now the spectacular revelation at Mount Sinai made it clear that this God was a holy God. That in itself created all kinds of barriers to approaching him; but his desire to dwell among his people necessitated the provision of ways to do just that.

With the formation of the sanctuary, God would be able to dwell among his people, just as he had done in Eden. And where God dwelt there was life and light, blessing and glory, and the provision of all good things necessary for life. But because people were sinful and defiled by this fallen world, they would not have unmediated access to God or his sanctuary. While one portion of the prescribed ritual explained how such worshippers could celebrate communion with God, another portion of it provided the way to enter. Accordingly, God installed a holy priesthood to ensure that the sacrificial provisions and the worship itself were done properly. It was up to those leaders to teach the laws about the sacrifice and the ritual and in so doing proclaim the nature of the holy LORD God they served.

The New Testament unveils the fulfillment of all this legislation in the Holy One himself, Jesus Christ our Lord. His perfect and complete sacrifice not only sanctified us so that we could come to his table and have fellowship with him, but it also fit us for glory and service in the heavenly sanctuary. The Paradise that is promised in the new covenant is not in an earthly tabernacle or temple, not even in a return to the garden, but in a heavenly sanctuary, in a heavenly city, in a glorious new creation. That is the hope of all true worshippers and has been from the beginning when the sinners were expelled from the presence of God. That hope is realized in the person of the Son of God who is both the Holy One and the one who makes people holy. Thus, sacrifice is still absolutely essential to worship, for the sacrificial death of the Lamb that the Father has provided is the basis of our salvation, the means of our sanctification, the focus of our fellowship, and our hope of glory. And proper leaders of worship are also essential if worship is to be pleasing to God and meaningful in the lives of the worshippers.

# PART 5

# WORSHIP *as* PRAISE

*The Provision for Celebration in Worship*

# Introduction

ON THE EASTERN SHORE OF THE Sea the Israelites sang and danced in celebration of their deliverance. Their jubilation was spontaneous and unbounded, but it proved all too brief, for as they made their way into the desert, the music gave way to murmuring over hardships and general dissatisfaction. They had yet to learn how those who live by faith may worship with thanksgiving in times of difficulty as well as deliverance. They would realize that life was going to be a varied course of experiences that would prompt different responses in their cycle of prayer and praise.

At Sinai the Law taught the people how they should live and worship in order to maintain communion with the LORD who was dwelling among them. Their sin with the golden calf made them painfully aware of how much they needed his forgiveness. Thereafter their worship would not only celebrate their deliverance from bondage, but also their restoration by God's grace (Pss. 32:5; 122:4).

Accordingly, a pattern of prayer and praise developed to complement the sacrificial ritual and the proclamation that had come to characterize worship. It was through praise that the enthusiastic celebration of being in the presence of God was most clearly expressed. Genuine praise became the measure of true worship, for it indicated that the one praising had been accepted into the presence of God through sacrificial atonement, was enjoying a life with the blessing of God, was depending on the LORD for all things through prayer, and had come to the sanctuary to share with the community. In praising God worshippers would recapture the glory of Creation when the angels shouted for joy, and the wonder of redemption when their ancestors sang the song at the sea, and the relief for forgiveness when intercession prevented the wrath of God from destroying a disobedient nation. Praise for such displays of glory, power, and grace could be given spontaneously at any time. Or, their praise might celebrate

221

the LORD's gracious provisions in daily life—an abundant harvest, flourishing flocks, or the blessings of the family. Thus praise was expected at the scheduled seasons of worship when the people gathered in the presence of the LORD of heaven and earth to give thanks.

# CHAPTER 13

# Seasonal Celebrations

## Scheduled Worship

### Worship and Time

The worship of devout believers was to be characterized by praise and thanksgiving at all times (Ps. 33:1; cf. Eph. 5:19–20). Accordingly, the law scheduled worship for different hours of the day, days of the week, months and seasons of the year, and years of the Jubilee period. The Lord of eternity created time so that all his works could fulfill his plan in the seasons and sequences of this life. He then stepped into time to redeem his fallen creatures from death and receive them into his eternal rest. Every celebration in the sanctuary was a participation in the Sabbath rest of the Creator, for Leviticus 23 designates all the festivals as times of special Sabbaths. By using each day, week, month, and season as an occasion for worship, people could truly appreciate the LORD as the creator and sustainer of all life. And because the LORD's saving acts had taken place in time, each appointed time of worship enabled the people to celebrate him as their Redeemer as well. Then, in the fullness of time God sent forth his Son into the world (Gal. 4:4), and time came to its focal point. The appearance of the Lord of Glory late in time now guides the Christian view of time, not only in its understanding of the plan of God, but also in its seasons of worship.[1]

Time-regulated worship has always had numerous benefits for the people of God. First, it helps people subordinate all the experiences of life to the Lord. Because the day belonged to God, worship was daily; because the week belonged to God, there was Sabbath worship; because

---

1. See Stuhlman, *Redeeming the Time.*

the month belonged to God, there were new moon observances; and be-cause the years belonged to God, there was seasonal worship, festivals, Sabbath years, and a Jubilee. In time-regulated celebrations, the people acknowledged that God was sovereign over all things, even time itself, and that those times were gifts from God. Many in the church also have kept hours, days, weeks, and seasons for various occasions of prayer and thanksgiving.[2]

Second, scheduled worship preserves the heritage of the faith. In addi-tion to being harvest festivals, Israel's appointed festivals commemorated the development of the faith in history. As time progressed, worshippers needed to relate their experience as the people of God to God's deal-ings with their ancestors, in order to preserve the historic faith and to be identified with it. Year by year the ancient events might have faded from memory, but through the festivals those events were kept alive. The festivals did this through drama and ritual; they retold the history of the acts of God from the beginning and anticipated a glorious culmination. Likewise, in the church feasts have preserved the great events of the his-tory of the faith.[3]

Third, a slate of scheduled worship helps make the believing commu-nity distinct from the world. The secular world follows its cycle of life, but the people of God have a holy calendar. Certainly there was some overlap when both systems were tied to the agricultural year, but the re-ligious year followed the festivals, beginning in the spring with Passover. The faithful were inclined to refer to dates by the festivals rather than by other references (e.g., Acts 20:6, 16). It was a way of saying that one's life was ordered more by God's dealings in human affairs than by secular timetables. Likewise, in the church when there is a calendar of religious observances, worshippers can relate their lives to a balanced worship of God throughout the year.

Fourth, scheduled worship provides believers with the opportunity of fulfilling their religious duties regularly. With Israel's three festivals, the tithes for each harvest could be paid at intervals. Perhaps more impor-tantly, several appointed times of worship ensured that the priests and

---

2. See Talley, *Origins of the Liturgical Year;* and R. Nelson, *Companion to the Festivals and Fasts.*

3. For a study of how the feasts of Israel were used in the Gospels, for example, see Yee, *Jewish Feasts and the Gospel of John.*

their families, as well as the poor, would be able to live off God's bounty at the harvests.

Fifth, prescribed communal gatherings at regular intervals foster unity among the people. They draw people out of their individual pursuits and bring them together at the right times. As one people, having one Lord and one faith, Israel would gather in the presence of their God at shared occasions, and there they would renew their common identity as they prayed together, praised together, and ate together from the holy food. And there they would be reminded of their covenant responsibilities to each other under God. The struggle today is to keep worship from being a private and individual activity, which undermines what worship is all about.

Sixth, scheduled convocations provide opportunities for greater praise and glory. In Israel, as today, at such occasions the celebration was greater, the ritual more elaborate, the music more glorious, and the opportunity for service almost unlimited. Just being in the sanctuary would have lifted the people up out of the world, so to speak, but the blasts of the trumpets signaling the beginning of the festivals, the grand choirs of Levites singing psalms and playing musical instruments, and the abundance of the sacrifices and foods in the courtyard would have been thrilling if not overwhelming. The priests would have been there in great number in their flowing white garments, and the high priest in his glorious robes would have stood out even before he pronounced the blessings. The place would have been alive with activity! Every once in a while, a prophet like Isaiah or Jeremiah might have been present to deliver an oracle or a stirring exhortation. Everything would have come together in grand style and given people a glimpse of the power and the glory of the LORD (Ps. 63:2). Such times stayed in the memory of the people when they went back to their little villages and their ordinary routines, or when they found themselves in isolated places (42:4). Individual prayers and praises were important to the spiritual life of the believer, but they were to be given full expression in the celebrations in the presence of the assembly.

It was always wonderful to have glorious convocations, and the timing of those gatherings in Israel made them even more beneficial. The welcome rest and relief from the labor (whether the labor of the week or the season), the joy of the harvest, and the dramatization of their common heritage all worked together to rejuvenate their spirits. But the proclamations at the altar, whether oracles or blessings or praises, ensured that the LORD was the focus of their celebration and the inspiration for their faithfulness. This should be the experience of the church as well. Special services and festivals provide glorious times for worshippers and a glimpse of glory when all the saints will be gathered into his presence.

## Holy Days

*Daily worship* claimed every day for God. The ritual of the sanctuary included offering a lamb for a burnt offering in the morning, and another at twilight, along with an offering of flour and oil, and a libation of wine (Exod. 29:38–42; 30:7–8; Num. 28:2–8). In the Exile there were no morning and evening sacrifices, so people offered prayers to continue the tradition. Daniel customarily prayed three times a day facing Jerusalem (Dan. 6:10).

The church adapted morning and evening prayers as well as hours of prayers through the day. While there were instructions for each of these, and Books of Hours produced for the devotional life, only the first and last hours were long enough to have services, although in the religious orders services were conducted for each of the times.[4]

*Weekly worship* acknowledged that the whole week belonged to God. Sanctuary worship on the Sabbath required two lambs, the dedication offering, and a libation in addition to the daily sacrifices (Num. 28:9–10). Apart from this prescribed ritual, we do not know what form the services took. The superscription of Psalm 92, "For the Sabbath day," indicates that specified prayers and praises came to be used.[5] Sabbath services seem to have been better attended than daily services because according to 2 Kings 11:5–8 the temple guard was doubled on Saturday. But the observance of the day did not require attendance at the sanctuary—people observed it all over the land.

Sabbath *(shabbāt)* is normally defined as a day of rest, the reasonable assumption being that by stopping work people would have opportunity to rest and refresh themselves. But since the law commanded that the day

---

4. See Trenholme, "The Lesser Hours," 685–89; and Taft, *Liturgy of the Hours in East and West.* See also the provocative article by Bradshaw, "Whatever Happened to Daily Prayer?"

5. The liturgy for Sabbath services grew up in the talmudic period when the liturgy of the church was also being developed. This was roughly from A.D. 300 to A.D. 700. See Millgram, *Jewish Worship,* 162; and Andreason, *The Old Testament Sabbath.*

be sanctified, whatever was done on the Sabbath had to harmonize with the LORD's design for the day. Accordingly, purely physical recreation would not have satisfied this purpose; neither would simple idleness.[6] It was a holy day, not a holiday.

The pattern for the Sabbath day was the Sabbath that God instituted and enjoyed at Creation (Gen. 2:1–3). God did not need physical rest and refreshment; his rest meant that he had finished his work and was able to enjoy how everything he had done had found its perfect place in the harmonious universe. In this light the Sabbath day was to be a joyful time when people could share God's celebration of Creation (although Israel oten missed the meaning; see Isa. 1:13; Hos. 2:11). It was like entering the garden of the LORD, there to commune with the living God and enjoy his bounty. They were able to recall what the original intent of creation had been and to renew their hope for a better world. To enter God's rest was a reminder that there yet remains a Sabbath rest. By recalling God's plan for creation, people would commit themselves to serving God and one another.

The New Testament teaches that we who have believed in Jesus the Messiah have entered into the Sabbath rest, the spiritual and eternal rest that the Sabbath day anticipated (Heb. 4:3–11; cf. Matt. 11:28). For Christians, every day, and not one in seven, is to be set apart for the worship and service of the LORD.[7] Nevertheless, it was right and necessary for the early church to set a time for weekly worship.[8] Sunday, the first day and not the seventh,[9] was the appropriate choice because it commemorated the resurrection. Most Christians recognize that it is important to have one day a week, at least, for the congregational worship of God.[10] Christian worship remains largely a Sunday activity in countries where

---

6. In time the sages of Israel taught that certain amusements were acceptable: recreation for enjoyment was fine but not for commercial purposes and not done to fatigue; playing chess was acceptable, but poker was not; attending a poetry reading was approved, but going to a wrestling match was not. See Klein, *Guide to Jewish Religious Practice*, 89–90.

7. See my comments on the Sabbath in *Holiness to the LORD*, 396–407.

8. Talley discusses when and how the early church began making Sunday, the resurrection day, its time of worship (*Origins of the Liturgical Year*, 18–27). Apparently it was well in place around A.D. 150, and perhaps in apostolic times.

9. They are very different: the seventh day ended the week and looked back to Creation; the first day began the week and emphasized the new creation.

10. See Edwards, "The Christian Sabbath," 2–15.

Christianity has influenced that to be a free day; but other times for worship work just as well.

*Monthly worship* was set for the beginning of each month. The prescribed ritual called for the sacrifice of two bulls, a ram and seven lambs, tributes and libations, and a goat for a sin offering (Num. 28:11–15). On Israel's lunar calendar, this occasion was called the New Moon (cf. Isa. 1:13–14); it was designed to declare the sovereignty of the Creator over the month's activities.[11]

In the New Testament the significance of these times for Christianity was more important than outward conformity to them. Paul writes: "Therefore do not let anyone judge you by what you eat or drink, or with regard to a religious festival, a New Moon celebration or a Sabbath day. These are a shadow of the things that were to come; the reality, however, is found in Christ" (Col. 2:16–17). Meticulously observing the rules of holy days is no longer required, for in Christ every day and every hour is to be sanctified. But some congregations follow the principle behind the regulations and try to mark the times with special worship. This at least impresses worshippers that the days and the months belong to God.

## Appointed Seasonal Festivals

The festivals in Israel's worship were times of exultation that elevated life above its earthbound routine to its more glorious aspects, as the Creator had intended it. Abraham Karp says,

> They add beauty to the life of a people whose vocation is to proclaim the sovereignty of God. . . . They elevate man above the rest of creation, liberating him from the chains of nature which bind him to unceasing labor and the chains of time which bind him to the here and now. He desists from labor and soars through heart and mind to spheres of spiritual delight. He breaks the bonds of time as he relives experiences of ages past and envisions with the prophets the end of days.[12]

---

11. The feast may have lasted two days, for King Saul invited people to come and dine on the New Moon and the day after (1 Sam. 20:5, 18, 24–27). It was considered a holy meal, for when David did not show up, Saul assumed that he was ceremonially unclean (v. 26).

12. Karp, *The Jewish Way of Life*, 149.

The festivals were not only appropriate times for the people to praise the LORD for the bounty of the harvests and the flocks, but also occasions for them to preserve the memory of their historical events. They recognized that their celebration of them anticipated the final ingathering of the righteous at the end of the age. In this way all the festivals had a prophetic meaning as well. The spiritual and prophetic significance of the festivals was acknowledged by the church as part of God's eternal plan of redemption fulfilled in the work of the Savior. Thus, the holy calendar of the church made substantial use of this material.[13]

The festivals were clustered around three seasons in the year—spring, early summer, and fall—during which times the Israelites were to go to Jerusalem to worship the LORD (Exod. 23:14–17). Accordingly, these "festival pilgrimages" were pilgrimages to the shrine for sacrificial worship (*khag*, s.v. *khāgag;*[14] see Exod. 5:1; 10:9); they culminated in processions into the sanctuary itself. One psalmist recalls how he "used to go with the multitude, leading the procession to the house of God, with shouts of joy and thanksgiving among the festive throng" (Ps. 42:4b; see also Ps. 100:4).

These festivals were also called "appointed times"; the word (*môʿēd*) means "a fixed meeting time" or "place" appointed for worship. The word was also used in the description of the tabernacle as the "Tent of Meeting" (*ʾōhel môʿēd*). The festivals also were referred to as "holy convocations" (*miqrāʾ qādôsh*), or "Sabbaths of complete rest" (*shabbat shabbātôn*). We also find expressions such as "days of awe," "fasts," and then simply "ascents" as in the "pilgrim psalms," 120–134 (psalms of "ascents" or "goings up" [to Jerusalem]).

And the people were truly glad when they heard others say, "Let us go to the house of the LORD" (Ps. 122:1), because that meant the labor of the harvest was over and the celebrations were about to begin. There would be singing and dancing and feasting and enjoying time together. But it would also be a time for giving thanks to God, fulfilling duties, and renewing spiritual commitments. In short, it was worship with celebration, or worship because of celebration.

---

13. Van Goudoever in *Biblical Calendars* studies the feasts to see how they were celebrated in the early church. See also Caird, *Notes on the Feasts of the Lord.*
14. W. A. Heidel, *The Day of Yahweh.*

### *Festival Worship in the Spring*

Israel's holy calendar began with Passover and the Feast of Unleavened Bread. This was the great festival of deliverance from the bondage to Egypt, and because it was instituted in the spring in Egypt, in the land of Canaan it coincided with the first harvest of the year, the barley harvest.

The spring festal worship began with Passover on Nisan 14;[15] it was then followed by the week of Unleavened Bread, and during that week was the Feast of Firstfruits. Therefore, the people had three feasts to celebrate in one week.

Passover would have been a complete experience for the faithful worshippers, drawing the whole person into the drama. And drama it was, for the people were to observe it "as if" they had been there that night in Egypt.[16] According to Exodus 12, in the full moon of the first month of spring, the people were to slaughter a lamb at twilight, roast it, and eat it together, along with unleavened bread and bitter herbs.[17] In Egypt they were to eat it quickly, burn the leftovers, and smear the blood on the lintel to avert supernatural harm when the Angel passed over their house. It was this aspect that provided the popular understanding of the word *pesakh* as "Passover."[18] Along with the sacrificial ritual and communal meal, there was a liturgy to explain the meaning of this event to the children. Over time this part was expanded to include the telling of the whole Exodus story, prayers, and the singing of selected psalms (Pss. 113–118).

For the following week the people were to eat unleavened bread, and on the first and last days of that week they were to observe complete Sabbaths. This was the Feast of Unleavened Bread.[19] How simple that bread must have seemed to people now used to finer foods—and how boring after a few days! But eating bread without leaven, while instructive in its own right, would have made the people appreciate God's bounty all the more when they could return to tasty breads and cakes.

---

15. Because Israel's festivals used the lunar calendar, the harvests did not always line up with them. Occasionally an extra month had to be added to the calendar to ensure Passover would come at the barley harvest. Nisan 14 can therefore fall in March or April.
16. Chaim, *A Feast of History.*
17. Haran, "The Passover Sacrifice."
18. For suggestions for the actual meaning of the word, see J. B. Segal, *Hebrew Passover;* and for a full discussion of the feast, see Bloch, *Biblical and Historical Background,* 211–44.
19. See Atkinson, "Ordinances of Passover-Unleavened Bread," 70–85.

What had begun as a simple religious ritual in the homes in Egypt, over the years changed into a national celebration held in the sanctuary: on each day of the week there was to be offered one male goat for the sin offering, and continual burnt offerings of two bulls, one ram, and seven lambs, along with cereal and drink offerings (Num. 28:17–24). In addition, the first sheaf of the new harvest and a lamb were offered as the firstfruits (Lev. 23:9–14). Israel therefore, by God's guidance, greatly enhanced the festival without changing the meaning.

Passover was celebrated most gloriously at the great revivals. When Hezekiah (2 Chron. 30) and Josiah (2 Chron. 35) wanted to turn the nation back to its historic faith, they chose Passover to unite the people in their allegiance to the LORD. Their revivals did not go back to restore the simple home Passovers; rather, they were the most glorious Passovers ever held.

Because Jesus celebrated the Passover with his disciples in the Upper Room and related it to his sacrificial death, his followers came to understand that he fulfilled Passover. Thus, Paul declares, "For Christ, our Passover lamb, has been sacrificed. Therefore let us keep the Festival, not with the old yeast, the yeast of malice and wickedness, but with bread without yeast, the bread of sincerity and truth" (1 Cor. 5:7b–8). By "Festival" Paul was referring to the Feast of Unleavened Bread: just as the Israelites would scour their houses for leaven, so too the redeemed in Christ are to purge sin from their lives. From its beginning the church has recognized that the death of Christ is the new center of worship, and that Holy Communion is the new ritual. All Christians celebrate in some way the memorial of his death by eating unleavened bread and drinking the fruit of the vine. And Christians everywhere set aside a holy week in the springtime in which they memorialize the events culminating in the death and resurrection of Christ on Good Friday and Easter Sunday.[20]

The Feast of Firstfruits was included in Israel's springtime holy week. On the morning after the Sabbath after Passover—Sunday morning— the sheaf of the firstfruit of barley was presented to the LORD in the sanctuary (Lev. 23:9–14). This added a new element of joy to the Passover celebration.[21] During Passover the people would recall their bondage and

---

20. See further M. R. Wilson, *Our Father Abraham*, 237–55; and McQuaid, *The Outpouring*.
21. Throughout the agricultural year there were other firstfruits offered. But this was the first of the year.

deliverance, but with Firstfruits they looked to the future, to the harvest to come.

There is a well-developed ritual for the Feast of Firstfruits recorded in Deuteronomy 26. The Israelites were to take some of the firstfruits in a basket and go to the sanctuary and say to the priest in charge:

> I declare today to Yahweh your God that I have come to the land Yahweh swore to our forefathers to give to us. (v. 3)

The priest would then take the basket and set it down in front of the altar . Then the worshipper would declare:

> My father was a wandering Aramaean, and he went down into Egypt with a few people and lived there and became a great nation, powerful and numerous. But the Egyptians mistreated us and made us suffer, putting us to hard labor. Then we cried out to Yahweh, the God of our fathers, and Yahweh heard our voice and saw our misery, toil and oppression. So Yahweh brought us out of Egypt with a mighty hand and an outstretched arm, with great terror and with miraculous signs and wonders. He brought us to this place and gave us this land, a land flowing with milk and honey; and now I bring the firstfruits of the soil that you, O Yahweh, have given me. (vv. 5–10)

Then after placing the basket before the LORD, the worshippers were to bow down before him. Then they and the Levites and even the foreigners in the land were to rejoice over the bounty of God.

The passage continues with the liturgy for the tithes that were to be offered in the third year; these were the tithes given to the Levites, the foreigners, the fatherless, and the widows so that they might eat and be satisfied. The worshippers professed their obedience to the faith and prayed for God's continued blessing on the people and the land (vv. 13–15).

By offering the firstfruits and by paying the special tithes, the devout believer fulfilled the duty of giving thanks to God (Ps. 122:4). The little basket of firstfruit offerings to God was merely a token, but if offered in faith it expressed true allegiance to the Lord of the harvest. In addition, the paying of this particular tithe would have been the genuine expression of gratitude to God, acknowledging that what was given by God was not to be hoarded up but was to be shared with those who had great needs.

The fulfillment of Firstfruits, according to Paul, came in the resurrection of Jesus. Christ died on the Friday of Holy Week, but he arose from the dead on the first day of the week, Sunday ("the morning after the Sabbath"). In teaching the doctrine of the resurrection, Paul declared, "But Christ has indeed been raised from the dead, the firstfruits of those who have fallen asleep" (1 Cor. 15:20). Christ's resurrection was the guarantee of a great harvest to come at the final resurrection (v. 23). This reality should inspire the saints to greater praise and thanksgiving, just as the harvest in Israel was an occasion for great joy. But the Christian praise has the greater moment: it can be broad enough to praise God for all the bounty of life, but it inevitably will focus on the resurrection of our Lord. The church has rightly made the celebrations of Easter Sunday the most glorious, for it celebrates Christ's victory over sin and death, opening the way to Paradise.

### Worship in the Early Summer

Fifty days after Firstfruits (thus the Greek name "Pentecost") came the Feast of Weeks (*shābū'ōt*; see Exod. 34:22).[22] This feast celebrated the harvest of wheat and the ripening of the firstfruit in the land; it also commemorated the giving of the law at Sinai, which took place shortly after the Exodus.

The worship activities at this festival included the same offerings that were given on each day of Unleavened Bread (Lev. 23:16–20; Num. 28:26–31). But unique to this feast was the presentation of the two loaves that represented what the harvest provided. The ritual culminated with the offering of two male lambs for peace offerings. Later in time the book of Ruth came to be read at the festival, for its central events took place between the barley and the wheat harvests.

In the New Testament the fulfillment of this feast was identified with the wording of Acts 2:1, which says literally, "Now when *the* day of Pentecost had fully come." The apostles saw the analogy between what the harvest grain produced—loaves of bread—and what the resurrection produced—the church; so on the Day of Pentecost, when God sent his

---

22. Its date was set for Silvan 6–7, which occurs in May or June.

Spirit to unite believers into one body, they thought of God's plan to write the law on the hearts of believers (Jer. 31:33; Ezek. 36:26) as he had given it at Sinai.

The instructions for Israel's Feast of Weeks also speaks to the Christian community today in another way. It instructed the people to leave the wheat in the corners of their field for the poor and the foreigners to glean (Lev. 23:22). Harvest festivals called for the people of God to give thanks to God for his blessings on life; but their gratitude had to be expressed by their sharing with the poor. The church has failed by and large to make this connection.

### Worship in the Fall Season

Scheduled worship in the fall included three festivals: Trumpets, Atonement, and Tabernacles.[23] The seventh month Tishri (September–October) began with the convocation of Trumpets (cf. Lev. 23:23–25), announcing the time to celebrate the end of the year and the beginning of a new year.[24] It was to be a Sabbath observance, a holy convocation, and a memorial. As a "memorial" *(zikrôn)* trumpets reminded the people of the changing of the season and the year in accordance with the order of creation and also awakened them to the season of repentance, pardon, and restoration. A "memorial" at a worship festival prompts the worshippers, and God as well, to act on what was being called to mind;[25] and what was called to mind was the message of the Word of God (Neh. 8:8).

Trumpets were to be blown on the first day of every month to call people to worship, but in the seventh month there was a great festival of the sound of trumpets. The number seven often signified completion, here the completion of the year.[26] But when the people assembled in the fall in response to the trumpets, they did so with the anticipation that at the end of the age, the completion of God's program, they would be gathered into the very presence of God in glory to sing their praises with choirs of angels. What better way was there to celebrate the beginning

---

23. Glaser and Glaser, *The Fall Feasts of Israel* (note the bibliography and glossary).
24. Snaith, *Jewish New Year Festival.* Snaith traces the change from the celebration of the new year at Passover to the fall.
25. See Childs, *Memory and Tradition in Israel,* 1–8.
26. In the book of Revelation, the destinies of the age are sealed in a book with seven seals, and the events of the seventh seal are ushered in by the sound of seven trumpets.

of the new year than in the presence of the one who someday will make everything new?

Because the trumpets signaled things to come, the motif has been used by prophets and apostles for the announcement of the end times: the LORD will gather his saints to himself with the sound of the trumpet (see 1 Cor. 15:51–52; 1 Thess. 4:16). The fact that this festival occurred at the end of the agricultural year made the imagery of the harvest for the final judgment even more obvious.

Ten days after the convocation with trumpets, Israel kept the holiest day of the year, the Day of Atonement (Tishri 10). This was the day on which all the ritual of worship came to its climax; this was the day on which the high priest actually entered into the very presence of the holy and glorious LORD God, signifying the way back to God. Thus, the ritual of worship (especially on this day) dramatized the reality of redemption.

The day began with ritual for the preparation of the high priest (Lev. 16:3–5). A young bull was offered for a purification offering and a ram for a gift; then the high priest was clothed with the simple linens of the priesthood. Then he was properly prepared to carry out the ritual of atonement—and what an amazing sight it must have been (Lev. 16:6–28). Two goats were chosen, one for the LORD and one to carry the sin outside the camp (called *Azazel*).[27] Then, the high priest sacrificed a bull for his own sin offering. From the altar he took a censer of burning coals and with it two handfuls of incense and the blood of the offering, and then he entered the Most Holy Place. He put the incense on the coals so that smoke with its sweet aroma filled the place above the ark; he then sprinkled the blood on the cover of the ark, the place of propitiation, and seven times before it. After this ritual for himself, he sacrificed a goat for the people and repeated the ritual to make atonement for the uncleanness and rebellion of the people. Then he sanctified the tent and the high altar with blood. Next came the ritual with the live goat— the "ritual of riddance." He pressed both hands on the goat's head and confessed all the wickedness and rebellion of the people—all their sins, accidental or premeditated. The imposition of the hands signified

---

27. ʿĂzāʾzēl has been translated "scapegoat" from the earliest days of English translations. Although there have been many suggestions for the etymological analysis, "goat for going" (into the wilderness) is probably the basic idea.

openly that the sins would be carried away symbolically when the goat was led away.[28]

For such an important day of worship, the people had to prepare themselves carefully. They were to "afflict" (KJV) themselves, meaning deprive themselves of the comforts and pleasures of life that would be distracting (Lev. 16:29–31),[29] and give themselves over completely to spiritual reflection and the acknowledgment of their sin before God. Without this spiritual preparation, the day's activities would be of little benefit to them.

When the Israelites participated in the ritual of this day with genuine faith, they were made acceptable to God—they were "atoned." It marked a new spiritual beginning in their continuing relationship with the LORD as it wiped clean the failures and follies of the previous year. But they knew that it was a temporary provision, for it had to be repeated the next year, and every year after—until in the fullness of time God would resolve the problem once and for all. We know that he did that by the sacrificial death of his Son, Jesus the Messiah. His atoning death fulfilled all the rituals of Israel's sacrificial worship. His being led outside the city to die fulfilled the ritual of the scapegoat; and by his entering into the heavenly sanctuary to complete the work of atonement, he became our eternal High Priest. All Christian worship is based on the atonement, and all Christian worship focuses on the atonement. Both Israel's keeping of the Day of Atonement and the Christian commemoration of Holy Week point to God's provision, the one symbolic of what was to come, and the other commemorative of what happened.

Some Christians prepare for Holy Week with a season of Lent, a time of spiritual preparation. By doing this they relive the experience of turning from sins to receive the forgiveness that God provided at the cross; but they also focus on the significance of living the spiritual life in the light of God's provision of atonement, which will be celebrated annually as well in Holy Week. Even though self-examination should be a regular feature of the spiritual life throughout the year, many find a designated season helpful for ensuring that it is done at all. Unfortunately, without

---

28. For an explanation of how this was all done, especially in the days of the second temple, see the tractate Yoma in the Mishnah.

29. The Targum, the official synagogue interpretation, says that they were to refrain from food, drink, bath, rubbing, sandals, the practice of bed, and all work (see also Acts 27:9).

any focus on this in the church's schedule, little if any attention will be given to this kind of spiritual reflection by the people.

If the Day of Atonement was the most holy day of the year, the Feast of Tabernacles was the greatest celebration. This festival, called "Booths" (*sukkôt;* Lev. 23:34), came five days after the Day of Atonement (on Tishri 15). Because it was a harvest festival of summer crops and fruits, the final harvest of the year, it was also called "Ingathering" (*ʾāsîph;* Exod. 34:22). It began on the full moon of the month and was observed for seven days followed by an eighth day, the great day of the feast (Num. 29:12, 35; Neh. 8:18). The people came to the sanctuary to praise God for the harvest and to present their thank offerings. During their thanksgiving they prayed for the rains of the winter months that would ensure good crops in the following year. Apparently they also renewed the covenant with a service that included both reading the law, probably Deuteronomy, and their response with vows to fulfill their religious obligations.

The worship ritual was the most elaborate at this festival (Num. 29:12–40). On each day of the feast, several young bulls, two rams, fourteen lambs, and one goat were offered—some two hundred animals in the week. All this sacrificial ritual plus the singing of psalms and the reading of Scripture demonstrated the greatness of the festival and signified the culmination of the appointed festivals of the year.

The value of Tabernacles for preserving the historic faith was captured by the observance of the "booths." Here was the drama of worship, the most effective way of remembering the temporary dwellings of the ancestors in the wilderness. The people built little booths, perhaps originally harvesters' shelters made of branches and palm leaves, and then dwelt in them for the week to reenact the earlier Israelites' experience. Then, on the final and great day of the feast, they left their shelters and returned to their comfortable homes, commemorating the fulfillment of the promises when their ancestors settled in the land. This provided even greater reason for rejoicing.

Tabernacles also had a prophetic meaning, signifying the consummation of the promises in the future. There was coming a great "ingathering" of the people that would be a time of great rejoicing because the LORD would fulfill all his promises. The prophets predicted that people would come from all over the world to keep the Feast of Tabernacles in the Holy City (Zech. 14:16). It was with this tradition in mind that Peter wanted to build three "tabernacles" when he saw Christ transfigured (Matt. 17:4). But the fulfillment of the promises would also bring judgment on the world. Accordingly, harvest motifs are used throughout the Bible for the judgment that will mark the end of the age and the beginning of the age to come, when the Lord of the harvest will gather the good grain into the barn and burn up the chaff (Matt. 3:12).

It would be wonderfully helpful for the church to include in its calendar of worship something more in line with this Feast of Tabernacles.[30] The point of such a celebration would be the anticipation of the fulfillment of the promises of God, beginning with the coming of the Lord to judge the world and to gather all his saints into his kingdom; in other words, it would be a time to celebrate the hope of glory. Without a regular and growing emphasis on the hope of glory, or the appearance of Christ in glory, or the kingdom of righteousness and peace, or any other way the Bible describes those wonderful promises, there will be insufficient motivation and inspiration for the saints to persevere in their worship and service.

## Unscheduled Worship

In the history of the faith, worshipful acts have always taken place independent of the scheduled times of worship, or within the times of worship without necessarily becoming a fixed part of that ritual.

### Spontaneous Worship

As we shall see later, an Israelite could enter the courts of the sanctuary at any time to worship God, whether to pray or praise, to hear the teachings of the priests, to offer freewill offerings, to make and pay vows, or to seek the LORD for any number of reasons. The sanctuary was always open, priests were always on duty, the altar was always ablaze, and the Levitical choirs were always there—so "spontaneous services"[31] could occur at any time between the morning and the evening oblations.

---

30. Some churches use Advent to focus on the coming of the Lord, but the emphasis too often gets lost in the other interests of the Christmas season.
31. For a service to be "spontaneous" does not mean it was not planned (they had to prepare the sacrifices for it); it means that bands of worshippers could come and worship whenever they felt inspired to do so, and that their worship was genuine and fresh.

Christians have to remove from their thinking that Israel's worship was scheduled for a set time each week in which people sat down for the service and then left as soon as they could. The great festivals lasted for days on end, and day-in-and-day-out there were worshippers meeting and doing the many things necessary for their spiritual needs. The courtyard was a hive of activity.

## Special Occasions

There were many celebrations in Israel that, although not holy convocations, were religious in nature. The Bible refers to marriages (Gen. 29:22; Judg. 14:10; Ps. 45), funerals (Gen. 23:2; 2 Sam. 1:11–12), and the weaning of a child (Gen. 21:8), but no details are given. A sheep-shearing festival could have been part of an agricultural celebration (Gen. 38:12; 1 Sam. 25:2–38), as was the festivity with winnowing (Ruth 3). The crowning of a king (Ps. 2), ordaining priests (Lev. 8), praying for victory in battle (Ps. 20), celebrating victory in war (Pss. 21; 24), and other concerns required religious services as well (Gen. 35:14; Judg. 21:19–21; 1 Sam. 1:3–20), services that were no doubt more grand than ordinary events.

Fasts also were occasions for worship. A worshipper might fast at any time it seemed appropriate for giving greater attention to spiritual matters. In fact, prophetic instructions to proclaim a fast were almost synonymous with a call for repentance (Joel 1:13–15). The idea in fasting is the denial of normal bodily appetites, for it is difficult to concentrate on spiritual matters while indulging in physical pleasures (Lev. 16:29–31; Zech. 8:19).[32]

Fasts that were proclaimed at a time of crisis often became fixed festivals for later generations. Judaism and Christianity have certain times set aside for the commemoration of sad events in their histories. In the Bible the Feast of Purim in Esther is the prime example. It has survived through the centuries, and today Purim is a wonderful celebration, especially for the family, as the book of Esther is read dramatically with enthusiastic audience responses.

---

32. For a survey of the occasions and circumstances of fasting, see Brongers, "Fasting in Israel in Biblical and Post-Biblical Times," 1–21.

## Conclusion

God established times of worship in order to give the people opportunity to perform their religious duties regularly and to dedicate all
aspects of life to him. But among the scheduled times of worship, the
appointed festivals carried even greater spiritual meaning. Those times
called for thanksgiving for the harvests, preservation of the historic
faith, and renewal of the covenant. In all the worship activities connected with these set times, the people would be made aware of the fact
that the LORD was the glorious Creator of all life, the almighty God of
history, the wonderful Redeemer, and the Sovereign Lord of the earth.
The powerful impressions that the holy convocations made on the worshippers inspired them in their private worship as well, for the year was
also filled with unscheduled worship activities that met the individual
needs of the people.

The features that made the great celebrations so meaningful were a
prolonged time away from mundane activities and ordinary labor, a large
gathering of all the people together rather than little separated groups,
great music (Scripture) by massive choirs and a wide variety of musical
instruments, spiritual edification from the praises offered by the people,
messages from the prophets, teachings by the priests, dramatic reenactment of events from tradition, special feasts with all kinds of foods and
drink that were not part of the normal diet, solemn ritual with sacrifices,
the scapegoat, the priestly blessing, and family gatherings and fellowship
with friends. In all of this there were the sounds, sights, impressions, and
experiences that were unique to the occasions. The people truly did come
up higher when they went up to Jerusalem, and for that prospect they
eagerly anticipated the journey.

Christian worship has lost much in relinquishing the full use of the
holy calendar as a means to worship and reducing the special occasions
to special but similar services rather than developing more glorious periods of celebrations. Such observances throughout the year help worshippers relive events in the heritage of the faith and develop a sense of
communion with the saints of all ages. Only when worshippers begin to
see how creation and redemption inform their use of time will they fully
appreciate what it means to enter into the Lord's rest and enjoy fellowship
with the holy God, and with one another in Christ. When this happens,

worship will find new life through the greater variety of experiences and occasions for celebration. When worship becomes a celebration in every sense of the word, then people might actually be glad when it is time to go to the house of the Lord.

# CHAPTER 14

# A Place *for* Praise

FROM THE BEGINNING GOD HAD made his presence central to the life and worship of his people,[1] and the symbol of this presence was the Holy Place, the central sanctuary (Deut. 12:10–26). We have studied the sanctuary as the place of sacrificial ritual; now we must observe how it was also a house of prayer and a place of praise. Of course, people could pray and praise anywhere, anytime; but it was in the central sanctuary that prayer and praise achieved their fullest expression and intended purpose.

## Preparation by David

Under David a permanent resting place for the ark was sought in Jerusalem. The plan to build a temple there began with the purchase of the threshing floor of Araunah (2 Sam. 24:16–25). This was no ordinary place. The Chronicler identified the area as Mount Moriah where Abraham had sacrificed Isaac (2 Chron. 3:1). Moreover, Jerusalem originally had been known as Salem, the seat of Melchizedek (Gen. 14), who was a priest of the Most High God. His holy place probably was on the crown of the hill—in the area that David purchased for the sanctuary. The place was appropriate because it was revered as a holy place in the tradition of the old city, as well as in Israel's ancestral traditions.[2]

The acquisition of this property came about after David's sin of numbering the people (2 Sam. 24; 1 Chron. 21–22). The LORD chose this spot to announce the punishment;[3] and then, when the LORD stopped the plague, David was instructed by the prophet Gad to make an altar there. The account in Chronicles is more detailed. At that time the ark was in

---

1. See further Polan, "Divine Presence," 13–21. Polan relates Genesis 1–3; Exodus 3; and 1 Kings 8.
2. Merrill, "Royal Priesthood," 50–61.
3. See Lindblom, "Theophanies in Holy Places in Hebrew Religion," 91–106.

Gibeon, but David was too terrified of the Angel who had brought the plague to go there, so he sacrificed on this new site. When David offered his sacrifices, he called out to the LORD and the LORD answered with fire from heaven. The Angel of the LORD then sheathed his sword as a sign that the plague was over. This episode symbolized the drama of worship that would unfold here: sinful people who would appeal to God's grace on the basis of the sacrifices would find true peace with God, and even if they had to endure brief times of divine discipline, through the provisions in this holy place they would find a lifetime in God's favor (Ps. 30:5). Psalm 30, written for the dedication of the temple, is a psalm of praise for the restoration to divine favor. David's praise psalm was appropriate for the dedication of the house of the LORD because it was to be a place where sinful people would find spiritual renewal.[4]

Araunah wanted to donate the land, but David insisted on buying it, saying, "I will not . . . sacrifice a burnt offering that costs me nothing" (1 Chron. 21:24). He understood the essence of sacrifice. Therefore, he bought the spot, built an altar, and offered burnt and peace offerings to God. He announced that "the house of the LORD God is to be here, and also the altar of burnt offering for Israel" (22:1). But he was not permitted to build the temple (vv. 7–10). If the LORD's resting place was to recall the memory of God's rest in the garden, then a man of blood was not to be the one to build it.

But David did as much as he could to prepare for the temple: in addition to acquiring the land, he collected the materials, hired the artisans and craftsmen, and raised the money (1 Chron. 22:2–16).[5] It was David who drew up the plans by divine inspiration and then instructed Solomon in the construction (1 Chron. 28). But most significantly, David moved the ark of the covenant from its location in the woods to its permanent resting place, the place that would for ages be known as the temple mount.[6]

---

4. Likewise, the episode of the golden calf was recorded prior to the building of the tabernacle, forever reminding the people of how much they needed the tabernacle, where atonement and intercession were provided.

5. The amount of gold, silver, bronze, and iron was enormous—thousands of tons of material. It may be that our translation of the word for "thousand" might need to be reconsidered (J. W. Wenham, "Large Numbers in the Old Testament," 19–53), or that we may not fully understand the weight of a talent. Be that as it may, the point of the text is that gold, silver, bronze, and iron were given in abundance.

6. For patterns used in the texts of the ancient Near East, see Hurowitz, "The Priestly Account of the Building of the Tabernacle," 21–30.

Such a time-consuming and costly building project was possible because it occurred in a time of peace and prosperity. Accordingly, the fund-raising was voluntary and generous: the leaders of families and the overseers gave willingly (1 Chron. 29:6–7); and whoever possessed precious stones gave them to the treasury (v. 8). The generosity of the people was so amazing that David exemplified their spirit in a psalm. In it he blessed the LORD for his greatness, power, glory, and majesty, acknowledging that everything in heaven and earth belonged to him. He confessed that he and the people were not in themselves able to give so generously, but they did so because they realized that everything comes from God and they had only given back to him what he had provided. They could not take credit for it in any way; they could only be thankful that God inspired them to give willingly. David then prayed that such a willing spirit would remain with the people and that Solomon would remain obedient (vv. 10–19). True praise must exalt the LORD in this way; and even faithful giving must be turned into praise for the LORD.

In response to David's invitation, all the assembly praised God and fell prostrate before him in recognition of his sovereignty, holiness, and goodness (v. 20).

This blessing of the LORD by David is one of the best examples we have of humility coupled with gratitude; and it set the tone for the spirit of giving for all ages by formulating the appropriate words. There is little emphasis on praising the individuals who provided for the building of the temple, other than acknowledging that their offerings were willingly brought. What is stressed is that it all belonged to God to begin with— what they had came from God, and their gifts were acknowledging this.

## The House of the LORD

### Solomon's Preparation

Solomon began construction in the fourth year of his reign, about 966 B.C. (1 Kings 6:1). The fact that the plans had been drawn up by David in accordance with what the Spirit put in his mind (1 Chron. 28:10–19) recalls how God had given the pattern for the tabernacle to Moses (Exod. 25:9).

Solomon contracted with Hiram, king of Tyre, for workers to cut timber and help in the construction (1 Kings 5:2–12).[7] He conscripted 30,000

---

7. See among other sources in the bibliography, Kapelrud, "Temple Building," 56–62.

laborers from Israel to work in Lebanon in monthly shifts; he had 70,000 transporters and 80,000 stoneworkers in the mountains (v. 15); and he appointed 3,300 overseers (v. 16). This was a massive project—but then it was for the LORD of all creation.

## The Basic Construction

The temple complex was elaborate and majestic. At its center was the temple building itself, a construction approximately[8] 104 feet long, 34 feet wide, and 52 feet high, with walls that were ten feet thick. The building was divided into the two compartments, the Holy Place, which was the open part of the sanctuary where the priests served (70 feet long), and the Most Holy Place, the place where the presence of the LORD dwelt on earth (the "shrine" or *d*ᵉ*vîr*). It was an exact cube of 34 feet (the ceiling being lower here). At the front of the temple there was a "porch" or "entrance hall" (*'ûlām*),[9] 34 feet wide and about 17 feet deep. The entire building stood on a platform 10 feet high.

The courtyard was bounded by chambers and galleries for the Levites, the musicians, singers, and the servants—as well as for storage. These chambers were constructed in three stories with massive outer walls. This provision of lodgings ensured that there would always be ministers on hand for any service.

## The Furniture and Equipment

The same basic furnishings that were in the old tabernacle were also present in the temple but on a grander scale. For example, in contrast to the portable altar, Solomon's altar was thirty-four feet square and seventeen and a half feet high. Another stunning feature was Solomon's laver for water, the "molten sea," seventeen feet in diameter and eight and a half feet deep, holding about ten thousand gallons of water. The whole reservoir was held up by twelve bronze bulls in groups of three, each facing a different direction.[10] There were ten carts of bronze, each able to carry two hundred gallons of water (1 Kings 7:23–26; 2 Chron. 4:1–6).

---

8. These calculations are based on the interpretation that a royal cubit was 20.9 inches in length.

9. In Mesopotamian temples there is also an entrance, called *ellamu*, "front."

10. The use of images like this were not considered a violation of the Decalogue as long as they did not serve as the objects of worship. For more on the laver, see Wylie, "On King Solomon's Molten Sea," 86–90.

The other basic elements first introduced in the tabernacle in the wilderness were also included in the temple. A smaller altar of cedar decorated with gold was placed in front of the Most Holy Place (1 Kings 7:48; 2 Chron. 4:19). The table for the bread was also in the Holy Place. But rather than one lampstand, Solomon had ten of them. Finally, it was the original ark of the covenant that was placed in the Most Holy Place.

## The Art and the Symbolism

The temple and all its furnishings provided everything that was needed for the dramatic approach to God through sacrifice and intercession. Moreover, the way it was designed and decorated reminded people that they were drawing near to the sovereign God of creation. At the entrance stood two large pillars forty feet high with a circumference of twenty feet covered with bronze; they were named "Jachin" and "Boaz" (1 Kings 7:13–22; 2 Chron. 3:15). The pillars may have represented the dynastic covenant God made, giving Solomon and his successors dominion over his creation.[11] But perhaps they stood for the foundations of the earth, giving a cosmic dimension to the domain of the LORD.[12] In fact, they were decorated with carvings of lilies and pomegranates, symbolic of creation and therefore fitting for the sanctuary of the Lord of creation.[13] Moreover, calling the laver a "sea" indicated that it also symbolized the sovereign domain of God. But this "sea" was calm and controlled in the LORD's presence, not a force of chaos (see Job 38:4–11). The laver was held up by figures of animals as noted above, and around its rim were carved various arboreal designs. All these symbols suggested to the worshipper that this temple was like a new creation.[14] Solomon's ten lampstands must have

---

11. The descriptions of the pillars are not always the same, suggesting that the writers are describing different aspects of their position. "Jachin" means "he establishes," and "Boaz" means "in his strength." These words appear in dynastic passages, e.g., 2 Samuel 7:12–13 ("I will establish the throne of his kingdom") and Psalm 21:1 (in the "strength" of the LORD will the king rejoice).

12. The poetic image is that of the earth, the land, being supported by pillars over the subterranean waters (see Ps. 24:2).

13. See further Cope, *Symbolism in the Bible and the Church.*

14. In Egyptian temples a "sacred lake" was formed in the precincts to be life-giving and purifying. The symbolism of ancient sanctuaries that seems to be represented in some of the things that Solomon did does not represent a paganization of Israel's worship but rather the claim that it is Yahweh who is the Lord of creation, and not these other gods.

seemed like a garden of trees, giving light and life in the presence of the LORD.[15]

Inside the Holy Place the walls were covered with cedar and the floor with cypress, so that no stonework could be seen (1 Kings 6:14–18). Much of the woodwork was decorated with inlaid gold;[16] and the inside walls were filled with carvings of gourds, palm trees, and open flowers, as well as the cherubim who guard the way to the LORD (vv. 18, 29). There were large double doors made of olive wood that led into the temple proper as well as the Most Holy Place; both these sets of doors also were decorated with fine carvings and gold inlay. God was truly a God of beauty and glory, as this sanctuary, and all creation, reminded the worshippers.

Inside the Most Holy Place, where the ark of the covenant was, there were two huge carved cherubs about seventeen feet high made of olive wood and trimmed with gold, symbolically representing the angelic presence with the LORD. They faced the entrance, so that their touching wings spanned wall to wall (1 Kings 6:23–28). The representations of angels in the embroidery, inlay, and now the images were reminders that the LORD was also the Lord of heaven, attended to by angels who supported the throne of God.[17]

## The Impression of God's Dwelling Place

The temple in Jerusalem was built as the dwelling place of God among his people, but only in a representative sense.[18] When Solomon dedicated the temple, he said:

> But will God really dwell on earth? The heavens, even the highest heaven, cannot contain you. How much less this temple I have

---

15. See further Yarden, *Tree of Light.*
16. The translation "overlaid" should be understood as "inlaid" (1 Kings 6:19–22, 30). It would be strange to cover such fine woodwork with gold. Archaeology from places like Samaria and Megiddo show samples of beautiful inlaid materials, although using ivory and not gold.
17. Even a general survey of the archaeological data confirms that the basic plan of the temple was similar to but distinct from temples in the Fertile Crescent. See the following articles in Wright and Freedman, *Biblical Archaeologist Reader, 1*: Harold Nelson, "The Egyptian Temple," 147–59; A. Leo Oppenheim, "The Mesopotamian Temple," 158–68; G. Ernest Wright, "The Temple in Palestine-Syria," 169–84; and Floyd F. Filson, "Temple, Synagogue and Church," 185–200.
18. See Haran, "Divine Presence in the Israelite Cult and Cultic Institutions," 251–67.

built! Yet give attention to your servant's prayer and his plea for mercy, O LORD my God. . . . May your eyes be open toward this temple night and day, this place of which you said, "My Name shall be there," so that you will hear the prayer your servant prays toward this place. Hear the supplication of your servant and of your people Israel when they pray toward this place. Hear from heaven, your dwelling place, and when you hear, forgive. (1 Kings 8:27–30)

So Solomon himself repudiated any idea that the temple localized God. God could not be so confined, and neither had he need of such a place; but his people needed a place where they could find him, where others would pray with them, and where their communion with him would be most meaningful and beneficial.[19] The temple, then, was "the house of the LORD" because his "name" was there; in other words, it was where all the aspects of his nature could be fully realized.[20]

## The Majesty of God

It is easy to see how the temple reflected Israel's belief in the majesty of God. Not only was everything made in perfect harmony and symmetry, but also the richest products were used, all of which were from God's creation. Worshippers would have been struck immediately by the beauty and the wealth: the colors of the hangings (blue, purple, and scarlet) belonged with royalty, divine royalty in this place; the beautifully inlaid wood represented the love and adoration of the nation for this sovereign; the precious metals used in the sanctuary, the bronze, the silver, and the gold, witnessed to the honor due the one who was worshipped there.

All of that, however, was for the one national shrine. Religious communities throughout the land, like local assemblies today, had to work within their means when they built their places of worship (such as synagogues in the later period). Nevertheless, if worshippers want their building to be a place where people can come up out of their mundane routines

---

19. See Haran, *Temples and Temple Service in Ancient Israel;* see also Andre Parrot, *The Temple of Jerusalem.*
20. Recall that the "name" of Yahweh refers to his character or nature, all the perfections and attributes that belong to God and are manifested in his mighty works. By witnessing these works in the lives of people, the worshippers could see his power and his glory.

and catch a glimpse of glory, then how they build the sanctuary and with what materials it is constructed has to be given careful thought. The place of worship, after all, reflects not only the priorities and procedures of the worshippers who assemble there but also the value they place on the holy God they worship (most synagogues were some of the finest constructions in the towns). No matter how humble the place of worship, the preparation and the care of it should say to all worshippers that this place is special, that it is a place that has been set aside for communion with the Majesty on high and that he deserves the best they have.

## The Salvation of God

The temple also reflected Israel's belief in the salvation of God. The courtyard was a garden enclosed from the world, and entrance into it was controlled by the Levitical gatekeepers who helped the worshippers prepare spiritually for their journey into God's presence. The worshippers first approached the high altar where the sanctifying sacrifice was made. They then proceeded to the laver for washing with water, symbolizing the purification of life that follows atonement. Further access to God's presence was guided by the light of the lampstands and promoted by the intercessory prayers of the priest at the little altar of incense. But final entrance into the very presence of God was realized vicariously as the high priest entered one day a year. When the priest emerged from that room and declared grace and peace to the people in his blessing, the worshippers rejoiced that their spiritual quest in the worship was complete. This was the drama of Israelite worship: in tracing the approach to God in worship it was also unfolding the drama of redemption. Therefore, the sanctuary service declared not only that God is the sovereign Creator but also that he is Savior.

Churches that include symbolism and drama in their worship also have sought to use the architecture and the furnishings to convey this spiritual movement of the worshippers through the order of the service from the call to worship to the communion with the Lord, reflecting both their redemption in Christ and their ongoing maintenance of their relationship with him in sanctification.

## The Kingdom of God

As stated earlier, the holy sanctuary was the place that God manifested his sovereign presence on earth.[21] This was his domain; this was his throne room in the midst of his people. Everything here reminded people that this was a special place, a new creation of God in a world that was corrupt and contaminated. This was his other Eden, the place where heaven and earth met, the earthly replica of the heavenly sanctuary of God.[22] But this earthly dwelling place of God was also a revelation of the new order. The emblems of cherubs told of the great company of angels that surround the throne of God in glory and from the creation of the world have never ceased to praise him for creation. This kingdom of God on earth was a place where the people of God could come to find refuge from the world outside, to find peace, security, and wholeness. It was, in every sense of the word, a sanctuary.

The symbolism of the temple art and architecture must have been truly striking. Rarely have sanctuaries approximated such a grand vision of glory as this.[23] On the contrary, many places of worship witness to the fact that there has been little thought given to what is being communicated by the features, even though almost every one of them has something symbolic present. Churches that incorporate more of the drama of worship attempt to have symbolism for the details of the ritual.[24] Then when the service also dramatizes this movement of the worshipper through the entire process of approaching God, which in itself is symbolic of the process of salvation in Christ,[25] the total impact can be powerful.[26]

A study of churches that have attempted to do this is instructive and inspiring.[27] Although many of them have comprehensive decorative

---

21. I. Wilson argues that Deuteronomy clearly presents God as present on earth and not eliminated from the earthly sphere. Deuteronomy 4:36 presents God as both in heaven and on earth (*Out of the Midst of the Fire*).
22. See again Levenson, *Sinai and Zion;* and idem, "The Temple and the World," 275–98.
23. But see K. Barth, "The Architectural Problem of Protestant Places of Worship."
24. For a general introduction to the subject, see Irvine and Dawtry, *Art and Worship;* Dillenberger, *Theology of Artistic Sensibilities;* Rouet, *Liturgy and the Arts;* and E. D. Martin, *Art and the Religious Experience.*
25. See D. Brown and Loades, *The Sense of the Sacramental.*
26. See Ladner, *God, Cosmos, and Humankind.* See also Addleshaw and Etchells, *Architectural Setting of Anglican Worship;* and A. Anderson, "Building and Cherishing: Cathedrals and Buildings."
27. For example, the church of St. Michael in Munich, Germany demonstrates how the architecture and the art in a church can work together to develop a comprehensive scheme. This is not an ordinary parish church. It functions as a church, of course, but

schemes that are far beyond the means of most congregations, they may at least serve as a motivation to other churches to make every area, every furnishing, and every decoration useful in the spiritual activities that take place in their sanctuaries. This is especially important in view of the fact that the symbolism of these grand churches was inspired by the way God revealed the heavenly pattern for the earthly tabernacle and temple, in which everything was functional for the various aspects of worship but also symbolic of the doctrine that was taught. If there is also a proper emphasis on teaching, the more features that are present to remind the worshippers of these truths, the greater will be the inspiration to praise. Without proper teaching or proclamation, the symbols can easily be misunderstood and the course of worship altered.

## Conclusion

The temple was a visible reminder of God's presence among his people and of his saving dominion over all creation. It was where God would make himself known and permit his people to find union with him in their worship. Everything about it ministered to the aesthetic sense of the worship—God was a God of order, beauty, and perfection. God also was a sovereign God—everything used actually belonged to him anyway. Moreover, the temple design came from God in the first place, so that no one could claim the credit or affix blame on the king. Everything about the temple reminded people that the LORD was a holy God and filled them with the hope of glory.

In the New Testament the meaning of this temple provides several important sets of teaching. First, the idea of the temple in Israel housing the glory of the LORD foreshadowed the body of Christ that veiled his glory (John 1:14; 2:19). Three days after the opposition destroyed that "temple," Jesus arose from the dead. Not only was the true temple, the body of Christ, raised up, but also a new dwelling place was established for his presence on earth—the mystical body of Christ, or the church. Thus, according to the New Testament, believers become the temple of the Holy Spirit as the Lord dwells within (1 Cor. 6:19). Everything about their lives must be fitting for the Holy One who dwells in them.

---

it was designed from the outset as a teaching church to assist the worshipper in following the teachings of the church, i.e., the Jesuits with their emphasis on Ignatius's *Spiritual Exercises*. See J. C. Smith, *Sensuous Worship*, 77–97.

Second, as we noted with the tabernacle, the temple with its symbolic features was used by the apostles to teach the doctrines of the faith as well as Christian life and service.

Third, while we do not have biblical instructions for building churches, nevertheless a number of practical lessons from this material are reflected in the New Testament. When Christianity grew so rapidly, it became necessary to have better places for believers to meet. Practicality required that these places have the appropriate features for the ritual. Symbolism was helpful, if not necessary, to identify these places as special places, places where the Lord's presence was manifested in special ways. They were to be recognized as places in which the central focus was on sacrificial atonement as the basis of worship and the condition for participating in Holy Communion, which in itself reflected Israel's celebration of being at peace with God in the eating of the meal in the temple precincts. Thus crosses and other Christian symbols of the faith became more prominent. The setting and surroundings of places of worship always speak volumes about the beliefs and practices of the people who worship there.

The earliest churches for which we have any archaeological data show a deliberate attempt to reflect the structure and order of Israel's sanctuaries, albeit with adjustments to Christian symbols and services.[28] God's revealed plan for the tabernacle was enhanced in the temple and in turn influenced the structures of synagogues and churches. What better plan to follow than that which was given as the earthly copy of the heavenly sanctuary, the hope of glory we share.

---

28. See for diagrams and discussion Webber, *Worship: Old and New,* 151–60.

# CHAPTER 15

# Musical Guilds, Sanctuary Choirs, *and* Congregational Singing

## Music in Ancient Israel

The law laid out the occasions and the ritual for worship, but it was David who prepared the way for the full and glorious praise of God in that worship, not only by organizing the guilds of singers and musicians, but also by writing many psalms that became part of the hymnbook.

Songs of praise were used prior to the time of David of course. For example, in the "Song of the Sea"(Exod. 15:1–21), Moses and Miriam used poetic verse with musical accompaniment. Deuteronomy 32 records the "Song of Moses"; 33, the "Blessing." It is impossible to say if these were set to music, but the poetic form would have lent itself to that. We also have the Song of Deborah at the victory over the Canaanites (Judg. 5). But Hannah's song of praise is the first example of an Israelite song delivered at the sanctuary (1 Sam. 2:1–10).[1]

In other cultures there were fully developed musical guilds, no doubt performing the myths, hymns, and laments of those religions. The Canaanite texts not only list singers and musicians among the guilds, but they also record their myths in a poetic form similar to the patterns of early Hebrew poetry.[2]

---

1. The composition is clearly a praise psalm, even though the text says that she "prayed and said" these words (cf. Jonah 2:1). The verb *prayed* may refer to the earlier prayer, and not the praise to follow.
2. For more information on Ugaritic singers, see Albright, *Archaeology and the Religion of Israel,* 209; and for the whole mythic cycle, see Craigie, *Ugarit and the Old Testament,* 44–66; and A. Curtis, *Ugarit, Ras Shamra,* 66–106.

Of course secular music and singing were common. Genesis (4:21) says that the making of musical instruments occurred at the very dawn of civilization, but this tells us nothing about their nature or their use other than what we can gather from later evidence.[3] When "music" was used in battle, both to muster troops and terrorize the enemy, it included trumpet blasts as well as noise-making instruments (Judg. 7:18–20; 1 Kings 1:39–40; 2 Kings 11:14; 2 Chron. 13:14; 20:28). Popular singing at celebrations would have been more pleasing since it had verbal content and was accompanied by stringed instruments and various horns or flutes. Songs were common at weddings (Song of Songs; Ps. 45), during the harvest (Isa. 16:10; Jer. 48:33), and at the digging of wells (Num. 21:17). They were also useful in making ridicule more memorable (Job 30:9; Isa. 14). Besides songs at family functions (Gen. 31:27; see also Luke 15:25) and at work projects (Isa. 16:10; Jer. 31:4–7; 48:33), there were songs of praise for heroes (Judg. 11:34; 1 Sam. 18:6), harem and court music (2 Sam. 19:35; Ps. 45:14–15; Eccl. 2:8), banquet music (Isa. 5:12; 24:8–9), funeral dirges and laments (2 Sam. 1:17–18; 2 Chron. 35:25; cf. Matt. 9:23), and various incantations (Josh. 6:4–20; 2 Kings 3:15). In David's time, women came out singing and dancing with tambourines and musical instruments (1 Sam. 18:6–7). David himself could play the harp as a young man and soothe the troubled spirit of the king (1 Sam. 16:23). Because of his musical abilities and his many compositions, David was called "Israel's beloved singer" (2 Sam. 23:1 [NIV note]).

The use of music in worship is a natural extension of its force in life. It elevates the singers above their mundane experiences by heightening the tone and expression of their speech and thereby increases the celebration. It also intensifies the pathos of prayers and laments, serving as a powerfully therapeutic way of dealing with the dark riddles of life.[4] Bells on the priest's garments (Exod. 28:34–35), trumpets at the festivals (Lev. 23:24), lamentations and dirges in times of sadness and grief (Lamentations), animated songs of the prophets (1 Sam. 10:5–6), demonstrations of prophetic inspiration through minstrels (2 Kings 3:15), or the regular singing and playing of music in the sanctuary (Ps. 150) all witness to the power of music on religious activities. Without the religious ritual and

---

3. See J. Braun, *Music in Ancient Israel/Palestine,* for a study of the archaeological findings about ancient music and musical instruments by a musicologist.
4. See Eaton, "Music's Place in Worship," 85–107.

proclamation, the music would not have had the great meaning it did; but without the music, with its rhythm, the lofty and evocative words, and the rich poetic forms, the religious ritual and the prophetic messages would have been less effectual and certainly less memorable.

## Musicians and Music in Israel's Worship

David's contribution to the use of music in worship began with his moving the ark of the covenant to where the temple was to be built (1 Chron. 15:11–16), although psalms he had written earlier were added to the worship. For the procession he appointed Levites as singers and musicians, notably Asaph, Heman, and Ethan (v. 19).[5] The Levites used cymbals and stringed instruments with different arrangements (for women's voices [*'ălămôt*, v. 20], or with harps of eight strings [*sh*ᵉ*mînît*, v. 21]). Still others were to blow trumpets (v. 24). The leader was Kenaniah, a skillful instructor of music (v. 22). He and all the singers and musicians were clothed in fine linen for this procession (v. 27).

This organization of musicians and singers was then retained for temple worship. David appointed Levites as ministers (*m*ᵉ*shār*ᵉ*tîm*, s.v. *shārat*) "to remind, and to acknowledge, and to praise the LORD God of Israel" (1 Chron. 16:4).[6] Their ministry thus had different purposes, as these infinitives suggest. The first infinitive, "to remind" (*l*ᵉ*hazkîr* [s.v. *zākar*]) fits the lament psalms, because in them the people reminded the LORD of their dilemmas and petitioned for intervention. The petition frequently called God to hear, to see, or to remember his servants (e.g., Pss. 13:3; 132). The tone and substance of music on such an occasion would be more solemn than festive, perhaps a liturgical lament or a dirge.

The second infinitive, "to acknowledge" (*l*ᵉ*hôdôt* [s.v. *yādāh*]; related to the word "thanksgiving," *tôdāh*), is the key word for a declarative praise psalm in which the worshipper declared what God had done (e.g., Ps. 118:1, 21). This had an entirely different tone from the lament, one that would be appropriate for rejoicing and dancing (Ps. 30:11–12). The third infinitive, "to praise" (*l*ᵉ*hallēl* [s.v. *hālal*]) refers to the psalm of pure praise to God, the descriptive praise or hymn (e.g., Pss. 33; 113). One

---

5. See additionally Polk, "The Levites in the Davidic-Solomonic Empire," 3–22.

6. A. E. Hill notes that music is both worship and an aid to worship. And judging from the variety of songs in the Psalter, singing was a favorite response of the worshippers to the person and work of the LORD (*Enter His Courts with Praise!* 114–15).

would expect the presentation of praise for the greatness and the grace of God to be more majestic than other types of psalms. Hymns, therefore, do not report personal experiences but tend to be more doctrinal. So the singers and musicians were assigned the ministry of presenting or accompanying the various expressions of the faith of the people.

The various musical instruments mentioned in this and other biblical passages indicate a wide variety of sounds to accompany the praise and singing.[7] Cymbals and timbrels are simple percussion instruments.[8] Among the wind instruments there is the "trumpet" (*khătsōts'rāh* [Ps. 98:6]), "ram's horn" (*shōphār* [Ps. 47:5]), the "flute" (*khālîl* [1 Kings 1:40]), and the "pipe" (*'ûgāv* [Ps. 150:4]). The major stringed instruments included the "lyre" (*kinnôr* [Ps. 33:2]), the "harp" (*nēvel* [Ps. 150:3]), "strings" (*minnîm* [Ps. 150:4]), "ten strings" (*'āsôr* [Ps. 33:2]), and "lute" (*shālîsh* [three strings? 1 Sam. 18:6]).[9] Moreover, the word commonly used for a "psalm" (*mizmôr*, s.v. *zāmar*) indicates that a psalm is a poetic composition to be sung to the accompaniment of stringed instruments.[10]

Among the divisions of the Levites (1 Chron. 23), four thousand were assigned to praise with instruments.[11] When they were on duty in the temple, they were to stand every morning to thank and praise the LORD, and at every evening, as well as at every worship service (vv. 30–31). Thus, sounds and voices of singers and musicians filled the house of the LORD every day; and worshippers took part in the musical celebration in whatever ways they could.

Interestingly, the division of gatekeepers, the sons of Jeduthun, are list-

---

7. In addition to J. Braun's, *Music in Ancient Israel/Palestine,* see Sellers, "Musical Instruments of Israel"; and Finesinger, "Musical Instruments in the Old Testament," 21–76; and idem, "The Shofar," 193–228.

8. For the cymbals the Bible uses several words: *m'tsiltáyim* (1 Chron. 16:5, 42), *tselts'lîm* (Ps. 150:5), and *m'na'an'îm* (rattles? castanets?) (2 Sam. 6:5, "sistrums" in NIV). For the timbrel the Hebrew word is *tōph* (Ps. 81:2).

9. There are other instruments mentioned in the Old Testament that will be discussed in the dictionaries and commentaries. It is not possible to go into greater detail here; this survey should be sufficient to show how rich and varied the musical accompaniment would have been.

10. The modern trend toward using guitars recaptures some of the sounds, but the stringed instruments in the ancient cultures were very different—they were along the order of lyres and harps, which would have been simpler and softer in sound.

11. See also Williamson, "The Origins of the Twenty-Four Priestly Courses."

ed among the musicians and singers. According to 1 Chronicles 26 gate-keepers were to serve as watchmen as well as porters, permitting qualified worshippers to the sanctuary (vv. 12–16). But they aspired to sing and praise as well. Jeduthun was a singer, and his son wished to be one too (1 Chron. 16:38–42). Likewise the sons of Korah, originally gatekeepers, were also singers (see 2 Chron. 20:19, and the heading "sons of Korah" for twelve psalms).[12] Gatekeepers had a musical part in the liturgy, for some of the Psalms are liturgies for the entrance to the sanctuary (see Pss. 15; 24:3–6; 118:19–27).

But a number of these Levites were more than musicians. According to 1 Chronicles 25, Asaph, Heman, and Jeduthun were "prophets" using harps, strings, and cymbals, and they wrote psalms for the hymnbook, which ultimately became Holy Scripture. Because Asaph was the chief choir director, many compositions were deposited with him for use in the sanctuary (hence, the headings "to the chief choir director" in the Psalms). These psalms were understood to be God's word to the people, that is, prophetic compositions; and their elevated poetic form was harmonious with divine prophecy. In addition to preserving such works, Asaph also wrote inspired works for the service (e.g., Ps. 50). Asaph's "sons" (a guild?[13]) were under the supervision of their father, who prophesied (1 Chron. 25:2); the "sons" of Jeduthun (v. 3) performed with harps; and the "sons" of Heman (vv. 4–5), who was the king's seer, also performed in the temple services with instruments. The order that emerged apparently had David over all sanctuary music, perhaps also as the royal patron, then Asaph the prophet as director of music, then Heman and Jeduthun, who were prophets and seers over the musical guilds who performed their words. At the time that David organized the musicians and singers, he began their ministry of music by writing a psalm to be sung in thanksgiving to the LORD (1 Chron. 16:7–36).[14] This inspired composition set the tone for the psalms that would be collected for sanctuary service.

In the Old Testament, singing or rhythmic chanting was considered

---

12. J. M. Miller, "The Korahites of Southern Judah," 58–68.
13. There is no reason to doubt that "sons" here refers to the sons, for families can indeed be musical from generation to generation. But the term could also mean guilds that these men formed (Gen. 4:21).
14. See Butler, "A Forgotten Passage," 142–50.

the most powerful form that prophecy could have and a form of prophecy itself.[15] Thus, when the Chronicler used the verb "prophesy" for the work of temple singers, he was signifying that their singing, and especially what they were singing, was due to prophetic inspiration.

Poetic composition is also used throughout the Old Testament for all the major prophetic books, and at times in specific genres of poetic writing. When messages were delivered in such a majestic and powerful form, their character as divine inspiration was beyond question. Because David, Asaph, Heman, and perhaps Jeduthun wrote biblical psalms, they were also considered "divinely inspired" prophets as well as being "inspired" musicians and poets (see 2 Sam. 23:2). There is a level of artistic skill in music and poetry that deserves to be called "inspired"; it is truly evidence that the human spirit shares something of the divine work of creating. But when those gifts are used by God to communicate his eternal word, the description "inspired" takes on a more specific and in many ways more ominous meaning. The content is the eternal Word of the LORD. For the very words from God to be put into beautiful poetry and set to musical accompaniment is not only one of the most powerful and glorious expressions of the celebration of the people of God, but also a memorable form of the revelation of God. Not only does it lift the spirits of the worshippers as they lift their voices, taking them out of the mundane, daily form of communications, but it also unites them harmoniously in their spiritual service more than at almost any other time. While such harmony and unity can be true of secular singing and musical events as well, in the worship of God the unity and harmony is with heaven, for in those moments the worshippers join the company of angels and archangels in praising the one true and living God, the Lord of all creation, their Redeemer and their King.

## Singing in Israel's Worship

In addition to the praise offered by the official singers (1 Chron. 15:27; Ps. 68:25), there was also singing by the congregation (Num. 21:17; Ezra 3:11) and by individuals (Exod. 15:20–21; Ps. 51:14). The Psalms themselves frequently call other worshippers to "sing to the LORD" (*shîr;* Ps. 30:4);[16] and the worshipper's response of "I will sing to the LORD" records

---

15. See Guillaume, *Prophecy and Divination Among the Hebrews and Other Semites.*

16. See Gunn, *Singers of Israel;* J. A. Smith, "Ancient Synagogue, the Early Church, and Singing," 1–16; and then for a practical use, *The Psalter: The Psalms and Canticles for Singing.*

the natural and expected response to the call. Singing is not, therefore, an optional embellishment of worship; it is a necessary requirement of it. By singing, the worshippers lift up their voices in beautiful words and memorable sounds appropriate to the beauty of the holiness of God. Psalm 33:1 says, "Sing joyfully to the LORD, you righteous; it is fitting for the upright to praise him." Singing songs of praise was, and is, the appropriate and enthusiastic way for the people to tell of the glorious and gracious works of the LORD: "He put a new song in my mouth, a hymn of praise to our God" (Ps. 40:3).

Congregational singing may have been antiphonal at times (recall Exod. 15:21). It would be fairly easy for a congregation to sing a psalm in this way, following the lead of a cantor or choir. Some psalms indicate that parts were taken by the priestly singers and some by the congregation. Psalm 121 lends itself nicely to this arrangement, for judging from the change in pronouns, the pilgrim-psalmist would have sung verses 1 and 2, and an accompanying priest (or pilgrim) would have answered with verses 3 through 8. In Psalm 20 the pronouns indicate that the congregation sang verses 1 through 5 as an intercession for the king, the king proclaimed his confidence with verses 6 through 8, and the congregation prayed verse 9. Such arrangements not only reflected the details of an earlier event but also preserved them for a dramatic reenactment in worship. Writing psalms in this manner made it easy to adapt them to responsive or antiphonal singing.

There were many litanies as well. A litany is a series of petitions or praises in worship, recited or sung by those leading the services and responded to in recurring formulas by the people. This is by far the easiest to incorporate in a service. The earliest example is recorded in Deuteronomy 27:12–26, where the Levites read each curse, and all the people responded with "Amen!" Psalm 136 is more for worship; it follows every line of the text with "His [loyal] love endures forever." It would have been easy for the congregation to take this part while listening (more carefully) to what the singers were singing or saying. Psalm 118:1–4 employs this same litany; it calls for the Israelites, then the priests, and then all worshippers in turn to exclaim "His [loyal] love endures forever!"

There are other descriptive words for the celebration and praise in the sanctuary that are more ecstatic—cultic shouts and ringing cries. The ringing cry *(rānan)*, often translated "sing, shout, cry aloud," refers to

the shrieking cry made in the back of the throat with the tongue dart-
ing from side to side. Obviously, a cultural shift is preferred in modern
services when following the biblical call to shout for joy, otherwise its use
would startle most Western congregations and distract from the desired
intent. But the point is that there were times when the congregation could
not contain their joyful enthusiasm and so shouted words or sounds of
acclamation in their worship. In Leviticus 9:24 when the people saw the
glory of the LORD they "shouted for joy" and worshipped (cf. Ps. 2:11,
"give a cultic shout [NIV "rejoice"] with trembling"). The shouts or ringing cries hardly qualify as music, but they were congregational responses
of great joy. Shouts of *"amen"* or *"hallelu-yah"* would have been common
in the assembly (cf. 1 Kings 18:39; 1 Chron. 16:36; 2 Chron. 7:3; Neh.
8:6). With these the spontaneous praise of the people would be most notable, especially when they saw or heard something new and wonderful.
Likewise, in heaven the shouts of acclamation and praise will accompany
the culmination of the ages (Rev. 19:1–7).

The celebration of praise accompanied by music and singing would
also at times inspire people to dance before the LORD, as David did at
the moving of the ark to the Holy City (2 Sam. 6:14). In fact, Psalm 150:4
calls for people to worship God with dancing and tambourines, and accordingly there appears to have been regular dancers for the sanctuary
(Ps. 87:7; s.v. khûl). The dancing was in no way the dancing of profane
pagan practices, then or now; it was the natural joy of the human spirit
in response to God. The words used indicate that it consisted of whirl-
ing and turning, probably a round dance in which the dancers danced in
circles.[17]

## Conclusion

In the sanctuary the Israelite worshippers could have singers and musicians sing a psalm for any occasion, or they could join the singing in
unison or antiphonally, or they could respond with short expressions,
or they could shout doxologies and words of praise, or they could dance.
In any event they were active participants in the musical praise in the
sanctuary, for they knew that it was appropriate to praise God in every

---

17. See further C. L. Meyers, "Drum-Dance-Song Ensemble," 49–67; J. G. Davies,
*Liturgical Dance, An Historical, Theological, and Practical Handbook;* and Seasoltz,
"The Dancing Church," 253–61.

way (Pss. 92:1; 147:1; 150). And the sanctuary was the most fitting place for God to be praised, for it was where he made his presence known most frequently through the praises of the people. When the people of God were faithful to give him thanks (Ps. 122:4), the sanctuary was filled with praise from morning to evening, so much so that David could say that God dwells "in the praises of Israel," meaning that he dwells in the sanctuary where praises are given (Ps. 22:3).

It would be difficult to think of worshipping God without musical instruments and singing, for these forms of praising were not only instructed by God, but also inspired by heaven as well. Creation was celebrated by the angels who sang and shouted for joy; and in glory there are and always will be choirs of angels and saints singing God's praises for his wondrous power and glory. In the meantime we who are his new creation must sing our songs as well and play our instruments skillfully, reclaiming the glory and honor that is due him and anticipating the great day of redemption when all creation will sing.[18] The New Testament does not go into a detailed description of praise and music and musical instruments for the early church; it did not have to because all of that was so much a part of the Israelite's worship of God. The writers simply assume that such praise should continue and will continue in glory. When Paul instructs Christians to speak to one another with psalms, hymns, and spiritual songs, he is at the least referring to the types of psalms in the temple hymnbook (Eph. 5:19). By using the word "psalm," he is including musical instruments, because a psalm is a poetic composition sung to the accompaniment of stringed instruments. Through music and singing God is exalted and glorified in ways that unembellished speech could not do, and in ways that are fitting for his holy and glorious nature.

---

18. It is significant that the Israelites took the horns of dead rams and turned them into instruments that would sound forth the glory of the LORD.

# CHAPTER 16

# The Psalms *in* Worship

## The Development of the Temple Hymnbook

The book of Psalms is a collection of the prayers, praises, meditations, and liturgies of ancient Israel that were set to poetic form and deposited in the sanctuary for use by individual worshippers and choirs.[1]

Most of the Psalms were originally individual compositions written about a variety of personal experiences in the faith. We have some compositions that were never added to the sanctuary collection but were recorded in other biblical books that provided the historical settings that inspired them.[2] The Psalms, however, do not retain that specific orientation since they were intended for a wider application in the lives of the faithful.

As individual psalms were deposited in the sanctuary, they were periodically arranged into collections. Psalm 72 apparently stood at the end of an earlier collection because verse 20 notes that the prayers of David end, when in fact more follow in our present collection. A couple of centuries later Hezekiah instructed the Levites to sing the psalms of David and Asaph (2 Chron. 29:30), indicating that there may have been two collections in his day. Asaph's psalms are Psalms 50 and 73–83, the latter grouping perhaps preserving an original collection, and Psalm 50 (an indictment of sinful worshippers) was moved by a later editor to its place next to Psalm 51 (a confession for sin). Some groups of psalms may

---

1. Mowinckel focuses on the use of the Psalms in sanctuary worship (*The Psalms and Israel's Worship*).
2. E.g., the Song of Moses (Exod. 15), the Song of Deborah (Judg. 5), the Song of Hannah (1 Sam. 2), the Song of the Bow (2 Sam. 1), Hezekiah's praise (Isa. 38), Jonah's praise (Jonah 2), and the prayer of Habakkuk (Hab. 3).

have been kept together from earlier collections with similar psalms added later to the group: the pilgrim psalms, 120–134; the Korahite psalms, 42–49 and 84–88; and the Hallel psalms, 113–118 and 145–150. Whatever arrangements may have existed earlier, the temple hymnbook appears to have been given its final form by the time of the Chronicler.[3] It included doxologies after Psalms 41; 72; 89; and 106. The present order of the Psalms shows signs of being the work of one editor or editorial school, because it groups the collection into five books and because it follows an arrangement that leads from one psalm to the next by links in motifs or words, indicating that there was a plan for stitching them together.

## The Use of the Psalter in Worship

Since a text of the Psalms would not have been available to the worshippers, they had to rely more on memory and prompting by Levitical singers. As in congregations today, people would have learned the pieces that were sung regularly fairly easily and so could participate enthusiastically in the celebrations of the great festivals.[4] The literary forms of the Psalms, the parallel expressions in them, and the musical accompaniment all aided their learning of the Psalms. The instruments marked the time with simple rhythms, probably consisting of a few notes to cover a line, with the last measure rising or falling, which meant that the singing probably took the form of a rhythmic recitation.

### Reflections of Experiences

Most of the Psalms came out of significant experiences and crises that the people faced in their lives. People wrote psalms to express their experiences in greater intensity and beauty, and other worshippers who had similar experiences could draw on them to express their faith as well and gain comfort and encouragement. The confession of sin, Psalm 51, is one passage that has been used by almost everyone.

One of the most commonly shared experiences would have been the

---

3. The final collection included a number of psalms that were written after the Exile (e.g., Ps. 126). Of course most modern critical scholars would place the completion of the whole collection much later than the time of the Chronicler and credit few if any of the Psalms to David.
4. According to Matthew 21:9, the people going into Jerusalem at the Triumphal Entry were familiar with the lines of Psalm 118 because it was regularly sung at Passover.

*payment of vows* in the sanctuary, such as the firstfruits, or the dedication offering, or the tithes. After these were presented to God and the priestly ritual enacted, the worshippers would attest to their faith with the appropriate words (Deut. 26:1–11), giving thanks to God for the good gifts of life, especially the harvest. For that, a harvest song like Psalm 65 may have been used. They then would swear that they had fulfilled their obligations (Deut. 26:12–15), and perhaps renew their dedication to do God's will, using the words of Psalm 40:6–8.

A second experience that called for prayer and praise was *personal illness.* Faced with a physical crisis, and possibly death, the devout would pray to God for healing, promising to praise him if and when he was delivered. The lament psalms in which the sufferer cried to God for healing and restoration of life would have been widely used by others (see Pss. 6; 38); they included the lament and the cry for help, but also the praise to be given to God once the prayer was answered. This section of praise, a rehearsal of what would be said, formed a vow to God. Once fully recovered the worshippers would bring the appropriate offerings (Lev. 12–15) and then pay their vows by offering thanksgiving to God for healing them and restoring them to life (Pss. 30:2; 118:13–18; Isa. 38:9–20).

Another experience that prompted psalm writing was *deliverance from danger.* Various psalms tell how the worshipper found a place of safety in the sanctuary, perhaps fleeing from enemies, thus making the temple truly a sanctuary (for God's provision of sanctuary, see also Exod. 21:12–14; Deut. 19:1–13; 1 Kings 1:49–53; 2:28–35). Some would speak of taking refuge in the LORD so that their life was spared from harm and danger (Pss. 91; 142); and even though the psalmists might not have been completely free from their danger when they wrote, they had faith in God's ultimate protection. But besides being a place of safety, the sanctuary enabled the troubled soul to regain a proper perspective on the inequities of life (Ps. 73).

*False accusations* provided another reason for prayer. People frequently cried out to God for vindication and then recorded with their prayers their confident trust for others to share. For example, Psalms 43 and 26 call on God to vindicate the psalmist; others express the hope that righteous leaders will plead the cause of the widow and the orphan (Ps. 72). This frequent theme in the Bible indicates that there were serious legal problems in the land, and very often only through prayer could people find hope, and only by hearing the praises of others could they be encouraged to keep on praying.

Another spiritual crisis that prompted the writing of psalms concerned *sinful acts*. From such occasions come a number of penitential psalms (e.g., 32; 51; 130) that focus on the need for forgiveness, or the request for divine discipline to end, or the expression of the joy of being forgiven. These prayers and praises were written from the pain of guilt or the joy of forgiveness by individuals, but when they were deposited in the sanctuary, they found a wide currency among the people who likewise needed forgiveness regularly. Such psalms would have found a regular use in the sanctuary ritual of sin offerings (Lev. 4:1–6:7).[5]

There were many other occasions for which psalms were written and used over the years apart from these kinds of individual experiences. For example, several formed part of the royal liturgy—a king's coronation (Ps. 2), his wedding (Ps. 45), or the charter by which he would reign (Ps. 101).[6] Other psalms were written in the genre of wisdom literature, reminding people of the important choices in life (e.g., Pss. 1; 49; 73). Historical psalms in the form of hymns were probably used at the festivals when the history of the people was rehearsed (e.g., Pss. 105–106). And prophetic psalms also may have accompanied the great festivals when the people renewed the covenant with their God who someday would establish his dominion with the power and the glory he displayed at Sinai (Pss. 93; 97–98; 110). These and a number of other types of psalms in the Psalter, written by individuals out of their triumphs and their tragedies, made it possible for the collection to receive a wide and varied use by other believers, as well as the whole congregation in its scheduled convocations.

## Set Prayers and Praises

Once the Psalms were deposited in the temple, they provided set prayers and praises for the scheduled times of worship. It is hard to know exactly how the Psalter was used in organized worship, but from later Jewish traditions we learn how many of them were assigned for daily worship. For instance, on Sunday, Psalm 24 was used; on Monday, Psalm 48; on Tuesday, Psalm 82; on Wednesday, Psalm 94; on Thursday, Psalm 81; on

---

5. For a study of the various prayers, see P. D. Miller, *They Cried to the Lord;* see also B. Anderson, *Out of the Depths.*

6. See J. H. Walton, "The Psalms," 21–31.

Friday, Psalm 93; and on Saturday, Psalm 92 (see its title).[7] In addition to daily offices, the Psalms also were appointed for the festivals. The pilgrim psalms, 120–134, were to be sung when the people went up to Jerusalem for the three main festivals. Because of frequent use, the pilgrims would have known these songs fairly well, especially since they were accompanied by priests or Levites going up to Jerusalem.[8]

But the Psalter also was put to liturgical use during all the great services,[9] especially to accompany the ritual of the sacrifices.[10] The evidence for this comes mostly from later Jewish tradition, but it more than likely reflects ancient traditions. For example, Oesterley summarizes this tradition about the Psalms at Passover:

> The great importance of the "Hallel"[11] in the temple worship can be seen by its place during the great Festivals. When the Passover lambs had been slain, two rows of priests were drawn up in the Court of the Priests, in which the great altar stood; they received into gold and silver bowls the blood from the lambs which the head of each family had to offer at this feast. These bowls were passed up to the officiating priest at the great altar; as he received each bowl he emptied it at the base of the altar, and then handed the empty bowl back. The ceremony lasted from the ninth until the eleventh hour (i.e., 3–5 PM), and during it the "Hallel" was sung by the Levites. The congregation repeated the first clause of each of the six psalms, and after every other clause or line they shouted "Hallelujah"; when they came to the last of the six (Ps. 118), they repeated not only the first clause, and shouted "Hallelujah" after each clause, but they also repeated after the Levites the three clauses contained in verses 25–26:

---

7. This arrangement reflects the practice during the time of the second temple, but on the basis of this evidence it can be concluded that such a use of some psalms was quite ancient (Hayes, *Understanding the Psalms*).

8. See Crow, *The Songs of Ascent (Psalms 120–134)*; and Keet, *Study of the Psalms of Ascents*.

9. See the liturgical arrangements in Psalms 118 and 132.

10. Oesterley, "Worship in the Old Testament," 52–59.

11. "Hallel," meaning "praise," refers to Psalms 113–118 and others that have the oft-recurring expression "Hallelujah."

"Save now, we beseech thee, Yahweh;
Yahweh, we beseech thee, send us now prosperity.
Blessed is he that cometh in the name of Yahweh."

The "Hallel" was repeated in this way until the whole ceremony was completed.[12]

Other texts from Jewish tradition show that a large number of the Psalms were used for all the festivals and therefore are in the fullest sense songs of praise.[13] While prayers seem to reflect individual yet shared experiences, the praise psalms were intended to be delivered in the assembly. Thus, the cycle of prayer and praise would be completed in the assembly of worshippers.

## Conclusion

The church could use the Psalter much more effectively than it does. It is true that some churches read a psalm or two in the daily readings, and others use parts of psalms set to contemporary music. Psalms used to be sung as the hymns of the church well into the modern times, but then they were gradually replaced by modern hymns and songs. Now even these great hymns of the church are being replaced by shorter songs and repetitious choruses. In each period the hymns and songs have been a reflection of the circumstances of the times in which they were written.[14] If the Psalter were restored to a prominent place in worship, it would put more of the Word of God on the lips of worshippers, teach people how to pray and praise, and strengthen and encourage their faith.[15] With proper instruction and guidance, the Psalms could be read creatively, used appropriately with ritual, prayed as prayers, sung or said as prayers and praises,[16] and adapted to creeds, litanies, and exclamatory responses as frequent parts of a worship service.[17] Church leaders must teach people

---

12. Oesterley, "Worship in the Old Testament," 56.
13. For example, see J. Gray, "A Cantata of the Autumn Festival: Psalm LXVIII," 2–26.
14. See the books on hymns reflecting their social circumstances; for example, Coddaire and Weil, "Use of the Psalter in Worship," 342–48; Hoffman, *Sacred Sound and Social Change*; Thompson, *The Seventeenth-Century English Hymn*; and Watson, *The English Hymn*.
15. Merton says, "If we have no real interest in praising him, it shows that we have never realized who he is" (*Praying the Psalms*, 11).
16. See Saliers, "The Integrity of Sung Prayers," 290–303.
17. J. A. Lamb, *Psalms in Christian Worship;* and Holladay, *Psalms Through Three Thousand Years*.

how to pray and to praise, and what better way to do it than to study the divinely inspired prayers and praises in the Bible. Moreover, the use of the Psalter would ensure that worshippers would regularly contemplate the holy God of glory, the Creator, Redeemer, and King, in the beautiful and powerful ways that he chose to reveal himself.

# CHAPTER 17

# Offering *the* Sacrifice *of* Praise

WITH THIS SURVEY OF THE PRAYERS and praises found in the hymnbook now in mind, we can begin to assemble the complete picture of Israel's worship. We can bring together in our thinking the many-faceted ministry of the altar and the array of proclamations that made up the ministry of the word. No ritual act in the sanctuary would have been performed, whether at a great festival or a simple assembly, without the words of interpretation and proclamation. And none of it would have been worth doing without a vision of God's glory. All the aspects of Israel's worship came together in the full communion with the living God, best exemplified in the sacrifice of praise (Ps. 50:14; see also Heb. 13:15).

Now, from the biblical writings themselves, we can capture the spirit of the people as they ascended the hill of Zion to behold the power and the glory of God, to praise him, to pray to him, to hear from him, to eat at his table in communion, and to renew their covenant commitments to him. With all these reasons to go to the sanctuary, that Holy Place became the central focus of the people of God.

And what a focus it was! There in the sanctuary—that other Eden— worshippers would have been caught up with the dramatic ritual of sacrificing animals, the smell of roasting meat and the sweet aroma of the incense ascending to heaven, the startling sight of blood being dashed at the side of the altar, the refreshing feel of pure water running over their hands and their feet, the scores of baskets of fresh produce, grains, and breads, olive oil in abundance for the sanctuary, and the glorious music of the skilled musicians and singers. It was all part of the Israelites' cycle of life, beginning with their anticipation of ascending to Jerusalem to commune with God and culminating in his blessing through the words of the high priest.[1] This was their life. Everything else was secondary.

## Anticipation of and Preparation for the Worship of God

When the worship of the LORD was right and good, the faithful earnestly desired to be there (Ps. 63:1). To join the procession to the sanctuary for the great celebrations was a delight eagerly anticipated. When people found themselves separated from the sanctuary, they fondly recalled how they used to go with the multitudes to the house of God with shouts of joy, and they longed to be able to do that again (Ps. 42:2). The more they reflected on all the blessings that were in store for them there, the more they desired to return and remain there for the rest of their days (Ps. 23:6).

This happy longing was present even when they were not prevented from going. When it was time to go to the festivals for worship, the people were filled with joy (Ps. 122:1). When their souls yearned for the living God, thoughts of his lovely dwelling place intensified their anticipation (Ps. 84:1–2). How lucky the sparrow that could live near the altar of the LORD! How blessed the Levites who remained in the courts to praise (vv. 3–4)! If only they could be doorkeepers for the sanctuary, the pilgrims thought, they would be more than satisfied in his presence (v. 10)!

As the people of God made their way to the city of God with their families and friends, they would sing the pilgrim psalms and the songs of Zion in praise of their God and as witness to their faith and hope.[2] These songs give us some wonderful glimpses of their thoughts and feelings as they went up to Jerusalem every year to worship the LORD: their apprehension at the thought of traveling through the dangerous hills (Ps. 121:1–2) and the welcome assurance of divine protection (vv. 3–8); their thrill at actually standing within the gates of Jerusalem (Ps. 122:2); the sense of security in the LORD, vividly illustrated by the hills surrounding Jerusalem (Ps. 125:1–2); the joy in the providence of God and his provision of children (Ps. 127:3–5); the comfort in knowing that in this holy

---

1. See Liebreich, "Songs of Ascent and the Priestly Blessing," 33–36.
2. The songs of Zion extol the qualities of the city of God. Psalm 46 says that the city where the Most High dwells remains secure, because God is there with his people. See Viviers, "The Coherence of the *ma'ălôt* Psalms (Pss. 120–134)," 275–89.

place one could find forgiveness from God (Ps. 130:4), hope in the LORD (Ps. 131), and unity among believers (Ps. 133); the expectation that righteous priests and a triumphant king would again be present, worshipping in God's presence (Ps. 132); and in it all the joy of lifting hearts and hands to heaven in praise of God. The celebration was even greater after seventy years in exile and the painful but successful labor of encouraging others to join them (Ps. 126).

They came in throngs to enter his gates with thanksgiving and his courts with praise (Ps. 100:4–5), because they believed that "he is good" and that his loyal love "endures forever" (Pss. 118:1–4; 136). They would approach the sanctuary as the righteous had done time after time, calling for the Levites to open the gates so that they could enter and give thanks to the LORD (Ps. 118:19, 21). But first they would be reminded by the gatekeepers' liturgy that only those who had clean hands and pure hearts could enjoy immediate communion with the holy God (Pss. 15; 24:4). So they needed to come with a sacrifice if they were to seek his face, that is, find favor from the LORD (Ps. 24:6), for no one could claim to be good enough to enter into the presence of the holy God. So with humility and gratitude their sacrifice would be bound to the horns of the altar (Ps. 118:27 MT). Then, and only then, would they be free to celebrate being at peace with the Holy One of Israel, the God of all creation.

## Celebration and Communion in the Presence of the Living God

Communion with God is a multifaceted gem. We can begin to understand this when we survey the many purposes the people had for coming to the sanctuary.

### To Give Thanks to the LORD

Perhaps the most common reason for the Israelites to enter the sanctuary was to give thanks to God. This was not an option; it was a binding statute for the tribes to go up to Jerusalem three times a year "to give thanks" to the name of the LORD (Ps. 122:4)

"To give thanks" may sound simple today, because we say "thanks" so easily, but it was not simple for the Israelite worshippers. It involved the full sacrificial ritual culminating in the peace offering, and that offering was explained to the assembled congregation through the public declaration of thanks to God (Ps. 22:22). The worshipper would deliver the praise while the sacrifice was on the altar so that the people would know why it was being offered. He might say,

> I will come to your temple with burnt offerings
>     and fulfill my vows to you—
> vows my lips promised and my mouth spoke
>     when I was in trouble.
> I will sacrifice fat animals to you
>     and an offering of rams;
>     I will offer bulls and goats.
> Come and listen, all you who fear God;
>     let me tell you what he has done for me.
>                                             (Ps. 66:13–16)

Then the thankful worshipper would tell his story; and the Levites were always to be prepared to "give thanks" in song when the person finished. Then the worshipper, family and friends, priests and singers, and any poor people present would eat the peace offering as a communal meal (Lev. 7:11–18; Ps. 22:26–29; cf. Exod. 24:11). But they would know why they were eating!

In biblical studies psalms of thanksgiving are called "declarative praise" psalms. The translation of the noun *(tôdāh)* and verb *(yādāh)* as "thanksgiving" and "give thanks" needs clarification.[3] The words indicate that this form of praise was a public acknowledgment, what we might call a testimony except for the fact that it required an elaborate ritual to go with it. It was an offering to God called "the sacrifice of thanksgiving," with the thanksgiving delivered to the congregation for edification and encouragement (Ps. 22:22–26); and the congregation was to respond to the invitation to praise (*hallelû-yāh* is an imperative—"praise the LORD") and share the worshipper's joy as well as the meal.

The greatest opportunity for worshippers to express their faith in the midst of the congregation was through this public praise. Although such

---

3. To be taken into consideration is the fact that this verb is also used for the confession of sin (e.g., Lev. 5:5; Ps. 32:5). The church uses the word *confess* in a similar way for both the confession of the faith and the confession of sin.

praise has been abandoned by most churches,[4] it was required by God. It was never a supplement to the ordinary worship; it was the life of that worship. And it was not replaced by the choirs or the singing; they complemented it and responded to it (Ps. 30:4).

It was up to the priests to teach the people how to do this so that the time was not wasted by self-promotion or unnecessary talk. And this was easy to do because the Psalms provided the pattern for people to express their own thanksgiving, and the structure of the *tôdāh* is not complicated. The opening declaration ("I will give thanks to the LORD") contains the reason for the praise ("because he is faithful"); then there is a report of the dilemma that was faced ("I was surrounded by enemies") and the deliverance ("he heard my prayer" and "he delivered me"); this is followed by the full declaration of praise ("God is faithful to those who love him"); and finally, the conclusion offers a word of encouragement to others ("Seek the LORD while he may be found"). It is not difficult to train folks to construct their own thanksgiving with such a pattern.[5]

The cycle of prayer and thanksgiving that emerges would follow this sequence: (1) During the time of need the believer prayed to the LORD and vowed to give thanks to him when the prayer was answered (e.g., Ps. 51:13–17).[6] (2) When it was time for this praise, a peace offering (as well as the sin and burnt offerings) had to be brought to be shared with the congregation—it cost people to praise. (3) The public thanksgiving was declared in the congregation while the peace offering was being roasted for the communal meal. In this way the vow was paid.[7] (4) All those present benefited from the thanksgiving by sharing this meal, but they first had to hear why they were going to eat together. This was not a common meal; it was a holy meal in a holy place. It is easy to see how individual praise was the heart and soul of communal worship.

Westermann explains why this biblical idea of praise is superior to the

---

4. No doubt individual praise was abandoned because it was abused and often time consuming. It was easier to replace it with a set time of singing than it was to teach people how to do it.

5. For a study of the type and its forms, see Westermann, *Praise of God in the Psalms*.

6. This was a spiritual vow and not crass bargaining; in confidence the individual rehearsed what praise would be given when the prayer was answered, and this gave God a reason to answer the prayer.

7. Many churches use "pay your vows to the LORD" when taking the offering, but the command meant to give a public thanksgiving along with the gift of gratitude.

modern practice of saying "thanks."[8] First, praise is offered in a public forum, whereas expressing "thanks" does not necessarily have or need this
forum. To the Israelites, it was a sin to fail to acknowledge God publicly,
for God had blessed them in order that they might do just that.

Second, praise elevates the object of the praise, but thanksgiving may
not. Genuine praise looks away from the self and focuses on the LORD—
he is to be exalted and his works are to be described and lauded ("He
lifted me up from the miry pit") so that people will be drawn to him. But
the person saying "thank you" is the subject of the sentence ("[I] thank
you, LORD"). The less focus there is on the speaker and the more there is
on the object of the praise, the greater the praise.

Third, true praise is never routine. Lewis observed that people naturally talk about things that they enjoy because that is part of the enjoyment. Therefore, when the teaching of the church reminds us that our
chief end is to glorify God and enjoy him forever, we understand that
these are one and the same.[9] If people glorify God, they are enjoying him;
and if they are not enjoying him, they will not glorify him—except when
compelled to do so in congregational singing.

Fourth, individual praise is edifying. It should encourage and instruct
other people in the light of what the one praising has learned through the
experience.

Fifth, praise is magnanimous. In offering the sacrifice of praise, the
Israelite would share the bounty of God with others, especially those yet to
be blessed, because the evidence of gratitude is generosity. After all, what
he received, what he was praising for, was a gift from God. Therefore, if
praise is being given properly, the needs of others will not be overlooked.
The same connection between praise and sharing is reiterated in Hebrews
13:15–16.

This kind of praising is almost nonexistent in today's churches. It has
been replaced by artificial times of "fellowship" and set times of "worship
music" (although some have tried to approach it with smaller groups).
A service with the routine singing of formal hymns and old favorites,
or a steady diet of repetitious, experiential songs, or the performance of

---

8. The point is not that the words "thank you" or "thanksgiving" should not be used,
   but rather that the praise expressed through their use should be on a par with biblical
   praise.

9. Lewis, *Reflections on the Psalms,* 97.

a good choir, no matter how meaningful these might be, falls short of God's design for believers to express their faith by offering individual praise to God in public so that a spiritual community might develop.

## To Pay Vows

People also went up to the sanctuary to make vows to the LORD (1 Sam. 1) or to pay their vows in the public forum (as in Deut. 26:1–15; Acts 21:20–26). Giving an individual acknowledgment, the sacrifice of praise, was one way to fulfill a vow, as we have seen. But there were other kinds of vows that were to be completed properly in the presence of the LORD with the same ritual of the peace offering for a communal meal (Lev. 7:16).

There is no formally worded statement to be used in the sanctuary when one fulfilled a vow, but it is hard to imagine such moments without something significant being said. Hannah gives us the type of declaration that would have been made (1 Sam. 1:11, 21–28). She had vowed to give the child Samuel to the LORD, so when she brought him to Eli, she said, "I prayed for this child, and the LORD has granted me what I asked of him. . . . For his whole life he will be given over to the LORD" (vv. 27–28). Likewise the fulfillment of the Nazirite vow would have included a declaration of some sort (Num. 6:13–21).

## To Offer Praise to God

A third reason people went up to the sanctuary was to praise God. This was not the individual thanksgiving *(tôdāh)* given for an answer to prayer but a hymn of praise *(hālal)* to God.[10] The hymn, whether said or sung, is a more general description of who God is and what he has done; hence, it is called the descriptive praise psalm. Even though it differed in form and content from the *todah*, the nature of biblical praise applies here as well.

The hymn begins with the worshipper calling others to join in praising God (this could be as brief as "praise the LORD" *[hallᵉlû-yāh]*); then it focuses on the reason for the praise, which is almost always some demonstration of the greatness and the grace of God; and it concludes with a prayer, a lesson, or a renewed call to praise. The devout Israelites never

---

10. The word *hālal* conveys a natural and enthusiastic response to something that is immediately worthy of praise (e.g., the princes of Pharaoh raving about the beauty of Sarai in Gen. 12:15). It may be related to a word for shining, suggesting a glowing report.

tired of singing hymns to God's majesty as Creator (Pss. 8; 33), Redeemer (Pss. 105–107; 111), Lawgiver (Ps. 19), Provider (Ps. 113), and the like; and they loved to extol his gracious dealings with them in faithfulness, righteousness, and unfailing love (Ps. 33). The value of hymns is that they preserve crucial doctrinal ideas of the faith in a way that nothing else in the life of the believing community could. The thanksgivings often included similar descriptions of God, but these hymns focus on those descriptions.

This kind of praise is also being lost in the modern worshipping communities because people do not know doctrine. Even in the music, doctrinally rich hymns are being replaced with shorter experiential songs and choruses.

## To Proclaim Their Faith

It was a natural development from such hymns that creeds developed. When people went up to the sanctuary to praise God, they were proclaiming what they believed about God, because hymns that are descriptive of the person and work of God provided people with the proper things to say. Psalm 111, for example, enumerates God's glorious and majestic works, his righteousness, his grace and compassion, his faithfulness to the covenant, his power, his trustworthiness, his uprightness, and his redemption—in summary, his holy and awesome name. Such lists of divine attributes recalled the proclamation of the attributes of the LORD to Moses on Mount Sinai in Exodus 34 and provided the people of God with a rich description of the God they worshipped.

If worship is ever going to recapture the vision of the holy God of glory, it must begin with the knowledge of the person and works of the Lord. The divine attributes found in so many creedal expressions open a way for the people of God to speak about God. The significant point about these early creedal statements is that God gave them to his people to be used as a means of preserving the historical faith and maintaining their allegiance to him.

## To Behold God's Power and Glory

A fifth and related reason that people went up to the sanctuary was to see God, that is, to behold his power and his glory. Yes, they went to give thanks, pay vows, sing hymns, and proclaim their faith, but all these would be hollow if God did not make his presence known to them. Thus, David writes, "O God, you are my God, earnestly I seek you; my soul thirsts for you, my body longs for you. . . . I have seen you in the sanctuary and beheld your power and your glory" (Ps. 63:1–2). And again he says, "One thing I ask of the LORD, this is what I seek: that I may dwell in the house of the LORD all the days of my life, to gaze upon the beauty of the LORD and to seek him in his temple" (Ps. 27:4). God desires to be seen, which is why he has revealed himself. But since God is a spirit, he must be seen spiritually.

All believers share this desire to see him in all his glory and beauty. And our Lord Jesus Christ himself desires that we see him, for he prayed, "Father, I want those you have given me to be with me where I am, and to see my glory" (John 17:24a). This prayer, and our desire, will be realized in heaven; but in the meantime, to "see the Lord" is to see the evidence of his presence.

When the faithful declared to the assembly what God had done in their lives through answers to prayer or supernatural intervention, the assembled worshippers witnessed his power and his glory at work; when the choirs praised God, rehearsing his marvelous works from creation through redemption, the worshippers realized the majesty of God; when the sacrifices were placed on the altar and the fire of the LORD consumed them, or when the high priest came out of the Holy of Holies and declared God's blessing on them, the worshippers who came seeking God, that is, seeking his face (Ps. 24:6), knew that he had revealed his gracious presence to them. As the worshippers saw him by faith, they knew that some day they would truly behold him (Pss. 17; 73). Even if their life was troubled, and in most cases because it was troubled, their faith would be emboldened to anticipate seeing this God: "I myself will see him with my own eyes—I, and not another. How my heart yearns within me!" (Job 19:27). Thus, on Mount Zion the ancient proverb would be realized again and again, that "on the mountain of the LORD it will be seen [NIV, provided]"[11] (Gen. 22:14). At the sanctuary worshippers would see again and again how the LORD provides, and in those provisions that they witnessed, or heard about in the praises, they beheld his glory and power in their midst.

---

11. The verb can also be rendered "it will be provided," meaning God would see to it, or provide; and so in that provision "he will be seen"—another possible translation of the words.

They also would recall God's powerful presence in the reenactments of their traditions. As they relived the Passover night, or as they dwelt in booths as their ancestors had, or as they retraced the movement of the ark up to Jerusalem, they sang the songs of Zion and the great historical psalms; and in those moments they saw how the God of glory revealed himself, and they were thereby inspired with the hope of greater glory in his presence (Pss. 17; 68; 113–118; 132). If they never saw evidence of God at work in their midst, there was not much reason to go to the assemblies. That is an observation we are forced to make today as well.

This kind of spiritual perception leads to meditation. Although people could meditate any time and any place (Pss. 42; 63:6), their meditation would be more focused in the sanctuary. The writer of Psalm 73 found comfort for his troubled, doubting thoughts when he entered the sanctuary, where he was able to think through his spiritual crisis about the injustices of life—the ungodly would be brought to nothing, but he and the saints would be received in glory (Ps. 73:15–28).

Several words are used for the spiritual discipline of meditation. One conveys the idea of speaking in a low, muted tone *(khāgāh)* as one might speak under one's breath while studying and learning the Word of the LORD (Ps. 1:2; Josh. 1:8). Another term is based on the verb "remember" *(zākar)*; it can mean "to remind, keep in memory," and thus "to ponder" (Ps. 20:7; NIV, "trust"). A third word for "meditate" is one that also means "lament" *(sîakh)* and so would reflect the thoughts of a troubled worshipper.

Meditation makes a powerful contribution to worship because it forms the Word in the heart of the worshipper. The process begins with acquiring a thorough knowledge of a portion of the Word, preferably memorizing it so that it can be recalled anywhere at anytime. But this demands disciplined study in order to understand the text for its application to life. Then, during the meditation this reflection on God's Word is intertwined with prayer. One talks to God about what God said, but one also speaks to oneself in meditation. Here it takes the form of a soliloquy, certainly self-exhortation—"Why are you downcast, O my soul?" (Pss. 42:5, 11; 43:5). The intent is to strengthen one's commitment to the faith. The worshipper contemplates how to plead the case of a biblical idea with his own soul. As Ignatius would say, meditation engages the will and pours out the affections, all for the purpose of maintaining a constant, lively apprehension of the presence of the Lord. Naturally, the circumstances need to be right for meditation. If they are not, if the setting is disturbing with noise and distracting with clutter, then spiritual reflection is almost impossible. In many churches it is difficult for worshippers to meditate before or after the service for these very reasons.

## To Pray to the LORD

Believers also went up to the sanctuary to talk to God. They could pray at any time and in any place, but they preferred to go to the sanctuary to pray, for in that holy place their prayers were both inspired and confirmed as they heard the prayers and thanksgivings of others in God's presence. There they would find other people to pray with them and encourage them in their faith; and when all the people assembled in the great assemblies, the prayers of the people would be strengthened by their unity. This is how it was supposed to be. After all, the temple was to be a house of prayer. When Solomon dedicated the place, he stood before the altar and spread his hands to heaven, calling on God to hear the prayers that were to be made in this place (1 Kings 8:22–61; cf. Matt. 21:13).[12]

Praying is essentially asking God for something. Prayer forms the essence of a personal devotional life that ultimately leads to praise, and it is the substance of sanctuary worship itself in which the people of God gather to seek his favor (Pss. 24:6; 31:16). In this sense, sacrifice was itself a form of prayer; in fact the sacrifices were often accompanied by prayer, whether a supplication, confession, or intercession. And some of these prayers were recorded and set in forms that could be adapted to singing or appropriated by others in the congregational praying.[13] Thus, the book of Psalms was also the temple prayer book.

*Supplication* is the basic form of prayer, a simple request for a need to be met. There are a number of words used with this sense. One is a legal term that means "to seek arbitration for oneself" or "pray" *(hitpallēl,* s.v. *pālal);* its noun "prayer" is *t<sup>e</sup>phillāh.* Another has the idea of "seeking favor for oneself" *(hitkhannēn);*[14] it is related to the word "grace" *(khēn)* and the verb "to be gracious" *(khānan).* Accordingly, this word for supplication signifies that what is requested is undeserved. The noun

---

12. See Knoll, "Between Voice and Silence," 17–30.
13. Merton, *Praying the Psalms;* and Saliers, "The Integrity of Sung Prayers," 290–303.
14. Ap-Thomas, "Some Aspects of the Root *HNN* in the Old Testament," 128–48.

"supplication" is *t<sup>e</sup>khinnāh*, "a petition for divine favor or grace." A third term for prayer means "to entreat the favor" of God *(khālāh)*; it has the sense of "mollify, appease, smooth down" (like a child's stroking a parent's face [Zech. 8:21–22]) in order to gain favor. And in addition to these specific terms, we also find "to lament" *(sîakh)*, "to entreat" *('ātar)*, "to ask" *(shā'al)*, "to call out, cry out" *(qārā', tsā'aq, zā'aq)*, and "to cry out of distress" *(tsiwwā')*. These words, and a few others, show how important prayer was to the believers, how dependent they were on God for help. Accordingly, true worshippers are people who pray.

Because of all this, several basic observations are in order. First, those who prayed to the LORD (actually prayed, as opposed to saying prayers) were "the righteous," the members of the covenant who had come to trust God for all their needs. As such their spiritual posture was that of a servant—the LORD is the Master.

Where did they pray? In the Old Testament, prayers could be offered to God anywhere and at anytime. For example, Psalm 3 was an urgent prayer by David in flight from his enemies and away from the sanctuary. However, if it was at all possible, Israelites would go to the sanctuary to pray (Pss. 5:7; 28:2; 63:1–2; 84:1–2, 10–11; 138:2; Isa. 37). Even in the Gospels we read of people going up to the temple to pray. The point was not that prayer had to be made in the temple, but rather that the temple was more conducive to prayer in that it was the holy place where so many prayers were made and so many people were praying.

How did they pray? There is a wide variety of postures for prayer exhibited in the Old Testament. The passages are descriptive and thereby exemplary, but they do not prescribe specific ways to do it. The gestures and postures that were most appropriate to the culture and the occasion were followed. At times people prayed standing up *('āmad, "to stand,"* in 1 Sam. 1:26; 1 Kings 8:22; Jer. 18:20); this custom was used in New Testament times as well, because people stood on the steps of the temple to pray. But the verb "stand" may have a different meaning in some places; for example, Solomon went up to the platform and stopped *('āmad,* stood still) "and then knelt down" (2 Chron. 6:13). He then remained kneeling on the platform and looked to heaven with outstretched arms.

In the days of Nehemiah, the people knelt down to confess sin (Neh. 9:3); the verb used is the one often translated "to worship" *(hishtakhăwāh),* which literally means "to bow oneself low to the ground." Such a posture in prayer was to exhibit humility and submission before God (Ps. 95:6), and so people often prayed on their knees (1 Kings 8:54; Isa. 45:23; Dan. 6:10), either with their hands raised or more often palms spread out on the ground (Ps. 28:2; Lam. 2:19). At times they prostrated themselves on the ground (Pss. 5:7; 99:5, 9). The physical posture of falling to the knees, putting the face to the ground, and spreading the palms out on the ground would indicate the earnestness of the prayer. None of this was to be done for show, although it often was; but nothing would ruin the spirit of the moment more than being self-consciously posturing oneself for the greatest effect.[15]

When the Israelites came to pray in the temple, they had to bring sacrifices to gain access. Psalm 20:3 records the congregation's intercession for David with the words, "May he remember all your sacrifices [dedication offerings] and accept [make fat] your burnt offerings." Joining worship with praying was natural, for by the ritual of the burnt offering the worshipper was seeking access to God, and by the dedicatory offering he was trying to please God with his commitment.

For what did they pray? A study of the prayers in the canon shows that they were offered for just about every situation and every need common to human experience.[16] But in making their petitions known to God, they were conscious that informed and spiritual people pray for the will of the LORD to be done—their own will being made to harmonize with the divine will as far as they understood it. They were not trying to talk God into doing something that was contrary to his nature or his plan. They could ask for almost anything as long as it was in accordance with what they knew God to be willing to do, either from past experience or divine revelation. So ultimately prayer is the expression of the believer's submission to the will of God in times of need.

To what purpose did they pray? We may observe from the biblical teachings on prayer that those who pray share in the outworking of God's will through faith, that they prompt greater faith in God among other believers, that the one praying receives divine approval for the obedience (prayer is never just an option), and that the one praying will have occasion to praise God for working through the lives of the faithful.

---

15. Ap-Thomas, "Some Notes on Old Testament Attitude Toward Prayer," 75–90.
16. See B. Anderson, *Out of the Depths.*

Thus, a major part of the temple worship was given over to prayer—it was a house of prayer, after all. While the aroma of the sacrifices ascended to God as a pleasing aroma, and while the incense burned and added to the fragrances before God, the worshippers and the priest on their behalf would make supplication to the LORD. If it was a shared need, then the congregation would join in a communal lament.

One very specific form of supplication is the *confession* of sin with its consequent prayer for forgiveness.[17] The main term used in Leviticus for confession has more of the idea of "acknowledge."[18] When worshippers brought their sin offerings to the sanctuary, they confessed their sin before the LORD (Lev. 5:5). Confession probably was made when the guilt was first uncovered (2 Sam. 12:13), but it still would have to be acknowledged in the assembly so that the sacrifice would be identified with the sin and atonement completed. A confession may not seem like a prayer for forgiveness, but a simple acknowledgment of sin to the LORD was sufficient to find forgiveness (Ps. 32:5; Isa. 6:5–7). Nevertheless, the existence of penitential psalms like Psalms 6, 51, and 130 indicates that more detailed prayers for forgiveness grew out of the simple acknowledgment. Nehemiah 9 records a confessional service that indicates how such a service was conducted. It must be noted, however, that this service was not for an ordinary sin but for the sin of the nation that had caused the Exile. But the pattern of the service would work on any level. It began with the reading of the Book of the Law, for which the people stood ("rose up" [*qûm*]); then came the confession of sins, during which the people knelt or bowed down to the ground *(hishtakhăwāh);* and then the singing of a psalm in response to the Levites' instruction, with the people standing again (Neh. 9:3–5; cf. 1 Kings 8:54–55). It is interesting to note that the reading took a fourth of the day and the confession and praise another fourth.

To be sure, the prayer of confession is a private matter between the worshipper and God; but in Israel there was definitely something public about it because of the ritual. When the priest began the service with a sin

---

17. R. J. Thompson, *Penitence and Sacrifice in Early Israel.*
18. There is a connection between confessing sin and praising the LORD ("confess" is *hitwaddāh,* s.v. *yādāh,* and so cognate to *tôdāh,* "thanksgiving" or "acknowledgment"). One cannot confess sin without acknowledging the provision of the LORD; and one cannot praise the LORD without acknowledging sin. The translation "acknowledge" fits both categories, as does "confess."

offering for himself, the congregation knew that he was making confession—they did not need to know what was being confessed, only that he too was confessing. This act by the leader would have strengthened the sense of unity in the congregation, because they knew they all shared the same need as sinners.

The confession was made to God, but God usually communicated forgiveness by the words and actions of the priest (or a prophet as in 2 Sam. 12:13) and then dramatically by the fire consuming the sacrifice.

Supplication offered on behalf of others is *intercession*. The greatest acts of intercessory prayer, those by Abraham (Gen. 18; 20) and Moses (Exod. 32; and then countless times in the wilderness), left their mark on the nation. Naturally, priests were to be about this duty regularly as they made the morning and evening prayers; but individual worshippers also were responsible to uphold one another in prayer, whether they knew the exact nature of the need or not.

Intercessory prayer is not a matter of saying a short prayer or merely mentioning someone's name at prayers. Effective intercession requires the interposing of oneself between God and those for whom the prayers are made. Moses' act of intercessory prayer shows what the cost of it could be. His powerful intercession involved his willingness to take the place of those in trouble and in that way made the appeal more urgent and compelling—he understood what was at stake. And he remained in his intercession for forty days! When intercessory prayer reaches this intensity, the one praying actually becomes absorbed in the lives of those for whom the prayer is given.[19] The plight of the needy cannot be forgotten as soon as the prayer ends with "amen."

## To Renew the Covenant

Seventh, the people went up to the sanctuary to renew the covenant with God. Through all the worship in the LORD's presence, the people would already have renewed their spiritual relationship with him. But more was required—to renew their commitment to God. Other parts of their worship addressed this issue when they went to hear from God and to respond to God.

---

19. Jesus is the best example of this dimension of intercession. Isaiah 53 says that by his vicarious sufferings he made intercession for sinners. He did more than pray for us—he took our place.

*Divine Instruction*

How do worshippers hear from God? The normal way is through his Word. Therefore, the public reading of Scripture formed an integral part of worship (see Exod. 24; Neh. 9). In Nehemiah 8 we learn how Ezra the scribe read the Book of the Law before the people at an appointed gathering. When he opened it up, the people stood up (v. 5). "Ezra praised the LORD, the great God; and all the people lifted their hands and responded, 'Amen! Amen!' Then they bowed down and worshipped the LORD with their faces to the ground" (v. 6). Several Levites then caused the people to understand the law while they stood in their place. "They read from the Book in the Law of God, making it clear and giving the meaning so that the people could understand what was being read" (v. 8). This public reading had become a fixed part of Israel's convocations; when the congregation gathered to worship God, they expected to hear from God, and hearing from God's Word would have been the basis of their communion with God and commitment to him (cf. Josh. 8:30–35, esp. vv. 34–35).[20]

In conjunction with the reading of the Word, worshippers expected to hear God's instruction through others in the sanctuary. This would normally be expected from the priests, who as the LORD's shepherds were to feed (i.e., teach) the flock and lead them into righteousness (Ezek. 34:1–2; and see the divine pattern for shepherds in Ps. 23:1–3). But there may have been a special message from one of the staff, such as Asaph (Ps. 50) or another worshipper who would speak out of his own experience (Ps. 32:8–10).[21] And on occasion the people would hear a powerful word of instruction and exhortation from a prophet.[22]

Since the primary duty of the priests was to teach God's commandments, God held them accountable for that. God said,

> My covenant was with him,[23] a covenant of life and peace, and
> I gave them to him; this called for reverence and he revered me
> and stood in awe of my name. True instruction was in his mouth

---

20. From the setting of prophetic oracles as well as the later structure of synagogue services, there is evidence to show that the law was read at communal worship.
21. Psalm 95 offers such instruction: "Today if you hear his voice. . . ." See Renz, "Come, Let Us Listen to the Voice of the Lord," 140–53.
22. For example, see von Rad, "The Levitical Sermon in 1 and 2 Chronicles."
23. The reference is to Levi, meaning the tribe from Levi when it became a priestly tribe.

and nothing false was found on his lips. He walked with me in peace and uprightness, and turned many away from sin.

For the lips of a priests ought to [must] preserve knowledge, and from his mouth men should seek instruction—because he is the messenger of the LORD Almighty [LORD of hosts]." (Mal. 2:5–7)

The priests, then, had the charge of living and teaching the law—the Word of God—so that worshippers could expect to hear from God through them. But when this part of the worship broke down, the people fell into all kinds of disobedience, which ultimately destroyed their worship.

At times God spoke in unexpected and sometimes spectacular ways. The "divine oracle" could be symbolic or verbal; and it could come through the priest or the prophet or directly from the LORD himself.

A few times God revealed himself through an appearance at the altar with verbal communication. Isaiah 6 is the most notable example (but this was to a prophet, not the worshipping community). Gideon likewise received a revelation from the Angel of the LORD (Judg. 6:11–24), and in the New Testament Luke describes a revelation through an angel at the altar to the father of John the Baptist (Luke 1:11). Judging from the responses of the people involved, all of these were extraordinary communications, and so we may conclude this was not the normal way that God communicated with his people during worship.

Similarly, prophets, priests, or Levites occasionally spoke for God in declaring an oracle of salvation, that is, the Word of the LORD, to the person or persons praying. For example, in 2 Samuel 12:13 Nathan declared the oracle of forgiveness to David, and in 2 Chronicles 20:14–17 the Spirit came upon a Levite to declare that the king's prayer was answered. These too would not be the normal expectation of worshippers going up to the temple, although everyone might have hoped for such a dramatic revelation.

Another way that God spoke to the worshipping community was through a prophet's message. Prophets were powerful because they spoke for God. And because their messages were perceived to be direct communication from God, many of them were preserved in the collections of the holy books. Consequently, God still instructs believers through the words of the prophets.

Worshippers themselves had the responsibility to exhort one another in their assemblies; and if this was done properly by God's guidance, then it too became a way for God to speak to the congregation. The best evidence for this comes from the didactic portions of the Psalms (and later the Pauline teaching on the spiritual gifts). Psalm 32 celebrates forgiveness from God but adds instruction for the non-repentant person not to be stubborn like the mule (vv. 8–9). Psalm 34 has a heavy didactic content growing out of the psalmist's experiences. And Psalm 22:26c exhorts people not to give up but to continue to pray.[24]

### Faithful Commitments

When God speaks, he demands a response. The kind of response he wants was exemplified by the Exodus community, who made a commitment to obey the Word of the LORD (Exod. 24:3, 7). Such commitments are necessary in worship; they express compliance with specific teachings from God. Other responses like "Amen," or some creedal statement, or shout of acclamation, declare agreement with and loyalty to the covenant God in general.

But there are more formal attestations of devotion prescribed in the Bible. David's reads: "Here I am, I have come—it is written about me [prescribed for me] in the scroll. To do your will, O my God, is my desire; your law is within my heart" (Ps. 40:7–8). He recognized that worship ritual without commitment was worthless and that dedication without direction was delusion. With such a declaration, the devout acknowledged dedication to God and his direction in the Word of God and a desire to please God. Now their sacrifices would mean something.[25]

As time passed the words of Deuteronomy 6:4 became a fixed statement of commitment as well as faith—"Hear O Israel: Yahweh is our God, Yahweh alone." Then the worshippers were instructed to love the

---

24. "May your hearts live forever" in this psalm means "don't give up; keep on praying," because earlier in the psalm the psalmist said his heart had melted, meaning he had almost given up.

25. In the New Testament these words have their fullest meaning. God had prepared a body for His Son, and the Scriptures had prophesied about the Son, and the Son came to do the will of God (Heb. 10:7). It was the greatest commitment ever made.

LORD wholeheartedly.[26] Love for the LORD was clearly the primary motivation for the faith and obedience of Israel; the true worshipper loved the LORD. Without the commitment to obey, any celebration of praise meant nothing; with it, the worshippers committed themselves to living out their faith in society, championing righteousness and justice, and meeting the needs of the widow, the orphan, the needy, and the stranger (see Isa. 1:16–20).

In this statement from Deuteronomy, as well as in others, it is almost impossible to distinguish the creedal formula from the commitment vow. Even in the rustic setting of Elijah's altar, when the people cried, "Yahweh—He is the [true] God; Yahweh—He is the [true] God!" they were reconfirming their faith (after having wavered between two opinions) and renewing their commitment to do his will (1 Kings 18:39). When Josiah renewed the covenant in 2 Kings 23:1–3, all the people "pledged themselves to the covenant." This implies a verbal commitment, at least, to join the king in rooting out idolatry and leading the nation back to righteousness.

## To Receive the LORD's Blessing

Eighth, the people went up to the sanctuary to receive the LORD's blessing.[27] Throughout the worship activities, the people would know that the living God was with them and speaking to them, both directly and indirectly. But the communication from God that they waited for, the word that completed the ritual and comforted their souls, was the final blessing. According to Numbers 6:22–27, the LORD declared that he would bless the people through the words of the high priest:

> Yahweh bless you
>    and keep you;
> Yahweh make his face shine upon you,
>    and be gracious to you;

---

26. The text is "*Shᵉmaᶜ Yiśrāʾēl, YHWH ʾĕlōhēnû, YHWH ʾekhād.*" The line may be rendered: "Hear, O Israel! Yahweh [is] our God, Yahweh [is] one"; or "Hear, O Israel! Yahweh [is] our God, Yahweh alone." The traditional English rendering using LORD is a little confusing, saying "The LORD our God is one LORD." In the original the name is used and not this title.

27. Liebreich, "Songs of Ascent and the Priestly Blessing," 33–36.

Yahweh turn [lift up] his face toward you,
    and give you peace.[28]

(Num. 6:24–26)

With these words the priest declared that God's grace and peace were bestowed on the worshippers.[29] It is called a blessing because God said that when this oracle was pronounced, he would put his blessing on the people. A blessing *(bᵉrākāh)* is a declaration of an enrichment of some kind, whether spiritual, physical, or material—it is a gift from God but a gift that often includes empowerment.[30] Here the high priestly blessing announced protection, grace, and peace. That the granting of grace and peace are central can be seen from the fact that they each receive a line and are expressed with the addition of an anthropomorphic image, the shining face of God signifying grace and the uplifted face signifying peace.[31]

This declaration was to be made by the priest on various occasions but primarily after he came out of the Most Holy Place, where he made atonement for the people. Thus, on the basis of the atoning sacrifice, the blessing of God granted the people grace and peace. This was no mere greeting or wish; it was not a prayer.[32] The high priest was instructed by God to use this blessing when he saw the faith and the ritual combined in the proper way, and he had the word from the LORD promising that

---

28. I have used the holy name "Yahweh" here instead of the traditional substitution of "the LORD" because that is what the text actually has, of course, but also because in the Mishnah the standard Jewish teaching says that on the Day of Atonement when the high priest said this, he actually said the holy name—God commanded him to say these words (see tractate Yoma).

29. For a detailed study, see P. Miller, "The Blessing of God," 240–51.

30. For example, when God blessed Adam and Eve, saying, "Be fruitful and multiply," he provided the enablement to do so. And the blessing of the patriarchs was not just a statement of hope—it was an incontrovertible oracle from God. It was a communication from heaven, a visible sign of God's favor. See C. W. Mitchell, *The Meaning of BRK;* and Westermann, *Blessing in the Bible and in the Life of the Church.*

31. Later, Paul would use these two motifs for his salutations in his epistles, because on the basis of our High Priest's atonement, God has given us grace and peace. See Lieu, "Grace to You and Peace," 161–78.

32. In some English translations it sounds like a prayer or a wish. The type of verb used (jussive) can in certain contexts be prayers and wishes (Ruth 4:11), but in others it has the force of a decree (Gen. 1:3). If the words of the blessing are from God, directly or indirectly, they are efficacious.

they would be blessed—for sure! The worshippers would go away knowing they had received grace and were at peace with God. The words were efficacious only because they were God's words being communicated to the worshippers under the proper circumstances. The priest himself did not have the power to bless otherwise.

So when the high priest pronounced the blessing as a part of the ritual, he was declaring the Word of God to the people. In Leviticus 9 Aaron lifted his hands toward the people and blessed them after the sacrifices had been made (v. 22) and then again after he and Moses came out of the tent (v. 23). Then the glory of the LORD appeared to the people (v. 23). Through the sacrifices and the intercession of the high priest, the people would realize God's grace and peace. Worshippers desperately needed to hear these promises from God when they came to worship. Likewise today, when people leave the sanctuary after a time of worship, they need to leave with an overwhelming sense that they are at peace with God, because they have seen God, heard from God, renewed their spiritual relationship with God, and eaten with God at his holy table.

# Conclusion *for* Part 5

THE WORSHIP OF GOD WAS intended to be a joyful celebration of communion with the sovereign and holy Lord God, the Creator and Redeemer. When the Israelites ascended the holy hill of Zion for any reason, they were acknowledging that they owed the LORD their thanksgiving and praise; and when they assembled for their great convocations, they were acknowledging that all time and every season belonged to him. Whenever they entered that sanctuary, they hoped to see his power and his glory; but they expected to hear from his Word that was read or used in the instructions and exhortations, to commune with him through the atoning ritual and the shared meal, and to be blessed by him. All their worship was greatly enhanced by the majesty and beauty of the temple, the powerful ritual, and the glorious music and singing that filled its courts daily.

At the heart of their worship, though, was the cycle of prayer and praise, reflected so regularly in the book of Psalms. From it we may learn a good deal that is important for worship.

# PART 6

# WORSHIP REFORMED

*Prophetic Rebukes and Reforms*

# Introduction

ONE WOULD EXPECT THAT ONCE the temple was built and the rich slate of worship activities were underway, the people of God would have been so moved by their glorious celebrations in the presence of the living God that they would have treasured it all forever, at least for a few generations. But they did not, as hard as that may be to understand. Whatever the reasons, pure worship soon deteriorated into a lifeless participation in ritual and a growing interest in the baser practices of pagan idolatry. This should not come as a complete surprise. From the very beginning the human race was not satisfied with the good things given to them by the Creator but soon followed the prompting of the Evil One, that old Serpent, to oppose the divine will and turn their devotion to the creature.

Such rebellion even surfaced in Israel at its very beginning. At Sinai while the LORD was revealing his law on the mountain, the people down below were fashioning an idol.[1] They survived that, but after they settled in the land they constantly embraced false religions, and God had to raise up leaders who would renew loyalty to the covenant (Judg. 2:10–23).[2] The debased worship of the pagans had not been eradicated, and so paganism became a viable option to many Israelites for satisfying their religious needs (Isa. 57:3–10). The door opened wide when the worship of pagan gods was sanctioned by the monarchy, beginning with Solomon's building pagan temples in Jerusalem and coming to full expression with succeeding kings making the worship of false gods the state religion. The honor and glory that rightfully belonged to the LORD, the only true God,

---

1. See Zipor, "The Deuteronomic Account of the Golden Calf," 20–33.
2. The need to defend the covenant was dramatically anticipated in Abram's driving away the birds of prey from the sacrificial animals. For another application, see further Knowles, "Abram and the Birds in Jubilee 11," 141–51.

had been handed over to grotesque and perverse deities, who were but outward embodiments of all that is base and low in this fallen creation.[3]

Because of these corrupt practices, prophets came on the scene with greater frequency to call the people back to God, warning them that if they persisted in their rebellion they would be expelled from the land. To the prophets it did not matter that such a glorious temple had been built. If the LORD was going to be robbed of his honor and glory, it would not be allowed to happen in the house of the LORD. If the worship remained corrupt, the building was useless and would be destroyed. And if corrupt worship still persisted, God would turn to the nations to raise up a people who would worship him in spirit and in truth (Hos. 1:10; 2:23; Mal. 1:11–14; John 4:21–24).

The proper setting and forms of worship, no matter how grand they may appear or how precisely they may be followed, cannot guarantee true worship. That depends on the spirituality of the worshippers. So God laid out the spiritual qualifications for worship—and they remain valid for our worship today. We too may have grand buildings with all kinds of services filled with lively music and enthusiastic expressions about the faith with a full array of ritual acts, but without true spirituality inspired by the realization that we are entering into the presence of the holy God in a special way, these trappings will be worthless and may even divert our attention from true worship. Concerning worthless and hypocritical practices, Tozer says, "My first [reaction] is that I believe the very last thing God desires is to have shallow-minded and worldly Christians bragging about Him."[4] He then adds, "But God in His revelation has told us that He is spirit and those who worship Him must worship Him in spirit and in truth. God takes the matter of worship out of the hands of men and puts it in the hands of the Holy Spirit."[5]

But even before the nature of true worship was so clearly prescribed by Jesus (John 4:24), the Old Testament had in various ways recorded God's spiritual requirements for worshippers. When these qualifications were ignored, worship became corrupt very quickly; and when worship became corrupt, the prophets were there to rebuke the people and to

---

3. See Buck, "Worship, Idolatry, and God," 68–82.
4. Tozer, *Whatever Happened to Worship?* 23.
5. Ibid., 44.

call for the renewal of the spiritual life and the reformation of worship.[6] These powerful people had nothing to fear because they spoke for God. Although they were at times persecuted and killed for their efforts, God held the people accountable for their words. And because the prophets spoke for God, their rebukes of worship clearly expressed the divine condemnation of it, and their calls for reform clearly expressed what God wanted the people to do.

6. See R. R. Wilson, "Early Israelite Prophecy," 3–16; and Rabe, "The Origins of Prophecy," 125–28.

# CHAPTER 18

# Qualifications *for* Worshippers

WHEN GOD REVEALED HIS PLAN for Israel to become a kingdom of priests and a holy nation (Exod. 19:3–6), he was informing them that they were not simply another nation with their own God and their own worship but that they were given the responsibility of serving God in his sanctuary and proclaiming the faith to the world.[1] In God's sanctuary there was to be no audience—there were to be no spectators—not then, not now. The worshipping community has always been a priestly community, for which God laid down very clear spiritual qualifications.[2] And although these were most directly applicable to worship in the sanctuary, they applied fully to all worshipful acts in private as well, for coming into God's presence spiritually in private was the initial step to coming into God's presence in his sanctuary. How spiritual the people were over the years is impossible to say. No doubt, down through the centuries there have been scores of people who participated in worship but who had no right to be there. Nevertheless, God's Word reveals what was expected of those who gathered to worship, that is, to celebrate being in fellowship with him.

## True Worshippers Are Faithful Believers

### They Are to Profess Their Faith

The worshipper was expected to be a believer, a member of the covenant community, one of "the faithful people of God." This assumption forms the basis of all the instructions for worship.[3]

---

1. See Senn, *The Witness of the Worshiping Community*. Worshippers exist for the world, which is a way of stressing that worship is proclamation.
2. See Harper, "Old Testament Spirituality," 63–77.
3. This is so self-evident that it is often overlooked. But it is important to state it because there is a good deal of confusion over the matter. Many people assume that in the Old

In time, short statements of faith and commitment were developed for use, the most basic one being Deuteronomy 6:4. But we also find other professions of faith embedded in the hymns and prayers. For example, believers confessed that God was their God (Pss. 22:1, 10; 63:1) and that they were his people, the sheep of his pasture (Ps. 95:6–7); they declared that by his grace they were able to take refuge in him and that he had provided them access to his courts (Ps. 36:5–9); they affirmed that they were the "righteous" who could enter the sanctuary and worship him (Ps. 118:20); and they acknowledged that their first loyalty was to God and his righteous people (Pss. 26:1–8; 27:4; 42:4). These, and many other passages, make it clear that devout worshippers were true believers in the LORD who rightly participated in the celebration of being the people of God. They were worshippers because they were believers, and their living faith opened to them a spiritual illumination for all the things of God.[4]

Because the people of God professed faith in the LORD, they lived on a higher level than unbelievers. When people came to faith in the LORD, they, like Abraham, were credited with righteousness (Gen. 15:6; Rom. 4:3–5). Accordingly, the Bible describes them as "the righteous," meaning that they were believers who sought to live according to God's standard of righteousness.[5] As Israelite understanding grew over the years with additional revelation, believers found different ways to express their faith. For example, they affirmed that Yahweh was the one true living God of the universe (Ps. 95:3–7), the almighty Creator and Sustainer of the universe (Pss. 33:6–11; 96:4–13), the Lawgiver (Ps. 19:7–14), and the righteous Judge of the whole world (Ps. 9:7–8). Accordingly, they knew that he was the Holy One, whose presence required sanctification through the forgiveness of sins, which his grace freely provided to all who believed (Ps. 130:3–4). So they would confess their sins to him as they prepared to enter his courts with their sacrifices and offerings (Pss. 6; 32; 51), trusting that he would forgive them, receive them with favor, and continue to bless them (Deut. 26:1–15; Ps. 30:4–12). And they committed their lives

---

Testament all the Israelites were believers because they are called the people of God (his chosen nation). But the Bible is clear that the true believers were a remnant of the population. See on this theme Allmen, *Worship: Its Theology and Practice,* 184–212.

4. See Erickson, *Participating in Worship,* 5.

5. In contrast the Bible refers to unbelievers and unfaithful people as "the wicked," or as the AV had it, "the ungodly." These were people who did not believe in the Lord and so remained guilty before him, even though they might have appeared decent and good.

to praising and serving him (Pss. 27:4; 63:1–5). This is not to say that they did not doubt or falter (Ps. 73:2–14), but when they did they knew they would regain their proper perspective when they focused on glory in the sanctuary (Ps. 73:16–28).

The New Testament carries these characteristics of faithful worshippers forward but adds God's full revelation in Christ to the content of the faith (Heb. 1:1–2).[6] A true Christian worshipper is one who has come to faith in Christ and has received the righteousness of God (Rom. 3:22–26; 10:9–10; Eph. 2:8–9). We may not know exactly when it happened or how it happened, but there was a time when we ceased to be alienated from God and were born into the family of God. Although the "righteous" may spend the rest of their lives growing in the faith, and even struggling with the faith, the truth remains that when they came to faith in Christ they became members of the new covenant, embarking on a new course of worship and service as the people of God. Paul is very clear in Romans that there is a righteousness that comes from God, and those who believe in Jesus Christ as Lord have received this righteousness, but those who do not believe do not have it (Rom. 3:20–26). And since without faith it is impossible to please God (Heb. 11:6), those who do not have faith in Jesus Christ cannot legitimately participate in the worship of the church.[7]

## They Are to Proclaim Their Faith

Faithful believers have always proclaimed their faith through their worship and service. In the Old Testament they proclaimed their faith to a listening world, not only by their distinctive worship at the altar, but also by their ritual observance of the stipulations of the covenant, beginning with the signs of the covenant. The sign of the Abrahamic covenant was circumcision, a special act of initiation into the covenant family (Gen. 17:9–14, 27).[8] The ritual was a sign that they shared the faith of Abraham.

---

6. Believers will accept further revelation from the LORD. Jesus himself said that if the people had believed in God, they would have believed in him also (see John 8:42–47; 14:1).

7. Churches are happy for everyone to attend a service to hear the Word of God read and proclaimed; but only those who are "in Christ" by faith are welcome to participate in Holy Communion. Unbelievers are not in communion with God; they have nothing to celebrate and so must refrain from full worship.

8. The ritual act of circumcision would be a public witness by the faithful family; the practical effect of circumcision would be a private reminder that in their marriage relationships they were to produce a godly seed.

This was not a trivial matter either, for failure to comply brought judgment from God (17:14), as even Moses, the head of the covenant people, discovered (Exod. 4:24–26). While it was primarily a witness of the parents that they were committed to love and serve the Lord with their whole heart (Deut. 30:6),[9] through the proper teaching of their children the faith would be carried forward from generation to generation.

The sign of the covenant made at Sinai was the observance of the Sabbath day, and this was to be a regular demonstration of their commitment to the faith. If the people remained loyal to the covenant, that is, if they kept the law, they would be blessed by God and be the blessing God wanted them to be (Gen. 12:1–3). Keeping the Sabbath was not to be a mechanical observance of a holy day, a day "off" from work. Observing the Sabbath days was a reminder to keep the whole covenant with the LORD, their Creator, so that they might enter into his rest.

Unfortunately, keeping covenant signs like circumcision and Sabbath observance is no guarantee that there is genuine faith or that the worship accompanying these signs was genuine. Paul explains that simply being circumcised was never sufficient; circumcision was to be a sign that the person was set apart to God, a sign of sanctification (Rom. 2:28–29; cf. Deut. 30:6 for the same point made by Moses). Faith had to come alongside the ritual to confirm it. The church has the same problem with its signs of baptism and Holy Communion,[10] which for many nominal Christians is all there is to "church." They assume that because they were baptized, perhaps as children, they are Christians, assured a place in heaven and welcomed to the Lord's Table. Paul's point applies to the new covenant as well as the old. Unless there is faith, the signs and the rites mean nothing; but when there is faith, keeping the signs in the setting of worship witnesses to the fact that the participant is a faithful believer.

---

9. The Law taught that circumcision signified the circumcision of the heart, that is, setting the will of the believer apart from the world. It later was clear that many who had been circumcised outwardly had not been circumcised in their hearts—that is, they were not set apart to God by faith.

10. The signs of the old covenants find their fulfillment in the new covenant, that is, they have to be explained in the light of Christ's fulfillment of the Law and the Prophets. True circumcision is of the heart, meaning that the old way of the world is put away and a new life of holiness is begun. Christians have entered into this new life by faith and have been sanctified by the blood of Christ (Rom. 3:21–31). And, having received Christ, they also have entered into the true and eternal Sabbath rest (Heb. 4:3).

For the new covenant believer, the first sign is baptism, done once, indicating identification with Christ and therefore initiation into the body of Christ.[11] The second is Holy Communion, or the cup, observed regularly by the worshipping community to make proclamation of the Lord's death until he comes (Luke 22:20; 1 Cor. 11:26). These signs witness to the faith of the worshippers. They are not merely special additions to worship services; they are an integral part of the worship. This means that they should be given much more attention so that the meaning is not lost in the rite.

## They Are to Demonstrate Their Faith by Their Works

The signs of the covenant reminded the faithful of their covenant obligation—obedience to the Word of God. It was obedience that kept their worship from being hypocritical and therefore meaningless.

Those who were truly committed to the faith desired to live obediently day in and day out (Ps. 1:1–3). Their commitment was a natural response to God's revelation of redemption: "I am the LORD your God, who brought you out of Egypt, out of the land of slavery. You shall have no other gods before me" (Exod. 20:2–3). Because he was their God, they owed him their wholehearted allegiance: "Love the LORD your God with all your heart and with all your soul and with all your strength" (Deut. 6:5).[12] Their love for God prompted their obedience to his commandments, which they were to learn (v. 6), teach to their children, talk about daily, write on their door frames, and bind on their hands and their foreheads (vv. 7–9), so that they would remember to fear God and serve him only (vv. 13–14). In short, the demonstration of their faith was to be a life of obedience to God—they were to live by every word that proceeded from him (8:3).

Acts of worship without the obedience of faith were not pleasing to God. Early in Israel's history, Samuel declared: "Does the LORD delight in burnt offerings and sacrifices as much as in obeying the voice of the LORD? To obey is better than sacrifice, and to heed is better than the fat

---

11. Some Christian traditions insist that baptism is an act of obedience and therefore to be done by faith; other traditions include the baptism of infants but require (at least in theory) the rite to be confirmed when the child comes to faith.
12. See Moran, "Ancient Near Eastern Background of the Love of God in Deuteronomy," 77–87.

of rams. For rebellion is like the sin of divination, and arrogance like the evil of idolatry" (1 Sam. 15:22–23a). God also spoke through Hosea, saying, "For I desire mercy, not sacrifice, and acknowledgment of God rather than burnt offerings" (Hos. 6:6). Proverbs added: "The LORD detests the sacrifice of the wicked, but the prayer of the upright pleases him" (15:8), and "To do what is right and just is more acceptable to the LORD than sacrifice" (21:3).

Compliance with the commandments for purity, holiness, and righteousness was the expected evidence of faith (Lev. 19:2, 37). This is still true (1 Tim. 2:8; James 2:17–26; 1 Peter 1:13–16). People who attend worship services with no commitment to obey God's Word have failed to see that worship is not a time to merely profess faith with some creed and ceremony but a time to affirm their devotion to the Lord and renew their commitment to live out their faith. For the Israelites to enter the Holy Place and worship the living God required not only their separation from all that was incompatible with his holy nature, but also their pursuit of all that harmonized with it.

## True Worshippers Are Confessing Believers

Devout worshippers are not sinless people; they are confessing believers. The Israelites certainly knew this. They knew that because God's requirements of holiness and righteousness were so high, whenever they wished to enter his Holy Place they first had to deal with their faults and their failures. They knew that no matter how hard they tried to live righteously, they had not done all that they should have done and they had done things they should not have done. If anyone, even the best of them, was going to enter God's presence to worship, there had to be a provision for forgiveness.

To remind people of this, priests would meet them at the gates with a little ritual, a "liturgy at the gate." For example, Psalm 15 begins by asking who was qualified to enter the sanctuary of the LORD. It then records the priestly answer, a checklist of ten characteristics of practical righteousness. One could enter the sanctuary only if one had a blameless life, spoke the truth, slandered no one, did no wrong to a neighbor, cast no slur on anyone, despised those who are vile, honored the God-fearers, kept oaths, lent money without interest, and took no bribes. Who could ever claim to have lived so perfectly?

The purpose of such a list would have been to make the worshippers aware of sins that they may have overlooked—the little, everyday attitudes and acts. Upon hearing these things, they would have realized their need to confess their sins and offer the appropriate sacrifices if they were to gain entrance into the presence of God. Most people who went to the sanctuary would have taken such offerings in anticipation of the need, but psalms like this would have assisted them in focusing their confessions. The point is that God would not accept worship from people who were defiled by sin, even if they were the "righteous" people of the land. What God was looking for from the worshipper was not routine ritual and perfunctory service but obedience. And for any disobedience, no matter how small, confession had to be made. Therefore, the real sacrifice to be brought was a broken and a contrite heart (Ps. 51:16–17). Then there could be communion, for the holy LORD God who dwells in the highest heaven also dwells with the one who is contrite in heart (Isa. 57:15).

There was no reason for people not to confess their sin, other than stubborn pride. Once they acknowledged their sin, they found his forgiveness so immediate and so wonderful that they wondered why they had waited so long (Ps. 32:1–2, 5, 9)!

The New Testament also teaches that sin destroys fellowship with the Lord and ruins worship and service. Jesus himself told people to take care of their sin before trying to bring gifts to God (Matt. 5:23–24). Peter warned that even friction in marriage could hinder prayers (1 Peter 3:7). And Paul reported that some actually had died prematurely for taking Holy Communion in an unworthy manner (1 Cor. 11:30). Before enjoying full communion with the Lord, believers still must acknowledge their sins and failures. But because forgiveness is based on the blood of Christ, they can be confident that they will be cleansed of all unrighteousness. Therefore their confession will quickly turn from guilt and remorse to relief and gratitude.

The worship service itself should inspire this: if the service confronts people with a glimpse of the glory of God, if people are made aware of the holiness of God, if they truly hear his Word, then like Isaiah they will be struck with their own sinfulness and their uncleanness and immediately repent and seek forgiveness.

## True Worshippers Follow After Holiness

A related prerequisite for Israel's worship in the sanctuary was holiness, that is, living a life set apart from the world and all its defilements. The Israelites were to remain pure in body and spirit, as the laws of ceremonial cleanness and ritual purification make clear. No believing Israelite would (or could with a clear conscience) enter the sanctuary with physical impurities or worldly defilements. These were not sins, and so no confession was required or forgiveness declared. But that which was "unclean" was prohibited from God's presence in the temple, as it will be in the heavenly temple (Rev. 21:27). This label covered anything wrong with this life—disease, contamination, forbidden food, contact with corpses, bodily emissions, or the like.[13] Accordingly, if there had been any defilement or common uncleanness, even if unavoidable, a ritual purification was necessary before worship could begin.[14] People with lifelong illnesses, such as hemorrhages or leprosy, were never permitted inside the sanctuary. For them, the hope of glory would have to sustain them.

New Testament believers no longer have the temple and its ceremonial laws. But the revelation of the nature of God that informed those regulations remains for us, namely, that he is holy. This means that any worldly defilement of body, spirit, or mind, even if through simple contact with the world system, is incompatible with the holiness of God and interferes with the purity of worship. The New Testament does not prohibit the physically diseased or defiled from joining the worship in the assembly (although wisdom would dictate if it was safe); but it does require sanctification, which we now normally think of as spiritual cleansing (see passages such as 1 Cor. 5:6–8, 13; 11:17–22, 28). But sanctification includes separation from the world and all its defilement. Spiritual cleansing should include at least an acknowledgment that defilement, disease, death, and all other earthly things, whether physical or mental, have a troubling effect on our hearts and minds, hindering our full contemplation of and service for the Lord. Although in this life we have to endure such things,

---

13. For a more thorough study of the laws of uncleanness in Leviticus 11–15, see my work, *Holiness to the Lord.*

14. It should be noted that the laws for purification applied to the sanctuary, the dwelling place of the holy LORD God. Where worship activities were held away from this sanctuary, the purity laws of the temple did not apply in the same way; there may have been quarantine for serious infections and daily uncleanness, but people would not be prohibited from their personal worship.

they will have no place in the world to come (Rev. 21:27). Since worship invites us to lift up our hearts and enter the presence of God spiritually, any worldly influences or physical defilements must be seen for what they are and not allowed to distract us from communion with God. Therefore, as people prepare for worship, they should purify their hearts and minds from the disturbing and defiling images and noises of the world, as well as the troubling circumstances of their lives in so far as that is possible. Some things cannot be easily left behind; but in moments of spiritual reflection, the hope of glory becomes a welcome respite. This is why the worship service must recall such a hope.

As people prepare for worship, they should recall how perfectly God created this world and everything in it and how God has promised to make everything whole and perfect in the glorious age to come. When meditating on such things, they should acknowledge that they have shared not only in the sins of the world but also in the corruption and contamination that came with the Fall. The illnesses and weaknesses that they must endure in this mortal body should prompt in them a greater anticipation of glory. In this way the awareness of the holiness of God will once again become a dominant influence in their lives, prompting them to try to live a life that is holy and pure, a life that is above the curse (see Phil. 4:8).[15]

## True Worshippers Are Spiritually Motivated

The Bible records various aspects of personal piety that prepared the devout for communion with the living Lord.[16] The devout would meditate on God's Word during the night on their beds (Pss. 16:7–8; 63:6) and throughout the day wherever they were (Ps. 1:2). They made it their desire to please the LORD (Pss. 63:1–5; 66:8–20), and to that end they listened for his voice (Ps. 95:6–7). Their memory of God's Word provided spiritual strength that would guard against sin (Ps. 119:9–16). And when they sinned, they immediately sought forgiveness with true repentance (Ps. 6:1–7). In other words, preserving a spiritual life based on meditation and

---

15. If their perception of God is defective, then their lives will not be what they are supposed to be. See McCullough, *The Trivialization of God.*
16. In his discussion of the evidence of personal piety, A. E. Hill surveys repentance and avoidance of sin, praise and thanksgiving, prayer, glorifying God, and covenant obedience (*Enter His Courts with Praise!* 18–23).

prayer throughout the year prepared believers for those glorious times of worship in the presence of God. What, then, were the main characteristics of a heart that was spiritually ready to commune with God?

One characteristic is genuine *humility*.[17] Truly humble worshippers understood God's grace; they depended on God for everything, knowing that everything they had came from him and everything belonged to him (1 Chron. 29:14).[18] This understanding left no room for independence or self-promotion. This pleased the LORD, for he was looking for worshippers who were broken of all self-will and rebellion (Ps. 51:9–12). He still is.[19]

A second spiritual characteristic was *devotion* to the LORD. The godly person's desire to please God (Pss. 63:1–5; 66:8–20) was displayed in a number of ways: they would make sure their sacrifices were without blemish (Lev. 1:3), their flour and incense was the finest they could prepare (2:1), and their gifts to God were the best they had (3:3; 7:30, 34). And on great holy days they would "afflict their souls" so that nothing worldly would interfere with their fellowship with the LORD (16:29–30). This kind of devotion is not possible without humility. For example, without humility Abraham never would have agreed to give up his son to God, David never would have danced so freely to the LORD in the street, Solomon never would have prayed for wisdom, and countless others never would have been willing to lay aside personal prestige and possessions in order to please God (see Heb. 11:32–39). God was looking for worshippers who desired his honor and glory above all else.

A third characteristic was a *generous spirit* that manifested itself in the active involvement in the life of the community.[20] Worshippers who were spiritually motivated would be in the sanctuary at times other than those prescribed by the law—it was their life. They so enjoyed living in communion with God that they would go to the temple anytime they could to offer their freewill offerings and in the process provide food for the poor and the needy who would be there (Lev. 7:15–16). When separated

---

17. The kind of prayers and praises given in the assembly may reveal whether or not genuine humility is present—it is the difference between "God be merciful to me a sinner" and "I thank God that I am not a sinner like other men."

18. D. R. Thomas, "Some Notes on the Old Testament Attitude to Prayer," 422–29.

19. R. J. Thompson, *Penitence and Sacrifice in Early Israel.*

20. Harper writes, "The Old Testament knows nothing of authentic spirituality apart from community, and several Old Testament theologies make 'community' the central concern of the OT" ("Old Testament Spirituality," 63–77).

from the sanctuary, they felt a genuine loss (Pss. 42:1–4; 63:1–8); and when they could join the festal throng, they would be arrayed in holiness (Ps. 96) and shout and sing and dance enthusiastically to show their love for the LORD (Ps. 98). When other people received an answer to prayer, or made a vow, those who were spiritual would be there to share in the celebration. When others were in need, they would be there to pray with them and, if possible, help meet their needs. The truly spiritual worshipper was part of a community, and apart from the community there was no course for the spiritual life to follow.[21] If through selfishness or indifference people disrupted or destroyed the value of the community, worship became a lifeless regimen.[22]

## Conclusion

These basic qualifications of the spiritual life are still applicable today for all forms of worship and service. We may conclude with the apostle that those who are spiritual discern all things: they fully understand who God is and what they are, what it means to be in his presence, how they should prepare for it, and what should come from the experience.[23] There is no secular life for devout worshippers, not for those who in genuine humility (Phil. 2:5–11) make pleasing God their goal (2 Cor. 5:9). They are filled with joy in their worship and ready to meet the needs of others (Heb. 13:15–16). For the devout every moment is an opportunity for the spiritual life.[24]

But when pride takes over and selfish ambition is the rule of the day so that the needs of the community are ignored, then the words of the prophetic rebukes and warnings that first came to Israel resound in our sanctuaries as well: God still rejects such worship and warns that if it does not change he will remove the witness (Rev. 2–3).[25]

---

21. Jeske notes that in the book of Revelation to be "in the Spirit" is a relational term, for the work of the Spirit is related to the life of the community, and nowhere is it connected to the experience of an individual apart from the community ("Spirit and Community in the Johannine Apocalypse," 452–66).
22. See further on this Wainwright, *Worship with One Accord*. The fifteen articles develop the theme that praise is marred by division. See also Donnelly, "Preem," 39–53.
23. The spiritual life not only prepares a person for worship but is inspired by the worship. See Seasoltz for the practical implementation of peace ("Peace: Belief, Prayer and Life," 152–72).
24. Dyrness, *Themes in Old Testament Theology*, 125.
25. We will return to this theme in the section on worship in the book of Revelation. For God to remove the lampstand would mean that the church would lose its light and its usefulness to God.

# CHAPTER 19

# The Prophetic Denunciation *of* Corrupt Worship

## Warnings Against Idolatry

Idolatry, the devotion to alien gods usually represented by physical images or statues, robs God of his glory and therefore destroys true worship.[1] The very first commandment unambiguously declared that God would have no rivals: "You shall have no other gods before me" (Exod. 20:3; Deut. 5:7).[2] This first prohibition finds its corresponding positive statement in Deuteronomy 6:5, which says, "Love Yahweh your God with all your heart and with all your soul and with all your strength."[3] It was appropriate and right that Yahweh, who redeemed Israel from bondage and proved himself to be the one, true living God, should lay claim to their allegiance. But if that was not reason enough, the fact that he was the Creator of all things eliminated all possible rivals (Isa. 44:6–9).

Accordingly, Yahweh was not going to let his people defect: "Do not worship any other god, for Yahweh, whose name (i.e., nature) is Jealous, is a jealous God" (Exod. 34:14). The word "jealous," perhaps better expressed as "zeal," signifies God's passionate intensity to protect what rightfully belongs to him.[4] He would confront any threat to his relationship with his people (cf. John 2:14–17).

---

1. Buck, "Worship, Idolatry, and God," 68–82.
2. The phrase "before me," or "beside me," may have a hostile sense, literally "against my face," meaning "in defiance of me" (*'al-pānāy*; see Gen. 16:12; 25:18; and Deut. 21:16). B. Jacob, *Second Book of the Bible: Exodus,* 546–47.
3. See Fretheim, *Exodus,* 224.
4. The word may have a positive connotation of zeal, but it also may have a negative connotation of envy, especially when the object of the jealousy does not rightly belong to the person.

The second commandment builds on the first: "You shall not make for yourself an idol *(pésel)*. . . . You shall not bow down to them or worship them" (Exod. 20:4–5; this is variously restated in Exod. 20:23; 34:17; Deut. 27:15). The prohibition includes any image that would be venerated, whether in a pagan religion or the worship of Yahweh. Accordingly, pure worship was the worship of the invisible and therefore image-less God—a unique phenomenon in antiquity. The only symbol of God's presence was the ark of the covenant, a box, and the only images attached to it were of angels.[5]

The problem with images, as Fretheim explains, is that they fix the deity in place and time as well as in form and substance. But God is living and active and not confined to any place, or form, or time; he is the eternal God of heaven, the Lord of time and space. To make and worship an image denies these basic attributes of God.[6] Moreover, in the ancient world making an image was part of the way of controlling the deity.

This second commandment qualified the prohibition further with the addition of "or any likeness" (NIV, "in the form of anything" *[t°mûnāh]*) of anything that is "in heaven above or on the earth beneath or in the waters below" (Exod. 20:4). This law might be interpreted to rule out a good deal of artistic creativity were it not for the fact that God himself had the Israelites embroider and carve images of cherubs in the sanctuary. In fact, the tabernacle and especially Solomon's temple used decorations in plant and animal motifs. The prohibition concerned making images to be worshipped: "You shall not bow down *(khāwāh* [s.v. *shākhāh* in BDB]) to them or worship *('āvad)* them" (Exod. 20:5).[7] If the law prohibiting idolatry was not strong enough, the preaching of the prophets left little doubt about this spiritual folly. The prophets had always played a significant role in the worship of Israel, providing it with ethical content and exhorting greater devotion.[8] But when idolatry became so pronounced,

---

5. For an extensive discussion on the subject, see Keel, *God, Goddesses, and Images of God in Ancient Israel.*
6. See Fretheim, *Exodus*, 227. Furthermore, the one who revealed God most decisively was a living, active human being—Jesus Christ. He is the image of God (Heb. 1:3).
7. The combination of these verbs is used in contexts that refer to offering worship to pagan divinities rather than the worship of Yahweh (see Josh. 23:7, 16; 2 Kings 17:35).
8. Gordon says the prophets were more involved in the cult in spite of their rhetoric (Gordon, *The Israelite Prophets in Recent Scholarship*, 112).

they appeared in the assemblies to declare the words of the LORD to the priests and the people alike, denouncing all practices that violated the law and all false prophets and priests who sanctioned the inclusion of pagan rituals.[9] For example, in the eighth century, Hosea ridiculed the process of making a calf idol out of silver or gold, saying that it would only bring destruction. God's anger burned against the people because of this impurity, and as a result it would be destroyed because it was man-made (Hos. 8:4–6).

A little later Isaiah offered a scornful and sarcastic description of idol making; it reduces the activity to spiritual blindness and self-glorifying stupidity (Isa. 44:9–20). He declared that all who make a graven image are worthless (*tōhû*, v. 9)—idolatry reverses the order of creation and reduces the worshipper to a *"waste"* (*tōhû wābōhû* in Gen. 1:2). The folly of idolatry is that the idol-maker, a mere mortal, gets tired and thirsty in the process of making a god in his image and according to the form and beauty of a human being (Isa. 44:12–13)! God created human beings to be his image. But now, in the confusing kingdom of darkness, people were making gods in their own image.

Isaiah could only marvel at their blindness. The idol-maker uses half of a log to burn a fire (a log from a tree that he did not cause to grow), and from the other half of the log he makes a god that he will worship! How could anything that a mere mortal makes be a god? If people cannot solve their own problems, then nothing that they can make will be able to do so, for what they make will be inferior to them (cf. Ps. 115:2–8). To find deliverance from the problems of life, people need a God who is greater than they, a God who created them (Isa. 44:21–22).

Of course, in the ancient world images were perceived to be the localizations of gods. It was not the material any more than the form that was believed to make the difference, but the spirit power behind it.[10] But the prophets knew that even though the worship of spirit forces was a threat,

---

9. There was a great variety of prophets in ancient Israel; some had a cultic role to perform with music, psalms, or exhortations, but others were independent and in fact not welcome in the sanctuary. See A. R. Johnson, *Cultic Prophet and Israel's Psalmody*, esp. 58–59; and Rowley, "The Prophets and the Cult," in *Worship in Ancient Israel*, esp. 144–75.

10. E.g., the prophets of Baal cried out to their god to send the fire from heaven, even though they had statues of Baal (1 Kings 18). And when the LORD brought the plagues on Egypt, he was destroying their gods (Num. 33:4).

it was doomed to failure because Yahweh was, and is, the only true, sovereign of all creation. Even false gods will have to submit to his authority when he appears (Ps. 97:7).

Idolatry was very complicated. Pagan idols represented the religious, social, and political values of their respective cultures.[11] To worship these gods was to exalt the ideas of those cultures and live by their values. Most importantly, though, idolatry was the ultimate rejection of the sovereignty of God.

The modern world, at least in the West, is not plagued by a vast array of idols as was the ancient Near East.[12] But the spirit of idolatry remains, for anything that rivals God in his rightful place as Sovereign Lord is a violation of the first principle of the faith. It does not matter if the object is Baal, or science, or money. If it robs God of his proper glory, then it diminishes any devotion offered to him.

The label "idolatry" may be affixed to anything that fills our desires and devotions instead of God, anything that replaces God as the source of security and satisfaction in our lives, or anything that robs God of his proper place in our affections and commitments. Paul writes, "Put to death, therefore, whatever belongs to your earthly nature: sexual immorality, impurity, lust, evil desires and greed, which is idolatry" (Col. 3:5).[13] Accordingly, John warns Christians to keep themselves from idols (1 John 5:21). The way to avoid idolatry in any form is to have a wholehearted devotion to the Lord that finds expression in pure worship and righteous service.

## Israel's Refusal to Heed the Warnings

The folly of idolatry began early in Israel's history, and it remained throughout its history until it eventually destroyed them. To study the historical accounts in the Old Testament is to study the record of spiritual defection, and to read the prophetic books is to read oracle after oracle against the corrupt worship of strange gods. A brief survey of some of the

---

11. See Watts, "Babylonian Idolatry in the Prophets," 115–22.
12. But there are movements to bring forth ancient deities and rites in an attempt to reimage God; see for example A. B. Spencer et al., *The Goddess Revival.*
13. The meaning of the word for "greed" here is the ruthless desire for, and seeking after, material things. This attitude is the same as that found in idolatry, which puts self-interest and things in place of God (Vaughan, "Colossians," 2:212).

most blatant periods of Israel's unfaithfulness will be sufficient to show how it ruined their worship and ended their existence as a nation.

## Anticipation of Idolatry

Moses knew that after he was gone Israel would turn and worship other gods in spite of his warning that if they did they would be destroyed (Deut. 4:25–28). Deuteronomy 32, written in the prophetic form of historical recollection,[14] records a panorama of the nation's future spiritual history. Verses 15–18 tell how once the nation ("Jeshurun") became affluent, it forsook God, its Creator and Redeemer, and provoked him to jealousy with abominable gods, gods they did not know, new gods their fathers did not fear. They even sacrificed to demons.

Even without this divine revelation, Moses would have had reason enough to foresee that the nation would not be able to preserve the purity of the faith, not only because of their idolatry with the golden calf (Exod. 32; Deut. 9:7–29), but also because of their constant rebellion in the wilderness. Because of these sad events, the Israelites themselves should have been aware of how dangerous it was to rob God of his rightful place—the prophets would call it treachery, unfaithfulness, and fornication.[15] But the people seemed to heed the warnings only when they were on the brink of annihilation.

## Early Defection

When the Israelites settled in the land, they showed no signs of overcoming pagan forms of worship. Psalm 106 summarizes their idolatrous activities to warn all subsequent worshippers. Basically it says that they adopted the customs of the nations and worshipped pagan idols, which became a snare to them; they sacrificed their sons and daughters to demons, shedding innocent blood and desecrating the land;[16] and by defiling themselves in this way they prostituted themselves (Ps. 106:35–39; cf. Ps. 78:54–64).

---

14. Because the poem is written in this form, and because it is so accurate, many biblical scholars believe that it was written after the fact and not as a prophetic oracle.
15. See Zipor, "The Deuteronomic Account of the Golden Calf," 20–33. Zipor follows the view that the event is a variant of the sin of Jeroboam, but he has helpful insights into the nature of idolatry.
16. Green, *Role of Human Sacrifice in the Ancient Near East.*

It appears that the Israelites were simply caught up in the idolatry all around them. In some ways their defection in the time of the judges is easy to understand, for they had to deal with a priesthood that was quickly becoming corrupt and they had very little access to God's word (1 Sam. 3:1). But later, say in the time of Hosea, when the people had the benefit of centuries of temple worship, frequent prophetic preaching, and countless experiences of divine intervention in their history, *and they still chose false gods,* this was completely inexplicable and inexcusable.

The early Israelites had seen the gods of Egypt, grotesque gods usually characterized by animal or half-animal forms. But when they arrived in Canaan, they found gods that were very human in form and nature—too human. They still found some ancient symbolism: both the Canaanite god El and Baal were at times portrayed as bulls. The bull was the ancient symbol of fertility and procreative powers.[17] The goddess Asherah was represented by her cult object, a wooden pole.[18] And the goddess Astarte (biblical Ashtaroth) was portrayed at times as a lioness.[19] But for the most part, the gods and goddess were portrayed in human form and oftentimes engaged in the baser activities of humans.

It was no time at all before the Israelites embraced Canaanite religion with its popular fertility cult (e.g., Judg. 3:7). It is sometimes hard for modern believers to understand this defection, but the worship of Baal and Asherah appealed to the baser human instincts and satisfied the natural desire to have and manipulate the deity to obtain fertility. It seemed to make sense that the way to achieve fertility and immortality was through the ritual of sympathetic enactment in a local shrine, that is, participating in fertility rites to induce the gods and goddesses to act. All of this was shamelessly displayed before them, in striking contrast to their worship of only one God who remained invisible and who had a strict code of ethics and morality. Moreover, as the tribes spread out through Canaan, they lost the immediate contact with the center of their worship. They were simply not able to resist the temptation to eat of this

---

17. Oswalt, "Golden Calves and the 'Bull of Jacob,'" 9–18.
18. Patai, "The Goddess Asherah," 37–52.
19. The Bible also uses human and animal descriptions for God; but the biblical figures of speech never use descriptions that are base and low, sexual or immoral. And it is clear that they are merely figures of speech because the Bible makes it clear that God is a Spirit.

forbidden fruit. In fact, the times of the judges comes to a close with the priests themselves being judged for their fornication at the very entrance to the house of the LORD, perhaps an adaptation of cult prostitution at the shrine (1 Sam. 2:22).

At a time when there were few bright spots, Gideon stands out as the first reformer. He tore down the altar of Baal and cut down the wooden Asherah the people had been worshiping (Judg. 6:25) and used the wood for a burnt offering to Yahweh (v. 26). When the men of the city demanded punishment for the deed, Gideon's father, apparently brought to his senses by his son's zeal, challenged them: "If Baal really is a god, he can defend himself" (v. 31). But as the psalmist says, idols may have mouths, but they cannot speak; eyes, but they cannot see; noses, but they cannot smell; hands, but they cannot handle; feet, but they cannot walk; neither can they utter a sound. And, those who make them and those who trust in them are as worthless as they are (Ps. 115:4–8).

## Growing Apostasy

There were many who brought idolatry into Israel's religious life in a number of ways. The theme gets old quickly, but it bears repeating, for God chose to delineate the various failures in Scripture for our instruction. We shall make only a brief survey of the major defections and the LORD's responses to them.

### The LORD Judged Solomon's Disobedience

Solomon tolerated the gods of his many wives and thus opened the way for state-sanctioned idolatry (1 Kings 11:1–13).[20] But he also went after Ashtoreth and Milkom and built high places to Chemosh and Molech.[21] These "abominations" were a snare to the people's faith and the sin that spoiled Solomon's service. Yahweh was angry with Solomon and announced that most of the kingdom would be given to a subordinate (vv. 9–13).

### The Man of God Denounced Jeroboam's Idolatry

Even though this subordinate, Jeroboam, had been established by God in the northern kingdom of Israel, he quickly set up idolatrous worship.

---

20. See R. Dillard, "The Chronicler's Solomon," 289–300.
21. Weinfeld, "The Molech Cult and Its Ancient Near Eastern Background," 21–27; and idem, "The Worship of Molech and the Queen of Heaven," 133–54.

Reasoning that his subjects could not remain loyal to him and worship in the other kingdom of Judah, he built rival places of worship (1 Kings 12:25–33) and set up golden calves in Dan and Bethel to represent Israel's God(s). The prophets were clear—this was the idolatry that started at Sinai (1 Kings 14; Amos 4:4, etc.).[22] Jeroboam also burnt offerings at the high place himself (1 Kings 13:1) and formed his own staff of priests to serve at Bethel, people he gathered from the lowest of the people (v. 33).

This sin was so great that it was sufficient to cut off the house of Jeroboam from the face of the earth—as God had almost done with the generation at Mount Sinai. God sent a man from Judah to cry out against the altar and prophesy that Josiah, a future king of Judah, would destroy the false priests and burn their bones on this false altar. As a sign that the word was from God, the altar was split in two (1 Kings 13:1–5).[23] There could be no doubt that God was condemning Jeroboam's false religion.

### Rehoboam Defied the Word of the LORD

Under the reign of Rehoboam, the people of Judah built high places, made images and Asherah poles, worshipped under every green tree, installed shrine prostitutes, and engaged in all kinds of detestable pagan practices (1 Kings 14:22–24). To judge them God used Shishak of Egypt, who invaded Jerusalem and plundered the treasury of the temple (vv. 25–26).

### Elijah Challenged the Worship of Baal

A few decades later the weak king Ahab married Jezebel, a Phoenician princess, and under her powerful influence established Baal worship and set up the Asherah pole (1 Kings 16:29–33). First Kings records that Ahab did more to provoke God's anger than all the kings before him.

The task of confronting this new wave of idolatrous practices fell to Elijah and then Elisha.[24] Elijah (*ʾĒlîyāhû* means "Yah is my God") was

---

22. Oswalt says that the evidence indicates that there existed the worship of Yahweh as a bull. The prophets held tightly to boundaries that differentiated them from the pagans: they had a king, but he was not deified; they had sacrifices but not to feed God; and they described God as the bullish [mighty] one of Jacob, but he was not a bull ("Golden Calves and the 'Bull of Jacob,'" 9–18).

23. In conjunction with this study, see R. R. Wilson, "Early Israelite Prophecy," 3–16.

24. For a detailed discussion of the works of Elijah and Elisha against the backdrop of Canaanite religion, see Bronner, *The Stories of Elijah and Elisha as Polemics Against Baal Worship*. For supplementary information and some corrections, see Battenfield, "Yahweh's Refutation of the Baal Myth," 19–37.

to oppose Baalism in the most dramatic way, forcing the confrontation on Carmel (1 Kings 18:21). Elijah's challenge was direct: if any god could bring fire from heaven, surely it would be the storm god Baal. So the prophets of Baal cried out all day, but there was no answer whatsoever (v. 29). Elijah, however, knew that Yahweh was the true God and that he alone was to be worshipped. So after a brief prayer, fire fell from the clear skies and consumed the sacrifice and the altar.[25] The point was that there could be no shared allegiance with other gods, no halting between two opinions. This challenge became the theme of all prophetic preaching to follow.[26]

### Elijah Condemned Inquiring of Baalzebub

Ahab's legacy of apostasy continued into the reign of his son Ahaziah, who enquired of Baalzebub, the god of Ekron, whether or not he should recover from his injury (2 Kings 1). Yahweh sent Elijah to him to ask, "Is it because there is no God in Israel that you are going off to consult Baal-Zebub, the god of Ekron?" (v. 3). The judgment for this spiritual defection was that he would die in his bed.

### Jehu Purged Israel of Baalism

King Jehu was anointed by Elisha to destroy the dynasty of Ahab and avenge the blood of those slain by Jezebel (2 Kings 9:4–13). This he did with a vengeance, slaying Joram of Irsael and Ahaziah of Judah in war (vv. 22–29), then Jezebel herself (vv. 30–37), and then Ahab's sons (10:1–7). Finally, he destroyed the prophets of Baal, their idols, and their temple while they were sacrificing to their gods (vv. 20–27). It was ruthless and violent, and God would remember it; but Jehu did destroy Baal worship in Israel (v. 28). Yet, Jehu retained the golden calves that were in Bethel and Dan, giving added life to the idolatry of Jeroboam.

### Jehoiada Restored Yahwism

The worship of Yahweh was restored in Judah after a crisis almost ended the Davidic line. When Athaliah, the daughter of Jezebel, tried to destroy the royal family (2 Kings 11), the priest Jehoiada hid the young Joash. Jehoiada then made a pact between Yahweh, the king, and the

---

25. Cohn, "The Literary Logic of 1 Kings 17–19," 341.
26. J. A. Thompson, *The Book of Jeremiah*, 8.

people, that they should be loyal to the God Yahweh (vv. 17–21). As a result they destroyed the temple of Baal, smashed the idols, and slew the priest of Baal at the altar. The king began the work of restoring the temple to its original purpose (2 Kings 12). Funds were raised so that all the necessary repairs could be made to the house of Yahweh. Unfortunately, when faced with war, the king looted the gold of the temple that had been dedicated to God to buy off the king of Damascus. He died at the hands of assassins.

### Isaiah Exposed the Unbelief of Ahaz

After a time of weak and corrupt kings, the wicked King Ahaz came to power in Jerusalem. When in Damascus, paying tribute to his overlord the king of Assyria, Tiglath-Pileser, he saw an altar and sent the pattern to his priest to copy for temple use (2 Kings 16:10–18).[27] This was symptomatic of the man's religious syncretism—he followed the detestable ways of the nations, burned incense in the high places and under every spreading tree, and even sacrificed his son in the fire (vv. 3–4).[28]

The kinds of horrible practices that Israel adopted from the Canaanites are catalogued in Isaiah 57. It tells how the rebellious people ran after false gods, burning with lust under the spreading trees and sacrificing their children in the ravines (v. 5). They poured out drink offerings and offered grain offerings to the idols among the smooth stones of the ravines (v. 6). They replaced the law on the doorposts with grotesque symbols of the fertility cult (v. 8a), and because they entered into covenant with the false gods (v. 8b), they opened their beds to the gods they loved and sent emissaries to inquire from the dead (v. 9). Amazingly, in all of this corrupt practice, they found renewal for their weary lives (v. 10)—probably in the way a modern pagan would on a wild weekend. But if they were not going to be faithful to Yahweh, they had no right to exist as his nation.

### The Prophets Announced the Doom of Samaria

The blow came to Samaria (722 B.C.) earlier than to Jerusalem (586 B.C.). The northern kingdom of Israel was utterly destroyed because of its idolatrous practices, building high places, setting up idols, worshipping Baal and the host of heaven, using enchantments and divination,

---

27. McKay, *Religion in Judah Under the Assyrians.*
28. See Green, *Role of Human Sacrifice in the Ancient Near East.*

and even sacrificing children (2 Kings 17:7–20).[29] These practices had replaced the pure worship of the one sovereign and holy LORD God of heaven, who had redeemed them and brought them to the land and given them every kind of blessing.

To Hosea the nation's defection was the same as adultery and fornication, for the people had left Yahweh for other lovers.[30] Because of their spiritual defection, his only conclusion could be: "You are not my people, and I am not your God" (Hos. 1:9).[31]

### The Beginning of the Samaritans

It was shortly after this critical time that an ethnically mixed group of people came into existence, a people who would develop their own form of worship—the Samaritans. When Assyria deported people from Israel, they also settled other exiled tribes in the vacant regions of Samaria, hoping intermarriage would break down nationalism (2 Kings 17:24–33). Those Israelites who married the foreigners were looked on as impure and their descendants as not really Jewish. Consequently, the Samaritans formed their own religious practices based on the Pentateuch and the tradition of Joshua's confirming the covenant in Samaria. A racial problem had become a religious one.

### Hezekiah's Reforms of Worship

In the nation's long history, there had been reforms and revivals, but Hezekiah's stands out as one of the greatest.[32]

Hezekiah saw how idolatry destroyed the northern kingdom of Israel; so with the guidance of the prophet Isaiah, he determined to bring about major reforms in Judah. In his first year he set about restoring the temple and its worship. He opened and repaired the doors of the sanctuary,

---

29. Along this line see Lapp, "The Ritual Incense Stand from Taanach," 16–17.
30. The choice of the image no doubt reflects the reality of the situation, for Canaanite worship did involve all manner of fornication in the groves and the high places.
31. God in his faithfulness to his covenant did announce through Hosea and the other prophets that Israelites would be regathered and replanted in the land. But this generation had excluded themselves by their idolatry.
32. See further Todd, "The Reforms of Hezekiah and Josiah," 288–93; Rosenbaum, "Hezekiah's Reform and Deuteronomic Tradition," 23–43; and Rowley, "Hezekiah's Reform and Rebellion," 395–431.

which had been closed in the days of Ahaz (2 Chron. 29:3).[33] When several Levites took charge, the temple was cleansed, restored, and sanctified in sixteen days.[34] The king then reorganized the temple staff to revive worship (vv. 30–36). Appropriate sacrifices were offered to make atonement, singers and musicians were stationed to sound praises to the LORD, and all the congregation worshipped the LORD, joyfully participating in peace offerings and burnt offerings.

But revival needed to mark a new beginning for the worship of the LORD. Therefore Hezekiah proclaimed in all the land that Passover would be held once again.[35] Most of the people in the north, Israel, laughed them to scorn. Not even conquest and exile had gotten through to them. Some responded, however, and they, along with the people of Judah, came with singleness of heart to do the will of the LORD (2 Chron. 30:11–12). Things were slow in starting: the priests were unprepared to serve, and the corrupt altars had to be removed. But the Levites took charge of the sacrifices in the place of those who were not sanctified to lead the worship.[36] The festival lasted two weeks, with the people praising the LORD with enthusiasm and sacrificing to God and the priests sanctifying themselves to the LORD and standing to bless the people (vv. 23–27).

The worship of the LORD in Jerusalem could not allow rival gods and competing shrines to exist, as the LORD had declared and history had proven. Hezekiah, therefore, set about to destroy the idols and altars and pillars throughout the land (2 Chron. 31:1). After that he reestablished the divisions of the priests and the provisions for their support from the tithes and offerings (vv. 2–21).

---

33. When the Israelites had been restored to their land, the Chronicler tried to recapture the glory that had been lost. The book, therefore, focuses on the temple and its welfare. The Chronicler believed the king was necessary for the maintenance and functioning of the cult. See Moriarty, "The Chronicler's Account of Hezekiah's Reform," 399–406.

34. One thing that Hezekiah removed was the bronze serpent Moses had made because people were beginning to worship it. See Joines, "Bronze Serpent in the Israelite Cult," 145–56.

35. It was to be held in the second month, because there were not enough sanctified priests to do it in the proper time and because the people had not had time to assemble in Jerusalem (2 Chron. 30:1–5).

36. It was more important to have the Passover without the properly prepared priests than to follow the letter of the law and cancel the worship.

### The Final Undoing of Judah

Unfortunately, Hezekiah's piety had no influence on his son, Manasseh (2 Kings 21:1–18). As incredible as it seems, he built up the high places that his father had torn down, raised again the altars to Baal, made the Asherah, and served the host of heaven. He built pagan altars in the two courts of the house of the LORD. But worse than this, in his religious observances he made his son pass through the fire, used enchantments, dealt with familiar spirits and wizards, and put up an Asherah in the temple. For his sins he was carried off in shackles to Babylon, but there he repented and was restored by the LORD (2 Chron. 33:10–13).[37] He then tried to restore the pure worship of the LORD, but the people continued to follow the pagan practices he had initiated.

And so the prophet Jeremiah, among others, denounced Judah for its sins.[38] In an extended oracle (Jer. 2:1–3:5), he declared that a great apostasy had taken place without warrant (2:5–8)—the people had gone after idols and no longer enquired of the LORD. It was no surprise that the people forgot the LORD, for many of those entrusted with teaching the law did not even know the LORD.

He then marveled at such apostasy, that the nation had actually traded the living God for no gods (Jer. 2:9–13). They had forsaken "the spring of living water" and made "cisterns" that easily cracked and could not hold water. The point of this imagery is that with all the natural resources available to them from God (living water from springs), they chose unreliable religions that were made by man (cisterns). This apostasy was like leaving Eden's rich provisions to scratch out a subsistence from the dust of the ground.

Jeremiah's oracle then elaborated on the folly of choosing helpless gods. The people and the princes say to a tree, "You are my father," and to a stone, "You gave me birth"; yet, in a time of trouble, they cry again to the LORD for help but to no avail (Jer. 2:26–28).

---

37. The pseudepigraphal prayer of Manasseh was probably written by a Jewish theologian about A.D. 70, who was trying to supply the prayer referred to in the Bible. Although not Scripture, it has genuine religious value for the Day of Atonement or other acts of contrition; thus, it is included in the Book of Common Prayer and used in services.

38. There have been a number of studies to show that his messages were cast in literary forms that were used in worship. See Lundbom, *Jeremiah;* Stulman, *The Prose Sermons of the Book of Jeremiah;* and K. M. O'Connor, *The Confessions of Jeremiah* (confessions of Yahweh's power).

Finally, the prophet implored the people to acknowledge their iniquity and idolatry (Jer. 3:12–13), but they would not even admit that they had sinned (2:35). So God warned them of judgment: if they were so enamored with worshipping the Babylonian god Tammuz[39] and the goddess, the Queen of Heaven,[40] then to Babylon they would go.

Jeremiah's writings also condemned immoral activities, which had always been connected to idolatry (Jer. 3:1; 5:1–9; 23:10–13). He denounced the priests and prophets in particular as immoral (5:30–31; 6:13–15; 14:14), for they were at the heart of the problem. But most dramatically Jeremiah had come to the conclusion that under the circumstances the temple was no longer essential. If communion with God had been ruined by disobedience, sacrifice in a sanctuary would not restore it. Temple worship had always been a means of pointing people to God. Now, as Thompson puts it, it had become an empty parade and God rejected it.[41] There would be a new covenant and a rebuilt sanctuary for pure worship, but in his day all Jeremiah could see was the judgment of God on an apostate nation—the temple had to go!

This promise of the new covenant probably was overshadowed by the chaos of the destruction and the Exile. But it was intended to give the people hope—there was coming a great spiritual renewal and restoration (Jer. 31:31–40).[42] Others delivered similar revelations from God. Zephaniah prophesied that the LORD was going to purify the lips of the people[43] so that all of them might "call on the name of the LORD"[44] and serve him. He was going to regather them to the land and renew the proper spirit in them to worship at his holy mountain (Zeph. 3:9–11).

---

39. See Gurney, "Tammuz Reconsidered," 147–60.
40. See Olyan, "Some Observations Concerning the Identity of the Queen of Heaven," 161–74.
41. J. A. Thompson, *The Book of Jeremiah*, 67–68.
42. Jeremiah enumerates the basic promises of the new covenant: the LORD will forgive them and restore them to their land; he will write his laws on their hearts; they will all know the LORD; and they will rebuild the ruined city as a holy place to the LORD.
43. The miracle of Pentecost in Acts 2 is often seen as a harbinger of the complete fulfillment of this promise.
44. The Hebrew expression uses the same words that were used in the description of Abram's calling on the name of the LORD; it refers to proclamation of the faith through the worship and service of the LORD *(liqrōʾ kullām bᵉshēm YHWH)*.

### The Reform of Josiah

In the days of Jeremiah, a good king ascended the throne, one who earnestly desired to restore the pure worship of the LORD. He was the one that God had raised up to do it (1 Kings 13:2).

Josiah began his reforms in the eighth year of his reign, when he was just sixteen years old, but it took ten years to enforce them throughout the land (2 Kings 22–23; 2 Chron. 34).[45] He sent men to remove all idolatrous elements from the temple, the images for Baal and the host of heaven, and all their vessels, and he burned them in the fields of Kidron and carried their ashes to Bethel. He put down the idolatrous priests who burned incense to the sun,[46] moon and stars; he brought out the Asherah, burned it, stamped it to powder, and sprinkled it on the graves; he destroyed the houses of the cult prostitutes by the temple, where women had been making hangings for the Asherah;[47] he defiled the high places, where abominable offerings were made, Topheth in the Hinnom valley in particular; he took away the little statues of the horses for the chariots of the sun and burned the chariots; the altars that had been built in the upper chambers he broke down; the high places that had been there from Solomon's day he defiled and purged of images; he desecrated the altar at Bethel with the burning of the bones of the wicked and then destroyed Jeroboam's altar; he also destroyed all the temples in Samaria and on the borders,[48] drove out the spiritists, and slew the wicked priests and burned their bones on the altars of their high places in fulfillment of the three-hundred-year-old prophecy. From this list of the reforms of Josiah, we may get a fairly detailed picture of how corrupt and perverted worship had become in the land.[49]

Everything in the king's reforms intensified in the eighteenth year of his reign when in the rebuilding of the temple Hilkiah the high priest

---

45. See D. Robinson, *Josiah's Reform and the Book of the Law.*
46. Taylor, *Yahweh and the Sun,* 85–99.
47. See further, Dion, "Did Cultic Prostitution Fall into Oblivion in the Postexilic Era?" 41–48.
48. The archaeological work at Arad in the desert corroborates the biblical witness that in these shrines pagan worship had been included. See Mazar, "The Sanctuary of Arad and the Family of Hobab, the Kenite," 297–303; Ahlstrom, "Heaven on Earth," 67–83"; and Aharoni and Amiran, "Arad," 1–32.
49. See Ogden, "The Northern Extent of Josiah's Reforms," 26–34.

found the Book of the Law (2 Chron. 34:14–18).[50] When the king heard the law read to him, he rent his clothes and commanded the spiritual leaders to enquire of the LORD, because the nation was in jeopardy for its sin (vv. 19–21). They went to Huldah the prophetess,[51] who confirmed that judgment was coming on the nation. Josiah responded quickly by calling a convocation in the temple and renewing the covenant with God (2 Kings 23:1–3; 2 Chron. 34:29–31). Because he humbled himself, tore his clothes, and wept, Huldah revealed that the judgment would not take place in his lifetime.

In that same year Josiah ordered that the Passover be kept in accordance with the Book of the Law (2 Chron. 35). Josiah provided 30,000 animals from the flock and 3,000 cattle for the people. His leaders gave 2,600 sheep and 300 cattle, and their brethren gave 5,000 sheep and 500 cattle. When the time came, they sacrificed the animals to the LORD, the priests sprinkled the blood, and the people ate the boiled portions. The priests were busy well into the night, and the singers and the gatekeepers kept their positions too throughout the time of celebration. It truly was the greatest Passover since the days of Samuel (v. 18).

## Final Abominations

These great reforms were not enough to turn the tide of corruption in Judah's worship. The LORD had sent messengers again and again to warn the people, but they mocked them and despised the message until the wrath of the LORD arose against the nation (2 Chron. 36:15–16). Even when the people found themselves in exile, they still did not fully understand why God had not saved them. Ezekiel had to remind them of their depravity, primarily their abominations in the temple, explaining that because they made no attempt to meet God's requirements of holiness, they brought the destruction on themselves (2:1–10; 8:7–18; 13:1–12; and 20:1–29).

---

50. See D. Robinson, *Josiah's Reform and the Book of the Law.* The law that was found may have been some form of the book of Deuteronomy because it fits so well the reforms that the king made in centralizing worship and purging idolatry. It is untenable to say that this passage means that the book of Deuteronomy was actually written at this point.

51. Huldah's role seems to have focused on the spiritual direction of the nation; she was to make sure that God's message was correctly received (see Handy, "The Role of Huldah," 40–53; and Priest, "Huldah's Oracle," 366–68).

God clearly had warned the nation that because of their idolatry he would destroy their corrupt altars and cast down their slain before their idols (Ezek. 6). The people had become so blind to the truth that it would take a judgment of this severity to get through to them. So God said, "[Then] they will know that I am the LORD" (v. 13).

Ezekiel reported that in his visions he saw the "image of jealousy" in the inner court of the temple (Ezek. 8:3). By making such images, Israel was rejecting their God Yahweh, the only one who could save them. But worse than that, inside the sacred precincts were idols portrayed on the walls, creeping things and abominable beasts, and seventy elders stood before them with incense burners. At the north gate Ezekiel observed women weeping for Tammuz, the Babylonian god. And even worse, twenty-five men were worshipping the sun in the east, with their backs to Yahweh. God asked, "Is it a trivial matter for the house of Judah to do the detestable things they are doing here?" (v. 17). If people choose to reject the holy God Yahweh and worship grotesque and vile creatures and demons, they forfeit their privilege to live in God's blessing and commune with him in his sanctuary. All they have to look forward to is life without God's presence.

As a sign of God's judgment, the brilliantly shining glory of the LORD departed from the Most Holy Place, then from the temple, then from the city, and finally from the land itself.[52] Because the divine presence had left the temple, there was no protection for the people. So they went into exile because of their corrupt worship.

Klutsko observes how the structure of the book of Ezekiel parallels the book of Exodus.[53] In Exodus 25–31 we have the instructions for building the tabernacle, and in chapters 35–40 the report of its construction. Between these two sections is the sin of idolatry and the restoration through Moses' intercession (chaps. 32–34). The book of Ezekiel is similarly divided between the glory of God's presence in the temple (chaps. 1–11) and the restoration in a newly built temple with the glory present (chaps. 40–48), but the sin had to be purged from the nation before the glory could return. Ezekiel becomes the new Moses, forcing the people to face their sin of idolatry and instructing them in the plan to construct the

---

52. May, "The Departure of the Glory of Yahweh," 309–21.
53. Klutsko, *Between Heaven and Earth*, 95–96n. 62.

temple.[54] The irony was that God's absence was a powerful argument for his presence and his power, for he was acting to purge the nation of false worship. Conversely, the presence of the idols in the house of the LORD became a clear indication of their absence or impotence.[55]

Ezekiel also held out the promise of the new covenant for the people. As the Creator and Sustainer of Israel, Yahweh is infinitely superior to those idols that had to be created and carried by their devotees (cf. Isa. 46:1–2). So when the promised restoration comes, God will regather his people to their land, remove their sins, give them a new heart, and put his Spirit in them (Ezek. 36:26–27). He will cause them to be fruitful and multiply (v. 11) and the crops and the trees to produce in abundance (v. 30). He will cause all the waste places to be rebuilt (vv. 33–34) so that people will say, "This land that was laid waste has become like the garden of Eden" (v. 35a). No longer will the people be dwelling in captivity by the Tigris and Euphrates rivers, but in their land, in Jerusalem, where God's provision of living water will supply their needs. God will prepare the landscape for their return to the worship and service of him, just as he had prepared the original setting in Paradise.[56] The new covenant, of course, was inaugurated by Jesus in the Upper Room.

But Ezekiel continues to draw upon the motifs of Creation in his description of Israel's renewal (Ezek. 37:1–14). God will regather them (the dry bones) from the nations and will "set them" in their land (Ezek. 37:14; Gen. 2:8); then he will breathe his breath (*rûaḵh*) into them so that they may live (cf. Gen. 2:7, 15).[57] In other words, the nation will be physically regathered to the land and then subsequently receive God's Spirit to bring them to spiritual life. Ultimately, God's plan is to re-create the people as pure worshippers. Then the glory of the LORD will be present in a new and far more glorious sanctuary (Ezek. 40–48).

Simply restoring the people to old Jerusalem and life in a devastated land would not satisfy the promises of the new covenant—dramatic changes had to accompany the spiritual renewal of the people of God on

---

54. See also Levenson, *Theology of the Program of Restoration of Ezekiel 40–48*, 38.

55. Klutsko, *Between Heaven and Earth*, 100.

56. Ibid., 130–31.

57. Jeremiah 10:14 notes that there is no spirit in idols. For a discussion of Isaiah 6:9–13 as a polemic against idols, see Beale, "Isaiah VI 9–13," 257–78.

every hand.[58] One of the motifs that the prophets develop in discussing the new creation is that of Zion as the source of flowing water.[59] Isaiah 35:5–7 portrays salvation as water that is both cleansing and life giving. Ezekiel, who earlier alluded to the garden of God and the holy mountain (Ezek. 28:1–19), sees the river flowing from Zion (47:7–12). And to reinforce the allusion to Creation, the prophet tells how the fresh water will swarm with fish and living creatures.[60]

But it will not simply be Paradise restored; it will be the beginning of a new creation, far more glorious and perfectly righteous—and eternal.

## Conclusion

The LORD God will have no rivals for the worship and service of his people and will permit no images to be made of himself or any of his creatures for the purpose of worship.[61] Any attempt to include the perverse practices of the world and its false religions in the worship of God will corrupt the worship and the morals of the participants and will incur the judgment of God. The reason for such exclusivity is that the man-made religions of the world, with all their pagan practices, represent a vast and unclean spirit world that is in antagonism and rebellion to God. Idolatry in any form is the ungrateful rejection of the true God to follow the ways of the deceiver and destroyer, that old Serpent.

The history of Israel's religion is tragic and tedious in its constant theme of defection to idolatry. But the message of the prophets was clear: there would be no true worship as long as idols were present to compete for the people's devotion, and if idols were present there would be no worship in the house of the LORD at all.

After the return from the Exile, idolatry never again dominated the religion of the Jews. It was still a threat, though, due to the presence of

---

58. See Weinfeld, "The Design and Theme of Ezekiel's Program of Restoration," 181–208.
59. For a full development see Kwon, "The Zion Traditions and the Kingdom of God," 84–99.
60. Kwon interprets Ezekiel's intention to be that the temple was not a self-contained holy place but a place allowing life and healing to flow out to the land (ibid., 97).
61. For centuries Christians have disputed the meaning and use of sacred objects. Many reject them outright as idols; and others explain them as important parts of worship. For some background, see Limouris, *Icons: Windows in Eternity*; and for the history of the veneration of the cross, see Regan, "Veneration of the Cross," 2–12.

foreign powers in the lands of Persia, Greece, and Rome. But now the Jews would suffer persecution for their opposition to pagan culture. The same was true of the early church. Idolatry was not present in the Jewish church; but when the church spread to the pagan lands, it became an issue that had to be addressed.[62] The apostles emphasized without any equivocation that fellowship with the Lord Jesus Christ excludes any communion with idols or demon powers (2 Cor. 6). Not only did the church reject pagan idols, but it also refused to worship the emperor as a god, a refusal that cost many their lives.

Amazingly, an urge to embrace the religious impulses of the ancient polytheistic societies has resurfaced today, as if that were some kind of progress in religious thought toward a more magnanimous pluralism.[63] As in the days of the prophets, those who hold to the authority of the Word of the LORD in such matters are seen as outdated and narrow-minded, and sometimes even branded as "un-Christian." For those who would corrupt Christian worship by re-imaging God (making a god in their image), or by reintroducing ancient deities like the Queen of Heaven, or by redefining doctrines to make them more acceptable to other religions, the way has been prepared by decades of liberal theology that has discredited and marginalized the written Word of God, the Holy Scriptures. Once this was done, it was easy for people to address the clear-cut commands of God in the familiar words of the deceiver, "Did God really say?"

By setting aside the revealed faith in favor of a man-made religion (that is in fact ancient paganism reborn), many false teachers have made it easy for the morality of the people to deteriorate in the name of tolerance and inclusivity so that what the Bible labels as sin is no longer sin and may actually receive the approval and blessing of churches. Of course forgiveness and redemption cease to matter if sin no longer exists. What has happened is that the sovereignty of the holy LORD God has been set aside, and that has always been the first step to false worship and pagan idolatry.

---

62. The warning appears in the letter to the church of Thyatira, using the name Jezebel for the idolatry and immorality that will ruin the witness of the church (Rev. 2:20–25).
63. Keel, *God, Goddesses, and Images of God in Ancient Israel,* suggests that the original popular religion of Israel was a rich polytheism and that the reformers suppressed the images and ideas to form a rigid monotheism in the nation out of their own communities (391, 408–9).

All of this is possible because of the ignorance of the people: they do not know the Scriptures, doctrine, or the history of the paganization of the faith. And that ignorance prevails even in congregations that have become satisfied with their own experiential forms of worship. A great conflict lies ahead, a challenge over the historic faith from very liberal groups within Christendom and intolerant non-Christian religious groups without. Too many people have turned a blind eye to it all, choosing to believe unity (i.e., no dissension) is more important than truth. Believers must know the revelation of the God of glory thoroughly and safeguard the proper forms of worship and spiritual service that he has ordained.

# CHAPTER 20

# The Prophetic Rebuke *of* Hypocritical Worship

THE PROPHETIC DENUNCIATION of idolatry was important because of the serious consequences of rejecting the sovereign God to embrace idolatry. It was not merely a sanctuary matter but affected every aspect of society. If there were no sovereign God, then there was no absolute law to obey. The breakdown of morality and ethics and the neglect of social justice, Oswalt explains, is the result of refusing to entrust oneself to the sovereign, loving, and just God.[1] He adds that when people believe that the cosmic order is uninterested in human welfare and that those who succeed are those who know how to capture these forces for their own purposes (which is the underlying attitude of idolatry), the more helpless and vulnerable in society are crushed.

In ancient Israel the people were called to worship and serve the sovereign, holy God. True worship is not simply a celebration of God's provision of atonement but a celebration of being in covenant with the Lord—and being in covenant carries responsibilities. Every *memorial* act in worship was a reminder to remain faithful to God, promote justice in the land, and show mercy to those in need.

But when Israel began to worship like pagans, they offered sacrifices to appease and manipulate God, or other gods, hoping by the operation of sympathetic magic to prosper in their lives. The whole orientation of pagan worship was for personal gain, not to serve the Lord; and without submission to the sovereign God at the core of their worship, there was no compelling reason to keep the laws. Thus, disobedience to the Word of God results from weak and corrupted worship.

---

1. Oswalt, *Isaiah, Chapters 1–39*, 106.

This is a growing problem in the church today. It is not that the church is idolatrous (for the most part), but it has been influenced by the attitudes and practices of the prevailing culture. With little or no emphasis on the sovereignty of God as Creator and Lord, or on the authority of his Word, worship is weakened and covenant responsibilities are ignored. At the same time the influence of the world is manifested in a number of ways: people are more interested in their own personal success than in service to others and more desirous of receiving a blessing than being a blessing; they want some experience but show little interest in spiritual growth; they gravitate to entertainment and leisure and are indifferent to the needs of people; and they are excited about being healed but do not comprehend what it means to count it joy that they suffer so that they can minister to others who are suffering. These may seem like little things to some, merely different emphases, but they reflect a drift from the biblical call for submission and service, dedication and obedience.

A self-serving form of religion is not far from the spirit of idolatry, for idolatry has always been a selfish form of religion.[2] In idolatry the devotee always seeks to manipulate the deity for personal advantage; it puts the control in the will of the idolater. But in the true, historic faith, God is sovereign; he will not be manipulated by gifts and ritual, and he demands that his people obey his commands.

Disobeying the commandments of God is not always tied to idolatry, as everyone would acknowledge. People who claim to be worshippers of the Lord also can be guilty of sins against their neighbors, indifference to those in need, and continuing social injustice at large. But such acts do have this in common with idolatry: they deny God his sovereign authority and make a mockery of worship.

## Prophetic Denunciations of Sins

### The Rebuke of Amos: Injustice and Immorality

From Amos we gain a glimpse of life in Israel just before it was destroyed in 722 B.C. (Amos 2:6–8).[3] Although Amos's day was a time of

---

2. When people ignore the universal moral order, they first overestimate their own importance and fail to keep their appointed place in the world, seeking wealth and power instead; and second, they fail to see where their trust and confidence should be, and so they rely on resources other than God (Barton, "Ethics in Isaiah of Jerusalem," 88).

3. See additionally Bentzen, "The Ritual Background of Amos i 2–ii 16," 85–99.

affluence, it was also a time of spiritual defection and social injustice. The wealthy abused the poor and deprived them of their rights, all for personal gain (v. 6)—they would take advantage of the poor in any way. In fact, verse 7 says that "they trample on the heads of the poor" (cf. Isa. 3:15; Prov. 22:22) and, literally, "pervert the course *(dérek)* [of justice]" (see Prov. 17:23), bullying and oppressing the poor and thus depriving them of the privileges and prerogatives to which they were entitled.[4] Then Amos says, "Father and son use the same girl and so profane my holy name" (Amos 2:7), a reference to the lack of moral conduct in the land. The wording suggests that the women were defenseless and exploited. Finally, in verse 8, Amos says, "They lie down beside every altar on garments taken in pledge.[5] In the house of their god they drink wine taken as fines." So the wealthy creditors violated the law that was given to protect the poor, and even at the altar they remained unmoved by their consciences. How reprehensible!

True worship will lead people to acknowledge that God must be honored through the way the poor are treated (Prov. 14:31; 17:5). If the poor are ignored, the worship will be hypocritical! What this means is that those who are truly righteous will seek every opportunity to protect the oppressed and the underprivileged, even if they are technically guilty, recognizing that it is God who has put the opportunity before them.[6]

## The Exhortation of Isaiah: Care for the Needy and Oppressed

Isaiah was concerned with the holiness of the people who claim to worship a holy God. The way the book begins sets the tone for the messages to follow: the people were completely sinful, and therefore their worship was hypocritical. It must have come as quite a shock to the leaders and the people of Judah when the prophet referred to them as rulers of Sodom and Gomorrah. After all, they had comforted themselves with the thought that they were the people of God and that their worship in the temple

---

4. Paul, *Amos,* 81.
5. The law prohibited the seizing of garments to cover unpaid debts (Exod. 22:25–26)— it was like taking the shirt off the back of a poor man to cover a debt.
6. Willimon suggests that rather than trying to convince people that they are really miserable and that Christ is "the answer," we should take a positive approach by urging them to use their gifts in gratitude and service *(The Gospel for the Person Who Has Everything;* see further, Hoffman and J. R. Walton, *Sacred Sound and Social Change).*

secured for them divine approval. But the word from God was that he hated everything about their worship because they were not right with him. The need was clear: "Wash and make yourselves clean. Take your evil deeds out of my sight! Stop doing wrong, learn to do right! Seek justice, encourage the oppressed. Defend the cause of the fatherless, plead the case of the widow" (Isa. 1:16–17). There could be no acceptance of their worship as long as they were failing in these matters. To care for the oppressed, the widow, the orphan, or the foreigner in the land is an integral part of righteousness, for such care is in the heart of God. Since he cares for them and champions their cause, how could his people, who claim to be in communion with him, ignore such needs? As long as these things are left out of a worshipping community's mission, their worship is not valid.

Other oracles in the book condemn people for social injustice and personal indulgences in the same manner that Amos did.[7] Isaiah 29:17–21 focuses on the miscarriage of justice in court. People were laying traps for those seeking justice, verbal traps designed to put them down with empty lies; they used false testimony to make the innocent appear guilty; and if there were those who sought to champion the cause of the oppressed, these shrewd culprits were ready to trip them up with legal niceties (cf. Amos 5:12). They even used empty platitudes to confuse the issue so that the person who was in the right did not get his day in court.

Legal manipulation like this is still very much alive and still depriving people of justice. Those in power have the means of manipulating legal matters and business arrangements and even nullifying the efforts of others who seek to champion justice.[8] But if they do these things and show up for services, their worship is the kind of worship God hates.

## The Charge of Hosea: Unfaithfulness

Hosea's prophecies cut right to the heart of the matter and do not mince words: Israel was an adulterous nation. The people were unfaithful to God and therefore unjust to one another. How corrupt they had become—they had no faithfulness and no love (Hos. 4:1), only cursing, lying, murder,

---

7. The book of Isaiah also condemns people for lives of excessive self-indulgence and impious behavior: they mocked God (5:21; 10:5–15), delighted in prestige (22:15–19), sought excessive luxury and personal adornment (3:16–4:1; 22:15–19; 32:9–14), were guilty of drunkenness (5:11–17, 22; 28:1–14), and turned to mediums instead of trusting God (8:19–22).

8. Wildberger, *Isaiah 28–39*, 114.

stealing, and adultery (v. 2); in fact, there were so many violent crimes that one murder simply flowed into another. Hosea says that mutual charges and accusations could not remedy their problems, for it would just be one lawsuit after another (v. 4). Rather, he suggests that they bring the charges against the priests, for they were the ones to blame for the problem (vv. 5–11). Such was the shameless depth to which the nation had fallen. But it is no wonder that the people lived this way. By following after Baal, they would live on the same base level that the Canaanites and their gods did.

## The Condemnation of Ezekiel: Self-Indulgence and Perversion

When Ezekiel explained to the exiles from Judah why their temple was destroyed and they were exiled, he included the fact that their sins were as great as those of Sodom and Samaria (Ezek. 16:47–52). What a revolting thought that must have been to them—the epitome of perversion! Sodom was arrogant, overfed, and unconcerned with the needs of others; her people were filled with pride and self-exaltation; their abundant materialism and luxury brought apathy and disdain for the poor on the one hand, and on the other hand fostered all kinds of sexual perversion. Eichrodt describes their condition as "the godless self-security of a rich worldly city" with an "unsympathizing attitude to those menaced by hunger and want."[9] The people of Judah had a self-righteous contempt for the Sodomites, but in every way they were worse, because to have the revelation of the LORD and reject it is the greater sin (cf. Jer. 23:14; cf. Jesus' comparison of Capernaum with Sodom [Matt. 11:23–24]).

What is amazing about all these prophetic oracles is that the people to whom they were delivered had assumed that because they worshipped in the house of the LORD and claimed to be God's people, they had his approval. For those who were guilty of hypocritical worship, the preaching of the prophets seemed to them more of a nuisance than something to be heeded. Jeremiah preached for years that the LORD was going to judge the nation, but as long as the people lived comfortably and had their routine of worship, his message was ridiculed (Jer. 20:6–9)—until the sad day he sat on the ruins of the once holy city and wept.[10] When all was said and

---

9. Eichrodt, *Ezekiel*, 215.
10. For a discussion of the literary form of the material as classic city laments, see Dobbs-Allsopp, *Lamentations*.

done, God had proved to be faithful to fulfill his word of judgment. The only good news was that God also would be faithful to his promise of redemption (Lam. 3:23).

There could be no mistaking the message of the prophets. Righteousness attends worship. Worship that pleases God is the worship of the righteous, and that worship produces a greater righteousness. This was not to be limited to personal avoidance of sin. For their worship to be valid they were to care for the widow and the orphan, relieve the oppressed and persecuted, seek justice in the courts for the poor and the needy, and see to it that the underprivileged of society as well as the foreigner in their midst share in God's bounty.

As we read these prophetic rebukes, it becomes painfully clear that they also fit our society to the letter. The "Christianized" modern, affluent societies have the personal and physical resources to meet the needs in society, and the churches have the responsibility to inspire this by leading the way. But they have failed to do so. In a crisis they rise to the occasion, but throughout the year they ignore the needs all around them. They are more concerned with preserving their way of life than fulfilling their obligations as members of the covenant. Yet, they expect their prayers to be heard and their hymns to strike the same pleasing notes in heaven as those of the angelic choirs.

## Rejection of Hypocritical Worship

Scripture is clear: God does not accept hypocritical worship. He hates it! Ritual acts of worship, no matter how beautiful and correct in form, can never conceal unconfessed sin. Of the many passages that speak to this issue, the following are the most powerful.

### Prophetic Preaching

#### Amos

Amos was particularly repulsed by the worship of sinful people. With biting sarcasm he called them to go to Bethel to continue their corrupt worship (Amos 4:4–5). The people thought that greater prosperity would come from increasing the offerings. But the more numerous the offerings were, the greater their transgressions were. Hypocritical worship is not merely worthless; it is a sin. Amos's message was that they had ritual without righteousness, and their only course of action was to return to the LORD and follow righteousness, especially in the courts (5:14–15). But because they had refused, all that was left was for them to prepare to meet their God (4:12).[11]

The people were satisfied with their form of worship, but if they had been truly seeking God in it, their way of life would have been different. Because of their hypocrisy, God declared that he hated their religious feasts and assemblies, rejected their offerings, and refused to listen to the noise of their music (5:21–23).

What were the sins that kept their worship from being pleasing to God? Amos highlights taking advantage of the poor (2:6), oppressing the poor and the needy (4:1), extortion of the poor (5:11), taking bribes to pervert justice for the poor in the gates (i.e., the courts [5:12]), immorality (2:7), abuse of rights (2:8), desecration of vows and obstruction of prophets (2:11–12), and violence and robbery (3:10). Because they had destroyed righteousness in every aspect of life, Amos's cry was all-encompassing: "Let justice roll on like a river, righteousness like a never-failing stream!" (5:24).

God desired pure worship. But because none was taking place in Bethel, Amos declared that the altar would crumble and the people would be judged (9:1).

### Isaiah

A generation or so later, Isaiah picked up the same theme, the denunciation of hypocritical worship by the people of Judah (Isa. 1:11–15).[12] Isaiah 1 appears to be an oracle delivered at a general convocation in a time of crisis, when people had rushed to the sanctuary to pray. They did not expect the prophetic response they received. The words are harsh, to say the least. God was fed up with their worthless worship and took no delight in their sacrifices. He did not want them in his courts, could not endure their hypocritical worship, hated their appointed feasts, and refused to listen to their prayers—all because their hands were full of blood. People cannot live self-indulgent and sinful lives and then in a crisis stampede into God's courts with their frantic prayers and manipulative sacrifices. God does not respond to that kind of worship.

---

11. Matthews, "Theophanies Cultic and Cosmic," 307–18.
12. For an analysis of the oracle with parallels to the Deuteronomic material, see Rignell, "Isaiah Chapter 1," 140–58.

What exactly were the sins that made their worship so contemptible? In addition to those indicated in Isaiah's instructions to care for the poor and needy, we now have a more direct enumeration: the faithful city of Jerusalem, once full of justice and righteousness, was now full of assassins and rebellious princes who were companions of thieves, easily bribed, and unwilling to defend the fatherless or hear the case of the widow (1:21–23).[13] Religion served these people as a means of sanctioning their self-indulgent lives, rather than a means of purifying them. God's demand was that they fulfill the true purpose of sacrificial worship, that is, receive the LORD's provision of forgiveness by genuine repentance, and then live out the righteousness of God in their daily lives.

### Jeremiah

A century later Jeremiah also stressed that obedience was essential if sacrificial worship was to be acceptable. He reminded the people that when the LORD brought their ancestors out of Egypt, he commanded them to obey before he instructed them in the ritual (Jer. 7:21–23; cf. Exod. 19:5–6). Jeremiah was not denying the validity of religious ritual; he was reminding the people that obedience had to come first.

What acts of disobedience did Jeremiah single out as the cause for the destruction of the temple and the doom of the nation? Jeremiah was to stand in the gate and declare them to all who came to worship (Jer. 7:2–11): they had failed to execute justice; they had oppressed the stranger, the widow, and the orphan; shed innocent blood; stolen, murdered, committed adultery, and sworn falsely; and worshipped other gods. The LORD asked through Jeremiah if the people would do all these things "and then come and stand before me in this house, which bears my Name, and say, 'We are safe'—safe to do all these detestable things? Has this house, which bears my Name, become a den of robbers to you? But I have been watching! declares the LORD" (vv. 10–11).

### Ezekiel

In the days of Ezekiel, the message was the same: even though there was a whole array of worship activities underway in the temple, the sins of the priests and the people had made them ineffectual (Ezek. 22). Those

---

13. This theme is repeated in James 1:27 for the church. See also Isaiah 10:1–2.

sins included treating parents with contempt, oppressing the stranger, mistreating the widow and the orphan (v. 7), despising holy things and Sabbaths (v. 8), slandering to cause bloodshed (v. 9), committing adultery and incest (vv. 10–11), as well as prompting bribery, extortion, and usury (v. 12). Once again the prevailing sins were social injustices borne by a spirit of self-gratification and characterized by an indifference to the needs of others. Not only did this nullify worship, but it also brought God's judgment on the nation.

For a sinful people there is only one course of action—repentance. David had stated that a broken heart was the sacrifice to bring to God first (Ps. 51:17). Isaiah called for people to demonstrate their repentance by changing their ways (Isa. 1:16–18). Joel called for the people to blow the trumpet and call a sacred assembly, to fast, and to pray that the LORD would spare them (Joel 2:15–17). Individual sin required contrition and confession; national sin called for a congregational fast and collective repentance, not just to make the people fit for worship—not now—but to avert national disaster.

## Instructions in the Psalms

Some of the prophetic rebukes and exhortations were preserved in psalms so as to become a regular and poignant part of the official hymns and prayers. This was an effective way of reminding people that worship had to be accompanied by faithfulness.

For example, David acknowledged that God did not desire sacrifices and offerings (Ps. 40:6). Obviously, this statement is not a repudiation of sacrificial worship since God had legislated it. The passage is looking at the proper spirit of the worshipper, without which the sacrifice would be futile. God wants a willing heart of obedience rather than a gift (vv. 6–9). God desires worshippers who surrender themselves to him and commit themselves to a life of obedience and service. Without the life of the worshipper, the act of worship is worthless.

This dedication to obedience always took priority over ritual. Samuel had rebuked Saul for trying to cover his disobedience with sacrifice, declaring for all time that "to obey is better than sacrifice" (1 Sam. 15:22–23a). God desires a submissive will that will be obedient; when he has that, he has a true worshipper.

In Psalm 50 Asaph presented God's evaluation of the worship of his day, and sadly of ours as well. The first six verses envision a court scene with God as Judge and the covenant people as defendants. He was raising the question, What if the Lord came and examined our worship today? There follows two indictments.

The first charge is worshipping for the wrong reasons, that is, going through the forms but without the proper spirit. Israel was performing the ritual perfectly, so there was no criticism of that. But they did it for the wrong reason. They had come to think that God was dependent on them and their sacrifices, as in the gods of the pagan world. But God did not need them. They were to bring sacrifices to God because they needed him. The ritual without the proper meaning is empty formalism.

The corrective? Asaph called for them to offer God "the sacrifice of praise" (Ps. 50:14–15). This was the heart of true worship, bringing to God a peace offering and declaring publicly how God had met their needs and then sharing the common meal. If they praised God this way, then their sacrifices would be offered for the proper reasons—to express their dependence on God and their gratitude for his deliverance. The solution for empty formalism or misguided ritual is still genuine praise, for this assumes that the worshipper is completely dependent on God.

The second charge concerns hypocrites in the congregation who profess the faith and say all the appropriate words of the covenant but whose lives give the lie to their words of worship.[14] Their sins were subtle—they consented with a thief, they partook with adulterers, and they slandered their brother. These sins, while not appearing to be blatant violations of the code, represented a tolerance for sin that leads to participation in it. Here too the psalmist gives advice: they must consider their ways and begin living as true worshippers. Genuine praise is also the solution for hypocrisy, for it represents a heart of obedient trust in the LORD.

People therefore must worship the Lord with the proper spirit and not an empty form or ritual; and they must worship him in obedience and not in hypocrisy (cf. John 4:24).

From David's great confession of sin, we learn that disobedience destroys any possibility of performing meaningful worship or service. Psalm 51 is essentially a theological reflection on why people must find

---

14. There is probably a sequence here: if the worship becomes a meaningless ritual, then disobedience will follow. If the worshippers do not love the LORD as they should, then they will not love other people righteously.

forgiveness if they are going to worship or serve the Lord. The sinful and still unforgiven worshipper is not free to teach other sinners God's ways, since he has not fully experienced them; he is not free to praise the LORD or join the singing in the sanctuary, since he has no reason to praise if he is not yet forgiven; and he is not free to sacrifice peace offerings to the LORD in the Holy Place, since he is not at peace with God (vv. 13–19). In fact, in Israel such a person was not even welcome in the sanctuary. His only recourse was to pray for forgiveness and cleansing, because God did not want his sacrifices or praises until he was forgiven. David acknowledged that "the sacrifices of [appropriate for] God are a broken spirit; a broken and contrite heart, O God, you will not despise" (v. 17).[15]

Unforgiven sin renders worship impossible. Of course, an individual can perform the ritual and say the words in a sinful condition, as Israel's history and our own experience shows, but it is not acceptable to God. The beginning point of worship for a sinful believer is a broken heart. In this the significance of sacrifice is plainly seen: the worshipper is the sacrifice! It is the only broken and damaged sacrifice that God will accept. The one who comes to God in deep contrition[16] and with sincere dedication is the kind of worshipper God delights in.

---

15. The expression "you will not despise" is an understatement. It means that God will joyfully receive the penitent worshipper. But David states it this way because the opposite is also true, that God will despise worship from an unrepentant sinner.
16. The word *contrition* describes the spiritual condition of one whose self-will and rebellious attitude has been broken. The Hebrew word behind it means "crushed."

# Conclusion *for* Part 6

THERE ARE SEVERAL IMPORTANT points to be made in the light of these prophetic messages. First, true worship is an expression of the believer's dependence on the Lord and submission to his will. Second, sinful people must find forgiveness and restoration before they can expect God to accept their worship. Third, unrepented sin in the would-be "worshipper" nullifies the worship and brings divine discipline. Fourth, worldliness—living according to the priorities and practices of the pagan world system—denies everything that worship is designed to do; it is the opposite of the life of holiness, purity, and love that worship inspires.

The clear point is that people cannot worship and give God his proper glory if they refuse to do his will. They have forgotten that worship is in part a covenant renewal ceremony. When the Israelites made the sacrifices, their dedication offering was to include a memorial given to the LORD. Through it they were not simply reminding God of his promises to them; they were reminded of their covenant duties as well. Those duties were to ensure righteousness, justice, mercy, and love. Such worship honors God because it seeks to extend the blessings of his presence among his people to the world at large.

The solution to hypocritical, formalistic ritual is not simply to get rid of the forms and the ritual. Some have tried that, only to find that groups with no ritual at all can be guilty of the same things. The solution lies in spiritual reform: contrition, repentance, confession, spiritual growth, and genuine praise. Only when faith is operating in this way will there be the proper spirit in worship, no matter what forms are being used; and only when genuine faith is operating will the worshippers be striving to live righteously. But as long as the poor and the needy, the widows and the orphans, or the foreigners in the land are abandoned, as long as religion serves to secure the comfortable lifestyle we desire, as long as money, power, and lust continue as the gods we serve, then there can be no hope that God is pleased with our worship, no matter how well we sing or how much we give. Worship must transform us into the image of Jesus Christ.

# PART 7

# WORSHIP TRANSFORMED

*The New Setting of Worship and the New Covenant*

# Introduction

THE DISARRAY AT THE TIME OF the Captivity created new challenges for the people of God. The Holy City was destroyed, the temple was reduced to rubble, and many people were carried off to a completely idolatrous country. The way back seemed hopeless, but God promised that he would restore them and their worship in Jerusalem. Out of this judgment God would begin a new work, a new covenant, and eventually a new creation. Out of the darkness of the chaos and confusion (Isa. 8:22), a light would shine and people who walked in darkness would see it (9:1–2). This light would be the Messiah, Immanuel, "God with us" (7:14; 9:6–7). The worshipper's desire to see God would now be realized in a most unexpected way, for God's plan to be with his people was about to come to a dramatic reality in the Incarnation.

In view of the fact that the desire of the idolatrous people had been to have a god like them, in their image—hands and feet and eyes and ears, just as the pagan religions had—one would have thought that when the divine Son of God became flesh that they would have responded enthusiastically. After all, Jesus had hands and feet, he had eyes and ears and lips. He was in so many ways like them. But no, they nailed those hands and feet to a cross, thinking that they could silence those lips with death. Why? Because he did not dance to their tune but made demands on their lives (Matt. 11:16–19). In the spirit of idolatry, the god is made to serve the whims and will of the people. Jesus did not do that.

In what must remain a mystery of the faith, God used even their rejection of the Messiah as the turning point of worship. They may have crucified Jesus by their wickedness, but it was also the eternal plan of God (Acts 2:23). By his death Jesus fulfilled the old provisions of atonement through sacrifice—he was the scapegoat, the sin offering, the ram caught in the thicket, and the Passover Lamb; and by his blood we have been set free from sin and death. Because Christ fulfilled the ritual of the law, because he is the Redeemer, and because he is the incarnate God dwelling among his people, all worship now must be in him. Everything that God had revealed about his plan of salvation in the Old Testament came to reality in Christ, and everything that God instructed about worship in the Old Testament was brought to complete clarity in the Incarnation. The patterns and principles of worship would not be done away with; rather, they would now be transformed by the full revelation in the Son (Heb. 1:2).

After the Jews returned from the Exile, they anticipated a glorious new beginning based on the promises of God. But it soon became obvious that the way back would not be easy. The promises of the new covenant seemed to lag seriously, even though the people were back in their land to rebuild the temple. The attempts to restore the old worship, that is, patching it up with new patches on old cloth (Luke 5:36), only made people realize that they could not go back and recapture the glory. The way had to be forward. Thus, they developed new structures, new laws, and new patterns of worship that would hasten the transformation, but they missed the sign for the new direction that God was going to open with the coming of the divine Lord, the Messiah, to his temple.

# CHAPTER 21

# The Need *for* Transformation

## Worship After the Destruction of the Temple

Because the people did not listen to the warnings of the prophets but persisted in their idolatrous and hypocritical activities—not for a few years but for a few centuries—the judgment of God finally came. For those taken into captivity there would be no pilgrimages to the festivals, none of the songs of Zion, and no reason to rejoice in the salvation of the LORD (cf. Ps. 137:1–6). For most of them it seemed like God's plan for Israel was finished: God apparently had abandoned them to a ruthless people whose gods were triumphant, and their God was unable or unwilling to deliver them (see Isa. 40:27; 50:1–3). Was there to be no more worship of the LORD?

But in the nation's darkest hours, the prophets spoke of a new beginning: the LORD would not leave the Israelites scattered among the nations but would regather them to their land, enable them to rebuild the temple, and reconsecrate them as a priestly people. It would be a new covenant that the LORD would make, not unlike the old, but better in all its provisions. It would not only provide for their restoration to the land and their spiritual renewal as the people of God, but it would also guarantee the reign of their King, the Messiah, or "anointed one," over a kingdom or righteousness and peace in a whole new creation (see primarily Isa. 54; Jer. 31; Ezek. 36). Those who waited on the LORD received this word with gladness and looked for the day of deliverance when the LORD would again say, "You are my people," and they would say "You are my God" (Hos. 2:16–23). Yes, after the restoration they could expect great changes to their worship. But until then, their worship was in ruins.

## Worship Among the Ruins

Even though the war left the temple in ruins, the site remained a holy place, and people continued to offer sacrifices there (Jer. 41:5). But because the center of their worship was in shambles and their leaders exiled (cf. Isa. 57:3–13; Ezek. 33:24–29), it is not surprising that their worship took on a decided note of lamentation and mourning. There had been laments offered before in the sanctuary (Jer. 41:4–6), but now a number of passages in Jeremiah were structured as liturgies of lamentation over the national devastation. And we read that by the time Zechariah returned, official lamentation in the worship had been going on in the fifth month ever since the destruction (Zech. 7:3–5). Hillers suggests that the poems in Lamentations may have been used almost immediately in public mourning in Jerusalem:[1] both the poetic forms and their organization fit the use of laments for "ritual" in the broad sense, that is, a poem is an abstraction from experience that invites contemplation, repetition, and the participation of others. But also in the narrower sense the poems are eminently suited for ritual in that they contain elements common in religious rites, such as petition, lament, confession, and imprecation, and draw on ancient native traditions of composition for common worship, such as the psalms of lament.[2]

What a contrast this was to the great celebrations that had filled the Holy Place before. If the people had lamented over their sins before the judgment (Joel 2:12–17), they would still have been rejoicing.

## Worship in the Exile

During the last chaotic days of Judah, many people had fled to Egypt (cf. Jer. 42), some just inside the border (43:7) but others much farther into Egypt (44:1).[3] The settlement on the northern coast grew into one of the major centers of Judaism (later Alexandria), but we do not know much of their immediate practices. Those who settled at the first cataract of the Nile (called Elephantine) became syncretistic in their religious practices.[4]

---

1. Later, some of Lamentations was used by the church in the worship of Holy Week.
2. Hillers, *Lamentations,* 6.
3. The Exile lasted fifty years, from 586, when the temple was destroyed, to the decree to return in 536 B.C. However, the full Exile was seventy years, counting from the first exile in 605 B.C.
4. Merrill, *Kingdom of Priests,* 486–87.

The Jews who were deported to Babylon[5] were allowed to live and assemble as they wished, but for the first time in their national existence their worship had to be non-sacrificial. There was no temple, no functioning priesthood, and no festival. Their captors even taunted them over this (cf. Ps. 137:3; Isa. 52:5). The believers had to rely on their holy books and traditions for their identity, so the study of Scripture and prayer became the focus of their gatherings.

The faithful held fast to the Torah (Dan. 1), refused to bow to pagan images (Dan. 3), and prayed openly to the LORD (Dan. 6). People gathered in the house of the prophet to hear the word of the LORD, although they often came just to hear a pleasing speaker (Ezek. 33:30–32). Eventually, teaching and preserving the teachings no longer remained the prerogatives of the priests. Scribes became active in copying, codifying, and explaining Holy Scriptures and so were seen to stand in the tradition of the prophets.

Out of the Exile there emerged a worshipping community that held more strictly to the law and the traditions than before. For them Sabbath observance became a crucial test for the faith (Jer. 17;19–27; Ezek. 20:12). Circumcision was adhered to carefully as the sign of their covenant, and their standards of clean and unclean foods were maintained in spite of being at odds with the diet of the East (Ezek. 4:12–15; 22:26; 44; Dan. 1).

So the devout came away from the Exile with something positive—a greater emphasis on the teaching and study of the Word of the LORD, more involvement of the people in the prayers and blessings, and a renewed appreciation of the importance of community. Never again would the nation be idolatrous as before; on the contrary, they immersed themselves in the texts and became rigidly legalistic.[6]

## Worship in the Restoration

### The Edict of Restoration

In the year 536 B.C. Cyrus allowed the Jews to return to their land and rebuild their temple with money from the royal treasury (Ezra 1:2–4;

---

5. The number was not large, 4,600 men (Jer. 52:28–30) plus the women and children.
6. Albertz suggests that the Torah scholars of the third century B.C. saw no possibility of remedying the social disorders they faced and so immersed themselves in the Torah (*A History of Israelite Religion in the Old Testament Period,* 563). The same thing happened from time to time in the history of the church. Out of such times great works were often produced.

6:3–5).[7] For many Jews this seemed to be the beginning of the fulfillment of the new covenant. As they returned they were filled with joy over what the LORD had done (Ps. 126:1–3) and that this was the day of deliverance that the LORD had made (Ps. 118:22–24). So grateful were they that when they arrived in the land they gave freewill offerings toward the rebuilding of the temple before settling into their own towns (Ezra 2:68–70).

## The Restoration of Worship

Under Zerubbabel the temple was to be rebuilt. But first the altar was built and worship was restored (Ezra 3:1–6). In the seventh month, the people came together to celebrate the Feast of Tabernacles. The priests offered sacrifices according to the law, especially for the requirements of the festival. From this beginning, then, sacrificial worship was reinstated for the regular worship as well as for appointed feasts. This they began to do even before the foundations had been laid.

When the laying of the temple foundation actually began about 534 B.C., the priests and Levitical singers and musicians stood by to praise and thank God by saying, "He is good; his love to Israel endures forever" (Ezra 3:10–11). There followed a great shout of praise from all the people, because the foundation had been laid. Older members who recalled the former temple now wept aloud since the new foundation was a far cry from the glorious place that Solomon had built (v. 12). Ezra says that no one could distinguish the sounds of the shouting for joy from the weeping (v. 13).

After about twenty years the temple was completed (March, 515 B.C.) with the help of the exhortations of Haggai[8] and Zechariah (Ezra 6:13–15).[9] The dedication services included the sacrificing of one hundred bulls, two hundred rams, four hundred lambs, and for a sin offering for all Israel, twelve male goats (v. 17). God had restored temple worship after almost a century of waste and void, and the people rejoiced in it, although, in view of the prophetic vision of a glorious city made with gold

---

7. The prayer of Daniel (chap. 9) was certainly instrumental (see Lacocque, "The Liturgical Prayer of Daniel 9," 119–42; and B. W. Jones, "The Prayer of Daniel 9," 488–93).

8. See E. M. Meyers, "The Use of *Tora* in Haggai 2:11," 69–76. See also Verhoef, *The Books of Haggai and Malachi.*

9. Baynes, "Zerubbabel's Rebuilding of the Temple," 154–60.

and precious stones (Isa. 54:11–12), they realized that this was not yet the fulfillment of the promise.

Then almost immediately the exiles celebrated the Feast of Passover (Ezra 6:19–22) as a sign that the return was a second exodus. The priests and Levites had purified themselves, and the Israelites "ate together with all who had separated themselves from the filth of the nations of the land in order to seek the LORD God of Israel" (v. 21 NKJV). It was confirmation to them that they were the people of God and that they were on the verge of receiving the promised golden era.

## Spiritual Direction for a New Beginning

### Ezra and the Exposition of Scripture

It was a full generation later that Ezra came to Jerusalem (458 B.C.; Ezra 7:8). He was a descendant of Aaron through Phinehas, but he was also a skilled scribe in the law (v. 6). He came prepared to study the law, teach it, and enact it (vv. 12–26).[10]

The main functions of the scribe were the study, arrangement, and interpretation of the text. As far as we know, the public exposition of Scripture in congregational worship, first seen with Ezra, became the privilege of these learned men. This was certainly necessitated by the failure of the priests to study or teach the law (Mal. 2:5–9). By the first century before Christ when houses of study (the *bêt hammidrāsh*) began to spring up throughout the land, scribes were usually present to teach and exhort. Thus, the religious education of the people was largely entrusted to them, and they eventually became a powerful religious aristocracy.[11]

When Ezra came to Jerusalem, he found a number of serious violations that needed to be addressed if worship was to be valid. The greatest difficulty concerned mixed marriages, even within the high-priestly family. Ezra wept and confessed the sin of the people before the LORD until it affected the conscience of the people (Ezra 10:1–5), and they rallied to the

---

10. Koch, "Ezra and the Origins of Judaism," 173–97.
11. The influence of scribes and lawyers in the leadership of the religious community was great. Under their leadership the authoritative "traditions" and teachings (some attributed to Ezra [*Baba Kamma* 82a]) were preserved. In the time of Antiochus the Great (223–187 B.C.), a senate was formed, also referred to as the eldership (1 Macc. 11:23), or later the Tribunal of the Hasmoneans (*Sanhedrin* 82a), and finally the Sanhedrin.

right course of action (vv. 6–15). Malachi also had to face this problem of men putting away their wives and marrying women who worshipped other gods (Mal. 2:10–16). For those who were guilty of this, the prophet declared, God would pay no attention to their worship—all he could see was the pain that they inflicted on their proper wives. No doubt some of these violations were due to the failure of the priests to teach the law correctly (Mal. 2:8).

Even later when Nehemiah came to be the governor, Ezra led the covenant reforms.[12] Nehemiah 8 reports that on the first day of the seventh month, Ezra read from the Law all morning and the people listened intently. He stood on a high wooden platform. When he opened the Book, the people stood up; and when he praised the LORD, the people responded with "Amen, Amen," and then bowed down and worshipped the LORD. In order to make sure that the people understood, Ezra and his assistants read clearly and gave the meaning of the Law so that the people could understand what was read.[13] The response was emotional as the people wept when they listened to the words. But the reformers encouraged them to rejoice and not to grieve, because the day was sacred—the joy of the LORD would be their strength (vv. 9–11).

On the second day they learned in their readings that they were to live in booths during the seventh month to commemorate their ancestors' wilderness experience. So they went out and collected the branches and made their booths. Day after day they listened to the Word being read as they celebrated the Feast of Tabernacles.

That same month the people assembled to fast, wearing sackcloth and having dust on their heads (Neh. 9:1–2). They confessed their sins and the sins of their fathers.[14] They read from the Law for a quarter of the day and spent an equal amount of time in confession and worship. The day concluded with their renewing their commitments to the covenant.

---

12. Throntveit observes that what is new for Ezra as the second Moses is the serious attention paid to the process by which the written Word functions authoritatively (*Ezra–Nehemiah*, 110). See also Duggan, *The Covenant Renewal in Ezra–Nehemiah*.

13. Childs points out that Ezra did not read the Law to reform Israel into becoming the people of God; he read it to reformed people (*Introduction to the Old Testament as Scripture*, 636).

14. See Fensham, "Nehemiah 9 and Psalms 105, 106, 135 and 136," 35–51; and Liebreich, "The Impact of Nehemiah 9:5–37 on the Liturgy of the Synagiogue," 227–37.

## Nehemiah's Glorious Celebration

Under Nehemiah the walls of Jerusalem were finally rebuilt, and the people committed themselves to obedience to the LORD and the stability of the Holy City (Neh. 10:28–39).[15] At the dedication of the walls, there was a great celebration of worship that took place (12:27–47). All the Levitical singers and musicians in the countryside were brought to Jerusalem so that the praise would be magnificent. But the celebration also had to be sanctified; so once they were in the Holy Place, the priests and Levites purified themselves as well as the people, the gates, and the wall.

Nehemiah appointed two large choirs with their instruments to go up onto the walls in different directions, one group led by Ezra and the other by Nehemiah. In the temple precincts, they sang loudly and the people rejoiced with great joy as the sacrifices were being offered.

It was also critical for them to read the Book of Moses because they wanted to make sure their worship was right. When they came to the curse on the Moabites and Ammonites, they decided it best to separate the mixed multitude from them (Neh. 13:1–3), no doubt recalling how their ancestors' tolerance for other people and their religious ideas had opened the door for corrupt worship. It appears that the believing community was trying to recapture the spirit and the form of worship as it was legislated by Moses, developed by David, and reformed by Hezekiah and Josiah. In fact, we know that 1 and 2 Chronicles were written about this time for this very purpose—to inform the Jewish people of what was supposed to be by reminding them of the history of the faith and especially temple worship, and to show them what it would take to restore it. The reformers and prophets tirelessly called the people to the kind of worship that had filled these holy courts with the celebration of communion with the holy LORD God.

## Malachi's Rejection of Worthless Worship

In addition to some of the same sins of the people, Malachi faced a different kind of problem in the worship in his day:[16] people were giving

---

15. See Clines, "Nehemiah 10 as an Example of Early Jewish Biblical Exegesis," 111–17.
16. If, as tradition says, Malachi's ministry came near the end of the Old Testament era, then the reforms of Ezra and Nehemiah were short-lived. See Dumbrell, "Malachi and the Ezra–Nehemiah Reforms," 42–52.

worthless gifts to God and so were actually despising him (Mal. 1:6–14). They were sacrificing animals that were crippled, blind, or diseased. By sacrificing worthless animals, they made their worship convenient but contemptible. They may have reasoned that the animals were only going to be burnt up on the altar anyway and that the performance of the ritual would be enough to please God. But what kinds of gifts people bring to the LORD indicates what they think of him. Malachi said these people despised the LORD.

In his message Malachi was addressing the priests because the whole mess was their fault. They had not upheld the standards of worship, probably because they were not teaching the Word of God correctly (Mal. 2:1–9). Accordingly, to them the whole sacrificial ritual had become a drudgery. They went through the ritual, but their hearts were not in it. Did God accept this? Absolutely not. Acceptable worship from the beginning had always required that God receive the best, no matter what was being offered to him. And that has not changed. The Lord lays claim to the best we have to offer, for he is to receive the preeminence in all things (Col. 1:18).

Malachi was so incensed by this that he wished that someone would shut the doors to the sanctuary and keep these people out! No worship at all would be better than kindling the fires of the altar for such a sham (Mal. 1:10).[17] If the priests did not change their teachings and the worship, God would reject them as unclean (the image used is to smear offal across their faces so that they would be carted out of the sanctuary; 2:3). If Israel would not worship him properly, he would turn to the Gentiles who would honor his name in pure worship (1:11, 14).[18] They probably took this as rhetorical excess, for they were a belligerent lot. Little did they expect that this would actually happen.

## Conclusion

After the disaster of the Exile, there were healthy efforts to transform worship into something honoring to God and meaningful for the people. The reforms and the reestablishment of worship, all with the memory of glorious worship in the days of David and Solomon and Hezekiah and Josiah, were necessary and meaningful steps forward. The greatest re-

17. See S. W. Gray, "Useless Fires," 35–41.
18. Vriezen, "How to Understand Malachi 1:11?" 128–36.

vival of the period, though, was of the importance of the Word of God in the worship and service of the people. And if the priests would not do it, or could not do it, then the scribes would. Because if the Word of God was not read, taught, and explained, the worship would easily be corrupted, not necessarily in the direction of idolatry, but in disobedience in general. It was clear that if proper worship was to be recaptured, the spiritual condition of the people had to be changed. That would have to be addressed by the faithful teaching of Scripture and addressed quickly, because the Lord was going to come like a refining fire (Mal. 3:1–5).

# CHAPTER 22

# The Change *in* Worship

## *The Focus on the Word of God*

THE RELIGIOUS LEADERS WERE now determined to give full attention to the law in their daily activities as well as their religious ceremonies. Piety was determined by obedience to the law; religious practices were based on the law; and their future hope was based in part on compliance with the law. Gradually, a strict legalism began to emerge, designed to safeguard Judaism from the errors of the past.

There was a renewed commitment to carrying out to the letter what the law said. So all the festivals were restored, along with a new one from the Exile. The Day of Atonement came into great prominence because of the realization that the Exile and the present condition were the result of disobedience to the law. Over the years other special rituals were added to the calendar to strengthen the concern for confession, including days of awe and lamentation preserved from the Exile.

Since the law was supreme, those who knew it best emerged as authorities. The scribes began to think of themselves as standing in the tradition of the prophets, because they knew God's Word, sometimes by heart. Acceptable interpretations of the law by the greatest teachers and sages were prepared by the schools of the scribes to form a "hedge" around the law to protect its meaning.[1] This gradually expanded to include the massive oral law of the sages. Every law was given detailed definition and prescribed adjustments to situations in order to preserve the right conduct under the law in every area of life and worship. Thus, by the time Jesus appeared on the scene, the worship of Israel was being zealously guarded

---

1. In time the teaching became authoritative as well. The Jewish leaders accused Jesus' disciples of sinning against the traditions of these leaders (Matt. 15:2; Mark 7:5).

by a whole new religious order, an order that sought to prevent the catastrophe of the Exile from happening again, while hoping for the promised deliverance from all oppressors. The basic traditions of the worship of ancient Israel were carried forward but with significant new developments and a different spirit.

## Worship in the Synagogue

### Origins

The origin of the synagogue is still obscure, but literary and archaeological clues continue to surface.[2] It is certainly older than Gospel times, because in Jesus' day synagogues dotted the land and had a fairly well-developed, if basic, order to their religious activities. The inspiration, if not the idea, for synagogues may go back to Ezekiel's time, when people met to hear the Word of the LORD taught, to pray, and to receive the blessings, encouragements, and oracles from the prophet (Ezek. 8:1; 14:1; 33:30–33). Eventually there developed a system for the scheduled reading and explanation of Scripture on Sabbaths and other special occasions. Deuteronomy was important to the liturgy because it had numerous expressions that could be adapted easily to worship. In fact, its emphasis on instruction in the law probably contributed to the development of synagogue worship.[3]

While there is very little information about early synagogue worship, it is clear that homilies of the passages of Scripture that were read formed an important part of the service.[4] There are homilies[5] in the early collections of rabbinic teachings that probably originated in this worship; and there are later homilies in the Midrash *Pesikta Rabbati* that reflect first-century homilies from worship services. There is also an oration on the power of reason in 4 Maccabees, which may be an early exposition, and

---

2. See for full discussion Levenson, "From Temple to Synagogue," 143–92.
3. Levertoff, "Synagogue Worship in the First Century," 60–77.
4. This would be expected in view of the long history of prophetic preaching in the temple (Stulman, *The Prose Sermons of the Book of Jeremiah*). But without the temple, these homilies became more prominent. See von Rad, "The Levitical Sermon in 1 and 2 Chronicles."
5. The name for this is *haggādāh,* an explanation and application of Scripture (s.v. *nagād*). It refers to sections that are expositional or homiletical in nature, as opposed to the sections of legal instruction. See Stegner, "The Ancient Jewish Synagogue Homily," 51–69.

a fragment of Philo's sermon on Samson. The New Testament records sermons or interpretations that were independent of the readings (Luke 4:15–21; Acts 13:16–41).

With regard to prayer in the synagogue, we have the same kinds of evidence. Matthew 6:5 indicates that prayer was a part of synagogue worship (albeit abused on occasion). But there are also pre-Christian set prayers in the Greek text of Daniel inserted between 3:23 and 3:24 (e.g., the litany of penitence, vv. 3–22; and a eucharistic litany, vv. 29–68), as well as rabbinical writings that reach back into earlier writings to support their set prayers.

Apparently, then, the reading of Scripture, probably the Law and the Prophets, interpretations and exhortations based on the readings, and a basic liturgy of set blessings, prayers, and benedictions formed the early worship of the synagogue.

## Organization

Synagogues came to be the most visible buildings in the towns. The simple ones were mere halls that had a few basic things like a chest ("ark") for the scrolls, some benches around the walls for the elderly, and perhaps a seat for the teacher.[6] The synagogue in Alexandria, Egypt, was patterned after the temple (see *Tos. Suk.* 4:20) and therefore was more elaborate. Most synagogues had some symbolism, such as carvings of vine leaves and grapes, paschal lambs, and seven-branched candlesticks on the columns or walls. But most importantly they had water reservoirs for ritual baths[7] in the courtyard or nearby.

There is no evidence that women had a special isolated gallery in the synagogue as has been commonly assumed.[8] That practice appears to have been brought into some centers of Judaism centuries later under Islamic influence or pressure. In the early periods women may have been

---

6. This prominent seat was called "the seat of Moses" (Matt. 23:2). One was found in the ruins of the synagogue at Chorazin from a later period.

7. The ritual bath *(miqweh)* had to be a substantial size because the worshippers would completely immerse themselves in the water before entering the synagogue. These were built for temple use as well; the area at the southern end of the temple had numerous ritual baths. It is likely that the baptisms recorded in Acts 2 took place in these baths.

8. See Safrai, "The Place of Women in the First Century Synagogues," 1–5. Lepers did have a special gallery (see *Tos. Neg.* 13:12).

asked to read the lessons in the services (see *Tos. Meg.* 4:11), and a few were teachers.

Early Jewish believers in Jesus continued to go to synagogues until near the end of the first century, when there was a special enactment to prevent them.[9] As a qualified teacher from Jerusalem, Paul made it his practice to find the synagogue and preach there. His homilies on the readings were met with varied responses.

Our information about the leaders of the synagogue begins to emerge with the New Testament, although it is still not clear how these positions came into existence or how their duties may have changed.

*Elders* held a prominent role in the synagogues, as well as in the early churches, because they had been so important in the Old Testament.[10] Elders also could be rulers or ministers of synagogues; they were also at times scribes and scholars, for they were the knowledgeable leaders of the communities and their worship. As in the Old Testament, elders were to be mature and wise and have the respect of the community.[11]

One was chosen *ruler over the synagogue* (*Sot.* 7:7; Mark 5:22), although the office was hereditary in places (*Kid.* 4:5; *Dem.* 3:1). In addition to the care of the synagogue, his duties included choosing the readers (Acts 13:15) and collecting alms for the poor (*Pe'ah* 8:7).

The *minister* of the synagogue (*Sot.* 7:7; *Shab.* 1:3; Luke 4:20) carried out the orders of the ruler, especially in getting the scrolls for the reader. Like deacons in the early church, he served tables (see Acts 6:1–6).[12] But he also was the elementary teacher (*Tos. Pe'ah* 4:10) and at times wielded the scourge (*Makk.* 3:12).

Additionally, there were people *designated* to lead the prayers, or read the lessons, or provide the interpretation in Aramaic[13] (or at times Greek) for the people (see *Meg.* 4:4; *Tos. Meg.* 4:20–21; see esp. 1 Cor. 14:27–28).

---

9. A response to the liturgy (the *Birkat HaMinim,* "the blessing of the heretics" [*Ber.* 12a]) was said aloud in order to detect the Christians, who would say the name of Jesus (*Pes.* 56a).

10. See McKenzie, "The Elders in the Old Testament," 522–40.

11. For their ordination, see *Tosephta Sanhedrin* 1:1. See also *Berakoth* lla, *Yoma* 18b, and *Shabbath* 23a. Compare Paul's list of qualifications for elders in 1 Timothy 3:1–7.

12. Goodman, *The Synagogue and the Church.*

13. These are called the Aramaic *Targums.* Later they were gathered into collections that became the standard synagogue interpretations.

We do not have much information about the *congregations* either.[14] From the later period (at least after the destruction of the temple in A.D. 70), the congregation said the responses, the most important of which were the "Amens" after the benedictions. The congregation also participated in saying the great Shema (Deut. 6:4): "Hear *(sh^ema‹)*, O Israel: the LORD our God, the LORD is one." At morning prayer, except on Sabbaths and festivals, men wore two symbolic little cases called *t^ephillîn* (*phulaktēria* in Matt. 23:5), one on the arm and one on the forehead. The cases contained parchment on which were written Exodus 13:1–10 and 11–16 and Deuteronomy 6:4–9 and 11:13–21. Moses had instructed the people to bind the law on their hands and their foreheads, and so the pious did this in order to remind themselves to keep the law on their minds and obey it (Deut. 6:8–9).

In the days of Jesus, some people apparently wore these all day and not only during prayer. The same may be true of the so-called prayer shawl (*tallît; himation* in the Gospel), that is, the upper garment with the fringes of hyacinth-blue and white wool at its corners (Num. 15:37–39; Deut. 22:12; cf. Matt. 9:20; 14:36; 23:5; Mark 6:56; Luke 8:44). Jesus criticized those who did this for show, feigning piety in public.

There is no mention of the congregation's singing, but it is probable that those parts of the liturgy that were connected with the temple worship, like the recitation of psalms, the Aaronic blessing, and that connected with processions on the Feast of Tabernacles, were sung or chanted rhythmically.[15]

## Prayers and Benedictions

In the Old Testament there is no specific commandment concerning prayers in worship. There are references to benedictions (Num. 6:24–26; 2 Chron. 30:27) and prayers proper (Lev. 16:21; Deut. 26:10, 13; 1 Kings 8:22–53), but they are not set forth as elements of a regulated divine service. Eventually there were two congregational prayer services, morning

---

14. According to *Megillah* 6:3, ten male members were required for an assembly of prayers and blessings. Whether these rules for the size of a congregation were in use in the days of Jesus is hard to say. But when Jesus said that where two or three came together in his name, there he would be with them (Matt. 18:20), he was announcing that it was his presence that now mattered for a congregation.
15. Werner, "The Doxology in Synagogue and Church," 275–351.

and afternoon prayers, with full "liturgical" worship taking place on Sabbaths and appointed festivals.

The earliest and most important prayers are those connected to the saying of the Shema and the benedictions. Again, it is important to stress that precise dating for the introduction and development of these set prayers is not always possible. But we can say that some of them, and some form of them, were likely in place by the time of the early church. Their inclusion here at least gives the reader an idea of what synagogue worship became.

### "Hear, O Israel"

The Shema was said in obedience to the precept, "You . . . shall talk of them [the commandments] . . . when you lie down and when you rise up" (Deut. 6:7 NASB). The ruling was that everyone was to say twice daily three paragraphs of Scripture, beginning with the Shema (Deut. 6:4–9) and adding Deuteronomy 11:13–21 and Numbers 15:37–41. According to tradition, this "creed," together with the benedictions and the Decalogue, formed a significant part of the temple liturgy (*Tamid* v. 1). Thus it was in use before A.D. 70.

### Benedictions

There were four liturgical pieces to be said with the Shema, two before and one after the morning Shema, and two before and two after the evening Shema (*Ber.* 1:4). The first is called *Yôtsēr*. It extols the LORD as the former (*yôtsēr*) of light. Its present form cannot belong to the first century because it contains medieval liturgical pieces. But the benediction emphasizes Creation and messianic redemption, drawing directly from Isaiah 45:7. Two of the themes match sayings of Jesus, God's daily renewal of creation (Matt. 5:45; cf. Luke 6:36) and his work in Creation and redemption, even on the Sabbath (John 5:10–18).

The second benediction is known by its opening word *ʾĂhăvāh* ([with] "love"). It praises the LORD for his unchanging love manifested in many ways, most importantly in redemption. Tradition claims that this prayer was recited by the priests in the temple before saying the Decalogue and Shema (*Mid.* v. 1). But there is some uncertainty about the date of its inauguration since it seems to contain polemical elements against Christian teachings.[16]

The concluding benediction (*'Ěmet wᵉ-Yatsîv,* "true and constant") blesses God for his faithful word that is worthy of acceptance (see 1 Tim. 1:15) because it endures from generation to generation. It may come from the time after Jesus and before the destruction of the temple in A.D. 70.

The *Hashîvēnû* ("cause us to lie down") is the second prayer to be said in the evening. The ending suggests that it was inaugurated after the destruction of Jerusalem in A.D. 70. It is a prayer for divine protection, weaving together a number of biblical praises on the theme.

In addition to these four prayers, there were "Eighteen Benedictions" *(shᵉmōneh ʿesrēh),* a group of prayers characterized mostly by praise. The collection is also called *tᵉphillāh,* "Prayer," and *ʿamîdāh,* "Standing," because it is recited standing. It is difficult to determine the earliest form of the benedictions, or their dates, but several were probably in use in Jesus' time. At first they probably numbered only about six prayers for weekdays and seven for Sabbaths and festivals.

For example, *Benediction 1* blesses the LORD as the sovereign God who shields his people from age to age. This may be earlier than the time of Jesus.

*Benediction 2* either precedes the Sadducean influence or opposes it, because it blesses the LORD who quickens the dead.

*Benediction 6* prays for forgiveness and blesses God who forgives; it may be from the beginning of the Christian era.

*Benediction 12* comes at the turn of the century (A.D. 110–117); it prays that apostates and Rome be rooted out and the Nazareans and Minim [heretics] perish in a moment (probably aimed at Jewish Christians[17]). It blesses the LORD for humbling the arrogant.

*Benediction 17* may be pre-Christian; it blesses God for his benefits, grace, and love that he has shown to his people Israel.

There was always an aversion among the Jewish teachers to letting prayer become a fixed duty with fixed formulas. To avoid this one could

---

16. The prayer emphasizes, for instance, God's unchangeable love to Israel, the eternal significance of the law, and the divine unity. For this see the first ten chapters of Romans, Galatians 4:21–31, and especially Ephesians 2:4.

17. Whenever the sovereignty of the LORD God or the eternal significance of the law is emphasized in any prayer, it carries an anti-Christian emphasis.

include something new in the prayer each day (*Ber.* 29b). But the set prayers and benedictions guided the faithful in their prayers, assisted them in articulating their faith, and preserved them from following new sects. The Jewish community was trying to preserve its identity in the face of the expanding new faith in Jesus.

## Services

All the uncertainties expressed so far show how difficult it is to reconstruct what a first-century synagogue service would have been like. The earliest information comes from Luke (4:15–21), and it, of course, is very brief and concerned with Scripture—reading and exhortation.[18] That prayers, especially in connection with the readings from the Law and the Prophets, were said, is, however, most likely. Benedictions like the following may have been said in the time of Jesus:

The one asked to read the Law would say:

> Bless the LORD, the Blessed One!

The congregation would respond:

> Blessed are you, O LORD,
> who gave us the Torah of truth
> and plants eternal life in our midst;[19]
> Blessed are you, O LORD, the Giver of the Torah!

The reader would then read the section from the Law and say:

> Blessed are you, O LORD our God,
> who has chosen us from among all the nations,
> and has given us the Torah!
> Blessed are You, O LORD, the Giver of the Torah.

---

18. Descriptions and references from later times about the earlier times are not to be disregarded. We look at what the synagogue service became and then work back to see what might have been in place earlier.

19. John 5:39, which we can translate, "Search the Scriptures, of which you think that in them you have eternal life," may allude to this benediction.

Before the prophetic lesson, the following benedictions also were probably already said, in substance, at any rate, in the first century:

> Blessed are You, O LORD our God,
>     who has chosen good prophets,
>     and has found pleasure in their words which
>         were spoken in truth.

> Blessed are you, O LORD our God,
>     who has chosen the Law,
>     and Moses your servant, and Israel your people,
>     and the prophets of truth and righteousness.

> Gladden us, O LORD our God,
>     with the prophet Elijah, your Servant,
>     and with the Kingdom of the house of David,
>         your Messiah.
> May he come soon and gladden our hearts.

> Do not permit a stranger [Herod?] to sit upon his throne,
>     nor let others any longer inherit his glory;
>     for by your holy Name you did swear unto him (David)
>         that his light should never be quenched.

> Blessed are you, O LORD, the Shield of David.

So if we fit the readings and the benedictions into the whole synagogue
service, we may reconstruct an order. The ruler summons the minister
to invite someone from the congregation to recite the Shema and the
benedictions connected with it. That person would begin by saying to the
congregation, "Bless the Lord, the Blessed One," to which the congregation would respond, "Blessed be the Lord, the blessed One, for ever and
ever." Then the leader would say (perhaps an early form of) the *Yôtsēr*
and the *'Ăhāvāh*, while standing in the midst of the congregation, who
were probably seated on the floor (elders and various others had seats).

The Shema proper would be said antiphonally: the leader would say,
"Hear, O Israel," and the congregation would respond by repeating that

and then continuing to the end. The leader would respond at once with "Blessed be the Name of the glory of his Kingdom for ever and ever."

After this, the *'Ĕmet wᵉ-Yatsîv* was probably said in unison. The Shema now ended, the ruler again would bid the minister to call upon someone to lead the Eighteen Benedictions. The congregation would rise to their feet, and the one chosen would ascend the platform where the ark for the Law was kept. Standing there before the ark, he would begin to recite the benedictions, to each of which the congregation would respond with "Amen." If a priest was present, between the sixth and seventh parts, he would pronounce the blessing, facing the congregation.[20]

This liturgy would be followed by the reading of the lesson from the Law (in portions) with its appropriate benedictions before and after. And because Hebrew was not fully understood by all, a designated translator gave the meaning in Aramaic.

This was followed by the lesson from the Prophets (called the *haphtôrāh*, "dismissal," because this ended the service) with its benedictions. This was also read in Hebrew and translated three verses at a time.

Then, if there was a qualified person present, the ruler would invite him (through the minister) to speak: "If you have any word of exhortation for the people, say on."[21]

That psalms were said or chanted especially at festivals and on Sabbaths is also likely since the synagogue services came to reflect temple worship. Because the original purpose of the synagogue was reading and explaining Scripture and praying, it was probably only after the fall of Jerusalem that it began to be considered a little sanctuary (based on Ezek. 11:16; cf. *Meg.* 29a), a substitute for the temple. If that is the case, in the time of Jesus there would not have been a lot of fixed liturgy, only the benedictions before and after the readings from the Law and the Prophets. We may assume that in the provincial synagogues psalms and prayers were chanted by those who could not go up to Jerusalem, but there is no direct evidence for this. After the death of Jesus and the beginning of the growth of the church, however, the Shema probably became a little creed,

---

20. The priests were not synagogue officials; their only function was this "raising of the hands." It is uncertain whether this was a synagogue function before the destruction of the temple, or after, when the priests were deprived of other functions.

21. See Acts 13:15. Paul apparently made this his main platform, taking the opportunity to preach the gospel based on the readings of the day.

and special prayers were formulated in connection with it to emphasize the divine unity, the permanency of the law, and Israel's identity. The other prayers would have been added later, so that by the middle of the second century the liturgy acquired a set form.

Jewish Christians apparently took part in all that was available to them for various reasons. They continued to go to the temple for worship activities until it was destroyed (see Acts 20:16). The meetings with Christians in homes were probably regarded as supplementary to and clarifying of the worship they were used to at the central sanctuary. But now they had come to realize that Christ fulfilled the purpose and the types of the temple, making their participation in temple worship very different at least, if necessary at all. Jewish believers also continued to attend synagogue services, for they were keenly interested in the interpretation of Scripture and prayer. However, that eventually came to an end as well.

Perhaps if we knew more about the synagogue services of the time we might see how Christian prayers (as in Acts 2:42) replaced synagogue prayers and the apostles' teaching replaced that of the scribes. Certainly Paul's letters are filled with expressions that reflect Jewish traditions and synagogue ritual; he was able to bring it all forward to show how Jesus the Messiah was God's answer to the longings of worshipping Israel.

## Sectarian Worship

The religious scene often seems like a bazaar with all the factions and sects clamoring to promote their claims to the historic faith. It was no different in the days of Jesus.[22]

### Samaritans

One of the oldest sects was the Samaritans. The pious Jews considered the Samaritans an impure race with a corrupted religious tradition and thus would have nothing to do with them. The Samaritans, of course, told a different story. They claimed the division with the Jews went back to the time that Eli set up an apostate shrine at Shiloh, abandoning the original setting at Mount Gerizim, where Joshua ratified the covenant. According to Samaritan teaching, "the accursed Ezra" falsified the sa-

---

22. Of the numerous works on this subject, see Gowen, *Bridge Between the Testaments;* Bronner, *Sects and Separatism During the Second Jewish Commonwealth;* and Bruce, *New Testament History.*

cred text to present the Samaritans as impure. The Samaritans set up their own worship; they built their temple on Mount Gerizim (between 335–330 B.C.)[23] and followed the law of Moses very carefully,[24] observing the Sabbath and the festivals. For the Day of Atonement they followed the Mosaic traditions, but they had their own high priest. One peculiar festival was held sixty days before Passover (the Day of *Simmuth*); it commemorated the day when the people obtained a calendar worked out by Phinehas from the meridian of Mount Gerizim. This mountain was therefore uppermost in the minds of the Samaritans, as we see in the case of the Samaritan woman (John 4:20). But Jesus said that true worship would be neither on Gerizim or on Zion in Jerusalem because it would be transformed by him forever (John 4:21–24).

## Major Jewish Sects

### The Pharisees

The Pharisees were a religious sect that held to the historic faith,[25] but often in self-righteous and hypocritical ways.[26] The name *Pharisee* means "separated one."[27] The Pharisees certainly did separate themselves from Gentiles, from "sinners" such as the people of the land, and the illiterate or unrefined who did not observe religious duties and purity laws. They did not think that people could be pious if they did not study the law (*'Avoth* 2:5; Matt. 9:11; John 7:49).

In their strict observance of the law, the Pharisees gave greatest attention to laws concerning Sabbath days, uncleanness and ritual washing, and

---

23. John Hyrcanus razed it in 129 or 128 B.C.; before that was the "era of favor," a period of a little over two hundred years of their temple's existence.
24. They still follow the Law today, even offering animal sacrifices. There are several hundred Samaritans living in Samaria and Tel Aviv. See MacDonald, *The Theology of the Samaritans.*
25. *Antiquities* 13.5.9. See further Saldarini, *Pharisees, Scribes, and Sadducees in Palestinian Society;* Finkel, *The Pharisees and the Teacher of Nazareth.*
26. The negative references to Pharisees concern a particular group of them, and not all of them (cf. Nicodemus). Even in the rabbinic literature there is a critical listing of the different types of Pharisees.
27. Perhaps their opponents, the Sadducees, gave them the name for their legalistic views of separation (*Yadaim* 4:6–7). Some think that the Pharisees applied the name to themselves; they were formerly called the *Hasidim* ("beloved" or "pious"; not to be confused with the modern group) because they fought hellenization.

tithing. Their teaching of the law often included detailed requirements that were intended to guide people in keeping the law but proved only to be burdensome (Matt. 23:4). There could be little joy in worship if no one could keep their rules. They had almost placed their traditions on a par with the law, at least in practice.[28] To violate them was a serious offense, which they were quite ready to point out (Mark 7:1–5). This has been a frequent tendency in the church too, as well-intended traditions—more so than Scripture—have become the defining features of different groups.

### The Sadducees

The Sadducees arose in reaction to the Pharisees in the early second century B.C. The name may have been taken from Zadok, the priest of Solomon's time who became the father of the main priestly line, for many priests and high priests belonged to the Sadducees (Acts 4:1; 5:17).[29] The Pharisees and Sadducees often engaged in vigorous debates (Acts 23:6–7; *Yad.* 4:6–7), but the Pharisees enjoyed popular support and were more powerful (*Yoma* 19b says the Sadducees were a little afraid of them). The Sadducees rejected the Pharisees' emphasis on oral tradition as authoritative, but since they represented the smaller, wealthy class, they were often forced to go along with the rulings and observe the oral traditions of the Pharisees (*Yoma* 1:5).

By and large the Sadducees were held in low esteem.[30] The *Psalms of Solomon* (mid-first century B.C.) calls them "sinners." One text in the Mishnah ranks the Sadducee with the deaf mute, imbecile, and minor (*'Eruv.* 3:2), and another compares the daughters of Sadducees to Samaritan women (*Nid.* 4:2) because they were lax on the law of purity.

The two religious parties differed on doctrine. Pharisees believed in the immortal soul, the resurrection of the dead, and the world to come. Sadducees denied the resurrection[31] (Matt. 22:23; Acts 4:1–2; 23:8), the

---

28. *Antiquities* 13.10.6.
29. Ibid., 20.9.1; 13.10.6. Several references point to Pharisees in those positions as well (John 1:19, 24; *Shek.* 4:4; *Avoth* 2:8; *Eduy.* 8:2).
30. It is true that all we know about them comes from their enemies, but the few descriptions of them in Scripture supports the general consensus.
31. Compare *Sanhedrin* 90b in the Talmud with Matthew 22:32. The argument for the resurrection in the Law based on the promises to the patriarchs was not that the patriarchs still exist, for that would not teach resurrection, but that God made promises to them that demand a resurrection.

existence of angels as presented by the Pharisees (Acts 23:8), the immortality of the soul, and future rewards or punishments. Consequently, the spiritual leadership in the temple, the high priest and the majority of the priests, often were men who did not believe in all that the historic faith had included.

Confrontations between the parties in Jesus' time were mild compared to what they had been for a century and a half before. Under Greek rule from Antioch, the office of high priest was sold to different people. The pious Jews, the Hasidim, opposed this and all hellenizing efforts. Finally, in 168 B.C. the Jews, under the leadership of the Maccabean priests, rebelled against Antioch because of the pagan practices at the altar in Jerusalem—the offering of a pig in particular. They won their independence and established the Hasmonean dynasty.

But the faithful soon found themselves with a new problem. In 140 B.C. the Hasmonean ruler Simon also became the high priest. Even though Simon was murdered, Hyrcanus I also became king and high priest (135 B.C.). The Pharisees objected vigorously to the priest (from Levi) having temporal power (from Judah). When Alexander Janneus (103–76) came to the throne, he not only became high priest but also married his brother's widow Salome, which was against the law for rulers. Janneus had such contempt for ritual law that once in a "worship" service he poured the sacred libations out on his feet. The Pharisees had come prepared—they pelted him with fruit. If that was not disgraceful enough, civil war broke out. Janneus was defeated initially, but in the end he managed to retain his power. Hundreds of Pharisees were crucified and their wives butchered, and thousands of people left the land.[32] The vision of entering the presence of the LORD for glorious worship must have seemed especially remote now.

After a time of struggle over these issues, Salome became political ruler (76–67). She made Hyrcanus II (a Pharisee) the priest, but his brother Aristobulus (a Sadducee) took over (67–63). Rome stepped in to bring peace to the land, and Pompey made Hyrcanus II, the Pharisee, priest and ethnarch. Under the cruel reign of Herod, and probably at his instigation, Hyrcanus was mutilated and had to be replaced as priest. Herod, as a half Jew, an Idumean (i.e., Edomite), and a friend of the Romans, continued

---

32. Josephus *Bellum Judaicum* 1.93–9; *Antiquities* 13.14.2.

to alienate the Pharisees. He yielded to pressure to put Aristobulus in the priest's office, only to have him drowned in his swimming pool. How people could continue to worship in the temple with all this confusion is amazing. We can certainly appreciate that the political and religious leadership of the land had become so corrupt that people were ready for a prophet with true spiritual authority.

To appease the Jews Herod began building the temple in Jerusalem. He wanted to build it exactly as the law and traditions dictated, using only Levites who were sanctified. But he also wanted it to be the greatest temple ever built; thus, construction had been ongoing for forty-six years when Jesus started his ministry. It was destroyed in A.D. 70 as Jesus predicted. Like Jeremiah, Jesus taught that true worship did not need a sanctuary. In fact, as things stood, worship would be better off without it.

### The Essenes

The Essenes were a sect that firmly believed they were better off without the temple. They could not abide the wicked high priest, so they left the temple to form their own communes, some of them in the desert.[33] The Essenes, whose name is from Aramaic *hasya*, "pious," apparently began with a "Teacher of Righteousness" who rejected the chaotic struggle in Jerusalem and encouraged living righteously away from it (about 160–143 B.C.). The early references identify their colony at the north end of the Dead Sea, but later there were different orders of Essenes in the land.

The Essenes in Qumran by the Dead Sea were ascetics, solitary men, searching for spiritual contentment rather than luxury. They held all things in common, each man surrendering all his possessions for everyone to use as the need arose. Moreover, they were somewhat of a secret society; they practiced celibacy, but they did take in orphans (some groups apparently allowed marriages). They emphasized ritual baths, regular study of Scripture, and a very strict discipline. Their organization was hierarchical, controlled by a leader and elders.[34]

---

33. Our primary sources are Philo of Alexandria (*Quod omnis liber probus sit* and *Hypothica* [known through Eusebius]), Josephus (*Bellum Judaicum* 2.7.2–13; 8.2–13; and *Antiquities* 13.5.9; 18.1.5), Pliny (*Natural History,* 5.17.4), Hyppolytus (*Refutation of All Heresies*) and the Dead Sea Scrolls (*Manual of Discipline; Habakkuk Commentary; War Scroll; Temple Scroll*).

34. John the Baptist was not an Essene because he was out preaching while the Essenes were a secret society. Moreover, his baptism was very different than their ritual baths.

They worshipped in strict obedience to the law. For six days of the week there was instruction, all of the members sitting in order with one man reading and another explaining. The seventh day was kept holy. But they were in disagreement with offering sacrifices in the temple in Jerusalem; they sent offerings to the temple but no sacrifices since their purification rites differed.

Their ideal was to live a life of righteousness untarnished by society's evil. They vowed piety to God, justice to man, hatred of the wicked, and love for the just. And their life was a life of discipline. Each day they arose in silence, prayed an ancestral prayer facing the sun, worked until about eleven in the morning, bathed in cold water (purity), put on sacred garments and assembled to eat. The priest prayed, ate, and then prayed again and blessed God. They would return to work until the evening meal, which followed the same routine.

They worked in the fields, the commune itself, or the *scriptorium*. They prepared natural healing products (often using stones and roots). They were good at predicting events and interpreting dreams. In fact, the Essenes ministered as prophets and scribes, zealously preserving the scrolls and the teachings. They thought they were in the last days and anticipated the final battle with the forces of evil. Their participation in the wars against Rome brought their communities to an end.

## Conclusion

After the destruction of Solomon's temple in 586 B.C., the devout life had to be sustained through careful compliance with Scripture, the reading and teaching of the Law, and prayer—aspects of worship that had been neglected in the past. And this renewed emphasis on the Word of the LORD was so helpful that when the temple was rebuilt it was retained as a part of the life of worship. In time the synagogue developed and became the dominant center of daily religious activities throughout the land, but without supplanting the temple as the place for sacrifices and festivals.

Although gross idolatry was never a national problem again after the Exile, there were other problems that in some ways were more difficult. The failure of the priests to teach the law opened the door for a host of sinful practices and contempt for worship. Scribes and teachers tried to restore obedience to the law but in time ended up adding rulings and traditions by their own authority. Corruption in the Jewish royal family and priesthood, which were often united, led to the conflicts between different religious groups and the confusion of the people. The Sadducees fought to hold the seats of power; the Pharisees sought to maintain a rigid compliance with the law; the Essenes left for the desert; and the common person was left with little hope because he was considered a sinner. Into this mix Jesus came with the truth.

Amazingly, in the church down through its history and even today, positions of leadership have often been controlled or influenced by those who believe even less than the Sadducees. They are rightly opposed by traditionalists, even though like the Pharisees these traditionalists' activities often display self-righteousness and hypocrisy. Some groups have walked away from the conflicts and formed their own communities, groups such as monastic orders and Christian communes. But the gates of hell have not prevailed against Christ's church; believers have always found ways to preserve the faith through the worship of the Lord. Whenever religious leadership has failed, God has raised up new leaders to transform the worship and service of the people of God. The faithful worship of the living God will always eclipse the difficulties and disagreements in the institutions with their positions of power.

CHAPTER  23

# The New Center *of* Worship

## *The Incarnate Word*

INTO THE MIDDLE OF THIS spiritual confusion stepped Jesus. And like
the prophets of old he rebuked false and hypocritical worship, from the
top down. He charged that many religious leaders not only had missed
the spirit and purpose of worship but also had perverted it. Jesus was no
ordinary prophet, for his words had an authority never heard before and
his works authenticated his message. And such authentication was necessary, for his message revealed, among other things, that he was both the
means and the object of true worship.

### Jesus' Ministry in Worship Settings

Jesus did much of his teaching and many of his works in settings of
worship. This should be no surprise since Jewish life was filled with services and festivals in synagogues and the temple.

He set the tone for his mission when at the age of twelve he was in
Jerusalem for Passover (Luke 2:41–50). Separated from his family in the
vast temple precincts, he was eventually found among the teachers, listening to them and asking questions that amazed them. Judging from
similar discussions at festival time, the dialogue probably concerned the
meaning of Passover, which Jesus' mission would fully reveal. Doeve says,
"Their amazement must relate to his deducing things from Scripture
which they had never found before."[1] Here, too, were Jesus' first recorded
thoughts about his identity—the temple was his Father's house, the place
where the Son should be (v. 49).[2]

---

1. Doeve, *Jewish Hermeneutics in the Synoptic Gospels and Acts,* 105.
2. Barrois, *Jesus Christ and the Temple;* Yee, *Jewish Feasts and the Gospel of John.*

After the long years of silence, Jesus chose the synagogue service in Nazareth, his hometown, to announce his mission. After all, it was his custom to go the synagogue on the Sabbath (Luke 4:16). The passage notes several aspects of the synagogue service: an attendant gave him the scroll when he stood up to read; and when he finished reading the passage from Isaiah, he handed it back to the attendant and then took the customary seated position (in Moses' seat) to deliver his comments, which on this occasion concerned the prophecy of his divinely ordained ministry (Luke 4:18–21; from Isa. 61:1–2) and how it was rejected in his hometown (4:23–27; cf. Matt. 13:54). The crowd in Nazareth expelled him, but he continued his teaching and preaching in the synagogues in Capernaum (Luke 4:31, 38; cf. John 6:59) and Judea (4:44).

In order to authenticate his claims, especially that of fulfilling Isaiah's prophecy, Jesus performed many miracles, some of them in the synagogue services and on the Sabbath day. In the presence of assembled worshippers, he cast out a demon (Mark 1:21–28), healed a shriveled hand (Luke 6:6–11), and ended a woman's years of infirmity (Luke 13:10–17). Nothing barred people with such infirmities from synagogues. In fact, people came to find God through prayer and his Word. But with Jesus present, synagogue worship had new life. People wanted to see his power and his glory, and when they did, they praised God. By doing these wonderful works on the Sabbath, however, he incensed some religious leaders who thought they should have been done on one of the other days. Nevertheless, when Jairus, the ruler of a synagogue had a dying daughter, it was Jesus whom he called (Luke 8:40–56).

When Jesus made the temple the center of his activities, the powerful religious leaders there saw him as a threat to their authority. His cleansing of the temple early in his ministry clearly aligned him with the reforming prophets: he made a whip out of cords and drove out the dishonest moneychangers, saying to those who sold doves, "Get these out of here! How dare you turn my Father's house into a market!" (John 2:16). Thus, Jesus revealed his passion for the sanctity of the temple; it was his Father's house, a place of prayer.[3]

When he healed a leper, he said, "Go, show yourself to the priest and offer the gift Moses commanded, as a testimony to them" (Matt. 8:4; cf.

---

3. Trudinger, "The Cleansing of the Temple," 329–30.

Mark 1:43). The expression "as a testimony to them" indicates that the miracle would attest to his messiahship. The Law specified that the priest would have to declare the man clean (and therefore authenticate the miracle) and then conduct the appropriate ritual (Lev. 14). Thus, Jesus shows that he did not come to do away with the law but to fulfill it (Matt. 5:17). By touching the unclean leper, Jesus actually superseded the law; by cleansing him, he fulfilled the law; and by sending him to the priest, he followed the law. Leprosy had prevented this man from full communion with God in the temple, but Jesus made that communion possible by removing the effects of sin. The Father was seeking worshippers (John 4:23)—and Jesus was providing them. A similar account is the cleansing of the ten lepers in Luke 17:11–19. Jesus instructed them to go and show themselves to the priest, and as they went they were healed. Again he demonstrated that he was able to make people, even society's outcasts, fit for God, and the only prerequisite was faith—they had to start for the temple before they were healed (v. 14).

The woman with the issue of blood had faith. She believed that if she could only touch Jesus she would be healed (Luke 8:43–48). For twelve years she had not been able to enter God's courts with singing or eat the peace offering in his presence. But what the law prevented, Jesus could provide. He could restore those who were by sickness or sin separated from communion with God, not just to the temple in Jerusalem, but to glory as well. By his words and his works, Jesus revealed that he was much more than a prophet. He was Immanuel, the Lord of creation, the Redeemer of the world, the promised Messiah—and he is worthy of all our praise.

According to John 7:1–10 Jesus went up to Jerusalem alone for the Feast of Tabernacles.[4] That festival provided him with two symbols for his teaching—water and light. On the eighth and great day of the feast, he declared that if people were thirsty they should believe in him and rivers of living water would flow from them. By this he meant the Spirit, whom believers would receive (John 7:37–39). Ever since Creation rivers symbolized the provision of life from God. Jesus was claiming that he could give worshippers the fullness of eternal life. And then, using the backdrop of the festival of lights in the temple ritual, Jesus also declared that it was he

---

4. Yee, *Jewish Feasts and the Gospel of John.*

who would provide people with access to the presence of God because he was the Light of the World (John 8:12). This would require a major shift in the focus of their worship away from the ritual and onto him.

John 10:22 reports that Jesus was in the temple at the Feast of Dedication, winter's Hanukkah. When the Jewish leaders pressed him to say that he was the Messiah, he went further and declared equality with the Father (v. 30). This would mean that he had the right to receive their worship and obedience. Understandably, they wanted to stone him for blasphemy.

Of course, Passover in Jerusalem was the setting for the Last Supper and the death of Jesus. The activities began several days before Passover when people came to the temple to present their lambs for approval. It was probably this procession that became the Triumphal Entry. Normally the liturgy of the temple would call for the priests to bless each worshipper: "Blessed is he who comes in the name of the LORD" (Ps. 118:26), but the followers of Jesus knew that he was the promised Messiah who was coming into the world (John 11:27). Therefore they chanted the lines of the Passover hymn with reference to him, praising him with "Blessed is he who comes in the name of the LORD," and calling on him to deliver them, literally saying, "Save now" (*hôshî'āh-nnā* [Greek *hōsanna*], Matt. 21:9; see Zech. 9:9).

During the days leading up to the Passover, what the church now calls Holy Week, Jesus taught in the temple each day (cf. Matt. 21–25; Luke 19:47; 20:1; 21:37). The people hung on his words (Luke 19:48) because he was teaching with authority and acting with authority in the temple (Luke 19:45). But a group of religious rulers challenged him, asking, "By what authority are you doing these things?" (Matt. 21:23). If they did not know, it was because unbelief had blinded them to God's revelation, for the prophets said that the Lord of the covenant would come to his temple (Mal. 3:1–5). Unbelief had turned the house of prayer into a den of thieves and left the nation blind to the truth.[5]

---

5. The healing of the two blind men just before the Triumphal Entry therefore has even greater meaning in the flow of the argument (Matt. 20:29–34). Unbelief is spiritual blindness; and when people do not acknowledge who Jesus is, their worship becomes religious activities. And yet, there are those who want to see (v. 33).

The Passover meal was the setting for the Last Supper and the explanation of Jesus' death. Jesus had come to fulfill his mission, and to that end, he was eager to eat this Passover with his disciples before he suffered (Luke 22:15). The evening followed the basic pattern of a Passover meal, except for the new teachings. But the major transformation in worship occurred here, for from this point on worship would focus on Christ, the fulfillment of the Passover (1 Cor. 5:7–8).

## Jesus' Rebuke of Worthless Worship

Jesus had much to say about the way people were performing acts of worship. His criticisms were not hypocritical, for he was perfectly righteous and devout in his own spiritual life. Perhaps one of the best windows into this aspect of Jesus' life is his discipline of prayer (Matt. 26:36–42; Mark 1:35; John 17).[6] Out of this deep communion with the Father came his painful disappointment in what the people were doing in his name.

### Ostentatious Displays

Jesus warned people not to do righteous acts in order to impress other worshippers. It is far better to be concerned with pleasing God in heaven than with what others think.[7]

#### Almsgiving

Jesus said that when people give to the needy, they should not "sound the trumpet" as the hypocrites do (Matt. 6:2–4).[8] Giving is a sincere act of worship when it is silent and inconspicuous. People who are not interested in giving anything to God but in drawing attention to themselves are hypocrites. Such people thrive on the praise of those who perceive them to be spiritual.

---

6. See Jeremias, *The Prayers of Jesus.*
7. Righteous deeds must be done with righteous intentions; God's reward is for those who care not about what others think but about what is right in heaven (W. D. Davies and Allison, *Gospel According to Saint Matthew,* 1:575).
8. This may be a reference to proclaiming public fasts in which prayers were recited in the streets and alms were given to ensure the efficacy of the prayers and fasting. But Jesus may be speaking metaphorically, alluding to the *"shôphār"* (horn) shaped chests in the treasury.

### Prayer

The hypocrites loved to be seen by others (Matt. 6:5)—they wanted everyone to know that they prayed. Jesus was not criticizing public prayer, only its use for self-exaltation. Prayer requires no audience but God. The hyperbole of going to a closet to pray stresses this point (though if people brag about praying in private, they are no different than the hypocrites).[9] One could say that if people are eager to pray in front of others but never pray in private, then they are probably just like these folks.

In another place Jesus spoke of a self-righteous Pharisee who went up to the temple "and prayed about [or to] himself; 'God, I thank you that I am not like other men—robbers, evildoers, adulterers—or even like this tax collector. I fast twice a week and give a tenth of all I get'" (Luke 18:9–14). The tax collector in humility prayed, "God, have mercy on me, a sinner." Jesus said that the self-righteous man would not be justified by God, for worship that is acceptable to God is self-abasing, not self-exalting.

Jesus also criticized the pagan babblings people used, thinking that they would be heard for their many words (Matt. 6:7). He was not speaking against long prayers or repetition in prayers, both of which can be found in the Psalms (see also Deut. 9:18; Matt. 26:36–46; John 17). He was talking about the pagan attitude that God could be induced to answer by repeated incantations and continuous babbling. Prayer is not a way of manipulating God; it is an expression of faith in seeking the will of God.

### Fasting

Jesus criticized the act of disfiguring the face in fasting in order to be seen by others as spiritual (Matt. 6:16). The law commanded fasting at the Day of Atonement (Lev. 16:29–31; 23:27–32; Num. 29:7), and after the Exile other fasts were added (Zech. 7:3–5; 8:19). Private fasting could be engaged in any time special petitions were offered. But the Old Testament already rebuked the hypocritical fast (Isa. 58:3–7; Jer. 14:12; Zech. 7:5–6). When people adopt a somber, downcast disposition (see the use in Luke 24:17) and walk about with ashes on their heads or sackcloth on their backs for the purpose of conveying to others that they are deeply pious—this is worthless to God. According to Isaiah 58, the kind

---

9. W. D. Davies and Allison, *Gospel According to Saint Matthew,* 1:585.

of fasting that pleases God is that in which his people spend themselves helping the poor and afflicted. So, with fasting, people are to turn their attention away from self-indulgence toward spiritual things.

## Legalism

Naturally there followed open conflict with the religious leaders of the day. On several occasions Jesus "violated" their traditions about the Sabbath but not the spirit or the letter of the law itself. In his disputations he reminded them of the true meaning of the Sabbath and thereby uncovered their inconsistencies.[10]

In one place Jesus healed a man with a withered hand on the Sabbath (Matt. 12:9–14; Mark 3:1–6; Luke 6:6–11). This brought an immediate challenge about the lawfulness of healing on the Sabbath. Jesus reasoned that they would pull a sheep out of a pit on the Sabbath, but the life of a human is far more valuable.[11]

In another incident (John 7:21–24) Jesus pointed out that if it was valid to circumcise on the Sabbath, as the religious leaders taught, it was valid to make someone whole on the Sabbath (cf. *Shab.* 18:3; 19:1ff.).[12]

On one occasion, Jesus not only healed a man on the Sabbath but also told him to carry his bed—a work (John 5:8–18). The Jewish leaders taught that one could carry a sick person on this day but not furniture (*Shab.* 10:5–6). Christ applied the law against Sabbath labor differently.

When Jesus healed the woman with an infirmity (Luke 13:10–17), he explained that since people would lead an ox to water on the Sabbath, why should he not set this woman free on the Sabbath (cf. *Shab.* 18:2; 24:2–4; 5:1–4)? Jesus was making comparable exceptions but on a higher level.

There was also the grain controversy (Matt. 12:1–8; Mark 2:23–28;

---

10. Many teachings on the Sabbath are recorded in the Mishnah. Even though this collection was put together a couple of centuries after Christ, it preserves ancient teachings. And the fact that Jesus referred to many of these teachings proves they were in existence in his time.

11. This is *qal wā-khōmer* reasoning, from the lesser to the greater. See in the *Mishnah Yoma* 8:6 (and its *Gemara*), *Shab.* 14:3–4; 18:3; and 22:6.

12. *Shab.* 132a in the Talmud says, "How do we know that saving a life supersedes the Sabbath? R. Eliezer b. 'Azariah said, 'If circumcision, which is performed on but one of the limbs of man supersedes the Sabbath, the saving of a life, *a minori,* must supersede the Sabbath.'"

Luke 6:1–5). The disciples apparently violated a Sabbath tradition by plucking grain—which was unlawful harvesting. Jesus could have responded with various arguments, but here he elevated the discussion to his identity. He reasoned that if David, on a holy mission, was able to violate the law by eating the sacred bread, and that if priests on their holy mission could work on the Sabbath (*Pes.* 5–6), then the disciples had the right to pick and eat because they were on a mission with him, the Holy One—and he was greater than the temple. As Lord of the Sabbath, the day was under his authority, not theirs.[13]

In all these disputes with the religious leaders, Jesus was showing that the Sabbath was made for people to share and enjoy with the Creator. The good works that Jesus did on this day were in complete harmony with the spirit of Creation. By claiming to be the Lord of the Sabbath, he affirmed that it had its full meaning in his presence—he was responsible for it and he would work to restore it (John 5:17). There was much to do to enable people once again to enter into the joy of the Sabbath. But rigid rules inconsistently applied turn the true meaning of worship into a laborious work. Because they turn the attention inward to personal compliance with traditions, they kill the joy of worship. It is simply hypocritical to be preoccupied with man-made rules about religious activities and ignore the crying needs of people.

## Hypocrisy

Jesus also rebuked the hypocritical lives of religious people.[14] The oracle in Matthew 23 provides the best example of this aspect of his teaching.[15] And the point is clear from the beginning: the religious leaders were hypocrites, and even though when they read and explained Scripture the people had to listen, they were not to pattern their lives after such hypocritical teachers (vv. 2–3).[16]

---

13. Two other incidents had similar meanings, the healing of the blind man on the Sabbath (John 9:14–16) and the healing of the man with dropsy (Luke 14:1–6).
14. For comparison with the prophets, see Winkle, "The Jeremiah Model for Jesus in the Temple," 155–72.
15. See Garland, *The Intention of Matthew 23.*
16. This makes it clear that the authority is the Word of God, not the religious leader. On hypocrisy, see Weinfeld, "The Charge of Hypocrisy in Matthew 23 and in Jewish Sources," 52–58; and Powell, "Do and Keep What Moses Says," 419–35.

Jesus once again denounced those who were more interested in public displays than in pleasing God: they put on the elaborate garments and phylacteries to appear devout, they loved the seats of honor in synagogues, and they enjoyed being addressed with titles (Matt. 23:5–8). Jesus made it clear that he is the true teacher, the one who generates truth, not them. No one should be carried away with titles and adulation in an effort to be seen as the spiritual authority.[17]

There then follows a series of "woes," or denunciations or judgments, for those who followed hypocritical practices. These rebukes harmonize with Jesus' earlier words applied from Isaiah: "These people honor me with their lips, but their hearts are far from me. They worship me in vain; their teachings are but rules taught by men" (Matt. 15:8–9 from Isa. 29:13).

The first woe is for the leaders who refused to enter the kingdom and hindered others from entering also (Matt. 23:13). Religious activity that diverts attention from what is needed for salvation is evil; if it does not lead to faith in Jesus, the Messiah, it is hypocritical— you cannot have the kingdom without the king. A congregation today where the gospel is never presented is not much better, and those who try to worship God while denying the deity of Christ are hypocritical and their worship is false.

Jesus' second judgment concerns the zeal people had for Judaism (Matt. 23:15).[18] Jesus was not criticizing zeal, but a zeal that locked converts into a religious system that left no room for him (e.g., the zeal of Saul of Tarsus). Zealous proselytizing that converts people to religious systems taught by men and not to Christ is misguided, for he is the divine Lord of all. Promoting arrogant denominational loyalty over the unity of the church (for which Christ prayed) comes dangerously close to this.

The third judgment concerns mishandling Scripture. The leaders were blind guides (Matt. 23:16–22), for they tried to fight abuses in oaths by differentiating what wording was binding and what was not and in the process ended up encouraging lying. Jesus declared that people must tell

---

17. "Father" was reserved for the greatest teachers who formulated teachings to be followed. W. D. Davies and Allison observe that today "one could scarcely find a biblical text so little heeded" (*Gospel According to Saint Matthew*, 3:275). See also Barbour, "Uncomfortable Words VIII," 137–42; and Derrett, "Mt 23.8–10 a Midrash on Isa 54.5 and Jer 31.33–34," 372–86.

18. Verse 14 is from Mark 12:40 and Luke 20:47. There Jesus rebuked the practice of taking money from wealthy widows and making lengthy prayers the foil for the greed.

the truth; to nullify an oath by manipulative interpretation of the wording is dishonest and therefore hypocritical. Likewise today, when people do not keep their word, the witness of the church suffers; but more seriously, when the meaning of the Word of God is skewered to condone disobedience, then truth is lost and worship nullified.

The fourth woe addresses the great imbalance in righteous acts (Matt. 23:23–24). It is hypocritical to be concerned with meticulous details of religion and neglect the greater matters of justice, mercy, and faithfulness. Jesus was not saying that details like careful tithing were to be set aside; rather, they were to be subordinated to the more important things. Self-righteous legalism that has ignored justice, mercy, and faithfulness is abhorrent to God.

The fifth woe rebukes external religious acts without inner spiritual cleansing (Matt. 23:25–26). Jesus used the metaphor of cleansing a cup to teach that the appearance of purity is hypocritical if there is no inner cleansing.[19] Even today in preparing for church, people spend their time cleaning up their outward appearance while often neglecting what is in their hearts.

The next judgment on hypocritical religious leaders is one of the most serious: even though they may appear righteous, they are defiled by sin (Matt. 23:27–28). Whitewashed caves prevented pilgrims from entering to lodge for a night because they were actually tombs, and entering them would have defiled the travelers. The Pharisees were obsessed with avoiding any kind of defilement, but they themselves were sources of defilement because of sin. It is utter hypocrisy to pursue religious rules to prevent worldly defilement while harboring unbelief and sin.

The seventh and last judgment against the Pharisees is that they were the sons of those who killed the prophets (Matt. 23:29–32). By using the word "sons" (v. 31 NASB), Jesus was not just saying that they were descendants of those murderers but that they had the same nature. They claimed to be pious, religious leaders, but they were plotting to get rid of Jesus. To give honor to the righteous in public while being filled with hatred against them and seeking to ruin them was blatant hypocrisy. It still is.

The restored temple had given the Jews a secure focal point for their worship, but many of them were primarily concerned with the appearance

---

19. See Maccoby, "The Washing of Cups," 3–15; and R. J. Miller, "The Inside Is (Not) the Outside," 92–105.

of piety and the security of the place—as their ancestors had been. The magnificence of Herod's temple focused everyone's attention on externals. It had been under construction for decades and was admired for its size and beauty, as well as for the elaborate ritual performed in it (Luke 21:5). But Jesus prophesied that not one stone would be left on another (Luke 21:6; cf. Matt. 24:2). The coming judgment was on the people, not the building; but God would take away their security and the symbol of his presence. Like Jeremiah, Jesus taught that the temple would no longer be necessary for worship. In fact, it was getting in the way of true worship.

These judgments began with a pronouncement against empty spiritual acts and culminated with the charge that the leaders intended to murder God's messengers. This arrangement mirrors the movement of events in the life of Christ in the Gospels: early religious disputes about righteous acts intensified until the enemies of Jesus sought to kill him.

The sum of the matter is that hypocrisy destroys the meaning of worship so that it is not worship at all and will eventually bring down the institutions and places of worship. Only the divine Son of God would be able to transform worship so that it would overcome sinful corruptions and lead to glory.

## Jesus' Instruction on True Worship

Throughout his ministry Jesus stressed the spiritual quality of true worship. For example, he taught that if someone was going to offer a gift on the altar and someone else had something against him, the worshipper first had to be reconciled to the other person before coming to worship God (Matt. 5:23–24; recall the requirements of the reparation offering in Lev. 5). So the ritual of worship should not be pursued if there is unresolved sin in the lives of the people.

We see the same focus when Jesus taught that giving for public attention showed a complete lack of humility. By way of contrast he observed spiritual giving in the widow who gave her two mites (Mark 12:41–44; Luke 21:1–4). There was no fanfare and no public praise; after all, the amount was nothing—by any estimation. But in proportion to her condition as a poor widow, she gave more than the wealthy. And her giving was sacrificial, theirs was not. Moreover, because it was not great in amount, her gift would please only God. And it was given for that reason.

## True Worship Is "in Christ"

While Jesus was talking to a Samaritan woman who raised the old issue of which mountain was the true place of worship, he announced that all of that was about to change because he, the Messiah, had come. He said:

> Believe me, woman, a time is coming when you will worship the Father neither on this mountain nor in Jerusalem. You Samaritans worship what you do not know; we worship what we do know, for salvation is from the Jews. Yet a time is coming and has now come when the true worshipers will worship the Father in spirit and truth, for they are the kind of worshipers the Father seeks. God is spirit, and his worshipers must worship in spirit and in truth. (John 4:21–24)

Genuine worship is not restricted to a place. Having a place to worship was necessary, of course; and God had chosen Jerusalem, thus making the Samaritan claims wrong. But now that the Father had sent the Son, worship would no longer be centered in a specific temple but in the Lord in a new way. Jesus had already spoken of himself as the temple when he predicted his resurrection (John 2:19). And John literally described his incarnation in terms of the glory of God "tabernacling" on earth (1:14) and exclaimed that he and others had beheld his glory! The glory of Christ was displayed in a number of ways but shone the brightest when through his death he opened the way to God, symbolized by the veil of the temple being torn (Matt. 27:51; Luke 23:45; John 1:14; 1:51; 17).

Jesus reminded the Samaritan woman that God is a spirit and cannot be confined to one place. Accordingly, true worship must be "in spirit and truth" (John 4:23). On one level "spirit and truth" define the qualification of true worshippers. Worship has to be genuine, not just an empty ritual or outward form. So the emphasis is on "spirit," as the description of God as spirit in the next verse indicates. God requires worshippers to be in accord with his nature. To worship in spirit is to worship in harmony with the Spirit of God,[20] and that means that it will be in truth as

---

20. Worshippers must be careful not to trivialize worship in the Spirit; to be in harmony with the Spirit of God will control the whole life and not just a few moments in a service.

well—not with deception or hypocrisy. If worshippers are truly spiritual, the place and the structure are not so important.

This, in itself, is not new revelation. What is new is the presence on earth of the divine Lord who would provide this spiritual life to those who believe in him (John 4:13–14). Genuine worship would now require faith in Jesus the Messiah, because he is the Lord who was to come to his temple (Mal. 3:1). And since the Lord is greater than the temple, he would be the center and means of worship. So on another level, to worship "in Spirit" means that one has to be born by the Spirit into the new covenant and live by the Spirit (John 3:5; 7:37–39); to worship "in truth" means that one must confess that Jesus is Lord, that he is the way, the truth, and the life (John 14:6), and then walk in the truth.[21] When Jesus told the woman that the Father was seeking true worshippers, he was indicating that with his presence now on earth the age-old quest for worshippers would be fulfilled in him and not on some mountain. Jesus' mission was to bring people to the Father by faith in him (John 14:6–7). True worship is only in him because only he can provide eternal life—only through him can anyone come to the Father.

That this was the point of his ministry was clearly explained in the Last Supper. When Jesus ate this Passover meal with his disciples, he identified himself as the victim of the Passover sacrifice (Matt. 26:26–29). He had already taught that the "eating" (that is, the appropriating) of his body and blood was the means of eternal life (John 6:53–58). Now the institution of the Lord's Supper on the night that he was betrayed would transform the Passover, in fact all worship, forever; it established this meal as the central ritual observance of his church, because what it signified—his death for sin—is God's plan of redemption, the center of the historic faith.[22]

## True Worship Is Worship of Christ

If Jesus had taught only these things on worship, and done only the mighty works we have listed thus far, he would have been acclaimed as a prophet, perhaps the greatest prophet—and no more. But Jesus went much further than that. By his astounding claims and his greatest work,

---

21. In other words, one must worship in union with the Father, who is spirit, and according to the revelation of the Son, who is truth (Whitacre, *John,* 107).
22. See Routledge, "Passover and the Last Supper," 203–21.

the work of redemption, he made it clear that he is the divine Lord—God manifest in the flesh. Only the Son of God could transform worship because only he could fulfill all that had gone before, and only he could establish the form and contents of true worship for ages to come. The church, therefore, rightly worships him.

In what may be the key passage in Matthew, Jesus called people to put their faith in him and learn from him so that they might find the rest for their souls that the Lord had promised (Matt. 11:25–30). Here we have the message of the book in capsule form: Jesus is the only one who knows and reveals the Father; he is the one who embodies the wisdom of God and fulfills the law of God; and he is the one who fulfills the calling of Israel.[23] With his invitation for the weak and the weary to come to him, Jesus was calling the people to make a radical break from their religious allegiances by putting their trust in him and learning from him.[24]

And why should they do this? Because Jesus alone is able to give them rest, that redemptive and eternal rest that the LORD promised through the prophets (cf. Jer. 31:25). Thus, Jesus is far greater than Moses and the prophets. It is important that we appreciate the authority in his invitation: he was not saying that he could teach the people about that rest or show them how to find it; he announced that he would give it to them. That is an astounding claim. By what right could Jesus guarantee that he could provide eternal rest for those who came to faith in him? The answer is clear from the wider context: Jesus can guarantee access to the Father because he alone knows the Father—he is the Son of God. No one else would dare make such a promise.

Jesus called people to follow him because of who he was and what he was able to do. Early in Jesus' ministry, Nicodemus visited him at night (John 3:1–18). In the course of the conversation, Jesus affirmed that everyone who believed in him would have everlasting life. Indeed, faith in Jesus would be a transforming faith, causing people to be "born again." By drawing on ideas from the prophets, Jesus was reiterating the need for spiritual renewal in order to find a share in the world to come.[25] That re-

---

23. W. D. Davies and Allison, *Gospel According to Saint Matthew,* 2:297
24. Stanton, "Matthew 11:28–30," 3–9. The passage is often compared to Ecclesiasticus 5:23–27, in which wisdom invites people to take her yoke; the yoke there refers to the Torah. Jesus is calling people to exchange yokes, and to receive and follow his teachings (Carson, "Matthew," 278).
25. For further study see Hodges, "Water and Spirit—John 3:5," 206–20.

newal would come by faith in him. If he, the Messiah, was to take away the sins of the world, then there was no forgiveness apart from him. Eternal redemption is not obtained through sacrificial offerings and ritual washing, or physical descent from Abraham, or the intense study of the law, or personal piety! It comes through repentance and faith in Jesus. And those who are thus identified with Christ in the new covenant (i.e., "in Christ") will build their lives on the teachings of Christ and worship and adore him.

By his works Jesus demonstrated that he was more than a good teacher; he demonstrated that he had the authority to forgive sins. In healing the paralytic (Matt. 9:1–8; Mark 2:1–12; Luke 5:17–26) Jesus made this point very clearly. He healed the man by saying, "Take heart, son; your sins are forgiven" (Matt. 9:2). This immediately angered some teachers because it seemed blasphemous to them. Only God can forgive sins (Isa. 43:25; 44:22)! To claim to be able to forgive sins was to claim equality with God. The teachers' accusation of blasphemy, which grew stronger and stronger through the days of Jesus' ministry, was correct from their point of view—if he was a mere mortal he could not forgive sins.

But Jesus explained that he healed the man in order to show that he could also forgive sins. He came into the world not only to take away sins but also to take away the griefs and sorrows that result from the presence of sin (Matt. 8:14–17; from Isa. 53:4). It would have been easier *to say,* "Your sins are forgiven," for no one would know for sure; but to tell the man to get up and walk required supernatural power. If he could make the man whole, he could also take away sins. So by speaking the words of forgiveness first instead of the words of healing, Christ presented the deeper moral aspects of his healing miracles. The point is that the Judge of the whole world was with them; he could forgive because he had the authority to judge (John 5:27).

A greater demonstration of his power and glory was demonstrated in the raising of Lazarus from the dead (John 11). If the Lord Jesus could cure the physical results of sin, then death would be the greatest challenge. The devout believed in the resurrection at the end of the age, as Martha so admirably affirmed (v. 24). Jesus wanted them to know that "he alone under the express sanction of the Father would raise them up."[26]

---

26. Carson, *Gospel According to John,* 412.

Therefore he declared, "I am the resurrection and the life. He who believes in me will live, even though he dies; and whoever lives and believes in me will never die" (vv. 25–26). Faith in Christ, therefore, assures the believer of victory over suffering and death. To demonstrate these claims, Jesus raised Lazarus from the dead. The miracle was a revelatory act; it was a sign of who Jesus is and what he is able to do.[27] It also provided a foretaste of the great resurrection at the end of the age. The message was clear: Jesus alone can give eternal life through the resurrection from the dead. Rightly do Christians worship him.

Faith in Christ Jesus, therefore, brings assurance of eternal life through the forgiveness of sins because he is the resurrection and the life. To believe the claims of Jesus is to affirm that he is God manifested in the flesh (1 Tim. 3:16).

Throughout the Gospels Jesus used language that revealed his true nature. Most notable is his use of the Father-Son terminology (e.g., John 5:19–24).[28] These terms meant more than ordinary spiritual relationship with God. He taught us to pray "our Father," but he referred to God as "my Father" in a special sense. He explained again and again that he was from above, that he was not of this world, but that he was sent into the world (John 8:23). Finally, he simply declared, "I and the Father are one [and the same]" (John 10:30). It is no surprise that Jewish leaders tried to stone him (v. 31).

In reflecting upon the self-revelation of Jesus, John described him as the "only begotten Son" (3:16 KJV). In contrast to verbs like *make* or *create,* the verb *beget* is a special word here. To make or to create could refer to almost anything; but to beget means that one produces a child with his own nature. Since there is no procreation in the Godhead (God is a spirit), the word must be figurative. What it signifies is that Jesus shares the same nature as the Father—he is eternal and divine.[29] In short, he is the divine Lord.[30]

One of Jesus' favorite titles for himself is "Son of Man."[31] The expres-

---

27. See Tenney, "Topics from the Gospel of John, Part 2," 145–60.

28. Freed, "Some Old Testament Influences on the Prologue of John," 145–61.

29. The Nicene Creed states it very well: Jesus is "true God from true God, begotten, not made, of one Being with the father." Because "begotten" means that he shares the nature of the Father, John adds a prefix—"only" *(mono-).* He is the *only* begotten Son—there is only one.

30. Among many works, see Marshall, "The Divine Sonship of Jesus."

31. Moule, "The Son of Man," 277–79.

sion certainly would describe someone as a human, but it also was a special designation for a prophet who spoke for God (Ezek. 2:1, 6, 8). With regard to the mission of Jesus, however, it was a title for the Messiah drawn from Daniel 7:13–14. In contrast to the string of ruthless, tyrannical and sinful world powers, portrayed as beasts (7:1–8), one like the Son of Man would come with clouds to judge the world and establish a kingdom of righteousness. The vision reveals that the Messiah existed before his appearance on earth (his goings were from everlasting; Mic. 5:2) and that he was sent into the world. It is no surprise then that when Jesus, during his trial, alluded to Daniel 7 by affirming that he was indeed the Messiah and that he would be seated at the right hand of the Majesty on high and come again on the clouds of heaven, that Caiaphas tore his robe and accused him of blasphemy (Matt. 26:63–65).[32]

And then there is the occasional "I am" language that Jesus used (e.g., John 8:58).[33] In the exchange with the Pharisees, Jesus claimed that Abraham rejoiced to see his day (v. 56), perhaps meaning that Abraham was given additional insight, if not revelation, concerning the fulfillment of the "sacrifice" of his son on Mount Moriah, which later became the temple mount.[34] When the opposition replied that Jesus had a demon because he was not yet fifty years old and Abraham had lived centuries earlier, Jesus declared, "Before Abraham was born, I am." This statement goes beyond the Messiah's preexistence; it clearly equates Jesus with the great I Am of the Old Testament, the LORD God who revealed himself to Moses and to all the true worshippers who came to know the LORD, this Yahweh, by faith (cf. John 12:41; 18:6). The enemies of Jesus knew what he was saying and consequently tried to stone him on the spot (8:59). What they should have done was fall on their knees before him and worship him.

## Conclusion

Jesus knew full well that he had come to transform the spiritual life and worship of the people by his sacrificial death. Before he could establish the new covenant with his blood, however, he had to restore the spirit

---

32. The implications of the answer were staggering; it is as if Jesus were saying, "You may be my judge today, but when I come again in the clouds I will be your judge."
33. Freed, "Who or What Was Before Abraham in John 8:58?" 52–59.
34. Moberly, "Christ as the Key to Scripture," 143–73.

of true worship by his teachings and his mighty works. Because he is the incarnate Son of God who came as the Messiah, the Lord of the covenant, the Savior of the world, and the resurrection and the life, access to the Father comes only through him. The glory of the LORD had been revealed in many ways over the centuries, but in Christ Jesus it is fully revealed; and in him the hope of glory will be realized. Therefore, worship in the new covenant must be in Christ and of Christ.

# CHAPTER 24

# The Turning Point *of* Worship

## The Last Supper

THROUGH HIS DEATH JESUS made the perfect and complete sacrifice for sin, and by his resurrection he guaranteed that his death set us free from sin and secured for us everlasting life. These events marked the beginning of Christianity, but it was at the Last Supper that Jesus announced the turning point of the faith, and thereby of worship. It was there that Jesus explained the divinely intended meaning of the Passover sacrifice and inaugurated the new covenant.

The passages that report the Last Supper are Matthew 26:26–30; Mark 14:22–26; Luke 22:19–20; and 1 Corinthians 11:23–25. In writing to the Corinthians, Paul used the rabbinical expressions of "receiving [the tradition] from" *(qibbēl min)* and "delivering [it] to" *(māsar lᵉ)* in order to affirm the reliable preservation of the tradition back to Jesus and the disciples who were eyewitnesses.[1] While there are some differences in the ways the event is reported by the different writers, all the accounts show that Jesus was completely in charge of not only the Passover meal but also what it signified and how that was going to work out.[2] By using the Passover to explain his sacrificial death, he transformed the paschal meal into what it is today, Holy Communion, the dramatic celebration of communion with God through the sacrifice of Christ. Holy Communion grew out of the meaning of this Passover, but it is not the Passover; it is the new center of the worship of God.[3]

---

1. See further Maccoby, "Paul and the Eucharist," 247–67.
2. Daly, "The Eucharist and Redemption," 21–27.
3. Routledge, "Passover and the Last Supper," 203–21.

## The Last Passover

There is some debate over the nature of the Last Supper in relation to the Passover meal.[4] Three Gospels say that the Last Supper was a Passover meal that Jesus ate with the disciples (e.g., Matt. 26:17–30), but the fourth notes that the death of Jesus was prior to the Passover (John 19:31). The apparent discrepancy may be resolved by the way that different groups reckoned the days.[5] Jews from Galilee reckoned the day from sunrise to sunrise, but those from Judea reckoned it from sunset to sunset (as is the view today). When Passover fell on Nisan 14, a Thursday in A.D. 33, the year that Christ died,[6] Jews from Galilee would have killed the animal in the late afternoon and eaten the meal that Thursday night. Jesus and his disciples did this; he was arrested in the middle of that night, tried in the early morning, and crucified from 9:00 AM to 3:00 PM. Jews in Judea, however, would have to wait until Friday afternoon to kill the animal.[7] The picture that begins to emerge is that Jesus ate the Passover meal with his disciples and then became the Passover sacrifice, as it were, when he died at 3:00 PM, the time the Judeans would have begun sacrificing their animals.

There is sufficient evidence to show that the meal Jesus ate with his disciples was a Passover meal.[8] First, the supper took place in Jerusalem, as the law required. People had to spend the night within the city precincts, so Jesus stayed in a garden rather than with his friends in Bethany a few minutes away. Second, the room was readily obtained (Mark 14:13–15); the owners may have known Jesus and willingly given the room, but citizens were expected to make rooms available to pilgrims because Jerusalem was a national possession. Third, Passover was eaten at night, whereas

---

4. See Keating, *The Agape and the Eucharist;* and Routledge, "Passover and the Last Supper," 203–21.
5. Hoehner, *Chronological Aspects of the Life of Christ,* 85–90.
6. Ibid., 60–63, 95–114. Hoehner demonstrates that John the Baptist began his ministry in the fifteenth year of Tiberias, or A.D. 29. Jesus' ministry started shortly after and covered at least three years, including four Passovers. The fourth Passover, the one in which he died, was April 3, A.D. 33.
7. The Law said that the animal was to be killed in the late afternoon ("between the evenings") on the fourteenth of Nisan. Judeans started the fourteenth day after Thursday afternoon was over.
8. The book by Jeremias, *The Eucharistic Words of Jesus,* provides a number of evidences in a very clear way. See also Bahr, "The Seder of Passover and the Eucharistic Words," 181–202.

ordinary meals were eaten much earlier. Fourth, the table companions at this meal were few in number—Jesus and his disciples. Although Passover was normally a time for the whole family, new legislation had provided for fraternities to have the meal together, as long as there were enough people.[9] Fifth, people normally sat on stools or chairs, but at this meal they reclined at a few round tables. In Egypt the Israelites ate standing up because they were slaves poised to escape (Exod. 12:11); but now as free people they reclined as the Romans did. Sixth, this supper was eaten in a state of purity, for Jesus made washing their feet a requirement for fellowship with him (John 13:3–10), and not just a sign that he was a gracious host. Through the ritual of footwashing, he taught the greater spiritual requirement of humility, service, and forgiveness. Seventh, Jesus broke the bread as they were eating (Matt. 26:21–26; Mark 14:18–22). At a Passover the head of the group would introduce Passover devotions in the middle of the meal, and this would prompt the children to ask about the different order of the meal (Exod. 12:26–27; *Pes.* 10.37d.4f. in the Jerusalem Talmud). Eighth, they drank wine (Mark 14:23, 25). Wine was used at festal occasions and not at ordinary meals (of common folk); red wine was prescribed for Passover to symbolize the blood (*Pes.* 10.1). Ninth, Jesus spoke words of interpretation over the bread and the wine. Interpretation was a fixed part of the ritual; in it the head of the family or group was required to mention the lamb, the unleavened bread, and the bitter herbs (*Pes.* 10:5) and to relate them to the nation's redemption. Jesus followed the structure of the Passover ritual but used his own words of interpretation. And tenth, the Last Supper ended with the singing of a hymn (Matt. 26:30), which is most likely a reference to the second half of the Hallel psalms (Pss. 113–118).[10]

If the Last Supper was a Passover meal, then we may look at the order of such a meal from the accounts in the New Testament, Philo, and rabbinical sources. The content of the ritual in the time of Jesus is far from

---

9. This would explain the apparent absence of women and children. It is possible that they were in the same place the disciples later gathered (Acts 1) but in a different area (later the Upper Room held 120 people).

10. Other activities of that evening fit a Passover as well. E.g., some of the disciples assumed that Jesus sent Judas to make some last-minute purchases, for it would have to be done quickly if the next day was a feast day. Some thought that Jesus commissioned Judas to give something to the poor (John 13:26–29), which was customary on Passover.

clear, but we can see that what happened according to the Gospels fits into the sequence of the full celebration that emerged later (see Jeremias).

When a Passover meal began with the preliminary course, the leader probably blessed the feast day and the first cup of wine (the cup of sanctification, the *qiddûsh* cup). This course included, among other things, green and bitter herbs. Next came the Passover liturgy in which the story (the *haggādāh*) was related by the leader.[11] Then the first part of the Passover "*hallēl*," Psalms 113–116, was said or sung. The participants drank from the second cup (the cup of interpretation, the *haggādāh* cup). The main course was then served, and a grace was said by the leader over the unleavened bread. The meal consisted of lamb, unleavened bread, bitter herbs (Exod. 12:8), fruit puree, and wine. After the meal the leader said a grace over the third cup (the cup of blessing). The ritual concluded with, among other things, the singing of the second part of the "*hallēl*," Psalms 117–118, and the drinking of the fourth cup of wine (the cup of consummation).

According to the New Testament, Jesus spoke the word of interpretation over the bread with the grace at the beginning of the main meal. The interpretation over the wine came at the grace after the meal (Mark 14:23, literally, "having given thanks") because it followed the bread and preceded the *hallēl*. Paul confirms this with his "after supper" (1 Cor. 11:25) and "the cup of blessing" (10:16 KJV). So Jesus used the prayers before and after the meal to give the words of interpretation over the bread and the wine. The cup that Jesus would not drink with them at that time would have been the fourth cup, the cup of consummation. He would drink that in the kingdom—at the real consummation. So they sang the Passover "*hallēl*" and went out to the garden.

Passover was a time of rejoicing, a festival of freedom. It looked back to the glorious deliverance from bondage through the blood of the lamb, but it also looked forward to the coming redemption through the Messiah, the hope of glory. But the heavy thoughts at this Passover meal must have surprised and troubled the disciples.[12] Later they came to understand and glory in it. Jesus' words provided the interpretation of Passover's true meaning, something that Israel should not have missed.[13]

---

11. See Flusser, "Some Notes on Easter and the Passover Haggadah," 52–60.
12. D. F. Ford observes that the festival was full of life—food, drink, singing, teaching, and such; but it was also a rehearsal for death (*Self and Salvation,* 147).
13. Daly, "The Eucharist and Redemption," 21–27.

## The True Passover

Jesus' words of interpretation are critical, of course, because they were to become the sanctifying words used in the celebration of Holy Communion.[14] A close analysis of the words reveals that Jesus was identifying himself as the true Paschal Lamb that was slain for the remission of sins. And that—what the Passover signified—would become the center of worship in the new covenant.[15]

### The Interpretation of the Bread

According to Matthew 26:26, Jesus took unleavened bread (Exod. 12:15), gave thanks, and broke it; he gave it to his disciples and said, "Take and eat; this is my body." The normal custom was to say a traditional prayer like: "Blessed are you, O LORD our God, King of the universe, who brings forth bread from the earth." But when Jesus broke the bread and distributed it to each of the disciples, he added his words of instruction and explanation.[16] Just as the Israelites identified with their ancestors who were redeemed from bondage by eating the Passover meal, so now Jesus' disciples were to identify with his redemptive death by eating this bread.

The statement "This is my body" is not part of the Passover ritual, but it was prompted by the description of the Passover bread as "the bread of affliction" (Deut. 16:3). In what became eucharistic language, Jesus had earlier claimed to be the Bread of Life that came down from heaven to give life (John 6:35). But now he explained further that his body was the bread of affliction, indicating that it would be given up for his disciples. In fact, he probably used the word "flesh" (*basar*) to express "body";[17] if so, then the language of the sacrifices would make it clear that he was identifying himself as the Passover Lamb. The fact that the bread was broken brings out the point of comparison—the bread that came down from heaven will give life only by being broken and then received by the followers of Jesus.

---

14. Schurmann, "Jesus' Words in the Light of His Actions at the Last Supper," 119–31.
15. D. F. Ford notes that this ritual of Holy Communion is the most participated in and most discussed in human history (*Self and Salvation*, 137).
16. One of the most powerful aspects of this is that with both the bread and the wine we have a face-to-face meal and command; this looks to the ultimate confrontation with the Lord in glory (ibid., 145).
17. Jesus would have said the words in Hebrew or Aramaic, which have no word for body. The Gospels translated the words into Greek and used the word *soma*.

## The Interpretation of the Wine

According to Matthew 26:27–28, Jesus "took the cup, gave thanks and offered it to them, saying, 'Drink from it, all of you. This is my blood of the [new] covenant, which is poured out for many for the forgiveness of sins.'" This is the third cup, the "cup of blessing" that followed the meal. The normal grace would have said something like, "Blessed are you, O LORD our God, King of the Universe, Creator of the fruit of the vine."

The Greek term translated "gave thanks" is *eucharistēsas;* from this the church designated the holy meal as *Eucharist*, "Thanksgiving." The choice of this particular term shows a proper understanding of the meal: the participants receive the bread and the wine with thanksgiving for what the Lord Jesus Christ has done for them, not in order to obtain peace with God. In this sense the Lord's Supper is exactly like the Israelite peace offering (Passover being a form of the peace offering because people ate from the sacrifice). In it the worshippers celebrated being at peace with God.

But after giving thanks Jesus added his interpretation. "This is my blood of the [new] covenant" (Matt. 26:28) confirms that he was appropriating sacrificial language to himself, for "body [flesh]" and now "blood" designated the two component features of Israel's sacrificial animals. And the use of the verb "poured out" is an obvious reference to the sacrifices with the blood being poured out at the altar. The declaration of Paul is the point: "Christ, our Passover, was sacrificed for us" (1 Cor. 5:7 NKJV).

In his words over the wine Jesus brought together three significant Old Testament passages. First, Jesus drew upon Exodus 24:8. There Moses inaugurated the old covenant at Sinai with sacrificial blood, saying, "This is the blood of the covenant." The Mishnah tractate *Pesahim* 10:6 also uses Exodus 24:8 to interpret the Passover wine as a symbol for blood that seals the covenant. By declaring "This is my blood," Jesus was clearly showing that he was doing what Moses had done—inaugurating a covenant. But this was a better covenant than the old one, for it would be sealed by Jesus' blood and not just the blood of an animal. It was the new covenant (see the wording in Luke and Paul).

Jeremiah 31:31–34, which prophesied that a new covenant would be instituted at the end of the age, is the second passage referred to in Jesus' words of interpretation. Although many of its promised blessings still await fulfillment, the Last Supper must be interpreted as the inauguration of this new covenant. Jesus fully understood that the violent, sacrificial death he was about to endure would ratify the covenant he was inaugurating (cf. Isa. 42:6; 49:8)—it would be sealed by the blood of the divine Lord.

Jesus also said that the blood of this covenant was to be poured out for many for the forgiveness of sins. He had already explained that he was the servant who was to suffer in accordance with the Scriptures; he said, "The Son of Man did not come to be served, but to serve, and to give his life as a ransom for many" (Matt. 20:28). He thus identified himself as the Suffering Servant of Isaiah 53. The third passage Jesus alluded to, then, is the fourth Servant Song of Isaiah (52:13–53:12). In the song the word "many" *(rabbîm)* figures prominently: "many were astonished at you" (52:14 NKJV), and "my righteous servant will justify many" (53:11), and "he bore the sin of many" (53:12). The verb "pour out" is also used in the song: "He poured out his life unto death" (53:12); his death was an "offering for sin" (53:10 NKJV). The suffering and death in the prophecy are clearly substitutionary and redemptive: "He was wounded for our transgressions, He was bruised for our iniquities; the chastisement for our peace was upon Him, and by His stripes we are healed. . . . And the LORD has laid on Him the iniquity of us all" (53:5–6 NKJV).[18]

Interpreters have tried to explain why the prophet, and Jesus, used the word "many." The community at Qumran, for example, understood "many" to mean the elect people of God, the eschatological community. The Jewish Targum and other rabbinical literature interpreted it as referring to Israel. But in the context of the Isaianic prophecies, the word "many" probably refers to the sinful people in the world, Gentiles as well as Jews, those for whom the Servant would die.

So when Jesus interpreted the wine as his blood of the new covenant poured out for many for the forgiveness of sins, he was explaining that his death would be a substitutionary sacrifice that would restore people to communion with God. With this clarification we also have the divine

---

18. The song cannot be interpreted as referring to Israel or even the righteous remnant of Israelites who had to suffer in the Captivity for the sins of others. Such suffering might be considered vicarious, but it was not redemptive. The wording of the song, in fact, draws upon the ritual of the Day of Atonement, when the sins were placed on the scapegoat.

explanation of the whole Israelite sacrificial system. If Jesus' "flesh and blood" fulfilled the Passover, then the full meaning of all the sacrifices is also to be found in him. It is no surprise, then, that in the visions of glory John saw seated on the throne the "Lamb" that had been slain (Rev. 5:6).

## The Memorial of the Lord's Supper

What should be the meaning and the impact of the celebration of the Lord's Supper on the worshippers? Jesus said, "Do this in remembrance of me" (Luke 22:19), which at least requires a faithful participation in the ritual. But Paul explained that observing it would also be a proclamation: "For whenever you eat this bread and drink this cup, you proclaim the Lord's death until he comes" (1 Cor. 11:26). This kind of living out of the faith in the eyes of the world would be with a view to the completion in glory. After all, Jesus set that eschatological goal by saying, "I will not drink of this fruit of the vine from now on until that day when I drink it anew with you in my Father's kingdom" (Matt. 26:29).

### Memorial

Believers are told to observe the Lord's Supper "in remembrance" of him. This injunction for a memorial *(anímnēsis)* usually prompts worshippers to focus their attention on the suffering and death of Jesus Christ for a few minutes in the service, to contemplate how the elements represent the body of Christ that was broken for them and the blood that was shed for them. Marcus Dods summarizes this part of the meaning by writing:

> Again, the form of this memorial is fitted to recall the actual life and death of the Lord. It is His body and blood we are invited by the symbols to remember. By them we are brought into the presence of an actual living Person. Our religion is not a theory; it is not a speculation, a system of philosophy putting us in possession of a true scheme of the universe and guiding us to a sound code of morals; it is, above all, a personal matter. We are saved by being brought into right personal relations. And in this Sacrament we are reminded of this and are helped to recognize Christ as an actual living Person, who by His body and blood,

by His actual humanity, saved us. The body and blood of Christ remind us that His humanity was as substantial as our own, and His life as real.[19]

If this were all that is involved in the remembrance of him, it would be powerful enough to inspire love and adoration. But the expression includes more than a simple remembering. The idea of a memorial had been introduced in the ritual of Israel's sacrifices with the term *'azkārāh* (s.v. *zākar*, "to remember,").[20] For example, a portion of the dedication offering (Lev. 2) was burnt on the altar as a token memorial. This gift *(minkhāh)* always followed the atoning sacrifice (Lev. 1), indicating that gratitude and dedication are the proper responses to atonement. But the word *'azkārāh* includes the meaning of acting on what is remembered.[21] When a dedication offering was made with a token given as a memorial, it was a way of keeping the covenant promises active. The believers reminded God of his covenant promises and their needs; but since it was an act of dedication, they also were reminding themselves of their covenant responsibilities. Worship always had this aspect of covenant renewal.

Regarding Christian worship, Dods says, "These symbols were appointed to be for a remembrance of Christ in order that, remembering Him, we might renew our fellowship with Him. In the Sacrament there is not a mere representation of Christ or a bare commemoration of events in which we are interested; but there is also an actual, present communion between Christ and the soul."[22]

If the Lord's Supper is such a communion with the living Lord who made an eternal covenant with us by his sacrifice for our sins, then the memorial aspect of it should be continually life changing.[23] It cannot remain a contemplative act. Rather, by doing this in remembrance of him,

---

19. Dods, *First Epistle to the Corinthians*, 270–71.
20. For a helpful word study, see Childs, *Memory and Tradition*, 1–8.
21. E.g., when God remembered Noah (Gen. 8:1), he began to reverse the Flood. The Psalms and Chronicles use "remember" in prayers for God to act on his promises (e.g., Ps. 132:1). And the thief on the cross asked the Lord to remember (=save) him when he came into his kingdom (Luke 23:42).
22. Dods, *First Epistle to the Corinthians*, 272.
23. D. F. Ford says that to identify with Jesus' death in this act of communion is "to discover an unimaginable fullness of life through death" (*Self and Salvation*, 148). See further Sykes, "The Eucharist as 'Anamnesis,'" 115–18; Dahl, "Anamnesis," 11–29; and Gregg, *Anamnesis in the Eucharist*.

we renew not only our confidence in the promises made to us through Christ but also our commitment to fulfill our covenant obligations. And these are many, if we but take the time to consider them. They include our responsibilities to other covenant members, such as loving them, forgiving them, encouraging them, and praying for them; they include our caring for the widow and the orphan, the poor and needy, and the stranger in our midst; they include providing hope to the world, body and soul, by meeting the needs of the oppressed and suffering in the world; they include finding our spiritual place of service and giving our lives to it; they include championing righteousness in society, opposing sin, contesting false teaching, and a host of other obligations we have to our Lord Jesus Christ. In other words, the exercise of this remembrance is for the purpose of transforming our perspectives and our activities; we remember that Christ has made us his own to fit us for service. Morrill says:

> The variety of practices—preaching, worship, prayer, and ethical action—whereby the Church keeps the memory of Jesus together comprise the praxis of faith whereby Christians know themselves as subjects in the presence of God. In the sacramental celebration of Eucharist this memory and identity converge in the Church's most compelling moment of knowledge. The Church's ritual action reveals the love unto death that made Jesus' words at the Last Supper true so that this truth might be realized in the ethical actions of believers until Christ comes again in glory.[24]

A large part of this understanding is the fact that it is communion. It is not an independent act of worship—we are not dining alone. We are to come to the Lord's Table as a community of believers who by God's grace are at peace with God and therefore at peace with one another. In this ritual act we are drawn out of ourselves to worship and serve the Savior. If this is what happens, then we have something genuine to offer the world, something worth proclaiming.

## Proclamation

Worship has always included proclamation in various forms. But the proclamation that is made through celebrating Holy Communion cap-

---

24. Morrill, *Anamnesis as Dangerous Memory,* 188.

tures the essence of the faith. From the very beginning, when sacrifices were made, the worshippers proclaimed the "name of Yahweh," that is, the nature and the saving acts of God. Over time these proclamations were put into the forms of psalms and creeds or expanded in prophetic messages. Now, if the ritual of Holy Communion is properly and fully explained and the ritual is observed with holiness and piety, the gospel will be proclaimed in the most effective way—its message of the remission of sins dramatized in the ritual of Communion.[25] Thus, this is a uniquely Christian ritual. Other religions have festivals, prayers, holy books, and hymns, but Holy Communion proclaims that in Christ there is forgiveness of sin, peace with God, and eternal life.

## Consummation

In the Passover ritual the fourth cup of wine, which ended the meal, was the cup of consummation. The four cups correspond to the four promises in Exodus 6:6–7, the fourth matching, "I will take you as my own people, and I will be your God." This cup, then, looks forward to life in the messianic kingdom; it was worship with the hope of glory. It makes sense that Jesus would not drink this cup until the kingdom in all its fullness came, meaning that the consummation of God's program of redemption lay in the future. Worshippers keep the Lord's Supper until he comes, but the consummation of their redemption will be celebrated in full communion with Christ at the messianic banquet (Isa. 25:6; Matt. 8:11). Holy Communion therefore must include this eschatological view, both to enable believers to endure this life and to expedite their commitment to serve the Lord until that time.

## The Passover Hymn

Jesus and his disciples sang a hymn and then went out to the Garden of Gethsemane (Matt. 26:30). Since this was a Passover meal, the reference is to the "*hallēl*" psalms that were sung, the last of them ending the meal. Psalm 118, the grand finale of the collection, is a liturgical psalm in which

---

25. The early church did not have to write developed treatises on salvation as it did with the Trinity or with Christology because the eucharistic liturgy was so rich in the doctrine (see McIntyre, *The Shape of Soteriology*, 8, 10). If more attention were paid to what was said at the celebration, the chief doctrines of the faith would be effectively reviewed in worship—the deity of Christ, the incarnation, the substitutionary, atoning death of Christ, justification by faith, the resurrection, and the hope of glory.

the singer tells of his[26] triumph over the nations who surrounded him. The victory did not come in normal ways but by the enemies' change of heart.[27] The second half of the psalm records the glorious procession up to the sanctuary to praise the LORD for the victory (vv. 19–29). The leader of the congregation is welcomed and blessed by the priests because he trusts in the LORD for salvation and comes to worship in the name of the LORD. In expressing his praise, the psalmist uses the imagery of the building stone (v. 22): the stone (the leader, meaning the nation) the builders (empire builders like Babylon) rejected (considered nothing and tried to destroy) has now became the head of the corner (the center of God's rebuilding of the theocracy), a work that was marvelous to behold (v. 23). So the psalm appears to have been written at the restoration from the Captivity.

Because this psalm was regularly sung at Passover, it found frequent application in Holy Week. First, when Jesus made his Triumphal Entry (Matt. 21:1–11), those who believed in him sang this song as he entered the city (it was one they sang on that occasion anyway, but now they saw it differently). He was not just a worshipper coming in the name of the LORD. He was the "coming One," the Messiah, so they blessed him, proclaiming, "Blessed is he who comes in the name of the LORD!" (cf. Ps. 118:26). They also cried out for complete salvation, using the psalmist's expression, "Save now" (*hôshî'āh-nnā'*, Ps. 118:25; in Greek, *hōsanna*).

Then, during the week Jesus interpreted this passage (Matt. 21:42–44). He was the *stone*[28] that the builders (Israel's leaders) rejected; but now he was to be the center of God's new covenant program. His victory over his enemies would be a spiritual and eternal victory, conquering sin and the grave. And so the Hebrew psalm ends with "Bind the sacrifice with cords to the horns of the altar" (Ps. 118:27 NKJV).

The third use of this psalm was in the Upper Room, when Jesus and his disciples sang the hymn. With this song's final words about the sacrifice, they went out into Gethsemane to watch and pray.

Because of the fulfillment of the Passover in the passion of Christ, the

---

26. That the psalmist speaks on behalf of the nation is clear from the circumstances of the deliverance recorded in the psalm. It was the nation, under the leadership of the king or governor, that was surrounded by other nations and finally delivered by God.

27. The verb "I cut them off" (Ps. 118:10) is the word "circumcise."

28. In the Gospel of Matthew Jesus is frequently presented as the true Israel; here, then, the psalm is typological of Christ. Other postexilic passages use the image of the stone for the Messiah (Dan. 2; Zech. 3).

church was absolutely correct to adopt the language of this hymn for its liturgy. Christians who use "Hosannah" and "Blessed is he who comes in the name of the LORD" in their worship liturgy are celebrating the fulfillment of the divinely inspired hymns used in Passover.

## Conclusion

There is an account of Jesus' meeting with two disciples from Emmaus that provides a wonderful summation of this essential feature of worship (Luke 24:13–35), so much so that it left its mark on the liturgy of the early church.[29] On the day of his resurrection, Jesus met the discouraged disciples as they were going home to Emmaus. Upon hearing the reason for their discouragement—the death of the one they had hoped was the Redeemer—Jesus rebuked them for their ignorance of the whole plan of God and their lack of faith. He then proceeded to expound from all the Law and the Prophets how the Messiah should suffer before entering into his glory (v. 27). Then, at the meal in Emmaus Jesus took the bread, blessed it, and broke it; and at that moment the eyes of the two men were opened—and they knew him! But then he vanished from their sight.[30] The power of the clear exposition of the Word of God and the celebration of the meal at the Lord's Table have formed the heart of Christian worship ever since.[31] Without the effectual exposition of Scripture, the meal will not be fully understood; and without the communal meal, the teaching will not be personalized and activated by faith.[32] Here in the experience of Cleopas and his friend we have the pattern: The experience of the burning heart when the Scripture is opened to us and the awareness of the reality of his presence in the breaking of the bread are absolutely essential to the vitality of our worship.[33]

This passage is a marvelous summation of the gospel itself. Thévenot

---

29. But see another explanation in Orlett, "The Influence of the Early Liturgy upon the Emmaus Account," 212–19.

30. The presence of the Lord in their midst and then his disappearance reflects the ancient motifs of the presence and the absence of the LORD—he is the living God and he is the absent God. In the Most Holy Place God was there, but he was not there. In Emmaus Christ made his real presence known, but he was not going to be restricted to that place or any place (see D. F. Ford, *Self and Salvation*, 104).

31. There is a parallel with the story of the Eunuch in Acts, but there the event ends with baptism. See J. M. Gibbs, "Luke 24:13–33 and Acts 8:26–39," 17–30; see also Rosica, "The Road to Emmaus and the Road to Gaza," 117–31.

32. Dupont, "The Meal at Emmaus," 105–21.

33. R. F. Smith, "Did Not Our Hearts Burn Within Us?" 187–93.

traces how the structure of the Emmaus account is similar to that of the Genesis account of the first sin (Gen. 2–3)—but in reverse.[34] The meeting with the risen Christ is thus a re-creation, a point that affects our view of the Eucharist. Through the symbolism of the meal, we experience a new relationship to seeing and hearing in worship, which leads to the recognition of otherness in spiritual service. The disciples who heard the Word and experienced the presence of the risen Lord could not wait to go back to Jerusalem and spread the good news.

The account also gives us a dramatic picture of how the gospel reverses the Fall. On the one hand, in Genesis God created humans and gave them his words of blessing and his warning not to disobey his words. But they missed God's clear meaning and went their own way from God. In disobedience they ate, and their eyes were opened! But rather than being like God as Satan had promised, they realized that they had opened up a world of evil and were now vulnerable, so in fear they hid themselves. Now they saw themselves as sinners, and their only prospect was death. But on the other hand, in the Gospels Christ died that death for all of us and opened the way for new life. Here on the road to Emmaus, he revealed God's plan fully and clearly so that the hearts of these disciples burned within them. And when they entered the house to eat the meal with this teacher, their eyes were supernaturally opened so that they recognized him as the risen Christ. He was alive, and the prospect of death forever lost its sting.

The differences between the two accounts explain how the gospel reverses the Fall. In the garden the Lord was invisible; but on the road to Emmaus he was visible, when he chose to be, and present with his people, thanks to the Incarnation. In Genesis only a few words from the Lord were revealed; but along the road to Emmaus, all the Scriptures about the divine plan were revealed because it was the fullness of time. And, in the beginning Adam and Eve ate in disobedience and broke their communion with God; but in the home in Emmaus, the Lord ate with his disciples as a sign of communion. Through his death and resurrection, Jesus reversed the curse of Genesis and re-created communion through his presence with his people. Is it any wonder that Christian worship should commemorate such a great redemption by the clear exposition of Scripture and the Communion meal?

---

34. Thévenot, "Emmaüs, une nouvelle Genèse? Une lecture psychanalytique de Genèse 2–3 et Luc 24, 13–35," 3–18.

# Conclusion *for* Part 7

DURING THE EXILE THE JEWISH people found themselves removed from every part of their formal religious life. As the years went by, the memory of the temple, the sacrifices, the festivals, and the Levitical choirs would have been very difficult to retain were it not for the Word of the LORD. As the holy books were read and explained by people like Ezekiel, the faithful were able to preserve their heritage, a heritage characterized by divine intervention throughout their history. And when the people returned to the land, now in ruins, it was that same revelation that inspired them to rebuild the temple and reinstitute worship. The prophets, as well as Ezra and Nehemiah, reminded the people of God's promise to restore communion with his people in a land at rest. That hope would never die out if the people held fast to the historic faith revealed in the Word of God.

Then, when God sent his Son into the world to fulfill the promises, the people were ready, eagerly awaiting that messianic age that had eluded them for centuries. Their form of worship now placed greater emphasis on the Word of God than it had before, so much so that legalism and self-righteous hypocrisy became the besetting sins of the religious people, and not idolatry. But the diligent study of Scripture kept alive in the memory the great works of God—Creation, the Exodus, Solomon's glorious temple, and more recently the deliverance from the Exile. They also memorialized with fasts and days of awe the great suffering that they brought upon themselves in the past. Jesus, however, transformed worship for all time by giving believers something greater to remember in their worship—his body and his blood that was poured out for the sins of the world. Jesus the Messiah of Israel was fulfilling the Scriptures, most immediately those that had directed Israelite worship for centuries and had held out the promise of forgiveness and redemption, and a share in the new creation. Now true spiritual worship would be in Christ, the divine Son of God. Now when believers recall the hope of glory as it was revealed down through the history of worship, they must interpret it in the light of the fulfillment in Christ Jesus.

# PART 8

# WORSHIP *in* CHRIST

*Patterns of Worship in the Early Church*

# Introduction

IN GENESIS THE HUMAN RACE that God created began life in the presence of God in a garden. But when Adam and Eve sinned by taking and eating from the forbidden tree, they were expelled from Paradise to live and die under the curse. Humanly speaking, since there was no way to return to the garden, they had to accept God's provisions for life in a world alienated from him and hope for an end to the struggle with evil.

In the Gospels the Son of God fulfilled God's Word and provided the way back to God. In the Upper Room he inaugurated the new covenant with the bread and the wine, commanding his followers to "take and eat"; and on the cross he sealed the covenant with his blood, taking on himself the sins of the world and opening the door to Paradise.

The followers of Jesus saw him on many occasions after his resurrection. He was truly alive! And they saw him ascend with clouds and angels into heaven. He was truly the exalted Lord of glory! And this was a great mystery, this godliness in which God was manifested in the flesh. As man he was one of them, the seed of the woman who gained the victory over the seed of the serpent for Adam's race. But he could not have done that if he had not also been divine. So as God he was worthy of their praise and devotion. It took a while for Christians to understand all this. But the careful search of Scripture and the remembrance of the interpreting words of Jesus in the ritual opened their eyes, just as it had done for the two disciples of Emmaus. The opening of the Scriptures and the breaking of the bread! This is how the Lord designed it to be; this is how it still is in worship.

# CHAPTER 25

# The Circumstances *of* Early Christian Worship

PEOPLE CAN WORSHIP AT ANY TIME, in any place. But it is practical and profitable for worshippers to have a place where they can worship in communion. Old Testament believers went to various places where God had made his presence known. They believed that his presence could be communicated more readily in such settings, even though they knew that he was not limited to those spots. And when God instructed that they build a holy place, great care was given (and required by God) for the appropriate decorum, the arrangement of space, and the placing of furnishings and symbols.

From their attention to the place of worship, we can make several observations. First, the place of worship must be functional. The physical surroundings must accommodate whatever forms of worship are to be followed. Second, the place for worship should be part of the communication of the faith. If worship is to reflect the hope of glory, the triumph of the LORD over sin and death, and the fellowship of the saints, then the structure and symbols should help convey these truths—or at least not get in the way of worship. Finally, the place of worship should be an expression of the congregation's love and devotion to God. It should be uplifting and unique, set apart from the world and honoring to God.

In the Old Testament the impact of the sanctuary and its service would have been exhilarating and transforming. People would have left the sanctuary knowing that they had been lifted up in body, mind, and spirit; they had come up out of the world and had all their senses engaged in the adoration of and communion with the LORD God.

For the early church the situation was a good deal more complex than what is normally assumed. It was a time of transition and new beginnings, and the setting of worship shows this. There were Christians who had been devout Jews, and they brought their culture with them to worship; there were Christians who had been hellenized, and they reacted against the Jewishness of the others; and there were Gentiles who were Christians, and they brought aspects of their cultures to worship. But since Christianity was the fulfillment of the Old Testament, it was impossible to do away with the circumstances of Old Testament worship.

## Places for Christian Worship

*Jewish Christian worship* retained some continuity with the temple and the synagogue as long as possible. The people continued to go to the temple daily as a part of their devout worship and new mission (Acts 2:46). And they continued to go up to the temple at the hours of prayer, for the temple was a house of prayer (3:1). Christians found the temple to be an appropriate place for proclaiming the good news about Jesus the Messiah as they praised and testified in the house of the LORD (3:11–26; 4:12–13, 19–26; 5:42).

But Christianity had started, so to speak, in the Upper Room, and that is where the early believers met for prayer (Acts 1:12–14). Luke tells us that they continued steadfastly in the teaching of the apostles, their fellowship in Christ, the breaking of the bread, and prayer (Acts 2:42).[1] In addition, when believers came together, they shared their earthly goods as well as their faith. Acts 2:46–47 tells of two arenas for their devotion: "So continuing daily with one accord in the temple, and breaking bread from house to house, they ate their food with gladness and simplicity of heart, praising God and having favor with all the people" (NKJV).

*Hellenistic Christians* had not been steeped in Hebrew customs, so their worship was different. Naturally tensions arose. The emphasis among these people was on a reinterpretation, if not renunciation, of Jewish practices. In many ways their attitude toward the law and the traditions had already been expressed by Jesus: for example, the temple was now the body of Christ (1 Cor. 3:16–17; Eph. 2:19–22), Christ was the true Passover (Rom. 3:25; 1 Cor. 5:7), and believers were priests (1 Peter 2:5, 9). These teachings became predominant in Christian worship, even though others in the early church held to Jewish customs as long as they could.

---

1. These are the rudimentary elements of worship that would take on a distinctively Christian nature in the early church: teaching the Word of God, fellowship in Christ, Holy Communion, and prayer.

*Gentile Christianity* had to overcome the Jewish thinking that Gentiles could become Christians only if they first became Jews (cf. Acts 10–11). According to Paul's first letter to the Corinthians, pagans had brought some customs with them, and these had to be relinquished in order to avoid problems with the Jewish converts. Thus the forms of worship were retained and Old Testament ideas reinterpreted. Gentiles had to be instructed in the Old Testament to understand the reasons for the forms of worship, not to mention the whole faith; and Paul never hesitated using the Old Testament in his teaching.

Interestingly, 1 Corinthians provides some of the most important information about worship for the middle of the first century. There are forms of blessings (1:3; 16:23); a great emphasis on the ministry of the Word with gifts of revelation, knowledge, prophecy, and words of instruction (14:6); responses of the people that included hymns (14:26), prayers, singing, saying amen, giving thanks (14:13–17); as well as preaching and observing the Lord's Supper (chaps. 10–11; 15). The old festivals of Passover and Pentecost were also brought forward for a new use in the church (5:7; 16:8).[2] And while there was a good deal of spontaneous participation in worship at Corinth, order (14:26–33a, 40) and discipline (5:5, 12–13; 6:1–6) were also needed.

Many early Christians were forced out of Jerusalem through persecution (Acts 8:1), and as they went they spread the gospel. When Paul began his ministry, he used the synagogue service as the opportunity to deliver the message of Jesus the Messiah (13:5, 14, 44; 14:1). In no time at all, churches not only were founded but also were flourishing, making continuance in small pockets in the synagogues difficult (13:1). Therefore, when churches were established, Paul appointed elders in every church, apparently following the pattern in the synagogues (14:23). The apostles apparently were based in Jerusalem (Acts 15; Gal. 1:18–19; 2:9), and from there they made rulings on the composition and customs of the church.

Paul continued to work within Jewish worship. He ministered in the synagogue on the Sabbaths (Acts 17:10; 18:4, 19), joined in prayer on the Sabbath as well (16:13), wanted to get to Jerusalem in time for Pentecost (20:16), and even fulfilled purification ritual at the temple (21:26).

So as the church and its forms of worship began, the Jewish heritage

---

2. Talley, *Origins of the Liturgical Year;* and R. Nelson, *Companion to the Festivals and Fasts.*

was not suddenly shaken off. On the contrary, because the full meaning of the Old Testament had been realized in Christ, it was easy for Paul to make the proclamation of the faith in the centers of Jewish worship. In time, of course, Christians had to separate entirely from those places, but then they had grown so large in number that it was almost impossible for them to meet in rooms or homes as they had done at the beginning (cf. Acts 12:12 and 19:9—from a home prayer meeting to the school of Tyrannus).

It is untenable to argue for a simple home setting as the only place of worship for the early church. Early Christians met in homes to be sure,[3] just as Israelite worship started in homes with Passover (Exod. 12); but just as the places and the practices of worship grew in ancient Israel, so too did the church need larger places of worship. Other spiritual needs of the Christians were met in other settings as well. The temple worship met their need for praise and glorious celebration—the singing of the Psalms enhanced their appreciation of the true faith even more. In the temple and the synagogues, they also met for prayer and the study of the Scripture— after all, it was their Bible too. So in the early period of the church, the places of worship were varied.

There is a gap in the information of about one hundred years before we find evidence for and descriptions of specified places of worship—church buildings.[4] With the preparation of places for worship came the use of symbols as well, usually a simple cross at first, but then more detailed symbols.[5] The ancient Syrian church seems to be a Christian version of the Jewish synagogue, the symbols, ark, veil, and candlestick all showing continuity with the Old Testament through Christian interpretation. But now a table for the Lord's Supper became the new most holy place, and the whole church pointed east in anticipation of the second coming rather than toward Jerusalem.[6]

By the time of Constantine (about 300), large churches were being built and Roman basilicas were being converted into places of worship.

---

3. Branick, *The House Church in the Writings of St. Paul.* See also R. P. Martin, *Worship in the Early Church.*
4. Hoppe, *The Synagogues and Churches of Ancient Palestine.*
5. Of the many works listed in the bibliography, see especially Cope, *Symbolism in the Bible and the Church;* Dillenberger, *Theology of Artistic Sensibilities;* and Stafford, *Christian Symbolism in the Evangelical Churches.*
6. See Webber, *Worship: Old and New,* 155–56.

This was due to the growing numbers who wished to attend and the developing hierarchy that was needed. Over the centuries the bishop's (overseer's) chair moved from the center of the congregation to a place behind the altar, becoming a throne of power. This cleared the way for the collective work of the people at worship to be replaced by the selective work of the clergy at worship, observed by the people. Moreover, the sevenfold candlestick was replaced by one candlestick, and the *bema* platform became the place where the ministers and the singers conducted the service, a congregation within the congregation. In time the separation of the basic worship activities from the people became more pronounced: a screen (sometimes filled with icons) separated the congregation from the altar where the priests (hidden) celebrated for them. Such practices, of course, were far removed from the biblical material, even from the Old Testament, and led to the need for the Reformation. But that is another study.[7]

## The Times for Christian Worship

The early Christians had to function within the calendar of the times. Sunday was not a holiday; it was an ordinary workday. In Jewish towns, Saturday was the day for participation in worship. Even though believers continued to meet on the Sabbath day and on festival days, they also came together on the first day of the week to break bread together (Acts 20:7). This was inspired by the resurrection and especially the appearance of Jesus at Emmaus in the breaking of the bread. Paul also instructed the Corinthians to lay aside their offerings on the first day of the week (1 Cor. 16:2). Now that the new covenant had begun, the Jewish Sabbath had lost its symbolic importance as part of the old covenant, for it was fulfilled in Christ (Col. 2:16–17; Heb. 4:3–13). Christians no longer were compelled to give merely one day a week to the Lord—every day belonged to him! However, the church found it profitable to have a day for the Christian community to assemble. So as time progressed Sunday, the resurrection day, became devoted to the service of the Lord.[8]

When Paul announced that Christ our Passover was sacrificed for us

---

7. For more information on the changes in worship reflected in the architecture, see ibid., 156–60.
8. The evidence indicates that this was in place by about A.D. 150. See Bauckham, "The Lord's Day," 221–50; and Beckwith and W. Stott, *This Is the Day.*

and that we should keep the Feast, he may very well have been referring already to a celebration of the death of Jesus Christ at the time of Passover in the spring. The instruction on the Feast (of Unleavened Bread), however, cuts through the ritual to the reality: righteousness results from the redemption through his blood, and this continues year round. At least by the second and third centuries, this time of the year was set apart in a special way to commemorate the death and resurrection of Christ. It also became the major time of baptism, preceded by a time of prayer and fasting.

By the fourth century a full church calendar had been developed to help in the worship of Jesus Christ by marking out the significant events in the faith. Advent marked the beginning of the year, eventually becoming the four-week period of preparation before Christmas. Epiphany, stressing the various ways that Jesus was manifested to the world (birth, wise men, first miracle), may have begun in Egypt to counter pagan days. Lent (in theory at least) goes back as early as the second and third centuries (see Justin Martyr [ca. 150], Didache [ca. 100], and Hippolytus [ca. 235]);[9] it was a time of preparation for baptism at Easter time.[10] The symbolism of forty in the Bible (Moses, Israel, Jesus) naturally supplied the time framework for Lent.[11] Pentecost, like Passover, seems to have been kept very early in the traditions of the church, perhaps even in the first century (witnesses for it are Tertullian and Eusebius). During the season of Pentecost the church concentrated on the power of the Holy Spirit and the ministry of the gospel.

Daily activities also may have been influenced by Jewish daily devotions. At nine in the morning, the Holy Spirit came on the disciples, and they began to minister at the temple (Acts 2:15); Peter went up to pray at about noon (10:9); and Peter and John were going up to the temple to pray at about three in the afternoon (3:1). These were the times of prayer in the Jewish system. Jewish believers who were accustomed to daily prayers continued in them but with greater insight and meaning. The information suggests that devotional daily prayer at these times was customary by the middle of the second century.

---

9. Justin, *First Apology,* 1.6 (see Duchesne, *Christian Worship,* 47–53). Easton, *Hippolytus.*
10. Talley, "The Origin of Lent at Alexandria," 594–612.
11. M. E. Johnson, "From Three Weeks to Forty Days," 185–200.

So as the early church grew, the leaders decided that certain times and seasons would serve their worship well. They recognized that these times had been set aside by the LORD for Israel in anticipation of the coming of Christ and that afterward those times could not be dissociated from the significant activities. Naturally, over the years the functions on these days changed; and it was not long before times and activities were divided into secular and sacred, a division that was supposed to have been broken down by Christ.

## Conclusion

Any place set apart for worship should be planned so that everyone can see and hear and participate with ease, directness, and propriety—choirs and congregation alike. But more than that, it should convey an atmosphere of peace and reverence, one that lifts the spirits above the chaos and confusion of the world. The worshippers should sense that they have come apart from the world and drawn closer to God in fellowship.

The furnishings, symbols, and vestments need to contribute to the worship by communicating aspects of the truth of Christianity. Whatever of these a congregation decides to use must be properly understood within the theology of the church. They must focus the worshippers' attention on the glories of Christ.

Celebrating different events in Christianity at regular times helps the worshippers retain the major events of the faith most vividly and develops a sense of continuity with worshippers of all times and places. A calendar reflects the belief that God created time for his plans, that Christ came in the fullness of time, and that worshippers have always set apart times for worship.

Sunday came to mark the manifestation in time of the reality of redemption. Most churches keep some special days—Christmas, Good Friday, Easter, Thanksgiving (in North America), and others include Advent, Epiphany, Ascension, and Pentecost. Paul's injunctions against keeping holy days (Gal. 4:10; Col. 2:16) are concerned with legalism and the occasion for judging. But if days are freely engaged as memorials and commemorations, then that is different. If the seasons and days are used to inspire spontaneous and genuine worship, they can be very effective.

# CHAPTER 26

# The Essentials *of*
# Worship *in the* Early Church

INSPIRED BY THE PATTERNS AND principles of worship recorded in Holy Scripture, and influenced by the helpful refinements of synagogue worship, the early church very quickly developed a full and rich form of worship centered in the person and work of Jesus the Messiah. Because Christ was the fulfillment of so much of the Old Testament ritual, it is important for us to survey worship in the early church to discern what aspects of worship came to an end in him and what aspects were changed through him. The study will show that the basic elements were carried over to the church but found their full meaning and spiritual reality in the new covenant.

## The Beginning of Participation in Worship

### Faith in Christ as the Basis of Worship

Jesus called people to come to him to find rest for their souls, and when they respond to his call by faith, they begin a new life of service and worship in him. This is the process by which the Father finds people to worship him in spirit and in truth. And before Jesus returned to the Father, he commanded his disciples to continue his work of bringing people to the Father so that they would become part of the new covenant community. He said, "Therefore go and make disciples of all nations, baptizing them in the name of the Father and of the Son and of the Holy Spirit, and teaching them to obey everything I have commanded you" (Matt. 28:19–20). The commission to make disciples, teaching them and baptizing them, is part of the priestly ministry of believers.[1] By obeying this

---

1. See Arndt, "A Royal Priesthood," 241–49; Torrence, *A Royal Priesthood;* and Best, "Spiritual Sacrifice," 273–99.

commission, Christians assume what had originally been the duty of the priests and Levites in the temple, but they do so with the clarity of divine revelation that faith in the Son of God restores the sinner to communion with the living God. And the full revelation of God is absolutely clear: if there is no salvation apart from Jesus Christ, then faith in Jesus Christ is certainly the basis of worship.

## Identification with Christ in Baptism

Part of the work of making disciples involves baptism, the ritual act of worship by which the believer is identified with Christ and begins a new life of worship. Water baptism was the most fitting rite to use, for it was developed from the use of ritual baths in Israel. In the Jewish practice the ritual bath was self-immersion with witnesses.[2] This was done regularly as part of the spiritual preparation for worship. But Christian baptism was different in that it was done only once to identify with the Christian faith.[3]

Jesus began his public ministry with baptism, and while this has inspired believers to be baptized, his baptism was unique (Matt. 3:13–17; Mark 1:9–11; Luke 3:21–22).[4] In fact, when he went to John to be baptized, John hesitated, saying that he should be baptized by Jesus. John knew that Jesus was greater than he, that he was the Messiah, the Lamb of God who would take away the sin of the world (John 1:29–34)—and the revelation at Jesus' baptism confirmed that. Because John's baptism was for repentance to prepare for the Lord—like a purification bath—John saw no need for Jesus to be baptized by him.

But Jesus said his baptism was needed "to fulfill all righteousness" (Matt. 3:15). It helps here to think of "righteousness" in the Hebrew sense of the word, for the term essentially means to conform to the will of God, which is the standard for all obedience. Jesus had come to fulfill God's will, and he would use baptism to begin that ministry. He had come into

---

2. It is not my interest to get into the issue of infant baptism in this study; the reader can study all the literature on the subject to learn when and why this was introduced into the church. But Jewish ritual baths were not for infants. See among the many resources the discussion in Rayburn, *O Come, Let Us Worship;* and see also McKenna, "Infant Baptism," 194–210.

3. There is a closer connection with the ritual bath for a proselyte who embraced the Jewish faith.

4. Besides the commentaries, see McDonnell, "Jesus' Baptism in the Jordan," 209–36.

the world to be the Suffering Servant that Isaiah described (Matt. 20:28; Phil. 2:5–11); and his baptism showed his willingness to take on the role of the servant (Isa. 42:1–4; 50:4–9; 52:13–53:12).[5] So Jesus' statement explains that he was committed to fulfilling the will of God for his life. By baptizing Jesus John would share in fulfilling all righteousness as well, for he was sent to introduce the Messiah to the world.

Jesus chose baptism to begin his ministry of doing the will of God because by it he was identifying with the nation. There was no need of a baptism of repentance for him, but he had entered the human race to take the sin of the world on himself. So it was necessary to inaugurate his ministry with an act that associated him with sinners.

After the baptism the voice from heaven witnessed to the fact that this was the beloved Son with whom God was well pleased. The word was confirmed by the sign of the Spirit of God descending on him like a dove.[6] The dove in Scripture can signify peace, as in the account of Noah; but the dove was also the sin offering of the common people and so a symbol of Israel's need. Jesus had come to fulfill God's plan to make a sacrifice for sin, and so to begin that journey he and John had to demonstrate their willingness to do God's will with the ritual of water baptism.

At the end of his earthly ministry, Jesus made baptism the initial ritual of the believer in the church. While there are a great number of different emphases drawn from this rite, in general it is a symbolic cleansing in which believers proclaim that through repentance and faith they have found forgiveness; and with it they also declare that they are following Christ in the water of baptism to be identified with his death and his life.[7] By being obedient to this rite, believers commit themselves to do the will of God.[8]

## Empowered by Christ for Worship

For worship to be spiritual, the Spirit of God must be at work in the worshippers; for worship to be life changing, worshippers have to be controlled by the Spirit. So when Jesus returned to the Father, he sent the

---

5. See further McDonnell, "The Baptism of Jesus in the Jordan," 98–109.
6. Lampe, *The Seal of the Spirit.*
7. See R. P. Martin, *Worship in the Early Church,* 98–109; and Whitaker, *The Baptismal Liturgy.*
8. As with circumcision the ritual without faith is worthless, but the ritual with faith is an act of obedience and a witness to the world of one's association with Christ Jesus.

Spirit to continue the work that he had begun. This means, on the one hand, that the Holy Spirit is part of everything that God does because God is one—Father, Son, and Holy Spirit. Nothing divine can happen without the Holy Spirit being the one who enables it to happen—Creation, redemption, the Incarnation, the Resurrection, or communion with God in worship.

Then, on the other hand, it means that the Holy Spirit indwells every genuine believer in Christ. This is what makes a person a Christian. At the time of regeneration, the Spirit of God somehow takes up residence in our spirits so that our bodies become the temple (the "most holy place") of the Holy Spirit (1 Cor. 6:19). Paul explains this identification with the body of Christ by declaring: "We were all baptized by one Spirit into one body" (1 Cor. 12:13). Once the Spirit has entered our lives and brought us into the family of God, he remains as the pledge or seal of eternal life (Eph. 1:13–14).[9]

The Holy Spirit does many things for us—he convinces us of sin, he guides us in righteousness, he focuses our attention on Christ, he produces in us the fruit of the Spirit, and he intercedes for us. All of these are marvelous and essential. But there are a couple of other ministries of the Spirit that influence our worship activities.[10] One is the anointing of the Spirit. All believers have this anointing and are therefore consecrated by the Spirit and enabled to serve the Lord (1 John 2:20). God expects us to use the anointing that we have to serve him; it is not necessary to pray for an anointing.

The other ministry of the Spirit involves spiritual gifts. Paul bases his teaching about spiritual gifts on the Old Testament image of the conquering king who distributes the spoils of war among his faithful followers. Since Christ's victory was spiritual, the gifts he gives are spiritual, so they come with the sending of the Spirit (cf. Ps. 68:18; Rom. 12:1–8; 1 Cor. 12:1–31; Eph. 4:7–13). Every Christian has at least one spiritual gift, and all believers are expected to use the gifts they have regularly. Spiritual gifts are not the same as natural abilities, although there may be some overlap; and they are not the same as offices in the church, although

---

9. Therefore, prayers for the Spirit to be given or to come upon Christians, need to be rethought to reflect the biblical theology; the prayer should be for the Spirit to make his presence known by moving in powerful ways in our lives.
10. R. P. Martin, *The Spirit and the Congregation.*

some gifts fit certain offices well. A spiritual gift is the exceptional and at times unexpected ability that the Holy Spirit gives a believer for spiritual service.[11] Most of the gifts overlap with ordinary Christian duties. For example, all believers are to give, but God the Spirit uses some people to give abundantly, naturally, and effectively. They have the gift of giving. People who do not have the gift are not absolved from giving. But the way for people to determine what gifts they have is to become obedient to all phases of Christian service. Then when the Spirit begins to bless in one area of service, that area should be cultivated by prayer, study, discernment of leaders, and increased service. It may be evidence of one's spiritual gift.

There are a good number of spiritual gifts listed by Paul. But what often happens is that at the mention of "spiritual gifts" people think of only two or three of them—the most spectacular ones, the ones that need no work or preparation or active involvement, and the ones that can easily appeal to pride. We must make sure that the other gifts are not ignored, for they are just as much indicators of the presence of the Spirit. Paul cautions his readers that not everyone has the same gifts, and for people to expect all others to express the gifts that they themselves have is not biblical. Paul reasons by analogy that the foot cannot be a hand; not everyone will have the gift of teacher (although everyone is supposed to teach), evangelist (although everyone is to be involved with evangelism), or administration (although here too many will have to do this whether they feel they have this gift or not).

Christian worship must incorporate the use of the spiritual gifts of the people, not only in the assembly but in the whole Christian life. People need to find places to use their gifts, and they need to cultivate them and improve their service through them; but they cannot manipulate or force the Spirit to work. Someone with the gift of teaching can cultivate the gift through study and prayer. However, how the Spirit chooses to use it cannot be dictated by the teacher. The teaching of Paul is clear: believers must find their spiritual gifts, use them in the service of the Lord with humility without envying or minimizing the spiritual gifts of others, and give all the glory to God. Paul instructed that in the worship service there must be Spirit-led participation, but it must follow order:

---

11. Ryrie, *The Holy Spirit*, 83–92.

> When you come together, everyone has a hymn, or a word of instruction, a revelation, a tongue or an interpretation. All of these must be done for the strengthening of the church. If anyone should speak in a tongue, two—or at the most three—should speak, one at a time, and someone must interpret. If there is no interpreter, the speaker should keep quiet in the church and speak to himself and God. Two or three prophets should speak, and the others should weigh carefully what is said. And if a revelation comes to someone who is sitting down, the first speaker should stop. For you can all prophesy in turn so that everyone may be instructed and encouraged. The spirits of prophets are subject to the control of prophets. For God is not a God of disorder but of peace. (1 Cor. 14:26b–33)

Paul was writing to address certain violations in the worship service in Corinth. Apparently with their newfound freedom in Christ and the coming of the Spirit, things had occasionally gotten out of control with many people clamoring for the right to speak. Paul's instruction was that order must prevail because God is not the author of confusion. Spirit-filled worship does not mean that planned forms of worship should not be used; the Spirit can be in the planning of those forms as much as in the participation itself. But with the new covenant, the church has to find ways for all the believers to use all their gifts within the body of Christ; if it does not, it is quenching the Spirit.[12]

Because there are many different views on this subject in the church today, Christians will have to be sensitive to the convictions of others.[13] They do not have to agree with them or join their worship, but they should not allow the different convictions to divide the body of Christ. They should study the Scripture for themselves and discover how the Spirit of God should be working in their lives. Worshippers dare not ignore the doctrine of the Holy Spirit because they think others are carried away with it. And those that emphasize the Spirit's work in their congregations must not consider those who do not agree with them on all points less spiritual. If the Spirit of God truly inhabits the lives of believers, then as

---

12. There is a good deal of literature on this, but for a start see Webber, *Blended Worship;* and R. P. Martin, *Worship in the Early Church,* 130–38.
13. See Senn, "'Worship Alive,'" 194–224.

they study the Word of God, yield their lives to the Lord, and worship him sincerely, the Spirit will lead in the way that they should go.

Christians, then, are commanded to be filled with the Spirit (Eph. 5:18), that is, be controlled by the Spirit.[14] To be filled means, in practical terms, to yield oneself to the Spirit, to be purged of sin and corruption, and to obey God's call on the life. Filling is not something to be prayed for—it is to be done.

The evidence of the Spirit's control of the life will be seen in a number of ways, most of which are not the brief and spectacular experiences. We should expect to see spiritual growth, obedience to the will of God, evidence of the development of the fruit of the Spirit, generous giving, and praise and thanksgiving in worship. When people are faithfully worshipping and serving the Lord and ministering to one another with their gifts, the Spirit will enable them to accomplish more than they could have imagined.

And if the Spirit of God is truly controlling our worship, it will be humble and devout. All too often we see the focus on the Spirit turned into a quest for worldly power. It may be an attempt to have power over other people rather than to serve them with humility. Or it may be unashamedly self-promoting, which is the first sign that the Spirit is not in it. It is presumptuous for anyone to say that others do not have the joy of the Spirit if they do not dance and shout in a certain way, or that others do not worship if they do not have their hands in the air, or that people do not have the Spirit if they do not have particular spiritual gifts. The Holy Spirit works differently in people, for not all have the same gifts, and not all have the same needs at the same time.

The point is that the kind of worship that pleases God will be Christ-centered and Spirit-led. To try to worship without faith in Christ is folly; to try to worship without the power of the Holy Spirit is hollow.

## Private Worship

One of the goals of the corporate worship of the church should be to inspire and instruct private worship. We would hope that as a result of

---

14. The Christian is instructed to be *filled* with the Spirit and is said to be *baptized* with the Spirit. But many have confused the two, calling filling baptism. I am not here contending with the phenomena; I am appealing for the proper use of Scripture to describe the phenomena.

participating in the assembly the people would have a much better sense of what it means to pray, to give praise and thanks, to meditate, and to develop community. We would hope that as a result of being in the assembly time and time again the patterns and principles of worship would become fixed in the individuals as the ways to live a life of worship.

It is the responsibility of the leaders of the congregation to try to guide and encourage the devotion of the people through the week. There are many ways this may be done. Certainly Bible classes can be effective; but they can become merely information-dispensing times that do not sufficiently lead to worship or service. Discipleship groups can be strong or weak, depending on the effectiveness of the people and the commitment to the process. The written word is one of the most effective methods— one that has been all but ignored. Earlier clergymen wrote devotional thoughts on the texts, prayers, praises, and applications for their people to use throughout the week. If this is done, then when it is time for the body of believers to assemble, people would begin coming with prayers and praises on their lips and the Word in their hearts, for their thoughts would be directed toward the corporate worship service.

## The Word of God in Worship

God's revelation formed a major part of Israel's services; Scripture was read and explained at Sinai, in the temple, and in the synagogue, primarily on the high feast days but at the regular assemblies as well. It became the task of the Levites and then later the scribes to teach the Scripture, giving the clear sense and the application. Often there were inspired prophetic messages delivered at the appropriate times in the sanctuaries. Truly, God was not silent; so the people of God have always gone to the sanctuaries expecting to hear from the Lord in one form or another.[15]

### The Public Reading of Scripture

By New Testament times, the reading of Scripture had become the mainstay of synagogue worship. A reader would read the portion from the Hebrew scroll, and another would interpret it for the people (cf. Acts 13:15, 27; 15:21; 2 Cor. 3:15). The emphasis was on the public reading of God's Word and its clear understanding.

Paul advised church leaders to give attention to the reading of Scripture

---

15. Renz, "Come, Let Us Listen to the Voice of the Lord," 140–53.

(1 Tim. 4:13). By this he primarily meant the Old Testament books, but of course he also recognized the growing body of new Scriptures. Accordingly, he instructed that his own epistles be read in the churches and then passed on to others (Col. 4:16; 1 Thess. 5:27), so that they could all continue in the apostolic teachings.

The earliest clear evidence from the church fathers of the importance of reading Scripture in worship comes from Justin Martyr.[16] He reported that Christians gathered on Sundays to read the Apostles and the Prophets—as long as time permitted—and then to receive exhortation for the imitation of these things (cf. Clement 13:1; 14:2; Barnabas 21:1, 6).

The reading of Scripture in the worship was increased so that by the third century portions of the Law, Prophets, Epistles, Acts, and Gospels were read, and Psalms were read or sung between the readings. It also became traditional to read the Gospel reading at the end of all the readings and to read it with the congregation standing. By the fourth century the church had attached liturgical prefaces and responses to the reading of the Word.[17] Common ones simply introduced the readings (such as "A reading from the book of the prophet Isaiah"), concluded them ("The Word of the LORD"), and prescribed the congregation's response ("Thanks be to God").[18]

Scripture was such an important part of the assembly because it was the inspired Word of God and therefore profitable for doctrine, correction, and instruction in righteousness (2 Tim. 3:16). A worship service dare not eliminate the public reading of Scripture.

Several observations come to mind for the implementation of public reading. First, schedules of readings (lectionaries) provide one good way to assure that all of Scripture will be read in a cycle and that related Scriptures will be read in a given service. Second, because the Word of God is so important to worship, readers must know how to read it well in public, not overly dramatic, but clearly, distinctly, and powerfully. Third, the form of the reading can be varied, especially with the Psalter, using responsive readings, antiphonal readings, readings in unison, litanies, as

---

16. Duchesne, *Christian Worship*, 54.
17. Old, *Reading and Preaching of the Scriptures.*
18. The response of Israel at Sinai might be more impressive: "All that the LORD says we are willing to do."

well as public readings, chants, choral presentations, and even dramatic presentations. And fourth, the translation used must be accurate, of course, and written in a proper and somewhat elevated style. It is, after all, the Word from God.

## Teaching and Exhortation from the Word

In the temple and synagogue the doctrinal and moral instruction based on God's Word was essential to the worship.[19] In the Old Testament, priests were responsible to teach the law (cultic and moral), and prophets came alongside them with exhortations from the Law and new revelation.

The early church followed the Lord in teaching the Word in the places of worship and in preaching the gospel wherever they went (Mark 1:14–15; Acts 8:4). And Paul preached Christ in the synagogues (Acts 9:20), taking the opportunities to give the Word of exhortation in the service (Acts 13:15).

One term that is used for the proclamation of the gospel is *kērussō*. It has the idea of heralding or proclaiming a message, and in the New Testament the message was the Christ event. This *kerygma,* or proclamation, was always designed to elicit a response; it was a call to repentance and commitment in faith, with God making the appeal through his Word that people be reconciled to him (2 Cor. 5:19–20; cf. Luke 10:16).

The message of this proclamation was new revelation to many who were accustomed to synagogue worship, so Paul had to make extensive use of the Hebrew Scriptures to show that God's plan of redemption was fulfilled through the Messiah, Jesus. The formulation of the gospel (1 Cor. 15:3–4), then, necessarily included "according to the Scriptures"—that "Christ died for our sins according to the Scriptures, that he was buried, that he was raised on the third day according to the Scriptures." The Christ event that formed the message of reconciliation is the death, burial, and resurrection of Jesus—as explained by the apostles from Scripture. Because this proclamation revealed the way to the Father, it also informed all of Christian worship. Its internal authority was the resurrection; so the apostolic kerygma constantly puts the resurrection of Jesus at the fore. Paul would not have preached this message if it were not for the resurrection (Rom. 8:34; 1 Cor. 9:1; 15:11–19; Phil. 3:10; 1 Thess. 1:9–10).

---

19. Stegner, "The Ancient Jewish Synagogue Homily," 51–69; and Mason, "Some Echoes of the Preaching in the Second Temple?" 23–49.

The resurrection can hardly be emphasized enough: without it there was no redemption; with it Christ's claims were authenticated. The death of Christ was indeed God's complete remedy for the ruin of the race.

The effectiveness of the proclamation of the risen Christ depended on the power of the Holy Spirit (2 Cor. 3:17–18). If the message was God's, then the intended results must also be by the power of God's Holy Spirit (1 Cor. 2:3–14). And this could never be manipulated or fabricated.

In addition to the proclamation of the Word, there was also an emphasis on edifying teaching—the early believers continued steadfastly in the apostle's doctrine (*didachḗ* in Acts 2:42). The main verb for "teach" is *didáskō,* and the important nouns are *didachḗ* and *didaskalía.* The teaching is, of course, the apostolic instruction, often in epistles, based on the Hebrew Scriptures but fully interpreted in light of their fulfillment in Jesus Christ. It is "sound doctrine" (1 Tim. 1:10) or "good teaching" (1 Tim. 4:6; cf. Mal. 2:1–10). Jesus began this new doctrine when he invited his followers to learn from him (Matt. 11:28–29) so that they might keep his commandments. When the Lord gave people spiritual gifts by sending the Spirit, he gifted some to be pastors and teachers. Now all Christians are supposed to teach (Heb. 5:12), but some have a gift in this area. A clear explanation of this function is in 1 Timothy 4:6–16, where Timothy is instructed to teach sound doctrine to others in the faith. This can take place anywhere, but the best arena is the assembly of worshippers.

Another word for teaching is *katechéō,* from which we get "catechism," referring to formal instruction in the basics of the faith (cf. Eph. 4:20–24; 1 Peter 2:2; 1 John 2:12–24). This emphasis probably came from the Jewish practice of training proselytes. One example in the New Testament is that Theophilus was a catechumen (one "being taught" in Luke 1:4).

Exhortation and encouragement are a necessary part of the exposition of Scripture. The word *paraklēsis,* best known for the designation of the Spirit as the Paraclete, has a wide range of meanings. Paul says that the one who proclaims God's message *(prophēteúōn)* speaks to people and gives them edification, "encouragement *(paraklēsis)* and comfort" (1 Cor. 14:3).

In the early church there were those who had a ministry of proclaiming God's message, or prophesying. Some actually predicted future events—Agabus (Acts 11:27–28; 21:10–11), John (Rev. 1:1–3), and of course Paul. But the ministry of prophecy, like the prophetic oracles in the Old Testament, was most often clear instruction and exhortation based on Scripture.[20] So in the assembly if any had a prophecy, he could deliver it, expounding the Scripture and exhorting the congregation to holy living and spiritual worship.

That the exposition of the Scriptures was a fixed part of worship assemblies can be demonstrated from the earliest extrabiblical sources. Justin[21] records how after reading the Old and New Testament sections, the "president in a discourse urges and invites to the imitation of these noble things." In time the sermon out of necessity turned from expounding the fixed lessons in the readings to topical discourses on doctrine. The exposition of Scripture became less and less a factor as ritual and liturgy took a more dominant role; and doctrinal discourses became more important when the Christological and Trinitarian disputes arose. The classic examples for this are John Chrysostom (374–407) and Augustine (354–430), whose sermons can be easily obtained.[22]

The conclusion of the matter is clear. Worship begins with the response to divine revelation. But if little time or attention is given to the revealed Word of God, read, proclaimed, or taught, then to what do people respond? The result is that worship becomes superficial or sentimental. If the church is truly interested in recapturing the spirit and nature of the prophetic and apostolic ministry of the Word in worship, then there will have to be a greater emphasis placed on reading, teaching, and preaching the Word of God, but it has to be with clarity, accuracy, power, and authority.[23]

Today, because of the way most churches are structured, the sermon time has to include what both the priests and the prophets did, that is, preaching and teaching. But most ministers do not have both of these abilities. If a church can make better use of the spiritual gifts in the congregation, some of these ministries can be shared and the worship made more effective. But whatever format is used, this part of the service must present solid doctrine with clear biblical exposition.[24] After all,

---

20. Wills, "The Form of the Sermon in Hellenistic Judaism," 227–99.
21. Justin, *First Apology,* 67.
22. Willis, *Augustine's Lectionary;* see also Hilkert, "Preaching and Theology," 398–409.
23. Keck, *The Bible in the Pulpit.*
24. Too often the sermon or homily has simply become a harmless composition on a current theme without power or seeming purpose; or it may be a shallow message veiled with passionate oratory and memorable phrases.

the sermon is also an act of worship in which the minister presents the message as a gift to God.

Without a return to the proper proclamation of the Word, the worship service—and the churches themselves—will lose authority and relevance. Proclaiming the Word must be restored, because all the evidence shows that the churches are filled with people who do not know doctrine or Scripture—and many of them are hungry for teaching! No matter how the ministry of the Word is developed in the life of the worshipping community, when the people assemble for a full worship service with Holy Communion, the risen Christ must be lifted up in the eyes of the people and glorified through it.[25] It will be the hope of glory revealed by God that will inspire adoration, obedience, and perseverance.[26] And the Spirit of God will burn the Word of God into the hearts and minds of the devout so that their loyalties will be renewed and their worship enriched.

## The Responses of the People in Worship

Because revelation demands a response, the people of God have found a number of ways to respond when they come together to worship God: they confess their faith; they proclaim their gratitude and devotion through praise; they demonstrate their loyalty by offering themselves and their gifts to God; they promise their commitments through vows; and they activate their faith in supplications and intercessions.

But in putting these responses into their proper forms, we have a tension. On the one hand, we want everything about our worship to be organized, pleasing, and theologically correct; but on the other hand, we want it to be spontaneous and free. It is possible to have both—at least Paul thought it was. But different congregations seem to lean one way or the other.

There are those who in their desire for spontaneous, free worship would minimize or eliminate any use of set forms—creeds, prayers, or liturgy. Some of this is a carryover from the early Congregationalists, Baptists, and Quakers. For example, John Smyth wrote,

---

25. Marshall, "The Divine Sonship of Jesus," 89–103; see also Breuggemann, *Finally Comes the Poet.*
26. Along this line consider Paul's inspiration for ministry; see Morray-Jones, "Paradise Revisited (2 Cor. 12:1–12)," 177–217.

> We hold that the worship of the New Testament properly so
> called is spiritual proceeding originally from the heart; and that
> reading out of a book (though it is a lawful ecclesiastical action)
> is no part of spiritual worship, but rather the invention of the
> man of sin, it being substituted for a part of spiritual worship.
> We hold that seeing prophesying is a part of spiritual worship:
> therefore in time of prophesying it is unlawful to have the book
> (i.e., the Bible) as a help before the eye. We hold that seeing sing-
> ing a psalm is a part of spiritual worship: therefore it is unlawful
> to have the book before the eye in time of singing a psalm.[27]

People who took this approach thought that set forms deprive people
of their own thoughts and words, could not meet all the needs, were idolatrous because they made liturgy equal with the Bible, led to overfamil-
iarity and lack of interest, and opposed the appropriate approach to the
Father; moreover, the imposition of set forms seemed to them a form of
religious persecution.[28]

One movement that exemplified this approach was Quakerism. It
abandoned the ordained ministry and the sacraments in favor of every
member's waiting on the Spirit. This meant that they rejected any external
aids or rites (the Spirit's revelation was supreme). Worship was inward,
and so all ceremonies were abolished—Spirit baptism superceded water
baptism, and the Eucharist was an inner spiritual reception of Christ
without external rite. In short, all participation in worship was through
the moving of the Spirit.

Out of this kind of interest in spiritual worship, the pietistic emphasis emerged. In arguing for free, spiritual worship to the exclusion of set
forms, some folks point to John 4 and Jesus' liberation from temple worship. There Jesus said that worship must now be in spirit and in truth,
but he said nothing of forms, times, or places of worship. Yet, he himself
taught his disciples how to pray, instituted the Lord's Supper by commanding his disciples to follow that manner regularly, and commanded
that baptism be used. And the apostle Paul, while describing Spirit-led

---

27. In many congregations today something akin to this in music is followed, namely,
   that it is better not to have to use a book to sing. For the survey of the literature referred to, see *A New Dictionary of Liturgy and Worship*, 78.
28. Ibid.

worship in the churches, established leaders to guide it, set rules for preserving order in it, required interpreters to be designated before someone
spoke in tongues, handed down the tradition of the Lord's Supper, counseled the leaders to study and prepare, and worked within the framework
of the normal time and place of worship. So apparently forms, structure,
and planning for worship in the assembly were not considered incompatible with spontaneous spiritual worship.

On the other end of the scale, there are congregations that rely on liturgy, creeds, and set forms for their worship. Although criticism of this is
valid in some places (where people never pray apart from reading a prayer
in a book, or cannot express their faith apart from reading a creed, for
example[29]), set forms can be a very helpful means of developing worship.
After all, they may be set forms, but they are mostly Scripture arranged
into patterns for worship.

Even in most "free" churches, ministers plan carefully for the sermon,
choirs practice diligently to offer their praise, leaders select in advance set
hymns from a book, a preferred order for Communion is followed, and
set words will be said at baptisms, weddings, funerals, and ordinations.

## Creeds or Confessions of Faith

One of the primary forms established for worship is the creed. Creeds
have always been controversial in the church—indeed, they grew up out
of controversies. Some people say they are too condensed and need more
clarification; others thinks they become too mechanical and routine.
But whether they use formal creeds or not, most churches hold to various doctrinal positions and expect their members to subscribe to them.
And many of those doctrinal statements are dependent on the wording
worked out so carefully in the early church councils.[30]

The word *creed* comes from the first word of the Apostles' and Nicene
Creeds, which, in the Latin, is *credo*, "I believe."[31] This in itself attests

---

29. It must be noted here that not using set forms of worship does not necessarily guar-
    antee that the worship will be spiritual.
30. See J. N. D. Kelly, *Early Christian Creeds*.
31. The Apostles' Creed, a statement of beliefs to which the church wished to attach ap-
    ostolic authority, probably began to be developed in Rome in the second century and
    was fully developed by the sixth or seventh (see Cranfield, *The Apostles' Creed*). The
    Nicene Creed, from the council of Nicaea in A.D. 325, grew out of the conflict with
    false teachings and served to help the bishops maintain orthodoxy. For further discus-
    sion, see Turner, *History and Use of Creeds*.

to a confession of personal faith. But it is also a condensed formula of Christian doctrine to be used in public worship. So on both counts it is a way that Christians have of declaring themselves.

Down through the ages believers have felt it worthwhile to express their faith in easily remembered and shared expressions. Statements of beliefs were included in passages such as Deuteronomy 26:5–9 and 6:4–5 and Joshua 24:2–13 to be used by people in their acts of worships. Likewise, lists of the attributes of God, such as that found in Exodus 34:6–7, formed the basis of creeds the Israelites used to affirm their faith. Even short acclamations such as "Yahweh reigns" from the Psalms would have been used at the festivals in the same way.[32]

There are creedal fragments in the New Testament that no doubt served early Christians well in their identification with and articulation of the faith. Some of these are listed here.

### The Gospel

The clear and poetically balanced statement of the gospel united the diverse groups in their basic Christian faith (1 Cor. 15:3–4; Col. 2:6–7). Any other gospel simply would not do (2 Cor. 11:4; Gal. 1:8–9).

### "Believe in the Lord Jesus Christ"

This is the prescription for joining the faith (Acts 16:31; Col. 2:6). The basic statement of faith is "Jesus is Lord" (cf. also Acts 11:19–21; 1 Cor. 8:5–6), which Paul affirms in Romans 10:9–10—"If you confess with your mouth, 'Jesus is Lord,' and believe in your heart that God raised him from the dead, you will be saved. For it is with your heart that you believe and are justified, and it is with your mouth that you confess and are saved" (cf. also Phil. 2:11). It is important to note that "Lord" in these statements means that Jesus is divine—he is God manifest in the flesh!

### "Jesus Is the Christ"

Related to this basic confession about Jesus are others that are more Jewish. The first is "Jesus is the Christ," that is, the Messiah. Peter said it early: "You are the Christ, the Son of the living God" (Matt. 16:16). Closely built on the *Shema* (Deut. 6:4) are statements like "There is one

---

32. Durham, "Credo, Ancient Israelite," *Interpreter's Dictionary of the Bible: Supplementary Volume,* 197–99.

God and one mediator between God and man, the man Christ Jesus"
(1 Tim. 2:5; cf. also 1 Cor. 8:4; James 2:19), or, Jesus is the "Son of David
and Son of God" (this may be behind Rom. 1:3–4). At the baptism of
the eunuch, Philip calls for a confession of faith, and the Ethiopian says,
"I believe that Jesus Christ is the Son of God" (Acts 8:37).[33] Others are
similar.

### Early Hymns

Creedal confessions may have formed the early hymns of the church,
especially those to be used at baptism or the Lord's Supper. Passages
that have the forms of hymns and are solidly doctrinal are John 1:1–18;
Romans 3:24–26; Philippians 2:6–11; and Colossians 1:15–20.[34] One of
the best samples of a doctrinal hymn is 1 Timothy 3:16, which speaks
about the mystery of godliness: "He appeared in a body, was vindicated
by the Spirit, was seen by angels, was preached among the nations, was
believed on in the world, was taken up in glory."

### The Incarnation

When John provided a test case to discern true teachers from false, he
summarized this important doctrine: "This is how you can recognize the
Spirit of God: Every spirit that acknowledges that Jesus Christ has come
in the flesh is from God" (1 John 4:2).

### Maranatha

This Aramaic expression, translated "Come, O Lord" in 1 Corinthians
16:22, was apparently a "creedal" prayer of the early church, for it was
taken into the liturgy (*Didache* 10:6).[35]

### Trinitarian Statements

The Christian Trinitarian faith found clear expression in the baptismal
formula, "baptizing them in the name of the Father and of the Son and
of the Holy Spirit" (Matt. 28:19), and the apostolic benediction, "May the
grace of the Lord Jesus Christ, and the love of God, and the fellowship of

---

33. This is the reading found in some of the later manuscripts of the passage and included
    in some English translations.
34. Bruce, "The 'Christ Hymn' of Colossians 1:15–20," 99–111.
35. Moule, "A Reconsideration of the Context of *Maranatha*," 307–10.

the Holy Spirit be with you all" (2 Cor. 13:14). The teaching of the Trinity appears in numerous other places, such as Ephesians 2:18.

Taking their inspiration from the confessions of faith in the Bible, the church fathers began to formulate ways for worshippers to affirm their faith, first at baptisms and then in the ordinary service.[36] Justin[37] indicates there was an interrogation or at least a reminder of the Trinitarian faith of the one being baptized; Irenaeus likewise stresses this essential part of the faith: "First of all, it bids us bear in mind that we have received baptism for the remission of sins in the name of God the Father, and in the name of Jesus Christ the Son of God, who was incarnate and died and rose again, and in the Holy Spirit of God."[38]

Hippolytus links a threefold interrogation concerning Trinitarian faith with threefold baptism:

> Do you believe in one God the Father Almighty?
> I believe in this way (baptism follows).

> Do you believe in Christ Jesus, the Son of God, who was born from the Holy Spirit from the virgin Mary, and was crucified under Pontius Pilate, and died, and rose again on the third day alive from the dead, and ascended into heaven, and sits at the right hand of the Father, and will come to judge the living and the dead?
> I believe (baptism repeated).

> Do you believe in the Holy Spirit and the Holy Church and the resurrection of the flesh?
> I believe (baptism a third time).[39]

And then in time the formal creeds were written to secure the cardinal doctrines of the faith, and these have stood the test of time.

In conclusion we may observe that there is always the danger in using creeds that worshippers will rely more on them than on the faithful study

---

36. Neufeld, *The Earliest Christian Confessions.*
37. Justin, *First Apology,* 46, 61.
38. Irenaeus, *Epideixis* 3.
39. Easton, *Hippolytus,* 21.1–23.2.

of Scripture, or that the creed might become an empty form for those who do not understand the doctrines. Nevertheless, they give devout worshippers a way to confess their faith in concise forms during a time of worship; and for the believer who is growing in the faith they provide a wonderful means of recalling the various passages of Scripture in a time of meditation. Without creedal forms and affirmations, little or no doctrine will be expressed.

It is the responsibility of the church to teach sound doctrine so that such confessions of faith will be genuine and meaningful. Even if creeds are not used, many of the hymns the church sings (as in the first century) are doctrinal creeds, and the people need to understand these as well. The church can prevent creeds from being routine by varying the ones to be used, or using the doctrinal passages in the Bible that express them, or by proclaiming them in different forms of expression. But the confession of faith has always been essential to worship—for clarification of the ritual, for the basis of fellowship, and for mutual edification and encouragement.

### Individual and Congregational Praise

In both the Old Testament and the New Testament, believers are commanded to offer God the "sacrifice of praise" (Ps. 50:14; Heb. 13:15). The fact that it is commanded means that it is not an option but an obligation, and the fact that it is called a sacrifice means that it is an offering to be given to God. Worship without praise is unthinkable; the devout Israelites would not think of receiving a benefit from God without praising him. When God gives blessings, he intends them to edify the assembly concerning the greatness and grace of God and to be an encouragement for prayer. So praise is central to the spiritual growth of the congregation; but more than that, it is essentially the public expression of covenant loyalty to the Lord—an acknowledgment that the Lord is the one who redeems his people, provides for them, and cares for them. It was to offer praise and thanksgiving that Israel went up to Jerusalem three times a year (Ps. 122:4). And by appearing before the LORD at those times and offering the sacrifices of praise, the Israelites preserved the historic faith in the midst of a pagan and corrupt world.[40]

---

40. Brueggemann, *Israel's Praise*; see also Power, "Doxology."

Beginning with the teaching of the apostles and concluding with the vision of the saints in glory, the New Testament confirms that praise is essential to the spiritual life and therefore to the life of the church. The church exists to show forth praise to God (1 Peter 2:9).[41] Indeed, when worshippers come to the assembly to worship, apart from whatever they expect to receive, there is something to be given—praise to God. And that praise must center on God (Rev. 19:10) and not on the self or other people (although people are at times praiseworthy [1 Cor. 11:2]).

When the Bible tells believers to offer the sacrifice of praise (Heb. 13:15), there is more to it than simply saying words of praise. By using the familiar Old Testament description the writer includes how offering a praise involved bringing a gift (an animal) as a thank offering to the Lord to share with the congregation as a communal meal. It cost the worshipper to praise the Lord (hence, a sacrifice). Now, even though Christ is the sacrifice, the writer still exhorts us to offer the sacrifice of praise; the exhortation carries the spirit of the law forward because generosity is part and parcel of biblical praise. So he adds, "And do not forget to do good and to share with others, for with such sacrifices God is pleased" (v. 16). Accordingly, we recall that in connection with praising God, the early Christians shared of their abundance with those in need (Acts 2:44–47).

One could say, then, that the measure of the spiritual vitality of a group is biblical praise. Either people will give God the glory, or they will not; and if they will not, they will live for themselves, satisfied with their own abilities and accomplishments (cf. Deut. 8:10–18). And if people have such independent and self-sufficient attitudes, they will almost certainly be indifferent to the needs of others. To give God the glory is an expression of dependence on God and so logically leads to generosity, for it recognizes everything as God's bounty. To "give praise to God" (cf. Josh. 7:19; John 9:24) is to acknowledge the truth that without him we have nothing and are nothing. So in the church, as in Israel, individual praise is essential to the true sense of community.

According to the New Testament, the entire Christian life is to be filled with praise and thanksgiving. Christians can praise the Lord informally, anytime, anywhere. Thus, benedictions and doxologies frequently appear in the New Testament apart from formal worship. "I thank my God"

---

41. See Wainwright, *Eucharist and Eschatology.* See also Ellsberg, *Created to Praise.*

(Phil. 1:3), or "We always thank God" (Col. 1:3), illustrates that praise and thanksgiving form a natural part of the believer's communication with God (as *bārûk ʾădōnāy* ["blessed be the LORD"] did in the Hebrew faith). But the fact that Paul used this language in his epistles gave it a liturgical function as well, for the Epistles were meant to be read in the assemblies.

These doxologies, benedictions, and invocations of praise express the character of God (at times in Trinitarian terms) as a gracious God who bestows blessing on his people. Naturally the greatest gift God has given is his "inexpressible gift" of salvation—"thanks be to God!" (2 Cor. 9:15; cf. Col. 1:12–14). The doxology of Ephesians 1:3–14 traces this benefit through the Trinitarian format (Father, vv. 3–6; Son, vv. 7–12; Spirit, vv. 13–14), ending each section with "to the praise of His glory."[42]

The New Testament blessings also attribute historical events to God. Thus, Paul could thank God for the generosity of certain Christians, just as Israel could praise God for working wonders in the world. Such blessing ascribes to him lordship of the whole world and everything in it.

In addition to the individual praises and thanksgivings that maintain the reality of the faith, the praise of God may be expressed through hymns and sacred songs. When the people come together to sing praises to God, they come out of themselves and elevate their voices above normal speech in celebration. Singing and making music was a major part of the temple worship of Israel and was gradually adapted for synagogue worship; it was only natural that it would be continued in the church as part of its communal praise since so much of early Christian worship was carried forward from temple and synagogue.[43]

Choirs were used in Israel for the singing of psalms, hymns, and other anthems.[44] These were made up of qualified people who gave their lives to such ministry. The rationale was that the worship of God must always have those there who are ready to praise God with music. The choir was a type of "firstfruits" of praise—the best (in voices) that the people of God could

---

42. See Westermann, *Blessing in the Bible and in the Life of the Church.*

43. The literature on this is extensive, but see J. A. Smith, "The Ancient Synagogue, the Early Church, and Singing," 1–16; Charlesworth, "Jewish Hymns, Odes, and Prayers," 411–36, and idem, "Prolegomenon to a New Study of the Jewish Background," 266–85; Flusser, "Jewish Roots of the Liturgical Trisagion," 37–43; Werner, *The Sacred Bridge;* and idem, "The Doxology in Synagogue and Church," 275–351.

44. Eaton, "Music's Place in Worship," 85–107; and Coddaire and Weil, "Use of the Psalter in Worship," 342–48.

offer to God; but it was also the inspiration for the worship and praise of the people, for they, following the pattern of the choir, were also instructed to sing praises to God. This is an essential ingredient of worship.

In Ephesians 5:19 Paul reminds the church that it too is to offer praise and thanksgiving to God with "psalms, hymns and spiritual songs" (cf. also Col. 3:16). His selection of words here draws clearly on the Old Testament worship. The first word Paul used is *psalms,* which certainly refers to the Hebrew Psalter.[45] James says, "Is any one of you in trouble? He should pray. Is anyone happy? Let him sing songs of praise" (5:13). It is entirely possible that these references to "psalms" included other, similarly constructed, musical pieces based on Scripture (like some of the extrabiblical psalms at Qumran), but the primary reference was to the canonical psalms, both in the Psalter and in the New Testament books (e.g., the Song of Zachariah in Luke 1:67–79).

The word "psalm" *(psalmos)* in Ephesians 5:19 is the Greek translation of the Hebrew word *mizmôr,* which refers to a poem sung to the accompaniment of stringed instruments. Thus, the use of this particular word assumes the use of musical instruments, so it is not completely accurate to say that the New Testament does not refer to musical instruments. Musical instruments were so widely used in Israelite worship that the early Christians would have felt very much at home with them.

The second word Paul uses is *hymn (húmnos).* The word was also used in the Greek Old Testament for special songs of praise addressed to the LORD directly. A hymn was more formal than, say, a psalm of thanksgiving; it was loftier and more universal in scope, focusing on one or more of the divine attributes and not on personal experiences. Luke records a number of hymns near the very beginning of his gospel: Mary's hymn of praise (1:46–55, "The Magnificat"[46]), the angelic praise (2:14, "The Gloria"), and the song of Simeon (2:29–32, "The *Nunc Dimittas*"[47]). As the church developed, the hymns naturally became strongly Christocentric (see John 1:1–18; Phil. 2:6–11; Col. 1:15–20; 1 Tim. 3:16);[48] they praise the Savior who came to redeem that which was lost.

---

45. The early Christians loved and used the Psalms in their worship and service (cf. Acts 4:24–26).
46. The name is drawn from the Latin beginning of "My soul magnifies the Lord."
47. "Now let your servant depart."
48. See Harvey, "A New Look at the Christ Hymn in Phil. 2:6–11," 337–39.

Finally, Paul mentions the *spiritual song (ōdē)*. "Spiritual songs" (Eph. 5:19) could also refer to specific psalms in the Psalter, because the word *ōdai* is used in the Greek version of the Psalms as a heading for some of the songs. But it has been more commonly interpreted to refer to new songs that set forth the believer's spiritual enjoyment of life under God. But in the church these songs were to be spiritual as opposed to worldly; that is, they were to be songs inspired by the Spirit, as in 1 Corinthians 14:26 (see Eph. 5:14 for a possible baptismal song).

Although there may be some question about the precise meaning of these "psalms, hymns and spiritual songs," or what they include, it is clear that they are all part of Spirit-led worship. Paul writes, "Be filled with the Spirit, speaking to one another with psalms, hymns, and spiritual songs, singing and making music in your hearts to the Lord, always giving thanks to God the Father for everything, in the name of our Lord Jesus Christ, submitting to one another out of reverence for Christ" (Eph. 5:18b–21). I have translated this passage more literally to show that the participles in each clause express the result of being filled with the Spirit. In other words, giving thanks for everything, singing and making music, and speaking to one another with psalms, hymns, and spiritual songs come from the power of the Holy Spirit controlling the life. Of course, people can sing and give thanks without being spiritual, but that is not what God wants. Our Lord said that those who worship must worship in Spirit and truth. So the primary instruction here is to be filled with the Spirit, meaning, be controlled by the Spirit. The Spirit will then inspire in the worshipper such praise. This passage, therefore, is central to the spiritual life of the faith and cannot be minimized in any way. Ford analyzes this text in his discussion of how the community of worshippers are to face each other in their praise and thanksgiving; he writes,

> For a community of worship, this coming together before God in song is the fullest facing of all, explicitly acknowledging the reality of which they are all part, and adding their energies to enhance it. The specific contribution of music to the building up of community in worship includes its encouragement of alertness to others, immediate responsiveness to changes in tone, tune and rhythm, and sharing in the confidence that can come from joint singing. Singing together embodies joint responsibility in which

each singer waits on the others, is attentive with the intention of serving the common harmony.[49]

The sum of the matter is that the overall mood of worship should be celebration in community. After all, the church exists to praise God in the world: believers are instructed to offer the sacrifice of praise to God, and the Spirit of God produces it in those who are spiritual. Words of gratitude and praise and blessing must be on the lips of believers daily. For this to happen, they must be living in the reality of the goodness and grace of God, for praise is the spontaneous expression of what is enjoyed.

Several principles emerge from the biblical teachings on praise. First, individual believers must have the opportunity to praise God in the congregation, not just in the singing or in spontaneous acclamations, but in the carefully prepared individual praises—public testimonies. Second, praise must exalt the object of the praise, the Lord, and must not focus too much attention on people. Third, praise is edifying and therefore is a communal act—it is to be delivered in a forum. Fourth, generosity is the evidence of sincere gratitude expressed in praise; therefore churches need to find ways to combine praise with sacrificial gifts and provisions for people in need. Fifth, praise should be well prepared because it is an offering given to God; it would also be beneficial to write the praises for the encouragement and instruction of future believers. For all this to happen, there will have to be a good deal of effective teaching in the church on how to praise God as well as careful planning of the services to accommodate such praise. But the absence of individual biblical praise is one of the reasons that worship seems irrelevant and routine—people need to hear what God is doing in the lives of other believers.

Even though churches have hymns and songs as a regular part of their services, praise through music needs constant if not urgent attention.[50] Music must meet the same requirements as other forms of praise: it is to be biblically accurate, spiritually uplifting, honoring to God, and edifying

---

49. D. F. Ford, *Self and Salvation*, 122. See also Routley, *Church Music and the Christian Faith*.

50. I would start with a survey of the development of music in worship; the literature is vast, but see among others works like Blume, *Protestant Church Music*; Bishop, *Isaac Watts Hymns and Spiritual Songs*; Dean, *A Survey of Twentieth Century Protestant Church Music in America*; and Plank, *"The Way to Heaven's Doore."*

for the congregation.[51] The music is supposed to lift the worshippers out of their mundane experience, focus their attention on Christ, and transport their spirits to realms of glory. But if the music draws attention to the musicians rather than the Lord, centers on human experience instead of divine acts, mimics the style of entertainment that the world offers, or becomes routine and predictable so that the mind and soul are not engaged, then it fails to be an effective means of praising God. The desire today to be casual, informal, and relevant has in many cases made the music of praise shallow and superficial, which, unfortunately, goes hand-in-hand with the already weakened knowledge of biblical theology in the church. It will take a concerted effort to reverse this trend in the church. Our congregations must be guided in the use of music in worship by properly trained spiritual leaders who can develop the theology of music and use it in the organization of the services.[52]

The kind of music to be used will differ from congregation to congregation or country to country. But there are several principles in the biblical text that should guide the church in its musical praise.[53] First, all forms of praise, whether proclamation, music, or dance, must focus on the Lord and glorify him, not on the performers or the culture. Second, musical praise should elevate the praise to be a glimpse of glory, not an imitation of the world; music is essential for worship because it makes the praise grand and glorious and unites the worshippers in harmony in the expression of their faith. Third, church music should have a balance of hymns, praise songs, doxologies, choruses, and litanies. A steady run of subjective, experiential songs without the doctrinal hymns will not be as edifying as the music should be; and an absence of the songs will not help the congregation express their spiritual experiences in harmony with the historic faith. Fourth, the music must be done well, not because it is a performance, but because it is an offering given to God, the best that the worshipping community can do. Fifth, musical praise must harmonize with the spirit and substance of the service, for the services will change throughout the spiritual seasons of the year.

---

51. The series of articles on music in the church by D. Hustad that are listed in the bibliography are well worth reading, even though they are a little out of date.
52. See further Berger, *Theology in Hymns?* A. Burton, "Till in Heaven . . . ," 309–17; and R. A. Lamb, *J. S. Bach as Preacher.*
53. Eskew and McElrath, *Sing with Understanding.*

Music must serve several spiritual purposes: it should enable the worshippers to become articulate in the doctrines and spiritual matters of their faith; it should contribute to the call for commitment and edification of the saints; it should be therapeutically effective in calming troubled spirits (as when David played for Saul); and it should be inspirational so that the worshippers will go away uplifted and encouraged in their lives. Singing and playing musical instruments should communicate the Word and the worship, without overshadowing them. To do all this the music must be sacred; it must be set apart to God and be distinctly worshipful— holy in its content, holy in its sound, holy in its presentation.

## Offerings and Gifts

Stewardship has always been a part of worship. The Israelites went up to the temple to give thanks to the LORD *at the harvest times* because that was when they would pay their tithes and offerings. When the Israelites brought their tithes, offerings, and sacrifices to the sanctuary, they were acknowledging that everything they possessed came from God and that they needed to express their gratitude and devotion with these things. Whatever offerings the worshippers brought to God in response to the manifestation of his grace and glory were always regarded as gifts of devotion to him. However, any such offering or gift would be considered worthless and hypocritical if the person was living in sin (Isa. 1:10–20) or if the gifts were less than the best they could offer (Mal. 1:6–14).

The New Testament teaches that everything that we have—our possessions, our time, and our abilities—is a gift from God and a trust— and as faithful stewards we are to use it all for his glory. But in our worship we are instructed to give a portion of what we have to him in gratitude and devotion.[54] The basic principle is the same as in the Old Testament; the difference is that more is expected of the Christian because of the value of the new covenant.

One major difference between the Testaments is the content of the offering. Whereas in Israel worshippers actually brought the animals for the sacrifices, in the new covenant God gave his Son to be the perfect sacrifice for us. Christians bring offerings but not *the* offering (unless in the spiritual sense of coming to God with or on the basis of the sacrifice

---

54. See the discussion of stewardship in R. P. Martin, *Worship in the Early Church,* 77–86.

of Christ). In the early church, however, giving included bringing the elements for the breaking of bread ritual, in addition to bringing food for the common meal. In token they were reflecting the tradition of the Israelites bringing sacrifices from the flocks that God had given to them.

For giving to be part of true worship, the New Testament lays down a number of qualifications. First, it is to be a regularly prepared stewardship based on the Lord's blessing (1 Cor. 16:1–4). The early church began laying up their gifts to God on the first day of the week. This carried forward the routine of scheduled giving in the Old Testament but set the time now on the Christian celebration of resurrection day. Second, it is to be done willingly (2 Cor. 8:1–8). This emphasis is also carried over from the Old Testament, for the willing offering is the spiritual offering. Third, it is to be generous (9:11). This brings greater praise to God because it follows the pattern of Christ: "You know the grace of our Lord Jesus Christ, that though he was rich, yet for your sakes he became poor, so that you through his poverty might become rich" (8:9). Because Christ held nothing back in his love for us, we ought to respond with self-sacrificing love. Therefore, fourth, spiritual giving may involve sacrifice (2 Cor. 8:9; Phil. 4:10–20). To give beyond one's means expresses true spiritual giving. Fifth, it is to be done with humility (Matt. 6:2–4). Giving as a part of worship must be concerned only with pleasing God and not with being praised by people.

The early church, under Paul's direction, took responsibility for meeting the needs of the people. He took up offerings wherever he went for the poor in Jerusalem (Rom. 15:27–29; 1 Cor. 16:1–4; 2 Cor. 8–9; Gal. 2:10). It is a fixed duty for the church to rally to the support of those in need. The welfare of the people in Jerusalem was a major concern for Christians because of the debt they all owed to the "mother church." In fact, the generous support for Jerusalem by Gentile believers certainly helped unite the church.

Giving is an outward expression of gratitude and devotion to the Lord, an appropriate response to his goodness and grace. But it also should be a solemn act of worship in which believers not only offer their gifts but also have opportunity to declare publicly their gratitude and faith (as in Deut. 26:12–15).

Thus giving should be handled by the church in such a way that it would resound to the praise of God in the congregation. It must not lose its value as a part of worship. Naturally, leaders must ensure that the offering is carefully used to the glory of God, clearly and openly before all the people, and that praise for the offering and its use goes to God and not the generous giver. (It is very hard not to praise generous people, and therefore it is hard for givers to have pure motives; but Jesus warned not to get caught up in the ostentatious show of giving.)

If giving is conducted properly, not only will the needs of the church be met, but so also will the needs of the poor. Then the congregation will be unified and God will be glorified.

## Vows and Commitments

The vow was a solemn way of strengthening a commitment or promise to do something in the worship or service of God. The Israelites regularly used vows in their religious services, most of them being vows of praise (promising to praise God when he answered their prayers) and vows of devotion (promising to serve God in some way). Occasionally someone would make a Nazirite vow for some purpose or for a life of service (Num. 6:1–21; 1 Sam. 1:11, 27–28; cf. also Acts 21:20–26).

Unfortunately, as with so many other things, vows were frequently misused, perhaps overused or made foolishly (cf. Lev. 27). Sometimes people were not able or willing to perform their vows, so they found clever ways to get out of them by contending that they were not actually binding in the way they were said. Jesus warned that it would be better for people not to vow at all—they should just keep their word (Matt. 5:33–37).

But there are times when vows are necessary or desirable. Jesus himself was put under oath to answer the high priest's question (Matt. 26:63–64), and Paul went to Jerusalem to fulfill a vow in the temple (Acts 21:20–26). But because of Jesus' warning the vow received limited use in the church. Instead of always making vows, Christians simply are to keep their word (2 Cor. 1:17–20). If they say emphatically and clearly that they will do such and such, then come what may they must keep their word (cf. also Ps. 15:4).

Traditionally the church has promoted vows for various religious duties. But because they have been overused and their significance has not been communicated clearly enough, the same thing has happened that happened in Israel—people have not taken their vows seriously enough to keep them. The most disgraceful example of this is the failure of believers to keep their marriage vows—and the church tolerates this! In a Christian marriage (i.e., holy matrimony), the man and the woman vow in the presence of God and other witnesses to sanctify and preserve their marriage and in the words of Jesus be joined inseparably as one in Christ.[55] Judging from the statistics on divorce, these vows are no longer considered binding—they have simply become an expression of hope or desire to make the marriage work. That is not a vow. Obviously the church must reassert the importance of vows and the seriousness of violating them.[56]

Baptismal vows also have been in use since the days of the early church, because the rite called for a public commitment to follow Christ.[57] Baptismal vows promise obedience to Christ based on the confession of faith (see the earlier discussion of baptism). This formula of faith and commitment is parallel to the Israelites' words of allegiance: "Everything the LORD has said we will do" (Exod. 24:3). The idea of having the witnesses of the baptism reaffirm their baptismal vows is a good one, for it is a way of calling people to do what they have promised. Moreover, renewing these vows immediately unites the one being baptized with the congregation in the fellowship.

Churches also use vows when infants are presented to the Lord (based on such passages as Hannah's presentation of Samuel). Some congregations use infant baptism and others simply dedication services. Apart from that issue, the point is the same: the parents and the congregation make vows to work together to bring the child up in the faith. But it is rare to find congregations that actually follow through on this commitment.

Vows are used for the ordination of clergy as well. This is a good idea, even if there is no direct biblical instruction for such ordination in the church. It is common for those who enter full-time ministry through ordination to take vows to preach the gospel, defend the faith, live obediently, and minister to the people. Here too we find that for many these vows are a formality, given the way that the clergy have so easily lived

---

55. Marriage was always viewed as a covenant and so includes the idea of vows. Malachi uses the terminology of a covenant treaty witnessed by God in his message on divorce; to break the covenant of marriage is treachery (Mal. 2:10–16).

56. The commandment not to take the name of the LORD in vain refers to oaths and vows; to invoke the LORD's name to a false purpose or to violate an oath made in his name was a capital offense.

57. Kasemann, "A Primitive Christian Baptismal Liturgy," 149–68.

in violation of Scripture and introduced heresy into the church. But if the vows are taken in a powerful and glorious worship service, then the proper motivation will be in place to impress the meaning of the vows on the ordinands.

One very popular use of vows or pledges concerns tithing. This practice does not follow biblical procedure because in Israel no one could vow to the LORD what already belonged to him—the tithe (Lev. 27:26, 30). A vow to give was to be a magnanimous spiritual act, and this was not possible if they were merely keeping the law. They could make vows to give things to the LORD *above* the normal tithes and offerings due to him. In such cases what they promised had to be paid in addition to their tithes and offerings (Lev. 27). The point is that vows should be used very sparingly because God's name is invoked, and he takes that very seriously even if we do not.

Apart from all these types of vows, people must have the opportunity in worship to respond with commitments to serve and obey. There must be that initial act of commitment by the believer (Rom. 12:1 2); but there also should be various commitments made in response to the Word of God delivered in a service and inspired by communion with the living Lord.

## Prayer

One of the most neglected aspects of corporate worship (and no doubt the spiritual life in general) is prayer. The time spent in prayer in a worship service is minimal, but prayer has always been one of the main reasons believers have assembled, both in the Old Testament and in the early church. Just as private prayer is basic to the spiritual life, so corporate prayer is at the heart of the worship and service of the congregation.[58]

We may recall how the temple in Jerusalem was to be a house of prayer, a place for people to find God. This should have made it clear for all time how important prayer is to worship. People came to the temple at different times of the day to pray, and in their great assemblies they joined in the prayers that were made for various occasions. The book of Psalms witnesses to the variety of supplications and intercessions that were made,

---

58. See Bounds, *The Complete Works of E. M. Bounds on Prayer.* Even though the works are somewhat dated, they are still very helpful reading on the subject in general.

and as prayers were added to the book, the collection provided other believers with prayers that could be applied to their own situations.

The synagogues also became places of prayer, but without sacrificial offerings and officiating priests. The great teachers debated over set prayers as opposed to free prayers, eventually concluding that set prayers in the worship provided uniformity and order. But they warned against making prayer a fixed duty. Thus, a balance was attempted between carefully planned, congregational praying and spontaneous praying. As would be expected, the prayers were heavily influenced by the Psalms; they joined prayers and praises together and repeated the major themes of the Psalms—forgiveness, redemption, deliverance from evil opposition, healing of the nation, fruitful seasons, establishment of the kingdom, and the triumph of righteousness.[59] These are the constant concerns of the people of God in this world.

It would be hard to read the New Testament and miss the point that the life of the believer is a life of prayer. But with specific reference to the beginning of Christian worship, we may note that the early Christians met regularly for prayer (Acts 2:42). They had been accustomed to doing this in the temple and the synagogues, but sadly prayers in those services did not embrace the person and work of Jesus the Messiah (even though the Psalms properly understood did speak of Christ). So the followers of Jesus also met in homes for their worship, and those meetings included prayer (Acts 16:15, 40; 21:8). Of course they also gathered to pray wherever the occasion called for it, such as by the harbor (20:36) or on the shore (21:5). Among other things they prayed for guidance (1:24), preservation from trouble (4:24–30), deliverance from immediate persecution (12:5, 12), and wisdom in ministry (13:1–3; 14:23).

The early believers knew how to pray generally; the tension came now that they knew Jesus to be the Son of God. This undoubtedly changed their perception of praying to God. Indeed, Jesus instructed them to continue to pray to the Father but in the name of the Son. Their prayers often combined prayers used in the temple and synagogues (which were drawn from Scripture) and the book of Psalms but included the full understanding and significance of the prayers now that Christ had come.[60]

---

59. Blank, "Some Observations Concerning Biblical Prayer," 75–90.
60. See Cunningham, "Origen's *On Prayer*," 332–39; and Merton, *Praying the Psalms*.

Some of the remnants of Hebrew prayers appear in the New Testament writings. For example, "ʾAbbaʾ" (Aramaic, "Father") is used in Mark 14:36. Contrary to popular thinking, the word ʾAbbaʾ does not mean "daddy."[61] There is no doubt that the word stresses the personal relationship that members of the covenant have with God, but it was always understood in a way that was appropriate to the sovereignty of God the Creator and Redeemer.

Besides the clear reports about prayer in the early church, there are other indirect references to them. Galatians 4:6 and Romans 8:15 may refer to the time in worship when believers confessed God as Father and approached him in prayer through Jesus Christ. The use of *"amen"* ("so be it," or "truly") was common in the Old Testament and was certainly appropriate in the church as well, for the custom in the synagogue and the church was for people to use it to express in faith their agreement with the prayer just said (1 Cor. 14:16; 2 Cor. 1:20; Rev. 3:14). Another prayer from the Psalms that was commonly used in Israel's festivals is *"Hosanna."* It was taken over by the church because of its connection to Christ. "Hosanna" simply means "Save [us] now we pray" (Matt. 21:15; Ps. 118:25). This soon was added to other Hebrew forms, such as *"Halleluyah,"* to become more of an expression of praise, although it never lost its meaning as the most important prayer anyone could pray. Even for the believer it is still valid as a prayer for the final deliverance. Along this line there is also the old prayer *"Marana tha,"* "Come, O Lord" (1 Cor. 16:22; cf. Rev. 22:20; *Didache* 10:6).

The place of prayer in the lives and teachings of Jesus and the apostles was sufficient to inspire the widespread use of prayers in worship in the early church, prayers of thanksgiving, supplication, intercession, and confession (for forgiveness), and most notably the Lord's Prayer.[62]

The model prayer that Jesus gave to his disciples, commonly known as the Lord's Prayer, has become the most important prayer in Christian liturgy—at least the best known.[63] A careful reading of the prayer will show

---

61. When the New Testament writers translated the word into Greek, they used "the father" and not words that would mean "daddy." For a thorough discussion of this issue, see J. Barr, "ʾABBAʾ Isn't 'Daddy.'"
62. See Stuhlman, *Redeeming the Time.*
63. Manson, "The Lord's Prayer"; and Bahr, "The Use of the Lord's Prayer in the Primitive Church," 153–59.

the proper perspective in prayer: we are the needy and the sinful, and he is the provider and sustainer; the glory and the honor belong to him, and the submission and dependence are ours. To forget this in praying is to reduce the Lord to a servant who must do our bidding. The spiritual "posture" of prayer is humility and submission; and the words of prayer are asking, not commanding. Moreover, this prayer reminds us that we are a community: it uses the pronouns "our" and "we," not "me" or "I." Its use is not limited to an assembly; but its use must make us mindful that we are part of a community with shared needs, expectations, and responsibilities. And the wording and the requests included in this prayer draw upon the prayers and the experiences of the Israelites and transfer them into the new life of faith in the Messiah.[64]

The prayer begins with the address, "Our Father in heaven" (Matt. 6:9). The wording is clearly designed for us, for Jesus always used either "the Father" or "my Father." The pronoun reminds us at the outset that we are a community, a family, that we all have one Father (cf. Mal. 1:6; 2:10). To call God "Father" is basic to the faith; the use of this figure contains at least three important ideas that are essential for praying. First, to call God "Father" is to refer to him as the Sovereign Lord and Creator. In the literature of ancient Canaan, the high god was referred to as the father of the gods, meaning he was sovereign over them. No other word would have stressed the Lord's sovereignty.[65] To use the word *Father* in praying is to acknowledge that God produced everything by himself and is therefore absolutely sovereign over it all. And since God sustains his creation, everything in it is totally dependent on him for life.

Second, the title "Father" is covenant language. Israel in the old covenant was called God's son (Exod. 4:22–23; Hos. 11:1); the king in the Davidic covenant is called God's son (2 Sam. 7:14; Ps. 2:7); and in the church believers are the children of God and thus God is our Father (John 1:12–13). Prayer, then, is to the Lord of the covenant by the covenant community.

---

64. Petuchowski and Brocke, *The Lord's Prayer and Jewish Liturgy*; Cyster, "The Lord's Prayer and the Exodus Tradition," 377–81.

65. The metaphor "mother" would not have signified anything like this; goddesses in the pantheons were consorts of the gods. In Hebrew there is not even a word for "goddess." Feminine descriptions are used for God but not feminine titles. See E. Achtemeier, "Female Language for God," 24–30.

Third, to call God "Father" is to use the language of a family relationship. Because we have been declared to be his children by adoption, we can come boldly and openly before the throne of grace with all our petitions, knowing that as a father pities his children, so the Lord pities us—and loves us, and cares for us, and is intimately aware of each of us personally.[66] But in calling God "Father" there is one important qualification: he is our Father *in heaven.* The title "Father" cannot be reduced to mean what we know from our human fathers; our heavenly Father is God—there is no fault or failure with him, no abuse or abandonment from him, only all that a father should be. He is God described with a human term "father"; he is not a human father who is called God.

The Lord's Prayer itself can be divided into two parts: the first three requests are for the culmination of God's glorious plan of the ages, and the last three (or four) are for our needs in the meantime.[67] The first request is for God's name to be hallowed, or sanctified. This prayer draws upon the passage in Ezekiel 36:16–36. Because of sin the people had been sent into captivity, and it looked like God had abandoned them, or was unable to deliver them—it looked like his reputation (name) was no good. But in spite of their sin, God promised to fulfill his word for his name's sake. He will rescue his reputation and prove himself sovereign and trustworthy. When the Lord appears and fulfills all the promises that he has made, then everyone will know that he is not weak or indifferent, that he does not lie and fill us with false hopes, but that he is the holy God and his name will be holy. It is that for which we pray. But in praying for that, we should be reminded that we are also to sanctify the name of the Lord in everything we do so that no shame or discredit comes to the faith through us.

The second request—that God's kingdom will come—falls right into line with the first. This appeal focuses directly on the consummation of the ages, for although the kingdom of God is here in Christ in one form, it is not yet fully what God intends it to be (Heb. 1:8–9). It is true that day by day people enter his kingdom and his reign is extended. But this prayer, and the prayers of the early church, focus on the coming of the

---

66. See Bondi, *To Pray and to Love.*
67. The closing benediction (Matt. 6:13 KJV) is generally considered a later addition, even though appropriate and beautiful. There is really nothing wrong with using it since it unites doxologies from other parts of the Bible.

Lord and his great kingdom. That is why it is worded "your kingdom come." This request, then, is for the coming of the Lord, who will come to judge the world and establish his reign of righteousness and peace. Prayer always has this element of eschatological hope.

The third request is for God's will to be done on earth as it is in heaven. This too looks forward to the culmination of God's program when God's righteous demands will be fulfilled. It is true that the will of the Lord is being fulfilled on earth in a number of ways now—but not as it is in heaven. The eternal plan of God, begun in Paradise but interrupted by sin and death, will yet find its fulfillment in the new heaven and earth. Of course praying for this should also remind the people of God that they should be doing his will if they are praying for it. God's will now appears to be thwarted constantly by sinfulness, but that will end.

The remaining requests are for the shared needs of the people of God as they await the consummation. The first is for daily bread, that is, sufficient provision for daily needs (using the description of the daily manna in Exod. 16).[68] It is hard for people living in an affluent culture to see the urgency of this request, but they should be reminded of Israel's folly in forgetting God (Deut. 8). They must not take for granted what they have. To pray for it daily is to maintain faith and reliance on God day by day; to pray for it at all is to acknowledge dependence on him.

The next requests are linked by conjunctions, as if to say that receiving daily provisions for life is not enough. After all, one must not live by bread alone (Deut. 8:3). So we have "Forgive us our debts, as we also have forgiven our debtors" (Matt. 6:12). The wording recognizes that we all owe a debt of gratitude to God for the forgiveness of sin. It is natural, then, for people who have been forgiven to adopt the spirit of forgiveness toward one another.[69] For people to refuse to forgive someone else is to play the role of God, to act as if they had not needed forgiveness themselves. Jesus seems to be saying that there is no forgiveness for those who are unforgiving, because they do not understand the first thing about forgiveness. If they pray for forgiveness but do not forgive others, their prayer is hypocritical because they do not have a humble and contrite heart. And we know what God thinks of that. The point is that the need for forgiveness

---

68. Yamauchi, "The 'Daily Bread' Motif in Antiquity," 145–56.
69. J. M. Ford, "The Forgiveness Clause in the Matthean Form of the Our Father," 127–31; and idem, "Yom Kippur and the Matthean Form of the Pater Noster," 609–19.

is the primary constant that binds believers together into a community. Christians are the forgiven, and the forgiving—or should be!

The last request is that we be spared in the time of trial. The prayer asks not to be led into temptation but to be delivered from evil, or the Evil One. People often find themselves in places of testing, and if they do not respond correctly, they can fall into sin. But the trials in life should also be an occasion for spiritual victory. This petition probably includes all these ideas, that is, that God not lead us into a place of trials that would be so severe that our integrity would be destroyed by sin (cf. Ps. 125:3) but that he would deliver us (cf. Dan. 3:16–18). Even though there will be trials and tests in life, God's people can pray that he will deliver them out of the hand of the Evil One, the Devil. But again, the prayer is communal; it may be used to address personal trials and troubles, but any difficulty in the body of Christ is a test for the whole community and calls for this prayer.[70]

One of the most meaningful and necessary prayers in worship is the confession of sin. Some congregations encourage times of silent confession, while others have a few set confessions in the liturgy; but others ignore it entirely, thinking that it is not necessary for Christians. When the matter of the believer's sin is not dealt with properly, people will have a poor understanding of the seriousness of sin with regard to worship and service and fellowship and a diminished appreciation for the grace of God.

It would be wonderful if everyone knew how to pray such confessions and knew the Scriptures that assure forgiveness, but they do not. So down through history the church has written prayers of confession based on the penitential psalms to help people think through the wording and use and build on it. The problem with such prayers is that they are often used without explanation and with no time provided to think about what is being said. If they are used properly, they can be most beneficial for the spiritual life. When the confession is made, the people also need to be assured that God has forgiven them. Human ministers do not have the power to forgive sins, but they do have the responsibility to declare the words of forgiveness that God has given. People need that, for when they have guilty

---

70. There is an enormous amount of literature on prayer and especially the Lord's Prayer; but one source that would be most helpful is Thielicke, *Our Heavenly Father.*

fears, they do not feel very confident. They need to know that there is a constant provision for forgiveness in the blood of Christ. They need not wait until Sunday to confess their sins, but the worship service is the appropriate place to remind people of their need to maintain their spiritual relationship with the Lord and to assure them of the Lord's forgiveness. But we must be clear: if there is genuine repentance and confession, then the sin is gone, off the record, forgotten as it were. God will not bring it up again, not in this life or the life to come.[71] That is certainly reason for praise and thanksgiving, especially as we approach the Lord's Table to celebrate communion with him and with one another.

The evidence from the Bible and the literature on the early church attests to the widespread use of prayers in worship. We will see more of this material in the next section on the Lord's Supper, but it will be worthwhile making a few observations here.

First, God expects his people to pray with holiness and faith. Paul called for prayer to be given with "holy hands, without wrath and doubting" (1 Tim. 2:8 NKJV). And Peter even warned that difficulties between husbands and wives might hinder prayers being answered (1 Peter 3:7; cf. Mal. 2:13–14). It is the prayers of the righteous that are most effectual.

Second, powerful prayers are filled with expressions of confidence in the Lord. The psalmists even rehearsed the praise they would give once the prayer was answered. In their prayers people need to build their confidence and strengthen the faith of others by including descriptions of who the Lord is and what he can do. By doing this the one praying will also be more likely to pray according to the revealed will of God.

Third, in worship services set prayers draw the entire congregation into the time of prayer. They give worshippers the opportunity to pray when otherwise they might not (either because of ignorance or inexperience).[72] If set prayers are prayed with conviction and supplemented with personal and spontaneous prayers, they can be a powerful way of uniting the church in prayer.

Fourth, such prepared prayers provide a wonderful opportunity to teach people how to address God, how to confess sin as a believer, how to use Scripture in prayer, and how to appeal to the will of God. They incor-

---

71. But on the other hand, many sins have natural consequences, and those will remain with us for some time, reminding us of our sin.
72. Bradshaw, "Whatever Happened to Daily Prayer," 10–23.

porate biblical doctrine as the foundation for the prayer and include the proper motivations. Accordingly, they will help people to see that the goal of praying is to seek God's will in their lives. As Ralph Martin says, "Prayer 'succeeds' when it melts into commitment and obedience; it fails when it is treated as a recital of our needs and an attempt to force God to act."[73]

Fifth, these planned prayers need not destroy Spirit-led worship, but if done badly they can. It is important to remember, however, that a worshipper can be just as indifferent and unbelieving in a free prayer as in a set prayer, because ultimately it is a matter of the heart and not the form used. The one praying simply must prepare his or her heart and meditate on what is said in the prayer. Praying in the assembly not only must be spiritual, but it also must be honoring to God and edifying to the congregation. A blend of set prayers and free prayers in worship is most effective and easily developed for the congregational time of worship.[74]

It will take a transformation of worship in most churches before prayer becomes an integral part of the service and not just an obligatory token. But the inspiration for this will come only with a renewed vision of the Lord of glory and the importance of being in communion with him.

## The Table of the Lord in the Worship of the Early Church

### The Breaking of the Bread

The early Christians followed the lead of the Last Supper by meeting together for the breaking of the bread (Acts 2:46). At first this seems to have supplemented the other worship activities of the temple and synagogue, but very quickly it became the center of Christian worship, being celebrated frequently, if not daily, by believers. Jesus himself encouraged this by his postresurrection appearances, for he appeared to his followers several times at the breaking of the bread and table fellowship (e.g., in Emmaus in Luke 24:30; then with the disciples in v. 43; again with the Eleven in Mark 16:14; and on the shore in John 21:13). The disciples then naturally continued this fellowship together.[75]

The text of Acts 2:46 makes it clear that the "breaking of the bread" was

---

73. R. P. Martin, *The Worship of God*, 31.
74. See Saliers, "The Integrity of Sung Prayers," 290–303.
75. See further Rordorf et al., *The Eucharist of the Early Christians*.

done with great joy. The disciples remembered that Jesus had said that he would not drink with them again until the kingdom; and now they had seen the risen Christ break bread with them. So by continuing the ritual of the Last Supper, the followers of Christ celebrated the presence of the risen Christ with anticipation of the glorious union in the kingdom. Only the resurrection faith with the hope of glory can explain the great celebration that characterized their observance of the ordinance—this was no routine ritual for them. Moreover, the expectation of the Lord's imminent return probably prompted them to celebrate daily, an expectation inspired by the outpouring of the Holy Spirit.

It appears that the early believers combined their common fellowship meals with the celebration of the "breaking of the bread." Or, in other words, the *eucharist* at first was a part of the *agapē* or "love" meal. The evidence for this comes from hints in Scripture as well as from later extrabiblical witnesses to early worship. For example, Paul says that in Corinth the wealthier members disregarded the rest, beginning to eat before the others arrived, and that certain members went to excess in the ceremonial rite, perhaps confusing the two meals (1 Cor. 11). Paul insisted that they all eat together, for the spiritual character of the meal was far more important than the social character. A shared common meal was a natural occasion for fellowship and perhaps necessary when persecution began; and it was easy to add the ritual of the breaking of the bread at the beginning and the drinking of the cup at the end to put the focus on worship.

We also learn from Pliny, the governor of Bithynia, in his letter to Trajan (10:96), that the Christians met together to eat but that they gave this up after he issued an edict (A.D. 113) against unlicensed clubs. Apparently the Christians of Bithynia had to abandon their common meal when the *lex Julia* was enforced. As a result the *Eucharist* was separated from the meal and held in the predawn liturgy (as we find in Justin Martyr). The Christians did not give up the *eucharist*—it was too important a part of their worship.[76]

Eating together had always been recognized as the quintessential sign of fellowship. To eat together spoke of peace, of common interests, and of

---

76. For a survey see the three articles by George Dollar on the Lord's Supper in the early church. See also Murphy-O'Connor, "Eucharist and Community in First Corinthians," 56–69.

shared possessions. So as the early Christians broke bread together, they carried on the table fellowship that some of them had enjoyed with Jesus. The *communal* meal was the occasion for continuing fellowship together, but the *Communion* meal included in it reminded them of Christ and the inauguration of the new covenant. In this sense the Emmaus story is probably exemplary. They came in to eat the regular meal together, but because Jesus was there it included the more significant Communion aspects—it was all very different from an ordinary meal.

Acts 20:7–11 also may provide a glimpse of early Christian eucharistic fellowship. People came together on the first day of the week to break bread, and Paul spoke to them late into the night. After the episode with Eutychus, Paul broke bread and ate and then continued to talk a long while—until daybreak. From this it may be concluded that the early Christians, many Gentiles as well as Jews, on occasion may have continued their services on the Saturday well into the evening (sundown marking the beginning of the first day of the week).[77] Then, early in the morning on Sunday the breaking of the bread would celebrate the Lord's resurrection. Gradually, the Sunday morning service became predominant for the celebration of the meal, especially as the *agapē* meal ceased or lost its urgency.

Throughout the Epistles there are hints that the early church included a sermon with the breaking of the bread (Acts 20), which would be comparable to the inclusion of apostolic teaching mentioned in Acts 2. The general prayers of 1 Timothy 2:1–2 and 8 could have been part of the service, since Acts 2 also refers to prayers. And Scripture reading, at least the apostolic letters (Col. 4:16), would have no better setting than this assembly. Moreover, some blessings, doxologies, creeds, and hymns probably formed a part of the meal-service, just as they had with Passover.

More details of early worship emerge from the book of Revelation. Some parts of Revelation have been cast in the forms of worship, much in the manner that the Psalms and prophets drew on temple imagery. For example, in the description of the setting of Revelation 4–5 the throne corresponds to the bishop's chair and the seats of the elders to those of the presbyters on either side of the bishop. The Lamb of course would be the reality behind the communal bread and wine, the book, the gospel

---

77. Unless this was a special occasion with Paul present.

text, and the refrains the early Christian hymns (Sanctus in 4:8 and the Amen in 5:14). John is disclosing for us the pattern for the worship that was being developed by the apostles out of Israel's divinely given institutions. In those institutions there was a foretaste of worship in glory; the church now could see the pattern more clearly. This confirms that the type of service known from the second century had been taking shape in the first.

## Apostolic Instructions

We have noted so far that the "breaking of the bread" became the central ceremonial part of Christian worship, that it was the cause of great joy, and that it was very early joined with apostolic teaching.

It was probably inevitable that in time there would be violations of the Lord's Supper, given its frequent and widespread use. Paul found it necessary to correct the excesses in the celebration at Corinth. Not only were they eating before others arrived, as we have noted, but some were taking the feasting to excess, missing the solemnity of the bread and wine altogether. After all, many of them had come from pagan backgrounds where Bacchian feasts were commonplace. So Paul stressed the significance of the meal—it is the *Lord's* Supper. To participate in the Communion meal was to proclaim the death of Christ that brought forgiveness from sins and established the fellowship of the saints. No one should take the wine to excess, for the bread is the body of Christ and the wine the blood, and both were given for all; and no one should go without either, for as the sacrifice of Christ it was to extend to all.[78]

This problem, as well as others, made it obvious that there had to be people to oversee worship. Thus the apostolic instruction for church order included an "overseer" (*episkópos* is often translated "bishop"), "elders" *(presbuteros),* and "deacons" *(diakonos).* But even though these were there to ensure proper service, Paul is silent on who actually should lead the communion meal or say the appropriate words. Certainly, if an apostle like Paul were present, he would be expected to lead the service. In Antioch there were prophets and teachers who were leading the ritual for the church there (Acts 13:1–3). From the time of Ignatius (A.D. 110),

---

78. For a very thorough and helpful discussion of the entire biblical theme, see Maurice, *The Doctrine of Sacrifice Deduced from the Scriptures;* see too Packer, *Eucharistic Sacrifice;* and H. M. Davies, *Bread of Life and Cup of Joy.*

the overseer customarily presided over the celebration and gave the consecratory prayers. In his absence he would appoint one of the elders to oversee the rite. Deacons by this time received the communal offerings and served the meal, even to the sick and the absent. We also learn from Didache 15 and 1 Clement 44:4 that it was the overseer who conducted the eucharistic meal, offering the gifts and saying the thanksgiving. So it seems that very early the leading of corporate worship, that is, directing the official apostolic teaching and overseeing the communal meal, was reserved for the properly authorized overseer or elders, to be assisted by deacons and deaconesses.

## Communal Worship

The words *communion* and *communal* worship sometimes slip by us without impressing on us their deep significance. Communal worship goes hand in hand with communal living. We see this most powerfully exhibited in Acts 4:32–37, which describes the believers as united and sharing what they had with one another. Some, like Barnabas, sold what they had and gave the proceeds to the apostles for the needs of the community. This is true communal living, or community, or what we call fellowship. The text makes it clear that it is a result of the control of the Spirit of God.[79] Communion, or fellowship, refers to what we share in Christ, or because of Christ. It may refer to sharing our possessions; or it may refer to sharing in the sufferings of Christ. The point for worship is that if this communion is not in place, then celebrating the ritual of Holy Communion will be hollow—unless the celebration of Holy Communion reminds us of our covenant responsibilities to each other and changes the way we live.[80]

For more specific information about Christian communal worship in the early church, we must look to the witnesses in the second century. While this material is removed some decades from any apostolic presence, it does reveal a continuity with and development of what was done earlier.

---

79. In stark contrast we have the account in Acts 5 of a couple who were controlled by Satan. They held back some money in their giving and lied about it to the church.

80. Recall that the word *remember* meant to bring into actuality what is remembered and that in Communion this would be our covenant obligation. As Rayburn says, "The Lord's Supper has never been a solemn wake held in sorrowful remembrance of a dead person" (*O Come, Let Us Worship*, 257).

One source of information already mentioned is the letter of Pliny to Trajan about the church in Bithynia (A.D. 113). He says Christians "were accustomed on a special day to assemble before day light and to sing antiphonally a hymn to Christ as if he were a god, and to bind themselves by an oath not for any wrong purpose, but not to commit theft, or robbery or adultery, not to break their word or to deny a deposit when asked for. After this it was their custom to depart, and to meet together again to take food, but ordinary and harmless food. Even this they gave up after my edict." Pliny thus describes an early morning meeting that had antiphonal singing or liturgy, perhaps messianic psalms or new Christian hymns, and the recitation of the law in the form of commitments to obedience. This service corresponds in some ways to the synagogue service. Later in the day (Sunday), they reassembled for a communal meal that included the Lord's Supper. When the edict came down, the Communion was transferred to the early service and the common meal ceased. The reason for a predawn service and a late evening meal was probably practical, for Sunday was not a holiday and most of the people had to attend to their businesses.[81]

The clearest information on the Christian communal worship comes from Justin Martyr's description of the church in Rome of A.D. 150.[82] The Sunday service began with the reading of the Scriptures. The overseer ("president" for Gentiles) then delivered a sermon while seated in a chair, which was the manner of the synagogue (Luke 4:20). After he finished, the people stood, some with outstretched arms, and offered prayers. They may have been long intercessions like those in 1 Clement 59 (A.D. 110) but with the Roman liturgy. A deacon would call for prayer on a subject, individuals would then pray silently, and then the bishop would sum up the prayers on that matter (a "collect"). Sometimes, if not always, the prayers would be intoned. The prayers would end with an enthusiastic "Amen" from the congregation (Justin describes it as "shout in applause"). "Amen" came to mean more than "so be it," because Paul had said that Christ is the "Amen" to all the promises of God (cf. 2 Cor. 1:20). The kiss of peace followed the prayers (in Oriental practice men

---

81. For similar practical reasons we began to meet later in the morning for services to allow farmers to do their chores before assembling.
82. Justin, *First Apology,* 65–67. See Flanigan, "The Roman Rite and the Origins of the Liturgical Drama," 263–84; and King, *Liturgies of the Past.*

would not kiss women) and expressed the fellowship that they shared as members of the body of Christ.

The Eucharist celebration concluded the service. The offering of bread and wine was taken up (believers bringing the elements). After the deacons arranged these gifts on the table, the bishop offered the prayer of consecration, a series of thanksgivings for Creation,[83] redemption, and deliverance from evil. The prayer was to be prayed to the best of his ability (apparently it was not a set prayer at this time) and could be extended. The people would respond with "Amen." Within the time of the thanksgiving, there was a dialogue between leader and people modeled after the Jewish dialogue before grace. It probably concerned the institution of the Lord's Supper.[84] After the appropriate words had been said, the deacons served communion to the people (standing before the table). The deacons would then take portions of it to those who were absent.

The nature of the bread and the wine were early interpreted to represent the presence of the risen Christ. Justin is not clear, but he draws the analogy with the incarnate Word: just as the Word was made flesh, so here the bread and wine were in some sense the body and blood of Jesus. It is doubtful that the early church held to transubstantiation—that came later; but they did see the Eucharist as something stronger than symbolism. The bread and the wine were no longer part of a meal; they now took on a totally different significance to the worshipper.[85]

The three emphases of the celebration were (and are) offering, remembrance, and communion. The idea of the bread and wine being an offering draws on the nature of the death of the sacrifice as an offering for sin against the background of the Old Testament. The early Christians brought bread and wine for the communal meal to signify that the basis of their acceptance by God was the body and blood of Christ; Clement (A.D. 110), Justin (A.D. 150), and Hippolytus (A.D. 235) all called it an offering. The worshipper brings it in submission to the Lord, the deacon presented it to the overseer, and the overseer offered it

---

83. In addition to sources mentioned before, for more information, see J. G. Davies, *A New Dictionary of Liturgy and Worship;* and Bradshaw, *New SCM Dictionary of Liturgy and Worship.*

84. Easton, *Hippolytus,* 6.3.

85. Luis Alonso-Schoekel, *Celebrating the Eucharist;* and Wolterstorff, "The Remembrance of Things (Not) Past."

with the prayers of thanksgiving. Didache 14:2–3 (A.D. 100) first called it a sacrifice, perhaps incorporating the terminology of Hebrews 13:15–16 for the "sacrifice of praise," or 1 Peter 2:5 for the "spiritual sacrifices." At any rate, the early church conducted the Last Supper on the order of a Passover, and they saw it altogether appropriate to incorporate the language of Passover in it.

## The Development of the Liturgy

The words that are said with ritual and the acts that are done must be precise and meaningful. Therefore, in the early church the Lord's Supper was described and clarified by a developed liturgy.

This word *liturgy* is a perfectly good biblical word and need not be avoided as something foreign to historic Christianity. The noun is *leitourgia,* literally "the work of the people"; it means a service or a ministry. The related verb means "to minister" or "to serve." In Acts 13:2 the verb form is used to describe the church's worship: they were "ministering" to the Lord and fasting.[86] The New Testament uses these words for various aspects of Christian service: for giving money for the poor (Rom. 15:27; 2 Cor. 9:12), the ministry of the people (Phil. 2:17), and the service of carrying an apostolic message (Phil. 2:25). It is no surprise, then, that the early church used the word *liturgy* for the worship and service of God by the people and in time developed prayers and blessings to guide that worship.

A study of the liturgies of the early church reveals some common features that were not only appropriate for the celebration but also quite biblical. The most complete liturgy may be found in *The Apostolic Tradition* by Hippolytus, but other sources supplement our understanding of the development of the liturgy.

---

86. Rackham notes that the word was originally used among the Greeks to denote a service to the state rendered by an individual (see Rom. 13:6). Then the Greek translators of the Old Testament adopted it for the service in the temple; from this Old Testament use, it naturally passed to the New Testament (e.g., for Zacharias in the temple, Luke 1:23; or the priest's duties, Heb. 8:6; 10:11). Paul speaks of the service of faithful Christians with this word and refers to himself as the servant *(leitourgos)* of Christ (Rom. 15:16). The true work of the people is the service of God in its many forms. In time the word came to refer to the worship service (especially in Greek services), and specifically the part that the people played in the worship (Rackham, *The Acts of the Apostles,* 189–90).

The entire service is a dramatization of the Lord's own Last Supper, with the addition of Christianized blessings and responses. At its core are the details of the drama in the Upper Room. The first part of the early liturgies dramatizes the fact that the celebration is a symbol of the offering ("he took"). All the people readied themselves and presented the offering of bread and wine, which the overseer offered to the Lord as a thanksgiving in remembrance of Christ. By the fourth century a ceremonial washing of the hands was included according to Cyril (from Ps. 26:6). The practice of the offering and the washing were dropped by the Reformers, probably because of the way the church had changed their meanings.

The entire celebration was characterized by giving thanks ("he blessed"). The church got away from the Jewish blessings given at the Passover and developed a Christian blessing.[87] The first part of Communion liturgy was the dialogue. It began with the *sursum corda* (named after the first line; Hippolytus). This opening dialogue stresses that true worship takes place in the heavenlies (Eph. 2:6–7), and the bidding of the congregation to lift up their hearts calls for them to ascend to that realm in their spirits (Rev. 4–5). The development of liturgies took place over the first few centuries, and so it is difficult to know what was said in the earliest periods (as it was with synagogue worship). But Christians knew that words had to be proclaimed with the ritual, and so to guarantee that the right words, the best words, were said, they formed their various prayers and narratives. Some of the earliest pieces had this kind of service:

LEADER:    Up with your hearts
PEOPLE:    We have them with the LORD
LEADER:    Let us give to the LORD
PEOPLE:    It is fitting and right.

Then came the *preface,* a brief proclamation as to why thanksgiving is to be offered. Hippolytus's preface was brief: "We render to you, O God, through your beloved Son Jesus Christ, whom in the last times you sent to us as Savior, Redeemer, and Angel of your will." The preface of John Chrysostom (A.D. 380) is much longer:

---

87. See Oesterley, *Jewish Background of Christian Liturgy;* and Taft, *Liturgy of the Hours in East and West.*

LEADER: It is fitting and right to hymn you, to bless you, to praise you, to give thanks, to worship you in all places of your dominion. For you are God, ineffable, inconceivable, invisible, incomprehensible, existing always and in the same way, you and your only-begotten Son and your Holy Spirit. You brought us out of not being to being; and when we had fallen, you raised us up again; and did not cease to do everything until you had brought us up to heaven, and granted us the kingdom that is to come. For all these things we give thanks to you and to your only begotten Son and to your Holy Spirit, for all that we know and do not know, your seen and unseen benefits that have come upon us. We give you thanks also for this ministry; vouchsafe to receive it from our hands, even though thousands of archangels and ten thousands of angels stand before you, cherubim and seraphim, with six wings and eyes, flying on high, singing the triumphal hymn, proclaiming, crying, and saying:

Then came the *sanctus,* the response of the congregation (taken from Isa. 6:3; Rev. 4:8; and the Psalter). By responding with this, the congregation joins the heavenly assembly in singing eternal praise.

PEOPLE: Holy, Holy, Holy, Lord of hosts; heaven and earth are full of your glory. Hosanna in the highest. Blessed is He who comes in the name of the LORD. Hosanna in the highest.

Finally, the congregation was led in the prayer of *thanksgiving.* Once again more elaborate prayers come from the Eastern churches, but this sample from Hippolytus will serve:

LEADER: Who is your inseparable Word, through whom you made all things, and in whom you were well pleased. You sent him from heaven into the Virgin's womb; and, conceived in the womb, he was made flesh and was manifested as your Son, being born of the Holy Spirit and the Virgin. Fulfilling your will and gaining for you a holy people, he stretched out his hands when he should suffer, that he might release from suffering those who have believed in you.

> And when he was betrayed to voluntary suffering that he might destroy death, and break the bonds of the devil, and tread down hell, and shine upon the righteous, and fix the limit, and manifest the resurrection . . .

Then came the breaking of the bread ("he broke"); it had first served as a means of distribution, but also took on the meaning of Christ's broken body. This part of the liturgy began with the *narrative*, which is simply the repeating of the words of Jesus from the Gospel account. Hippolytus continues, recording the early form:

LEADER:   He took bread and gave thanks to you, saying, "Take, eat; this is my body, which shall be broken for you." Likewise also the cup, saying, "This is my blood, which is shed for you; when you do this, you make my remembrance."

The more detailed *memorial* was used instead to help the worshippers in their remembrance of Christ. *The Apostolic Constitutions* (A.D. 375) records:

LEADER:   Remembering therefore what he endured for us, we give you thanks, Almighty God, not as we ought but as we are able, and we fulfill His commands. For in the night he was betrayed, he took bread in his holy and blameless hands and, looking up to you, his Father, he broke it and gave it to his disciples, saying, "This is the mystery of the new covenant; take it and eat; this is my body which is broken for many for forgiveness of sins." Likewise also he mixed the cup of wine and water and sanctified it and gave it to them, saying, "Drink from this, all of you; this is my blood which is shed for many for forgiveness of sins. Do this for my remembrance; for as often as you eat this bread and drink this cup, you proclaim my death, until I come." Remembering then his passion and death and resurrection from the dead, his return to heaven and his future second coming, in which he comes to judge the living and the dead, and to reward each according to his works, we offer to you, King and God. . . .

The "memorial" activates the event in the past so that it is a present experience in its effects.[88] It was not simply a mental act of remembering; it was a present proclamation of the reality of Christ's sacrifice and a dramatic reenactment of receiving Christ; it was a means of calling to mind the stipulations of the covenant—a call to service as it were.

Then came the *epiclesis,* the prayer for the empowerment by the Holy Spirit. Hippolytus has:

LEADER:    And we ask that you would send your Holy Spirit upon the offering of your holy church; that, gathering them into one, you would grant to all who partake of the holy things (to partake) for the fullness of the Holy Spirit for the confirmation of faith in truth.

This led into intercession. In the West the full intercession came earlier in the service, with only the Lord's Prayer being said here. In the Eastern church a full intercession is included here, because here the congregation is at the throne of God in their worship. After the intercession the breaking of the bread took place in a way for all to see and to hear.

With the blessings, narratives, and breaking of the bread completed, the elements were distributed to the worshippers ("he gave"). The early church followed the pattern of Christ in the Upper Room; the minister handed the bread and the cup to each person and said either the exact words or a paraphrase of them. *The Apostolic Constitutions* records this:

MINISTER:       The body of Christ
WORSHIPPER:   Amen
MINISTER:       The blood of Christ, the cup of life
WORSHIPPER:   Amen

This, of course, is the heart of the Communion. Paul said, "Is not the cup of thanksgiving for which we give thanks a participation in the blood of Christ? And is not the bread that we break a participation in the body of Christ?" (1 Cor. 10:16). Giving the elements personally to the worshipper

---

88. Likewise in the Passover Gamaliel said that each participant was to eat the meal as if he had been in Egypt with the ancestors (*Pesahim* 10).

and speaking personally to the worshipper the words of Christ, followed by the worshipper's eating the bread and drinking the wine, heightened the great spiritual effect of the moment.

For the conclusion, the benediction was inspired by the high priestly benediction of Numbers 6:22–27, the one that Aaron pronounced after the sacrificial blood had been presented to God on behalf of the worshipper. But in the new covenant the wording of the blessing changed to become clearly Trinitarian:

> May the grace of the Lord Jesus Christ,
>> and the love of God, and the fellowship of the Holy Spirit
>> be with you all.
>
>                    (2 Cor. 13:14)

The recessional hymn was one of great joy and celebration, a triumphant shout of *"alleluia"* and *"amen."* The early church used such pieces as "Lamb of God," modeled after "the Lamb of God, who takes away the sin of the world" (John 1:29). With the end of the service the people would go forth to fulfill their service of the Lord, inspired by the Word and the Eucharist.

## Faithful Obedience

It should be clear by now that true worship leads to a life of faith and obedience. It is the purpose of worship, on the human side, to inspire faith and devotion to the Lord, not just for an hour, but for the whole week and for the whole life. This was the emphasis of the preaching of the prophets and the teaching of Jesus and the apostles; and this emphasis was based on the significance of worship as a covenant renewal, a ritual that not only celebrated the blessings that God has bestowed on his people through Christ but also reminded the people of their own covenant responsibilities.

At the heart of faithful obedience is personal holiness and righteousness. True worship has no place for gossip, slander, malice, envy, strife, control, or any other sin that destroys worship. Our celebration of being at peace with God must issue in living in peace with other believers. Our covenant obligations do not stop with our purging out the leaven from our lives. There is a positive side of righteousness that calls for action. If the church claims to be worshipping but has no interest in helping the poor and the homeless, the widow and the orphan, the oppressed and the foreigner, or in championing justice and equity in society, then the worship is empty. And if the worship does not prompt the work of evangelism and missions, or simply sharing the faith, then the worship has not been led by the Spirit of God. With these and many other serious matters we may test whether worship has fully achieved what God has designed it to achieve.

In many worship services the hour ends with a dismissal along the lines of "Go in peace to love and serve the Lord." This is followed by a time of silent prayer, presumably to allow individuals the opportunity to make commitments and decisions. But who gives it much thought? Maybe something more specific, more in line with what has just happened in the service, could be said at that moment.

## Conclusion

The Eucharist, Communion, or the Lord's Supper, is the central act of Christian worship. It is the celebration of communion with the risen Christ and the true fellowship of the saints. Every Christian group observes it at different times, and every Christian group has liturgy of some kind in order to make it part of the worship.[89] But every congregation must be constantly seeking ways to make sure that it is the meaningful and powerful part of worship it was intended to be.

There is no need at this point to offer suggestions on how to celebrate Communion or how to explain it; there is a good deal of literature on this aspect of the subject. But there are some additional observations that can be made that often fall by the wayside.

First, the observance of Communion should lead to celebration; it may start with solemn meditation, self-examination, and prayer; but it should end with triumphant joy and praising. Since opportunities for individual biblical praise are missing in most worship services, this could be one of the best times for it, especially when it comes at the end of the service.

Second, this is a holy meal. Therefore, the church must impress this fact on the people by the way it is observed. The time should not be trivi-

---

89. E.g., see Byars, "Eucharistic Prayers in the Reformed Tradition," 114–32; and H. M. Davies, "Response," 371–78.

alized or abbreviated so that proper attention cannot be given to the rite. The words and the elements should not be made commonplace or popular so that the uniqueness of it is lost. And inappropriate music and conversations should be avoided because this can divert the meditation.

Third, liturgy is important for the Communion because the extemporaneous words offered in many services run the risk of being incomplete or inaccurate. Churches need not allow the words to become an empty formula, however; there are so many liturgies available that have been in use for centuries and are sound and rich that there is no reason for churches to limit themselves in worship.

Fourth, if Holy Communion is properly explained and spiritually observed, then the sound doctrine it has always conveyed will strengthen the faith of the people and provide an excellent opportunity for the church to clarify the gospel.

Fifth, if the church is properly taught along the way, then all the words of Communion will be effectual in transforming believers' lives. One part that has been all but ignored over the years is the full meaning of doing this in remembrance of Christ, that is, as an occasion for renewing commitments to fulfill covenant obligations. That alone should prompt the church to become a vital Christian community and a living witness to the world.

# Conclusion *for* Part 8

TOO MANY CHRISTIANS HAVE settled into a familiar routine called worship; they are not comfortable with change, and they are afraid to do things that might look like what other denominations do. But worship is one of those aspects of the Christian faith that must continue to grow and flourish, or it will cease to have the dynamic impact it can have on believers who must cope with life in this world. There is no reason for individual congregations to change everything they have been doing; but there is every reason for all congregations to evaluate everything they are doing to see how they can do it better. And the test for this evaluation is how well the worship activities transform the lives of believers for service in this life and fit them for glory.

There is no need to reiterate here all the things that Jesus and the apostles taught and all the ways that the early church tried to develop biblical and meaningful worship. All that remains to be said here is what James said to the early church: "Be doers of the word, and not hearers only" (James 1:22 NKJV). To assist us in finding more and more ways to do what pleases God, God has given us a revelation of things to come, and especially a revelation of what worship will be like when we actually enter into the presence of our holy Lord.

# PART 9

# THE PERFECTION of WORSHIP in GLORY

# Introduction

GOD, BY HIS GRACE, HAS GIVEN his people a final revelation of glory. It is a vision that we desperately need as we find our way through the confusion of this age and prepare for the dark days that will fall upon our world before the coming of Christ in glory. It is possible when reading the book of Revelation to get caught up in the drama on earth, the raging of the forces of evil against the kingdom of God and the fantastic judgments that fall upon them. But to focus primarily on those things is to miss a most significant part of the prophecy, namely, the vision of the fulfillment of God's plan of redemption in glory.[1] After all, it is the vision of glory that inspires the people of God to persevere in their faith, even at the cost of their lives should that become necessary.[2] When believers fix their thoughts on things that are eternal, then they are able to keep everything in proper perspective.

But this glimpse of glory also inspires and directs the people of God in their worship here on earth.[3] As we read these passages, it will become clearer and clearer how worship on earth foreshadows heavenly worship. We do not have to be in the midst of Roman persecutions like the early church to appreciate the value of being lifted out of this world in our spirits to realms above. To lift up our hearts to that transcendent glory

---

1. Bauckham, *The Climax of Prophecy*. For the contexts of the visions, see the general works as well as Collins, "Reading the Book of Revelation in the Twentieth Century," 229–41; and Boring, "The Theology of Revelation," 257–69.
2. Martyrdom is one of the major themes in the book (see Rev. 6:9–11; 12:11; Trites, "*Martus* and Martyrdom in the Apocalypse," 72–80).
3. There is a good deal of literature that discusses how the visions influenced or reflected the worship of the early church. Otto Piper studies the liturgy of the book with early writings of *1 Clement* (34:5–7) and the *Didache* and concludes that the descriptions of worship in the book correspond to the liturgy of the early church ("The Apocalypse of John," 10–22).

for even a moment will have a definite impact on the way we worship. If we even begin to comprehend the risen Christ in all his glory, or faintly hear the heavenly choirs that surround the throne with their anthems of praise, or imagine what life in the presence of the Lord will be like, then we can never again be satisfied with worship as usual. We will always be striving to make our worship fit for glory; and we will always be aware that our efforts, no matter how good and noble, are still of this world and not yet of that one.[4]

Accordingly, we must appreciate that there are several major differences between worship in glory and worship below. For example, in heaven worshippers are in the actual presence of God—they are caught up in the fullness of his glory and respond to that presence with undiminished joy. But here for now, for the most part, we have to rely on the written records of past visions and appearances and on our spiritual perceptions of God's mystical presence. Frequently God reveals his presence in miraculous ways, but it is not glory. Another difference with worship in heaven is that it is with pure angelic choirs and glorified saints. Here on earth it is hard to imagine what worship would be like without human frailties and pride hindering it, but that will be glory. This reminds us of yet another difference. Worshippers in heaven can give themselves completely to praise and adoration, because a number of aspects of worship that belong to this life will no longer be present—confession of sin, prayers of the people, and exhortations to combat evil, avoid idolatry and hypocrisy, pursue righteous living, develop evangelistic endeavors, and address pain and suffering in the world. So the revelation of worship in heaven has been given to us, not only to inform us of how good it will be, but also to remind us of what worship must still do here on earth.

Although there are differences, worship in glory will continue the basic aspects of worship that have been present from the very beginning— and perfect them. First, for example, worship is the response to divine revelation. In the book of Revelation, from the initial vision of Christ in glory to the acclamations that he is worthy of praise because he created everything and has redeemed his creation, every living creature responds appropriately and perfectly. Christ's glorious works were revealed before,

---

4. See Kooy, "The Apocalypse and Worship," 198–209; and Cabaniss, "A Note on the Liturgy of the Apocalypse," 78–86. See also D. Barr, "The Apocalypse of John as Oral Enactment," 243–56.

but in glory they are displayed with a reality and clarity that has never been witnessed on earth.

Moreover, each new act of worship is a response to something new that God does. At each step of the way in the consummation of the ages—the taking of the scroll (5:9), the breaking of the seal (8:1), the sounding of the trumpet (11:15),[5] or the casting down of Satan (12:10)—there is a response of amazement and adoration. And it builds through the book to the grand climax when Babylon is overthrown (18:20) and all the multitudes and heavenly hosts acclaim God's power and dominion (19:1–5). Then, there follows the sound of the great multitude, like the roar of rushing waters and loud peals of thunder, shouting "Hallelujah," because the wedding of the Lamb has come (19:6–8). In the book of Revelation, the things that the LORD does are truly beyond human comprehension; he fulfills all of his promises and creates a new heaven and a new earth, so that the celebration of God's work in the heavenly Paradise far exceeds that which occurred at the creation of the earthly one. In short, the worshipful responses of God's creatures in heaven transcend anything imaginable on earth.

Another aspect of worship is that it is a communal activity.[6] Whether it is the letters to the churches, or the souls under the altar, or the thousands who fall before the Lord, worshippers are portrayed as united in one body from every nation, tribe, and tongue on earth, proclaiming greater praise and devotion than is possible here below.

Third, worship in glory still involves the whole person. We do not know what all the circumstances will be like in glory, but it is obvious that worship is not simply an act of the spirit or the mind but also of glorified bodies responding to God's presence. People may choose not to kneel or bow in worship here, for example, but there they will fall on their faces before him in deep humility and reverence. The heavenly scenes of worship are very lively, with trumpets blasting, people shouting and praising and singing, and a number of dramatic acts being carried out in the celebration of communion with the living Lord. In addition,

---

5. See Finesinger, "The Shofar," 193–228; and Bockmuehl, "The Trumpet Shall Sound," 199–225.
6. Jeske, "Spirit and Community in the Johannine Apocalypse," 452–66. In Revelation the work of the Spirit is related to the community as a whole; nowhere in the book is it connected to the experience of an individual apart from the community.

Revelation communicates with familiar symbols—altars, lavers, scrolls, lamps, and the like, as well as with elements like fire and wind and blood.[7] Sounds, posture, dramatic ritual, and symbols are all an important part of Christian worship because they reflect the patterns of the spiritual reality in the heavenly sanctuary.

With this involvement of the whole person, glorified and perfected by the blood of Christ, participation will be fully in communion with all the saints and angels, as indeed it must now be. And that communal worship will focus on the Lord, the one who created everything by his will and has redeemed us for himself. In that realm not a word that he speaks will be ignored or left unfulfilled, and not an act that he performs will pass without his creatures marveling at such wonders and spontaneously acclaiming his surpassing glory. Thus should it be here below; thus must it be.

---

7. Cody, *Heavenly Sanctuary and Liturgy.*

# CHAPTER 27

# Christ *in* Glory *with* Choirs *of* Angels

## The Vision of Christ in Glory

Because the last book in the Bible is the revelation of Jesus Christ, he has the preeminence throughout. Fittingly, after the brief prologue and the salutation,[1] John begins with a *doxology:*

To him who loves us and has freed us from our sins by his blood, and has made us to be a kingdom of priests[2] to serve his God and Father— to him be glory and power for ever and ever! Amen. (Rev. 1:5b–6)

Here, at the outset of the prophecies in this book, a doxology reminds us of the love of Christ for us.[3]

Then John adds a short *acclamation:*

Look, he is coming with the clouds,[4]
and every eye shall see him,
even those who pierced him;
and all the peoples of the earth will mourn because of him.
So shall it be! Amen.[5]

(Rev. 1:7)

---

1. Lieu, "Grace to You and Peace," 161–78.
2. S. Brown, "The Priestly Character of the Church in the Apocalypse," 224–31.
3. Cruz, "The Beatitudes of the Apocalypse: Eschatology and Ethics," 269–83.
4. R. B. Y. Scott, "Behold He Cometh with Clouds," 127–32.
5. This is the first occurrence in the book of the amplified oracle, that is, a prophetic saying is appended to another one for the purpose of expanding or interpreting it (see also 13:9; 14:13; 16:15; 19:9; 21:5–8; 22:12–15; 22:18–20; Aune, *Revelation 1–5,* 58–59).

What John, or perhaps the early church, has done is combine Daniel
7:13, Zechariah 12:10, and Matthew 24:30 in a paean of praise.[6] The significance of the acclamation is absolutely clear—if the risen Christ is
coming and everyone will see him, then he ought to be the focus of our
devotion and service now![7]

This opening doxology and acclamation is followed by a magnificent
but terrifying revelation of Christ in glory. John was in the spirit on the
Lord's Day,[8] the first day of the week, when he heard a loud voice, turned,
and saw the vision of the Lord[9] among the seven[10] golden lampstands.[11]

> [He was] "like a son of man," dressed in a robe reaching down
> to his feet and with a golden sash around his chest. His head and
> hair were white like wool, as white as snow, and his eyes were like
> blazing fire. His feet were like bronze glowing in a furnace, and
> his voice was like the sound of rushing waters. In his right hand
> he held seven stars, and out of his mouth came a sharp double-
> edged sword. His face was like the sun shining in all its brilliance.
> (Rev. 1:13b–16)

This vision is the foundation upon which everything that follows is
based. It is a vision that brings comfort and hope, for John saw Christ living, Christ supreme, Christ aware and caring for his churches—holding
them in his hand as it were.[12]

In the revelation Christ is "like a son of man"[13] (cf. Dan. 7:13), a description of the Messiah as a human figure, but in view of the setting,
both here and in Daniel, it is one of a supernatural being in human form.
The fact that his face was shining like the sun and his head and hair were
pure white is evidence of his incomparable divinity in human form. It

---

6. Collins, "The 'Son of Man' Tradition in the Book of Revelation," 536–68; and Beale,
*The Use of Daniel in Jewish Apocalyptic Literature.*

7. See Boring, "The Theology of Revelation," 257–69.

8. See Bruce, "The Spirit in the Apocalypse," 333–44. See also Bauckham, "The Lord's
Day," 221–50.

9. Lindblom, "Theophanies in Holy Places in Hebrew Religion," 91–106.

10. Varley, *Seven;* C. Abrahamowitz, "The Number Seven."

11. See Yarden, *Tree of Light,* and C. L. Meyers, *The Tabernacle Menorah.*

12. C. A. Scott, *The Book of the Revelation,* 147.

13. Moule, "The Son of Man," 277–79.

reveals that Jesus who walked on earth is the immortal and eternal God of glory. Thus, he must be worshipped.

His eyes were like blazing fire, penetrating and consuming in their knowledge and perception. His voice was strong and powerful, like rushing waters; and from his mouth his word, like a two-edged sword, was able to divide between soul and spirit and cut to the heart. And his feet, like bronze glowing in a furnace, were ready to tread the winepress of the wrath of God. All of this reveals him as the righteous Judge of the whole earth (see Gen. 18:25; John 5:22).

John was completely overcome by the vision. But Jesus set his heart at ease with comfortable words: "Do not be afraid" (Rev. 1:17). With these words the Lord turned his terror into adoration.[14] This revelation is a reminder that the key to time is eternity, that human life finds its meaning and destiny only in the reality of glory, for Christ declared, "I am the First and the Last. I am the Living One; I was dead, and behold I am alive for ever and ever! And I hold the keys of death and Hades" (Rev. 1:17b–18).

Without the vision of Christ in glory, our worship, in fact our faith, would be impoverished and easily threatened.[15] From time to time God has allowed people to catch a glimpse of this glorious scene in order to enliven their faith and devotion. Moses saw the glory of the LORD on Sinai. Isaiah saw the LORD enthroned in glory and surrounded by angelic choirs. Ezekiel also saw the heavenly throne guarded by the cherubim. Daniel witnessed the Son of Man receiving the kingdom from the Ancient of Days in the heavenly court. And some of the disciples beheld his glory at the transfiguration. But now John peered into the realms of glory, and there as clear as could be was the risen and glorified Christ, assuring the churches of his sovereign care.

Because of the power and the glory of our Lord and Savior Jesus Christ, all our adoration and praise and thanksgiving and devotion belongs to him. It is such revelations of the heavenly glories that fill us with hope and inspire uplifting worship.

## The Vision of the Heavenly Choirs

If there is any doubt that worship is celebration, the description of the angels and saints in heaven joyfully praising the one who is worthy

---

14. Simcox, *Revelation of St. John,* 9.
15. Bauckham, "The Worship of Jesus in Apocalyptic Christianity," 322–41.

should dispel it.[16] What it comes down to is this: To the degree that we see the God of glory as real and worthy of praise, we shall be prepared to participate fully in true celebration; and to the degree that we appreciate the redemption that we have in his blood, we shall respond with enthusiastic thanksgiving and praise.[17]

## The Throne of God

In the Spirit John was transported to the heavenly court before the throne of God (Rev. 4:1–2).[18] Of the one who sat on the throne, Scott says,

> His presence scintillating with the brilliance of a diamond, glowing like a carnelian, with the concentrated redness of a furnace, and yet overarched with fresh and living green as of an emerald. Blinding brilliancy, the glowing of a consuming fire, the soft radiance of rainbow promise, these were the contrasted elements in the impression made upon the heart of the seer by the vision of Him who sat upon the throne.[19]

From the throne came flashes of lightning, rumblings and peals of thunder. And in this heavenly realm there were seven blazing lamps, which are the seven spirits (or sevenfold Spirit) of God.[20] Before the throne there was a sea of glass, clear as crystal. It reflects the creation of the waters in Genesis, which were also represented by the "sea" in the temple that symbolized the LORD's control over nature. So under God's sovereign dominion, the sea is not chaotic but calm and untroubled.

The vision of such things in the heavenly realm was intended to intensify the impression of the reality of God's sovereign rule over all creation. The spontaneous response to this vision is the great anthem of praise that is the climax of the chapter.

Revelation 4 and 5 corresponds to some of the earliest forms of

---

16. In chapter 1 a vision of Christ as the Lord of the church set the stage for the letters to the churches. Now the vision of the Lord on the throne will set the stage for the events to follow (see Mowry, "Revelation 4–5 and Early Christian Liturgical Usage," 75–84).
17. Ibid.
18. For a parallel study, see Morray-Jones, "Paradise Revisited (2 Cor. 12:1–12)," 177–217; and Collins, "The Seven Heavens in Jewish and Christian Apocalypses," 21–54.
19. C. A. Scott, *The Book of Revelation*, 156–57.
20. Rowland, "The Visions of God in Apocalyptic Literature," 137–54.

Christian worship.[21] According to the *Didache,* Sunday became the day of liturgy, characterized by the public reading of Scriptures, as well as letters and documents, and the delivery of a homily interspersed with singing and doxologies. That was inspired in part, no doubt, by John's experience of being drawn into heavenly worship.[22] The pattern is as follows:[23] first there was the invitation to participate ("Come up here," 4:1);[24] then, after a description of the setting that John enters, there was the singing of the *trisagion* (4:8);[25] this was followed with a brief ascription of praise to God as the Creator of all things (4:11) with the participants prostrating themselves before him. Then the scroll was brought forth to be opened by the one who reveals the whole plan of God (5:1–7),[26] more prayers were offered with praise psalms interspersed (5:8–10),[27] followed by the congregational response with appropriate versicles concerning the worthiness of Christ (5:12). Finally the congregation and the angelic hosts together sang the great doxology to God and to his Christ, concluding with the choral "Amen" of the living creatures (5:13–14). Worship would be greatly enhanced if more churches followed this heavenly pattern.

## Worship at the Throne of God

In the fourth and fifth chapters of Revelation, there are five hymns sung by heavenly choirs.[28] The first two are addressed to God, the next

21. This should not come as a surprise because the church was following the patterns of worship that had been developed down through history, patterns that were inspired by the revelation from heaven.
22. See Cabaniss, "A Note on the Liturgy of the Apocalypse," 78–86.
23. The general outline is taken from Mowry, "Revelation 4–5 and Early Christian Liturgical Usage," 75–84.
24. This has been reflected in worship through the centuries in the call for Christians to "lift up" their hearts, meaning, be transported into the heavenly throne room.
25. Variations of "Holy, Holy, Holy" have been sung as part of the liturgy of the church from its beginning. Usually lines from Revelation are combined with the words in Isaiah 6.
26. The opening of the Scriptures and the proper interpretation of life in the light of the full revelation of God in Christ, i.e., the reading and proclamation of God's Word, are at the heart of Christian worship.
27. The offering of the prayers of the saints before God has found a regular place in Christian worship; what must be included, though, are the words of the new song to encourage people in their prayers as a kingdom of priests who serve the Lord and who will reign on earth.
28. The hymns provide a link in the structure of the book. See O'Rourke, "The Hymns of the Apocalypse," 399–409. See also Mowry, "Revelation 4–5 and Early Christian Liturgical Usage," 75–84.

two to the Lamb, and the last to both. Also, from hymn to hymn the choirs become larger and larger, building to the climax when every creature sings to God and to the Lamb.

### The Praise of the Four Creatures

In recording the praise and glory in the presence of God almighty, John focuses on four living creatures, angelic beings (Rev. 4:6b–9).[29] Day and night they never stop saying:

> Holy, holy, holy is the Lord God Almighty,
>     who was, and is, and is to come.

Once again the response to the awesome presence of God is the ascription of holiness to him—three times, as in Isaiah's vision (Isa. 6:1–3). Their praise is fitting for the Lord God almighty, for there is no one like him in power, and there is no one like him in eternity, for he was, and is, and is to come. If angels constantly proclaim God's unique power in his past, present, and future activities, then how much more should we who benefit from them!

### The Acclamation of the Twenty-Four Elders

Whenever the four living creatures give glory and honor to God who sits on the throne and who lives for ever and ever, twenty-four elders fall down and worship him.[30] These elders are distinguished from saints in the book and thus may well be another order of heavenly beings (see Isa. 24:23). Whoever they are, their worshipful response is exemplary:

> You are worthy, our Lord and God,
>     to receive glory and honor and power,
> for you created all things,
>     and by your will they were created
>     and have their being.
>                                                   (Rev. 4:11)

---

29. R. G. Hall, "Living Creatures in the Midst of the Throne," 609–13. For a comparable description of the cherubim, see Ezekiel 1.
30. Frequently the elders are taken to be humans and their number representative. Simcox, for example, thinks they are the glorified representatives of the people of God (*Revelation of St. John*, 31).

Several things are instructive here for our worship—their posture as they fall down before God almighty, their submission to his absolute authority as they lay their crowns before him, and their continuous praise. Whereas the first anthem praised God for his holiness, this one praises him for his worthiness. He is worthy to receive such adulation because he sovereignly created everything that exists and by his will allows them to continue to exist (cf. Job 38:4–7). No one has this kind of power and majesty except God.[31] No one else could even understand it!

With such praise, humility and submission are indispensable: when these high orders sing their praise to God, they fall before him and relinquish all their honor to him. No one can acclaim God to be worthy of all glory, honor, and power and yet cling to one's own bit of honor and power, no matter how well deserved it may be.

### The Praise of Saints and Angels

In chapter 5 the focus of praise is on the Lamb, and the reason for it now includes redemption.[32] Therefore, the saints join the choir to praise him for creation and redemption (Rev. 5:9–10). Both themes look to the future but draw on the past: he who created all things by his pleasure will yet make a new heaven and earth; and he who purchased us by his blood and made us a new creation will perfect that marvelous work.

In this vision Christ, the King (as the titles stress), is worthy to open the seven-sealed scroll of judgment because as the spotless Lamb of God he has paid for sin with his blood. He appears here as a Lamb, looking as if it had been slain, but standing.[33] Moreover, the Lamb has seven horns and seven eyes, signifying that he has absolute power and perfect knowledge and understanding. Not only is he worthy to judge the world, but he alone has the ability to do so.

---

31. Those in the churches who accept the idea that creation came about by chance and that the biblical accounts of creation are mythological texts have little reason to offer praise to the Creator.

32. P. J. Achtemeier, "Revelation 5:1–14," 283–88. See also Charles, "An Apocalyptic Tribute to the Lamb," 461–73; and idem, "Imperial Pretensions and the Throne-Vision of the Lamb," 85–97.

33. P. J. Achtemeier says that because the Lamb stands there is absolutely nothing now that can stand between us and God's love for His reconciled creation ("Revelation 5:1–14," 283–88).

## The Creatures and Elders Sing a New Song

The Lamb is authorized to take the book and execute its judgments on the earth, for in him and through him the Godhead was at work in history for salvation.[34] Now the larger choir of the living creatures and the elders falls down before him. Each of them has a harp, and each has a bowl full of incense, which are the prayers of the saints. They sing this new song:

> You are worthy to take the scroll and to open its seals,
>> because you were slain,
>>> and with your blood you purchased men for God
>>>> from every tribe and language and people and nation.
>> You have made them to be a kingdom
>>> and priests to serve our God,
>>> and they will reign on the earth.
>>>>>>>>>>> (Rev. 5:9–10)

Primarily because of its circumstances, this is one of the most significant songs ever to be sung. It comes at the time of the fulfillment of the prophecies, the coming of the Lord in judgment. Because Christ is the Lamb of God who takes away the sins of the world, he is worthy to judge the world. Because he, the Lord, paid the penalty for the sins of the world, the world must answer to him. Not only did his death purchase people from every nation and language, but it also defeated all powers over creation and cleared the way for the new creation and the new order, in place of the old that was ruined by the Fall. God's people will serve him as they rule and have dominion on the earth.

Here is the center of Christian worship explained—Christ is to be worshipped because he is the Creator, Redeemer, and Sovereign Lord of all the world. In short, he is to be worshipped because, like the Father, he is divine. Now the background of the first-century church was a strict Jewish monotheism, which meant that only God could be worshipped—not the angels (who refuse worship) and certainly not mere mortals. But in the historic faith the Son of God is part of the Godhead: He is the giver of revelation, whereas the angels are merely instruments; he is the Creator,

---

34. R. D. Davis, *The Heavenly Court Judgment of Revelation 4–5.*

whereas all creation sings to him; and he is the Redeemer who alone conquered the grave. Thus, through the focus of worship, the message is clear that the Lamb is divine. The book of Revelation makes a clear line of distinction between who worships and who should be worshipped. It does not endorse the tendency to worship intermediary beings, whether angels or saints. Only God can be worshipped—and this book, as indeed the whole Bible, puts Christ on the divine side of the line. But as Bauckham observes, the language of this chapter is very sensitive to the theological issue: God and the Lamb are praised in joint worship, or, as he puts it, "their 'functional unity' is such that Christ cannot be an alternative object of worship but shares in the glory that is due God."[35] And this is important because the theme of the whole prophecy is the distinction between true worship of God and false or idolatrous worship.[36]

### Myriads of Angels Sing in a Loud Voice

John witnessed hosts of angels, thousands upon thousands, and ten thousand times ten thousand, encircling the throne and the living creatures and the elders, and in a loud voice singing,[37]

> Worthy is the Lamb, who was slain,
>> to receive power and wealth and wisdom and strength
>> and honor and glory and praise!
>>> (Rev. 5:12)

The choirs of angels sing out their song to the Lamb, their sevenfold acclamation ringing like the sound of a huge bell (cf. Dan. 7:10). And what they proclaim are all intrinsic qualities of Jesus Christ the Son of God, except the last one, which is praise that is due him. Human beings cannot begin to contemplate infinite power, wealth, wisdom, strength, honor, and glory; but when these properties are seen in the way that God the Son brings everything to its intended conclusion, we are given a glimpse of their meaning, albeit just the hem of the garment as it were.

---

35. Bauckham, "The Worship of Jesus in Apocalyptic Christianity," 331.
36. Ibid., 322–41. The human race is divided between those who worship the Beast (the symbol of false religious systems) and those who worship God. There are two visions of this division with parallel conclusions, 19:10 for false worship and 22:8 and following for true.
37. See McKinnon, *Music in Early Christian Literature.*

### All Creation Worships God and the Lamb

The last song of praise in this section of the book is the grandest, both in scope and in content. John saw that far beyond the immediate precincts of the throne there arose a volume of praise from the whole creation. Every creature in heaven, and on earth, and under the earth, and on the sea, and all that is in them, joined in this universal acclaim, this doxology to God the Father and God the Son. They said,

> To him who sits on the throne and to the Lamb
>   be praise and honor and glory and power,
>     for ever and ever![38]
>                                         (Rev. 5:13)

The four living creatures said, "Amen," and the elders fell down and worshipped. This ending doxology is the grand acknowledgment that God the Father and God the Son deserve praise from every creature.

## Conclusion

In these five hymns of praise, we can observe an ascending might in the number of voices, as well as a movement in the contents of the praise from creation to redemption and to both Father and Son.[39] This is what has been happening, and yet is what is going to happen in glory; for when all the saints are gathered in and see him as he is, then shall praise of this magnitude be realized. Achtemeier correctly notes that we are to praise the Lamb who got us the victory, because the vision recorded here will achieve reality as surely as there is a God who promised it.[40] Scott adds,

> And it is not a little significant that in each of these chapters the situation becomes clear, the meaning of the vision steals into our hearts, when we hear the burst of praise. Is not this the reason why praise forms so important a part of worship, not only that it

---

38. The doxology seems to acclaim the fulfillment of passages like Psalm 47:6–8 and Psalm 48:10. Likewise, many of the enthronement psalms call for all of creation to praise the LORD who reigns above.
39. The fact that the Spirit is not mentioned here as receiving praise seems to harmonize with the work of the Spirit to direct attention to the Father and the Son (John 16:12–15). None of it is possible otherwise.
40. P. J. Achtemeier, "Revelation 5:1–14," 287.

is our due to God, but that it is the vehicle for expressing, and so of realizing, thought and emotion which lie too deep for words, "fancies which break through language and escape," high pulsations of joy, for which the utmost that words can do is to lend them wings."[41]

The heart of the believer should race with anticipation for that day in glory when praise and worship will be so magnificent. But until then, we may draw inspiration from these visions of the hope of glory as the Holy Spirit continually draws us into the presence of God. Among other things we learn that praise for our God and Savior will be, and must now be, boundless, endless, universal, majestic, and devout. True apprehension of the glory of the LORD is now and always will be overwhelming—devout worshippers fall before him in wonder and surrender.[42]

It was before the Lord revealed to John the scenes of devastation that were yet to come that he gave him this comforting vision of the power and the glory of the Lord declared through the praise in heaven. Like John, the saints of all ages need to embrace this vision of the Lord's ability and determination to bring everything to its glorious culmination. They have no idea what catastrophes lie ahead in this world, but they know that eventually it will be wave upon wave of trouble, forces of evil raising themselves to power and causing confusion and distress among the people of God and possibly even the abandonment of the faith, but certainly a constant struggle between good and evil culminating in one final conflict.[43] But to be held by the power of the One who was dead and is alive forevermore, the one who holds the keys to death and hell, is cause for unending praise and adoration.

But there is one other thing that we learn from the order of these two chapters. The great song of creation, a song that has not ceased since the first day the morning stars sang together, is a song that humans cannot take part in until they have learned to join triumphantly in the song of redemption. We join the heavenly choirs because of the Lamb that was slain; then we can truly participate in all the praise that belongs to God.

---

41. C. A. Scott, *The Book of Revelation*, 165.
42. See further Piper, "The Apocalypse of John and the Liturgy of the Ancient Church," 10–22; Unnik, "Worthy is the Lamb," 445–61.
43. C. A. Scott, *The Book of Revelation*, 167.

This is because by entering the new creation through redemption, we see in all creation the working of one supreme and holy will; we may see life as it is, with all that threatens it and all that limits it, and yet we can be filled with praise for our Creator and Redeemer. When we who are redeemed realize that in praise we are joining companies of angels whose praise transcends all that runs counter to God, then we begin to understand the reality that makes sense out of life. Then our worship will celebrate victory over the world.

# CHAPTER 28

# The Glorious Celebration
## *of the* Fulfillment *of the* Promises

IN ADDITION TO GIVING ATTENTION to the ways that we celebrate being in covenant with the sovereign and holy Lord God of glory, we must also keep the goal in mind. All of our worship is done in anticipation of the fulfillment of the covenant promises in glory. Therefore, worship must also be eschatological, that is, concerned with things yet to come. If we keep our eyes on things spiritual and things eternal, we will be better able to overcome the world, and especially the way that the world worships.

## The Celebration of the Redeemed in Glory

In Revelation 7 John received a vision of the redeemed in glory worshipping before the throne. The vision came in the midst of judgment—six judgments had been poured out on the earth, but the seventh was delayed until the redeemed on the earth could be sealed from it (7:1–4). Those sealed were from all the tribes of Israel (see Ezek. 9:4).[1] After this John saw an enormous multitude of people that no one could count, from every nation, tribe, people, and language. The contrasts between the two groups is striking: the first group is said to be from all the tribes of Israel, but the second group is from every nation on earth; the first group is given a definite number, but the second is said to be innumerable. The vision, therefore, starts with the company of Israelites sealed from the judgments but expands as heaven opens to display the greater company of the redeemed.

---

1. The 144,000 has been the subject of much study. The use of complete numbers, 12,000 from each of the twelve tribes, was a symbolic way of reaffirming what Paul said to the Romans, that when the fullness of the Gentiles has come in then "all Israel will be saved" (Rom. 11:26).

But of greater interest to our study is the worship that takes place
in this setting in glory. John saw this innumerable company of the redeemed wearing white robes and holding palm branches in their hands
(Rev. 7:9),[2] praising God and crying out,

> Salvation[3] belongs to our God,
>     who sits on the throne,
>     and to the Lamb.
> (Rev. 7:10)

All the angels were standing around the throne and around the elders
and the creatures, and they fell down on their faces and worshipped God
as well,[4] saying,

> Amen!
> Praise and glory
>     and wisdom and thanks and honor and power and strength
>     be to our God for ever and ever.[5]
> (Rev. 7:12)

John also learned that

> they are before the throne of God
>     and serve him day and night in his temple;[6]
> and he who sits on the throne will spread his tent over them.
> Never again will they hunger; never again will they thirst.
>     The sun will not beat upon them, nor any scorching heat.

---

2. Kelly notes that at the least the white robes and the palm branches are images of victory, as in 1 Maccabees 13:51 and 2 Maccabees 10:6–7 (B. H. Kelly, "Revelation 7:9–17,"
   290).
3. These are the redeemed who have come out of the Great Tribulation, who have
   washed their robes and made them white in the blood of the Lamb (Rev. 7:14).
4. This gives a liturgical air to the whole scene. See further Shepherd, *The Paschal Liturgy
   and the Apocalypse.*
5. Like 1:6 and 5:13 this is a doxology.
6. Christians thus become ministering priests in the heavenly sanctuary. S. Brown, "The
   Priestly Character of the Church in the Apocalypse," 224–31.

> For the Lamb at the center of the throne will be their shepherd;
>     he will lead them to springs of living water.
> And God will wipe away every tear from their eyes.[7]

(Rev. 7:15–17)

There are some fascinating symbols used in this vision: the saints are robed in white, they carry palm branches, they sing praise for God's salvation, the LORD spreads his tent over them, and they enjoy the bounty of life—without scorching heat, hunger, or thirst. The hunger, thirst, heat, and tears are the characteristics of life in a fallen world, especially in the wilderness. But not only will God remove the difficulties of this life, but he also will provide a place for his own, signified here by God's spreading his tent over them, leading them to springs of living water, and being their shepherd. In other words, they will pass from this human, earthly life into the new order. What is clear is that the Feast of Tabernacles provides the background for this chapter, as indicated by images such as palm branches, the provision of water, the tent spread over them, and the consummation of the ages.[8] This harmonizes with Zechariah 14, which predicts that at the end of the age saints from all lands will come to the Holy City and celebrate the Feast of Tabernacles (vv. 12–16). While interpreters may differ on how this prophecy will be fulfilled exactly, we do know that the point of the festival in Israel was the anticipation of the fulfillment of the promises.

A close study of Revelation 6 and 7 against the backdrop of Zechariah 14 will show a good number of parallel themes, but at the center is the Feast of Tabernacles. That feast was for Israel a remembrance of their wilderness sojourn, which eventually led to the joy of settlement in the land. It also celebrated the fact that the harvest was in and the new year had begun. But in their celebration in this life, they knew that the harvest for the next year required God's provision of water and light; so they developed a water ritual and a light ritual for Tabernacles. We may recall how Jesus used the images of the water and the light at this feast to declare

---

7. O'Rourke thinks that John borrowed from liturgical sources for the hymns and praises in this collection (1:4–5, 8b; 4:8b; 7:12, 15–17; 11:15, 17–18; 19:5, 6b–8). But this raises the question of what he actually saw and heard ("The Hymns of the Apocalypse," 409). See also Siegman, "Apocalypse," 1:659.

8. J. A. Draper, "The Heavenly Feast of Tabernacles," 133–47.

that he was the provision of life to come (John 7–8). Thus, in the world to come, all God's provisions for life, a whole new life, will be made secure by Christ's final victory.

Revelation 7 describes the great celebration in glory at the end of the age when the covenant promises have been fulfilled; in it the saints celebrate because they have been redeemed from the judgment and enjoy the eternal blessings of a new world order. Set in the midst of unrelieved horrors, the vision John receives is a vision of God's vindication that is always ready to break in upon the human scene. And it is this future certainty that forms the hopes and inspires the actions of the saints in the present.[9] This is why the church at worship is a celebration of victory over the world, no matter what the current situations might be. Wesley based his hymn of triumph on this passage: "Ye servants of God, your master proclaim, and publish abroad His wonderful name." If Christian worship does not sound this eschatological note regularly, this anticipation of heavenly worship that will celebrate Christ's victory over the world and the fulfillment of all the promises, then life as we know it will continue to be oppressive and worship will not overcome it.

## Union with the Lord of Glory

The greatest hope for us in glory is complete communion with the living Lord. Therefore, John also received a vision of the marriage of the Lamb in glory and all the praise and adoration associated with it. Here is the realization of the plan of creation and the purpose of redemption; here is fulfilled the desire of the Savior that we might be with him (e.g., John 14:3, 20; 17:24). The vision is recorded in chapter 19 amidst the great shouts of celebration for the victory over the pagan world and its false system of religion.[10] As the chapter opens John tells of the roar of a great multitude in heaven shouting with joy over the defeat of Babylon:

> "Hallelujah!
> Salvation and glory and power belong to our God,
>     for true and just are his judgments.

---

9. B. H. Kelly, "Revelation 7:9–17," 293–94. Kelly shows how Isaiah 25:8; 49:10; and Psalm 23:1–2 all form the biblical background of these songs of victory.

10. Here at long last the age-old struggle with idolatry comes to an end. Throughout the Bible Babylon was the symbol of antagonistic pagan worship.

He has condemned the great [harlot] who corrupted the earth by her adulteries.
  He has avenged on her the blood of his servants."

And again they shouted:

> "Hallelujah!
> The smoke from her goes up for ever and ever."
>                     (Rev. 19:1b–3)

This is a different kind of celebration, more of a victory song now that the outcome of the struggle on earth is secured. The multitudes are joined by the twenty-four elders and the four creatures, who fall down and worship God, crying,

> "Amen, Hallelujah!"
>                     (v. 4)

Then a voice came from the throne, saying:

> "Praise our God,
>   all you his servants,
>   you who fear him, both small and great!"
>                     (v. 5)

Then John heard what sounded "like a great multitude, like the roar of rushing waters and like loud peals of thunder," shouting:

> "Hallelujah!
>   For our Lord God Almighty reigns.
>   Let us rejoice and be glad and give him glory!
>     For the [marriage] of the Lamb has come,
>     and his bride has made herself ready.
>     Fine linen, bright and clean,
>     was given her to wear."
>                     (Rev. 19:6–8)

John explains that "fine linen stands for the righteous acts of the saints" (Rev. 19:8). Then the angel said, "Blessed are those who are invited to the marriage supper of the Lamb!" (v. 9). This scene in heaven is then followed by a vision of the Lord coming in glory to judge and to rule (19:11–20:5). He and his armies are shown to be holy (white linens) and victorious (white horses).[11]

The imagery of a wedding feast is not surprising. Throughout the Bible union with God is portrayed as a marriage, or a betrothal, and the relationship as that of a husband and wife, to indicate the close, intimate, personal union between God and his people. Revelation 19 and 20 envision the fulfillment of the messianic Psalm 45, which combines the motif of the marriage of the king with the anticipation of the king's conquest of his enemies and his righteous reign. The psalmist extolled the king as one who loves righteousness and hates wickedness and therefore as one who will reign in righteousness forever. Because the writer of Hebrews saw the psalm as a prophecy of the reign of Jesus the Messiah after his return in glory (Heb. 1:6–9), the additional themes of his coming to establish justice and mercy and righteousness on the earth and his union with his bride are properly applied to him as well. Both the marriage feast and the riding on a horse convey the clear meanings those images have carried throughout the Bible. Jesus Christ will be united, actually, spiritually, and eternally, with his people and will come in power and with great glory with his saints and angels to put down all wickedness and to reign with righteousness forever. Our worship today must anticipate these things, for our Lord's instructions for worship included the anticipation and preparation for the coming of his kingdom (Matt. 26:29).

In the wedding song the poet also gave advice to the bride before she was ushered into the throne room: "Since the king desires your beauty; because He is your Lord, worship him" (Ps. 45:11, author's translation). The beauty referred to here is of character and demeanor, not physical beauty, for that could not be achieved by devotion and obedience. The point is that the bride must do obeisance—must worship—the bridegroom because he is not just her husband, but also her Lord and her king. This instruction is carried forward to its fulfillment as well, for John says that the bride was instructed to be robed in white linen, meaning, righ-

---

11. R. B. Y. Scott, "Behold He Cometh with Clouds," 127–32.

teous acts. Every righteous act that a believer performs helps make up the perfect glory of the church as it shall be when it is presented to Christ.

Jesus used the same wedding image to exhort people to be properly prepared when the bridegroom comes for his bride (Matt. 22:2–14). And in the parable of the virgins he elaborated on the exhortation: those who by faith eagerly looked for his coming kept the lamps burning; they had oil in their lamps, meaning the Spirit of God was in them, preparing them for the union with the Lord of glory (Matt. 25:1–13). Paul also used the imagery of marriage for the union between Christ and the church (see Eph. 5:23). In fact, he "betrothed" people to the Lord (2 Cor. 11:2) with the hopes that he could present them as a pure bride. That union will take place in glory when believers are glorified.

The idea of a marriage feast provides an appropriate picture of the union of Christ and his people. Weddings are perhaps the most joyous occasions people have; they are celebrations of love and harmony, filled with excitement and anticipation of the beginning of a new life and a new identity. Similarly, down through the ages believers have longed to be with their Lord in perfect communion, to be caught out of their old life and ushered into his presence, where there is joy and peace and love. Until now, their worship has been with this hope, as they now come into his presence by the Spirit. In glory, though, all such hopes will be fulfilled—not for an hour or a season, but for all eternity.

## Worship in the New Creation

In the last two chapters of the Bible, John records a vision of things to come. Here is Paradise regained, or rather, Paradise re-created in the new heaven and new earth.[12] It is important to note that contrary to popular opinion the ultimate destiny of God's people is an earthly destiny. The Bible places the redeemed on the new earth and not only in a heavenly realm; they will reign with Christ on earth (Rev. 5:10).

The vision first unveils the new heaven and the new earth that is created, for the old had passed away, and there was no more sea (Rev. 21:1).[13]

---

12. As a related study, see Innes, "Heaven and Sky in the Old Testament," 144–48; and E. Levine, "Distinguishing 'Air' from 'Heaven' in the Bible," 97–99.

13. Before the new is inaugurated, the old order must be judged so that it flees away. In the Bible the judgment of nature and the creation of a new order is an important theme. At times the picture is of a simple regeneration (Isa. 11:6–9), and at times it is complete transformation (Isa. 65:17). Peter sees a dissolution of the heavens and the elements melting before a new order emerges (2 Peter 3:10–13).

Then it reveals the heavenly city, the New Jerusalem, descending out of heaven from God, prepared as a bride beautifully dressed for her husband (v. 2). Because the simile of the bride is used here and because the angel shows John the bride as he shows him this city, many take the view that this is a picture of the church descending from heaven to take up residence on the new earth.[14] That is certainly a possible interpretation. However, the context of the chapter with all the details of what the city is like suggests that a city, the spiritual center of the new creation for the righteous, may be what is meant.[15] At the end of the chapter, we read that only those whose names are written in the Lamb's Book of Life will enter this city. Thus, the dwelling of God with his people, so important to the history of worship, is central to the new order.

This is the point that must be stressed with regard to worship. What is "new" about all of this is the reality of the presence of God with his people. The waiting will finally be over, the alienation and separation ended. The people of God will no longer commune with God by image and symbol but in reality because his habitation will be with them.[16] This is the New Jerusalem, of which the earthly city is an imperfect copy (see on Rev. 4:6; 6:9). While this world lasts, this true Jerusalem remains above (Gal. 4:26); and we know its significance from the earthly copy of it, before Christ came, and the spiritual approach to it, because Christ came (Heb. 12:22).[17] But in the days here described, it will be realized in all its perfection.[18]

---

14. Ladd takes the view that it is a city but allows for the possibility that it is metaphorical because "Jerusalem" in the Bible can be used for people living in it (see Matt. 23:37; cf. 1 Cor. 3:16; Eph. 2:21;). So in the vision of the new world, the people of God and their capital city, the church and the New Jerusalem, are so closely connected that the same figure, a bride, is used for both (*Commentary on the Revelation of St. John,* 249).

15. In the pagan world the ancient city of Babylon was so great that the Babylonians claimed it was prepared in heaven by Anunaki gods and lowered to earth. Here, in the end of Revelation, Babylon has just been destroyed, and the heavenly Jerusalem descends to earth from heaven.

16. Raber, "Revelation 21:1–8," 296–301. Raber examines the church's anticipation and preparation for this under the images of "bride, consort, lover, homemaker."

17. The New Testament conceives of a heavenly Jerusalem as the dwelling place of God (Gal. 4:26; Phil. 3:20; Heb. 12:22). This heavenly city is also the dwelling place of departed saints but not their final destiny (2 Cor. 5:8; Phil. 1:23). In the consummation the heavenly Jerusalem will descend to its permanent place on the new earth (Ladd, *Commentary on the Revelation of St. John,* 276).

18. Simcox, *Revelation of St John,* 130.

But however our attempts to interpret the vision may differ, the point is made clear from the word from heaven: "Now the dwelling of God is with men, and he will live with them" (Rev. 21:3). He will have his "tabernacle" among "his people." The same language is used in John 1:14. The word for "people" in Revelation 21:3 is plural, indicating that all the nations are God's people (see Ps. 67:7). The dwelling of God with his people began in the Garden, was interrupted by sin, continued in the Old Testament sanctuary, found full expression in the Incarnation, and now is with his people in the Spirit—by faith and not sight. In the coming age, the people of God will behold him in glory. This direct, unmarred communion between God and his people is the goal of all redemption, the motivation for our perseverance, and the focus of our worship.

## Conclusion

John's prophetic book brings forward the imagery of the Garden of Eden, with which we began this journey. The river of the water of life, as clear as crystal, flows from the throne of God and from the Lamb, down through the city of God. And on either side of it stands the Tree of Life, bearing its fruit regularly and providing healing for the nations (22:1–2).[19] The inclusion of the river of life reminds us that God is the source of life. And the emphasis on the Tree of Life tells us that the curse is over, that life has triumphed over death, that humans are no longer barred from living forever in the presence of God—for they are now righteous and glorified.

Down through the ages the prophets kept the hope alive that there would be a renovation of all of creation, a new world order, perfect and glorious, in which only righteousness would dwell. Perhaps we may take our cue from the analogy of the new condition of the saints, for in this life the mortal body is corrupt and corruptible, but in the resurrection it will be a far more glorious body, incorruptible and perfect. But nonetheless real.[20]

In this new order on earth there will be perfect life—spiritual, physical, eternal. There will be no more night, no pain, no grief, and no death,

---

19. Wong, "The Tree of Life in Revelation 2:7," 211–26.
20. Ladd, *Commentary on the Revelation of St. John*, 284, notes that in the age to come we will not lose our identity; we will still be people from every nation and background (see Isa. 60:9; Rev. 21:24).

all of which are most visible in the present world order. But there the curse will be removed—no ignorance, no heartbreak, no wounding of spirits, and no separation from God. The second chapter of the Bible told us about human life before the curse; and the next to last chapter of the Bible holds out the prospect of life when the curse is gone. Between we have the drama of redemption, the work of God to remove the curse and bring us to glory in a new creation.

Under the curse, so long as it has existed, there was a temple, for the temple was a place where people might realize the presence of God and more clearly hear his voice. It was a place of mediated access to God, because the effects of the curse barred people from the sanctuary. But in the Holy City there is no need for a temple, for the Lord is there with his people. Scott says, "That which now has to be delimited from the world, and set apart for God—yes, and held with determination and force of will against invading hosts—has there expanded to cover the whole area of human experience and activity."[21]

In the city the redeemed of God will serve him, which is what people were created to do in the beginning. But in the age to come, life will be very different from what we cling to now. All earthly limitations will disappear: physical limitations of sickness and weakness; social hindrances with all the difficulties of human relationships; mental limitations that cause errors, mistakes, and misconceptions; and, of course, spiritual problems, the influence of sin—gone, forever. And we will see his face! This hope expresses all the joys of glory: the fulfillment and contentment of all our craving for love, which only God can satisfy; our desire for holiness, not less than the holiness of God; our longing for the capacity of an eternal spirit set free; and our desire to look back and see the meaning of it all and to look forward and know that time and change, grief and sin, pain and death, are not possible, not ever.

We will see his face, for we will have been restored to immediate access to God. And we will worship him in ways that we cannot even imagine now. This is the hope of glory that believers in all ages have shared and that true worship down through the years has kept alive in the faith of the people of God.

---

21. C. A. Scott, *The Book of Revelation*, 314.

# Conclusion *for* Part 9

THE BOOK OF REVELATION OFFERS us a glimpse of worship in glory as a counterbalance to the chaos and devastation on earth. The aspects of worship revealed here most certainly informed and inspired the worship of the early churches. But as is true of all devout worship, the book begins with a vision of the risen Christ in glory. All acts of worship are a response to this divine revelation. The vision not only prompts fear and adoration, but it brings comfort and encouragement as well, for the one who was dead is alive forevermore and glorified.

The immediate response of all who are near the heavenly Lord, and therefore everyone who expects to be in his glorious presence, is praise and adoration. The angelic praise is of his incomparable nature and his mighty works, most notably, creation. But with the addition of saints to the heavenly choirs, the praise also must include redemption through the blood of the Lamb. Praise is the natural and immediate response of those who see the Lord, either now in the Spirit or then face to face. And that praise is spontaneous, lavish, and continuous. Without such praise, we have not come close to worshipping the Lord.

The prophets and the apostles look forward to the fulfillment of the promises, and accordingly that time will be marked by an elaborate celebration of worship. And what better model to follow than Israel's Feast of Tabernacles, which recalled this earthly pilgrimage and celebrated the consummation of God's plan? A great festival of worship awaits the saints in glory; and while we will praise and worship him forever, the initial entrance into his presence will be of such a glorious nature that all the company of redeemed will extol and honor him in a way that no one has ever seen before.

The best metaphor for union with the living God throughout the Bible was marriage—as God intended it. And so the celebration of the union with the Lord in heaven is revealed to be a marriage supper. Since this is a spiritual union with Christ that will last forever and bring with it eternal bliss, the initial celebration of the union will be a time of worship in the purest sense. Accordingly, the saints will be there clothed with righteousness as they celebrate their complete communion with Christ and honor him with their adoration and obeisance.

But the ultimate picture of worship after the end of this age is one of eternal worship. It will be centered on the marvelous reality of the presence of the Lord with his people and his provisions for all their needs. It will be the true Paradise, of which the earthly was a mere shadow. And in this glorious new creation, the people of God will serve the Lord and worship him forever. That is the hope of glory.

# PART 10

# BASIC PRINCIPLES *for* MORE GLORIOUS WORSHIP

THE HEART OF CHRISTIAN WORSHIP is to recall and celebrate the hope of glory. Not only does it recall the beliefs and practices of the historic faith that inform this hope, but it also brings them forward to their fulfillment in Christ; and because of this Christians celebrate communion with the living God with confidence. Accordingly, worship in Christ encourages and enhances the Christians' spiritual journey through this world and ultimately to glory. But this hope of glory can be sustained and enlarged only through effective communal worship, which the Scriptures set forth in positive principles that recollect the traditional elements that form the very foundations of the faith. And these traditional elements start not with early Israelite worship, but with Creation itself, for it is in Paradise that we first see what it means to enter into the presence of the living God, something that the believers down through time have longed to enjoy again and now is made possible through Christ Jesus. To rightly honor, celebrate, and serve the holy Lord God, who in righteousness and mercy became incarnate to redeem human beings, is the highest calling and responsibility of Christians; and when it is done in humility and sincerity, with decorum and grace, it is well-pleasing to the Lord God.

There is no need to repeat the numerous ideas and implications of this study in a concluding chapter. In fact, because there is so much material on the patterns and principles of worship in the Bible, it will take some time to think it all through. And no matter how much we may apprehend, when we stand in glory we will realize how far short we fell. Nevertheless, the church, believers, must always be discovering more meaningful and more glorious ways to worship God, for worship is essential to the spiritual life. If the studies in this book assist people in that discovery, even in a small way, then the effort will have been worthwhile; and if the studies make people aware of the wonder and glory of the Lord and how the faithful of all time have responded by acts of devotion and commitment, then the motivation will be present for the transformation of their spiritual lives and their worship.

Nevertheless, there are several principles that surface again and again and therefore seem to me to be absolutely essential for developing the worship of God.

1.   **The revelation of the exalted Lord God in glory inspires glorious worship and fills us with the hope of glory.**

The proper motivation for worship has always been the revelation of the God of glory. It is this alone that lifts people out of their world and transports them in their spirits to the Paradise to come. Now that Christian worship centers on the reality of the risen Christ in glory, everything in worship should bring that revelation to bear on the worshippers—the setting and the circumstances, the service with all its aspects of worship, and most importantly the celebration of Holy Communion—all of it. But retaining this vision of glory is a constant struggle, because everything in the world steals our attention and staggers us with trouble and strife. Yet if we recall in our worship how this hope has enabled believers down through the ages to hold to their faith triumphantly, then we will be encouraged to live in the light of that hope too. When communal worship is inspired by the revelation of the Lord God of glory, then the worship will be spiritual, life-giving, and inspiring.

2.   **The evidence of the Lord's presence makes worship a holy convocation in a holy place that calls for holiness.**

Yes, we know that God is everywhere, that there is nowhere we can go from his presence. Nevertheless, the Bible says again and again that in certain places and at certain times God has made his presence known in more powerful ways. The Lord first demonstrated his desire to be with us and displayed the richness of his provisions by his very presence in the Garden of Eden. Accordingly, one of the most frequent occasions in which he has made himself known by coming near to us has been and still is in corporate worship, which in many ways reflects Paradise as it anticipates his coming presence. If the presence of the Lord is more of a reality in communal worship than in ordinary gatherings and regular activities, it will be a vital force in the life of the church and inspire holiness in worship: the time and the place will be set apart ("made holy") for the purpose of drawing near to God spiritually, especially in the Communion; and everything about that time and place will complement what is taking place in that holy hour; and everything in the worship service will give evidence that God is alive and manifests himself to his people. It is fitting, then, for the people of God to make their worship reflect the reality of God's presence through holy worship. Their praise, their fellowship, their liturgy, and their ritual must all be holy, as a witness to the fact that the Lord has demonstrated his presence among them in power and glory to bring them salvation, deliverance, comfort, and peace. The greater the sense of the holy presence of the Lord in worship, the greater will be the worshippers' understanding of the Lord God and their desire to develop a life of holiness.

### 3. Sacrifice is at the center of worship as the basis and expression of it.

Because of the pervasiveness of sin in the world, access to God must be mediated; God therefore spent hundreds of years teaching his people about atonement through sacrifice so that they would be able to draw near to him in communion. And in the fullness of time God sent his Son to be the perfect sacrifice for the sins of the world. Since the sacrificial death of Christ is the center of God's plan of redemption, it also must be the center of Christian worship. It is the focus of our praise, the content of our proclamation, and the meaning of our ritual and liturgy. In the celebration of Holy Communion, then, it is essential that the liturgy, or some comparable, carefully formulated prayers and proclamations based on the biblical teaching of the atoning death of Christ, accompany the ritual acts in order to remind the people of the meaning of the cross. If handled well, this will be a powerful way to instruct the congregation in the faith and thereby draw people closer to the Savior in love and adoration.

By remembering the death of Christ in worship and by basing all worship acts on the sacrifice of Christ, worshippers will come to realize that all worship itself is sacrificial, inspired by the Lord's own sacrifice. It is in this realization that worship becomes life changing. Our sacrificial service begins when we first bring to him the sacrifice of a broken heart, that is, when we surrender our wills to him so that we may properly dedicate our lives to him, offer our gifts to him, and share our possessions with those in need. Christian fellowship is possible only through sacrifice; it is based on our Lord's death on our behalf, and it is characterized by our sacrificial love for one another.

### 4. Sound biblical proclamation informs all worshipful acts.

Every act of worship by the faithful, no matter how small or great, must be properly explained by appropriate words, carefully chosen and said well. In the Bible when the people of God were faithful in their worship, they declared their faith in creeds and creedal formulas, testified to the historic faith as they brought their offerings and gifts, rehearsed the events of the faith in their drama and ritual, declared their walk with God when they offered thanksgiving, and expressed their convictions in their commitments to serve the Lord. Today, in an age that seeks to simplify everything—songs, sermons, readings, and ritual of the service—the clear and powerful proclamation of sound biblical doctrine and practice in every part of the service will give spiritual depth to worship and demonstrate the vitality of the faith in the lives of the worshippers. Without it, worship becomes empty ritual and the faith itself obscure. The proper words of worship must be on the lips of the worshippers as they come into the presence of the Lord.

### 5.   The ministry of the Word, an act of worship itself, is the key to coherent, corporate worship.

The reading of Scripture and the exposition of it are primary acts of worship in the church; they are offerings given to God in reverence and devotion. Reading God's holy Word in the assembly without understanding, interpretation, or enthusiasm undermines the foundation of all worship, which is to hear from God. When the reading of Scripture is with clarity, conviction, and power, it sets the Word of God before the people in a way that demonstrates its authority and demands a response. The reading of Scripture should be one of the most powerful parts of worship—every word spoken from the Word is from God.

The time for the sermon is also a holy time; the messenger speaks for God! The message, therefore, must be biblically sound and divinely directed in its application. After all, the Word from God is never boring or irrelevant. An effective sermon will take a good deal of study and prayer to ensure that every word, every sentence, every idea in the message is what God wants declared from the text being expounded. Anytime anyone opens the Bible to declare its message is a holy moment, and if it is done well it will transform the assembly into a holy convocation and draw greater worship and service out of the people.

6. **Individual public praise and thanksgiving is the evidence of the spiritual life that is alive in the church.**

For Christians to have the opportunity to tell publicly of God's blessing and help in their lives is necessary to proper spiritual growth. By sharing their faith this way, Christians are obeying the command of God, following the pattern of the inspired worship of the psalmists, and demonstrating that the Holy Spirit is at work in their lives, prompting them to give thanks and praise. Thus, individual public praise in the assembly which can be done effectively and movingly to the glory of God is the best measure of the spiritual vitality of a congregation. People must have the opportunity to tell of their faith—what they believe, what the Lord means to them, how he has answered their prayers, and how they would encourage others. Such praise is part of the cycle of prayer and praise; it recognizes that God blesses people so that they will tell of his works so that others in turn will be edified in the faith and encouraged in their prayers.

7. **Singing, chanting, playing musical instruments, and dancing done to the glory of God are a part of the praise of the people of God.**

In addition to individual thanksgiving, the worship of God includes several other ways of offering praise to God. Down through the history of the faith, hymns, songs, shouts of acclamation, playing musical instruments, and even jubilant dancing have been given full expression in the celebration of God.

When we think of the thousands of hymns that have been written, the grand musical compositions, and the variety of sounds and expressions, it is overwhelming. What devotion! What jubilation! There is so much available to make worship glorious, so much to make praise new every morning, if we would just step out of our set patterns and away from our favorite songs from time to time to discover it.

The basic principle in Scripture is that all of God's creation, everything that has life, must praise him. But whatever is done must exalt the Lord in the eyes of the people, focus attention on him and not the performers, and communicate truth about the Lord and not conceal or confuse it. In short, music used in worship must be accurate in its theology, glorifying to God, and prepared well, and it must minister to the needs of all the people. To be properly worshipful, music used in the public assembly of Christian worship must be guided by the theology of praise with its paradigm in Holy Scripture.

### 8.   Worship is the response of people to the divine revelation.

Worship confronts people with the divine revelation of God—read, preached, sung, prayed, or displayed in the art and architecture. It may be uplifting, encouraging, and delightful; but it is also challenging. If worship focuses on God the Creator, Redeemer, and sovereign Judge of all mankind, then there has to be some response by the people. When worship services provide opportunity for the responses of the people, the worshippers will, among other things, make commitments to obey, confess their sins and find forgiveness, be reconciled to one another as they forgive one another, renew their vows, and answer calls to serve the Lord. Since believers are a kingdom of priests placed here on earth to serve the Lord, then each worship service becomes a covenant renewal service in which we maintain our relationship with the Lord and with each other. The measure of the effectiveness of the worship service will be the life-changing responses to the divine revelation.

### 9.   Worship prompts moral and ethical acts.

This principle goes hand-in-hand with the previous one. There must be moral, ethical, and social change if we are truly confronted by the presence of the holy and righteous Lord. Part of this will concern our personal spiritual walk with the Lord, remaining faithful and pure in a corrupt world. But if worship is fully life changing, it will prompt positive acts of righteousness in the world, that is, caring for the poor and the needy and the widows and the orphans, providing for the homeless and the foreigners, championing justice and fairness in courts and businesses for those who have no one to help them, and working to do something for people who are dying from famine, disease, persecution, and war. The point cannot be missed if we study the Bible: such righteous acts were emphasized in the way that Israelites made their sacrifices so that the poor and needy could eat; and their neglect was evidence of corrupt, worthless worship, according to the prophets. This was an important part of the teaching of Jesus and the apostles as well; it was powerfully reiterated in the instruction of "remembrance" in celebrating Holy Communion as a covenant renewal service. Worship cannot remain a private, individual act of devotion. It was designed to be a sacrificial service. To give thanks to God, no matter how sincere, and yet ignore social injustice, poverty, hunger, and abuse is a travesty of worship itself. True communion with God based on the love of Christ will inspire the faithful to reach out to people with needs, people for whom Christ also shed his blood.

### 10. Great festivals preserve the heritage of the faith, unite believers, and gather resources for greater worship and service.

If the church wants to bring greater richness and vitality into the worship of the people, great seasonal celebrations and festivals are the most effective ways to do it. And these easily cut across denominational bounds—Israel's did, for all groups attended the festivals, because there was a higher allegiance that united them, even though they went their separate ways in ordinary worship. There is a place in the Christian community for purely social events, but a festival is more than this. If the church employs great festivals as part of its cycle of worship, it will not only claim the seasons and times for the Lord but will also keep the history of the faith alive in the minds of the people. In the special celebrations of the year, the church is reminded that it is part of a great company of saints and angels who love and adore and serve the Lord. And of all people on earth, Christians have the most reason to celebrate!

### 11. The household of faith preserves the purity and integrity of worship.

Every generation of worshippers is faced with the same difficulty—worshipping in a world that is religious but antagonistic to the truth. It has always been the desire of the tempter that religious people make unholy innovations in their worship, often subtle changes but always in the direction of the pagan world system, either in doctrine or practice. From the biblical and historical records of the spiritual conflicts in worship, we know that Satan often appears as a minister of light, questioning what God said, calling good evil and evil good, and prompting people to find ways to neutralize the ritual, or reimage God, or make their beliefs compatible with the world's standards. Idolatry in all its forms has always been a threat to the worship of the true and living God.

The time of worship is the place to distance the faith from the world system. By the clear declaration of the truth that carries authority and conviction and by the demonstration of the truth in worship and service, we will hold the historic faith in place. But in doing so the church must follow the pattern of Christ, who was both gracious and righteous in his dealings with the enemies of the faith; he was, after all, full of grace and truth. The worship of the church celebrates victory over the world and anticipates the final victory, but in doing so it also calls people in the world to come to the truth.

### 12.   Worship possesses a balance of form and spirit.

Achieving the proper balance in worship is a lifelong quest. There are times when we stand for the truth but do not have much grace or compassion; and there are times when we are full of compassion and love but perhaps have set aside the truth. Likewise, there are worship services that follow a strict form to preserve order; and there are others that abandon the forms to follow free worship. If worship is to be significant to all the people and remain honoring to God, it must seek a balance. The proper forms of worship have to be followed, especially in observing the divine institutions; but they should be followed in ways that allow genuine Spirit-led worship to flourish. The church is a body of believers who have different temperaments and traits, different needs and yet similar needs, different spiritual gifts and yet one Spirit. There is so much in the Bible about worship activities that there is no reason for any church to limit itself to a set pattern that appeals to only one segment of the congregation. Worship in the Bible, in both Testaments, was varied in form, content, purpose, and mood; if the church wants to draw out the richness of worship and meet the needs of all the people, it will strive for greater variation within the proper forms and a greater balance in structured and free worship.

### 13.   Worship is eschatological.

Prophecy makes up a great portion of Scripture and is therefore a significant part of the Christian faith. It is no surprise, then, that it also has a significant part in worship. All of our activities in worship are to be done in anticipation of the fulfillment of the promises in the ages to come. The book of Revelation provides a glimpse of what worship will be like in the glorious new creation when Christ comes to complete the plan of redemption. It is therefore appropriate that the acclamation "Christ will come again" is included in the liturgy of many services. If worship includes such an emphasis on the coming of the Lord, or the coming judgments, or the hope of glory, it will motivate the religious activities of the people of God with the urgency that prophecy expects.

### 14. Prayer enables all the acts of worship to achieve what God intended.

Prayer is essential for worship. It does not matter whether a church uses set prayers or not; what matters is that the people pray—throughout the week, before the service, and during the service. In a worship service, prayers of supplication, intercession, and confession must be offered to God if the worship is to be at all effective. This means that proper time be given for such prayers and that proper wording be used in leading prayers so that all the people can fully participate and learn to pray. But it is also important that prayer be seen as spiritual service in which the people of God humble themselves before the throne of grace. This is often difficult to do in a congregational service, for everything in us calls for us to perform well, to show that we can pray. But worship is most meaningful when the here-and-now, the present circumstances around us, cease to matter, and we are caught up into the presence of the Lord in our holy conversation. Prayer in communal worship should be the full expression of a life of prayer as well as the inspiration for private prayers. Prayer is the most significant aspect of the integration of private and corporate worship; and prayer is the source of the praise of God in the church.

### 15. Worship transcends time and space.

If the church truly begins to develop biblical patterns of worship, time and space will seem confining. When modern worship does not have transcendent moments, our minds often wander to immediate and pressing matters. But for those times in our lives when worship lifts us out of our concerns, mundane things do not matter. We are caught up with the hope of glory that enables us to keep everything in this life in proper perspective. The church must do everything it can to make times of transcendence a regular part of spiritual worship.

A church cannot possibly do all that the Bible reveals about worship in one hour a week, especially if it does not vary its program over the year.

Worship is too rich for that. The early church was a living community of worshippers—worship filled their lives, and they took every opportunity to worship. The church today is ready for some creative thinking about how and when to worship, while holding to the patterns and principles of worship that are found in the Bible. If worship is fresh, varied, and vital, while incorporating the necessary aspects of entering into the presence of the living God, then the worshippers will find it a life-giving and life-changing experience.

# Bibliography

## General Works on Worship

Allmen, J.-J. von. *Worship: Its Theology and Practice*. New York: Oxford University Press, 1965.

Brabant, Frank Herbert. "Worship in General." In *Liturgy and Worship: A Companion to the Prayer Books of the Anglican Communion,* edited by W. K. Lowther Clarke, 12–37. London: SPCK, 1932.

Carson, D. A., ed. *Adoration and Action.* Grand Rapids: Baker, 1993.

Davies, J. G., ed. *A Dictionary of Liturgy and Worship.* London: SCM, 1972.

———. *New Perspectives on Worship Today.* London: SCM, 1978.

Elkins, H. M., and E. C. Zaragoza, eds. *Pulpit, Table and Song: Essays in Celebration of Howard G. Hageman.* Lanham, MD: Scarecrow Press, 1996. See esp. A. Caspers Honders, "The Reformers on Church Music," 46–52; and H. M. Elkins, "On the Altar of the Gospel: Reforming Preaching and Worship," 218–33.

Erickson, Craig Douglas. *Participating in Worship: History, Theory, and Practice.* Louisville: Westminster, 1989.

Garcia-Rivera, Alejandro. *The Community of the Beautiful: Theological Aesthetics.* Collegeville, MN: Liturgical Press, 1999.

Hardin, H. Grady, Joseph D. Quillian, and James F. White. *The Celebration of the Gospel: A Study of Christian Worship.* Nashville: Abingdon, 1964.

Hislop, D. H. *Our Heritage in Public Worship.* Edinburgh: T. & T. Clark, 1935.

Hoornaert, Eduardo. *The Memory of the Christian People.* Translated by Robert R. Barr. New York: Orbis Books, 1988.

Huxtable, John. *The Bible Says.* Richmond, VA: John Knox Press, 1962.

Jenson, Robert. *Visible Words: The Interpretation and Practice of Christian Sacraments.* Philadelphia: Fortress Press, 1978.

Lang, Bernhard. *Sacred Games. A History of Christian Worship.* New Haven, CT: Yale University Press, 1997.

Martin, Ralph P. *The Worship of God.* Grand Rapids: Eerdmans, 1982.

Meland, Bernard Eugene. *Modern Man's Worship.* New York: Harper & Brothers, 1934.

Micklem, Nathaniel, ed. *Christian Worship: Studies in Its History and Meaning by Members of Mansfield College.* Oxford: Clarendon Press, 1936. [Essays on Old Testament by Wheeler Robinson, Jewish Background by T. W. Manson, the Lord's Supper by C. H. Dodd, Luther by James Moffatt, and others].

Old, Hughes Oliphant. *Themes and Variations for a Christian Doxology: Some Thoughts on the Theology of Worship.* Grand Rapids: Eerdmans, 1992.

Peterson, David. *Engaging with God: A Biblical Theology of Worship.* Grand Rapids: Eerdmans, 1993.

Rayburn, Robert G. *O Come, Let Us Worship: Corporate Worship in the Evangelical Church.* Grand Rapids: Baker, 1980.

Reed, Esther D. "Questions People Ask: What Is Worship All About?" *Expository Times* 107 (1995): 68–74.

Saliers, Don E. *Worship as Theology: Foretaste of Glory Divine.* Nashville: Abingdon, 1994.

Schaper, R. N. *In His Presence.* Nashville: Nelson, 1984.

Shepherd, Massey H. *The Worship of the Church.* Greenwich, CT: Seabury, 1952.

Stringer, Martin D. *A Sociological History of Christian Worship.* Cambridge: Cambridge University Press, 2006.

Tozer, A. W. *Whatever Happened to Worship?* Compiled and edited by Gerald B. Smith. Camp Hill, PA: Christian Publishers, 1985.

Underhill, Evelyn. *Worship.* Scranton, PA: Harper & Row, 1936.

Wakefield, Gordon S. *An Outline of Christian Worship.* Edinburgh: T. & T. Clark, 1998.

Webber, Robert E. *Blended Worship: Achieving Substance and Relevance in Worship.* Peabody, MA: Hendrickson, 1996.

―――. *Worship: Old and New.* Grand Rapids: Zondervan, 1982.

White, James F. *A Brief History of Christian Worship.* Nashville: Abingdon, 1993.

―――. *Introduction to Christian Worship.* Nashville: Abingdon, 1980.

―――. *New Forms of Worship.* Nashville: Abingdon, 1971.

―――. *The Worldliness of Worship.* New York: Oxford University Press, 1967.

Winward, S. F. *The Reformation of Our Worship.* London: Carey Kings Gate Press, 1963.

# General Theological Background

Balthasar, Hans Urs von. *The Glory of the Lord: A Theological Aesthetics.* 8 vols. New York: Crossroads, 1983.

Bloesch, Donald G. *Essentials of Evangelical Theology.* Peabody, MA: Hendrickson, 1998.

Dyrness, William. *Themes in Old Testament Theology.* Downers Grove, IL: InterVarsity, 1979.

Eichrodt, Walther. *The Theology of the Old Testament.* 2 vols. Translated by James A. Baker. Philadelphia: Westminster, 1961.

Fink, P. E. "Towards a Liturgical Theology." *Worship* 47 (1973): 601–9.

Freed, Edwin D. "Who or What Was Before Abraham in John 8:58?" *The Journal of New Testament Studies* 17 (1983): 52–59.

Gibbs, John G. *Creation and Redemption: A Study of Pauline Theology. Novum Testamentum Supplement* 26. Leiden: E. J. Brill, 1971.

———. "The Relation Between Creation and Redemption According to Philippians 2:5–11." *Novum Testamentum* 12 (1976): 270–83.

Habershon, Ada R. *Study of the Types.* Grand Rapids: Kregel, 1974.

Hoekema, Anthony A. *Created in God's Image.* Grand Rapids: Eerdmans, 1986.

Jacob, Edmond. *The Theology of the Old Testament.* Translated by Arthur W. Heathcote and Philip J. Allcock. New York: Harper & Row, 1958.

McIntyre, John. *The Shape of Soteriology.* Edinburgh: T. & T. Clark, 1992.

Roy, Louis. "Inclusive Language Regarding God." *Worship* 65 (1991): 207–15.

Soltau, Henry W. *The Tabernacle, the Priesthood, and the Offerings.* Grand Rapids: Kregel, 1972.

Thiselton, Anthony C. "The Supposed Power of Words in the Biblical Writings." *Journal of Theological Studies* 25 (1974): 283–99.

Vajta, V. "Creation and Worship." *Studia Liturgica* 2 (1963): 29–46.

Ward, K. *The Divine Image.* London: SPCK, 1976.

Wolff, Hans Walter. *Anthropology of the Old Testament.* Philadelphia: Fortress Press, 1974.

Wright, George Ernest. *The Old Testament Against Its Environment.* London: SCM, 1965.

# The Holy LORD God

Barr, James. "Theophany and Anthropomorphism in the Old Testament." *Vetus Testamentum* 7 (1959): 31–38.

Coggin, Donald F. *The Glory of God.* London: Church Missionary Society, 1950.

Gelander, Shamai. *The Good Creator: Literature and Theology in Genesis 1–11.* Atlanta: Scholars Press, 1997.

Habel, N. C. "He Who Stretches Out the Heavens." *Catholic Biblical Quarterly* 34 (1972): 417–30.

———. "Yahweh, Maker of Heaven and Earth." *Journal of Biblical Literature* 91 (1972): 321–37.

Labushchagne, C. J. *The Incomparability of YHWH in the Old Testament.* Pretoria Oriental Series 5. Leiden: E. J. Brill, 1966.

Moltmann, Jurgen. *God in Creation: A New Theology of Creation and the Spirit of God.* San Francisco: Harper & Row, 1985.

Otto, Rudolph, *The Idea of the Holy.* Translated by John W. Harvey. 2d ed. London: Oxford University Press, 1950.

Packer, J. I. *Knowing God.* Downers Grove, IL: InterVarsity, 1973.

Pink, Arthur W. *The Attributes of God.* Swengel, PA: Reiner Publications, n.d.

Stott, John R. W. "The World's Challenge to the Church." *Bibliotheca Sacra* 145 (1988): 123–32.

Tozer, A. W. *The Pursuit of God.* Harrisburg, PA: Christian Publications, 1948.

Trevethan, Thomas L. *The Beauty of God's Holiness.* Downers Grove, IL: InterVarsity, 1995.

Vawter, B. "Yahweh: Lord of the Heavens and the Earth." *Catholic Biblical Quarterly* 48 (1986): 461–67.

# Israelite Worship

## General Works

Albertz, Rainer. *A History of Israelite Religion in the Old Testament Period.* Vol. 2, *From the Exile to the Maccabees.* Translated by John Bowden. Louisville: Westminster John Knox, 1994.

Arzt, Max. *Justice and Mercy: Commentary on the Liturgy of the New Year and the Day of Atonement.* New York: Holt, Rinehart & Winston, 1963.

Bloch, Abraham P. *The Biblical and Historical Background of Jewish Customs and Ceremonies.* London: SCM, 1953.

Broadhurst, Donna and Mal. *Passover: Before Messiah and After.* Carol Stream, IL: Shofar Publications, 1987.

Buksbazen, Victor. *The Gospel in the Feasts of Israel.* Fort Washington, PA: Christian Literature Crusade, 1954.

Chilton, David. *Paradise Restored.* Tyler: Reconstruction Press, 1987.

Clines, D. J. A. "The Creation—Un-creation—Re-creation Theme of Genesis 1–11." In *The Theme of the Pentateuch,* 61–79. Journal for the Study of the Old Testament: Supplement Series 10. Sheffield, UK: University of Sheffield Department of Biblical Studies, 1978.

Davidson, Robert. *The Vitality of Worship: A Commentary on the Book of Psalms.* Grand Rapids: Eerdmans, 2000.

De Vaux, Roland. *Ancient Israel.* Translated by John McHugh. Leiden: DLT, 1961.

Edersheim, Alfred. *The Rites and Worship of the Jews.* New York: Revell, 1891.

———. *The Temple: Its Ministry and Services as They Were at the Time of Christ.* Reprint, Grand Rapids: Eerdmans, 1987.

Gaster, Theodore H. *Festivals of the Jewish Year.* New York: William Sloane, 1966.

Glaser, Mitch, and Zhava Glaser. *The Fall Feasts of Israel.* Chicago: Moody, 1987.

Guillaume, Alfred. *Prophecy and Divination Among the Hebrews and Other Semites: The Bampton Lectures, 1938.* London: Hodder & Stoughton, 1938.

Heidel, William Arthur. *The Day of Yahweh.* New York: Century Company, 1929.

Kraus, Hans-Joachim. *Worship in Israel: A Cultic History of the Old Testament.* Oxford: Basil Blackwell, 1966.

McKay, John. *Religion in Judah Under the Assyrians.* London: SCM, 1973.

McQuaid, Elwood. *The Outpouring: Jesus in the Feasts of Israel.* Chicago: Moody, 1986.

Merrill, E. H. *Kingdom of Priests.* Grand Rapids: Baker, 1987.

Oesterley, William Oscar Emil. "Worship in the Old Testament." In *Liturgy and Worship: A Companion to the Prayer Books of the Anglican Communion,* edited by W. K. Lowther Clarke, 35–59. London: SPCK, 1932.

Rowley, H. H. *Worship in Ancient Israel: Its Forms and Meanings.* Philadelphia: Fortress Press, 1967.

Sarna, Nahum M. *Understanding Genesis.* New York: Schocken, 1966.

Segal, M. H. *The Pentateuch: Its Composition and Its Authorship, and Other Biblical Studies.* Jerusalem: Magnes Press, 1967.

Van Goudoever, J. *Biblical Calendars.* Leiden, Netherlands: E. J. Brill, 1959.

Williams, Donald L. "The Israelite Cult and Christian Worship." In *The Use of the Old Testament in the New and Other Essays,* edited by James M. Efird, 110–24. Durham, NC: Duke University Press, 1972.

Wilson, Marvin R. *Our Father Abraham.* Grand Rapids: Eerdmans, 1991.

Wright, David P., David Noel Freedman, and Avi Hurvitz, eds. *Pomegranates and Golden Bells: Studies in Biblical, Jewish, and Near Eastern Ritual, Law, and Literature in Honor of Jacob Milgrom.* Winona Lake, IN: Eisenbrauns, 1995.

## Specific Topics or Passages

Aharoni, Yohanan. "The Solomonic Temple, the Tabernacle, and the Arad Sanctuary." *Alter Orient und Altes Testament* 22 (1973): 1–8.

Aharoni, Yohanan. "Arad: Its Inscriptions and Temple." *Biblical Archaeologist* 31 (1968): 2–32.

Andreason, Niels-Erik A. *The Old Testament Sabbath: A Traditional-Historical Investigation.* Society of Biblical Literature Series 7. Missoula, MT: Society of Biblical Literature, 1972.

Arden, E. "How Moses Failed God." *Journal of Biblical Literature* 76 (1957): 50–52.

Atkinson, C. W. "The Ordinances of Passover-Unleavened Bread." *Anglican Theological Review* 44 (1962): 70–85.

Barton, John. "Ethics in Isaiah of Jerusalem." In *The Israelite Prophets in Recent Scholarship,* edited by Robert P. Gordon, 80–97. Winona Lake, IN: Eisenbrauns, 1995.

Baynes, N. H. "Zerubbabel's Rebuilding of the Temple." *Journal of Theological Studies* 25 (1924): 154–60.

Beale, G. K. "Isaiah VI 9–13: A Retributive Taunt Against Idolatry." *Vetus Testamentum* 41 (1991): 257–78.

Bentzen, A. "The Ritual Background of Amos i 2–ii 16." *Old Testament Studies* 8 (1950): 85–99.

Ben-Uri, M. "The Mosaic Building Code." *Christian Research Quarterly* 19 (1982): 36–39.

Bokser, Baruch M. *The Origins of the Seder: The Passover Ritual and Early Rabbinic Judaism.* California: University of California Press, 1984.

Brichto, Herbert. *The Problem of "Curse" in the Hebrew Bible.* Philadelphia: Society of Biblical Literature and Exegesis, 1963.

Brongers, H. A. "Fasting in Israel in Biblical and Post-Biblical Times." *Old Testament Studies* 20 (1977): 1–21.

Bronner, Leah. *Sects and Separatism During the Second Jewish Commonwealth.* New York: Block, 1967.

Brooten, Bernadette J. *Women Leaders in the Ancient Synagogue.* Chico, CA: Scholars Press, 1982.

Chaim, Raphael. *A Feast of History: The Drama of Passover Through the Ages.* Tel Aviv: Weidenfeld and Nicolson Japhet Press, 1971.

Childs, Brevard S. *Introduction to the Old Testament as Scripture.* Philadelphia: Fortress Press, 1979.

Clark, W. M. "The Legal Background of the Yahwist's Use of 'Good and Evil' in Genesis 2–3." *Journal of Biblical Literature* 88 (1969): 266–78.

Clines, D. J. A. "Nehemiah 10 as an Example of Early Jewish Biblical Exegesis." *Journal for the Study of the Old Testament* 21 (1981): 111–17.

Cody, A. *A History of the Old Testament Priesthood.* Rome: Pontifical Biblical Institute, 1969.

Coggins, R. J. "The Interpretation of Ezra iv.4." *Journal of Theological Studies* 16 (1965): 124–27.

Cohn, Robert L. "The Literary Logic of 1 Kings 17–19." *Journal of Biblical Literature* 101 (1982): 333–50.

Costley-White, H. *Abraham of Ur.* London: Rich & Cowan, 1938.

Crenshaw, James L. "A Monstrous Test: Genesis 22." In *A Whirlpool of Torment: Israelite Traditions of God as an Oppressive Presence,* 9–29. Philadelphia: Fortress Press, 1984.

Cross, Frank Moore. "Notes on Psalm 93: A Fragment of a Liturgical Poem." In *A God So Near: Essays on Old Testament Theology in Honor of Patrick D. Miller,* edited by Brent A. Strawn and Nancy R. Bowen, 73–78. Winona Lake, IN: Eisenbrauns, 2003.

Crow, Loren D. *The Songs of Ascents (Psalms 120–134): Their Place in Israelite History and Religion.* Atlanta: Scholars Press, 1996.

Curtis, Edward M. "Ancient Psalms and Modern Worship." *Bibliotheca Sacra* 154 (1997): 285–96.

———. "Structure, Style and Context as a Key to Interpreting Jacob's Encounter at Peniel." *Journal of the Evangelical Theological Society* 30 (1987): 129–37.

Davies, G. Henton. "The Ark in the Psalms." In *Promise and Fulfillment: Essays Presented to Professor S. H. Hooke,* edited by F. F. Bruce, 51–61. Edinburgh: T. & T. Clark, 1963.

De Vaux, Roland. "The Revelation of the Divine Name YHWH." In *Proclamation and Presence: Old Testament Essays in Honour of Gwynne Henton Davies,* edited by John I. Durham and J. R. Porter, 48–75. London: SCM, 1970.

———. *Studies in Old Testament Sacrifice.* Oxford: University of Wales, 1964.

Dillard, Raymond. "The Chronicler's Solomon." *Westminster Theological Journal* 43 (1980): 289–300.

Dumbrell, W. J. "Malachi and the Ezra–Nehemiah Reforms." *Reformed Theological Review* 35 (1976): 42–52.

Emerton, John A. "The Etymology of *Hištaḥᵃwāh*." *Old Testament Studies* 20 (1977): 41–55.

————. "The Origin of the Promises to the Patriarchs in the Old Sources of the Book of Genesis." *Vetus Testamentum* 32 (1982): 14–32.

————. "Priests and Levites in Deuteronomy." *Vetus Testamentum* 12 (1962): 12–38.

Fensham, F. Charles "Koheleth's Use of Genesis." *Journal of Semitic Studies* 5 (1960): 256–63.

————. "Malediction and Benediction in the Ancient Near Eastern Vassal Treaties and the Old Testament." *Zeitschrift für die alttestmentliche Wissenschaft* 74 (1962): 1–9.

————. "Nehemiah 9 and Psalms 105, 106, 135 and 136: Post-exilic Historical Traditions in Poetic Form." *Journal of Northwest Semitic Languages* 9 (1981): 35–51.

Fishbane, Michael. "Form and Reformulation of the Biblical Priestly Blessing." *Journal of the American Oriental Society* 63 (1983): 115–21.

————. *Text and Texture: Close Readings of Selected Biblical Texts.* New York: Schocken Books, 1979.

Foh, Susan T. "What Is the Woman's Desire? (Gen. 3:16; 4:7)." *Westminster Theological Journal* 37 (1974): 376–83.

Fokkelman, J. P. "'On the Mount of the LORD There Is a Vision': A Response to Francis Landy Concerning the Aqedah." In *Signs and Wonders: Biblical Texts in Literary Focus,* edited by J. C. Exum, 41–58. Society of Biblical Literature, 1989.

Forman, Charles C. "Koheleth's Use of Genesis." *Journal of Semitic Studies* 5 (1960): 256–63.

Fox, Michael V. "Jeremiah 2:2 and the 'Desert Ideal.'" *Catholic Biblical Quarterly* 35 (1973): 441–50.

Fox, Michael V., et al., eds. *Texts, Temples, and Traditions: A Tribute to Menahem Haran.* Grand Rapids: Eerdmans, 1996.

Freed, Edwin D. "Some Old Testament Influences on the Prologue of John." In *Old Testament Studies in Honor of Jacob M. Myers,* edited by Howard N. Bream et al., 145–61. Philadelphia: Temple University Press, 1974.

Fretheim, T. E. "The Priestly Document: Anti-Temple?" *Vetus Testamentum* 18 (1968): 313–29.

Gispen, W. H. "Genesis 2:10–14." *Studia Biblica et Semitica: Festschrift für T. C. Vriezen.* Wageningen Veenman, 1966.

Goodman, Paul. *The Synagogue and the Church.* London: Routledge, 1908.

Gordon, Robert P., ed. *The Israelite Prophets in Recent Scholarship.* Winona Lake, IN: Eisenbrauns, 1995.

Graesser, C. F. "Standing Stones in Ancient Palestine." *Biblical Archaeologist* 35 (1975): 34–62.

Gray, S. W. "Useless Fires: Worship in the Time of Malachi." *Southwestern Journal of Theology* 38 (1987): 35–41.

Guilding, Aileen. *The Fourth Gospel and Jewish Worship: A Study of the Relationship of St. John's Gospel to the Ancient Jewish Lectionary System.* Oxford: Clarendon Press, 1960.

Handy, L. K. "The Role of Huldah," *Zeitschrift für die alttestmentliche Wissenschaft* 106 (1994): 40–53.

Hanks, T. D. "The Chronicler: Theologian of Grace." *Evangelical Quarterly* 53 (1981): 16–28.

Haran, M. "The Ark and the Cherubim: Their Significance in Biblical Ritual." *Israel Exploration Journal* 9 (1959): 30–38, 80–94.

———. "The Divine Presence in the Israelite Cult and Cultic Institutions." *Biblica* 50 (1969): 251–67.

———. "The Nature of the *'Ohel Mo'edh'* in the Pentateuchal Sources." *Journal of Semitic Studies* 5 (1960): 50–65.

———. "The Passover Sacrifice." In *Studies in the Religion of Ancient Israel. Vetus Testamentum Supplement* 23. Leiden: E. J. Brill, 1972.

———. "The Priestly Image of the Tabernacle." *Hebrew Union College Annual* 36 (1965): 191–226.

———. "The Religion of the Patriarchs." *Annual of the Swedish Theological Institute* 4 (1965): 30–55.

———. *Temples and Temple Service in Ancient Israel.* Oxford: Oxford University Press, 1978.

———. "The Use of Incense in Ancient Israelite Ritual." *Vetus Testamentum* 10 (1960): 113–25.

Harper, J. Steven. "Old Testament Spirituality." *Asbury Theological Journal* 42 (1987): 63–77.

Harrelson, Walter. "The Celebration of the Feast of Booths According to Zech. xiv 16–21." In *Religions in Antiquity: Essays in Memory of Erwin Ramsdell Goodenough,* edited by Jacob Neusner, 88–96. Leiden: E. J. Brill, 1968.

Heidel, Alexander. *The Epic of Creation and Old Testament Parallels.* Chicago: University of Chicago Press, 1949.

Heinz, Kruse. "Exodus 19:5 and the Mission of Israel." *North East Asia Journal of Theology* 24 (1980): 239–42.

Hillers, Delbert R. "The Ritual Procession of the Ark in Psalm 132." *Catholic Biblical Quarterly* 30 (1968): 48–55.

Horbury, W. "The Aaronic Priesthood in the Epistle to the Hebrews." *Journal for the Study of the New Testament* 19 (1983): 43–71.

Houtman, Cornelis. *Der Himmel im Alten Testament Israels Weltbild und Weltanschauung.* Old Testament Studies Deel 30. Leiden: E. J. Brill, 1993.

———. "What Did Jacob See in His Dream at Bethel? Some Remarks on Genesis xxviii 10–22." *Vetus Testamentum* 27 (1977): 337–51.

Huffman, Herbert B. "The Treaty Background of Hebrew *Yadaʾ*." *Bulletin of the American Schools of Oriental Research* 181 (1966): 31–37.

Innes, D. K. "Heaven and Sky in the Old Testament." *Evangelical Quarterly* 43 (1971): 144–48.

Janzen, Waldemar. "*ʾAshre* in the Old Testament." *Harvard Theological Review* 58 (1965): 215–26.

Johnson, A. R. *The Cultic Prophet and Israel's Psalmody.* Cardiff: University of Wales Press, 1962.

Joines, K. R. "The Bronze Serpent in the Israelite Cult." *Journal of Biblical Literature* 87 (1968): 245–56.

———. *Serpent Symbolism in the Old Testament.* Haddonfield, NJ: Haddonfield House, 1974.

Kalimi, I. "The Land of Moriah, Mount Moriah, and the Site of Solomon's Temple in Biblical Historiography." *Harvard Theological Review* 83 (1990): 345–62.

Keet, Cuthbert C. *A Study of the Psalms of Ascents: A Critical and Exegetical Commentary on Psalms cxx–cxxxiv.* London: Mitre Press, 1969.

Kingsbury, E. C. "The Theophany *Topos* and the Mountain of God." *Journal of Biblical Literature* 88 (1967): 208–9.

Klingbeil, Martin. *Yahweh Fighting from Heaven: God as Warrior and as God of Heaven in the Hebrew Psalter and Ancient Near Eastern Iconography.* Goettingen: Vandenhoeck and Ruprecht, 1999.

Klutsko, John F. *Between Heaven and Earth: Divine Presence and Absence in the Book of Ezekiel.* Winona Lake, IN: Eisenbrauns, 2000.

Knierim, Rolf P. "Conceptual Aspects in Exodus 25:1–9." In *Pomegranates and Golden Bells: Studies in Biblical, Jewish, and Near Eastern Ritual, Law and Literature in Honor of Jacob Milgrom,* edited by David P. Wright et al., 113–24. Winona Lake, IN: Eisenbrauns, 1995.

Knowles, Michael P. "Abram and the Birds in Jubilee 11: A Subtext for the Parable of the Sower." *New Testament Studies* 41 (1995): 141–51.

Koch, K. "Ezra and the Origins of Judaism." *Journal of Semitic Studies* 19 (1974): 173–97.

Konkel, A. H. "בהו [Void]." In *The New International Dictionary of Old Testament Theology and Exegesis,* edited by Willem Van Gemeren, 1:606–9. Grand Rapids: Zondervan, 1996.

Kwon, Hyuk Seung. "The Zion Traditions and the Kingdom of God in the New Testament: A Study of the Zion Traditions as Relevant to the Understanding of the Kingdom of God in the New Testament." Dissertation, Hebrew University, 1998.

Lawlor, J. I. "The Test of Abraham: Gen 22:1–19." *Grace Theological Journal* 1 (1980): 19–35.

Lee, A. C. C. "Genesis 1 and the Plagues Tradition in Psalm CV." *Vetus Testamentum* 40 (1990):257–63.

Leiser, B. M. "The Trisagion of Isaiah's Vision." *New Testament Studies* 6 (1960): 261–63.

Lemke, Werner E. "Circumcision of the Heart: The Journey of a Biblical Metaphor." In *A God So Near: Essays on Old Testament Theology in Honor of Patrick D. Miller,* edited by Brent A. Strawn and Nancy R. Bowen, 299–320. Winona Lake, IN: Eisenbrauns, 2003.

Levenson, Jon D. "From Temple to Synagogue: 1 Kings 8." In *Traditions in Transformation: Turning Points in Biblical Faith,* edited by B. Halpern and Jon D. Levenson, 143–92. Winona Lake, IN: Eisenbrauns, 1981.

———. *Theology of the Program of Restoration of Ezekiel 40–48.* Missoula, MT: Scholars Press, 1976.

Levertoff, Paul Philip. "Synagogue Worship in the First Century." In *Liturgy and Worship: A Companion to the Prayer Books of the Anglican Communion,* edited by W. K. Lowther Clarke, 60–77. London: SPCK, 1932.

Levine, B. A. "The Descriptive Tabernacle Texts of the Pentateuch." *Journal of the American Oriental Society* 85 (1965): 307–318.

Levine, E. "Distinguishing 'Air' from 'Heaven' in the Bible." *Zeitschrift für die alttestmentliche Wissenschaft* 88 (1976): 97–99.

Liebreich, Leon J. "The Songs of Ascent and the Priestly Blessing." *Journal of Biblical Literature* 74 (1955): 33–36.

Lundquist, John M. "Temple, Covenant, and Law in Ancient Near East and in the Old Testament." In *Israel's Apostasy and Restoration: Essays in Honor of*

*Roland K. Harrison,* edited by Avraham Gileadi, 291–305. Grand Rapids: Baker, 1988.

MacDonald, J. *The Theology of the Samaritans.* London: SCM, 1964.

Malul, M. "More on *paḥad Yiṣḥaq* (Gen. 31:42, 53) and the Oath by the Thigh." *Vetus Testamentum* 35 (1985):63–85.

May, H. G. "The Departure of the Glory of Yahweh." *Journal of Biblical Literature* 56 (1937): 309–21.

Mays, James Luther. "There the Blessing: An Exposition of Psalm 133." In *A God So Near: Essays on Old Testament Theology in Honor of Patrick D. Miller,* edited by Brent A. Strawn and Nancy R. Bowen, 79–90. Winona Lake, IN: Eisenbrauns, 2003.

Mazar, B. "The Cities of the Priests and the Levites." *Vetus Testamentum Supplement* 7 (1959): 193–205.

———. "The Sanctuary of Arad and the Family of Hobab the Kenite." *Journal of Near Eastern Studies* 24 (1964): 297–303.

McCarthy, Dennis J. "*Bᵉrît* in Old Testament History and Theology." *Biblica* 53 (1972): 110–21.

McKenzie, John L. "The Elders in the Old Testament." *Biblica* 40 (1959): 522–40.

Merrill, Eugene H. "Royal Priesthood: An Old Testament Messianic Motif." *Bibliotheca Sacra* 150 (1993): 50–61.

Meyers, E. M. "The Use of *Tora* in Haggai 2:11 and the Role of the Prophet in the Restoration Community." In *The Word Shall Go Forth: Essays in Honor of David Noel Freedman in Celebration of His Sixtieth Birthday,* edited by C. L. Meyers and M. O'Connor, 69–76. Winona Lake, IN: Eisenbrauns, 1983.

Milgrom, J. "The Paradox of the Red Cow (Num 19)." *Vetus Testamentum* 31 (1981): 62–72.

Miller, Patrick. "The Blessing of God: An Interpretation of Numbers 6:22–27." *Interpretation* 29 (1975): 240–51.

Mitchell, Christopher Wright. *The Meaning of BRK, "To Bless," in the Old Testament.* SBL Dissertation Series 95. Atlanta: Scholars Press, 1987.

Mitchell, T. C. "The Old Testament Usage of *Nᵉšāmâ.*" *Vetus Testamentum* 11 (1961): 177–87.

Moberly, R. W. L. *At the Mountain of God: Story and Theology in Exodus 32–34.* Journal for the Study of the Old Testament: Supplement Series 22. Sheffield, UK: JSOT Press, 1983.

———. "Christ as the Key to Scripture: Genesis 22 Reconsidered." In *He Swore an Oath,* edited by R. S. Hess, P. E. Satterthwaite, and G. J. Wenham, 143–73. Cambridge: Tyndale, 1993.

———. "The Earliest Commentary on the *Akedah.*" *Vetus Testamentum* 38 (1988): 302–23.

———. *The Old Testament of the Old Testament: Patriarchal Narratives and Mosaic Yahwism.* Minneapolis: Augsburg Fortress, 1992.

Moran, William L. "The Ancient Near Eastern Background of the Love of God in Deuteronomy." *Catholic Biblical Quarterly* 23 (1963): 77–87.

Morgenstern, J. *The Ark, the Ephod, and the Tent of Meeting.* Cincinnati: Hebrew Union College Annual, 1945.

Moriarty, F. L. "The Chronicler's Account of Hezekiah's Reform." *Catholic Biblical Quarterly* 27 (1965): 399–406.

Moule, C. F. D. "'The Son of Man': Some of the Facts." *New Testament Studies* 41 (1995): 277–79.

Nicholson, E. W. "The Covenant Ritual in Exodus XXIV 3–8." *Vetus Testamentum* 32 (1982): 74–86.

Nieman, D. "The Supercaelian Sea." *Journal of Near Eastern Studies* 28 (1969): 243–49.

North, Robert. *Sociology of the Biblical Jubilee.* Analecta Biblica 4. Rome: Pontifical Biblical Institute, 1954.

O'Connor, Kathleen M. *The Confessions of Jeremiah: Their Interpretation and Role in Chapters 1–25.* Atlanta: Scholars Press, 1988.

Oesterley, William Oscar Emil. *Sacrifices in Ancient Israel: Their Origin, Purposes and Development.* London: Hodder & Stoughton, 1937.

Ogden, G. "The Northern Extent of Josiah's Reforms." *Australian Biblical Review* 26 (1978): 26–34.

Olyan, Saul M. "Why an Altar of Unfinished Stones? Some Thoughts on Ex 20, 25 and Dtn 27, 5–6." *Zeitschrift für die alttestmentliche Wissenschaft* 108 (1996): 161–71.

Parker, S. B. "Possession, Trance and Prophecy in Pre-exilic Israel." *Vetus Testamentum* 28 (1978): 271–85.

———. "The Vow in Ugaritic and Israelite Narrative Literature." *Ugarit-Forschungen* 11 (1979): 693–700.

Parke-Taylor, G. H. *Yahweh: The Divine Name in the Bible.* Waterloo, ON: Wilfred Laurier University Press, 1975.

Parunak, H. Van Dyke. "A Semantic Survey of NḤM." *Biblica* 6 (1975): 512–32.

Phillips, A. "David's Linen Ephod." *Vetus Testamentum* 19 (1969): 48–87.

Polan, Gregory J. "Divine Presence: A Biblical Perspective." *Liturgical Ministry* 3 (1994): 13–21.

Polk, T. "The Levites in the Davidic-Solomonic Empire." *Studies in Biblical Theology* 9 (1979): 3–22.

Priest, J. "Huldah's Oracle." *Vetus Testamentum* 30 (1980): 366–68.

Proctor, John. "Fire in God's House: The Influence of Malachi 3 on the New Testament." *Journal of the Evangelical Theological Society* 36 (1993): 9–14.

Rabe, V. W. "The Origins of Prophecy." *Bulletin of the American Schools of Oriental Research* 221 (1976): 125–28.

Rainey, A. F. "The Order of Sacrifices in Old Testament Ritual Texts." *Biblica* 51 (1970): 485–98.

Rignell, L. G. "Isaiah Chapter 1." *Studia Theologica* 11 (1958): 140–58.

Robinson, D. *Josiah's Reform and the Book of the Law.* London: Tyndale, 1951.

Rodriguez, Angel Manuel. "Sanctuary Theology in the Book of Exodus." *Andrews University Seminary Studies* 24 (1986):132–34.

Rosenbaum, J. "Hezekiah's Reform and Deuteronomic Tradition." *Harvard Theological Review* 72 (1979):23–43.

Ross, Allen P. "Did the Patriarchs Know the Name of the LORD?" In *Giving the Sense: Understanding and Using Old Testament Historical Texts,* edited by David M. Howard Jr. and Michael A. Grisanti, 323–39. Grand Rapids: Kregel, 2003.

Rowley, H. H. "Hezekiah's Reform and Rebellion." *Bulletin of the John Rylands University Library of Manchester* 44 (1961–62): 395–431.

———. "Zadok and Nahushtan." *Journal of Biblical Literature* 58 (1938): 113–41.

Rudolph, David J. "Festivals in Genesis 1:14." *Tyndale Bulletin* 54 (2003): 23–40.

Sabourin, L. "The Biblical Cloud: Terminology and Traditions." *Biblical Theology Bulletin* 4 (1974): 290–311.

Safrai, Shmuel. *The Jewish People in the Period of the Second Temple.* Tel Aviv: Am Oved, 1970.

———. "The Place of Women in the First Century Synagogues." *Jerusalem Perspective* 40 (1993): 1–5.

Schwartz, J. "Jubilees, Bethel and the Temple of Jacob." *Hebrew Union College Annual* 56 (1985): 63–85.

Scott, R. B. Y. "A Kingdom of Priests (Exodus xix 6)." *Old Testament Studies* 8 (1950): 213–19.

Segal, J. B. *The Hebrew Passover from the Earliest Times to A.D. 70.* London: Oxford University Press, 1963.

Simpson, William W. *Jewish Prayer and Worship: An Introduction for Christians.* London: SCM, 1965.

Skinner, D. "Some Major Themes of Exodus." *Mid-America Theological Journal* 1 (1977): 31–42.

Snaith, Norman H. *The Jewish New Year Festival: Its Origins and Development.* London: SPCK, 1947.

Strawn, Brent A., and Nancy R. Bowen, eds. *A God So Near: Essays on Old Testament Theology in Honor of Patrick D. Miller.* Winona Lake, IN: Eisenbrauns, 2003.

Stroes, H. R. "Does the Day Begin in the Evening or Morning? Some Biblical Observations." *Vetus Testamentum* 16 (1966): 460–75.

Taylor, J. G. *Yahweh and the Sun: Biblical and Archaeological Evidence for Sun Worship in Ancient Israel.* Journal for the Study of the Old Testament: Supplement Series 3. Sheffield, UK: JSOT Press, 1993.

Thomas, D. R. "Some Notes on the Old Testament Attitude to Prayer." *Scottish Journal of Theology* 9 (1956): 422–29.

Thompson, R. J. *Penitence and Sacrifice in Early Israel.* Leiden: E. J. Brill, 1960.

Throntveit, Mark A. "Songs in a New Key: The Psalmic Structure of the Chronicler's Hymn (1 Chron. 16:8–36)." In *A God So Near: Essays on Old Testament Theology in Honor of Patrick D. Miller,* edited by Brent A. Strawn and Nancy R. Bowen, 153–70. Winona Lake, IN: Eisenbrauns, 2003.

Todd, E. "The Reforms of Hezekiah and Josiah." *Scottish Theological Review* 9 (1956): 288–93.

Van der Toon, K. "The Nature of the Biblical *Teraphim* in the Light of the Cuneiform Evidence." *Catholic Biblical Quarterly* 52 (1990): 203–22.

Vos, Clarence J. *Woman in Old Testament Worship.* Delft, N. V. Verenigde Drukterijen: Judels and Brinkman, n.d.

Vriezen, Th. C. "The Exegesis of Exodus xxiv 9–11." *Oudtestamentische Studien* 17 (1972): 100–33.

———. "How to Understand Malachi 1:11?" In *Grace upon Grace: Festschrift Lester J. Kuyper,* edited by J. I. Cook. Grand Rapids: Eerdmans, 1975.

Walters, S. D. "Prophecy in Mari and Israel." *Journal of Biblical Literature* 89 (1970): 78–81.

Waltke, Bruce K. "The Creation Account of Genesis 1:1–3," Part 3, "The Initial Chaos Theory and Procreation Chaos Theory." *Bibliotheca Sacra* 132 (1975): 216–28.

Weinfeld, Moshe. "The Design and Theme of Ezekiel's Program of Restoration." *Interpretation* 38 (1984): 181–208.

————. "Sabbath, Temple and the Enthronement of the Lord: The Problem of the *Sitz im Leben* of Genesis 1:1–2:3." In *Mélanges bibliques et orientaux en l'honneur de M. Henri Cazelles*, edited by A. Caquot and M. Delcor, 501–12. Alter Orient und Altes Testament 212. Kevelaer: Verlag Butzon und Bercker, 1981.

Wenham, Gordon J. "The Akedah: A Paradigm of Sacrifice." In *Pomegranates and Golden Bells: Studies in Biblical, Jewish, and Near Eastern Ritual, Law and Literature in Honor of Jacob Milgrom*, edited by David Noel Freedman et al., 93–102. Winona Lake, IN: Eisenbrauns, 1995.

————. "Attitudes to Homosexuality in the Old Testament." *Expository Times* 102 (1991): 359–63.

————. "The Religion of the Patriarchs." In *Essays in the Patriarchal Narratives*, edited by A. R. Millard and D. J. Wiseman, 157–88. Leicester: InterVarsity, 1980.

Wenham, J. W. "Large Numbers in the Old Testament." *Tyndale Bulletin* 17 (1967): 19–53.

Whitekettle, Richard. "Leviticus 12 and the Israelite Woman: Ritual Process, Liminality, and the Womb." *Zeitschrift für die alttestmentliche Wissenschaft* 107 (1995): 393–408.

Williams, A. J. "The Relationship of Genesis 3:20 to the Serpent." *Zeitschrift für die alttestmentliche Wissenschaft* 89 (1977): 357–74.

Williamson, H. G. M. "The Origin of the Twenty-Four Priestly Courses." *Vetus Testamentum Supplement* 30 (1979): 251–68.

Wilson, Ian. *Out of the Midst of the Fire: Divine Presence in Deuteronomy*. Atlanta: Scholars Press, 1995.

Wilson, Marvin R. *Our Father Abraham: Jewish Roots of the Christian Faith*. Grand Rapids: Eerdmans, 1991.

Wilson, R. R. "Early Israelite Prophecy." *Interpretation* 32 (1978): 3–16.

Wiseman, D. J. "Flying Serpents." *Theologische Bücherei* 23 (1972): 108–10.

Wylie, C. C. "On King Solomon's Molten Sea." *Biblical Archaeologist* 12 (1949): 86–90.

Yarden, L. *Tree of Light: A Study of the Menorah, the Seven-Branched Lampstand*. Ithaca, NY: Cornell University Press, 1971.

Yaron, K. "The Dirge over the King of Tyre." *Annual of the Swedish Theological Institute* 3 (1964): 28–57.

Young, J. B. de. "The Contributions of the Septuagint to Biblical Sanctions Against Homosexuality." *Journal of the Evangelical Theological Society* 34 (1991): 157–77.

Zipor, Moshe A. "The Deuteronomic Account of the Golden Calf and Its Reverberations in Other Parts of the Book of Deuteronomy." *Zeitschrift für die alttestmentliche Wissenschaft* 108 (1996): 20–33.

Zornberg, Avivah Gottlieb. *The Beginning of Desire: Reflections of Genesis.* Philadelphia: Jewish Publications Society, 1955.

## Polemics and Pagan Worship

Albright, William Foxwell. *Archaeology and the Religion of Israel.* Baltimore: Johns Hopkins Press, 1956.

———. *Yahweh and the Gods of Canaan.* Garden City, NJ: Doubleday, 1968.

Battenfield, James R. "YHWH's Refutation of the Baal Myth Through the Actions of Elijah and Elisha." In *Israel's Apostasy and Restoration: Essays in Honor of Roland K. Harrison,* edited by Avraham Gileadi, 19–38. Grand Rapids: Baker, 1988.

Bronner, Leah. *The Stories of Elijah and Elisha as Polemics Against Baal Worship.* Leiden: E. J. Brill, 1968.

Buck, Harry M. "Worship, Idolatry, and God." In *A Light unto My Path: Old Testament Studies in Honor of Jacob M. Myers,* edited by Howard N. Bream et al., 68–82. Philadelphia: Temple University Press, 1974.

Bullock, C. Hassell. "The Priestly Era in the Light of Prophetic Thought." In *Israel's Apostasy and Restoration: Essays in Honor of Roland K. Harrison,* edited by Avraham Gileadi, 71–78. Grand Rapids: Baker, 1988.

Cornelius, Izak. *The Iconography of the Canaanite Gods Reshef and Ba'al. Late Bronze and Iron Age I Periods (c. 1500–1000 B.C.E.)* Goettingen: Vandenhoeck & Ruprecht, 1994.

Craigie, Peter C. *Ugarit and the Old Testament.* Grand Rapids: Eerdmans, 1983.

Curtis, A. H. W. "The 'Subjugation of the Waters' Motif in the Psalms: Imagery or Polemic?" *Journal of Semitic Studies* 23 (1978): 245–56.

Curtis, Adrian. *Ugarit: Ras Shamra.* Grand Rapids: Eerdmans, 1985.

Dion, P. E. "Did Cultic Prostitution Fall into Oblivion in the Postexilic Era? Some Evidence from Chronicles and the Septuagint." *Catholic Biblical Quarterly* 43 (1981): 41–48.

Dozeman, Thomas B. *God on the Mountain: A Study of Redaction, Theology and Canon in Ex 19–24.* Atlanta: Scholars Press, 1989.

Fisher, L. R. "Creation at Ugarit and in the Old Testament." *Vetus Testamentum* 15 (1965): 313–24.

Gileadi, Avraham, ed. *Israel's Apostasy and Restoration: Essays in Honor of Roland K. Harrison.* Grand Rapids: Baker, 1988.

Green, Alberto Ravinell Whitney. *The Role of Human Sacrifice in the Ancient Near East.* Missoula, MT: Scholars Press, 1975.

Gurney, O. R. "Tammuz Reconsidered: Some Recent Developments." *Journal of Semitic Studies* 7 (1962): 147–60.

Heidel, Alexander. *The Babylonian Genesis: The Story of the Creation.* Chicago: University of Chicago Press, 1951.

———. *The Gilgamesh Epic and Old Testament Parallels.* Chicago: University of Chicago Press, 1946, 1949.

Hoffmeier, James Earl. *"Sacred" in the Vocabulary of Ancient Egypt: The Term DSR, with Special Reference to Dynasties I–XX.* Goettingen: Vandenhoeck & Ruprecht, 1985.

Jacobson, T. *The Treasures of Darkness.* New Haven: Yale University Press, 1976.

James, E. O. *Myth and Ritual in the Ancient Near East.* London: Thames & Hudson, 1958.

———. *Sacrifice and Sacrament.* London: Thames & Hudson, 1962.

Keel, Othmar, *God, Goddesses, and Images of God in Ancient Israel.* Translated by Thomas H. Trapp. Edinburgh: T. & T. Clark, 1998.

Kellermann, D. *"ˀAsham* in Ugaritic?" *Zeitschrift für die alttestmentliche Wissenschaft* 76 (1964): 319–22.

Kikawada, I. M. "Two Notes on Eve." *Journal of Biblical Literature* 91 (1972): 33–37.

Lambert, W. G. "Myth and Ritual as Conceived by the Babylonians." *Journal of Semitic Studies* 13 (1968): 104–12.

Lapp, P. "The Ritual Incense Stand from Taanach." *Qadmoniot* 2 (1969): 16–17.

Matthews, Victor H. "Theophanies Cultic and Cosmic: 'Prepare to Meet Thy God.'" In *Israel's Apostasy and Restoration: Essays in Honor of Roland K. Harrison,* edited by Avraham Gileadi, 307–18. Grand Rapids: Baker, 1988.

Moran, William L. "The Creation of Man in Atrahasis: 192–248." *Bulletin of the American Schools of Oriental Research* 200 (1970): 48–76.

Oden, R. A. "Divine Aspirations in Atraḫasis and in Genesis 1–11." *Zeitschrift für die alttestmentliche Wissenschaft* 93 (1981): 197–216.

Olyan, Saul M. "Some Observations Concerning the Identity of the Queen of Heaven." *Ugarit-Forschungen* 19 (1987): 161–74.

Oswalt, John N. "Golden Calves and the 'Bull of Jacob': The Impact on Israel of Its Religious Environment." In *Israel's Apostasy and Restoration: Essays in Honor of Roland K. Harrison,* edited by Avraham Gileadi, 9–18. Grand Rapids: Baker, 1988.

Parpola, Simo. "The Assyrian Tree of Life: Tracing the Origins of Jewish

Monotheism and Greek Philosophy." *Journal of Near Eastern Studies* 52 (1993): 161–208.

Patai, Raphael. "The Goddess Asherah." *Journal of Near Eastern Studies* 24 (1965): 37–52.

Paul, Shalom M. "Heavenly Tablets and the Book of Life." *Journal of the Ancient Near Eastern Society of Columbia University* 5 (1973): 345–53.

Reed, W. L. *The Asherah in the Old Testament.* Fort Worth, TX: Texas Christian University Press, 1949.

Speiser, E. A. *Oriental and Biblical Studies.* Edited by J. J. Finkelstein and Moshe Greenberg. Philadelphia: University of Pennsylvania Press, 1967. See esp. "*ʾĒD* in the Story of Creation" and "The Rivers of Paradise."

Spencer, Aida Besancon, Donna F. G. Hailson, Catherine Clark Kroeger, and William David Spencer. *The Goddess Revival.* Grand Rapids: Baker, 1995.

Tsumura, David Toshio. "The Earth in Genesis 1." In *"I Studied Inscriptions from Before the Flood": Ancient Near Eastern, Literary, and Linguistic Approaches to Genesis 1–11,* edited by Richard Hess and David Toshio Tsumura, 310–28. Winona Lake, IN: Eisenbrauns, 1994.

Veenker, R. A. "Gilgamesh and the Magic Plant." *Biblical Archaeologist* 44 (1981): 199–205.

Wakeman, M. K. *God's Battle with the Monster: A Study in Biblical Imagery.* Leiden: E. J. Brill, 1973.

Watts, John D. W. "Babylonian Idolatry in the Prophets as a False Socio-Economic System." In *Israel's Apostasy and Restoration: Essays in Honor of Roland K. Harrison,* edited by Avraham Gileadi, 115–22. Grand Rapids: Baker, 1988.

Weinfeld, Moshe. "The Molech Cult and Its Ancient Near Eastern Background." *Immanuel* 2 (1973): 21–27.

———. "The Worship of Molech and the Queen of Heaven and Its Background." *Ugarit-Forschungen* 4 (1972): 133–54.

Wright, G. R. H. "The Bronze Age Temple at Amman." *Zeitschrift für die alttestmentliche Wissenschaft* 78 (1966): 350–56.

Young, D. W. "With Snakes and Dates: A Sacred Marriage Drama at Ugarit." *Ugarit-Forschungen* 9 (1977): 291–314.

## Holy Places of Worship

Ahlstrom, G. W. "Heaven on Earth—at Hazor and Arad." In *Religious Syncretism in Antiquity,* edited by B. A. Pearson, 67–83. Missoula, MT: Scholars Press, 1975.

Clifford, Richard J. *The Cosmic Mountain in Canaan and in the Old Testament.*
  Harvard Semitic Monographs 4. Cambridge, MA: Harvard University, 1972.

———. "The Tent of El and the Israelite Tent of Meeting." *Catholic Biblical
  Quarterly* 33 (1971): 221–27.

Clines, D. J. A. "The Tree of Knowledge and the Law of God." *Vetus Testamentum*
  24 (1974): 8–14.

Cornelius, Isak. "עֵדֶן [Eden]." In *New International Dictionary of Old Testament
  Theology and Exegesis,* edited by Willem A. Van Gemeren, 4:555–56. Grand
  Rapids: Zondervan, 1996.

———. "גַּן [gan, Garden]." In *New International Dictionary of Old Testament
  Theology and Exegesis,* edited by Willem A. Van Gemeren, 1:875–78. Grand
  Rapids: Zondervan, 1996.

———. "The Garden in the Iconography of the Ancient Near East: A Study of
  Selected Material from Egypt." *Journal of Semitic Studies* 1 (1989): 204–28.

———. "Paradise Motifs in the 'Eschatology' of the Minor Prophets and the
  Iconography of the Ancient Near East." *Journal of Northwest Semitic Languages*
  14 (1988): 41–83.

Cross, F. M. "The Priestly Tabernacle." *Biblical Archaeology Review* 1 (1961):
  201–8.

Davey, C. "Temples of the Levant and the Building of Solomon." *Tyndale Bulletin*
  31 (1980): 107–46.

Dever, William G., et al. "Further Excavations at Gezer, 1967–1971." *Biblical
  Archaeologist* 34 (1971): 94–132.

———. *Did God Have a Wife? Archaeology and Folk Religion in Ancient Israel.*
  Grand Rapids: Eerdmans, 2005.

Engnell, Ivan. "'Knowledge' and 'Life' in the Creation Story." *Wisdom in Israel.
  Vetus Testamentum Supplement* 3 (1955): 103–19.

Fensham, F. C. "Thunder Stones in Ugaritic." *Journal of Near Eastern Studies* 18
  (1959): 273–74.

Habel, N. C. "Ezekiel 28 and the Fall of the First Man." *Concordia Theological
  Monthly* 38 (1967): 516–24.

Haran, M. *Temples and Temple-Service in Ancient Israel.* Oxford: Clarendon Press,
  1978.

Heller, J. "Der Name Eva." *Archiv Orientální* 26 (1958): 636–56.

Hoppe, Leslie. *The Synagogues and Churches of Ancient Palestine.* Collegeville,
  MN: Liturgical Press, 1994.

Hurowitz, A. "The Priestly Account of the Building of the Tabernacle." *Journal of the American Oriental Society* 105 (1985): 21–30.

Kapelrud, A. S. "Temple Building: A Task for Gods and Kings." *Orientalia* 32 (1963): 56–62.

Kearney, Peter J. "Creation and Liturgy: The P Redaction of Exodus 25–40." *Zeitschrift für die alttestmentliche Wissenschaft* 89 (1977): 375–86.

Levenson, Jon D. "The Paronomasia of Solomon's Seventh Petition." *Hebrew Annual Review* 6 (1982): 131–35.

———. *Sinai and Zion: An Entry into the Jewish Bible.* Minneapolis: Winston Press, 1985.

———. "The Temple and the World." *Journal of Religion* 64 (1984): 275–98.

Lindblom, J. "Theophanies in Holy Places in Hebrew Religion." *Hebrew Union College Annual* 32 (1961): 91–106.

Malamat, Abraham. "Mari." *Biblical Archaeologist* 34 (1971): 2–22.

Marcus, R. "The Tree of Life in Proverbs." *Journal of Biblical Literature* 62 (1943): 117–20.

May, H. G. "The King in the Garden of Eden: A Study of Ezekiel 28:12–19." In *Israel's Prophetic Heritage,* edited by B. W. Anderson and W. Harrelson, 166–76. New York: Harper, 1962.

McKenzie, John L. "Mythological Allusions in Ezekiel 28:12–28." *Journal of Biblical Literature* 75 (1956): 322–27.

Mealand, David. "'Paradisial' Elements in the Teachings of Jesus." In *Studia Biblica,* 1978. Journal for the Study of the New Testament: Supplement Series 2. Sheffield: JSOT Press, 1980.

Meyers, Carol L. *The Tabernacle Menorah.* American Schools of Oriental Research Dissertation Series 2. Missoula, MT: Scholars Press, 1976.

Millard, A. R. "The Etymology of 'Eden.'" *Vetus Testamentum* 34 (1984): 103–6.

Murray, Peter and Linda. *The Oxford Companion to Christian Art and Architecture.* New York: Oxford Press, 1996.

Parrot, Andre. *The Temple of Jerusalem.* 2d ed. New York: Philosophical Library, 1955.

Reicke, Bo. "The Knowledge Hidden in the Tree of Paradise." *Journal of Semitic Studies* 1 (1956): 193–201.

Robinson, Jeremy, and Patricia Markert, eds. *Religious Buildings.* New York: McGraw-Hill, 1979.

Scott, R. B. Y. "The Pillars Jachin and Boaz." *Journal of Biblical Literature* 58 (1939): 143–50.

Speiser, E. A. "ʾĒD in the Story of Creation." *Bulletin of the American Schools of Oriental Research* 140 (1955): 9–11.

———. "The Rivers of Paradise." In *Oriental and Biblical Studies,* edited by J. J. Finkelstein and M. Greenberg, 23–34. Philadelphia: University of Pennsylvania Press, 1967

Ussishkin, David. "The 'Ghassulian' Temple in Ein Gedi and the Origin of the Hoard from Nahal Mishmar." *Biblical Archaeologist* 34 (1971): 23–40.

Wallace, Howard N. *The Eden Narrative.* Harvard Semitic Studies 5. Atlanta: Scholars Press, 1985.

Watson, P. "The Tree of Life." *Restoration Quarterly* 23 (1980): 232–38.

Wenham, Gordon J. "Sanctuary Symbolism in the Garden of Eden Story." *Proceedings of the World Congress of Jewish Studies* 9 (1986): 19–25. Reprinted in *"I Studied Inscriptions from Before the Flood": Ancient Near Eastern, Literary, and Linguistic Approaches to Genesis 1–11,* edited by Richard Hess and David Toshio Tsumura. Winona Lake, IN: Eisenbrauns, 1994.

Woudstra, Marten H. *The Ark of the Covenant from Conquest to Kingship.* Philadelphia: Presbyterian & Reformed, 1969.

———. "The Tabernacle in Biblical Theological Perspective." In *New Perspectives on the Old Testament,* edited by J. Barton Payne, 88–103. Waco, TX: Word, 1970.

Wright, George Ernest, and David Noel Freedman, eds. *The Biblical Archaeologist Reader, 1.* Garden City, NJ: Doubleday, 1961.

## Christian Worship

Arndt, W. "A Royal Priesthood." *Concordia Theological Monthly* 19 (1948): 241–49.

Barbour, R. S. "Uncomfortable Words VIII: Status and Titles." *Expository Times* 82 (1971): 137–42.

Barrois, G. A. *Jesus Christ and the Temple.* New York: St. Vladimir's Seminary Press, 1980.

Bauckham, R. J. "The Lord's Day." In *From Sabbath to Lord's Day,* edited by D. A. Carson, 221–50. Grand Rapids: Zondervan, 1982.

Best, E. "Spiritual Sacrifice: General Priesthood in the New Testament." *Interpretation* 14 (1960): 273–99.

Branick, Vincent. *The House Church in the Writings of St. Paul.* Wilmington: Michael Glazier, 1989.

Bradshaw, Paul F. *The Search for the Origin of Christian Worship.* London: SPCK, 1992.

Bruce, F. F. *New Testament History.* New York: Doubleday, 1969.

Cabaniss, Allen. *Pattern in Early Christian Worship.* Macon: Mercer University Press, 1989.

Campion, L. G. *Benediction and Doxologies in the Epistles of Paul.* Oxford: Kemp Hall Press, 1934.

Clark, Kenneth Willis. "Worship in the Temple After 70 A.D." In *Kenneth Willis Clarke: The Gentile Bias and Other Essays.* Selected by John Lawrence Sharpe III. New Testament Supplement 54. Leiden: E. J. Brill, 1980.

Cullmann, Oscar. *Early Christian Worship.* London: SCM, 1953.

Delling, Gerhard. *Worship in the New Testament.* Philadelphia: Westminster, 1962.

Derrett, J. D. M. "Mt 23.8–10 a Midrash on Isa 54.5 and Jer 31.33–34." *Biblica* 62 (1981): 372–86.

Doeve, J. W. *Jewish Hermeneutics in the Synoptic Gospels and Acts.* Assen, Amsterdam: Van Gorcum Press, 1954.

Dunn, J. D. G. "Pharisees, Sinners and Jesus." In *The Social World of Formative Christianity and Judaism: Essays in Tribute to Howard Clark Kee,* edited by J. Neusner, 264–89. Philadelphia: Fortress Press, 1988.

Dupont, J. "The Meal at Emmaus." In *The Eucharist in the New Testament: A Symposium,* edited by J. Delorme. Translated by E. M. Stewart, 105–21. Baltimore: Helicon Press, 1964.

Easton, Burton Scott, ed. *Hippolytus: The Apostolic Tradition.* Hamdens, CT: Archon, 1972.

Finkel, Asher. *The Pharisees and the Teacher of Nazareth.* Leiden: E. J. Brill, 1964.

Flusser, David. "Some Notes on Easter and the Passover Haggadah." *Immanuel* 7 (1977): 52–60.

Garland, David F. *The Intention of Matthew 23. Novum Testamentum Supplement* 52. Leiden: E. J. Brill, 1979.

Gibbs, J. M. "Luke 24:13–33 and Acts 8:26–39: The Emmaus Incident and the Eunuch's Baptism as Parallel Stories." *Bangalore Theological Forum* 7 (1975): 17–30.

Gowen, Donald E. *Bridge Between the Testaments: A Reappraisal of Judaism from the Exile to the Birth of Christianity.* Pittsburgh: Pickwick Press, 1980.

Hahn, Ferdinand. *The Worship of the Early Church.* Philadelphia: Fortress Press, 1977.

Hamm, Dennis. "Acts 4:23–31—A Neglected Biblical Paradigm of Christian Worship (Especially in Troubled Times)." *Worship* 77 (2003): 225–36.

Hamman, A. *Early Christian Prayers*. Translated by Walter Mitchell. London: Longmans, Green and Co., 1961.

Hengel, Martin. *The Zealots*. Edinburgh: T. & T. Clark, 1989.

Hodges, Zane C. "Water and Spirit—John 3:5." *Bibliotheca Sacra* 135 (1978): 206–20.

House, H. Wayne. "Tongues and the Mystery Religions of Corinth." *Bibliotheca Sacra* 140 (1963): 135–50.

Jeremias, Joachim. *The Prayers of Jesus*. Translated by John Bowden. Naperville, IL: Alec Allenson, 1967.

Johnson, Maxwell E. "From Three Weeks to Forty Days: Baptismal Preparation and the Origin of Lent." *Studia Liturgica* 20 (1990): 185–200

Jungmann, J. A. *Public Worship*. Translated by Clifford Howell. London: Challoner, 1957.

Kasemann, Ernst. "A Primitive Christian Baptismal Liturgy." In *Essays on New Testament Themes*. London: SCM, 1965.

Keenan, Joseph. "The Importance of the Creation Motif in Eucharistic Prayer." *Worship* 53 (1979): 341–56.

La Piane, George. "The Roman Church at the End of the Second Century." *Harvard Theological Review* 18 (1925): 201–77.

Lee, Michelle. "A Call to Martyrdom: Function as Method and Message in Revelation." *Novum Testamentum* 40 (1998): 164–94.

Lieu, J. M. "'Grace to You and Peace': The Apostolic Greeting." *Bulletin of the John Rylands University Library of Manchester* 68 (1985): 161–78.

*The Liturgies of Sts. Mark, James, Clement, Chrysostom, and Basil and the Church of Malabar*. Translated with introduction and appendices by J. M. Neale and R. F. Littledale. London: J. T. Hayes, 1969.

Lohmeyer, Ernst. *The Lord's Prayer*. Translated by John Bowden. London: William Collins, 1965.

Maccoby, H. "The Washing of Cups." *Journal for the Study of the New Testament* 14 (1982): 3–15.

Marshall, I. H. "The Divine Sonship of Jesus." *Interpretation* 21 (1967): 89–103.

Martin, Ralph P. *The Spirit and the Congregation: Studies in 1 Corinthians 12–15*. Grand Rapids: Eerdmans, 1984.

———. *Worship in the Early Church*. Grand Rapids: Eerdmans, 1966.

Miller, R. J. "The Inside Is (Not) the Outside." *Forum* 5 (1989): 92–105.

Moran, William L. "A Kingdom of Priests." In *The Bible in Current Catholic*

*Thought,* edited by John McKenzie, 7–20. New York: Herder and Herder, 1962.

Morray-Jones, C. R. A. "Paradise Revisited (2 Cor. 12:1–12): The Jewish Mystical Background of Paul's Apostolate." *Harvard Theological Review* 86 (1993): 177–217.

Moule, C. F. D. "A Reconsideration of the Context of *Maranatha.*" *New Testament Studies* 6 (1959–60): 307–10.

———. *Worship in the New Testament.* Bramcote: Grove, 1977.

Orlett, R. "The Influence of the Early Liturgy upon the Emmaus Account." *Catholic Biblical Quarterly* 21 (1959): 212–19.

Peterlin, Davorin. *Paul's Letter to the Philippians in the Light of Disunity in the Church. Novum Testamentum Supplement* 79. Leiden: E. J. Brill, 1995.

Powell, M. A. "Do and Keep What Moses Says (Matthew 23:2–7)." *Journal of Biblical Literature* 114 (1995): 419–35.

Rosner, Brian. "Temple Prostitution in 1 Corinthians 6:12–20." *Novum Testamentum* 40 (1998): 336–51.

Ryrie, Charles Caldwell. *The Holy Spirit.* Chicago: Moody, 1965.

Sabourin, Leopold. *Priesthood: A Comparative Study.* Leiden: E. J. Brill, 1973.

Saldarini, Anthony J. *Pharisees, Scribes, and Sadducees in Palestinian Society: A Sociological Approach.* Wilmington, DE: Michael Glazier, 1988.

Sandmel, Samuel. *Judaism and Christian Beginnings.* New York: Oxford University Press, 1978.

Scharlemann, Martin H. *Stephen: A Singular Saint.* Rome: Pontifical Biblical Institute, 1968.

Smith, Morton. "Pauline Worship as Seen by Pagans." *Harvard Theological Review* 73 (1980): 241–49.

Smith, R. F. "Did Not Our Hearts Burn Within Us?" *Currents in Theology and Mission* 15 (1988): 187–93.

Snyder, Graydon F. *Ante Pacem: Archaeological Evidence of Church Life Before Constantine.* Macon, GA: Mercer University Press, 1985.

Stanton, G. N. "Matthew 11.28–30: Comfortable Words?" *Expository Times* 94 (1982): 3–9.

Talley, Thomas J. "History and Eschatology in the Primitive Paschas." *Worship* 47 (1973): 212–21.

———. "The Origin of Lent at Alexandria." *Studia Patristica* xvii (1982): 594–612.

Tenney, Merrill C. "Topics from the Gospel of John, Part 2, The Meaning of Signs." *Bibliotheca Sacra* 132 (1975): 145–60.

Thévenot, Xavier. "Emmaüs, une nouvelle Genèse? Une lecture psychanalytique de Genèse 2–3 et Luc 24, 13–35." *Mélanges de science religieuse* 37 (1980): 3–18.

Torrence, T. F. *Royal Priesthood: A Theology of Ordained Ministry.* Edinburgh: T. & T. Clark, 1955.

Warren, Frederick Edward. *The Liturgy and Ritual of the Ante-Nicene Church.* London: SPCK, 1912.

Warren, Frederick Edward, and Jane Stevenson. *The Liturgy and Ritual of the Celtic Church.* 2d edition. Studies in Celtic History 9. Woodbridge, Suffolk: Boydell Press, 1987.

Watkins, Oscar Daniel. *A History of Penance.* 2 vols. London: Longmans, Green, 1920.

Weinfeld, Moshe. "The Charge of Hypocrisy in Matthew 23 and Jewish Sources." *Immanuel* 24–25 (1990): 52–58.

Whitaker, E. C. *The Baptismal Liturgy.* 2d ed. London: SPCK, 1981.

Willimon, William H. *Sighing for Eden: Sin, Evil, and the Christian Faith.* Nashville: Abingdon, 1985.

Willis, G. G. *Augustine's Lectionary.* Alcuin Club Collections 44. London: SPCK, 1962.

Winkle, R. E. "The Jeremiah Model for Jesus in the Temple." *Andrews University Seminary Studies* 24 (1986): 155–72.

## Liturgy

Bedingfield, M. Bradford. *The Dramatic Liturgy of Anglo-Saxon England.* Woodbridge, Suffolk: Boydell Press, 2002.

Bouyer, Louis. *Liturgical Piety.* Notre Dame, IN: Notre Dame Press, 1955.

Bradshaw, Paul F., ed. *The New SCM Dictionary of Liturgy and Worship.* London: SCM, 2002.

Brock, Sebastian. "Studies in the Early History of the Syrian Orthodox Baptismal Liturgy." *Theological Studies New Series* 23 (1972):16–64.

Brueggemann, Walter. *The Creative Word: Canon as a Model for Biblical Education.* Philadelphia: Fortress Press, 1982.

Burlin, R. B., ed. *The Old English Advent: A Typological Commentary.* Yale Studies in English 168. New Haven: Yale University Press, 1968.

Byars, Ronald P. "Eucharistic Prayers in the Reformed Tradition." *Worship* 77 (2003): 114–32.

Clarke, W. K. Lowther, ed., assisted by Charles Harris. *Liturgy and Worship: A Companion to the Prayer Books of the Anglican Communion.* London: SPCK, 1932.

Cummings, Owen J. "The Liturgical Jeremy Taylor." *Worship* 77 (2003): 42–438.

Davies, Horton M. "Response: A Protestant Vindication of Liturgics." *Worship* 53 (1979): 371–78.

Davies, J. G., ed. *A New Dictionary of Liturgy and Worship.* London: SCM Press, 1986.

Day, Peter. *The Liturgical Dictionary of Eastern Christianity.* Tunbridge Wells, Kent: Burns and Oates, 1993.

Dix, Gregory. *The Shape of the Liturgy.* New York: Seabury, 1982.

Duchesne, Mgr. L. *Christian Worship: Its Origin and Evolution: A Study of the Latin Liturgy Up to the Time of Charlemagne.* Translated by M. L. McClure. London: SPCK, 1931.

Enders, Jody. *Rhetoric and the Origins of Medieval Drama.* Ithaca, NY: Cornell University Press, 1992.

Flanigan, C. Clifford. "The Roman Rite and the Origins of the Liturgical Drama." *University of Toronto Quarterly* 43 (1973–74): 263–84.

Fowler, Roger, ed. "A Late Old English Handbook for the Use of the Confessor." *Anglia* 83 (1965): 1–34.

Harper, John. *The Forms and Orders of Western Liturgy from the Tenth to the Eighteenth Century.* Oxford: Clarendon Press, 1991.

Harris, Charles. "Liturgical Silence." In *Liturgy and Worship: A Companion to the Prayer Books of the Anglican Communion,* edited by W. K. Lowther Clarke, 774–82. London: SPCK, 1932.

Hoffman, Lawrence A. *Beyond the Text: A Holistic Approach to Liturgy.* Bloomington, IN: Indiana University Press, 1987.

———. "Blessings and Their Translation in Current Jewish Liturgies." *Worship* 60 (1986):134–61.

———. "The Jewish Lectionary, the Great Sabbath, and the Latin Calendar: Liturgical Links Between Christians and Jews in the First Three Christian Centuries." In *Time and Community: Essays in Honor of Thomas Talley,* edited by J. Neil Alexander, 3–20. Washington: Catholic, 1990.

Idelsohn, Abraham L. *Jewish Liturgy and Its Development.* New York: Schocken 1975.

Jay, Nancy. *Throughout Your Generations Forever: Sacrifice, Religion, and Paternity.* Chicago: University of Chicago Press, 1992.

Jones, Cheslyn, Geoffrey Wainwright, and Edward Yarnold, eds. *The Study of Liturgy.* New York: Oxford University Press, 1978.

Kavanagh, Aidan. *On Liturgical Theology.* New York: Pueblo, 1984.

King, Archdale A. *Liturgies of the Past.* London: Longmans, Green and Co., 1959.

Klauser, Theodor. *A Short History of the Western Liturgy.* English Translation. Oxford: Oxford University Press, 1979.

Lathrop, Gordon W. *Holy Ground: A Liturgical Cosmology.* Minneapolis: Fortress Press, 2003.

———. *Holy Things: A Liturgical Theology.* Minneapolis: Fortress Press, 1993.

Liebreich, L. J. "The Impact of Nehemiah 9:5–37 on the Liturgy of the Synagogue." *Hebrew Union College Annual* 32 (1961): 227–37.

Marcheschi, Graziano, with Nancy Seitz Marcheschi. *Workbook for Lectors and Gospel Readers: Celebrating Liturgy.* Chicago: Liturgy Training Publications, 1989.

Mazza, Enrico. *The Origins of the Eucharistic Prayer.* Translated by Ronald E. Lane. Collegeville, MN: Liturgical Press, 1995.

McMichael, Ralph, ed. *Creation and Liturgy: Studies in Honor of H. Boone Porter.* Washington: Pastoral Press, 1993.

Morrill, Bruce T. *Anamnesis as Dangerous Memory.* Collegeville, MN: Liturgical Press, 2002.

Oesterley, William Oscar Emil. *The Jewish Background of Christian Liturgy.* Gloucester: Peter Smith, 1965.

Porter, Harry Boone. *Jeremy Taylor: Liturgist (1613–1667).* London: SPCK, 1979.

*The Promise of His Glory: For the Seasons from All Saints to Candelmas, Commended by the House of Bishops of the General Synod of the Church of England.* Collegeville, MN: Liturgical Press, 1991.

Ramshaw-Schmidt, Gail. *Christ in Sacred Speech: The Meaning of Liturgical Language.* Philadelphia: Fortress Press, 1986.

Seasoltz, R. Kevin. "Peace: Belief, Prayer and Life." *Worship* 56 (1982): 152–72.

Senn, Frank C. *The Witness of the Worshiping Community: Liturgy and the Practice of Evangelism.* New York: Paulist Press, 1993.

Taft, Robert. *The Liturgy of the Hours in East and West: The Origins of the Divine Office and Its Meaning for Today.* Collegeville, MN: Liturgical Press, 1986.

Thompson, Bard, ed. *Liturgies of the Western Church.* Philadelphia: Fortress Press, 1961.

Wainwright, Geoffrey. "In Praise of God." *Worship* 53 (1979): 496–511.

———, ed. *Worship with One Accord: Where Liturgy and Ecumenism Embrace.* Oxford: Oxford University Press, 1997.

Whitaker, E. C., trans. *Documents of the Baptismal Liturgy.* Alcuin Club Collections. London: SPCK, 1970.

Wolterstorff, Nicholas. "Liturgy, Justice and Tears." *Worship* 62 (1988): 386–403.

———. "The Remembrance of Things (Not) Past: Philosophical Reflections on Christian Liturgy." In *Christian Philosophy,* edited by Thomas P. Flint, 118–61. Notre Dame, IN: University of Notre Dame Press, 1990.

Woolley, R. M., ed. *The Canterbury Benedictional.* HBS 51. London: Harrison & Sons, 1917.

## Creeds and Confessions

Cranfield, C. E. B. *The Apostles' Creed: A Faith to Live By.* Edinburgh: T. & T. Clark, 1993.

Kelly, J. N. D. *Early Christian Creeds.* 3d ed. New York: David McKay, 1972.

Neufeld, Vernon H. *The Earliest Christian Confessions.* Grand Rapids: Eerdmans, 1963.

Turner, C. H. *The History and Use of Creeds and Anathe Mai in the Early Centuries of the Church.* London, SPCK, 1910.

## Reading and Preaching the Word

Achtemeier, Elizabeth. *Preaching About Family Relationships.* Philadelphia: Westminster, 1987.

Breuggemann, Walter. *Finally Comes the Poet: Daring Speech for Proclamation.* Minneapolis: Fortress Press, 1989.

Chandos, John, ed. *In God's Name: Examples of Preaching in England from the Act of Supremacy to the Act of Uniformity, 1534–1662.* London: Hutchinson of London, 1971.

Crenshaw, James L. *Prophetic Conflict: Its Effect upon Israelite Religion.* Berlin: Walter de Gruyter, 1971.

Hart, I. "Preaching the Account of the Tabernacle." *Evangelical Quarterly* 54 (1982): 111–16.

Hilkert, Mary Catherine. "Preaching and Theology: Rethinking the Relationship." *Worship* 65 (1991): 398–409.

Keck, Leander E. *The Bible in the Pulpit: The Renewal of Biblical Preaching.* Nashville: Abingdon, 1978.

Kelly, Timothy. "Reflections on Preaching and Teaching." *Worship* 53 (1979): 250–64.

Killinger, John. *Fundamentals of Preaching.* Philadelphia: Fortress Press, 1985.

Mason, R. "Some Echoes of the Preaching in the Second Temple?" *Zeitschrift für die alttestmentliche Wissenschaft* 96 (1984): 23–49.

Mellow, John Allyn. "Homily or Eulogy? The Dilemma of Funeral Preaching." *Worship* 67 (1993): 502–18.

———. "Publish or Perish: A Review of Preaching Literature, 1981–1986." *Worship* 62 (1988): 497–514.

Mitchell, W. Fraser. *English Pulpit Oratory from Andrewes to Tillotson: A Study of Its Literary Aspects.* London: SPCK, 1932.

Old, Hughes Oliphant. *The Reading and Preaching of the Scriptures in the Worship of the Christian Church.* Vol. 1, *The Biblical Period.* Grand Rapids: Eerdmans, 1998.

O'Meara, Thomas F. "Forum: What a Bishop Might Want You To Know." *Worship* 68 (1994): 55–63.

Parker, T. H. L. *Calvin's Preaching.* Louisville: Westminster John Knox, 1992.

Rad, Gerhard von. "The Levitical Sermon in 1 and 2 Chronicles." In *The Problem of the Hexateuch and Other Essays,* translated by E. Dicken, 267–80. New York: McGraw-Hill, 1966.

Renz, Christopher J. "Come, Let Us Listen to the Voice of the Lord." *Worship* 70 (1996): 140–53.

Richard, William A. "Preaching the Dark Side of the Gospel." *Worship* 61 (1987): 141–51.

Ridenhour, Thomas E. "The Old Testament and Preaching." *Currents in Theology and Mission* 20 (1993): 253–58.

Senior, Donald. "Scripture and Homiletics: What the Bible Can Teach the Preacher." *Worship* 65 (1991): 386–97.

Skudlarek, William. "Lay Preaching and the Liturgy." *Worship* 58 (1984): 500–506.

Sloyan, Gerard S. "Is Church Teaching Neglected When the Lectionary Is Preached?" *Worship* 61 (1987): 126–40.

———. "Some Thoughts on Liturgical Preaching." *Worship* 71 (1997): 386–99.

Stegner, William Richard. "The Ancient Jewish Synagogue Homily." In *Greco-Roman Literature and the New Testament,* edited by David E. Aune, 51–70. Missoula, MT: Scholars Press, 1988.

Stookey, Laurence Hull. "Marcion, Typology, and Lectionary Preaching." *Worship* 66 (1992): 251–62.

Waznak, Robert P. "The Homily Fulfilled in Our Hearing." *Worship* 65 (1991): 27–37.

———. "The Preacher and the Poet." *Worship* 60 (1986): 46–55.

Willimon, William H. *Preaching About Conflict in the Local Church.* Philadelphia: Westminster, 1987.

Willimon, William H., and Richard Lischer, eds. *Concise Encyclopedia of Preaching.* Louisville: Westminster John Knox, 1995.

Wills, Lawrence. "The Form of the Sermon in Hellenistic Judaism and Early Christianity." *Harvard Theological Review* 17 (1984): 277–99.

Wilson, R. *Prophecy and Society in Ancient Israel.* Philadelphia: Fortress Press, 1980.

## Prayer

Achtemeier, Elizabeth. "Female Language for God: Should the Church Adopt It?" *Transformation,* 24–30. Condensed from "Female Language for God: Should the Church Adopt It?" In *The Hermeneutical Quest: Essays in Honor of James Luther Mays on His Sixty-fifth Birthday,* edited by Donald G. Miller, 97–114. Allison Park, PA: Pickwick Publications, 1986.

Appleton, George, ed. *The Oxford Book of Prayer.* Oxford: Oxford University Press, 1985.

Ap-Thomas, D. R. "Some Aspects of the Root *HNN* in the Old Testament." *Journal of Semitic Studies* 2 (1957): 128–48.

———. "Some Notes on Old Testament Attitude Toward Prayer." *Scottish Theological Review* 9 (1956): 422–29.

Bahr, G. J. "The Use of the Lord's Prayer in the Primitive Church." *Journal of Biblical Literature* 84 (1965):153–59.

Barr, James. "'*ABBA*' Isn't 'Daddy.'" *Journal of Theological Studies* 39 (1988): 28–47.

Blank, Sheldon H. "Some Observations Concerning Biblical Prayer." *Hebrew Union College Annual* 32 (1961): 75–90.

Bondi, Roberta C. *To Pray and to Love: Conversations on Prayer with the Early Church.* Minneapolis: Fortress Press, 1991.

Bounds, E. M. *The Complete Works of E. M. Bounds on Prayer.* Reprint, Grand Rapids: Baker, 1990.

Bradshaw, Paul F. "Whatever Happened to Daily Prayer?" *Worship* 64 (1990): 10–23.

Cunningham, Lawrence S. "Origen's *On Prayer:* A Reflection and Appreciation." *Worship* 67 (1993): 332–39.

Cyster, R. F. "The Lord's Prayer and the Exodus Tradition." *Theology* 64 (1961): 377–81.

Fink, Peter E. "Public and Private Moments in Christian Prayer." *Worship* 58 (1984): 482–99.

Ford, J. Massyngberde. "The Forgiveness Clause in the Matthean Form of the Our Father." *Zeitschrift für die neutestamentliche Wissenschaft und die Kunde der älteren Kirche* 59 (1968): 127–31.

———. "Yom Kippur and the Matthean Form of the Pater Noster." *Worship* 41 (1967): 609–19.

Griffiss, James E. *Naming the Mystery: How Our Words Shape Prayer and Belief.* Cambridge, MA: Cowley, 1990.

Hughson, Shirley C. *Contemplative Prayer.* London: SPCK, 1935.

Janzen, J. Gerald. "Prayer and/as Self-Address: The Case of Hannah." In *A God So Near: Essays on Old Testament Theology in Honor of Patrick D. Miller,* edited by Brent A. Strawn and Nancy R. Bowen, 113–17. Winona Lake, IN: Eisenbrauns, 2003.

Jones, B. W. "The Prayer of Daniel 9." *Vetus Testamentum* 18 (1968): 488–93.

Knoll, I. "Between Voice and Silence: The Relationship Between Prayer and Temple Cult." *Journal of Biblical Literature* 85 (1966): 17–30.

Lacocque, A. "The Liturgical Prayer of Daniel 9." *Hebrew Union College Annual* 47 (1976): 119–42.

Manson, T. W. "The Lord's Prayer." *Bulletin of the John Rylands University Library of Manchester* 38 (1955–56): 99–113.

McDonnell, Kilian. "Prayer in Ancient Western Tradition." *Worship* 55 (1981): 34–61.

Merton, Thomas. *Praying the Psalms.* Collegeville, MN: Liturgical Press, 1956.

Miller, Patrick D. *They Cried to the Lord: The Form and Theology of Biblical Prayer.* Minneapolis: Fortress Press, 1994.

Mowinckel, Sigmund. "The Intercession of the Covenant Mediator (Exodus 33:1a,12–17)." In *Words and Meanings: Essays Presented to David Winton Thomas,* edited by P. Ackroyd and B. Lindars, 159–81. Cambridge: Cambridge University Press, 1968.

Nugent, Robert. *Prayer Journey for Persons with Aids.* Cincinnati: St. Anthony Messenger Press, 1989.

Petuchowski, Jakob J., and Michal Brocke, eds. *The Lord's Prayer and Jewish Liturgy.* London: Burns and Oates, 1978.

Rainsford, Marcus. *Our Lord Prays for His Own.* Chicago: Moody, n.d.

Reif, Stefan C. *Judaism and Hebrew Prayer. New Perspectives in Jewish Liturgical History.* Cambridge: Cambridge University Press, 1993.

Saliers, Don E. "The Integrity of Sung Prayers." *Worship* 55 (1981): 290–303.

Seasoltz, R. Kevin. "Peace: Belief, Prayer and Life." *Worship* 56 (1982): 152–72.

Steere, Douglas V. "Solitude and Prayer." *Worship* 55 (1981): 120–36.

Stuhlman, Byron D. *Redeeming the Time: An Historical and Theological Study of the Church's Rule of Prayer and the Regular Services of the Church.* New York: Church Hymnal Corporation, 1992.

Thielicke, Helmut. *Our Heavenly Father: Sermons on the Lord's Prayer.* Grand Rapids: Baker, 1960.

Trenholme, E. C. "The Lesser Hours." In *Liturgy and Worship: A Companion to the Prayer Books of the Anglican Communion,* edited by W. K. Lowther Clarke, 685–89. London: SPCK, 1982.

Viviers, Hendrek. "The Coherence of the *ma'ălôt* Psalms (Pss 120–134)." *Zeitschrift für die alttestmentliche Wissenschaft* 106 (1994): 275–89.

Yamauchi, E. M. "The 'Daily Bread' Motif in Antiquity." *Westminster Theological Journal* 28 (1966): 145–56.

## Holy Communion

Alonso-Schockel, Luis. *Celebrating the Eucharist: Biblical Meditations.* Translated by John Deehan and Patrick Fitzgerald-Lombard. New York: Crossroad, 1989.

Bahr, G. J. "The Seder of Passover and the Eucharistic Words." *Novum Testamentum* 12 (1970): 181–202.

Bynum, Caroline Walker. *Holy Feast and Holy Fast: The Religious Significance of Food to Medieval Women.* Berkeley: University of California Press, 1987.

Crichton, J. D. *Christian Celebration: The Prayer of the Church.* London: Chapman, 1976.

Dahl, Nils A. *Jesus in the Memory of the Early Church.* Minneapolis: Augsburg, 1976.

Daly, R. J. "The Eucharist and Redemption: The Last Supper and Jesus' Understanding of His Death." *Biblical Theology Bulletin* 11 (1981): 21–27.

Davies, Horton M. *Bread of Life and Cup of Joy.* Grand Rapids: Eerdmans, 1993.

Dollar, George. "The Lord's Supper in the Second Century." *Bibliotheca Sacra* 117 (1960): 144–54.

———. "The Lord's Supper in the Third Century." *Bibliotheca Sacra* 117 (1960): 249–57.

———. "Views on the Lord's Supper in the Fourth and Fifth Centuries." *Bibliotheca Sacra* 117 (1960): 342–49.

Emerton, J. A. "The Aramaic Underlying *to haima mou tes diatheke* in Mk xiv, 24." *Journal of Theological Studies* 6 (1955): 238–40.

Flusser, David. "The Last Supper and the Essenes." *Immanuel* 3 (1973): 23–27.

Gregg, D. W. A. *Anamnesis in the Eucharist.* Nottingham: Grove, 1996.

Heron, Alasdair I. C. *Table and Tradition: Towards an Ecumenical Understanding of the Eucharist.* Philadelphia: Westminster, 1983.

Jeremias, Joachim. *The Eucharistic Words of Jesus.* Philadelphia: Fortress Press, 1966.

Keating, J. F. *The Agape and the Eucharist in the Early Church: Studies in the History of the Christian Love-Feasts.* New York: AMS Press, 1969.

Keenan, Joseph. "Tea and Eucharist." *Worship* 56 (1982):365–84.

King, Archdale A. *Concelebration in the Christian Church.* London: A. R. Mowbray, 1966.

Lietzmann, Hans. *Mass and the Lord's Supper: A Study in the History of Liturgy.* Leiden: E. J. Brill, 1979.

Maccoby, H. "Paul and the Eucharist." *New Testament Studies* 37 (1991): 247–67.

Macy, Gary. *The Banquet's Wisdom: A Short History of the Theologies of the Lord's Supper.* New York: Paulist Press, 1992.

Marshall, I. Howard. *Last Supper and Lord's Supper.* Grand Rapids: Eerdmans, 1981.

Martmort, A. G., ed. *The Church at Prayer: The Eucharist.* Shannon: Irish University Press, 1973.

Maurice, F. D. *The Doctrine of Sacrifice Deduced from the Scriptures.* London: Macmillan, 1893.

Miller, Mark. "The Sacrificial Theology of Hans Urs von Balthasar." *Worship* 64 (1990): 48–66.

Murphy-O'Connor, Jerome. "Eucharist and Community in First Corinthians." *Worship* 51 (1977): 56–69.

Nelson, J. Robert. "What Methodists Think of Eucharistic Theology." *Worship* 52 (1978): 409–24.

Packer, J. I., ed. *Eucharistic Sacrifice.* London: Church Book Room Press, 1962.

Power, David N. "Words That Crack: The Uses of 'Sacrifice' in Eucharistic Discourse." *Worship* 53 (1979): 386–404.

Powers, Joseph M. *Eucharistic Theology.* New York: Seabury, 1967.

Rordorf, Willy, et al. *The Eucharist of the Early Christians.* Translated by Matthew J. O'Connell. New York: Pueblo, 1978.

Routledge, Robin. "Passover and the Last Supper." *Tyndale Bulletin* 53 (2002): 203–21.

Schurmann, H. "Jesus' Words in the Light of His Actions at the Last Supper." In *The Breaking of Bread. Concilium* 40, 119–31. New York: Paulist Press, 1969.

Stebbins, J. Michael. "The Eucharistic Presence of Christ: Mystery and Meaning." *Worship* 64 (1990): 225–36.

Sykes, M. "The Eucharist as 'Anamnesis.'" *Expository Times* 71 (1959–60): 115–18.

Wainwright, Geoffrey. *Eucharist and Eschatology.* London: Epworth Press, 1971.

Watkins, Keith. "Eucharist, American Style." *Worship* 56 (1982): 401–11.

Young, Francis M. *Sacrifice and the Death of Christ.* London: SPCK, 1975.

## Sacred Calendar

Beckwith, Roger T., and Wilfrid Stott. *This Is the Day: The Biblical Doctrine of the Christian Sunday in Its Jewish and Early Christian Setting.* London: Marshall, Morgan and Scott, 1978.

Caird, William R. *Notes on the Feasts of the Lord: As Prescribed to the Jews and Their Bearing upon the Faith and Hope of the Christian Church.* London: Thomas Bosworth, 1884.

Edwards, Tilden H., Jr. "The Christian Sabbath: Its Promise Today as a Basic Spiritual Discipline." *Worship* 56 (1982): 2–15.

Hoehner, Harold. *Chronological Aspects of the Life of Christ.* Grand Rapids: Zondervan, 1977.

Nelson, Robert. *A Companion to the Festivals and Fasts of the Church of England.* 1704.

Rowe, Barbara, et al. *Silent Voices, Sacred Lives: Women's Readings for the Liturgical Year.* New York: Paulist Press, 1992.

Talley, Thomas J. *The Origins of the Liturgical Year.* Collegeville, MN: Liturgical Press, 1986.

Yee, Gale A. *Jewish Feasts and the Gospel of John.* Wilmington, DE: Michael Glazier, 1989.

## Music and Praise

Adey, Lionel. *Class and Idol in the English Hymn.* Vancouver: University of British Columbia Press, 1988.

Anderson, Bernhard W. *Out of the Depths.* Philadelphia: Westminster, 1983.

Apel, Willi. *The History of Keyboard Music to 1700.* Bloomington, IN: Indiana University Press, 1972.

Bailey, Albert Edward. *The Gospel in Hymns.* New York: Charles Scribner's Sons, 1950.

Benson, Louis F. *The English Hymn.* Philadelphia: Presbyterian Board of Publications, 1915.

Berger, Teresa, *Theology in Hymns? A Study of the Relationship of Doxology and Theology According to a Collection of Hymns for the Use of a People Called Methodist.* Nashville: Abingdon, 1995.

Bicknell, S. *The History of the English Organ.* Cambridge: Cambridge University Press, 1996.

Bishop, Selma L. *Isaac Watts Hymns and Spiritual Songs (1707).* Ann Arbor, MI: Pierian Press, 1974.

Blume, Friedrich. *Protestant Church Music: A History.* New York: W. W. Norton, 1974.

Boyd, Malcolm. *Bach.* London: Dent, 1983.

Braun, Joachim. *Music in Ancient Israel/Palestine.* Grand Rapids: Eerdmans, 2002.

Brown, Deirdre. "The Contemporary Composer and Liturgical Reform." *Worship* 61 (1987): 16–24.

Bruce, F. F. "The 'Christ Hymn' of Colossians 1:15–20." *Bibliotheca Sacra* 141 (1984): 99–111.

Brueggemann, Walter. *Israel's Praise: Doxology against Idolatry and Ideology.* Philadelphia: Fortress Press, 1988.

Bumpus, John. *A History of English Cathedral Music.* London: T. Werner Laurie, n.d.

Burton, Adrian. "'Till in Heaven . . .' Wesleyan Models for Liturgical Theology." *Worship* 71 (1997): 309–17.

Burton, Gregory. "Music and Rhetoric in Early Seventeenth-Century English Sources." *Musical Quarterly* 66 (1980): 53–64.

Butler, T. C. "A Forgotten Passage from a Forgotten Era (1 Chron xvi 8–36)." *Vetus Testamentum* 28 (1978): 142–50.

Charlesworth, J. H. "Jewish Hymns, Odes and Prayers (167 B.C.E.–C.E. 135)." In

*Early Judaism and Its Modern Interpreters,* edited by R. A. Kraft and G. W. E. Nickelsburg, 411–36. Atlanta: Scholars Press, 1986.

————. "Prolegomenon to a New Study of the Jewish Background of the Hymns and Prayers in the New Testament." *Journal of Jewish Studies* 33 (1982): 266–84.

Childs, Brevard S. *Memory and Tradition.* Naperville, IL: Alec R. Allenson, 1962.

Coddaire, Louis, and Louis Weil. "The Use of the Psalter in Worship." *Worship* 52 (1978): 342–48.

Cone, James. *The Spirituals and the Blues.* Maryknoll, NY.: Orbis, 1991.

Crawford, Richard. *The Core Repertory of Early American Psalmody.* Madison, WI: A-R Editions, 1984.

Crichton, J. D. *Prayer and Singing.* London: Collins Liturgical, 1980.

Davidson, Robert. *The Vitality of Worship: A Commentary on the Book of Psalms.* Grand Rapids: Eerdmans, 1998.

Dean, Talmage W. *A Survey of Twentieth Century Protestant Christian Music in America.* Nashville: Broadman, 1988.

Dixon, Christa K. *Negro Spirituals: From Bible to Folksong.* Philadelphia: Fortress Press, 1976.

Dixon, Graham. "Handel's Music for the Carmelites." *Early Christian Music* 15 (1987): 16–29.

Donnelly, Doris. "Impediments to Praise in the Worshiping Community." *Worship* 66 (1992): 39–53.

Eaton, J. H. "Music's Place in Worship: A Contribution from the Psalms." *Old Testament Studies* 23 (1984): 85–107.

Ellsberg, Margaret R. *Created to Praise: The Language of Gerard Manley Hopkins.* New York: Oxford University Press, 1987.

Eskew, Harry, and Hugh T. McElrath. *Sing with Understanding: An Introduction to Christian Hymnology.* Nashville: Broadman, 1980.

*A Facsimile Reprint of the First Edition of the Bay Psalm Book.* New York: Burt Franklin, 1973.

Finesinger, S. B. "Musical Instruments in the Old Testament." *Hebrew Union College Annual* 3 (1926): 21–76.

————. "The Shofar." *Hebrew Union College Annual* 8–9 (1931–32):193–228.

Flusser, David. "Jewish Roots of the Liturgical Trisagion." *Immanuel* 3 (1973–74): 37–43.

Flynn, William T. *Medieval Music as Medieval Exegesis.* Lanham, MD: Scarecrow Press, 1999.

Foley, Edward. "The Cantor in Historical Perspective." *Worship* 56 (1982): 194–213.

Foote, Henry Wilder. *Three Centuries of American Hymnody.* Cambridge, MA: Harvard University Press, 1940.

Gelineau, Joseph, S.J. "Music and Singing in the Liturgy." In *The Study of Liturgy,* edited by Cheslyn Jones, 493–507. New York: Oxford University Press, 1992.

Gray, J. "A Cantata of the Autumn Festival, Psalm LXVIII." *Journal of Semitic Studies* 22 (1977): 2–26.

Gunn, George S. *Singers of Israel.* New York: Abingdon, 1963.

Halmo, Joan. "Advent Insights in Bach's Cantatas." *Worship* 64 (1990): 510–22.

———. "Hymns for the Paschal Traduum." *Worship* 55 (1981): 137–59.

Harvey, John. "A New Look at the Christ Hymn in Phil. 2:6–11." *Expository Times* 76 (1965): 337–39.

Hayes, J. H. *Understanding the Psalms.* Valley Forge, PA: Judson Press, 1976.

Hill, Andrew E. *Enter His Courts with Praise! Old Testament Worship for the New Testament Church.* Grand Rapids: Baker, 1993.

———. "Patchwork Poetry or Reasoned Verse? Connective Structure in 1 Chronicles xvi." *Vetus Testamentum* 33 (1983): 97–101.

Hill, Edmund. *Prayer, Praise, and Politics.* London: Sheed and Ward, 1973.

Hoffman, Lawrence A., and Janet R. Walton. *Sacred Sound and Social Change.* Notre Dame, IN: University of Notre Dame Press, 1992.

Holladay, William L. *The Psalms Through Three Thousand Years: Prayerbook of a Cloud of Witnesses.* Minneapolis: Fortress Press, 1993.

Hustad, Donald P. "Church Music: The Pastor's Responsibility." *Bibliotheca Sacra* 118 (1961): 8–22.

———. "Developing a Biblical Philosophy of Music," *Bibliotheca Sacra* 117 (1960): 108–22.

———. *Jubilate! Church Music in the Evangelical Tradition.* Carol Stream, IL: Hope, 1981.

———. "Music for Worship, Evangelism, and Christian Education," *Bibliotheca Sacra* 117 (1960): 301–22.

———. "Problems in Psychology and Aesthetics in Music," *Bibliotheca Sacra* 117 (1960):214–28.

Kelly, T. F. "Introducing the *Gloria in Excelsis.*" *Journal of the American Musicological Society* 37 (1984): 479–506.

Keyte, Hugh, and Andrew Parrott, eds. *The New Oxford Book of Carols.* Oxford: Oxford University Press, 1992.

Kleinig, John W. *The Lord's Song: The Basis, Function and Significance of Choral Music in Chronicles*. Sheffield, UK: Sheffield Academic Press, 1993.

Lamb, John A. *The Psalms in Christian Worship*. London: Faith Press, 1962.

Lamb, Robin A. "Bach and Pietism." *Concordia Theological Quarterly* 55 (1991): 5–22.

———. *J. S. Bach as Preacher: His Passions and Music in Worship*. St. Louis: Concordia, 1982.

Leaver, Robin A. "English Metrical Psalmody." In *The Hymnal 1982 Companion*, edited by Raymond F. Glover, 321–48. New York: Church Hymnal Corporation, 1990.

———. "Theological Dimensions of Mission Hymnody: The Counterpoint of Cult and Culture." *Worship* 62 (1988): 316–31.

Lewis, C. S. *Reflections on the Psalms*. New York: Harcourt, Brace, and World, 1958.

Luff, Alan. *Welsh Hymns and Their Tunes*. Carol Stream, IL: Hope, 1990.

McKinnon, James. "The Fourth Century Origin of the Gradual." In *Early Music History* 7, edited by Iain Fenton, 91–106. Cambridge: Cambridge University Press, 1987.

———. *Music in Early Christian Literature*. Cambridge: Cambridge University Press, 1987.

Meyers, Carol L. "The Drum-Dance-Song Ensemble: Women's Performance in Biblical Israel." In *Rediscovering the Muses: Women's Musical Tradition*, edited by Kimberly Marshall, 49–67. Boston: Northeastern University Press, 1993.

Miller, J. M. "The Korahites of Southern Judah." *Catholic Biblical Quarterly* 32 (1970): 58–68.

Minear, Paul S. *Death Set to Music: Masterworks by Bach, Brahms, Penderecki, Bernstein*. Atlanta: John Knox, 1987.

Moore, James H. "The Liturgical Use of the Organ in Seventeenth-Century Italy: New Documents, New Hypotheses." In *Frescobaldi Studies: Sources of Music and Their Interpretation*, edited by Alexander Silbiger, 351–83. Durham: Duke University Press, 1987.

Mowinckel, Sigmund. *The Psalms and Israel's Worship*. Nashville: Abingdon, 1960.

Newman, David R. *Worship as Praise and Empowerment*. New York: Pilgrim Press, 1988.

Pelikan, Jaroslav. *Bach Among the Theologians*. Philadelphia: Fortress Press, 1986.

Plank, Steven. *"The Way to Heavens Doore": An Introduction to Liturgical and Musical Style.* London: Scarecrow Press, 1994.

Pottie, Charles S., S.J. *A More Profound Alleluia! Gelineau and Routley on Music in Christian Worship.* Washington, DC: Pastoral Press, 1984.

Power, David N. "Doxology: The Praise of God in Worship, Doctrine, and Life." *Worship* 55 (1981): 61–69.

*The Psalter: Psalms and Canticles for Singing.* Louisville: Westminster John Knox Press, 1993.

Quasten, Johannes. *Music and Worship in Pagan and Christian Antiquity.* Translated by B. Ramsey. Washington, DC: Pastoral Press, 1983.

Reynolds, William Jensen. *A Joyful Sound: Christian Hymnody.* 2d ed. New York: Holt, Rinehart, and Winston, 1978.

———. *A Survey of Christian Hymnody.* New York: Holt, Rinehart, and Winston, 1963.

Routley, Erik. *Church Music and the Christian Faith.* Carol Stream, IL: Agape, 1978.

———. *The Church and Music.* London: Duckworth, 1978.

———. *I'll Praise My Maker: A Study of the Hymns of Certain Authors Who Stand In or Near the Tradition of English Calvinism, 1700–1850.* London: Independent Press, 1951.

Royal, Samuel. *A General Introduction to Hymnody and Congregational Song.* Lanham, MD: Scarecrow Press, 1991.

Schnoebelen, Anne. "The Role of the Violin in the Resurgence of the Mass in the Seventeenth Century." *Early Music* 18 (1990): 537–42.

Sellers, Ovid R. "Musical Instruments of Israel." In *Biblical Archaeologist Reader,* edited by George Ernest Wright and David Noel Freedman, 1:81–94. New York: Doubleday, 1961.

Smith, John A. "The Ancient Synagogue, the Early Church, and Singing." *Music and Letters* 65 (1984): 1–16.

Smolden, W. L. "The Melodies of the Medieval Church Dramas and Their Significance." *Comparative Drama* 2 (1968): 185–209.

Stackhouse, Rochelle A. *The Language of the Psalms in Worship: American Revisions of Watts' Psalter.* Lanham, MD: Scarecrow Press, 1997.

Sternhold, T. and I. Hopkins. *The Whole Book of Psalms Collected into English Meter.* London: Company of Stationers, 1618.

Thompson, Thelma B. *The Seventeenth-Century English Hymn: A Mode for Sacred and Secular Concerns.* New York: Peter Lang, 1989.

*In Tune with Heaven: The Report of the Archbishop's Commission on Church Music.* London: Hodder & Stoughton, 1992.

Van Deusen, Nancy. *The Harp and the Soul: Platonic Symbolism in Trecento Art and Music.* Lewiston, NY: Edwin Mellen, 1989.

Wainwright, Geoffrey. *Doxology: The Praise of God in Worship, Doctrine, and Life: A Systematic Theology.* London: Oxford University Press, 1980.

Walton, John H. "The Psalms: A Cantata About the Davidic Covenant." *Journal of the Evangelical Theological Society* 34 (1991): 21–31.

Watson, J. R. *The English Hymn: A Critical and Historical Study.* Oxford: Clarendon Press, 1998.

Werner, Eric. "'If I Speak in the Tongues of Men . . .': St. Paul's Attitude to Music." *Journal of the American Musicological Society* 13 (1960): 18–32.

———. "The Doxology in Synagogue and Church: A Liturgico-Musical Study." *Hebrew Union College Annual* 19 (1945–46): 275–351.

———. *The Sacred Bridge: The Interdependence of Liturgy and Music in Synagogue and Church During the First Millennium.* New York: Columbia University Press, 1959.

———. *The Sacred Bridge.* Vol. 2. New York: KTAV, 1985.

Wesley, John. *Collection of Psalms and Hymns.* Charlestown: Lewis Timothy, 1737. Facsimile reprint, Nashville: United Methodist Publishing House, 1988.

Westermann, Claus. *Blessing in the Bible and in the Life of the Church.* Philadelphia: Fortress Press, 1978.

———. *The Praise of God in the Psalms.* Translated by Keith R. Crim. Richmond: John Knox, 1961.

Westrup, J. A. *Purcell.* New York: Collier, 1962.

Wilson-Dickson, Andrew. *The Story of Christian Music.* Oxford: Lion, 1992.

Wituliet, John D. *Worship Seeking Understanding.* Grand Rapids: Baker, 2003.

Worst, John, and David P. Schaap, eds. *Hymns for Worship, Meditation, and Praise.* New Brunswick, NJ: Selah, 1989.

Zimmermann, Franklin. *The Anthems of Henry Purcell.* New York: American Choral Foundation, 1971.

## Art and Symbolism in Worship

Addleshaw, G., and F. Etchells. *The Architectural Setting of Anglican Worship.* London: Faber and Faber, 1948.

Anderson, A. "Building and Cherishing: Cathedrals as Buildings." In *Flagships of the Spirit: Cathedrals in Society,* edited by S. Platten and C. Lewis, 90–104. London: Darton, Longman, and Todd, 1998.

Barth, K. "The Architectural Problem of Protestant Places of Worship." In *Architecture in Worship*, edited by A. Bieler, 92–93. Edinburgh: Oliver and Boyd, 1965.

Benson, George Willard. *The Cross: Its History and Symbolism*. New York: Hacker Art Books, 1976.

Brown, D., and A. Loades. *The Sense of the Sacramental: Movement and Measure in Art and Music, Place and Time*. London: SPCK, 1995.

Cope, Gilbert. *Symbolism in the Bible and the Church*. London SCM, 1959.

Dillenberger, John. *A Theology of Artistic Sensibilities*. London: SCM, 1986.

Eco, U. *Art and Beauty in the Middle Ages*. New Haven: Yale University Press, 1986.

Finney, Paul Corby. *The Invisible God: The Earliest Christians on Art*. New York: Oxford University Press, 1994.

Freedberg, David. *The Power of Images: Studies in the History and Theory of Response*. Chicago: University of Chicago Press, 1989.

Guiver, G. *Pursuing the Mystery: Worship and Daily Life as Presences of God*. London: SPCK, 1996.

Hall, James. *Dictionary of Subjects and Symbols in Art*. Revised edition. New York: Harper & Row, 1979.

Irvine, Christopher and Anne Dawtry. *Art and Worship*. Collegeville, MN: Liturgical Press, 2002.

Kelly, J. "Church Architecture: Whose End Is Being Served?" *Church Building* 60 (2000): 54–55.

Ladner, Gerhart B. *God, Cosmos, and Humankind: The World of Early Christian Symbolism*. Translated by Thomas Dunlap. Berkeley: University of California Press, 1992.

Limouris, Gennadios, comp. *Icons: Windows in Eternity: Theology and Spirituality in Colour*. Geneva: WCC Publications, 1990.

Maltby, J. *Prayer Book and People in Elizabethan and Early Stuart England*. Cambridge: Cambridge University Press, 1998.

Martin, E. David. *Art and the Religious Experience: The "Language of the Sacred."* Lewisburg, NJ: Bucknell University Press, 1972.

Miller, Madeleine S. *A Treasury of the Cross*. New York: Harper & Brothers, 1956.

Milton, A. *Catholic and Reformed: The Roman and Protestant Churches in English Protestant Thought, 1600–1640*. Cambridge: Cambridge University Press, 1995.

Regan, Patrick. "Veneration of the Cross." *Worship* 52 (1978): 2–12.

Ross, Susan A. "The Aesthetic and the Sacramental." *Worship* 59 (1985): 2–17.

Rouet, A. *Liturgy and the Arts.* Collegeville, MN: Liturgical Press, 1998.

Smith, Jeffrey C. *Sensuous Worship: Jesuits and the Art of the Early Catholic Reformation in Germany.* Princeton: Princeton University Press, 2002.

Spencer, Aida. "The Bible as Apologetic for Art." In *God Through the Looking Glass,* edited by W. D. Spencer and A. B. Spencer, 17–28. Grand Rapids: Baker; Carlisle, Cumbriar, UK: Paternoster, 1998.

Stafford, Thomas A. *Christian Symbolism in the Evangelical Churches.* Nashville: Abingdon, 1942.

Viladesau, Richard. *Theological Aesthetics: God in Imagination, Beauty, and Art.* New York: Oxford University Press, 1999.

## Worship in Heaven

Achtemeier, P. J. "Revelation 5:1–14." *Interpretation* 40 (1986): 283–88.

Barr, David L. "The Apocalypse of John as Oral Enactment." *Interpretation* 40 (1986): 243–56.

Barrett, C. K. "The Lamb of God." *New Testament Studies* 1 (1954–55): 210–18.

Bauckham, R. J. *The Climax of Prophecy: Studies in the Book of Revelation.* Edinburgh: T. & T. Clark, 1991.

————. "The Worship of Jesus in Apocalyptic Christianity." *New Testament Studies* 27 (1980–81): 322–41.

Beale, G. K. *The Use of Daniel in Jewish Apocalyptic Literature and in the Revelation of John.* Lanham, MD: University Press of America, 1984.

Bockmuehl, Markus N. A. "'The Trumpet Shall Sound': *Shofar* Symbolism and Its Reception in Early Christianity." In *Templum Amicitiae: Essays on the Second Temple Presented to Ernst Bammel,* edited by William Horbury, 199–225. Journal for the Study of the New Testament: Supplement Series 48. Sheffield, UK: JSOT Press, 1991.

Boring, M. Eugene. "The Theology of Revelation: 'The Lord Our God the Almighty Reigns.'" *Interpretation* 40 (1986): 257–69.

Brown, S. "The Priestly Character of the Church in the Apocalypse." *New Testament Studies* 5 (1958–59): 224–31.

Bruce, F. F. "The Spirit in the Apocalypse." In *Christ and Spirit in the New Testament: Festschrift for C. F. D. Moule,* edited by B. Lindars and S. Smalley, 333–44. Cambridge: Cambridge University Press, 1973.

Cabaniss, Allen. "A Note on the Liturgy of the Apocalypse." *Interpretation* 7 (1953): 78–86.

Charles, J. D. "An Apocalyptic Tribute to the Lamb (Re 5:1–14)." *Journal of the Evangelical Theological Society* 34 (1991): 461–73.

———. "Imperial Pretensions and the Throne-Vision of the Lamb: Observations on the Function of Revelation 5." *Criswell Theological Review* 7 (1993): 85–97.

Cody, A. *Heavenly Sanctuary and Liturgy in the Epistle to the Hebrews.* St. Meinrad, IN: Grail Publications, 1960.

Coleman, R. E. *Songs of Heaven.* Old Tappan, NJ: Revell, 1980.

Collins, Adela Yarbro. "Reading the Book of Revelation in the Twentieth Century." *Interpretation* 40 (1986): 229–41.

———. "The Seven Heavens in Jewish and Christian Apocalypses." In *Cosmology and Eschatology in Jewish and Christian Apocalypticism,* edited by Adela Yarbro Collins, 21–54. Leiden: E. J. Brill, 1996.

———. "The 'Son of Man' Tradition in the Book of Revelation." In *The Messiah: Developments in Earliest Judaism and Christianity,* edited by J. H. Charlesworth, 536–68. Minneapolis: Fortress Press, 1992.

Cruz, V. P. "The Beatitudes of the Apocalypse: Eschatology and Ethics." In *Perspectives on Christology: Essays in Honor of Paul K. Jewett,* edited by Marguerite Shuster and Richard A. Muller, 269–83. Grand Rapids: Zondervan, 1991.

Davis, R. Dean. *The Heavenly Court Judgment of Revelation 4–5.* Lanham, MD: University Press of America, 1992.

Draper, J. A. "The Heavenly Feast of Tabernacles (Rev. 7:1–17)." *Journal for the Study of the New Testament* 19 (1983): 133–47.

D'Souza, J. *The Lamb of God in the Johannine Writings.* Allahabad: St. Paul Publications, 1968.

Hall, R. G. "Living Creatures in the Midst of the Throne: Another Look at Revelation 4:6." *New Testament Studies* 36 (1990): 609–13.

Hengel, M. "Hymns and Christology." In *Between Jesus and Paul: Studies in the Earliest History of Christianity,* edited by M. Hengel, 78–96. Philadelphia: Fortress Press, 1983.

Hillyer, N. "'The Lamb in the Apocalypse." *Evangelical Quarterly* 39 (1967): 228–36.

Jart, U. "The Precious Stones in the Revelation of John 21:18–21." *Studia Theologica* 24 (1970): 150–81.

Jeske, R. L. "Spirit and Community in the Johannine Apocalypse." *New Testament Studies* 31 (1998): 452–66.

Kelly, Balmer H. "Revelation 7:9–17." *Interpretation* 40 (1986): 290–94.

Kooy, V. H. "The Apocalypse and Worship: Some Preliminary Observations." *Reformed Review* 30 (1977): 198–209.

Mowry, Lucetta. "Revelation 4–5 and Early Christian Liturgical Usage." *Journal of Biblical Literature* 71 (1952): 75–84.

O'Rourke, J. J. "The Hymns of the Apocalypse." *Catholic Biblical Quarterly* 30 (1968): 389–409.

Piper, Otto. "The Apocalypse of John and the Liturgy of the Ancient Church." *Church History* 20 (1951): 10–22.

Raber, Rudolph W. "Revelation 21:1–8." *Interpretation* 40 (1986): 296–301.

Rowland, C. "The Visions of God in Apocalyptic Literature." *Journal of Semitic Studies* 10 (1980): 137–54.

Scott, R. B. Y. "Behold He Cometh with Clouds." *New Testament Studies* 5 (1958–59): 127–32.

Shepherd, Massey H. *The Paschal Liturgy and the Apocalypse.* Richmond: John Knox, 1960.

Siegman, E. "Apocalypse." In *The New Catholic Encyclopedia,* 1:659. New York: McGraw-Hill, 1967.

Trites, Allison A. "*Martus* and Martyrdom in the Apocalypse: A Semantic Study." *Novum Testamentum* 15 (1973): 72–80.

Unnik, W. C. van. "'Worthy Is the Lamb': The Background of Apoc. 5." In *Mélanges Bibliques en Hommage au R. P. Beda Rigaux,* edited by A. Descamps et al., 445–61. Gembloux: Ducolot, 1970.

Wong, Daniel K. "The Tree of Life in Revelation 2:7." *Bibliotheca Sacra* 155 (1998): 211–26.

## Variations of Worship

Adams, Doug. "Free Church Worship in America from 1620 to 1835." *Worship* 55 (1981): 436–40.

Bradshaw, Paul F., and Lawrence A. Hoffman, eds. *The Changing Face of Jewish and Christian Worship in North America.* Notre Dame, IN: University of Notre Dame Press, 1991.

———, eds. *The Making of Jewish and Christian Worship.* Notre Dame, IN: University of Notre Dame Press, 1991.

Carroll, Jackson W., ed. *Small Churches Are Beautiful.* New York: Harper & Row, 1977.

Davies, Horton M. *The Worship of the American Puritans, 1629–1730.* New York: Peter Lang, 1990.

———. *The Worship of the English Puritans.* London: Dacre Press, 1948.

Fleming, A. *Prayerbook for Engaged Couples.* Chicago: Liturgy Training Publications, 1990.

Fuller, Reginald, H. "Lectionary for Funerals." *Worship* 56 (1982): 36–63.

———. "Lectionary for Weddings." *Worship* 55 (1981): 244–59.

Greenberg, Irving. *The Jewish Way: Living the Holidays.* New York: Summit Books, 1988.

Halmo, John. "Planning Lent, Triduum, Eastertime: A Survey of Pastoral Guidebooks." *Worship* 56 (1982): 16–27.

Hinson, E. Glenn. "Reassessing the Puritan Heritage in Worship and Spirituality: A Search for Method." *Worship* 53 (1979): 318–26.

Hovda, Robert, ed. *This Far By Faith: American Black Worship and Its African Roots,* Washington, DC: Liturgical Conference, 1977.

Jong, James A. De. *Into His Presence.* Grand Rapids: Board of Publications of the Christian Reformed Church, 1985.

Karp, Abraham. *The Jewish Way of Life.* Englewood, NJ: Prentice Hall, 1967.

Klein, Isaac. *A Guide to Jewish Religious Practice.* New York: Jewish Theological Seminary of America, 1979.

Krapohl, Robert H., and Charles H. Lippy. *The Evangelicals: A Historical, Theological, and Bibliographical Guide.* Westport, CT: Greenwood Press, 1999. [See esp. chap. 13: "To God Be the Glory: Evangelical Worship and Music," 170–79.]

Lampe, G. W. H. *The Seal of the Spirit: A Study in the Doctrine of Baptism and Confirmation in the New Testament and the Fathers.* 2d ed. London: SPCK, 1967.

MacLeod, Donald. *Presbyterian Worship: Its Meaning and Method.* Richmond, VA: John Knox, 1966.

Martinez, German. "Marriage as Worship: A Theological Analogy." *Worship* 62 (1988): 332–53.

———. *Worship: Wedding to Marriage.* Washington: Pastoral Press, 1993.

McCullough, Donald W. *The Trivialization of God: The Dangerous Illusion of a Manageable Deity.* Colorado Springs, CO: NavPress, 1995.

McDonnell, Kilian. "The Baptism of Jesus in the Jordan and the Descent into Hell." *Worship* 69 (1995): 98–109.

———. "Jesus' Baptism in the Jordan." *Theological Studies* 56 (1995): 209–36.

McKenna, John H. "Infant Baptism: Theological Reflection." *Worship* 70 (1996): 194–210.

Melton, Julius. *Presbyterian Worship in America*. Richmond, VA: John Knox Press, 1967.

Middleton-Stewart, Judith. *Inward Purity and Outward Splendour: Death and Remembrance in the Deanery of Dunwich, Suffolk, 1370–1547*. Woodbridge, Suffolk: Boydell Press, 2001.

Miller, Paul M. "Worship Among the Early Anabaptists." *Mennonite Quarterly Review* 30 (1956): 235.

Millgram, Abraham. *Jewish Worship*. Philadelphia: Jewish Publication Society of America, 1971.

Old, Hughes Oliphant. *The Patristic Roots of Reformed Worship*. Zurich: Theologischer Verlag Zurich, 1975.

Phifer, Kenneth M. *A Protestant Case for Liturgical Renewal*. Philadelphia: Westminster Press, 1965.

Pottebaum, Gerard A., P. Freeburg, and Joyce M. Kelleher. *A Little Child Shall Lead Them: Guide to Celebrating the Word with Children*. Loveland, OH: Treehaus Communications, 1992.

Senn, Frank C. "Protestant Worship: Does It Exist?" *Worship* 64 (1990): 322–30.

———. "'Worship Alive': An Analysis and Critique of 'Alternative Worship Services.'" *Worship* 69 (1995): 194–224.

Sparkes, Robert, and Richard Rutherford. "The Order of Christian Funerals: A Study in Bereavement and Lament." *Worship* 60 (1986): 499–510.

Spinks, Bryan, and Iain Torrance, eds. *To Glorify God: Essays on Modern Reformed Liturgy*. Edinburgh: T. & T. Clark, 1999.

Stevenson, Kenneth. *Nuptial Blessings: A Study of Christian Marriage Rites*. London: SPCK, 1982.

Walker, Michael. "Baptism: Doctrine and Practice Among Baptists in the United Kingdom." *Worship* 52 (1978): 46–67.

Watkins, Keith. "Protestant Worship: Many Traditions or One?" *Worship* 64 (1990): 308–21.

White, James F. "The Teaching of Worship in Seminaries in Canada and the United States." *Worship* 55 (1981): 304–18.

## Supplementary Subjects on Worship

Abrahamowitz, C. "The Number Seven." *Dor le Dor* 15 (1986–87): 56–57.

Ahlers, Hans Peter. "Spiritual Rehabilitation: The Church's Mission to the Handicapped." *Worship* 55 (1981): 504–18.

Arnt, W. "A Royal Priesthood." *Concordia Theological Monthly* 19 (1948): 241–49.

Berger, Teresa. *Women's Ways of Worship: Gender Analysis and Liturgical History.* Collegeville, MN: Liturgical Press, 1999.

Betz, Hans Dieter. "The Logion of the Easy Yoke and Rest (Matt. 11:28–30)." *Journal of Biblical Literature* 86 (1967): 10–24.

Bradshaw, Paul. *Ordination Rites of the Ancient Churches of East and West.* New York: Pueblo, 1990.

Brown, Peter. *The Cult of the Saints: Its Rise and Function in Latin Christianity.* Chicago: University of Chicago Press, 1980.

Brown, William P. *Structure, Role and Ideology in the Hebrew and Greek Texts of Genesis 1:1–2:3.* Society of Biblical Literature Dissertation Series 132. Atlanta: Scholars Press, 1993.

Burton-Christie, Douglas. *The Word in the Desert: Scripture and the Quest for Holiness in Early Christian Monasticism.* New York: Oxford University Press, 1993.

Carruthers, Mary. *The Book of Memory: A Study of Memory in Medieval Culture.* Cambridge: Cambridge University Press, 1990.

Cawley, A. C., ed. *Everyman and Medieval Miracle Plays.* London: J. M. Dent & Sons, 1997.

Davies, J. G. *Liturgical Dance: An Historical, Theological, and Practical Handbook.* London: SCM, 1984.

Dillard, Annie. *Holy the Firm.* New York: Harper & Row, 1977.

Doran, Robert, trans. *The Lives of Simon Stylites.* Kalamazoo, MI: Cistercian Publications, 1992.

Driver, Tom F. *The Magic of Ritual: Our Need for Liberating Rites That Transform Our Lives and Our Communities.* San Francisco: Harper & Row, 1991.

Duffy, Regis A. "American Time and God's Time." *Worship* 62 (1988): 515–32.

Eastwood, C. *The Priesthood of All Believers: An Examination of the Doctrine from the Reformation to the Present Day.* Minneapolis: Augsburg, 1962.

Emmerson, Richard K., and Bernard McGinn, eds. *The Apocalypse in the Middle Ages.* Ithaca, NY: Cornell University Press, 1992.

Farmer, David Hugh. *The Oxford Dictionary of Saints.* New York: Oxford University Press, 1979.

Fink, Peter E. "The Challenge of God's Koinonia." *Worship* 59 (1985): 386–403.

Ford, David F. *Self and Salvation: Being Transformed.* Cambridge: Cambridge University Press, 1999.

Franklin, R. William. "Johann Adam Mohler and Worship in Totalitarian Society." *Worship* 67 (1993): 2–17.

Fredriksen, Paula. "Tyconius and Augustine on the Apocalypse." In *The Apocalypse in the Middle Ages,* edited by Richard K. Emmerson and Bernard McGinn, 20–37. Ithaca, NY: Cornell University Press, 1992.

Giakalis, Ambrosios. *Images of the Divine. The Theology of Icons at the Seventh Ecumenical Council.* Leiden: E. J. Brill, 1994.

Glen, M. Jennifer. "Sickness and Symbol: The Promise of the Future." *Worship* 55 (1981): 397–411.

Goldsmith, Margaret. *Joseph.* London: Rich & Cowan, 1937.

Graber-Miller, Keith. "Mennonite Footwashing: Identity Reflections and Altered Meanings." *Worship* 66 (1992): 148–70.

Greenburg, M. "The Biblical Concept of Asylum." *Journal of Biblical Literature* 78 (1959): 125–32.

Hanson, Paul D. *The People Called: The Growth of Community in the Bible.* San Francisco: Harper and Row, 1986.

Hardin, Grady. *The Leadership of Worship.* Nashville: Abingdon, 1980.

Harrington, Mary Therese. *A Place for All: Mental Retardation, Catechesis, and Liturgy.* American Essays in Liturgy Series. Collegeville, MN: Liturgical Press, 1992.

Havener, Ivan. "Monastic Priesthood: Some Thoughts on Its Future in America." *Worship* 56 (1982): 431–41.

Hayter, Mary. *The New Eve in Christ: The Use and Abuse of the Bible in the Debate About Women in the Church.* Grand Rapids: Eerdmans, 1987.

Holmes, Urban T. *The Priest in Community: Exploring the Roots of Ministry.* New York: Seabury, 1978.

Hughes, Philip Edgcumbe. "The Blood of Jesus and His Heavenly Priesthood, Part 3, The Meaning of the 'True Tent' and the 'Greater and More Perfect Tent.'" *Bibliotheca Sacra* 130 (1973): 305–14.

Hulse, E. V. "The Nature of Biblical 'Leprosy' and the Use of Alternative Medical Terms in Modern Translations of the Bible." *Palestine Exploration Quarterly* 107 (1975): 87–105.

Jart, Una. "The Precious Stones in the Revelation of St. John xxi. 18–21." *Studia Theologica* 2 (1970): 150–81.

Jeffery, Peter. "Mandatum Novum Do Vobis: Toward a Renewal of the Holy Thursday Footwashing Rite." *Worship* 64 (1990): 107–41.

Johnson, Todd E., ed. *The Conviction of Things Not Seen: Worship and Ministry in the Twenty-first Century.* Grand Rapids: Brazos, 2003.

Jones, Paul H. "We Are *How* We Worship: Corporate Worship as a Matrix for Christian Identity Formation." *Worship* 69 (1995): 346–60.

Kane, Thomas A. *The Dancing Church: Video Impressions of the Church in Africa.* New York: Paulist Press, 1992.

Krosnicki, Thomas A. "Dance Within the Liturgical Act." *Worship* 61 (1987): 349–57.

Lerner, Robert E. "The Medieval Return to the Thousand Year Sabbath." In *The Apocalypse in the Middle Ages,* edited by Richard K. Emmerson and Bernard McGinn, 1–71. Ithaca, NY: Cornell University Press, 1992.

Longenecker, Richard N., ed. *Community Formation in the Early Church and in the Church Today.* Peabody, MA: Hendrickson, 2002.

O'Loughlin, Thomas. "The Significance of Sunday: Three Ninth-Century Catecheses." *Worship* 64 (1990): 533–44.

Prest, John. *The Garden of Eden: The Botanic Garden, and the Re-Creation of Paradise.* New Haven: Yale University Press, 1981.

Ramshaw, Elaine J. "Ritual for Stillbirth: Exploring the Issues." *Worship* 62 (1988): 533–38.

Rosica, Thomas M. "The Road to Emmaus and the Road to Gaza: Luke 24:13–35 and Acts 8:26–40." *Worship* 68 (1994): 117–31.

Rouillard, Philippe. "From Human Need to Christian Eucharist, Part 1." *Worship* 52 (1978): 425–39.

———. "From Human Need to Christian Eucharist, Part 2." *Worship* 53 (1979): 40–56.

Seasoltz, R. Kevin. "The Dancing Church: An Appreciation." *Worship* 67 (1993): 253–61.

Thomas, Nicholas, and Caroline Humphrey, eds. *Shamanism, History and the State.* Ann Arbor, MI: University of Michigan Press, 1994.

Trudinger, Paul. "The Cleansing of the Temple: St. Johns Independent, Subtle Reflections." *Expository Times* 108 (1997): 329–30.

Varley, D. *Seven: The Number of Creation.* London: G. Bell & Sons, 1976.

Vogue, Adalbert de. "Eucharist and Monastic Life." *Worship* 59 (1985): 498–509.

Ward, Richard Finley. "Mourning at Eastertide: Revisiting a Broken Liturgy." *Worship* 71 (1997): 154–68.

White, Susan J. *Christian Worship and Technological Change.* Nashville: Abingdon, 1994.

Widengren, G. *The King and the Tree of Life in Ancient Near Eastern Religion.* Wiesbaden: Otto Harrassowitz, 1951.

Willimon, William H. *The Gospel for the Person Who Has Everything.* Valley Forge, PA: Judson, 1978.

———. *The Service of God: How Worship and Ethics Are Related.* Nashville: Abingdon, 1983.

Wilson, Ian. *Out of the Midst of the Fire: Divine Presence in Deuteronomy.* Atlanta: Scholars Press, 1995.

Wray, Judith Hoch. *Rest as a Theological Metaphor in the Epistle to the Hebrews and the Gospel of Truth, Early Christian Homiletics of Rest.* SBL Dissertation 166. Atlanta: Scholars Press, 1998.

Young, Karl. *The Drama of the Medieval Church.* 2 vols. Oxford: Clarendon Press, 1933.

## Commentaries Cited

Allen, Leslie. *Ezekiel 20–48.* Word Biblical Commentary 29. Dallas: Word, 1990.

Aune, David E. *Revelation 1–5.* Word Biblical Commentary 52. Dallas: Word, 1997.

Beasley-Murray, George R. *John.* Word Biblical Commentary 36. Waco, TX: Word, 1987.

Braun, Roddy. *1 Chronicles.* Word Biblical Commentary 42. Waco, TX: Word, 1986.

Bruce, F. F. *The Acts of the Apostles.* Grand Rapids: Eerdmans, 1968.

Budd, Philip J. *Numbers.* Word Biblical Commentary 5. Waco, TX: Word, 1984.

Carson, D. A. *The Gospel According to John.* Grand Rapids: Eerdmans, 1991.

———. "Matthew." In *The Expositor's Bible Commentary.* Edited by Frank E. Gaebelein, 8:3–599. Grand Rapids: Zondervan, 1984.

Cassuto, U. *A Commentary on the Book of Exodus.* Translated by Israel Abrahams. Jerusalem: Magnes Press, 1953.

———. *From Adam to Noah.* Vol. 1 of *A Commentary on the Book of Genesis.* Translated by Israel Abrahams. Jerusalem: Magnes Press, 1970.

———. *From Noah to Abraham.* Vol. 2 of *A Commentary on the Book of Genesis.* Translated by Israel Abrahams. Jerusalem: Magnes Press, 1970.

Childs, Brevard S. *The Book of Exodus.* Old Testament Library. Philadelphia: Westminster, 1974.

Cole, Alan. *Exodus.* Tyndale Old Testament Commentaries. Downers Grove, IL: InterVarsity, 1973.

Craigie, Peter C. *Psalms 1–50.* Word Biblical Commentary 19. Waco, TX: Word, 1983.

Davies, W. D., and Dale C. Allison. *The Gospel According to Saint Matthew: A Critical and Exegetical Commentary.* 3 vols. International Critical Commentary. Edinburgh: T. & T. Clark, 1997.

Dennett, Edward. *Typical Teachings of Exodus.* London: W. H. Brown and Rouse, 1889.

Delitzsch, Franz. *A New Commentary on Genesis.* 2 vols. Translated by Sophia Taylor. Edinburgh: T. & T. Clark, 1899.

Dillard, Raymond. *2 Chronicles.* Word Biblical Commentary 15. Waco, TX: Word, 1987.

Dobbs-Allsopp, F. W. *Lamentations: A Bible Commentary for Preaching and Teaching.* Interpretation. Louisville: John Knox, 2002.

Dods, Marcus. *The First Epistle to the Corinthians.* New York: A. C. Armstrong and Son, 1889.

Driver, S. R. *The Book of Genesis.* London: Methuen, 1913.

Duggan, Michael W. *The Covenant Renewal in Ezra-Nehemiah (Neh 7:72b–10:40): An Exegetical, Literary, and Theological Study.* Atlanta: Society of Biblical Literature, 2001.

Durham, John I. *Exodus.* Word Biblical Commentary 3. Waco, TX: Word, 1987.

Eichrodt, Walther. *Ezekiel.* Translated by Coslett Quinn. London: SCM, 1970.

Fokkelman, J. P. *Narrative Art in Genesis.* Assen Amsterdam: Van Gorcum, 1975.

Fretheim, Terence E. *Exodus.* Interpretation. Louisville: John Knox, 1994.

Gunkel, Herman. *Genesis ubersetzt und erklart.* Göttingen: Vandenhoeck & Ruprecht, 1922.

Hillers, Delbert R. *Lamentations.* Garden City, NJ: Doubleday, 1972.

Hagner, Donald A. *Matthew 14–28.* Word Biblical Commentary 33B. Dallas, TX: Word, 1995.

Houtman, C. *Exodus.* Kampen: Kok Publishing House, 1993–.

Jacob, Benno. *The Second Book of the Bible: Exodus.* Translated by Walter Jacob. Hoboken, NJ: KTAV, 1992.

Jantzen, J. Gerald. *Exodus.* Westminster Bible Companion. Louisville: Westminster John Knox, 1997.

Ladd, George Eldon. *A Commentary on the Revelation of St. John.* Grand Rapids: Eerdmans, 1972.

Leibowitz, Nehama. *Studies in Shemot.* 2 vols. Translated by Aryeh Newman. Jerusalem: World Zionist Organization, 1976.

Leupold, H. C. *Exposition of Genesis*. Grand Rapids: Baker, 1942.

Lundbom, Jack R. *Jeremiah: A Study in Ancient Hebrew Rhetoric*. Missoula, MT: Scholars Press, 1975.

Milligan, William. *The Book of Revelation*. The Expositor's Bible. London: Hodder and Stoughton, 1889.

Minear, Paul S. *I Saw a New Earth: An Introduction to the Visions of the Apocalypse*. Washington: Corpus Books, 1968.

Nolland, John. *Luke 18:35–24:53*. Word Biblical Commentary 35C. Dallas: Word, 1993.

Oswalt, John N. *Isaiah, Chapters 1–39*. New International Commentary on the Old Testament. Grand Rapids: Eerdmans, 1986.

Paul, Shalom M. *Amos*. Hermenia. Minneapolis: Fortress Press, 1991.

Rackham, R. B. *The Acts of the Apostles*. London: Methuen & Co, 1930.

Rad, Gerhard von. *Genesis*. Translated by John H. Marks. London: W. J. Mackay, 1961.

Ross, Allen P. *Creation and Blessing: A Guide to the Study and Exposition of the Book of Genesis*. Grand Rapids: Baker, 1986.

———. *Holiness to the Lord: A Guide to the Exposition of the Book of Leviticus*. Grand Rapids: Baker, 2002.

Ryle, Herbert E. *The Book of Genesis*. Cambridge: Cambridge University Press, 1921.

Scott, C. Anderson. *The Book of the Revelation*. London: Hodder & Stoughton, 1905.

Simcox, William Henry. *The Revelation of St John: The Bible for Schools and Colleges*. Cambridge: Cambridge University Press, 1890.

Skinner, John. *The Book of Ezekiel*. The Expositor's Bible. London: Hodder and Stoughton, 1895.

Stulman, Louis. *The Prose Sermons of the Book of Jeremiah*. Atlanta: Scholars Press, 1986.

Thompson, J. A. *The Book of Jeremiah*. New International Commentary on the Old Testament. Grand Rapids: Eerdmans, 1980.

Throntveit, Mark A. *Ezra–Nehemiah: A Bible Commentary for Teaching and Preaching*. Louisville: John Knox, 1992.

Vaughan, Curtis. "Colossians." In *The Expositor's Bible Commentary,* edited by Frank E. Gaebelein, 2:163–226. Grand Rapids: Zondervan, 1978.

Verhoef, Pieter A. *The Books of Haggai and Malachi*. New International Commentary on the Old Testament. Grand Rapids: Eerdmans, 1987.

Wenham, Gordon J. *Genesis 1–15*. Word Biblical Commentary 1. Nashville: Nelson, 1987.

———. *Genesis 16–50*. Word Biblical Commentary 2. Dallas: Word, 1994.

———. *The Book of Leviticus*. New International Commentary on the Old Testament. Grand Rapids: Eerdmans, 1979.

Westcott, B. F. *The Epistle to the Hebrews*. 1892. Reprint, Grand Rapids: Eerdmans, 1952.

Westermann, Claus. *Genesis 12–36*. Translated by John J. Scullion. London: SPCK, 1986.

Whitacre, Rodney A. *John*. Downers Grove, IL: InterVarsity, 1999.

Wildberger, Hans. *Isaiah 28–39*. Translated by Thomas H. Trapp. Minneapolis: Fortress Press, 2002.

Williamson, H. G. M. *Ezra, Nehemiah*. Word Biblical Commentary 16. Waco, TX: Word, 1985.

Woudstra, Marten H. *The Book of Joshua*. New International Commentary on the Old Testament. Grand Rapids: Eerdmans, 1981.

Wood, Leon J. "Hosea." In *The Expositor's Bible Commentary,* edited by Frank E. Gaebelein, 7:161–225. Grand Rapids: Zondervan, 1986.

## General Reference Works

Achtemeier, Paul J., ed. *Harper's Bible Dictionary*. New York: Harper and Row, 1985.

*The American Heritage Dictionary*. Second College Edition. Boston: Houghton Mifflin, 1991.

Brown, Francis, S. R. Driver, and Charles A. Briggs. *A Hebrew and English Lexicon of the Old Testament*. Oxford: Clarendon Press, 1907; reprint with corrections, 1962.

Buttrick, George A., ed. *The Interpreter's Dictionary of the Bible*. 4 vols. plus supplement. Nashville: Abingdon Press, 1962.

Catholic University of America. *The New Catholic Encyclopedia*. New York: McGraw Hill, 1987.

Davies, J. G., ed. *The Westminster Dictionary of Worship*. Philadelphia: Westminster Press, 1972.

Josephus, Flavius. *Josephus: Complete Works*. Translated by William Whiston. Grand Rapids: Kregel, 1960.

Kautzsch, E., ed. *Gesenius' Hebrew Grammar*. Translated by A. E. Cowley. 2d ed. Oxford: Oxford University Press, 1910.

Kittel, G., and G. Friedrich, eds. *The Theological Dictionary of the New Testament*. 10 vols. Translated by G. W. Bromiley. Grand Rapids: Eerdmans, 1964–76.

*Mishnayoth*. 6 vols. 3d ed. Revised, corrected, and enlarged by Philip Blackman. New York: Judaica Press, 1964.

Neusner, Jacob, and Richard S. Sarason, eds. *The Tosefta: Translated from the Hebrew*. Hoboken, NJ: KTAV, 1986.

Pritchard, J. B., ed. *Ancient Near Eastern Texts Relating to the Old Testament*. 3d ed. Princeton: Princeton University Press, 1969.

Roth, Cecil, ed. *The Encylopedia Judaica*. 16 vols. Jerusalem: Keter Publishing House, 1973.

*Septuaginta*. 2 vols. Stuttgart: Wurttembergische Bibelanstalt Stuttgart, 1965.

Tenney, Merrill, and J. D. Douglas, eds. *The New International Dictionary of the Bible*. Grand Rapids: Zondervan, 1987.

Van Gemeren, Willem. *The New International Dictionary of the Old Testament Theology and Exegesis*. 5 vols. Grand Rapids: Zondervan, 1998.

# Scripture Index

# Subject Index